NATIONAL GEOGRAPHIC
KiDS

ALMANAC
2023

A zebra foal runs through flowers in Etosha National Park in Namibia.

NATIONAL GEOGRAPHIC KiDS

ALMANAC
2023

NATIONAL GEOGRAPHIC
WASHINGTON, D.C.

National Geographic Kids Books
gratefully acknowledges the following people for their help
with the *National Geographic Kids Almanac*.

Stacey McClain of the
National Geographic Explorer Programs

Amazing Animals

Suzanne Braden, Director, Pandas International

Dr. Rodolfo Coria, Paleontologist,
Plaza Huincul, Argentina

Dr. Sylvia Earle, National Geographic
Explorer-in-Residence

Dr. Thomas R. Holtz, Jr., Senior Lecturer,
Vertebrate Paleontology,
Department of Geology, University of Maryland

Dr. Luke Hunter, Executive Director, Panthera

Nizar Ibrahim, National Geographic Explorer

Dereck and Beverly Joubert,
National Geographic Explorers-in-Residence

"Dino" Don Lessem, President, Exhibits Rex

Kathy B. Maher, Research Editor (former),
National Geographic magazine

Kathleen Martin, Canadian Sea Turtle Network

Barbara Nielsen, Polar Bears International

Andy Prince, Austin Zoo

Julia Thorson, Translator, Zurich, Switzerland

Dennis vanEngelsdorp, Senior Extension Associate,
Pennsylvania Department of Agriculture

Space and Earth
Science and Technology

Tim Appenzeller, Chief Magazine Editor, *Nature*

Dr. Rick Fienberg, Press Officer and Director of Communications,
American Astronomical Society

Dr. José de Ondarza, Associate Professor,
Department of Biological Sciences, State University
of New York, College at Plattsburgh

Lesley B. Rogers, Managing Editor (former),
National Geographic magazine

Dr. Enric Sala, National Geographic Explorer-in-Residence

Abigail A. Tipton, Director of Research (former),
National Geographic magazine

Erin Vintinner, Biodiversity Specialist,
Center for Biodiversity and Conservation at the
American Museum of Natural History

Barbara L. Wyckoff, Research Editor (former),
National Geographic magazine

Culture Connection

Dr. Wade Davis, National Geographic
Explorer-in-Residence

Deirdre Mullervy, Managing Editor,
Gallaudet University Press

Wonders of Nature

Anatta, NOAA Public Affairs Officer

Dr. Robert Ballard,
National Geographic Explorer-in-Residence

Douglas H. Chadwick, Wildlife Biologist and Contributor
to *National Geographic* magazine

Susan K. Pell, Ph.D., Science and Public Programs Manager,
United States Botanic Garden

History Happens

Dr. Sylvie Beaudreau, Associate Professor,
Department of History, State University of New York

Elspeth Deir, Assistant Professor, Faculty of Education,
Queens University, Kingston, Ontario, Canada

Dr. Gregory Geddes, Professor, Global Studies,
State University of New York–Orange,
Middletown-Newburgh, New York

Dr. Fredrik Hiebert, National Geographic Visiting Fellow

Micheline Joanisse, Media Relations Officer,
Natural Resources Canada

Dr. Robert D. Johnston,
Associate Professor and Director of the
Teaching of History Program, University of Illinois at Chicago

Dickson Mansfield, Geography Instructor (retired),
Faculty of Education, Queens University,
Kingston, Ontario, Canada

Tina Norris, U.S. Census Bureau

Parliamentary Information and Research Service,
Library of Parliament, Ottawa, Canada

Karyn Pugliese, Acting Director, Communications,
Assembly of First Nations

Geography Rocks

Dr. Kristin Bietsch, Research Associate,
Population Reference Bureau

Carl Haub, Senior Demographer,
Conrad Taeuber Chair of Public Information,
Population Reference Bureau

Dr. Toshiko Kaneda, Senior Research Associate,
Population Reference Bureau

Dr. Walt Meier, National Snow and Ice Data Center

Dr. Richard W. Reynolds, NOAA's National Climatic Data Center

United States Census Bureau, Public Help Desk

Contents

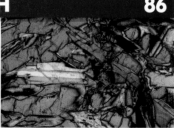

WONDERS OF NATURE 214

HISTORY HAPPENS 236

GEOGRAPHY ROCKS 268

NATIONAL GEOGRAPHIC KIDS
ALMANAC CHALLENGE 2023

THE RESULTS ARE IN!
**Which ocean animal won our
2022 Almanac Challenge?**
See page 113.

**Want to become part of the 2023 Almanac
Challenge?** Go to page 112 to find out more.

YOUR
WORLD
2023

Festivalgoers enjoy the swing ride at the Hamburg DOM, Germany's longest-running fair that happens three times a year.

3D-PRINTED JET SUITS

Ready, *jet*, go! With a jet suit, you may one day fly right into the future. The creation of British inventor Richard Browning, this suit is powered by arm-mounted turbine engines and a bigger engine that you wear like a backpack. The suit, which is controlled by body movement, can hit some 85 miles an hour (137 km/h) and fly for about five minutes. Browning, who holds a Guinness World Record for fastest speed in a body-controlled jet-engine–powered suit, used a 3D printer to design and create some of the parts that make up the 60-pound (27-kg) suit. But don't expect to see anyone soaring above your house in this suit anytime soon: Right now, it's being tested out by the military and police as a way to swiftly respond to emergencies or chase down criminals.

THE WORLD'S FIFTH OCEAN NAMED

THE SOUTHERN OCEAN IS OFFICIAL! Previously, the large body of water surrounding Antarctica—which is the place where the southernmost stretches of the Pacific, Atlantic, and Indian Oceans meet—was not recognized as a unique ocean. But National Geographic mapmakers ultimately decided to label the Southern Ocean as our planet's fifth ocean on all of their world maps. The new label isn't the only thing that's unique about the Southern Ocean: At some 34 million years old, it's one of Earth's "youngest" oceans. It's also colder and less salty than its four other ocean counterparts.

Welcome to
OTTER ISLAND

It's hard enough riding a bike on city sidewalks. But in addition to dodging people on walks, runs, or even skateboards, try dodging scampering otters, too! That's life for people in Singapore, a country in Southeast Asia, where smooth-coated river otters live alongside humans.

About 50 years ago, the rivers on the island country of Singapore were so polluted that these native otters could no longer survive there. But thanks to decades of programs that cleaned up the rivers, the otters have made a comeback in this urban environment.

Now biologists are studying the island's otters to learn how the species, found throughout much of Asia, is adapting to city life. For example, these otter pups live with their parents about a year longer than other smooth-coated otters do, since they don't have as much territory to spread out in. Instead of burrowing in the dirt, they make dens in concrete bridges; instead of sleeping in a forest, they snooze between slabs of pavement. This island is now *otterly* wild!

TWO OTTERS WALK NEAR MARINA BAY, SINGAPORE.

A GROUP OF OTTERS EXPLORES A RESIDENTIAL AREA.

A FAMILY OF OTTERS SWIMS IN MARINA BAY, SINGAPORE.

Wacky Tube Man
Scares Away Dingoes

Here's one way to keep dingoes away: Scare them off with a wiggly inflatable! Scientists in Australia are hoping to prevent the predatory wild dogs from hunting livestock by setting up inflatable objects on farms. In one study, researchers visited a dingo sanctuary, where they set up a bright yellow, 13-foot (4 m)-tall tube man nicknamed Fred-a-Scare near a bowl of dog food. The result? Three out of four times, the dingoes ran away as soon as they spotted Fred wiggling away. While not a foolproof plan—some experts think the dogs will stop fearing tube men after repeated visits— it may be an easy fix for the Australian farmers who routinely lose livestock to hungry dingoes.

BEE INSPIRED

LEMONADE COMPANY'S FOUNDER IS ON A MISSION TO SAVE THE HONEYBEES.

Talk about being buzz-worthy: 17-year-old Mikaila Ulmer has made a big business out of saving honeybees. In 2009, Ulmer created Me & the Bees Lemonade with a special recipe using flaxseed and honey that she plucked from her great-grandma's family cookbook. She eventually bottled it up and started selling it locally, and now, the drink can be found in stores all over the country. But Ulmer's not just about selling lemonade: Part of all Me & the Bees proceeds go to protect bees and their habitats. And aside from running her own company, Ulmer also heads up the Healthy Hive Foundation, a nonprofit organization that supports scientific research aimed at keeping honeybees buzzing around for a long time to come.

Pelican Rescue

Arvy the brown pelican isn't your average bird! When she was just a baby learning the ways of the world in Connecticut, U.S.A., she forgot she needed to fly south for the winter and found herself stranded on a frozen pond. Onlookers found Arvy and took her to a wildlife rehabilitation center in Florida, U.S.A. She was treated for pneumonia and severe frostbite on her webbed feet. Because Arvy lost 30 percent of her feet to frostbite, which impacts her balance, she is unable to return to the wild. So she's now spreading her wings as an ambassador for all brown pelicans at the Busch Wildlife Sanctuary in Florida.

RISE OF THE TITANS

WHEN RESEARCHERS IN AUSTRALIA unearthed fossilized dinosaur bones back in 2006, they didn't realize just how, well, *huge* their discovery was. Now, thanks to new 3D-scanning technology, they know the remains belong to the largest dinosaur species ever found in Australia. Scientists spent years analyzing 3D scans to compare the bones in a database of other species to this new dino, named *Australotitan cooperensis* (casually known as Cooper). Now, the team can say for certain that the dino, which was as long as a basketball court and as tall as a two-story house, is Australia's biggest. Cooper's other characteristics? A long neck and tail, four legs, and a preference for plants. Found in Australia's outback, Cooper's fossils are linked to a lineage of dinosaurs called titanosaurs that were named for their super size. Previously, titanosaurs of this size had only been found in South America's Patagonia region, but now Australia can claim its own titan.

VIKING SHIP
UNCOVERED

Beneath the ground in a spot near Oslo, Norway, sits a Viking ship more than 1,000 years old, and experts are doing everything they can to unearth it. The ship, believed to have been part of a Viking burial site dating back to the 10th century, was discovered by archaeologists using ground penetrating radar (GPR), which revealed that it's more than 60 feet (18 m) long and 16 feet (5 m) wide. Although much of the ship has mostly rotted away, experts hope to excavate the remains so they can use what's left to build a replica and learn more about ancient Viking culture and society. Bringing the boat aboveground is no easy feat, however: The painstaking process will require many hours of slow and careful digging to make sure that what is left of the ancient artifact remains intact.

Colosseum Makeover

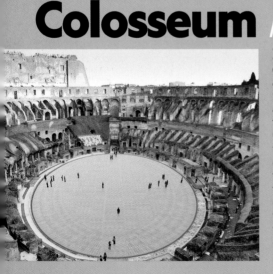

In Rome, Italy, a very old building is getting a new look. The Colosseum, the largest amphitheater in the ancient world, is undergoing renovations for a new retractable floor that will allow visitors a different vantage point of the famous landmark. An Italian architectural firm will lead the construction of the floor, which includes installing hundreds of wooden slats that can be rotated to let natural light and air into the chambers below. After archaeologists removed the original floor in the 19th century, visitors could only explore the underground network of tunnels in the ancient site. But once the floor is completed, people will be able to stand in the center of the Colosseum and get a gladiator's view of the surrounding arena.

YARN BOMB!

From street benches to city buses, from tree trunks to trains, nothing is truly safe from yarn bombing. And that's not necessarily a bad thing: Yarn bombing, the act of decorating a space with knitted projects, is a lively way to infuse ordinary objects with pops of color. A type of street art that dates back to the early 2000s, yarn bombing displays have been spotted around the world, from London to Paris to Australia to the United States. Sometimes, yarn bombing is done to bring awareness to hot-button issues, like one display calling for attention to climate change. But many yarn bombers do it simply to bring smiles and brighten up their community one colorful stitch at a time.

sports funnies
World Cup Edition

In 2023, the women's World Cup goes down under! Every four years, the best soccer players on the planet go head-to-head for a chance to claim the world title. In 2019, Team USA came out on top—who will win the 2023 final in Sydney, Australia? Tune in!

Ellen White of Great Britain scores a goal in a match against Chile at the Tokyo 2020 Olympic Games.

Canada's Deanne Rose delivers a penalty kick at the Tokyo 2020 Olympic Games.

Cool Events 2023

WORLD BICYCLE DAY

Spend some of your day on two wheels today—it's fun *and* good for the environment.

June 3

INTERNATIONAL SWEATPANTS DAY

GET COMFY! Throw on your favorite sweats and do something chill and relaxing while you're at it. You deserve it!

January 21

WORLD CHOCOLATE DAY

Need an excuse to eat chocolate? Here's one! Time to treat yourself.

July 7

INTERNATIONAL WOMEN'S DAY

Celebrate all of the amazing women on Earth on this day aimed at raising awareness for the importance of gender equality.

March 8

WORLD ELEPHANT DAY

Pledge to support a world that protects all the awesome elephants on Earth and their habitats.

August 12

EARTH HOUR DAY

Recharge the planet by powering down your electronics from 8:30 p.m. to 9:30 p.m.

March 25

WORLD SINGING DAY

TURN UP THE MUSIC and belt out your favorite tunes!

October 21

WORLD BEE DAY

Show your support for our planet's powerful pollinators, and get to know more about the threats they face.

May 20

INTERNATIONAL CHEETAH DAY

Celebrate the fastest land animal on Earth while helping to raise awareness for these amazing—and vulnerable—big cats.

December 4

MUPPET GEODE

Cookie Monster, is that you? Scientists were pleasantly surprised to crack open a geode and see a familiar face staring back at them. The rare rock, found in Brazil's Rio Grande do Sul region, sports a deep blue quartz crystal "face," along with two perfectly placed holes bearing an uncanny resemblance to the *Sesame Street* character. Experts say the geode may be worth $10,000. That can get you a lot of cookies!

NEW SUPERHERO: Ratman

MAGAWA, an African giant pouched rat who lived in Cambodia, had a nose for danger. The rodent could sniff out land mines, deadly devices hidden in the countryside. Left over from decades of war in the Southeast Asian country, the land mines are triggered when people accidentally step on them. But Magawa was trained to pick up the scent of the mines and scratch at the ground to signal that he found one so a human could disarm the device. Magawa passed away in 2022, but he found more than a hundred land mines and explosives in five years. What a hero!

Giant pouched rats get their name from the large, hamsterlike pouches in their cheeks, not their body size.

MAGAWA WEARS A MEDAL HE RECEIVED IN 2020 FOR HIS LIFESAVING ACTIONS.

DOG ART GALLERY

This art gallery is for the dogs—literally! In Hong Kong, one artist dedicated an entire collection to canines. The 50-piece collection was part of a temporary exhibit that included interactive pieces like a bouncy water bowl, a giant food bowl ball pit, and other features for pups to play on. There were also boldly colored portraits of dogs positioned close to the floor so the furry friends could get a better look. But humans were just as welcome to, um, *sniff* around.

KIDS vs. PLASTIC

Using rakes and a conveyor belt, Mr. Trash Wheel scoops hundreds of tons of trash out of the Inner Harbor in Baltimore, Maryland, U.S.A., each year.

WHAT IS PLASTIC?

>> **P**lastic can be molded, colored, and textured to make, well, just about anything. That begs the question: What precisely is this wonder product?

THE BASICS

Plastics are polymers, or long, flexible chains of molecules made of repeating links. This molecular structure makes plastic lightweight, hard to break, and easy to mold—all of which makes it extremely useful.

WHERE DO POLYMERS COME FROM?

Polymers can be found in nature, in things like the cell walls of plants, tar, tortoiseshell, and tree sap. In fact, nearly 3,500 years ago, people in what is today Central America used the sap from gum trees to make rubber balls for games. About 150 years ago, scientists began replicating the polymers in nature to improve on them— these are called synthetic polymers.

WHO INVENTED PLASTIC?

In 1869, an American named John Wesley Hyatt created the first useful synthetic polymer. At the time, the discovery was a big deal: For the first time, manufacturing was no longer limited by the resources supplied by nature like wood, clay, and stone. People could create their own materials.

WHAT IS SYNTHETIC PLASTIC MADE FROM?

Today, most plastic is made from oil and natural gas.

WHEN DID IT BECOME POPULAR?

During World War II, from 1939 to 1945, nylon, which is strong and light like silk but made of plastic, was used for parachutes, rope, body armor, and helmet liners. And airplanes used in battle had lightweight windows made of plastic glass, also known as Plexiglas. After the war, plastic became a popular material. Everything from dishes to radios to Mr. Potato Head hit the market. A few decades later, plastic soda bottles became a lightweight nonbreakable alternative to glass bottles, and grocery stores switched from paper bags to cheaper thin plastic ones.

THAT BRINGS US TO TODAY.

Look around: Are you more than a few feet away from something plastic? Probably not! Plastic is all around us.

AMERICANS use an average of ONE plastic grocery bag A DAY. People in DENMARK use an average of FOUR plastic grocery bags A YEAR.

WHERE DOES ALL THE PLASTIC GO?

Only a small percentage of all the plastic that has ever been made has been recycled to make other things. Most has been tossed out and left to slowly biodegrade in landfills, a process that can take hundreds of years. The other option for getting rid of plastic is to burn it. But because plastic is made from fossil fuels, burning it releases harmful pollutants into the air. Here is a breakdown of where all the plastic has gone since people started making it, and how long it takes to biodegrade if it does wind up in a landfill.

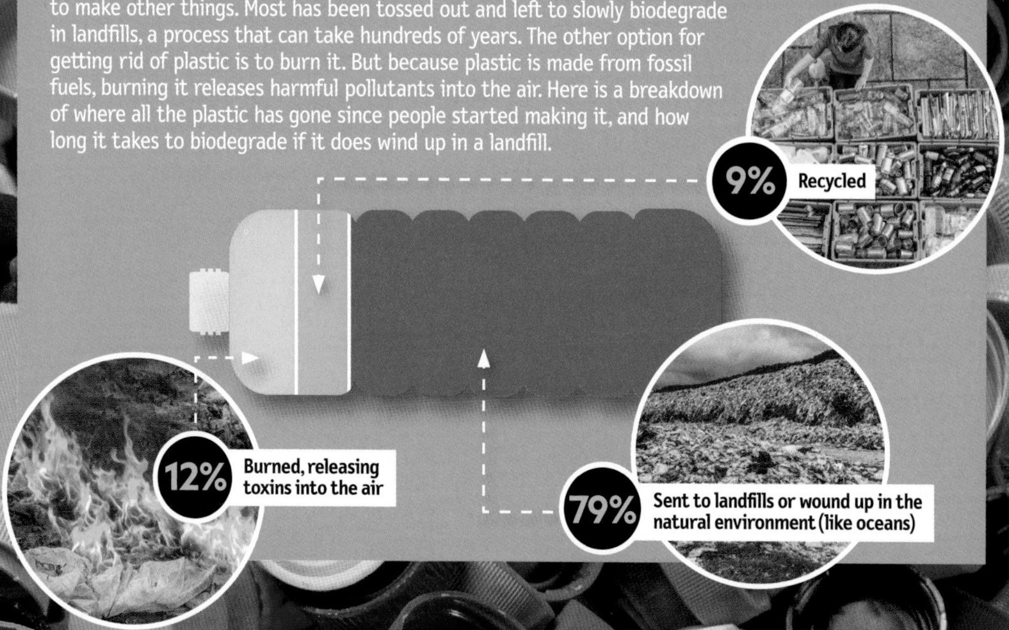

9% Recycled

12% Burned, releasing toxins into the air

79% Sent to landfills or wound up in the natural environment (like oceans)

THE LIFE SPAN OF PLASTIC

Plastic that's sent to a landfill doesn't just disappear—it stays there for a really long time. Different types of plastic take different lengths of time to biodegrade.

PLASTIC BAG
20 YEARS

PLASTIC-FOAM CUP
50 YEARS

STRAW
200 YEARS

BOTTLE
450 YEARS

SODA SIX-PACK RING 450 YEARS

FISHING LINE
600+ YEARS

DEADLY DEBRIS

THE INS AND OUTS OF THE (NOT SO) GREAT PACIFIC GARBAGE PATCH

On a map, the space between California and Hawaii, U.S.A., looks like an endless blue sea, but in person, you'll find a giant floating island—made up of plastic. Plastic can be found in all the oceans of the world, but currents and winds move marine debris around in certain patterns that create huge concentrations, or patches, of plastic in some spots. The biggest one is the Great Pacific Garbage Patch. Scientists estimate that there are about 1.8 trillion pieces of plastic in the patch, and 94 percent of them are microplastics. So, don't try walking on it; it's definitely not solid! Some of the patch is made up of bulky items, including fishing gear like nets, rope, eel traps, crates, and baskets. The patch is also made up of debris washed into the sea during tsunamis. A tsunami is a series of waves caused by an earthquake or an undersea volcanic eruption. It can pull millions of tons of debris—from cars to household appliances to pieces of houses—off coastlines and into the ocean. Scientists and innovators are working on ways to clean up the patch. But with more plastic constantly entering waterways, the effort will inevitably be ongoing.

TANGLED NYLON ROPE THAT HAS WASHED ASHORE OFF THE COAST OF PHUKET, THAILAND

SMASHED-UP SHIPS EVENTUALLY MAKE THEIR WAY TO A SWIRLING MASS OF DEBRIS CALLED THE GREAT PACIFIC GARBAGE PATCH.

GARBAGE PATCH ZONES

ARCTIC OCEAN

ASIA

NORTH AMERICA

ATLANTIC OCEAN

Great Pacific Garbage Patch

AFRICA

AFRICA

PACIFIC OCEAN

SOUTH AMERICA

INDIAN OCEAN

AUSTRALIA

Warm Ocean Current

Cold Ocean Current

ATLANTIC OCEAN

SOUTHERN OCEAN

ANTARCTICA

There are five large systems of circulating ocean currents around the world called gyres. Plastic and other trash travel with the currents and get trapped in the gyres. The gyre that the Great Pacific Garbage Patch swirls in is the largest of them all.

Garbage patch area with low concentration of plastics

CANADA

PACIFIC OCEAN

UNITED STATES

California

PACIFIC OCEAN

MEXICO

Hawai'i (United States)

Garbage patch area with high concentration of plastics

THE GREAT PACIFIC GARBAGE PATCH MEASURES 618,000 SQUARE MILES (1.6 MILLION SQ KM).

That's about:

3 TIMES THE SIZE OF FRANCE

2 TIMES THE SIZE OF TEXAS

There are **250 PIECES OF PLASTIC** in the Great Pacific Garbage Patch for **EVERY HUMAN** on Earth.

23

THERE ARE SOME 5.25 TRILLION PIECES OF PLASTIC WASTE FLOATING AROUND IN THE OCEAN.

In 2018, a group of volunteers removed **4,000 POUNDS** (1,800 kg) of **TRASH** from an **UNINHABITED VOLCANIC ISLAND** off the coast of Alaska, U.S.A.

One Oregon, U.S.A., organization **COLLECTS OCEAN TRASH** to make **COLORFUL SCULPTURES** of **SEA CREATURES.**

Some people take clever steps to sort this messy situation, like installing this giant fish-shaped trash can on a beach in Portugal. Others create art with plastic plucked from the sea, or simply spend time picking up trash to keep our shores clean—and safe.

A FIRE HYDRANT, GARDEN GNOMES, A SKI BOOT, and a RUBBER CHICKEN HAVE ALL WASHED UP ON BEACHES around the world.

FOOD WRAPPERS, CIGARETTE BUTTS, PLASTIC BOTTLES, and PLASTIC BOTTLE CAPS are among the TOP ITEMS COLLECTED during BEACH CLEANUPS.

kids
VS. PLASTIC

Do your part to help prevent single-use plastic items from reaching the ocean.
Parents and teachers:
For more information on this topic, you can visit **natgeokids.com/KidsVsPlastic** with your young readers.

CHOOSE THIS

NOT THAT

California, U.S.A., banned restaurants from handing out straws unless customers ask for them.

WHY?

Plastic straws might seem like a small part of the plastic pollution problem, but they can make big trouble for wildlife when they're blown into creeks or rivers and eventually end up in the ocean. A viral video showed rescuers working for nearly 10 minutes to pull just one plastic straw out of the nose of an olive ridley sea turtle—ouch!

So instead, ask your favorite restaurant to provide paper straws, bring your own reusable option, or just skip the straw altogether!

PICK YOUR PERFECT STRAW!

1 I don't want to buy a new straw.
HOLLOW DRY PASTA

2 I want something sturdy yet lightweight.
BAMBOO STRAW

3 I need one that's small and easy to carry.
COLLAPSIBLE STRAW

4 I like to chew on my sippers.
SILICONE STRAW

YOUR **PLASTIC-FREE** GUIDE TO

SNACKS

Chew on these three ideas for plastic-free snacking.

1
TRAIL MIX

Just mix all your favorite treats from the bulk section of the grocery store together in a bowl, and then eat! You can even sprinkle your mixture with sea salt, cinnamon, or another of your favorite spices for more flavor. Check out these ideas for ingredient inspiration.

- ☐ Pretzels
- ☐ Nuts like almonds, pistachios, or peanuts
- ☐ Pumpkin or sunflower seeds
- ☐ Dried fruit like apricots, raisins, or banana chips
- ☐ Chocolate chips
- ☐ Whole-grain cereal
- ☐ Shredded coconut

2
STOVETOP POPCORN

You'll need a paper bag full of popcorn kernels from the bulk section of the grocery store, some cooking oil, and a big pot with a lid. Make sure to get an adult's help with this recipe.

- ☐ Pour a splash of oil into the pot, using just enough to cover the bottom.
- ☐ Grab an adult and heat the pot on the stovetop over medium heat.
- ☐ Pour in enough popcorn kernels to create one layer along the bottom of the pot.
- ☐ Cover the pot with the lid.
- ☐ After a few minutes, listen for popping sounds. When the popping slows, remove the pot from the burner, take off the lid, and put the popcorn in a bowl.
- ☐ Top off your treat with salt, melted butter, or other spices.

3
BAKED APPLES

Turn this packaging-free fruit into a special snack with brown sugar, butter, and cinnamon. Make sure to get an adult's help with this recipe.

- ☐ Grab an adult and preheat the oven to 350°F (175°C). (You can also use the microwave.)
- ☐ Cut each apple in half, then scoop out its core.
- ☐ Put the apples in an ovenproof baking dish, and then spread a tablespoon of brown sugar and a tablespoon of butter on the inside of each apple half. Then sprinkle the apples with cinnamon.
- ☐ Bake the apples in the oven for about half an hour, or cook in the microwave for about three minutes or until the fruit softens.

DIY Granola Bar Goodies

Plastic food wrappers, like the ones on store-bought granola bars, are a common sight at beach cleanups. Here's a sweet solution: Help keep Earth healthy by ditching the plastic-wrapped snacks and making your own granola bars instead.

PLANET PROTECTOR TIP

Wrap your granola bars in paper or cloth instead of plastic wrap for an on-the-go treat.

YOU'LL NEED

- Medium-size mixing bowl
- Spoon
- 1½ cups (190 g) old-fashioned oats
- 1½ cups (190 g) puffed rice cereal
- ½ cup (65 g) roasted, unsalted sunflower seeds
- ½ teaspoon (1.3 mL) cinnamon
- Medium-size pot
- Knife
- 1 cup (125 g) brown sugar
- ½ cup (65 g) honey
- 3 tablespoons (45 mL) vegetable oil
- ¼ teaspoon (2.5 mL) salt
- ½ teaspoon (1.3 mL) vanilla extract
- ¼ cup (32 g) chocolate chips
- Wax paper
- Square glass baking pan

STEP ONE

Put oats, puffed rice cereal, sunflower seeds, and cinnamon in a mixing bowl and stir with a spoon.

STEP TWO

Grab an adult and combine the brown sugar and honey in a pot.

28

STEP THREE

Heat the mixture on low and stir for two minutes, or until the mixture is smooth.

STEP FOUR

Mix in oil, salt, and vanilla. Next add the chocolate chips and stir until the chips have completely melted. Then turn off the stove.

STEP FIVE

When the wet mixture in the pot is still warm, pour it into the bowl with the dry ingredients. Stir until the wet and dry ingredients are all combined.

STEP SIX

Place a sheet of wax paper into the glass baking pan so that the paper hangs over the sides of the pan. Pour the mixture on top of the wax paper in the glass pan.

STEP SEVEN

Use your hands to press the granola firmly into the pan. Wait a few hours for the granola to completely cool. (You can put the pan in the refrigerator to cool it more quickly.)

STEP EIGHT

When the granola mixture is fully cooled, carefully lift the wax paper out of the glass pan. Then ask an adult to help cut the snack into bars or bite-size squares. **Enjoy!**

SEA TURTLE RESCUE

RESCUERS SWOOP IN TO HELP A SEA TURTLE THAT SWALLOWED A BALLOON.

A young green sea turtle bobbed along the surface of the water off the coast of Florida, U.S.A. Young turtles usually don't hang out at the surface—that's where predators can easily spot them, plus their food is deeper underwater. But something was keeping this one-foot (30.5-cm)-long turtle from diving.

Luckily, rescuers spotted the struggling turtle and took it back to the Clearwater Marine Aquarium, where they named it Chex. Staff placed Chex in a shallow kiddie pool so that the turtle wouldn't waste energy trying to dive. They tested Chex's blood and ran x-rays but couldn't figure out what was wrong. "Then one day Chex started pooping out something weird," biologist Lauren Bell says. The weird object turned out to be a purple balloon and an attached string.

SOS (SAVE OUR SEAGRASS)!

Sea turtles often mistake floating trash for food. "Even some *people* can't tell the difference between a plastic grocery bag and a jellyfish in the water," Bell says. But plastic doesn't just hurt sea turtles: It also hurts their habitat.

Green sea turtles often hang out close to the shore near seagrass, one of their favorite snacks. Plastic trash left on the beach or coming from rivers that empty into the sea often ends up in this habitat. When it settles on the seagrass, the rubbish can smother the grass, causing it to die. That can mean trouble for green sea turtles like Chex that rely on the seagrass for food and shelter.

During one three-hour cleanup on a beach in Virginia, U.S.A., volunteers collected more than 900 balloons.

TURTLE POWER

BALLOON STRING

PIECE OF BALLOON

1 CHEX THE GREEN SEA TURTLE PROBABLY MISTOOK A TWO-FOOT (0.6-M)-LONG STRING FOR FOOD.

2 CHEX RECOVERED AT THE CLEARWATER MARINE AQUARIUM, SPENDING LOTS OF TIME IN A KIDDIE POOL. ONCE THE TURTLE STARTED EATING SOLID FOODS AGAIN, RESCUERS DECIDED CHEX WAS READY TO RETURN TO THE OCEAN.

GREEN SEA TURTLE
Redington Beach, Florida, U.S.A.

ARCTIC OCEAN

NORTH AMERICA
EUROPE
ASIA
PACIFIC OCEAN

ATLANTIC OCEAN
AFRICA
PACIFIC OCEAN

SOUTH AMERICA
INDIAN OCEAN
AUSTRALIA

Seagrass

SOUTHERN OCEAN

ANTARCTICA

BYE, BALLOON

After several days at the aquarium, Chex started to improve as the balloon made its way through the turtle's digestive system. Chex eventually passed the entire balloon, plus a two-foot (0.6-m)-long string. A few months later, after aquarium staff had successfully introduced solid food back into Chex's diet, rescuers declared the turtle ready to return to the sea.

Bell stood hip deep in the waves as another staff member handed Chex to her. She carefully placed the little turtle in the water and watched it paddle away. "Chex was like, 'Oh, there's the ocean! Okay, bye!'" Bell says. Chex's rescue is worth celebrating ... but maybe without the party balloons.

POLLUTION SOLUTION
PLASTIC PREDATOR

The ocean is full of trillions of pieces of trash called microplastics that are smaller than the period at the end of this sentence—which makes them really hard to clean up. But the solution might be in tadpole-like creatures called larvaceans (lar-VAY-shuns). These marine animals eat by filtering tiny food particles out of the water and through their bodies. The particles are first trapped in what's called a mucus house—a thin, see-through bubble of, well, mucus that surrounds the larvacean as it travels. Scientists are studying this behavior to see if a similar process could pull harmful microplastics out of the water.

3 BIOLOGIST LAUREN BELL PREPARES TO RELEASE THE LITTLE TURTLE BACK INTO THE SEA.

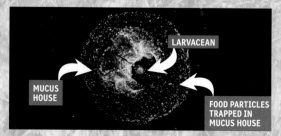

LARVACEAN

MUCUS HOUSE

FOOD PARTICLES TRAPPED IN MUCUS HOUSE

QUIZ WHIZ

What's your eco-friendly IQ? Find out with this quiz!

Write your answers on a piece of paper. Then check them below.

1 **True or false?** Of all plastic ever made, 90 percent has been recycled.

2 There are _____ pieces of plastic in the Great Pacific Garbage Patch for every human on Earth.

a. 2.5
b. 25
c. 250
d. 2,500

3 When was plastic invented?

a. 2009
b. 1769
c. 1969
d. 1869

4 What sea creature's unique way of eating may help pull microplastics out of the ocean?

a. larvacean
b. sea turtle
c. whale shark
d. stingray

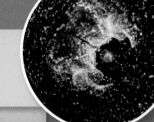

5 **True or false?** Shopping for your favorite treats from the bulk section of the grocery store can prevent plastic items from reaching the ocean.

Not **STUMPED** yet? Check out the *NATIONAL GEOGRAPHIC KIDS QUIZ WHIZ* collection for more crazy **ENVIRONMENT** questions!

ANSWERS: 1. False: Just 9 percent of plastic has been recycled; 2. c; 3. d; 4. a; 5. True

HOMEWORK HELP

Write a Letter That Gets Results

Knowing how to write a good letter is a useful skill. It will come in handy when you want to persuade someone to understand your point of view. Whether you're emailing your congressperson or writing a letter for a school project or to your grandma, a great letter will help you get your message across. Most important, a well-written letter makes a good impression.

CHECK OUT THE EXAMPLE BELOW FOR THE ELEMENTS OF A GOOD LETTER.

Your address

Date

Salutation
Always use "Dear" followed by the person's name; use Mr., Mrs., Ms., or Dr. as appropriate.

Introductory paragraph
Give the reason you're writing the letter.

Body
The longest part of the letter, which provides evidence that supports your position. Be persuasive!

Closing paragraph
Sum up your argument.

Complimentary closing
Sign off with "Sincerely" or "Thank you."

Your signature

Maddie Smith
1234 Main Street
Peoria, Illinois 61525

April 22, 2023

Dear Owner of the Happy Hamburger,

I am writing to ask you to stop using single-use plastic at the Happy Hamburger.

This is my favorite restaurant. My family and I eat there almost every Saturday night. I always order the bacon cheeseburger with mac and cheese on the side. It's my favorite meal, ever!

The other day, my dad brought home a to-go order from your restaurant. The order contained a plastic fork, knife, and spoon, all wrapped in plastic. It also came in a plastic bag. Now that's a lot of plastic!

I am concerned because plastic is a huge problem for the planet. Did you know that nine million tons of plastic waste end up in the ocean every year? Even worse, scientists think that the amount of plastic might triple by 2050.

Some other restaurants in town have cut back on their single-use plastic. The Hotdog Hangout uses paper bags instead of plastic bags for takeout. And servers at the Weeping Onion ask customers if they'd like plastic cutlery, instead of automatically including it in to-go orders.

These are simple changes that I hope you can make at the Happy Hamburger. That way, not only would you be serving the best burgers around, but you'd also be helping to protect the planet.

Thank you very much for your time.

Sincerely,

Maddie Smith

Maddie Smith

COMPLIMENTARY CLOSINGS

Sincerely, Sincerely yours, Thank you, Regards, Best wishes, Respectfully

AMAZING
ANIMALS

A close-up of a jumping spider in Turkey

EXTRAORDINARY ANIMALS

Silly Seal Sniffs Eel

Lisianski Island, Hawaii

This seal *nose* a thing or two about getting into trouble.

The Hawaiian monk seal pup was spotted lounging on the beach—with an eel hanging out of its nostril. Scientists approached the seal, gently held it down with their hands, and then pulled the two-and-a-half-foot (76 cm) dead eel out of its nose in about a minute. "The seal didn't feel any pain," says Charles Littnan, director of the Protected Species Division at the National Oceanic and Atmospheric Administration in Hawaii. "In fact, it didn't seem to care at all."

Scientists have since found three other young seals with eels in their noses—and they don't know why. But since eels are on the seals' menu, the mishap probably happened when the youngsters were hunting. "The pups aren't sure how to handle their food yet," Littnan says. "And they seem to be good at getting into trouble." Looks like these seals need to learn not to play with their food!

DO I HAVE SOMETHING ON MY FACE?

Ape Takes Boat for a Ride!

I WISH I HAD A MOTOR FOR THIS THING.

Tanjung Puting National Park, Borneo

Keep an eye on your vessel when Princess the orangutan is around. The boat-napping buccaneer steals canoes from the dock at Camp Leakey, the orangutan research station where she lives. Princess takes the boats so she can get to the tasty plants that grow downstream. But this sneaky great ape may have another motive: "If people are around, sometimes she does it to show off," says scientist Biruté Mary Galdikas, Camp Leakey's orangutan expert.

Princess's rides can be a royal pain for camp workers, who must retrieve the canoes she abandons. To discourage her, they store the canoes underwater. But Princess simply tips the boats from side to side until the water sloshes out.

All primates are intelligent, but Princess is especially brainy. "I'd say she's one of the smartest orangutans I've ever seen in my life," Galdikas says. Even when Princess is onshore, she eats like a queen: She figured out how to use a key to unlock the camp's dining hall!

I'M ALWAYS IN TUNE.

Singing Dingo

Alice Springs, Australia

He might not have been a famous pop star, but Dinky the dingo sure could belt out a tune! After innkeeper Jim Cotterill helped rescue the young wild dog from a trap in the Australian outback, he noticed that his new pet liked to "sing along" with the piano. When guests would play a song, Dinky would hop on top of the keys and howl a tune to match the notes. "A group of musicians told me that Dinky actually had pretty good pitch," Cotterill said. "When the notes went higher, so did Dinky's voice."

Hippo "Kisses" Hyena

South Luangwa National Park, Zambia

Pucker up! On a safari drive, guide Patrick Njobvu watched as a young hippopotamus emerged from the Luangwa River, walked over to a snoozing spotted hyena, and started to sniff. "The hyena didn't run, and both started sniffing each other, nose to nose, almost like kissing," Njobvu says. The two animals hung out together for about 20 minutes before walking away.

Experts don't know why the hyena didn't run away—some think it might have been too scared to move, while others believe that it could've been feeling very relaxed. And the hippo? It was likely just being curious. Behavioral ecologist Rob Heathcote says that young animals like this hippo are often more curious as they explore the world and learn how to behave.

The "kiss" wasn't true love, but it was definitely cute.

SORRY MY SMOOCHES ARE SANDY!

ANIMAL MYTHS BUSTED

Some people mistakenly think adult opossums hang by their tails or that porcupines shoot their quills. What other misconceptions are out there? Here are some common animal myths.

MYTH Elephants are afraid of mice.

HOW IT MAY HAVE STARTED People used to think that mice liked to crawl into elephants' trunks, which could cause damage and terrible sneezing. So it makes sense that elephants would be afraid of the rodents.

WHY IT'S NOT TRUE An elephant's eyesight is so poor that it could barely even see a mouse. Plus, if an elephant isn't afraid to live among predators such as tigers, rhinos, and crocodiles, a mouse would be the least of its worries!

Who are you again?

MYTH Goldfish only have a three-second memory.

HOW IT MAY HAVE STARTED While an adult human's brain weighs about three pounds (1.4 kg), an average goldfish's brain weighs only a tiny fraction of that. So how could there be any room for memory in there?

WHY IT'S NOT TRUE Research has shown that goldfish are quite smart. Phil Gee of the University of Plymouth in the United Kingdom trained goldfish to push a lever that dropped food into their tank. "They remembered the time of day that the lever worked and waited until feeding time to press it," Gee says. One scientist even trained goldfish to tell the difference between classical and blues music!

MYTH Touching a frog or toad will give you warts.

HOW IT MAY HAVE STARTED Many frogs and toads have bumps on their skin that look like warts. Some people think the bumps are contagious.

WHY IT'S NOT TRUE "Warts are caused by a human virus, not frogs or toads," said dermatologist Jerry Litt. But the wart-like bumps behind a toad's ears *can* be dangerous. These parotoid glands contain a nasty poison that irritates the mouths of some predators and often the skin of humans. So toads may not cause warts, but they can cause other nasties. It's best not to handle these critters—warty or not!

TOE WART CHIN WART NOSE WART FINGER WART BIG WART

WARTS

Cute Animal SUPERLATIVES

Funky features. Super senses. Sensational speed. No doubt, all animals are cool. But whether they've got goofy grins, funky hair, or endless energy, some species are extra adorable. Here are 15 of the cutest creatures on Earth.

FURRIEST

Thick, white fur helps polar bears blend in with the ice and snow of their Arctic habitat. This fur even grows on the bottom of their paws! It gives them a better grip on the ice and protection from frozen surfaces.

BEST ACROBAT

An inchworm has a funny way of walking: With legs at both ends of its body but none in the middle, it shifts from the front end to go forward, creating an awesome arch with its body as it moves.

MOST COLORFUL

The rainbow finch's funky feathers make this bird a standout on the grasslands of Australia. The hue of its head, which can be black, yellow, red, and orange, varies from bird to bird.

BEST STRETCH

The gerenuk, found in East Africa, is known to stand on its hind legs and stretch its slender neck to get hard-to-reach leaves on bushes and shrubs.

BEST COAT

Blizzard in the forecast? *Snow* problem! The golden snub-nosed monkey, found high in the mountains of central China, has a thick, furry coat and tail. They keep it warm in winter, making this primate ready for any weather.

BEST SPIKES

The lowland streaked tenrec may be tiny, but its spiky exterior poses a big threat to predators. Found only in Madagascar, this mini mammal is about the size of a hedgehog and will shoot its barbs into an animal when under attack.

BEST HAIR DAY

The Polish chicken sometimes goes by the nickname of "top hat" because of the funky feathers at the top of its head, or crest. Its unique appearance made it a prized bird among the rich and royalty in the 1700s. Despite its name, the breed known today comes from the Netherlands.

LONGEST DROP

Talk about a grand entrance: A baby giraffe falls about six feet (1.8 m) from its mom during birth before hitting the ground.

GREAT GLIDER

A Siberian flying squirrel can catch some major air. Using a flap of skin that stretches between its forelegs and hind legs like a parachute and its long, flat tail to balance, the squirrel can cover the length of a football field in one giant leap.

EARLY WALKER

Found in northern Canada, Greenland, Russia, Scandinavia, and Alaska, U.S.A., the sure-footed muskox can stand up, follow its mom, and keep up with its herd just hours after being born. This early start keeps the calf protected from potential predators.

BEST TRANSFORMATION

Think pink! The rosy maple moth may wind up with coloring that looks a lot like a fuzzy pink and yellow tennis ball, but it doesn't begin that way. It actually starts out as a caterpillar known as the greenstriped mapleworm.

BEST SNUGGLER

The smallest raptor in Africa, African pygmy falcons only grow to be about the length of a pencil. To stay warm in winter, these pint-size predators spend up to 15 hours a day snuggling together in their nests.

BEST STRIPES

The ribbon seal's unique black-and-white pattern sets it apart on the sea ice of Alaska, U.S.A., and Russia. Some scientists think the markings may act as camouflage, helping the seals blend into the shadows on ice floes.

BEST WARNING

If you spot a poison dart frog in the wild, watch out! These teeny amphibians are among the world's most toxic animals. Their brightly colored skin—which can be yellow, gold, copper, red, green, blue, or black—sends a message to predators to stay away.

SWEETEST RIDE

When common loon chicks hatch, they're almost immediately on the go—Mom carries her little ones on her back to protect them from predators. Once grown, loons can dive nearly 250 feet (76 m) and hold their breath for up to eight minutes as they fish.

WHAT IS Taxonomy?

Because our planet has billions and billions of living things called organisms, people need a way of classifying them. Scientists created a system called taxonomy, which helps to classify all living things into ordered groups. By putting organisms into categories, we are better able to understand how they are the same and how they are different. There are eight levels of taxonomic classification, beginning with the broadest group, called a domain, followed by kingdom, down to the most specific group, called a species.

Biologists divide life based on evolutionary history, and they place organisms into three domains depending on their genetic structure: Archaea, Bacteria, and Eukarya. (See page 197 for "The Three Domains of Life.")

SAMPLE CLASSIFICATION
RED PANDA

Domain:	Eukarya
Kingdom:	Animalia
Phylum:	Chordata
Class:	Mammalia
Order:	Carnivora
Family:	Ailuridae
Genus:	*Ailurus*
Species:	*fulgens*

TIP:
Here's a sentence to help you remember the classification order:
Did King Phillip Come Over For Good Soup?

Where do animals come in?

Animals are a part of the Eukarya domain, which means they are organisms made of cells with nuclei. More than one million species of animals, including humans, have been named. Like all living things, animals can be divided into smaller groups, called phyla. Most scientists believe there are more than 30 phyla into which animals can be grouped based on certain scientific criteria, such as body type or whether or not the animal has a backbone. It can be pretty complicated, so another, less complicated system groups animals into two categories: vertebrates and invertebrates.

HEDGEHOG

BY THE NUMBERS

There are 15,772 vulnerable or endangered animal species in the world. The list includes:

- 1,327 mammals, such as the snow leopard, the polar bear, and the fishing cat

- 1,481 birds, including the Steller's sea eagle and the black-banded plover

- 3,280 fish, such as the Mekong giant catfish

- 1,587 reptiles, including the Round Island day gecko

- 1,959 insects, such as the Macedonian grayling

- 2,444 amphibians, such as the emperor newt

- And more, including 218 arachnids, 743 crustaceans, 234 sea anemones and corals, 211 bivalves, and 2,123 snails and slugs

ROUND ISLAND DAY GECKO

Vertebrates
Animals WITH Backbones

Fish are cold-blooded and live in water. They breathe with gills, lay eggs, and usually have scales.

Amphibians are cold-blooded. Their young live in water and breathe with gills. Adults live on land and breathe with lungs.

Reptiles are cold-blooded and breathe with lungs. They live both on land and in water.

Birds are warm-blooded and have feathers and wings. They lay eggs, breathe with lungs, and are usually able to fly. Some birds live on land, some in water, and some on both.

Mammals are warm-blooded and feed on their mothers' milk. They also have skin that is usually covered with hair. Mammals live both on land and in water.

BIRD: MANDARIN DUCK

AMPHIBIAN: POISON DART FROG

Invertebrates
Animals WITHOUT Backbones

Sponges are a very basic form of animal life. They live in water and do not move on their own.

Echinoderms have external skeletons and live in seawater.

Mollusks have soft bodies and can live either in or out of shells, on land or in water.

Arthropods are the largest group of animals. They have external skeletons, called exoskeletons, and segmented bodies with appendages. Arthropods live in water and on land.

Worms are soft-bodied animals with no true legs. Worms live in soil.

Cnidaria live in water and have mouths surrounded by tentacles.

MOLLUSK: MAGNIFICENT CHROMODORIS NUDIBRANCH

SPONGE: SEA SPONGE

ARTHROPOD: PRAYING MANTIS

Cold-Blooded
versus
Warm-Blooded

Cold-blooded animals, also called ectotherms, get their heat from outside their bodies.

Warm-blooded animals, also called endotherms, keep their body temperatures level regardless of the temperature of their environment.

45

COMEBACK CRITTER:

GOLDEN LION TAMARIN

Scientists help these primates reclaim their forest home.

A family of golden lion tamarins is on the move. With two babies on his back and his mate beside him, the father tamarin reaches for a branch in Brazil's Atlantic Forest. Just a few years ago, this land was a treeless cattle pasture. But conservationists knew that if more forest was lost, then the golden lion tamarins— which live wild nowhere else on Earth—would be gone, too.

DISAPPEARING FORESTS

The Atlantic Forest was once about the size of Egypt. But in the 1500s, European traders and settlers started cutting down the trees to build ships and make room for settlements. Then, over the past century, farmers cut down more trees to clear land for crops until the forest was less than 10 percent of its original size.

Golden lion tamarins spend most of their time in the tree canopy, using branches to travel in search of food and mates. As the forest shrank, habitats became cut off from each other—and so did the primates. By the 1970s, concerned biologists estimated that only about 200 golden lion tamarins were left in the Atlantic Forest.

MONKEY BOOT CAMP

Conservationists gathered at the Smithsonian's National Zoo in Washington, D.C., in 1972 to develop a plan to save the species in the wild. Some zoos already had golden lion tamarins in captivity; all they had to do was breed more tamarins, then prepare some of the families to return to the wild. How? "We sent them to boot camp," says Kenton Kerns, assistant curator of small mammals at the National Zoo.

During several summers following 1972, zookeepers around the world let tamarins out of their enclosures to hang out in the trees. Staff provided each family with a nest to sleep in and sweet potatoes to munch on, and kept watch to

An adult golden lion tamarin is about the size of a squirrel.

GOLDEN LION TAMARIN FATHERS OFTEN CARRY THEIR BABIES ON THEIR BACKS IN BETWEEN FEEDINGS.

GOLDEN LION TAMARIN TWINS HANG ON TO THEIR FATHER AT GERMANY'S DUISBURG ZOO.

ATLANTIC OCEAN

SOUTH AMERICA

PACIFIC OCEAN

Where golden lion tamarins live

BRAZIL

BRAZIL

ATLANTIC OCEAN

ATLANTIC OCEAN

The golden lion tamarin is featured on a banknote in Brazil.

A GOLDEN LION TAMARIN LEAPS FROM ONE BRANCH TO ANOTHER IN ITS BRAZILIAN FOREST HOME.

make sure they didn't leave the grounds. "The free-range lifestyle taught the tamarins how to find insects and navigate branches," Kerns says. In 1983, the first group of tamarins was ready to return to Brazil's forests.

While the monkeys were in training, Brazil's Golden Lion Tamarin Association was busy restoring the tamarins' habitat. The group bought land from private owners and worked with farmers to plant trees on their property, connecting patches of forest and protecting more than 40 square miles (103 sq km) of habitat. The organization also gave local citizens jobs managing tree nurseries and trained teachers on environmental issues. "People were proud to have tamarins on their land," says Denise Rambaldi, former director of the Golden Lion Tamarin Association.

GOING GREEN

About 2,500 golden lion tamarins now live in the Atlantic Forest. About a third of them are descended from 147 captive-born tamarins from the zoo program.

But conservationists aren't done. They continue to reforest the land and inspire young people to protect the animals. Says Lou Ann Dietz, founding director of Save the Golden Lion Tamarin: "Seeing tamarin families chirping and jumping around in the trees overhead, their fur reflecting the sunlight like fire, makes it all worth it."

SUN BEAR RESCUE

How kind caretakers helped an orphaned cub return to the wild

These bears are named for the golden or white "rising sun" patch on their chests, which experts think might help the bears seem bigger than they are.

three-month-old sun bear huddles alone in a metal cage. A few days ago, poachers snatched the cub from the wild and brought her to a town in Malaysia, an island country in Southeast Asia, where she was sold as a pet, which is illegal. Now the orphan is stressed and hungry. If she stays in the cage, she may not survive.

BEAR AID

That's when caretakers from the Bornean Sun Bear Conservation Centre step in. They give the cub a name—Natalie—and take her in, giving her a special milk with extra protein, plus plenty of comfort and care. Within a few weeks, Natalie grows strong enough to head outside with a caretaker. She even climbs a tree! Soon, she joins three other bears in an outdoor enclosure. Together, the bears lounge, play, and learn to forage for their favorite treats of termites, earthworms, and honey.

WILD AGAIN

After five years at the rescue center, Natalie is ready to be released back into the wild. A team of veterinarians gives the hundred-pound (45-kg) bear one last checkup before fitting her with a tracking collar so that they can watch where she goes for the first few months. Her rescuers fly her by helicopter in a crate to a protected wildlife reserve where people don't live. They use a long rope to open Natalie's crate from afar. She bursts out into the woods—finally a free bear again.

Scientists have spotted mother sun bears cradling cubs in their arms while walking on their hind legs.

WONG SIEW TE FEEDS NATALIE A SPECIAL MILK TO HELP HER GAIN WEIGHT.

WONG WATCHES OVER NATALIE LIKE HER MOTHER WOULD HAVE IN THE WILD.

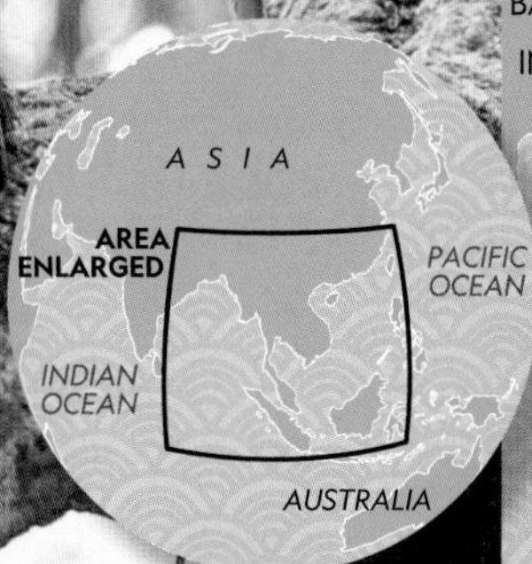

A S I A

BANGLADESH

INDIA

MYANMAR (BURMA)

LAOS

THAILAND

VIETNAM

CAMBODIA

South China Sea

INDIAN OCEAN

BRUNEI

MALAYSIA

INDONESIA

Where sun bears live

ASIA

AREA ENLARGED

PACIFIC OCEAN

INDIAN OCEAN

AUSTRALIA

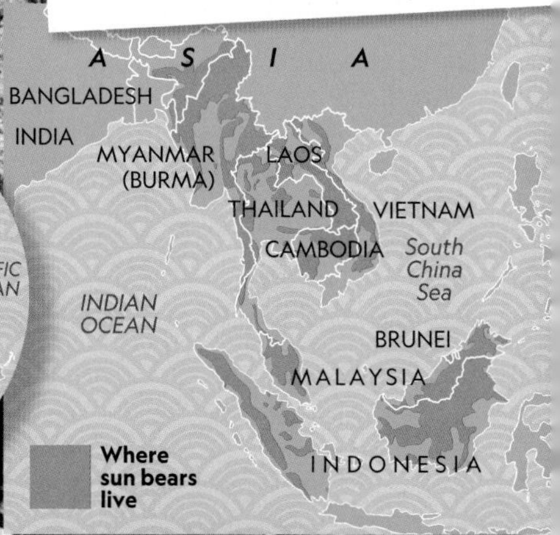

SharkFest

Dive in to join the party with these **5** surprising sharks.

Not all sharks are gigantic, toothy eating machines. Among the 500 species, there are a few surprising sharks. Some have teeth so small that they can't take a bite out of anything. Others are practically vegetarian! Discover five species of sharks with mind-blowing traits.

A group of sharks is called a shiver.

1 Fishy Friends: Lemon Sharks

TWO LEMON SHARKS HANG OUT NEAR THE BAHAMA ISLANDS.

Love hanging out with your BFF? So do lemon sharks! Young lemon sharks often stick together for protection from larger sharks and other predators. Scientists say this species hangs out with the same friends for years. And when scientists studied the pups in a predator-free environment, these sharks still chose to swim together rather than alone. Maybe these fish need matching friendship bracelets.

2 Green Glowers: Chain Catsharks

WHAT YOU SEE

WHAT CHAIN CATSHARKS SEE

TO CAPTURE THIS IMAGE, SCIENTISTS BUILT A CAMERA THAT SEES THE WORLD LIKE THIS CATSHARK DOES.

Through your eyes, the chain catshark seems to have brownish yellow skin with black chain-shaped markings. But to another chain catshark swimming 1,600 to 2,000 feet (488 to 610 m) below the surface, the fish glows in the dark! Pigments in the sharks' skin absorb the blue light in the ocean and reflect it as green. These sharks have special cells in their eyes—called receptors—to see it. Because the glow patterns are different for males and females, scientists think these shy sharks use this ability to attract mates.

3 Salad Snackers: Bonnethead Sharks

A BONNETHEAD SHARK EXPLORES THE WATERS OF THE FLORIDA KEYS.

Bonnethead sharks love their greens. Unlike almost all other sharks, which are carnivores, the bonnetheads' digestive system allows them to absorb nutrients from plants. Scientists aren't sure if bonnetheads intentionally snack on plants, or if they're accidentally ingested while scooping up shellfish hiding in the seagrass.

4 Ocean Oldies: Greenland Sharks

A Greenland shark swimming through deep, freezing Arctic water today might have been born when George Washington became the first president of the United States! This shark species can live for nearly 300 years—and possibly as many as 500 years. That's the longest of any vertebrate (an animal with a backbone). Experts think their icy cold habitat and slow lifestyle (a Greenland shark's heart beats only once every 12 seconds; yours beats about once a second) might be their secret to growing seriously old.

A GREENLAND SHARK SWIMS BELOW THE ARCTIC OCEAN ICE, OFF THE COAST OF CANADA.

Sharks have been on Earth longer than trees.

5 Gentle Giants: Whale Sharks

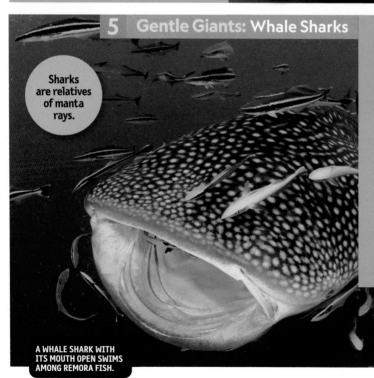

Sharks are relatives of manta rays.

A whale shark's mouth is so wide that a 10-year-old kid could fit inside. But don't worry: These easygoing sharks stick to a diet of tiny shrimplike plankton about as small as a few grains of sand. The largest fish in the world, whale sharks can be longer than a school bus and weigh 50,000 pounds (22,680 kg). They feed by swimming slowly with their mouths open, filtering plants and animals from the water.

A WHALE SHARK WITH ITS MOUTH OPEN SWIMS AMONG REMORA FISH.

UNIC☉RNS

OF THE SEA

SCIENTISTS TRY TO SOLVE THE MYSTERY OF THE NARWHAL'S GIANT TUSK.

Chilly water laps against an iceberg in the Arctic Ocean. Suddenly, a pod of narwhals—a species of whale that sports a unicorn-like horn on its head—emerges from the sea near the iceberg's edge.

Narwhals live in the Arctic Ocean. Like most whales, they're jumbo-size—up to 3,500 pounds (1,588 kg)—and surface to breathe. And like some whale species such as orcas, they live in pods. (Narwhals usually have 15 to 20 in a group.) But a narwhal has one thing that no other whale does: a giant tusk growing out of its noggin.

For centuries people have been trying to figure out what this tusk—actually an enlarged tooth—is used for. Scientists have come up with a couple theories that may help solve this gnawing puzzle.

TUSK, TUSK

A narwhal's swordlike tusk first pokes from its jaw through the animal's upper lip when it's about three months old. This is the only tooth the whale develops. Over time, the tusk can grow to be half the length of the whale's body. New research shows that narwhals may use these long appendages to snag prey like arctic cod, using quick jabs to stun the fish before they eat them.

TOOTH SLEUTHS

Another theory is that male narwhals use the tooth to attract females. Similar to a peacock's flashy feathers, the tusk makes them stand out to potential mates. The animals have been observed scraping their tusks together, as though they are in a fencing match. This may be a way for male members of the pod to identify one another.

There's still plenty that scientists don't know about narwhals, and they will continue to look for answers. In the meantime, it appears that these mysterious whales still have a few secrets up their tusks.

SURFACING ABOVE WATER, A GROUP OF NARWHALS TAKES A BREATH OF AIR.

THIS POD OF MALES SWIMS THROUGH ARCTIC WATERS.

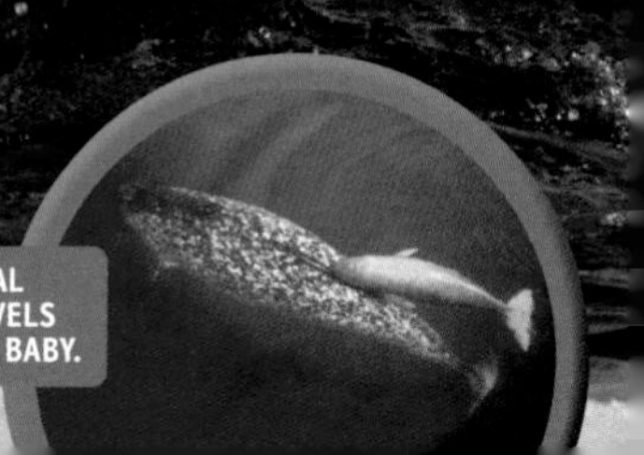

A NARWHAL MOM TRAVELS WITH HER BABY.

4 GNARLY NUDIBRANCHS

1 YOU ARE WHAT YOU EAT

Near the rocky shores of California, U.S.A., and Mexico's Baja California, a neon **Spanish shawl** nudibranch is hard to miss crawling on corals or fluttering through open water. This flashy finger-length slug gets its bright color by recycling pigments from its favorite food, tiny plantlike jellyfish known as hydroids.

LIKE OYSTERS AND CLAMS, NUDIBRANCHS ARE MOLLUSKS. BUT THESE SEA SLUGS DON'T HAVE SHELLS.

2 DEADLY SURFER

The thumbnail-size **blue dragon** cruises tropical oceans, using a stomach bubble to float on the surface while it searches for its favorite snack: Portuguese man-of-wars. But watch out! The dragon stores the poison it ingests from its prey in the tips of its frilly blue fingers.

3 PATTERN PLAY

Fluorescent stripes and polka dots turn the ***Nembrotha kubaryana***'s costume into a can't-miss warning sign for potential predators. Distinguished by its often orange edging, this nudibranch lives in tropical western Pacific and Indian Ocean waters and can grow up to 4.7 inches (12 cm) long.

4 SPOTS, HORNS, AND WINGS

Its frilly pigtails, mustache, and daisy-shaped spots make ***Bornella anguilla*** look more like a cartoon character than a pinkie finger–length sea slug. This nudibranch, named for its eel-like way of swimming (*anguilla* means "eel" in Latin), lives in the tropical waters of the western Pacific and Indian Oceans.

53

HUMPBACK WHALES RELY ON TEAMWORK TO HUNT, COORDINATING THEIR ACTIONS AS THEY CIRCLE IN ON THEIR PREY.

HUMPBACK WHALES typically **TRAVEL SOLO,** but they do join up during feeding sessions.

Known as the **"SONGSTERS OF THE SEAS,"** male humpback whales **SING COMPLEX SONGS** with repeated patterns.

This behavior, known as bubble-net feeding, allows the whales to disorient their prey by blowing bubbles in a spiral around a school of fish. The ring of bubbles forces the fish to the surface, where other humpbacks await and can then gulp the fish down.

Humpback whales eat up to **3,000 POUNDS** (1,360 kg) **OF FOOD A DAY,** including **SMALL FISH** and **TINY CRUSTACEANS.**

Each summer, Pacific humpbacks **MIGRATE FROM HAWAII, U.S.A.,** to their **FEEDING GROUNDS NEAR ALASKA, U.S.A.—** one of the longest migrations in the animal world.

Sit! Stay! Swim!

Surprising ways sea lions can seem like dogs

Sea lions use their whiskers, called vibrissae (pronounced VEYE-bree-see), to detect the movements of nearby fish.

A PAIR OF AUSTRALIAN SEA LIONS CHECK OUT A PHOTOGRAPHER'S CAMERA NEAR PORT LINCOLN, AUSTRALIA.

Hundreds of Australian sea lions have gathered together along the Australian coast. Some are sprawled out on the beach, sunning themselves. Others bark as they chase one another in the surf. Minus their flippers, these animals could fit right in at a dog park.

These marine mammals actually do remind some people of our furry pooch pals. "Sea lions are curious and playful, which is very doglike," says Deena Weisberg, a researcher who studies human and sea lion interactions on the Galápagos Islands in the Pacific Ocean. "Even when they're in the water, they behave very similarly to dogs." So should sea lions really be called sea *dogs* instead? Check out these five behaviors to decide.

They hang out in packs—er, rafts.

Hundreds of Steller sea lions are squeezed together on a beach in Alaska, U.S.A. Just when you'd think more sea lions couldn't possibly squish themselves into the group, called a raft, another pup wedges itself in. Sea lions are social animals that prefer to spend time in pairs or groups. And like dogs that share a home with cats, sea lions can interact with other animals in their ocean home. They've been spotted swimming with whales and sharing beaches with seals.

A GALÁPAGOS SEA LION BARKS ON A BEACH IN ECUADOR, A COUNTRY IN SOUTH AMERICA.

They bark—loudly.

If you've ever walked by a dog park, you know how loud a few barking dogs can be. When Galápagos sea lions bark, they sound similar—except there are hundreds of them! Like dogs, sea lions bark to get another animal's attention, or because they're excited or angry. But sometimes they bark to see which can be the loudest. The winning sea lion gets the best spot on the beach, which increases a male's chance of mating.

They play "fetch" (sort of).

Dogs chase tennis balls and chew on squeaky bones. Sea lions love to play, too, but their toys are colorful playthings found in the ocean. That could be anything from picking up sea stars, scooping up shells, trying to find an octopus hiding in the rocks, or chasing down fish for lunch. Sea lions love staying active ... just like dogs!

A CALIFORNIA SEA LION PLAYS WITH A SEA STAR IN THE SEA OF CORTEZ NEAR MEXICO.

A CALIFORNIA SEA LION CHECKS OUT A DIVER OFF THE COAST OF MEXICO.

They have a *lot* of energy.

When a dog needs to burn energy, its owner takes it for a long walk or a sprint around the yard. Sea lions "porpoise," or swim at fast speeds, zooming out of the water to dive like, well, a porpoise. One of the fastest marine mammals, sea lions go far. They'll swim several miles away and back again on the same day!

Male sea lions are called bulls, females are called cows, and babies are pups.

They ♥ humans.

Like dogs, sea lions, especially pups, are naturally curious. They'll waddle toward people on beaches or check out swimmers to get a better look. Underwater, sea lions will inspect scuba divers and their gear by nudging them. They can also be aggressive, so if one approaches you, stay calm and keep as much distance as possible until it gets bored and swims away.

FOXES ON ICE

Clever arctic foxes survive snow, ice, and freezing cold temperatures.

Not far from the North Pole, an arctic fox trots across the sea ice on a winter walkabout. It's been days since her last meal, and the whipping wind is relentless. She digs a hollow in the snow, curls up her cat-size body, and wraps her tail across her body and face to stay warm. Her fur acts like a warm sleeping bag, keeping her snug as temperatures dip below 0°F (-18°C). But warm fur alone might not keep this fox alive during the polar winter. Other freeze-defying strategies make this animal a champion of the cold.

FINDING FOOD

Arctic foxes prefer to eat small rodents called lemmings, but when times are tough, they'll take what they can get. This may be scraps of a seal that a polar bear has killed, or crabs and algae stuck to the bottom of ice. Sometimes, they'll stash dead lemmings near their dens for leaner times.

LEMMING

KEEPING WARM

In the toughest temps, this female fox digs a snow den and hunkers down for up to two weeks. She can slow her heart rate and metabolism to avoid burning energy—similar to hibernation but not as long lasting. The fox's short legs provide heat exchange between warm blood flowing down from the body and cold blood flowing up from the legs.

When the fox emerges, she listens for scurrying sounds under the snow. Quietly, she takes a few steps, and then dives into the snow. Her head emerges with a brown fur ball in her mouth. With the energy tank refilled, this arctic fox has a better chance of making it through the long, dark winter.

NINJA GIRAFFES

These animals have some seriously stealthy moves.

You might not think giraffes would have much in common with ninja, skilled combatants who prowled through 15th-century Japan on spy missions. After all, giraffes move awkwardly, and their superlong necks hardly seem stealthy. But these hoofed creatures are surprisingly sleek and agile. Discover how giraffes kick it up a notch, ninja style.

HIDE-AND-SEEK

Often hired by rulers who were competing for power, ninja would dress up as farmers or merchants to spy on their leader's opponent. Giraffes may have a distinctive appearance, but they sport the perfect camouflage for blending into their surroundings. Their brown spots look like the shadows created by sunlight shining through the trees, keeping them protected from predators.

THE NEED FOR SPEED

Ninja trained to become swift runners so they could easily slip away from foes during a chase. Giraffes are also excellent sprinters, using their long, muscular legs. At full gallop, these animals can reach 35 miles an hour (56 km/h), which helps them evade predators, like lions.

SPECTACULAR SENSES

People once believed that ninja could see in the dark and hear tiny movements. This likely wasn't true for ninja, but giraffes really do have superb vision and hearing. Using their keen eyesight, they can spot a moving animal more than a half mile (0.8 km) away. They also hear noises that humans can't detect. Could giraffes be even better warriors than ninja?

WEAPONS MASTERS

When ninja came face-to-face with their rivals, they used swords and daggers to defeat the enemy. Giraffes have their own built-in weapons: hooves with sharp edges. In fact, a giraffe kick can be deadly to other giraffes and predators. Two male giraffes might also fight for dominance by clubbing each other with their heavy heads and necks.

A RED-EYED TREE FROG SITS ON A PLANT SHOOT IN THE SOUTH AMERICAN COUNTRY OF COSTA RICA.

Earth is home to more than 6,000 species of frogs, many of which aren't much bigger than a coin. But these small amphibians possess some big surprises. Check out how five frogs use everything from their ears to their webbed feet to live their best life.

FROG Squad

These awesome amphibian features will turn you into a frog fan.

EYE SURPRISE

Appearing to have its eyes closed, a red-eyed tree frog sits on a branch. The frog, which lives in rainforests ranging from southern Mexico all the way down to the northwestern tip of Colombia in South America, may look like it's asleep, but it is observing its surroundings, thanks to a translucent eyelid. This allows the amphibian to spy on its habitat and look out for predators, like birds, snakes, and large spiders. When the frog senses movement, it opens its special eyelids to reveal its bright red eyeballs—in hopes of startling a hungry predator.

Closed

A SEE-THROUGH EYELID LETS RED-EYED TREE FROGS CHECK OUT THEIR SURROUNDINGS WHILE THEY REST.

Open

OPEN WIDE! RED-EYED TREE FROGS REVEAL THEIR BRIGHT RED EYES TO ALARM PREDATORS.

TINY EARS, BIG NOSE

It's almost impossible to hear anything over a thundering waterfall—unless you're a hole-in-the-head frog living in a rainforest in Southeast Asia. This frog is named for markings that look like, well, holes in its head. But the *actual* holes are for ears that give it super hearing.

The hole-in-the-head frog is one of just two frog species that can croak out and hear ultrasonic calls, or calls at a pitch too high to be heard by humans and other animals. This adaptation likely allows the frogs to communicate above rumbling rivers and streams in their habitat.

HOLE-IN-THE-HEAD FROGS CAN ONLY BE FOUND IN ONE PLACE ON THE PLANET: THE SOUTHEAST ASIAN ISLAND OF BORNEO.

MEGAMOUTH

African bullfrogs have huge mouths! When open, their mouths stretch approximately five inches (13 cm) wide, or over half the size of their eight-inch (20-cm)-long bodies. And these bullfrogs can fit plenty inside those mouths: Using their strong tongues to pull in prey like rodents, birds, and lizards, they pierce the animal with toothlike structures called odontodes, located on their lower jaws. Sharp teeth on the roof of a bullfrog's mouth keep the prey in place. Now the frog can take its time and enjoy the meal. Um, yum?

AN AFRICAN BULLFROG EYES ITS NEXT MEAL: A GIANT AFRICAN MILLIPEDE.

WEBBED FEET TO BEAT

In a rainforest in Southeast Asia, a Wallace's flying frog eyes a lower branch on a nearby tree. Rather than climbing down one tree and up the other to reach the branch, the frog simply takes flight. It splays out its four webbed feet as it leaps down. Membranes between its toes trap air from underneath to form tiny parachute-like shapes. Loose skin flaps on either side of the frog's body catch more air as it falls. It glides to the other tree before making a smooth landing.

Wide, sticky toe pads create cushions to soften the impact as Wallace's flying frogs land. These frogs have been spotted gliding 50 feet (15 m). "They probably glide that far to escape predators," said Phil Bishop, a scientific adviser for the Amphibian Survival Alliance. Traveling the extra distance beats becoming a snack.

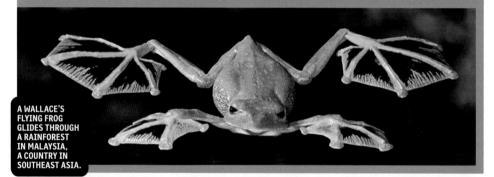

A WALLACE'S FLYING FROG GLIDES THROUGH A RAINFOREST IN MALAYSIA, A COUNTRY IN SOUTHEAST ASIA.

COOLEST SKIN FOR THE WIN

Up close, a dyeing poison frog's blue, yellow, and black hues are hard to miss. But this amphibian, found in the northeastern rainforests of South America, doesn't have to worry much about predators. Its skin is packed with poison that can paralyze or even kill other animals; the colors are a warning that the frog is toxic if eaten. The poison from certain species historically has been used on the tips of hunting darts, giving poison frogs their other common name, "poison dart frogs." *Yikes.*

AT CLOSE RANGE, IT'S HARD TO MISS A DYEING POISON FROG'S BOLD COLOR PATTERN.

SUPER SNAKES

Snakes are masters of disguise, skilled hunters, and champion eaters. More than 3,000 species of these reptiles slither around the world. Check out these surprising facts about snakes.

AMAZON TREE BOA

AFRICAN SAW-SCALED VIPER

SNAKES SMELL WITH THEIR TONGUES.

Smell that mouse? A snake uses its tongue to smell. It flicks its long, forked tongue to pick up chemical molecules from the air, ground, or water. The tongue carries the smelly molecules back to two small openings—called the Jacobson's organ—in the roof of the snake's mouth. Cells in the Jacobson's organ analyze the scent. Mmm, lunch!

SNAKE VENOM CAN KILL.

By sinking two hollow, pointy fangs into their prey, many snakes inject venom to paralyze or kill victims before devouring them. Africa's puff adder is thought to be one of the world's deadliest snakes. Up to six feet (1.8 m) long and weighing as much as 13 pounds (6 kg), the puff adder strikes fast. Its venom can cause severe pain, tissue damage, and even death in humans. It's a snake to be respected ... from a distance.

PUFF ADDER

SNAKES CHANGE THEIR SKIN.

Snakes literally grow out of their skin. Every few months, most start rubbing against the ground or tree branches. Starting at the mouth, a snake slithers out of its too-tight skin. Like a sock, the skin comes off inside out. Voilà—the snake has a fresh, shiny look. Nice makeover.

GOLDEN TREE SNAKE

CONSTRICTORS GIVE WICKED HUGS.

Boas, anacondas, pythons, and other snakes called constrictors are amazing squeezers. This kind of snake wraps its muscular body around a victim and squeezes until the animal suffocates. The twisted talent comes from muscles attached to 200 or more vertebrae in a snake's backbone. (Humans are born with only 33 vertebrae.)

DIONE RAT SNAKE

DEADLY CUTIES

JAVAN SLOW LORIS

Nine species of slow lorises live throughout Southeast Asia.

This adorable animal has some seriously KILLER traits.

Don't be fooled by the crazy-cute slow loris. The snuggly looking creature is the only venomous primate on the planet—and its bite packs enough toxin to kill prey in just a few seconds. The toxin is also powerful enough to kill or severely harm humans, but it's very rare for the slow loris to bite people without first being provoked.

And venom isn't the only killer move the slow loris has. Check out three ways the adorable slow loris is actually downright dangerous.

KILLER LOOKS
A slow loris's sweet face markings might say "Oh, he-ey!" to you, but they say "Danger!" to other animals. To a potential predator like a large snake or hawk-eagle, the markings are like flashing red lights near the loris's mouth, warning that the loris could fight back with its deadly venom.

HIDDEN HUNTER
Huge eyes make slow lorises look harmlessly huggable. But these peepers also make them effective hunters. A special layer behind the retina called a tapetum lucidum (pronounced tuh-PEE-tum loo-SUH-dum) reflects light back through the retina and gives lorises better nighttime vision for nocturnal hunting.

TWICE AS TOXIC
Unlike other venomous animals that produce venom in one place, slow lorises produce toxins in two places: in their saliva and in a gland in their underarms. When lorises lick that gland and mix it with their venomous saliva, they cook up an even more toxic mixture they can inject with a single bite.

A JAVAN SLOW LORIS HANGS OUT IN THE TREE CANOPY OF JAVA, AN ISLAND IN INDONESIA.

SURF Pups

5 WAYS COASTAL WOLVES THRIVE BY THE SEA

Coastal wolves are valued in many Indigenous cultures; some groups consider them ancestors.

Wolves often howl in a chorus.

A wolf steps out onto a sandy beach. Catching a scent, it paws at the wet sand in search of a buried clam. *Crunch!* The wolf crushes the clam in its jaws and swallows. Still hungry, it splashes into the ocean waves and swims to a nearby island to find more food. Wolves on the beach might sound strange, but these special gray wolves have been living seaside for thousands of years. Known as coastal wolves, about 2,000 of these individuals make their homes among the islands and coastal rainforest of western British Columbia in Canada. (Another population lives in Southeast Alaska, U.S.A.) "Their environment is so different from that of any other wolf," wildlife researcher Chris Darimont says. "So they've had to adapt to this unique place." Check out five ways these howlers are living their best life on the beach.

1

BEACH HAIR, DON'T CARE

Unlike most gray wolves, coastal wolves' fur is often streaked with reddish orange highlights. The color matches seaweed found on the shore, likely helping to camouflage these predators as they hunt on the beach.

Coastal wolves also have less underfur than other gray wolves. The cottony fluff helps wolves living in snowy places like Montana, U.S.A., keep warm, but coastal wolves' habitat is so mild that they don't need the extra layer.

2

SEA SIZE

About the size of a German shepherd, coastal wolves are about 20 percent smaller than gray wolves living in North American forests. Scientists think it could be because these seafood-eaters don't need the extra strength. After all, coastal wolves are wrestling otters, not gigantic moose like their gray wolf cousins. "They aren't chasing massive prey, so they don't need the large body size to take them down," Darimont says.

A wolf's sense of smell is about a hundred times more sensitive than a human's.

SWIM TEAM CHAMPS

One small island usually isn't big enough for coastal wolves to find and eat the seven pounds (3 kg) of food they need each day. So the canines dog-paddle from island to island in search of more food. "They swim between islands like we walk on sidewalks," conservationist Ian McAllister says. And these wolves really are super swimmers. Scientists have spotted them on nearly every one of the thousand islands and rocky outcrops in the area, McAllister says, sometimes swimming up to 7.5 miles (12 km) in between each strip of land.

3

Some coastal wolves can get 90 percent of their diet from the sea.

4

SPLASHY SURPRISE

Gray wolves that live in open habitats like the tundra often hunt by chasing big, hoofed animals across a wide plain, Darimont says. But that style of hunting doesn't work on a coast that's full of thick rainforest or tiny islands too small to run across. Instead, they often sneak up on prey—then pounce. "The seals haul out of the ocean to get away from killer whales," McAllister says. "But on land, they're not safe from ambushing wolves."

5

SEAFOOD, PLEASE!

What's to eat? Coastal wolves use their powerful sense of smell to find whatever snacks the ocean served up that day. They might dig in the sand for crabs and clams, feast on fish eggs stuck to kelp, or sneak up on larger animals like sunbathing seals or otters.

Others get their fill of fish just from salmon. "They wait in the shallows where the salmons' backsides are poking out, then snap up the tastiest-looking fish they can find," Darimont says. A coastal wolf might scarf down 10 salmon in one morning. Talk about fish breath!

Bet You Didn't Know!

7 Bee Facts to Buzz About

HONEYBEE

1 Bees have a special **stomach** for **carrying nectar.**

2 Some bees may **sleep** on **flowers.**

3 A bee beats its **wings** up to **12,000 times each minute.**

4 Male bees can't **sting.**

5 In summer, a single **hive** can house up to **80,000 honeybees.**

6 The **alkali bee** can visit up to **6,000 flowers** a day.

7 Sweat bees like the **taste** of human perspiration.

SPIDERWEB STATS

A single spider can eat up to 2,000 insects every year. How do spiders catch all those tasty treats? Using silk from special glands called spinnerets, spiders weave sticky webs to trap their delicious prey. But this silk can do much more than simply catch dinner. Stick around and learn more about the incredible spiderweb.

.00004–.00016

INCH (.001–.004 mm)
Thickness of silk a spider uses to build webs

-76°F TO 302°F

(-60°C to 150°C)

The extreme range of temperatures that a spider's silk can withstand

82

FEET (25 m)

Diameter of webs woven by Darwin's bark spiders—the largest spiderwebs in the world!

ORB WEAVER SPIDER

2–8

Pairs of spinnerets, the glands a spider uses to make silk

5

Number of times stronger a spider's silk is compared to steel of the same diameter

Age of oldest spiderweb ever found embedded in amber

140 MILLION

YEARS OLD

BIG CATS

Not all wild cats are big cats, so what are big cats? To wildlife experts, they are tigers, lions, leopards, snow leopards, jaguars, cougars, and cheetahs. The first five are members of the genus *Panthera*. They can all unleash a mighty roar, and, as carnivores, they survive solely on the flesh of other animals. Thanks to powerful jaws; long, sharp claws; and daggerlike teeth, big cats are excellent hunters.

A lion cub plays on a fallen tree in Botswana.

The National Geographic Big Cats Initiative's goal is to stop the decline of lions and other big cats in the wild through research, conservation, education, and global awareness.
Parents and teachers:
For more information on this initiative, you can visit natgeo.org/bigcats with your young readers.

WHO'S WHO?

BIG CATS IN THE *PANTHERA* GENUS MAY HAVE a lot of features in common, but if you know what to look for, you'll be able to tell who's who in no time.

FUR

SNOW LEOPARD

A snow leopard's thick, spotted fur helps the cat hide in its mountain habitat, no matter the season. In winter its fur is off-white to blend in with the snow, and in summer it's yellowish gray to blend in with plants and the mountains.

JAGUAR

A jaguar's coat pattern looks similar to that of a leopard, as both have dark spots called rosettes. The difference? The rosettes on a jaguar's torso have irregularly shaped borders and at least one black dot in the center.

TIGER

Most tigers are orange-colored with vertical black stripes on their bodies. This coloring helps the cats blend in with tall grasses as they sneak up on prey. These markings are like fingerprints: No two stripe patterns are alike.

LION

Lions have a light brown, or tawny, coat and a tuft of black hair at the end of their tails. When they reach their prime, most male lions have shaggy manes that help them look larger and more intimidating.

LEOPARD

A leopard's yellowy coat has dark spots called rosettes on its back and sides. In leopards, the rosettes' edges are smooth and circular. This color combo helps leopards blend into their surroundings.

LEOPARD
66 to 176 pounds
(30 TO 80 KG)
4.25 to 6.25 feet long
(1.3 TO 1.9 M)

BENGAL TIGER
240 to 500 pounds
(109 TO 227 KG)
5 to 6 feet long
(1.5 TO 1.8 M)

JAGUAR
100 to 250 pounds
(45 TO 113 KG)
5 to 6 feet long
(1.5 TO 1.8 M)

SNOW LEOPARD
60 to 120 pounds (27 TO 54 KG)
4 to 5 feet long (1.2 TO 1.5 M)

AFRICAN LION
265 to 420 pounds
(120 TO 191 KG)
4.5 to 6.5 feet long
(1.4 TO 2 M)

Weirdest. Cat. Ever.

THE SERVAL MIGHT LOOK STRANGE, BUT THAT'S A GOOD THING WHEN IT COMES TO HUNTING.

SERVALS CAN CATCH UP TO 30 FROGS IN THREE HOURS WHILE HUNTING IN WATER.

SERVAL KITTENS STAY WITH MOM UP TO TWO YEARS BEFORE LIVING ON THEIR OWN.

Servals can chirp, purr, hiss, snarl, and growl.

A serval sits patiently in a grassy field, swiveling its head back and forth like a watchful owl. The predator is scanning the savanna for a meal not with its eyes, but with its oversize ears. An unseen rodent stirs under the thick brush, and the wild cat tenses. It crouches on its legs and feet before launching up and over the tall grass. Guided only by sound, the serval lands directly on the once invisible rat.

Thanks to its extra-long legs, stretched-out neck, and huge ears, the serval is sometimes called the "cat of spare parts." This wild cat might look weird to some people. "But put together, their bizarre-looking body parts make them really successful hunters," says Christine Thiel-Bender, a biologist who studies servals in their African home.

In fact, servals catch prey in more than half their attempts, making them one of the best hunters in the wild cat kingdom. That's about 20 percent better than lions hunting together in a pride.

ALL EARS

The serval's big ears are key to the animal's hunting success. Servals rely on sound more than any other sense when they're on the prowl. Thanks to their jumbo ears—the biggest of any wild cat's relative to body size—a serval can hear just about any peep on the savanna. (If a person had ears like a serval's, they'd be as big as dinner plates!) To make the most of their super hearing, servals avoid creating noise while hunting. So instead of stalking prey like some cats do, servals squat in clearings and sit still—sometimes for several hours—as they listen for food.

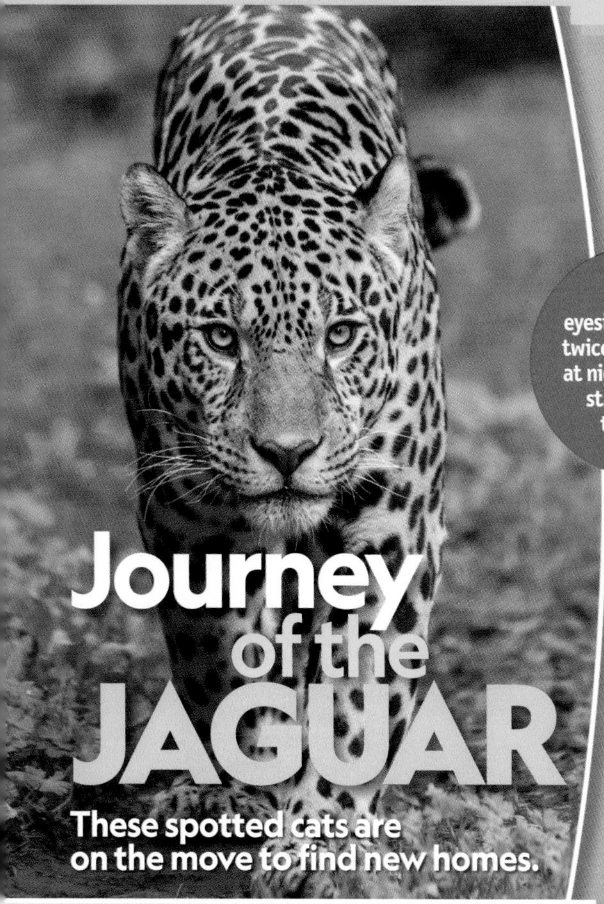

The jaguar once prowled through more than seven million square miles (18 million sq km) stretching through North and South America. But in the past century, things like cattle ranching and the growth of cities have cut this territory in half. Few jaguars have been seen in the United States, and their southern range now barely extends into Argentina. The separation of these pockets of jaguars means fewer mates will meet—and fewer cubs will be born each year.

A jaguar's eyesight is nearly twice as powerful at night to help it stalk prey in the dark.

Journey
of the
JAGUAR

These spotted cats are on the move to find new homes.

SAFE PASSAGE

Over the past decade or so, special corridors of land were set aside to allow jaguars to get from one habitat to another. But as humans have cleared trees, shrubs, and grass along these corridors, they've become more dangerous for the jaguars as they have nowhere to hide. As a result, wildlife ecologist Alan Rabinowitz launched the Jaguar Corridor Initiative (JCI) to protect the "superhighway" that the jaguars were using—and therefore their entire range.

HOME OF THE RANCH

Another key to keeping the jaguars safe? Educating farmers who live along the corridors. In the past, when jaguars traveled past a pasture of cattle, they may have tried to eat the easy prey, which would make the cats a target for ranchers protecting their herd. But thanks to new guidelines on keeping farm animals fenced in at night, both the cats and the livestock are safer.

A JAGUAR SWIMS ACROSS THE PARAGUAY RIVER IN BRAZIL.

Jaguar moms typically give birth to two to four cubs at a time.

A JAGUAR STALKS PREY IN BRAZIL'S CUIABÁ RIVER.

TIGERS in the Snow

These wild cats survive the cold of eastern Russia.

Many Amur tigers have beachfront access—they live in Russian forests on the edge of the Sea of Japan.

Silently moving through the trees, a tigress stalks her prey. Deep snow covers the ground, and with each step the big cat sinks to her belly. She knows the snow will muffle any sounds, so she can sneak up on a wild boar that is rooting around for pine nuts. A few yards away, the tiger pauses, crouches, and then launches her 280-pound (127-kg) body toward her prey. Snow sprays up with each leap as she prepares to pounce on the boar with her plate-size paws. A powdery cloud fills the air. Then the snow settles, revealing the three-foot (0.9-m)-long tail and orange, black, and white body. Now stained red, the tigress grasps the boar in her mouth.

She carries her catch behind some larch trees, and her two cubs join her from a nearby hill. Camouflaged in the trees, they were watching their mother hunt. Soon, they'll start hunting for themselves. But for now, they are content with the meal their mother has provided, followed by a nap.

These Siberian, or Amur, tigers live in the eastern reaches of Russia—farther north than any other tiger subspecies. A thick coat of fur insulates their bodies from the freezing winter temps. In summer, their coat blends in with the forest, making them nearly impossible to see.

HUNGER GAMES

The tiger trio is among some 600 Amur tigers that researchers think are left in the wild. As recently as 50 years ago, there were plenty of deer and wild boar, staples of a tiger's diet. Today, these prey animals are harder to find. People hunt

A TIGER CUB STICKS WITH MOM FOR AT LEAST 18 MONTHS.

them, and logging companies and fires destroy the forest where they live. Some tiger habitat is protected, but the cats wander beyond these safe zones in search of prey. Half of all tiger cubs die young because they are sick, killed by hunters, or orphaned. Cubs that survive leave Mom at about 18 months old, relying on the hunting skills they learned growing up. Sometimes a young male must travel far to find unclaimed land that has enough food. And odds are that his journey will take him through areas where people live.

TROUBLESHOOTING

It is late winter when the male tiger leaves his mother's care. When he scratches against a tree, he catches his paw on something. He's walked into a wire snare, and the more he moves, the tighter it gets. A little while later, he hears voices. People. They stay behind the trees, and one of them raises a gun. The tiger roars at the sharp pain in his backside, then lies down and falls asleep. He's been shot by a researcher's tranquilizer gun, not by a hunter. Unable to find enough food in the snowy forest, this tiger started taking livestock and dogs in a nearby town. Dale Miquelle and his team are called in to fix the problem. "Relocating them gives them a second chance," Miquelle says. Otherwise, the farmer would track down the tiger and shoot him.

The researchers quickly weigh and measure the tranquilized tiger. Then they fit a collar with a radio transmitter around his neck. This will let Miquelle's team keep track of the tiger's whereabouts for at least three years.

NEW TERRITORY

Two hours later, the tiger wakes up in the back of a truck about 150 miles (241 km) from the town. The cage gate opens, and the wild cat leaps out. Unfamiliar with the territory, he searches for signs of other tigers. He comes across a birch tree with a strong odor. Another male sprayed the tree and left scrape marks and urine on the ground to tell others "Occupied. Keep moving."

The young tiger walks on. Miquelle's team monitors his movements using signals from the radio collar. They hope he can find food, avoid other males, find his own territory, and eventually mate with a local female. The tiger spots a deer ahead. Melting snow drips from the trees, masking his footsteps as he ambushes his prey. His odds just got a little better.

THIS TIGER'S SCRATCHES ON TREES ARE MESSAGES FOR OTHER TIGERS.

In the 1930s, only about 30 Amur tigers were left in the wild.

ICE-COLD WATER QUENCHES THIS TIGER'S THIRST.

Naughty PETS

THE TUNA I ADDED TO THIS TEA MAKES IT VERY TASTY.

C'MON, LEMME IN. I DIDN'T ROLL IN THE GRASS THAT LONG.

NAME Bella

FAVORITE ACTIVITY
Fishing at teatime

FAVORITE TOY
Squiggly rubber worm bait

PET PEEVE Coffee

NAME Ed

FAVORITE ACTIVITY
Dyeing his fur green with grass stains

FAVORITE TOY Food coloring

PET PEEVE Brown winter grass

IT'S SO FUNNY WHEN THEY THINK I'M LOST IN THE COUCH.

REMOTE LEARNING ISN'T JUST FOR KIDS.

NAME Cullen

FAVORITE ACTIVITY
Playing hide-and-seek without his people knowing it

FAVORITE TOY Toilet paper tube to nibble on

PET PEEVE Locked cage

NAME Ito

FAVORITE ACTIVITY
Changing the virtual background

FAVORITE TOY
Mouse

PET PEEVE
Low battery power

PET TALES

Dog Protects Piglet

Do pets know their names?

Chew Barka

Hairy Pawter

Hörstel, Germany
Roland Adam wasn't sure what to do when he found an orphaned newborn Vietnamese potbellied pig alone and shivering on his farm. But Katjinga the Rhodesian ridgeback did. She snuggled up to the pint-size pig (now called Paulinchen), cleaning the pig with her tongue and nursing her as she would her own puppy. "Katjinga lay down, fed her, and kept her warm," Adam says. In fact, this isn't the first time Katjinga cuddled up with orphaned animals: She's also tended rabbits and ducks. "We even found her warming up one of our sheep that was sick," Adam says. Sounds like Katjinga was one protective pooch!

Yes—kind of. Pets don't speak human, but they do recognize sounds. One study has shown that pets know the difference between the names we've given them and similar-sounding words, even when said by a stranger. Scientists think that dogs and cats learn to listen for the sounds that make up their name because responding often means cuddles and treats. So why does your cat not always come when it's called? It likely knows its name—but it's probably ignoring you.

HoW TO
SPEAk
CaT

Come on, let's play!

Cats are on a roll. All around the globe, kitties now rank as the most popular pet. And no wonder: Everyone feels good when a friendly cat purrs, rubs against their legs, or snuggles in their lap.

But let's get one thing straight. Cats are not dogs! They look, act, and (we're pretty sure) think differently. Dogs depend on us to take care of them; cats maintain a lot of their wildness.

Because they're so independent, cats hide their feelings. Unless you know exactly what to look for, a happy cat and a miserable one can look very much the same. But cats do communicate. Check out how to read your cat's moods by recognizing four ways it "talks" to you.

Aah. This is the life.

THE PLAYFUL KITTEN

Kittens are always in the mood for fun. They spend almost every waking minute playing. They love to run and chase, pounce and wrestle, attack and retreat. At about seven weeks old, kittens learn the signs for inviting each other to play. Watch for a kitten with a relaxed, content look. That's its play face. Rolling onto its back or standing up on its hind legs are also signs that a cat's ready for fun. Holding its tail like a question mark and hopping sideways might be other ways of telling a playmate to let the games begin!

HAPPY CAT

You can tell a happy cat by its relaxed body, half-perked ears, and droopy whiskers. It'll greet you with a chipper "Hi, there" meow and a straight-up tail. Then it'll jump on your lap, purr loudly, and move its body under your hand. Keep your cat happy by petting it—just where it likes it.

Some of the best cat toys are free: a crumpled-up newspaper or a paper bag.

All cats, no matter the breed, are born with blue eyes. Their true color appears at about 12 weeks.

CAT ON THE HUNT

Shh! This cat is after something. You can tell by his intense stare, twitching tail, and forward-pointing ears and whiskers. All his senses are alert as he crouches low to the ground and pads silently toward his prey. Hunting is difficult, dangerous work. Humans have long admired cats for their courage and predatory skills. Without cats, early Egyptians would have lost much of their food supply to rats. So would sailors, who took the little rodent killers with them to sea, spreading the animals around the world. Your cat can hunt pesky houseflies or other insects that sneak into your home— keeping both you and your cat happy.

Cats hunt what they can get: rats in New York City; lizards in Georgia, U.S.A.; and baby turtles on Africa's Seychelles islands.

Heh, heh. He can't hear me coming.

Check out this book!

SPEAk CaT
A GUIDE TO DECODING CAT LANGUAGE

THE FRUSTRATED FELINE

A frustrated cat will have wide eyes and forward, pricked ears. It'll bat its paws, its teeth might chatter, and it may slowly thrash its tail. Like humans, cats get frustrated when they don't get what they expect. For instance, an indoor cat stares out the window at a bird, but she can't reach the prey outside. The longer the cat sits and watches, the greater her frustration, until she's ready to attack someone.

A cat can get frustrated often. But if you know the signs, you can turn your irritated cat into a contented kitty. When she's annoyed that she can't get to a bird, distract your feline by playing with a fishing-pole toy. Let your kitty catch the "mouse" at the end, and that bird will soon be forgotten.

The word for "cat" is *mao* in Chinese, *gatto* in Italian, *poes* in Dutch, and *kedi* in Turkish.

I'd rather be hunting.

77

Prehistoric TIMELINE

HUMANS HAVE WALKED on Earth for some 300,000 years, a mere blip in the planet's 4.5-billion-year history. A lot has happened during that time. Earth formed, and oxygen levels rose in the millions of years of the Precambrian time. The productive Paleozoic era gave rise to hard-shell organisms, vertebrates, amphibians, and reptiles.

Dinosaurs ruled Earth in the mighty Mesozoic. And 66 million years after dinosaurs became extinct, modern humans emerged in the Cenozoic era. From the first tiny mollusks to the dinosaur giants of the Jurassic and beyond, Earth has seen a lot of transformation.

THE PRECAMBRIAN TIME

4.5 billion to 541 million years ago

- Earth (and other planets) formed from gas and dust left over from a giant cloud that collapsed to form the sun. The giant cloud's collapse was triggered when nearby stars exploded.
- Low levels of oxygen made Earth a suffocating place.
- Early life-forms appeared.

THE PALEOZOIC ERA

541 million to 252 million years ago

- The first insects and other animals appeared on land.
- 450 million years ago (mya), the ancestors of sharks began to swim in the oceans.
- 430 mya, plants began to take root on land.
- More than 360 mya, amphibians emerged from the water.
- Slowly, the major landmasses began to come together, creating Pangaea, a single supercontinent.
- By 300 mya, reptiles had begun to dominate the land.

What Killed the Dinosaurs?

It's a mystery that's boggled the minds of scientists for centuries: What happened to the dinosaurs? Although various theories have bounced around, a recent study confirms that the most likely culprit is an asteroid or comet that created a giant crater. Researchers say that the impact set off a series of natural disasters like tsunamis, earthquakes, and temperature swings that plagued the dinosaurs' ecosystems and disrupted their food chains. This, paired with intense volcanic eruptions that caused drastic climate changes, is thought to be why half of the world's species—including the dinosaurs—died in a mass extinction.

DINO TIMES

THE MESOZOIC ERA

252 million to 66 million years ago

The Mesozoic era, or the age of the reptiles, consisted of three consecutive time periods (shown below). This is when the first dinosaurs began to appear. They would reign supreme for more than 150 million years.

TRIASSIC PERIOD

252 million to 201 million years ago

- The first mammals appeared. They were rodent-size.
- The first dinosaur appeared.
- Ferns were the dominant plants on land.
- The giant supercontinent of Pangaea began breaking up toward the end of the Triassic.

JURASSIC PERIOD

201 million to 145 million years ago

- Giant dinosaurs dominated the land.
- Pangaea continued its breakup, and oceans formed in the spaces between the drifting landmasses, allowing sea life, including sharks and marine crocodiles, to thrive.
- Conifer trees spread across the land.

CRETACEOUS PERIOD

145 million to 66 million years ago

- The modern continents developed.
- The largest dinosaurs developed.
- Flowering plants spread across the landscape.
- Mammals flourished, and giant pterosaurs ruled the skies over small birds.
- Temperatures grew more extreme. Dinosaurs lived in deserts, swamps, and forests from the Antarctic to the Arctic.

THE CENOZOIC ERA—TERTIARY PERIOD

66 million to 2.6 million years ago

- Following the dinosaur extinction, mammals rose as the dominant species.
- Birds continued to flourish.
- Volcanic activity was widespread.
- Temperatures began to cool, eventually ending in an ice age.
- The period ended with land bridges forming, which allowed plants and animals to spread to new areas.

DINO Classification

Classifying dinosaurs and all other living things can be a complicated matter, so scientists have devised a system to help with the process. Dinosaurs are put into groups based on a very large range of characteristics.

Scientists put dinosaurs into two major groups: the bird-hipped ornithischians and the lizard-hipped saurischians.

Ornithischian

"Bird-hipped"
(pubis bone in hips points backward)

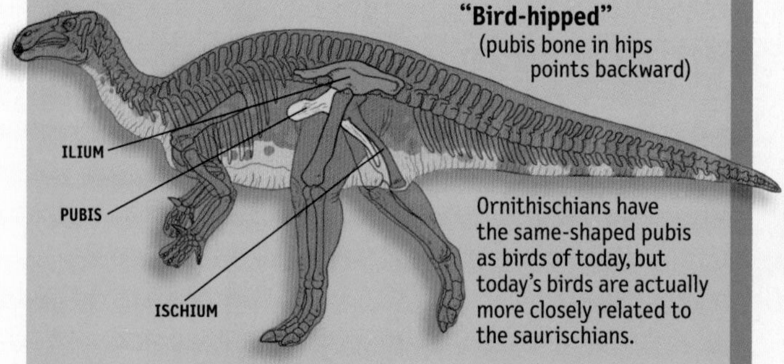

ILIUM

PUBIS

ISCHIUM

Ornithischians have the same-shaped pubis as birds of today, but today's birds are actually more closely related to the saurischians.

Example: *Styracosaurus*

Saurischian

"Lizard-hipped"
(pubis bone in hips points forward)

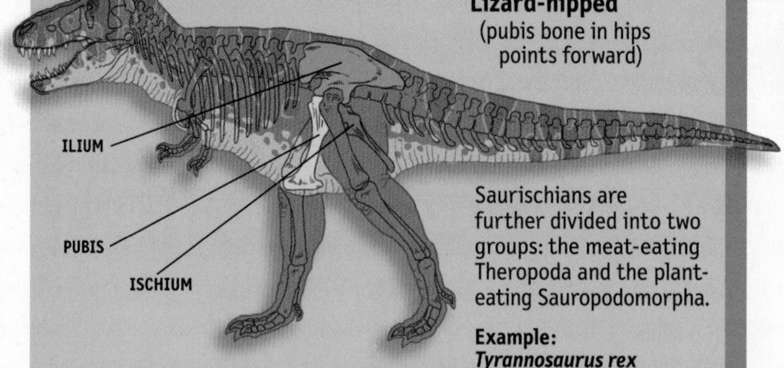

ILIUM

PUBIS

ISCHIUM

Saurischians are further divided into two groups: the meat-eating Theropoda and the plant-eating Sauropodomorpha.

Example: *Tyrannosaurus rex*

Within these two main divisions, dinosaurs are then separated into orders and then families, such as Stegosauria. Like other members of the Stegosauria, *Stegosaurus* had spines and plates along its back, neck, and tail.

VELOCIRAPTOR MEANS "SPEEDY THIEF."

THERE WERE NO T. REX IN SOUTH AMERICA.

TRICERATOPS HAD 800 TEETH.

IT TOOK A DINOSAUR EGG UP TO SIX MONTHS TO HATCH!

4 NEWLY DISCOVERED DINOS

Humans have been searching for—and discovering—dinosaur remains for hundreds of years. In that time, at least 1,000 species of dinos have been found all over the world, and thousands more may still be out there waiting to be unearthed. Recent finds include a *Yamatosaurus izanagii*, a hadrosaur discovered by an amateur fossil hunter in Japan.

1

Llukalkan aliocranianus
(Saurischian)

Name Meaning: *Llukalkan* means "one who causes fear" in the Mapuche Indigenous language.

Length: 16 feet (5 m)

Time Range: Late Cretaceous

Where: Argentina

2

Yamatosaurus izanagii
(Ornithischian)

Name Meaning: *Yamato* is the name for ancient Japan and *Izanagi* is the god who created the Japanese islands according to Japanese mythology.

Length: 23–26 feet (7–8 m)

Time Range: Late Cretaceous

Where: Japan

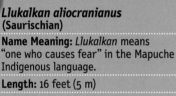

3

Tlatolophus galorum
(Ornithischian)

Name Meaning: *Tlatolophus* is a mix of two words—"word" in the Indigenous language Nahuatl and "crest" in Greek.

Length: 26.2–39.4 feet (8–12 m)

Time Range: Late Cretaceous

Where: Mexico

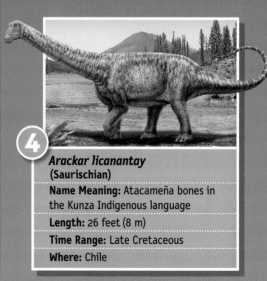

4

Arackar licanantay
(Saurischian)

Name Meaning: Atacameña bones in the Kunza Indigenous language

Length: 26 feet (8 m)

Time Range: Late Cretaceous

Where: Chile

DINO SECRETS REVEALED

Cool technology shows surprising discoveries about dinosaurs.

It's been 66 million years since the dinosaurs went extinct. And we're *still* learning new things about them, thanks to cutting-edge technology like lasers, 3D models, x-rays, and even robotics. For instance, experts are able to run extinct bones through a computer program to reconstruct missing bits and better understand how these animals actually functioned. Want to find out more? Check out three surprising dino discoveries that modern technology has helped scientists unearth.

SPINOSAURS HUNT PREHISTORIC SAWFISH.

River Beast

The Sahara seems like a strange place for a river-dwelling dinosaur. But more than 95 million years ago in what is now Morocco, a country in northern Africa, today's giant desert was actually lush with waterways deep enough for car-size fish to swim in. That's where *Spinosaurus*—a predator longer than *T. rex*—made its home.

At first, scientists believed that the sail-backed creature had some kind of watery lifestyle, perhaps hunting fish like a bear would. But after finding a partial skeleton in 2014, experts assessed that the dinosaur probably spent a lot of time in water.

And the paleontologists didn't stop there. Returning to the site in 2018, they dug up a 17-foot (5-m) *Spinosaurus* tail—one vertebra at a time. (These are the same bones that make up your spine.) Using high-speed cameras and robots, they created an eight-inch (20-cm)-long mechanical tail, which they watched paddle in an enclosed waterway.

They discovered that the beast swam through rivers like a crocodile and could propel itself with eight times more power than related land dinosaurs. In fact, *Spinosaurus* is the first large dino found that had a tail designed for swimming.

A YOUNG *MUSSAURUS* CHECKS OUT TWO RHYNCHOSAURS (PRONOUNCED REEN-KOH-SOARS) AS AN ADULT LOOKS ON.

Baby Steps

Dinosaurs lumbered on all fours like a *Stegosaurus* or scrambled around on two legs like a *Tyrannosaurus*. But not all dinosaurs moved the same way as they grew up.

Paleontologist Alejandro Otero found that out by using a high-tech machine called a CT scanner to take x-rays of *Mussaurus* bones (pronounced moo-SOAR-us). He then turned the x-rays into 3D models using a computer program and then simulated how the dinosaur stood at different ages.

What'd the simulations show? It turns out that, like human babies, *Mussaurus* hatchlings walked on all fours—but started walking on their two hind limbs as they grew older.

A NEWLY HATCHED *DEINONYCHUS* CHICK IS WATCHED OVER BY DAD.

Cracking the Case

A fossilized dinosaur egg looks kind of like a rock. So scientists were surprised to discover that the eggs of *Deinonychus* (pronounced die-NAHN-uh-kus) were probably blue!

When exposed to heat and pressure, microscopic dino remains can transform into stuff that can last for millions of years. This lets scientists take a closer look. When paleobiologist Jasmina Wiemann struck the *Deinonychus* eggs with a laser, the light reflecting back revealed compounds that give modern eggs bright colors and speckling.

This helped her figure out the blue color, but it also suggested something else: Like modern birds with similarly colorful eggs, *Deinonychus* likely sat on open-air nests to hatch its eggs.

QUIZ WHIZ

Explore just how much you know about animals with this quiz!

Write your answers on a piece of paper. Then check them below.

1 An adult golden lion tamarin is about the size of a _____ .
a. squirrel
b. golden retriever
c. beaver
d. hamster

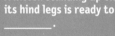

2 True or false? A pack of sea lions is called a raft.

3 Scientists think narwhals use their tusks to _____ .
a. jab and stun prey
b. stand out to potential mates
c. identify each other
d. all of the above

4 A kitten standing up on its hind legs is ready to _____ .
a. fight
b. play
c. run away
d. pounce

5 Which of the following is FALSE about arthropods?
a. They live in water and on land.
b. They have external skeletons, called exoskeletons.
c. They have segmented bodies with appendages.
d. They are the smallest group of animals.

Not **STUMPED** yet? Check out the *NATIONAL GEOGRAPHIC KIDS QUIZ WHIZ* collection for more crazy **ANIMAL** questions!

ANSWERS: 1. a; 2. True; 3. d; 4. b; 5. d

HOMEWORK HELP

Wildly Good Animal Reports

Seahorse

Your teacher wants a written report on the seahorse. Not to worry. Use these organizational tools so you can stay afloat while writing a report.

STEPS TO SUCCESS: Your report will follow the format of a descriptive or expository essay (see page 129 for "How to Write a Perfect Essay") and should consist of a main idea, followed by supporting details and a conclusion. Use this basic structure for each paragraph, as well as the whole report, and you'll be on the right track.

1. Introduction
State your **main idea.**
Seahorses are fascinating fish with many unique characteristics.

2. Body
Provide **supporting points** for your main idea.
Seahorses are very small fish.
Seahorses are named for their head shape.
Seahorses display behavior that is rare among almost all other animals on Earth.

Then **expand** on those points with further description, explanation, or discussion.
Seahorses are very small fish.
Seahorses are about the size of an M&M at birth, and most adult seahorses would fit in a teacup.
Seahorses are named for their head shape.
With long, tubelike snouts, seahorses are named for their resemblance to horses.
A group of seahorses is called a herd.
Seahorses display behavior that is rare among almost all other animals on Earth.
Unlike most other fish, seahorses stay with one mate their entire lives. They are also among the only species in which dads, not moms, give birth to the babies.

3. Conclusion
Wrap it up with a **summary** of your whole paper.
Because of their unique shape and unusual behavior, seahorses are among the most fascinating and easily distinguishable animals in the ocean.

KEY INFORMATION

Here are some things you should consider including in your report:
What does your animal look like?
To what other species is it related?
How does it move?
Where does it live?
What does it eat?
What are its predators?
How long does it live?
Is it endangered?
Why do you find it interesting?

SEPARATE FACT FROM FICTION: Your animal may have been featured in a movie or in myths and legends. Compare and contrast how the animal has been portrayed with how it behaves in reality. For example, penguins can't dance the way they do in *Happy Feet*.

PROOFREAD AND REVISE: As you would do with any essay, when you're finished, check for misspellings, grammatical mistakes, and punctuation errors. It often helps to have someone else proofread your work, too, as that person may catch things you have missed. Also, look for ways to make your sentences and paragraphs even better. Add more descriptive language, choosing just the right verbs, adverbs, and adjectives to make your writing come alive.

BE CREATIVE: Use visual aids to make your report come to life. Include an animal photo file with interesting images found in magazines or printed from websites. Or draw your own! You can also build a miniature animal habitat diorama. Use creativity to help communicate your passion for the subject.

THE FINAL RESULT: Put it all together in one final, polished draft. Make it neat and clean, and remember to cite your references.

A volcano erupts in
Geldingadalur, Iceland.

SPACE and EARTH

15 COOL THINGS ABOUT PLANETS

A billion Earths could fit inside one of SATURN'S **thousands of rings.**

A planet is a LARGE BODY of rock, gas, and other material that **travels** around a **star (like our sun).**

JUPITER is our solar system's BIGGEST PLANET— all seven of the other **planets** could **fit inside it.**

Pieces of MARS have been found on EARTH.

The **surface temperature** on **Venus** is hot enough to **melt lead.**

Earth's name comes from the **Middle English word** *ertha,* meaning *"ground."*

PLUTO used to be our solar system's ninth planet. But in 2006, scientists reclassified it as a **DWARF PLANET.**

EARTH was **created 4.5 billion years ago** from a **mass of DUST and ROCK.**

The Great Red Spot— a **hurricanelike storm** wider than **Earth—** has been blowing on **Jupiter** for **centuries.**

THE GREAT RED SPOT

EARTH moves around the **SUN** at **67,000** miles an hour— (107,826 km/h) that's more than **100 TIMES THE SPEED** of the fastest passenger airplane.

Uranus has only **two seasons: summer**

and **winter.** Each lasts **42 Earth years.**

EUROPA, one of **Jupiter's 79 known moons,** has **a salty, ice-covered OCEAN** that's almost 10 times deeper than **EARTH'S OCEANS.**

TITAN, one of **SATURN'S MOONS,** is LARGER than the planet MERCURY.

Olympus Mons— the highest peak on Mars— is **three times the size of** Mount Everest.

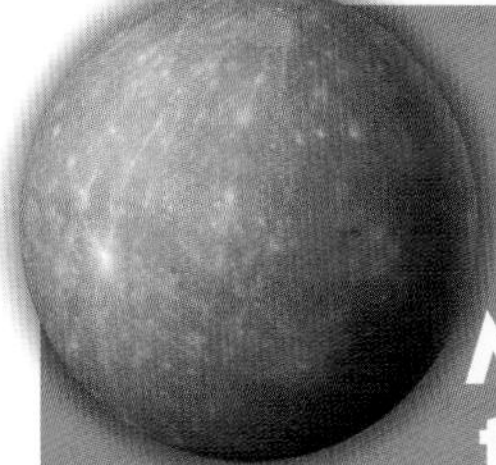

Because it's **closest** to the **sun, Mercury has the shortest year of our solar system's planets—** about **88 Earth days.**

PLANETS

CERES

MARS

EARTH

VENUS

MERCURY

JUPITER

SUN

MERCURY

Average distance from the sun:
35,980,000 miles (57,900,000 km)

Position from the sun in orbit: 1st

Equatorial diameter: 3,030 miles
(4,878 km)

Length of day: 59 Earth days

Length of year: 88 Earth days

Known moons: 0

VENUS

Average distance from the sun:
67,230,000 miles (108,200,000 km)

Position from the sun in orbit: 2nd

Equatorial diameter: 7,520 miles
(12,100 km)

Length of day: 243 Earth days

Length of year: 224.7 Earth days

Known moons: 0

EARTH

Average distance from the sun:
93,000,000 miles (149,600,000 km)

Position from the sun in orbit: 3rd

Equatorial diameter: 7,900 miles
(12,750 km)

Length of day: 24 hours

Length of year: 365 days

Known moons: 1

MARS

Average distance from the sun:
141,633,000 miles (227,936,000 km)

Position from the sun in orbit: 4th

Equatorial diameter: 4,221 miles
(6,794 km)

Length of day: 25 Earth hours

Length of year: 1.9 Earth years

Known moons: 2

This artwork shows the eight planets and five known dwarf planets in our solar system. The relative sizes and positions of the planets are shown but not the relative distances between them.

SATURN

URANUS

NEPTUNE

PLUTO
HAUMEA
MAKEMAKE
ERIS

JUPITER
Average distance from the sun:
  483,682,000 miles (778,412,000 km)
Position from the sun in orbit: 6th
Equatorial diameter: 88,840 miles
  (142,980 km)
Length of day: 9.9 Earth hours
Length of year: 11.9 Earth years
Known moons: 79*

SATURN
Average distance from the sun:
  890,800,000 miles (1,433,600,000 km)
Position from the sun in orbit: 7th
Equatorial diameter: 74,900 miles
  (120,540 km)
Length of day: 10.7 Earth hours
Length of year: 29.5 Earth years
Known moons: 82*

URANUS
Average distance from the sun:
  1,784,000,000 miles (2,871,000,000 km)
Position from the sun in orbit: 8th
Equatorial diameter: 31,760 miles
  (51,120 km)
Length of day: 17.2 Earth hours
Length of year: 84 Earth years
Known moons: 27

NEPTUNE
Average distance from the sun:
  2,795,000,000 miles (4,498,000,000 km)
Position from the sun in orbit: 9th
Equatorial diameter: 30,775 miles
  (49,528 km)
Length of day: 16 Earth hours
Length of year: 164.8 Earth years
Known moons: 14

*Includes provisional moons, which await confirmation
  and naming from the International Astronomical Union.

For information about dwarf planets,
see page 92.

DWARF PLANETS

Haumea

Eris

Pluto

Thanks to advanced technology, astronomers have been spotting many never-before-seen celestial bodies with their telescopes. One recent discovery? A population of icy objects orbiting the sun beyond Pluto. The largest, like Pluto itself, are classified as dwarf planets. Smaller than the moon but still massive enough to pull themselves into a ball, dwarf planets nevertheless lack the gravitational "oomph" to clear their neighborhood of other sizable objects. So, although larger, more massive planets pretty much have their orbits to themselves, dwarf planets orbit the sun in swarms that include other dwarf planets, as well as smaller chunks of rock or ice.

So far, astronomers have identified five dwarf planets in our solar system: Ceres, Pluto, Haumea, Makemake, and Eris. There are many more newly discovered dwarf planets that will need additional study before they are named. Astronomers are observing hundreds of newly found objects in the frigid outer solar system. As time and technology advance, the family of known dwarf planets will surely continue to grow.

CERES
Position from the sun in orbit: 5th
Length of day: 9.1 Earth hours
Length of year: 4.6 Earth years
Known moons: 0

PLUTO
Position from the sun in orbit: 10th
Length of day: 6.4 Earth days
Length of year: 248 Earth years
Known moons: 5

HAUMEA
Position from the sun in orbit: 11th
Length of day: 3.9 Earth hours
Length of year: 282 Earth years
Known moons: 2

MAKEMAKE
Position from the sun in orbit: 12th
Length of day: 22.5 Earth hours
Length of year: 305 Earth years
Known moons: 1*

ERIS
Position from the sun in orbit: 13th
Length of day: 25.9 Earth hours
Length of year: 561 Earth years
Known moons: 1

*Includes provisional moons, which await confirmation and naming from the International Astronomical Union.

BLACK HOLES

BLACK HOLE →

A black hole really seems like a hole in space. Most black holes form when the core of a massive star collapses, falling into oblivion. A black hole has a stronger gravitational pull than anything else in the known universe. It's like a bottomless pit, swallowing anything that gets close enough to it to be pulled in. It's black because it pulls in light. Black holes come in different sizes. The smallest known black hole has a mass about three times that of the sun. The biggest one scientists have found so far has a mass about 66 billion times greater than the sun's. Really big black holes at the center of galaxies probably form by swallowing enormous amounts of gas over time. In 2019, scientists released the first image of a black hole's silhouette (left). The image, previously thought impossible to record, was captured using a network of telescopes.

What's the farthest we've sent something into space?

About 13.8 billion miles (22.2 billion km)! In 1977, NASA scientists launched two spacecraft, Voyager 1 and Voyager 2, to study the outer planets of our solar system and beyond. Today, Voyager 1 is the farthest thing we've sent into the universe, while Voyager 2 is a still impressive 11.5 billion miles (18.5 billion km) away. Each far-flung vessel carries a gold-plated disc with messages for extraterrestrials. What would a traveling alien get out of us Earthlings? Music, whale calls, greetings in 55 languages, and photos of astronauts, airplanes, and kids in classrooms. Each disc also has playing instructions in case aliens ever find this high-tech message in a bottle.

93

DESTINATION SPACE

ALIEN SEA

Orange haze blurs the view outside your spaceship's window. You're descending to Titan, the largest of Saturn's 82 moons and 1.5 times bigger than Earth's moon. The smog beneath you thins, and you gasp in amazement: On the alien surface below, rivers flow through canyons. Waves crash in oceans. But Titan is nothing like home.

Your special spacecraft splashes down in Kraken Mare, Titan's largest sea. The pumpkin orange coastline is lined by craggy cliffs. Rocks dot the shore. But because it's a frigid minus 290°F (-179°C) here, the rocks are made of solid ice.

Rain begins to fall. It isn't water—it's methane and ethane. On Earth these are polluting gases. On Titan they form clouds and fall as rain that fills the rivers and oceans. You scoop up a sample of ocean liquid for a closer look: Scientists think there's a chance that Titan's seas might be home to alien life.

It'd be very strange if something did live here. On Earth everything living is partly made of water. Because there's no liquid water on Titan's surface, creatures here would be formed of methane or ethane. And because it's so cold, they'd move in slow motion.

Before you can get a good look at your sample, you hear a rumble. It's an ice volcano, thousands of feet tall. It shoots out a slurry of ice and ammonia (a chemical used as a cleaning product on Earth). You'd better get away before the icy blasts sink your spacecraft!

Destination
Titan

Location
Orbiting the planet Saturn

Distance
886 million miles
(1.43 billion km)
from Earth

Time to reach
3 years

Weather

At minus
290°F (-179°C),
Titan seems way too

Sky Calendar 2023

Jupiter

Annular solar eclipse

Supermoon

JANUARY 3-4
QUADRANTIDS METEOR SHOWER PEAK. Featuring up to 40 meteors an hour, it is the first meteor shower of every new year.

MAY 6-7
ETA AQUARIDS METEOR SHOWER PEAK. View about 30 to 60 meteors an hour.

JUNE 4
VENUS AT GREATEST EASTERN ELONGATION. Visible in the western sky after sunset, Venus will be at its highest point above the horizon in the evening sky.

JULY 3
SUPERMOON, FULL MOON. The moon will be full and closer to Earth in its orbit, likely appearing bigger and brighter than usual. Look for two more supermoons on August 31 and September 29.

AUGUST 12-13
PERSEID METEOR SHOWER PEAK. One of the best—see up to 90 meteors an hour! Best viewing is in the direction of the constellation Perseus.

OCTOBER 14
ANNULAR SOLAR ECLIPSE. The moon is too far away to completely cover the sun, so this eclipse appears as a ring of light around a dark circle created by the moon. Visible in southern Canada, the southwestern United States, Central America, Colombia, and Brazil. A partial eclipse can be viewed throughout most of North and South America.

OCTOBER 21-22
ORIONID METEOR SHOWER PEAK. View up to 20 meteors an hour. Look toward the constellation Orion for the best show.

OCTOBER 28
PARTIAL LUNAR ECLIPSE. Look for part of the moon to darken as it passes through Earth's penumbra—or partial shadow. It will be visible in Europe, Asia, Africa, and western Australia.

NOVEMBER 3
JUPITER AT OPPOSITION. This is your best chance to view Jupiter in 2023. The gas giant will appear bright in the sky and be visible throughout the night. Got a pair of binoculars? You may be able to spot Jupiter's four largest moons as well.

DECEMBER 13-14
GEMINID METEOR SHOWER PEAK. A spectacular show—see up to 120 multicolored meteors an hour!

2023—VARIOUS DATES
VIEW THE INTERNATIONAL SPACE STATION (ISS). Parents and teachers: You can visit https://spotthestation.nasa.gov to find out when the ISS will be flying over your neighborhood.

Dates may vary slightly depending on your location. Check with a local planetarium for the best viewing times in your area.

95

A LOOK INSIDE

The distance from Earth's surface to its center is some 4,000 miles (6,437 km) at the Equator. There are four layers: a thin, rigid crust; the rocky mantle; the outer core, which is a layer of molten iron and nickel; and finally the inner core, which is believed to be mostly solid iron.

The **CRUST** includes tectonic plates, land-masses, and the ocean. Its average thickness varies from 5 to 25 miles (8 to 40 km).

The **MANTLE** is about 1,800 miles (2,900 km) of hot, thick, solid rock.

The **OUTER CORE** is liquid molten rock made mostly of iron and nickel.

The **INNER CORE** is a solid center made mostly of iron and nickel.

What if you could dig to the other side of Earth?

Got a magma-proof suit and a magical drill that can cut through any surface? Then you're ready to dig some 7,900 miles (12,714 km) to Earth's other side. First you'd need to drill about 25 miles (40 km) through the planet's ultra-tough crust to its mantle. The heat and pressure at the mantle are intense enough to turn carbon into diamonds—and to, um, crush you. If you were able to survive, you'd still have to bore 1,800 more miles (2,897 km) to hit Earth's Mars-size core that can reach 11,000°F (6093°C). Now just keep drilling through the core and then the mantle and crust on the opposite side until you resurface on the planet's other side. But exit your tunnel fast. A hole dug through Earth would close quickly as surrounding rock filled in the empty space. The closing of the tunnel might cause small earthquakes, and your path home would definitely be blocked. Happy digging!

ROCK STARS

Rocks and minerals are everywhere on Earth! And it can be a challenge to tell one from the other. So what's the difference between a rock and a mineral? A rock is a naturally occurring solid object made mostly from minerals. Minerals are solid, nonliving substances that occur in nature—and the basic components of most rocks. Rocks can be made of just one mineral or, like granite, of many minerals. But not all rocks are made of minerals: Coal comes from plant material, while amber is formed from ancient tree resin.

Igneous

Named for the Greek word meaning "from fire," igneous rocks form when hot, molten liquid called magma cools. Pools of magma form deep underground and slowly work their way to Earth's surface. If they make it all the way, the liquid rock erupts and is called lava. As the layers of lava build up, they form a mountain called a volcano. Typical igneous rocks include obsidian, basalt, and pumice, which is so chock-full of gas bubbles that it actually floats in water.

ANDESITE

GRANITE PORPHYRY

Metamorphic

Metamorphic rocks are the masters of change! These rocks were once igneous or sedimentary, but thanks to intense heat and pressure deep within Earth, they have undergone a total transformation from their original form. These rocks never truly melt; instead, the heat twists and bends them until their shapes substantially change. Metamorphic rocks include slate as well as marble, which is used for buildings, monuments, and sculptures.

MICA SCHIST

BANDED GNEISS

Sedimentary

When wind, water, and ice constantly wear away and weather rocks, smaller pieces called sediment are left behind. These are sedimentary rocks, also known as gravel, sand, silt, and clay. As water flows downhill, it carries the sedimentary grains into lakes and oceans, where they are deposited. As the loose sediment piles up, the grains eventually get compacted or cemented back together again. The result is new sedimentary rock. Sandstone, gypsum, limestone, and shale are sedimentary rocks that have formed this way.

LIMESTONE

HALITE

Identifying Minerals

With so many different minerals in the world, it can be a challenge to tell one from another. Fortunately, each mineral has physical characteristics that geologists and amateur rock collectors use to tell them apart. Check out the physical characteristics below: color, luster, streak, cleavage, fracture, and hardness.

Color

When you look at a mineral, the first thing you see is its color. In some minerals, this is a key factor because their colors are almost always the same. For example, azurite, below, is always blue. But in other cases, impurities can change the natural color of a mineral. For instance, fluorite, above, can be green, red, violet, and other colors as well. This makes it a challenge to identify by color alone.

FLUORITE

AZURITE

Luster

"Luster" refers to the way light reflects from the surface of a mineral. Does a mineral appear metallic, like gold or silver? Or is it pearly like orpiment, or brilliant like diamond? "Earthy," "glassy," "silky," and "dull" are a few other terms used to describe luster.

ORPIMENT

DIAMOND

Streak

The "streak" is the color of a mineral's powder. When minerals are ground into powder, they often have a different color than when they are in crystal form. For example, the mineral pyrite usually looks gold, but when it is rubbed against a ceramic tile called a "streak plate," the mark it leaves is black.

PYRITE

Cleavage

"Cleavage" describes the way a mineral breaks. Because the structure of a specific mineral is always the same, it tends to break in the same pattern. Not all minerals have cleavage, but the minerals that do, like this microcline, break evenly in one or more directions. These minerals are usually described as having "perfect cleavage." But if the break isn't smooth and clean, cleavage can be considered "good" or "poor."

MICROCLINE

GOLD

Fracture

Some minerals, such as gold, do not break with cleavage. Instead, geologists say that they "fracture." There are different types of fractures, and, depending on the mineral, the fracture may be described as jagged, splintery, even, or uneven.

Hardness

The level of ease or difficulty with which a mineral can be scratched refers to its "hardness." Hardness is measured using a special chart called the Mohs Hardness Scale. The Mohs scale goes from 1 to 10. Softer minerals, which appear on the lower end of the scale, can be scratched by the harder minerals on the upper end of the scale.

RATING	MINERAL NAME	EXAMPLES
1	TALC	BAR OF SOAP
2	GYPSUM	FINGERNAIL
3	CALCITE	COPPER PENNY
4	FLUORITE	SOFT IRON NAIL
5	APATITE	STEEL POCKETKNIFE BLADE
6	ORTHOCLASE	WINDOW GLASS
7	QUARTZ	HARDENED STEEL FILE
8	TOPAZ	TOPAZ
9	CORUNDUM	RUBY, SAPPHIRE
10	DIAMOND	DIAMOND

A NEW TYPE OF ROCK
WAS RECENTLY DISCOVERED SOME
FIVE (8 KM) MILES
BENEATH THE SURFACE OF THE PACIFIC OCEAN.

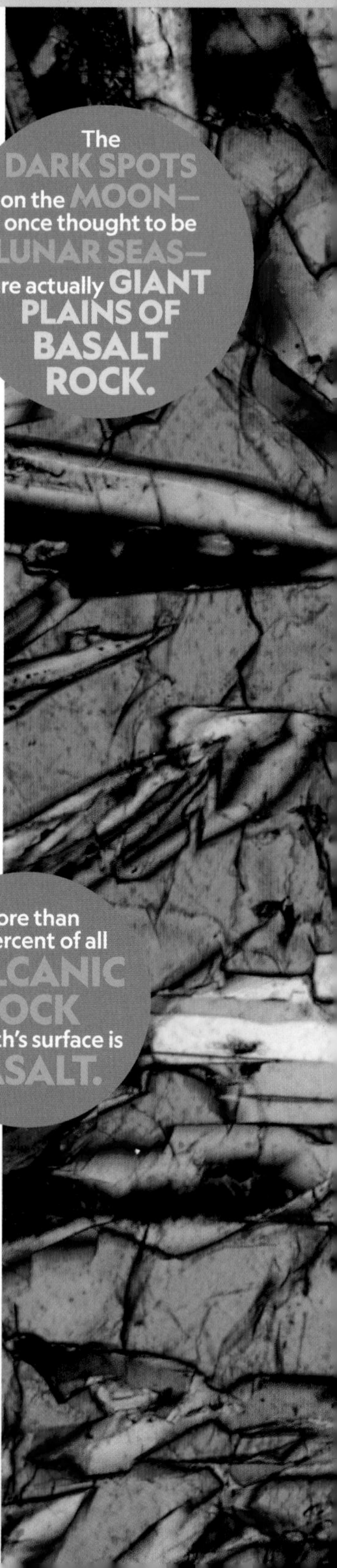

The **DARK SPOTS** on the **MOON**— once thought to be **LUNAR SEAS**— are actually **GIANT PLAINS OF BASALT ROCK.**

More than 90 percent of all **VOLCANIC ROCK** on Earth's surface is **BASALT.**

The never-before-seen basalt rock, found by drilling deep into the Pacific Ocean floor, has a different chemical and mineral makeup than anything ever discovered on Earth. Scientists think it was formed during huge and extra-hot volcanic eruptions some 50 million years ago.

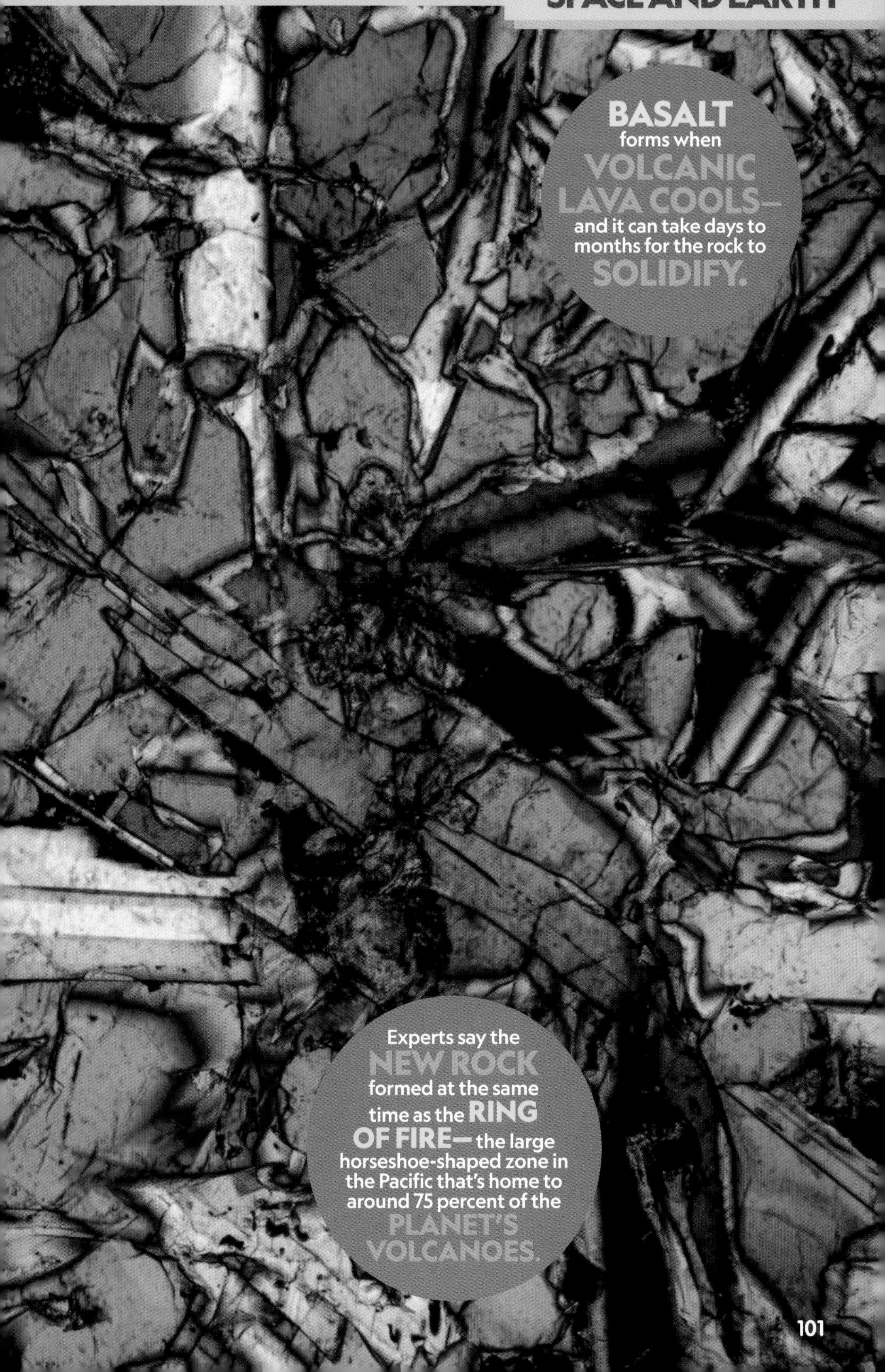

BASALT forms when **VOLCANIC LAVA COOLS—** and it can take days to months for the rock to **SOLIDIFY.**

Experts say the **NEW ROCK** formed at the same time as the **RING OF FIRE—** the large horseshoe-shaped zone in the Pacific that's home to around 75 percent of the **PLANET'S VOLCANOES.**

A HOT TOPIC

WHAT GOES ON
INSIDE A STEAMING, BREWING VOLCANO?

If you could look inside a volcano, you'd see something that looks like a long pipe, called a conduit. This leads from inside the magma chamber under the crust up to a vent, or opening, at the top of the mountain. Some conduits have branches that shoot off to the side, called fissures.

When pressure builds from gases inside the volcano, the gases must find an escape, and they head up toward the surface! An eruption occurs when lava, gases, ash, and rocks explode out of the vent.

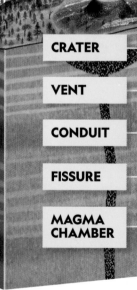

CRATER

VENT

CONDUIT

FISSURE

MAGMA CHAMBER

HARDENED LAVA AND ASH LAYERS

TYPES OF VOLCANOES

CINDER CONE VOLCANO
Eve Cone, Canada

Cinder cone volcanoes look like an upside-down bowl. They spew cinder and hot ash. Some of these volcanoes smoke and erupt for years at a time.

COMPOSITE VOLCANO
Licancábur, Chile

Composite volcanoes, or stratovolcanoes, form as lava, ash, and cinder from previous eruptions harden and build up over time. These volcanoes spit out pyroclastic flows, or thick explosions of hot ash that travel at hundreds of miles an hour.

SHIELD VOLCANO
Mauna Loa, Hawaii, U.S.A.

The gentle, broad slopes of a shield volcano look like an ancient warrior's shield. Its eruptions are often slower. Lava splatters and bubbles rather than shooting forcefully into the air.

LAVA DOME VOLCANO
Mount St. Helens, Washington, U.S.A.

Dome volcanoes have steep sides. Hardened lava often plugs the vent at the top of a dome volcano. Pressure builds beneath the surface until the top blows.

RING OF FIRE

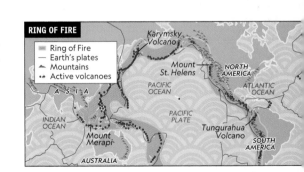

RING OF FIRE
- Ring of Fire
- Earth's plates
- Mountains
- Active volcanoes

Karymsky Volcano
Mount St. Helens
NORTH AMERICA
PACIFIC OCEAN
ATLANTIC OCEAN
ASIA
PACIFIC PLATE
INDIAN OCEAN
Mount Merapi
Tungurahua Volcano
SOUTH AMERICA
AUSTRALIA

Although volcanoes are found on every continent, most are located along an arc known as the Ring of Fire. This area, which forms a horseshoe shape in the Pacific Ocean, stretches some 24,900 miles (40,000 km). Several of the large, rigid plates that make up Earth's surface are found here, and they are prone to shifting toward each other and colliding. The result? Volcanic eruptions and earthquakes—and plenty of them. In fact, the Ring of Fire hosts 90 percent of the world's recorded earthquakes and about 75 percent of its active volcanoes.

BLUE VOLCANO

A strange eruption creates a dazzling light show.

The night is pitch-black. But the dark slopes of a hill inside the crater of Kawah Ijen volcano in Indonesia are lit up like a holiday light show. Tourists flock to the volcano to see what look like glowing blue rivers of lava. But they aren't rivers of lava. They're rivers of glowing sulfur.

Burning Blue

Glowing red lava flowing from an erupting volcano isn't unusual. Glowing sulfur is. Hot, sulfur-rich gases escape constantly from cracks called fumaroles in Kawah Ijen's crater. The gases cool when they hit the air. Some condense into liquid sulfur, which flows down the hillside. When the sulfur and leftover gases ignite, they burn bright blue and light up the night sky.

Scientists were told that sulfur miners on the volcano sometimes use torches to ignite the sulfur. The blue flames make Kawah Ijen popular with tourists, who watch from a safe distance. Scientists have also confirmed that some of the sulfur and gases burn naturally.

Volcano Miners

Sulfur is a common volcanic gas, and its chemical properties are used to manufacture many things, such as rubber. But sulfur is so plentiful in Kawah Ijen's crater that miners make a dangerous daily trek into the crater to collect it from a fumarole near an acid lake.

"The local people pipe the gases from the fumarole through ceramic pipes," says John Pallister, a retired geologist with the Cascades Volcano Observatory in Washington, U.S.A. He has walked into the crater himself, wearing a gas mask for protection against the clouds of acid that rise from the lake. "They spray the pipes with water from a spring," he says. This cools the gases and causes them to condense into molten sulfur. The sulfur then cools and hardens into rock.

Using this method, miners get more usable rock faster than if they just collected scattered pieces. They smash up the rock with metal bars, stuff the pieces into baskets, and carry them out of the crater on their backs. The loads are heavy—between 100 and 200 pounds (45 to 91 kg) apiece.

Reading the Danger Zone

Miners face another danger: a huge eruption. Kawah Ijen's last big eruption was almost 200 years ago, but the volcano is still active. A big eruption could endanger both miners and tourists.

Indonesian scientists want to find a way to predict a big eruption in time to keep everyone safe. But the deep acid lake makes it difficult to pick up the usual signals that warn of a coming volcanic eruption.

As scientists search for ways to predict this unusual volcano's behavior, Kawah Ijen's blue fires continue to attract audiences who appreciate the volcano's amazing glow.

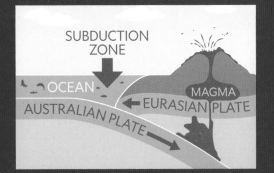

SUBDUCTION ZONE

OCEAN

AUSTRALIAN PLATE

EURASIAN PLATE

MAGMA

How Kawah Ijen Erupts

Earth's outer shell is broken into a jigsaw puzzle of several tectonic plates, or gigantic slabs of rock, that move constantly. In Indonesia, the oceanic **Australian plate** slips under the **Eurasian plate** at a **subduction zone**. As the Australian plate slides deep down, heat generated in Earth's interior makes the plate superhot, and parts of it melt. This melted rock, called **magma**, rises toward Earth's surface. Pressure on the magma lessens as it rises, allowing gases inside to expand, which can lead to explosive volcanic eruptions.

FUN FACTS ABOUT INDONESIA

Indonesia is a group of more than 17,500 islands off the coast of Southeast Asia. It's the largest country in the region.

When the volcano on the tiny Indonesian island of Krakatau erupted in August 1883, it could be heard thousands of miles away.

The *Rafflesia arnoldii,* the largest single flower in the world, grows in Indonesia. The flower smells like rotting meat, can grow to 3 feet (0.9 m) across, and weighs up to 24 pounds (10.9 kg).

Nearly 11 million people live in Jakarta, Indonesia's most populated city. That's almost 2.5 million more people than are living in New York City.

QUIZ WHIZ

Are your space and Earth smarts out of this world? Take this quiz!

Write your answers on a piece of paper. Then check them below.

1 **True or false?** Gravel, sand, silt, and clay are all ways to describe sedimentary rocks.

2 **In which ocean can you find the Ring of Fire?**
a. Pacific   c. Indian
b. Atlantic   d. Arctic

3 **Fill in the blank.** Indonesia is a group of more than 17,500 _____ off the coast of Southeast Asia.

4 **An annular solar eclipse occurs as a ring of light around a dark circle created by _____.**
a. the sun   c. Saturn
b. the moon   d. Venus

5 **True or false?** Earth moves around the sun at a pace that's more than 100 times the speed of the fastest passenger airplane.

Not **STUMPED** yet? Check out the *NATIONAL GEOGRAPHIC KIDS QUIZ WHIZ* book collection for more crazy **SPACE AND EARTH** questions!

ANSWERS: 1. True; 2. a; 3. islands; 4. b; 5. True

HOMEWORK HELP

ACE YOUR SCIENCE FAIR

You can learn a lot about science from books, but to really experience it firsthand, you need to get into the lab and "do" some science. Whether you're entering a science fair or just want to learn more on your own, there are many scientific projects you can do. So put on your goggles and lab coat, and start experimenting.

Most likely, the topic of the project will be up to you. So remember to choose something that is interesting to you.

THE BASIS OF ALL SCIENTIFIC INVESTIGATION AND DISCOVERY IS THE SCIENTIFIC METHOD. CONDUCT YOUR EXPERIMENT USING THESE STEPS:

Observation/Research—Ask a question or identify a problem.

Hypothesis—Once you've asked a question, do some thinking and come up with some possible answers.

Experimentation—How can you determine if your hypothesis is correct? You test it. You perform an experiment. Make sure the experiment you design will produce an answer to your question.

Analysis—Gather your results, and use a consistent process to carefully measure the results.

Conclusion—Do the results support your hypothesis?

Report Your Findings—Communicate your results in the form of a paper that summarizes your entire experiment.

Bonus!

Take your project one step further. Your school may have an annual science fair, but there are also local, state, regional, and national science fair competitions. Compete with other students for awards, prizes, and scholarships!

EXPERIMENT DESIGN
There are three types of experiments you can do.

MODEL KIT—a display, such as an "erupting volcano" model. Simple and to the point.

DEMONSTRATION—shows the scientific principles in action, such as a tornado in a wind tunnel.

INVESTIGATION—the home run of science projects, and just the type of project for science fairs. This kind demonstrates proper scientific experimentation and uses the scientific method to reveal answers to questions.

A woman climbs Grossvenediger, a glacier-covered mountain in the Austrian Alps.

AWESOME
EXPLORATION

THIS CLIFF

IS COVERED WITH

TENS OF THOUSANDS

OF DRAWINGS OF

ANCIENT ANIMALS

AND **HUMANS,**

DATING BACK MORE THAN

12,000 YEARS.

Experts say the **ARTWORK** was **COMPLETED** at the end of the **ICE AGE,** likely by the first humans to live in the western Amazon.

Scientists discovered the artwork on a cliff that extends for some eight miles (13 km) in the Amazon rainforest in Colombia. The drawings showcase now extinct animals that were alive and well at the time, as well as plants, humans, and geometric shapes.

There are also images of the **MASTODON,** the elephant's prehistoric relative, **GIANT SLOTHS,** and **ICE AGE HORSES.**

Also discovered in the area? The **REMAINS** of **FOOD** eaten by the artists, like **FRUITS, ALLIGATORS,** and **ARMADILLOS.**

Some of the **IMAGES** are so **HIGH ON THE CLIFF** that researchers **USED DRONES** to take pictures of them.

GET TO KNOW OUR
MIGHTY TREES!

NATIONAL GEOGRAPHIC KiDS
ALMANAC CHALLENGE 2023

As an "arbornaut," Dr. Meg Lowman spends much of her time in the treetops, studying life high in the branches. Here, the National Geographic Explorer and real-life Lorax shares more about her career and why she implores everyone to save the trees.

What is an arbornaut?

Like an astronaut explores outer space, an arbornaut explores the tops of the trees. It's a new science, but it's an essential one because half of the land species on our planet live in the treetops and never come to the ground. Trees are essential for our life in so many ways.

Have you always liked to climb trees?

Yes! As a kid, I built tree forts with my friends, and I have always just loved trees. Even though I do have a high respect for heights, I have an even bigger curiosity and amazement at the life up there.

What is one of your coolest discoveries in the treetops?

I have played a role in a lot of discoveries of new species of insects. I have even had some species named after me. There is a "Meg mite" out there, which is found in the forests of Ethiopia.

And it's not a discovery, but one of my proudest accomplishments is helping to create

and design canopy walkways, which can now be found all over the world. These walkways allow everyone, including people with mobility limitations, to have access to the treetops and discover their beauty.

Where is your favorite place to study trees?

The upper Amazon in Peru. It's so far from the mouth of the Amazon River that it is still fairly pristine. It hasn't been hit by poachers who cut down trees. I love it there because it has the highest biodiversity in the world.

What are your arbornaut essentials while in the field?

Water and Oreos! Just kidding, although I do love my cookies. I usually have a bucket dangling from my waist with a carabiner that holds tools like a tape measure, pencils, a notebook, a camera, binoculars, and little vials to collect important insects along the way. Oh, and I'll have a pooter, which is a tool that has a straw you suck on to grab bugs up without squishing them.

Why is it important to study trees?

They are the home to all of these species, and we have learned things like how leaves control climate for us, and how pollination occurs, and how it all impacts the environment. Trees literally keep us alive. We cannot survive on this planet without keeping our trees healthy.

THIS YEAR'S CHALLENGE

Trees take care of humans, so let's be good neighbors by taking care of trees in return! That starts by paying attention to them, which is the inspiration for this year's Almanac Challenge: Me as a Tree.

Discover your inner arbornaut! Have fun learning about different kinds of trees through reading, researching, and hands-on observation. Explore the arboreal world from roots to canopy to unearth the various features of different species. Think about which features you most appreciate and would want to have. Once you've imagined the kind of tree you'd want to be, tell us about your creation by writing a brief tree autobiography and drawing a tree selfie.

HINT: The more you understand trees, the more creative your tree autobiography can be!

Get details and the official rules at **natgeokids.com/almanac.**

LAST YEAR'S CHALLENGE

Kids care about the ocean and were eager to share the wonders of their favorite marine animals in last year's Our Awesome Ocean challenge. Here's what we learned from hundreds of stellar submissions:
• 86 percent were SHOW (drawing) and 14 percent were TELL (writing) and about half of those were both!
• The most popular creatures represented were dolphins, orcas, whales, sharks, sea turtles, sea otters, octopuses, and jellyfish.
• Less common favorites included coral, clown frogfish, flying fish, cuttlefish, catfish, snowflake clownfish, anglerfish, peacock mantis shrimp, and hermit crabs.
• Protecting ocean animals and their ecosystem is important to readers—and for the planet!

SHOW Grand Prize Drawing Winner, Aditi Sundar, age 10
TELL Grand Prize Writing Winner (featuring the vaquita),
Oola Breen-Ryan, age 10

See more entries online at **natgeokids.com/almanac.**

SEA TURTLE: ADITI'S DRAWING ENTRY INCLUDED A POEM ABOUT PRESERVING THE TURTLE'S OCEAN HABITAT.

DARE TO EXPLORE

How quick-thinking scientists help protect the planet

A SLOW LORIS SPENDS TIME IN ITS RAINFOREST HOME ON THE INDONESIAN ISLAND OF SUMATRA.

SCIENTISTS FIT THIS MATSCHIE'S TREE KANGAROO WITH A TRACKING COLLAR SO THEY CAN STUDY ITS MOVEMENTS.

THE BIOLOGIST

Lisa Dabek studies endangered Matschie's tree kangaroos to learn how to better protect them in the wild. She talks about tracking one on the island of New Guinea.

"Even the most difficult challenges always have solutions. I have asthma, but I figured out how to hike the mountains of Papua New Guinea."

"I was with our local research team, trying to capture a tree kangaroo in a cloud forest, which is a rainforest high in the mountains. Like regular kangaroos, tree kangaroos have pouches and can hop, but they live in trees. We wanted to put a camera on one so we could see what it did in the treetops.

"To find one, we looked for claw marks on bark and kangaroo poop on the ground. We finally spotted a kangaroo 60 feet (18 m) up in a tree. Then one of the locals climbed up. We knew the tree kangaroo would react by leaping down as if a predator were close. I held my breath. From way up high, the tree kangaroo spread its limbs, glided down, and landed on the soft, mossy ground. She let us gently put a camera collar on her before she hopped away. When the collar fell off five days later, we retrieved it and had footage of her munching on orchids and cleaning her pouch a hundred feet (30 m) up in a tree!

"Little is known about these animals, and I want more people to discover them so we can save them together."

WANT TO BE A BIOLOGIST?

STUDY   Biology, chemistry
WATCH   *FernGully: The Last Rainforest*
READ   *Quest for the Tree Kangaroo* by Sy Montgomery

THE WILDLIFE WARRIOR

Onkuri Majumdar is a wildlife conservationist who works to save animals stolen from the wild in parts of Asia and Africa. She recalls rescuing slow lorises seized by smugglers.

"When I was working in Thailand, my team heard that slow lorises—primates that live throughout Asia—were being poached, or illegally taken, from the wild. They were being sold so tourists could take photos with them and share the images on social media. Poachers also sell the shy, small animals as pets.

"To catch the criminals, we trained a local police team to track them. I was there for the arrest and rescue operation to make sure the animals were recovered safely. You could tell the lorises hadn't been well cared for. We wrapped them in blankets to keep them warm, but they were so stressed, they chewed up the cloth. I was relieved to deliver the animals to a wildlife rescue center where caregivers would help the lorises get healthy again.

"Moments like saving those lorises are why I do my job. I want to help catch poachers and encourage lawmakers to pass laws against these terrible crimes."

> "We should strive to make the world a better place, especially for wild animals that can't stand up for themselves."

WANT TO BE A WILDLIFE WARRIOR?

STUDY Veterinary science, law enforcement
WATCH *The Fox and the Hound*
READ *A Wolf Called Wander* by Rosanne Parry

THE ADVENTURER

Carsten Peter is a biologist who climbs sizzling volcanoes to photograph eruptions. He describes getting caught in the middle of a days-long eruption.

PHOTOGRAPHER CARSTEN PETER SNAPPED THIS PHOTO OF AN EXPLOSION ON MOUNT ETNA, A VOLCANO IN ITALY.

"A group of us were on an expedition on Mount Etna, a volcano in Italy. We hoped to photograph a paroxysm (pronounced puh-ROKS-ism). They're massive eruptions that produce fire mountains, or wild sprays of magma.

"We camped out halfway up the peak and waited. In the middle of the night a fissure, or crack, suddenly appeared in front of us. Ash and dust started swirling around, stinging our eyes. The smell of volcanic gases filled our noses, and volcanic lightning cracked in the air. The ground was so hot, the bottom of my friend's shoes melted.

"The eruption lasted for days. We decided to stay so we could document everything, even though we hadn't brought enough food. We saw several paroxysms. During calmer moments, we dug under cooled ash to find snow we could melt for drinking water.

"It's one thing to understand the science of volcanoes, but it's crazy to feel it up close. Not everyone can sleep on a volcano. That's why I do what I do—to show people the awesome power of nature."

> "Every volcano is as different as every human. Each one has its own character."

WANT TO BE AN ADVENTURER?

STUDY Photography, environmental studies, geography
WATCH The documentary *Volcanoes: The Fires of Creation*
READ *Extreme Planet: Carsten Peter's Adventures in Volcanoes, Caves, Canyons, Deserts, and Beyond!* by Carsten Peter and Glen Phelan

The Explorer's Lens

Meet conservation photographer Gab Mejia

As a conservation photographer and National Geographic Explorer, Gab Mejia shares powerful images of places, people, and animals in an effort to educate others on issues like climate change, pollution, and other challenges impacting Earth. Mejia was born and raised in the Philippines, and many of his images showcase his country—especially its endangered species and Indigenous people. Here, Mejia shares more about his message as a visual storyteller and what it's like being behind the lens.

PHILIPPINE EAGLE

Q: What inspired you to become a photographer?

A: When I was 13, my dad brought me on a trek in the rainforest in the Philippines, and it opened my eyes to a different world. One where I was able to witness nature and its beauty and rawness, and I wanted to share it with others. I also loved to travel and visit new places, and photography became my passport to see the rest of the world.

Q: What is the trickiest part of being a photographer?

A: Chasing the light! Many people don't realize that in order to get that perfect shot, you need the right lighting. So, I'll be up very early to get that golden light of the sunrise, or I'll wake up in the middle of the night to capture the stars. When I'm in the field, I don't get much sleep.

Q: What's one standout moment you've experienced in your career?

A: Photographing the Philippine eagle. It's such a beautiful creature, and the whole time I was taking photos I kept thinking, "I just can't believe I'm face-to-face with this majestic bird." Also, because they are on the brink of extinction, it gives my work more purpose. It's not just taking pictures of the eagle—it's capturing their images and showing everyone just how amazing they are.

Q: Any scary moments in the field?

A: One night, while I was shooting Monte Fitz Roy, a mountain in Patagonia, I went back to my tent late at night—and alone. Suddenly, I see these bright white, glowing eyes in the bush across from my tent. It was straight out of a horror movie. I thought for sure the eyes belonged to a mountain lion, and I freaked out. I grabbed my headlamp and shone it into the bush and saw it was actually a South Andean deer, which is a very rare species in Argentina. So what was a scary moment turned into a fascinating and memorable one.

Q: Part of your focus as a photographer has been to raise awareness about Indigenous communities. What has that experience been like?

A: They are private people, but they do want their story to be told. Their homes are being destroyed by logging and climate change—and they need our help. As far as actually being with the tribes, I spend time with them and gain their trust before I even bring out my camera. They respect that I am a fellow Filipino sharing their story, and I've become good friends with the tribe leaders.

Q: What message do you want to send through your photography?

A: Never stop exploring! I share my photos to inspire others to seek out their own adventures. To look for the wildlife, visit amazing natural places, and hopefully be inspired to use your voice to make a positive change. Also, I hope my photos are a reminder to all that our world is so beautiful, and we need to protect it for future generations.

117

EPiC SCIENCE FAiLS

Nat Geo Explorers spill their most embarrassing moments.

Even supersmart scientists mess up sometimes! These Nat Geo Explorers reveal some of their wildest slipups—and what they learned from them.

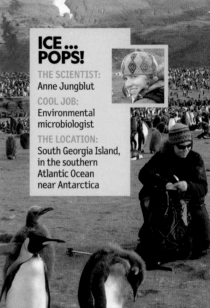

ICE... POPS!

THE SCIENTIST:
Anne Jungblut

COOL JOB:
Environmental microbiologist

THE LOCATION:
South Georgia Island, in the southern Atlantic Ocean near Antarctica

ANNE JUNGBLUT LOOKS FOR SOIL SAMPLES AMONG THOUSANDS OF KING PENGUINS ON SOUTH GEORGIA ISLAND.

LAZY LIONS

THE SCIENTIST:
Rae Wynn-Grant

COOL JOB:
Large carnivore ecologist

THE LOCATION:
Tanzania, a country in Africa

"I was studying the movement and hunting behavior of lions in the savanna. When I found my first subject, he was snoozing. I noticed that his belly was huge—he'd just eaten a big meal. I watched the lion do nothing but sleep for hours until it got dark. And then when I came back the next morning, the lion still hadn't moved.

"In four months, I found seven other lions ... just lying around, full of food. I never arrived in time to see the behavior I was there to study. Instead, I had to interview local people about the lions' movements for my paper—something I didn't need to spend months in Africa to do!

"I learned that wild animals don't always do things on my schedule. But at least I got to see these predators behaving naturally: Lions definitely spend most of their time asleep."

UNFORTUNATELY FOR RAE WYNN-GRANT, LIONS LIKE THIS ONE SLEEP OR REST UP TO 20 HOURS A DAY.

"I study too-small-to-see organisms that live in little pools of water on top of glaciers. I have to use special ice shoes, rope, and an ice axe to climb to collection sites since the ice sheet has deep cracks that could be deadly. So once I'm finally at the site, I'm eager to get started.

"One time I was so excited to gather as much evidence as possible and filled my sampling tubes to the top with water and sediment from the glaciers. Even though I'm an ice and soil scientist, I ignored the fact that water increases by 20 percent when it freezes. So when we put all my test tubes into the freezer for safekeeping, one totally shattered! Luckily, we quickly put the samples in new containers, but that day I learned to respect science—it's not going to change for me."

SNAKE MISTAKE

THE SCIENTIST: Ruchira Somaweera

COOL JOB: Herpetologist

THE LOCATION: Northern Australia

RUCHIRA SOMAWEERA HOLDS AN ARAFURA FILE SNAKE IN AUSTRALIA.

"I was catching snakes so I could study their health. We kept the snakes in fabric bags for the night so we could examine them the next day. Mosquitoes and ants were everywhere, and I didn't want the snakes to be uncomfortable, so I brought the bagged animals into my insect-proof tent.

"At about 3 a.m., I woke up to the most horrible smell. It turns out that a Stimson's python had escaped and crawled into my warm sleeping bag. I'd rolled over onto it, causing the snake to vomit parts of a half-digested frog!

"The snake was fine—we released it the next day—and now I always check that the snake bags are totally tied up."

MYSTERY BONE

THE SCIENTIST: Daniel Dick

COOL JOB: Paleontologist

THE LOCATION: Colombia, a country in South America

PALEONTOLOGISTS DANIEL DICK (LEFT) AND ERIN MAXWELL LOOK FOR ICHTHYOSAUR FOSSILS IN COLOMBIA.

"We were examining an eight-foot (2.4-m)-long skeleton of an ichthyosaur (a huge extinct marine reptile). It was my first day in the field, and I wanted to impress the other scientists. As I examined the skull, I spotted an unusual bone that the others had missed and began to describe it—the bone might be proof that this animal is an entirely new species!

"'That's mud,' my teacher said. I was so embarrassed, but science is about learning. And now I'm really good at spotting the difference between mud and bone."

SCRATCHY CHASE

THE SCIENTIST: Patrícia Medici

COOL JOB: Conservationist

THE LOCATION: Pantanal, Brazil

"We shot a tranquilizer dart at a large male tapir so that we could study its health. Sometimes, the animal sprints off into the forest, and we have to chase after it no matter where it goes. It can be dangerous for the tapir because if it falls asleep in water, we wouldn't be able to get it out. (An adult tapir can weigh over 500 pounds [227 kg]!)

"So we raced after this tapir straight into a sea of thorns and stickers. Most of us were wearing pants and long-sleeve shirts, but one member of the team was in shorts, and wound up covered in scratches by the time we caught up with the tapir. We named the tapir 'Band-Aid,' and I'm sure that my shorts-wearing teammate now always remembers to dress for a wild chase!"

PATRÍCIA MEDICI FEEDS A CAPTIVE BABY TAPIR AT A WILDLIFE REHABILITATION CENTER IN BRAZIL.

Keep Earth WILD

A National Geographic photographer gives you a behind-the-scenes look at his quest to save animals.

Joel Sartore has squealed like a pig, protected his camera from a parakeet, and suffered through a stink attack—all to help save animals through photography. "I hope people will look these animals in their eyes and then be inspired to protect them," says Sartore, a National Geographic photographer.

Sartore is on a mission to take pictures of more than 15,000 animal species living in captivity through his project, the National Geographic Photo Ark. During each photo shoot, he works with zookeepers, aquarists, and wildlife rehabbers to keep his subjects safe and comfortable. But things can still get a little, well, wild! Read on for some of Sartore's most memorable moments.

Moment of **SNOOZE**

GIANT PANDAS, *native to China*

Zoo Atlanta, Atlanta, Georgia, U.S.A.

"These giant pandas were just a few months old when I put the football-size twins in a small, white photo tent and snapped a few pics as they tumbled on top of each other. But the youngsters were tiring out, and I knew I was losing my chance to get a memorable photo before they drifted off to sleep. One cub put his head on the back of the other, and I managed to capture an awesome shot just seconds before the two cubs fell asleep."

> Some arctic fox dens are 300 years old.

Moment of **HA**

ARCTIC FOX, *native to the Arctic regions of Eurasia, North America, Greenland, and Iceland*

Great Bend Brit Spaugh Zoo, Great Bend, Kansas, U.S.A.

"Todd the arctic fox wanted to sniff everything, but he was moving too quickly for me to get a good picture. I needed to do something surprising to get his attention, so I squealed like a pig! The weird sound made the fox stop, sit down, and tilt his head as if he were thinking, What's the matter with you? Good thing I was fast, because the pig noise only worked once. The next time I squealed, Todd completely ignored me."

More **WILDNESS!** Photo Ark spotlights all kinds of animals. Meet some of Joel Sartore's strangest subjects.

BUDGETT'S FROG

ORANGE SPOTTED FILEFISH

MEDITERRANEAN RED BUG

NORTH AMERICAN PORCUPINE

Sartore uses black or white backgrounds because he wants the focus to be on the animals. That way a mouse is as important as an elephant.

Newborn giant pandas are about the size of a stick of butter.

A single colony of gray-headed flying foxes can include a million bats.

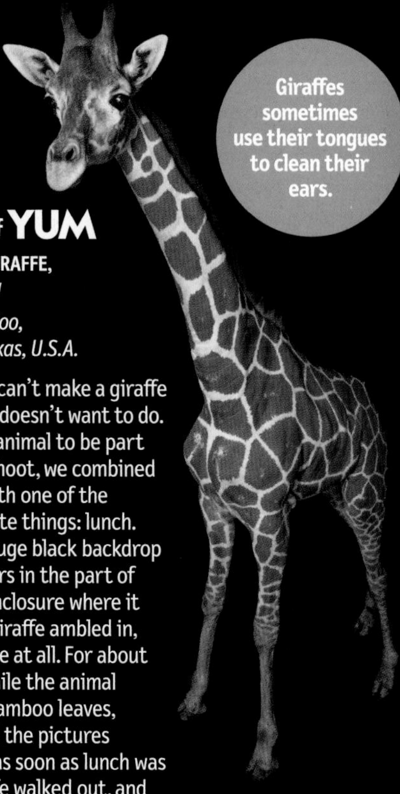

Giraffes sometimes use their tongues to clean their ears.

Moment of YAY

GRAY-HEADED FLYING FOX, *native to southeastern Australia*

Australian Bat Clinic, Advancetown, Australia

"When I arrived at the clinic, I was amazed to see all sorts of bats just hanging from laundry racks all over the rescue center. They sleepily watched me as I walked through the room and asked a staff member for a friendly flying fox to photograph. She scooped up a sweet bat and placed its feet on a wire rack in front of my backdrop. The calm bat didn't seem to mind being in front of the camera. The best part? This clinic rehabilitates bats that have torn their wings, and my subject was eventually released back into the wild."

Moment of YUM

RETICULATED GIRAFFE, *native to Africa*

Gladys Porter Zoo, Brownsville, Texas, U.S.A.

"You definitely can't make a giraffe do anything it doesn't want to do. So to get this animal to be part of our photo shoot, we combined the activity with one of the giraffe's favorite things: lunch. We hung the huge black backdrop from the rafters in the part of the giraffe's enclosure where it gets fed. The giraffe ambled in, not minding me at all. For about 10 minutes, while the animal munched on bamboo leaves, I could take all the pictures I wanted. But as soon as lunch was over, the giraffe walked out, and our photo shoot was done."

121

GETTING THE SHOT

Capturing good photographs of wild animals can be tough. To get amazing pictures of them, nature photographers often tap into their wild side, thinking and even acting like the creatures they're snapping. Whether tracking deadly snakes or swimming with penguins, the artists must be daring—but they also need to know when to keep their distance. Three amazing photographers tell their behind-the-scenes stories of how they got these incredible shots.

Check out this book!

GUIDE TO PHOTOGRAPHY

FANG FOCUS

PHOTOGRAPHER: Mattias Klum
ANIMAL: Jameson's mamba
SHOOT SITE: Cameroon, Africa

"The Jameson's mamba is beautiful but dangerous. It produces highly toxic venom. My team searched for weeks for the reptile, asking locals about the best spots to see one. At last we came across a Jameson's mamba peeking out from tree leaves. Carefully, I inched closer. It's important to make this kind of snake think that you don't see it. Otherwise it might feel threatened and strike you. At about four and a half feet (1.4 m) away, I took the picture. Then I backed up and the snake slid off."

SECRETS FROM
AMAZING WILDLIFE PHOTOGRAPHERS

Usually solitary creatures, oceanic whitetip sharks have been observed swimming with pods of pilot whales.

SHARK TALE

PHOTOGRAPHER: **Brian Skerry**
ANIMAL: **Oceanic whitetip shark**
SHOOT SITE: **The Bahamas**

"I wanted to photograph an endangered oceanic whitetip shark. So I set sail with a group of scientists to an area where some had been sighted. Days later, the dorsal fin of a whitetip rose from the water near our boat. One scientist was lowered in a metal cage into the water to observe the fish. Then I dived in. Because I wasn't behind the protective bars, I had to be very careful. These nine-foot (2.7-m) sharks can be aggressive, but this one was just curious. She swam around us for two hours and allowed me to take pictures of her. She was the perfect model."

LEAPS and BOUNDS

PHOTOGRAPHER: **Nick Nichols**
ANIMAL: **Bengal tiger**
SHOOT SITE: **Bandhavgarh National Park, India**

"While following a tiger along a cliff, I saw him leap from the edge to his secret watering hole and take a drink. I wanted a close-up of the cat, but it wouldn't have been safe to approach him. Figuring he'd return to the spot, I set up a camera on the cliff that shoots off an infrared beam. Walking into the beam triggers the camera to click. The device was there for three months, but this was the only shot I got of the cat. Being near tigers makes the hair stand up on my arm. It was a gift to encounter such a magnificent creature."

About 3,000 Bengal tigers are left in the wild.

123

WILD VET ADVENTURE
WITH ONE WILDLIFE DOCTOR

Animals can't tell their doctors when they aren't feeling well. So that makes the job of a wildlife veterinarian a little ... well, wild. Meet Gabby Wild, who travels the world to provide medical care for animals in zoos, shelters, national parks, and rescue centers. Here, the wildlife vet tells you how she treated one animal in need of a little medicine—and a lot of care.

KHUN CHAI (LEFT) NEEDED TO DRINK MILK FIVE TIMES A DAY.

ELEPHANT CALF GETS SOME TLC

"In Thailand, a country in Southeast Asia, people sometimes use elephants as work animals to help on their farms. One farmer illegally stole an elephant calf from the forest, which he thought would be cheaper than buying an adult elephant. But soon the calf was close to dying. The farmer realized the young elephant needed medical help.

"He brought the youngster to a wildlife hospital where I was working, and we named the calf Khun Chai, which means 'prince' in Thai. We observed that he didn't want to play with the other elephants and refused to drink the milk we offered him.

"I had studied some elephant behavior, and I thought that maybe he just didn't want to be bothered. So when I went into his enclosure, I sat quietly on the ground and only looked at him out of the corner of my eye. About a half hour later, I could feel a light tap on my shoulder—Khun Chai was patting me with his trunk!

"From that moment on, Khun Chai followed me all around the rescue center. I fed him milk five times a day, walked him three times a day, and bathed him a few times a week. As he ate and gained weight, he became a healthy elephant.

"We decided that because people had raised Khun Chai, it would be dangerous to release him back into the forest. So eventually we moved him to a local conservation center where he could live with other elephants. I'm glad I could help him grow up to be healthy and happy."

A male Asian elephant usually lives with its mother for about five years.

Extreme Job!

There's not much normal about John Stevenson's job. A volcanologist, Stevenson evaluates eruptions, follows lava flows, and travels to remote locations to learn more about volcanoes. Read on for more details on his risky but rewarding career.

TESTING NEW RESEARCH EQUIPMENT

SCIENCE-MINDED "As a kid, I really liked science and nature, and in college I pursued chemical engineering but studied geology as well. Having a background in all of the sciences gave me a better understanding of the bigger picture, from volcano monitoring to understanding eruptions."

BIG DIG "I once spent ten days collecting pumice and ash samples from a 4,200-year-old eruption in Iceland. We'd dig in the soil until we found the layer of ash that we wanted, then spend up to two hours photographing and taking samples. At night, we'd find a nice spot by a stream, eat dinner, and camp out."

DANGER IN THE AIR "Being exposed to the edge of a lava flow can be dangerous. The air is hot and can be thick with poisonous sulfur dioxide gas. Once, while working at the active Bárðarbunga volcano in Iceland, we had to wear gas masks and use an electronic gas meter as dust swirled around us."

RAINING ASH "When I worked at Volcán de Colima in Mexico, we camped a few miles from the crater. One night, I woke up to a whooshing sound. This quickly changed to a *patter-patter-patter* that sounded like heavy rain falling on the tent. When I put my hand out to feel the rain, it was covered in coarse gray sand. The volcano had erupted, and ash was raining down on us. We quickly packed up our stuff and headed to a safer spot."

JOB PERKS "I get to play with fun gadgets in cool locations. If I didn't have to work, I would still go hiking and camping and play with gadgets and computers in my spare time anyway. I enjoy trying to solve the problems of getting the right data and finding a way to process it so that it can tell us about how the world works."

WORKING IN THE FIELD

awes8me

Duh! Don't try these tricks on your own.

1 FLIPPING OUT

Freeride mountain biking sends riders down routes that look impossible to most people. Besides trails, bikers ride on wood planks, platforms, and even off cliffs! U.S. biker Cameron Zink impressed the crowd at a freeride mountain bike competition in Utah, U.S.A., when he completed a 78-foot (24-m)-long backflip, one of the longest in history.

THIS IMAGE IS A MASH-UP OF SEVERAL PHOTOGRAPHS OF CAMERON ZINK'S 78-FOOT (24-M)-LONG BACKFLIP.

SOARING SPORTS

YOU'D BETTER LIKE HEIGHTS IF YOU PLAN TO PLAY THESE GAMES.

TOKYO 2020

2 DEFYING GRAVITY

Gymnasts use strength, agility, coordination, and balance to leap and flip in the air. Considered the world's best gymnast, Simone Biles of the United States (left) won four gold medals, one silver, and two bronze after competing at two Olympic Games. She even has four original moves named after her. Go, Simone!

4 DIVE IN

Look out below! This cliff diver takes a big leap in Mazatlán, Mexico. People have been **cliff diving** for centuries: It's said that Hawaiian warriors jumped from cliffs on the island of Lanai to prove their loyalty and bravery.

5 FLIGHT OF THE FUTURE

Hoverboards might become old school if **flyboards** (like the one shown here) ever take off. Still in development, this flyboard has four engines operated by a handheld remote. It's fueled by kerosene and will be able to cover more than 7,000 feet (2,134 m) without stopping. Up next: flyboard races in the sky!

3 ALLEY-OOP

Now here's a way to guarantee a dunk—**trampoline basketball,** or basketball with some assists by trampolines. Sometimes going by the name SlamBall, the game has increased in popularity as more trampoline parks open across the United States.

SPRINGS FOR FEET 6

This super bouncer from California can jump more than six feet (1.8 m) in the air on his **pogo stick.** Traditionally, pogo sticks get their bounce from springs, but this one works with compressed air, which increases height.

7 OFF THE WALL

You literally bounce off the walls with this pastime. Part gymnastics, part parkour, **wall trampoline** jumpers improvise flips and twists midair. Some circus acrobats have been doing a version of wall trampoline for years, and now jumpers are hoping to turn it into a competitive sport.

TWO PEOPLE PRACTICE WALL TRAMPOLINE AT THE QUEBEC CIRCUS SCHOOL IN CANADA.

8 GO FLY A KITE

Talk about catching some air. A **kiteboarder** uses the wind to his advantage on the waters near the island nation of Mauritius, off the coast of Madagascar. Kiteboarders move along the water and make jumps of up to 50 feet (15 m) by using strength and coordination to control the kite that they're attached to.

QUIZ WHIZ

Discover just how much you know about exploration with this quiz!

Write your answers on a piece of paper. Then check them below.

1 Fueled by _____ , the flyboard can cover more than 7,000 feet (2,134 m) without stopping.
a. gasoline
c. plant power
b. kerosene
d. solar power

2 True or false? Poachers sell slow lorises as pets.

3 Oceanic whitetip sharks have been observed swimming with groups of what other sea animals?
a. walruses
b. greenback turtles
c. orcas
d. pilot whales

4 A cliff in Colombia is covered with some 70,000 drawings of ancient animals, including _____.
a. giant sloths
b. ice age horses
c. mastodons
d. all of the above

5 Male Asian elephants usually live with their mothers for about _____ years.

Not **STUMPED** yet? Check out the *NATIONAL GEOGRAPHIC KIDS QUIZ WHIZ* collection for more crazy **EXPLORATION** questions!

ANSWERS: 1. b; 2. True; 3. d; 4. d; 5. 5

HOMEWORK HELP

How to Write a Perfect Essay

Need to write an essay? Does the assignment feel as big as climbing Mount Everest? Fear not. You're up to the challenge! The following step-by-step tips will help you with this monumental task.

1 **BRAINSTORM.** Sometimes the subject matter of your essay is assigned to you, sometimes it's not. Either way, you have to decide what you want to say. Start by brainstorming some ideas, writing down any thoughts you have about the subject. Then read over everything you've come up with and consider which idea you think is the strongest. Ask yourself what you want to write about the most. Keep in mind the goal of your essay. Can you achieve the goal of the assignment with this topic? If so, you're good to go.

2 **WRITE A TOPIC SENTENCE.** This is the main idea of your essay, a statement of your thoughts on the subject. Again, consider the goal of your essay. Think of the topic sentence as an introduction that tells your readers what the rest of your essay will be about.

3 **OUTLINE YOUR IDEAS.** Once you have a good topic sentence, you then need to support that main idea with more detailed information, facts, thoughts, and examples. These supporting points answer one question about your topic sentence—"Why?" This is where research and perhaps more brainstorming come in. Then organize these points in the way you think makes the most sense, probably in order of importance. Now you have an outline for your essay.

4 **ON YOUR MARK, GET SET, WRITE!** Follow your outline, using each of your supporting points as the topic sentence of its own paragraph. Use descriptive words to get your ideas across to readers. Go into detail, using specific information to tell your story or make your point. Stay on track, making sure that everything you include is somehow related to the main idea of your essay. Use transitions to make your writing flow.

5 **WRAP IT UP.** Finish your essay with a conclusion that summarizes your entire essay and restates your main idea.

6 **PROOFREAD AND REVISE.** Check for errors in spelling, capitalization, punctuation, and grammar. Look for ways to make your writing clear, understandable, and interesting. Use descriptive verbs, adjectives, and adverbs when possible. It also helps to have someone else read your work to point out things you might have missed. Then make the necessary corrections and changes in a second draft. Repeat this revision process once more to make your final draft as good as you can.

FUN and GAMES

A tokay gecko grips onto a tree.

What do you get if you cross a pastry with a snake?

A pie-thon.

CRITTER CHAT

ARE YOU AMOOSED?

If animals used social media, what would they say? Follow this moose's day as it updates its feed.

Moose

LIVES IN: Northern regions of North America, Europe, and Asia
SCREEN NAME: OhDeer
FRIENDS: ⌄

SPRUCE GROUSE	CANADA LYNX	SNOWSHOE HARE
WoodBird	CoolCat	SnowHopper

START

7 a.m.

OhDeer: It's about time to say goodbye to my magnificent antlers. Before I shed them next month, let's all admire these six-foot-wide bad boys.

WoodBird: Those antlers seem like a lot of trouble just to fight for a mate. All my guy had to do was show off some fluffy feathers. (Isn't he handsome?)

CoolCat: I'll take my ear tufts over your 40-pound antlers—and I don't need them to impress a mate. I just found another lynx that lives nearby.

SnowHopper: You'll look so different without your antlers! But not as different as I'll look in a few months when I'm wearing my grayish brown summer coat. 😊

12:00 p.m.

OhDeer: Before this lake freezes over, I'm going to swim a few laps. #SwimSelfie

SnowHopper: I'll hop in the water to avoid @CoolCat when she wakes up at sundown, but I'd much rather take a bath in dust.

WoodBird: I bet wet moose smells pretty bad. I'll stick to the trees to keep safe from @CoolCat.

CoolCat: You guys are no fun. I just want to play hide-and-seek ... and eat. 😊

6:00 p.m.

OhDeer: First flurry of the season! Doesn't the snow look good on me?

WoodBird: Woot! If this keeps up, I'll finally be able to relax in a deep burrow under the snow. #SnowDaySleepIn

CoolCat: Hide all you want. But I'm more interested in where @SnowHopper's hanging out.

SnowHopper: Ha! Good luck—my winter coat matches the snow, so you'll never find me. #HareMagic

OhDeer: Hey, where'd @SnowHopper go?

132

WHAT IN THE WORLD?

SQUIRMY WORMY

These photos show close-up views of creepy little critters. On a separate sheet of paper, unscramble the letters to identify what's in each picture.

ANSWERS ON PAGE 354

DIEPSR

RCSOOINP

ELETEB

RETITMSE

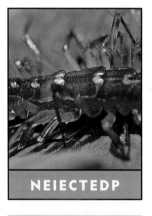

NEIECTEDP

HRACKCOCO

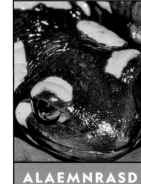

OMWSR

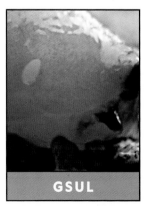

ALAEMNRASD

GSUL

133

SIGNS OF THE TIMES

Seeing isn't always believing. Two of these funny signs are not real. Can you spot which two are fake? **ANSWERS ON PAGE 354**

FUNNY FILL-IN

Ask a friend to give you words to fill in the blanks in this story and write them on a separate sheet of paper. Then read the story out loud and fill in the words for a laugh.

_____ and I set sail on the famous pirate ship the _____ _____ for
friend's name   _adjective_   _animal_

our summer vacation. After _____ out to sea, Captain _____ beard gave
                          verb ending in –ing   _color_

us a tour. Suddenly the sky turned dark and it started to _____ . A bolt of _____
                                                   verb   _noun_

streaked across the sky as a large wave filled with _____ crashed over the side of the
                                            noun, plural

ship. Fish were flying everywhere—one even landed on my _____ . The first mate,
                                                        body part

_____ , took cover with _____ . The captain was taking down the sail when a(n)
celebrity   _historical figure_

_____ gust of wind sent him flying through the air. He held on to the _____ but his
adjective   _noun_

trousers flew off the ship, showing _____-_____ underpants! After he landed back
                                           color   _noun_

on the deck, we all went below until the storm ended. But we didn't find the captain's pants until

_____ days later—when we spotted them on a(n) _____ 's fin.
large number   _ocean animal_

FUN STUFF
NOUN TOWN

This city is full of nouns, or people, places, and things. But 12 compound nouns—nouns made up of two or more words, or two words combined to make one word—have been drawn exactly as they're named. Can you guess the compound nouns illustrated in each of the numbered scenes? Here's a hint: The answer to number 1 is "sleeping bag."

ANSWERS ON PAGE 354

FIND THE HIDDEN ANIMALS

Animals often blend in with their environment for protection. Find each animal listed below in one of the pictures. On a separate sheet of paper, write the letter of the correct picture and the animal's name.

ANSWERS ON PAGE 354

1. stargazer (a type of fish)

2. arctic fox

3. pygmy seahorse

4. harlequin crab

5. katydid

6. common chameleon

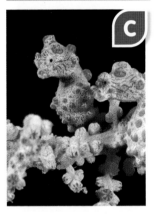

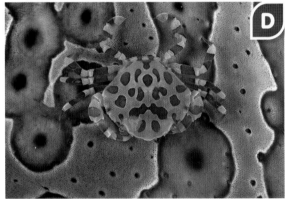

WHAT IN THE WORLD?

DOWN UNDER

These photographs show close-up and faraway views of things in Australia. On a separate sheet of paper, unscramble the letters to identify what's in each picture.

ANSWERS ON PAGE 354

DRSRBFUOSA

RTEGA ARERIBR FREE

ORNGAAKO

AWSCYSAOR

NREMBOGAO

RULUU

LAFG

OAAKL

DENYYS EORAP OESUH

FROM THE PAGES OF *QUIZ WHIZ:*

STUMP
YOUR PARENTS

Answer the questions on a separate sheet of paper. If your parents can't answer these questions, maybe they should go to school instead of you!

ANSWERS ON PAGE 354

1 Which of these wacky festivals is real?
a. the Lumberjack World Championships in Hayward, Wisconsin, U.S.A.
b. the Okie Noodling Tournament in Pauls Valley, Oklahoma, U.S.A.
c. the Rainbow Gathering in Santa Fe, New Mexico, U.S.A.
d. all of the above

2 _____ is the planet farthest from the sun.
a. Earth c. Mercury
b. Neptune d. Saturn

3 The first compasses were made in _____ .
a. China
b. Portugal
c. Peru
d. Zimbabwe

4 A person who studies trees is called a(n)_____ .
a. dendrologist
b. etymologist
c. treeologist
d. geologist

5 Before graduating high school, the average U.S. kid will have eaten _____ peanut butter and jelly sandwiches.
a. 800
b. 1,500
c. 2,600
d. 3,500

6 Which statement is false? Two-toed sloths _____ .
a. are often covered in algae
b. climb upside down
c. shiver
d. eat leaves

7 A group of grasshoppers is called a _____ .
a. cloud
b. pod
c. bloat
d. scrum

8 A _____ is the world's largest rodent.
a. chipmunk
b. New York City rat
c. capybara
d. marmot

9 Alfred Nobel, the man for whom the Nobel Peace Prize is named, invented _____ .
a. lightbulbs
b. sleeping bags
c. hot chocolate
d. dynamite

10 Match each country to the currency it uses:
a. Canada   1. metical
b. England   2. euro
c. Poland   3. dollar
d. Spain   4. pound
e. Mozambique 5. zloty

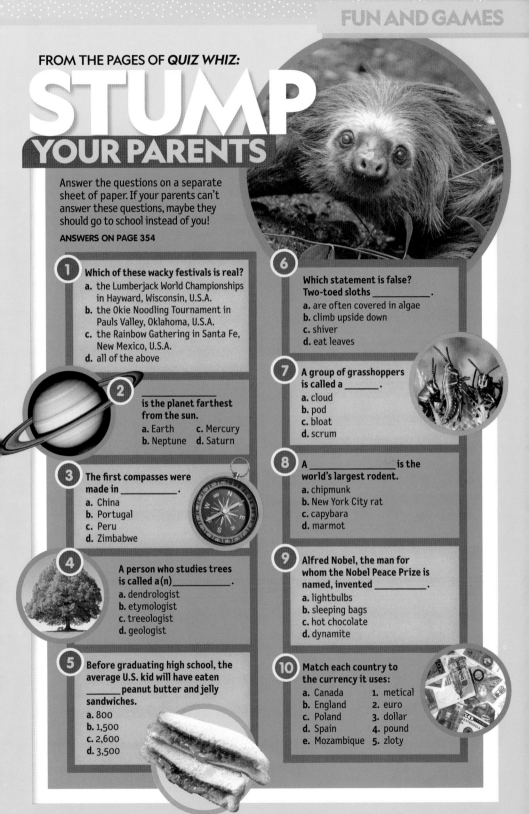

FUNNY FILL-IN

Ask a friend to give you words to fill in the blanks in this story and write them on a separate sheet of paper. Then read the story out loud and fill in the words for a laugh.

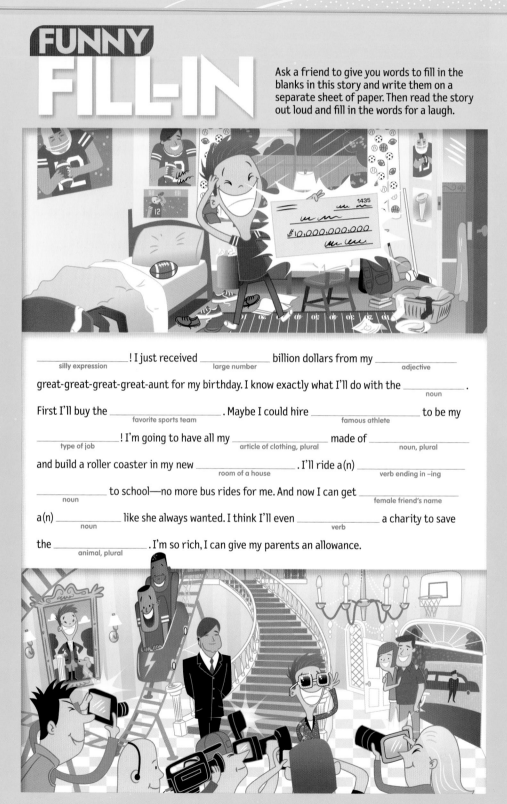

_____! I just received _____ billion dollars from my _____
silly expression   large number   adjective

great-great-great-great-aunt for my birthday. I know exactly what I'll do with the _____ .
                                                                                                                        noun

First I'll buy the _____ . Maybe I could hire _____ to be my
                            favorite sports team   famous athlete

_____! I'm going to have all my _____ made of _____
type of job   article of clothing, plural   noun, plural

and build a roller coaster in my new _____ . I'll ride a(n) _____
                                                            room of a house   verb ending in –ing

_____ to school—no more bus rides for me. And now I can get _____
noun   female friend's name

a(n) _____ like she always wanted. I think I'll even _____ a charity to save
           noun   verb

the _____ . I'm so rich, I can give my parents an allowance.
         animal, plural

LAUGH OUT LOUD

"NO THANKS."

"DO YOU HAVE ANYTHING
FOR DRY, SCALY SKIN?"

"I'M NOT OVER
HALLOWEEN YET."

Honk!

"I DON'T KNOW WHY HE DOESN'T
HONK LIKE THE REST OF US."

"I KNOW THIS IS GOING TO SOUND WEIRD
BUT ... I'M KINDA THIRSTY."

"FORGET THE GPS—LET'S
JUST FOLLOW THEM."

WHAT IN THE WORLD?

BEACH DAZE

These photographs show close-up views of objects you see at the beach. On a separate sheet of paper, unscramble the letters to identify what's in each picture.

ANSWERS ON PAGE 354

AMLP ETER

DASNELASCT

KOSLNER NAD KAMS

USMTIWSI

CABEH LABL

DEWAESE

LASLEHES

HEBAC WOLTE

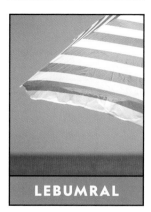

LEBUMRAL

FIND THE HIDDEN ANIMALS

Animals often blend in with their environment for protection. Find each animal listed below in one of the pictures. On a separate sheet of paper, write the letter of the correct picture and the animal's name.

ANSWERS ON PAGE 354

1. walking leaf insect
2. flounder
3. walruses
4. island fox
5. cowrie*
6. leaf-tailed gecko

***HINT:** A cowrie is a sea snail.

143

FUNNY FILL-IN

Ask a friend to give you words to fill in the blanks in this story and write them on a separate sheet of paper. Then read the story out loud and fill in the words for a laugh.

For summer break, my family took a trip to a(n) _____ town. I was excited to look
_____ historical era

for people wearing old-fashioned _____ and _____. My brother
_____ article of clothing, plural _____ noun, plural

only cared about seeing _____. We were _____ by a bank when a
_____ animal, plural _____ verb ending in –ing

man dressed in all _____ _____ out of the building. He threw some bags of
_____ color _____ past-tense verb

_____ over his shoulders before _____ off down the street. "Stop, thief!"
noun, plural _____ verb ending in –ing

a(n) _____ yelled behind us. I ran to the _____ next to the bank and
_____ type of job _____ animal, plural

_____ climbed on top of one. My brother tossed me a(n) _____ as I rode off
adverb ending in –ly _____ noun

after the crook. I twirled it in the air, _____ it around the _____ thief. I caught
_____ verb ending in –ing _____ adjective

him! The _____ gave my brother and me special badges as a thank-you for our help.
same type of job

Officer _____—I like the sound of that.
_____ your name

144

FROM THE PAGES OF *QUIZ WHIZ:*

STUMP
YOUR PARENTS

Answer the questions on a separate sheet of paper. If your parents can't answer these questions, maybe they should go to school instead of you!

ANSWERS ON PAGE 354

1 **What does mucus do?**
a. helps your lungs take in oxygen
b. makes flavors taste stronger
c. filters harmful bacteria from your body
d. stops your nose from collapsing

2 **Ostriches cannot do which of the following?** 
a. lay eggs
b. run
c. kick
d. fly

3 **Which is the world's highest waterfall?**
a. Niagara Falls, in Canada and the United States
b. Angel Falls, in Venezuela
c. Victoria Falls, in Zambia and Zimbabwe
d. Iguazú Falls, in Argentina and Brazil

4 **Which of these TV families first appeared in a 1938 magazine cartoon?**
a. the Addams family
b. the Flintstones
c. the Brady Bunch
d. the Munsters

5 **Which of the following terms would *not* be used to refer to a young lion?**
a. whelp
b. lionet
c. cub
d. calf

6 **Which ancestor do all dog breeds have in common?**
a. dinosaur
b. hyena
c. wolf
d. Scooby-Doo

7 **The scarab was a sacred insect in ancient Egypt. What is a scarab?**
a. a cockroach
b. a beetle
c. a wasp
d. a dragonfly

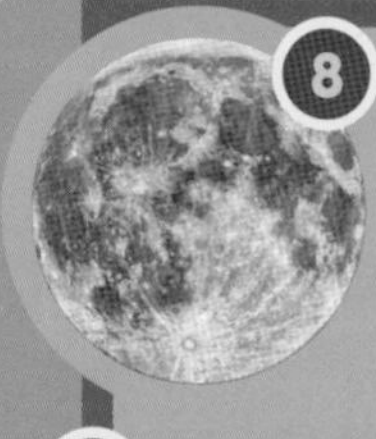

8 **What does Earth have that the moon does not?**
a. water
b. rocks
c. an atmosphere
d. aluminum

9 **In which century was the first macaroni and cheese recipe printed?**
a. 13th century
b. 15th century
c. 17th century
d. 21st century

10 **Which Disney princess kissed a frog?**
a. Ariel
b. Rapunzel
c. Tiana
d. Jasmine

145

WHAT IN THE WORLD?

RED ALERT

These photographs show close-up views of red things. On a separate sheet of paper, unscramble the letters to identify what's in each picture.

ANSWERS ON PAGE 354

ARESBIRSERP

IELCYBC

BYRU

EVSLGO

EDR XFO

PEPSRPE

EKRNAES

NAERGEMPAOT

AARDNLCI

CRITTER CHAT

I'M JUST THINKIN' ABOUT 'ROO!

If animals used social media, what would they say? Follow this eastern gray kangaroo's day as it updates its feed.

Eastern Gray Kangaroo

LIVES IN: Eastern Australia
SCREEN NAME: HopAlong
FRIENDS: ⌄

PLATYPUS	COASTAL PEACOCK SPIDER	COMMON BLUE-TONGUED SKINK
DuckBeaver	SparkleSpider	TongueSurprise

START

7 a.m.

HopAlong: Has anybody seen my joey? I just let him out of the pouch for the first time, and he's already hopped off on an adventure.

SparkleSpider: I'll keep all eight eyes out!

DuckBeaver: I remember when that little 'roo was the size of a cherry! That was when my lima bean–size babies were still in their eggs. (That's right, I'm a mammal that lays eggs!)

TongueSurprise: Oh yeah, I saw your joey not too long ago. He spooked me so much that I flashed my bright blue tongue at him to scare him off. #SorryNotSorry

HopAlong: Thanks, everybody! He's back in the pouch—and he's grounded.

3:00 p.m.

HopAlong: *Woot*—29 feet! My best long jump ever! #GoldMedalForMe

DuckBeaver: OK, but I'd lap you in a swimming contest. Meet me in the lagoon any time, any day.

SparkleSpider: That's nothing. Watch me shimmy-shake to impress a special lady spider.

TongueSurprise: That's one delicious-looking dance. 😊

4:55 p.m.

HopAlong: It's FINALLY cooling off. Time to feast on grass with my mob!

DuckBeaver: That sounds like too many party animals—I like to splash solo.

TongueSurprise: Bedtime for me. And since I just lost my tail to a falcon, I need my beauty sleep to start growing it back. TTYL!

SparkleSpider: Now that the lizard's snoozing, I can get in one last hunt without worrying. Look out, crickets!

147

20 THINGS
TO MAKE YOU
HAPPY

Looking at cute pictures of animals can make you happy, but there are other benefits, too! A study in Japan found that looking at pictures of cute baby animals may also boost your attention to detail and overall work performance.

What makes YOU HAPPY?

Rice Krispies Treats?
Jumping on a trampoline?
Reading comic books?

Make a "Happy List" of all the things that lift your spirits and refer to it when you need **a pick-me-up.**

PLAY WITH a puppy

There's actually a chemical reason you feel happier after snuggling a sweet pooch. When a person pets a dog, a hormone called oxytocin is released. It is a chemical that helps lower blood pressure and reduce stress.

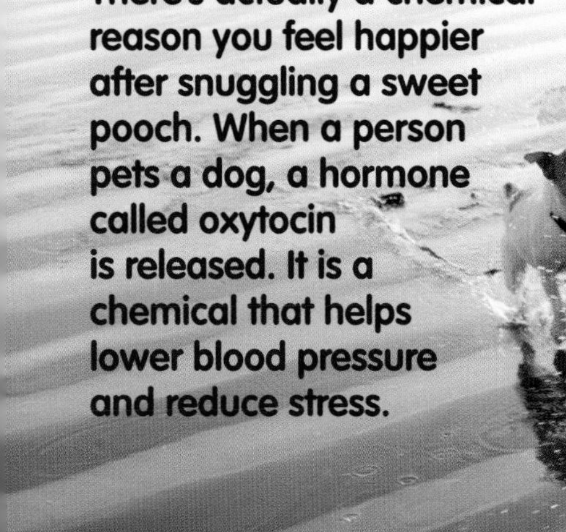

BECOME AN AWESOME LISTENER

TIP 1

TRY TO UNDERSTAND. Instead of thinking about what you'll say next, or whether you agree with the speaker, try to listen to what the person is telling you, why it's important to them, and how it makes them feel.

TIP 2

ASK FOLLOW-UP QUESTIONS. When someone is telling a story or sharing their feelings, don't immediately change the subject when they stop talking. To show that you're interested, ask questions about what they've told you. For example: Then what happened? How did that make you feel?

153

APPRECIATE SIMPLE PLEASURES

Take a bubble bath, watch the sun set, or eat a warm cookie.

Call a friend

GET MOVING!

- PLAY BASKETBALL
- ROLLER-SKATE
- RIDE A BICYCLE
- SWIM
- JUMP ROPE
- HAVE A DANCE PARTY
- JUMP ON A TRAMPOLINE
- PUNCH A PUNCHING BAG
- PLAY TAG, KICKBALL, OR CAPTURE THE FLAG
- TRY MARTIAL ARTS, LIKE KARATE OR TAE KWON DO

DON'T BE AFRAID TO FAIL!

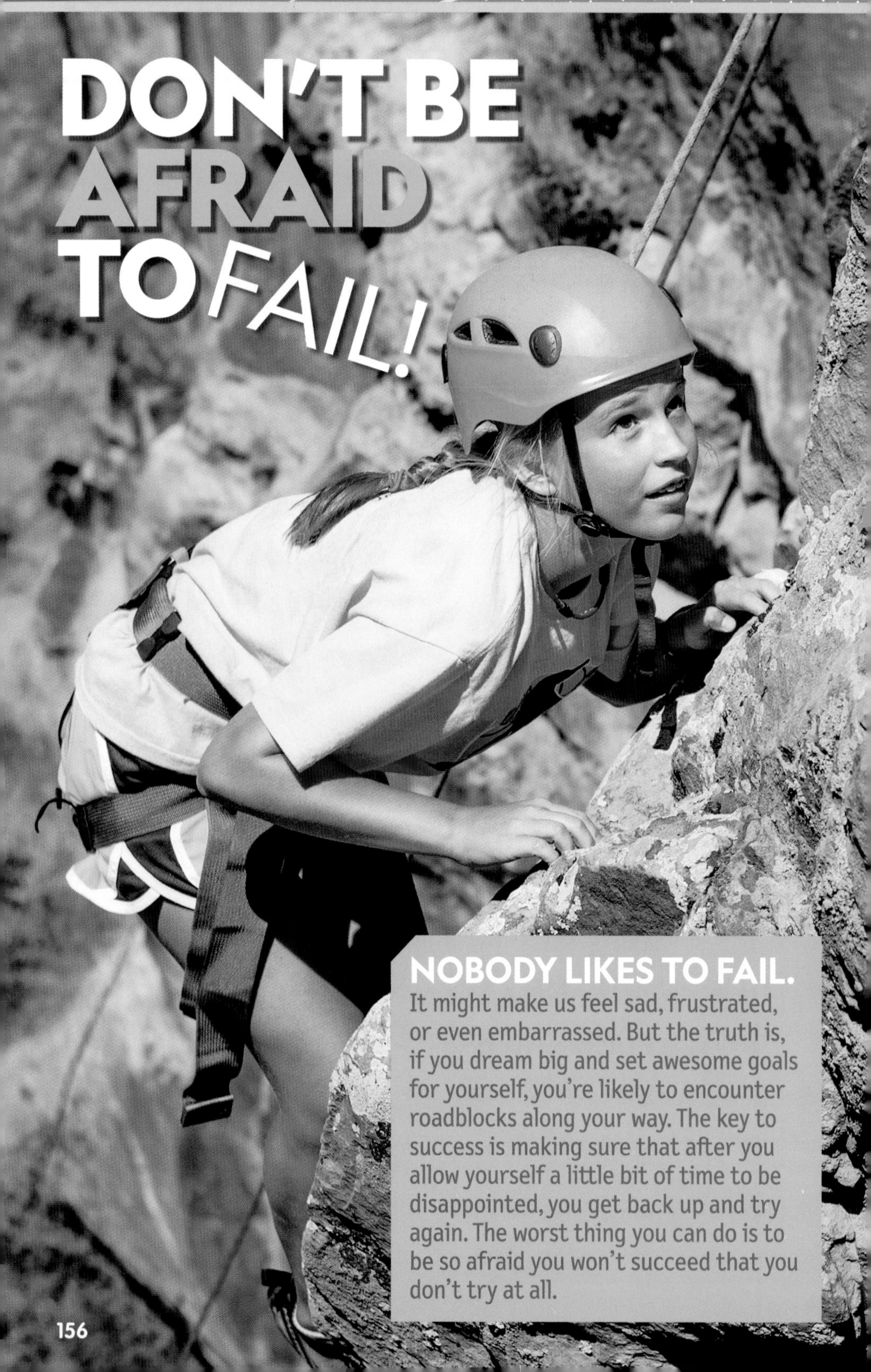

NOBODY LIKES TO FAIL.

It might make us feel sad, frustrated, or even embarrassed. But the truth is, if you dream big and set awesome goals for yourself, you're likely to encounter roadblocks along your way. The key to success is making sure that after you allow yourself a little bit of time to be disappointed, you get back up and try again. The worst thing you can do is to be so afraid you won't succeed that you don't try at all.

Meditate

5 Awesome Facts About Meditation:

 1 Meditation is a practice to train and quiet the mind.

 2 Studies have found that after eight weeks of meditating daily, people experience neuroplasticity, which means their brains physically change. So cool!

 3 Meditation has been shown to lower physical pain, anxiety, and blood pressure, as well as boost memory, alertness, and creativity.

 4 Meditation is not about clearing or ridding your mind of thoughts; in fact, thoughts are a normal part of practicing meditation. As the doctor, author, and meditator Deepak Chopra said, "Meditation is not a way of making your mind quiet. It is a way of entering into the quiet that is already there—buried under the 50,000 thoughts the average person thinks every day."

 5 Meditation isn't a religious practice—people from all different walks of life meditate.

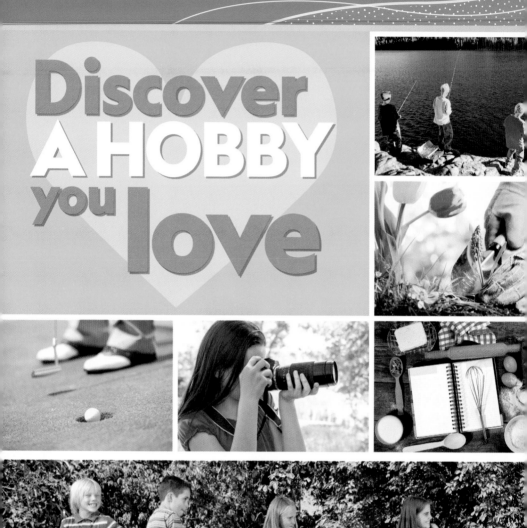

Discover A HOBBY you love

Be resilient.

THINK HAPPY THOUGHTS

JUST THINKING ABOUT HAPPY EXPERIENCES AND MEMORIES CAN MAKE YOU HAPPIER, SO WHY NOT GIVE THESE SOME THOUGHT?

The last time you laughed really hard

A time when you made someone else really, really happy

Something you're looking forward to in the future

The best meal you've ever eaten

Never, ever give up!

TRY yoga

WHAT IS YOGA?

Yoga is a practice that brings together our body, breath, and mind so that these different parts of us are all working together.

Happy Activity

Try the cat-cow yoga pose to get started and pump up your happiness.

STEP 1: To begin the pose, get down on your hands and knees. Place your hands right underneath your shoulders on the floor and your knees beneath your hips. Spread your fingers out nice and wide.

STEP 2: Inhale deeply and arch your back. Then pull your shoulders down while you look up at the ceiling so that your whole spine has a beautiful arch to it.

STEP 3: As you breathe out, round your back, spread out your shoulder blades, and look toward your belly.

STEP 4: Flow back and forth between these movements three to five times, or however many you like. Make sure you move slowly and breathe fully with each movement.

STEP 5: Check in with yourself to see if anything has shifted or changed. You've gotten oxygen into your system, regulated your breath and nervous system, and set the stage for happiness to unfold.

FORGIVE

WHEN SOMEONE HURTS
YOUR FEELINGS,

or treats you badly, it can be hard to move forward.
But holding on to that anger and bitterness is actually hurting *you*,
not them. And studies have found that forgiving someone
can reduce depression, anxiety, and anger. So for your health
and happiness, learn to let go and forgive.

KEEP
AN OPEN MIND

When you're willing
to see things from a
different angle, cool
things start happening—
you meet interesting
people, make amazing
discoveries, and
embark on awesome
adventures.

TAKE CARE
OF SOMETHING

Whether it be a puppy or a plant, if something relies on you to be there and nurture it, that gives you purpose. And having purpose makes people happy.

Pick Flowers

(though not from your neighbor's garden)!

LISTEN TO MUSIC

STUDIES HAVE FOUND THAT MUSIC CAN LESSEN ANXIETY, RELIEVE STRESS, AND BOOST LISTENERS' MOODS. SO TURN UP THOSE HAPPY TUNES!

Sleep soundly

Sleep is the body's way of recharging every night, and it's very important to your overall health. Sleep increases your ability to learn new things, improves your memory, and boosts your attention span. It also helps you be more alert, keep your emotions steady, and feel happier. With all of sleep's great benefits, it's no wonder experts recommend getting between 8½ and 9¼ hours of sleep a night.

Five Keys to Better Z's

) Turn off TVs, computers, cell phones, and other gadgets at least one hour before bedtime.

) Try to go to sleep and wake up around the same time each day.

) Avoid caffeine after noon each day.

) Exercise regularly.

) Try to decrease stress. If you are feeling anxious, try guided meditation, positive visualization, or a breathing exercise before bed.

BE GRATEFUL

Keep a Gratitude Journal

Every night, for about five minutes, take time to reflect on your day and all the parts of it that you're thankful for. If you're having trouble thinking of good things, try answering these questions.

- What went well today?
- Who are the people in my life I love? What do I love about them?
- What parts of my body are healthy and working well?
- What makes me laugh?
- Did I see anything, do anything, or eat anything today that made me smile?

Write a Thank-You Note

You know what's even better than thinking of why you're grateful? Telling someone that you're grateful for them or for something they did. Try writing someone a note, whether it be to a parent, teacher, sister, brother, or friend, and tell them that you appreciate them in your life, and why. Be specific about what it is they do that you're grateful for and how these things make you feel. Not only will you be making whoever you send it to feel happy, you'll feel happier, too!

GO outside

Humans need to be outside, in the sunlight, breathing fresh air into our lungs and being inspired by nature. So turn off that glowing screen and step outside!

5 THINGS TO DO OUTSIDE

1. Go for a hike or nature walk.
2. Climb a tree.
3. Roller-skate or in-line skate.
4. Make up a synchronized swimming routine, or play Marco Polo, in a pool.
5. Check out a field guide from the library and try to identify a flower, tree, or bird.

Costumed performers entertain a crowd with a traditional lion dance during a Lunar New Year celebration in London, England.

CULTURE CONNECTION

CELEBRATIONS

LUNAR NEW YEAR
January 22

Also called Chinese New Year, this holiday marks the new year according to the lunar calendar. Families celebrate with parades, feasts, and fireworks. Young people may receive gifts of money in red envelopes.

NAURYZ
March 21

This ancient holiday is a major moment on the Kazakhstan calendar. To usher in the start of spring, the people of this Asian country set up tentlike shelters called yurts, play games, go to rock concerts, and feast on rich foods.

EASTER
April 9†

A Christian holiday that honors the resurrection of Jesus Christ, Easter is celebrated by giving baskets filled with gifts, decorated eggs, or candy to children.

THE WHITE NIGHTS FESTIVAL
Second week of June through the first week of July

In St. Petersburg, Russia, during the "white nights" of summer the sun stays just above the horizon at night ... and the city comes alive. Festivities held under the midnight sun include the Scarlet Sails celebration, featuring a tall red-sailed ship and a brilliant fireworks display on the Neva River.

MEDELLÍN FLOWER FESTIVAL
(LA FERIA DE LAS FLORES)
Late July/Early August

Each year, Colombia showcases the work of local farmers by displaying their beautiful blooms throughout the city of Medellín. The weeklong festival is complete with competitions and a parade featuring flower-covered floats, horses, antique cars, and more.

ROSH HASHANAH
September 15*-17

A Jewish holiday marking the beginning of a new year on the Hebrew calendar. Celebrations include prayer, ritual foods, and a day of rest.

Around the World

THIMPHU TSHECHU
September 24-26

This colorful three-day Buddhist festival in Thimphu, Bhutan, features bustling markets, religious devotion, and entertainment that includes dances performed wearing traditional masks.

DIWALI
November 12

To symbolize the inner light that protects against spiritual darkness, people light their homes with clay lamps for India's largest and most important holiday.

HANUKKAH
December 7*-15

This Jewish holiday is eight days long. It commemorates the rededication of the Temple in Jerusalem. Hanukkah celebrations include the lighting of menorah candles for eight days and the exchange of gifts.

CHRISTMAS DAY
December 25

A Christian holiday marking the birth of Jesus Christ, Christmas is usually celebrated by decorating trees, exchanging presents, and having festive gatherings.

*Begins at sundown.
† Orthodox Easter is April 16.

2023 CALENDAR

JANUARY
S	M	T	W	T	F	S
1	2	3	4	5	6	7
8	9	10	11	12	13	14
15	16	17	18	19	20	21
22	23	24	25	26	27	28
29	30	31				

FEBRUARY
S	M	T	W	T	F	S
			1	2	3	4
5	6	7	8	9	10	11
12	13	14	15	16	17	18
19	20	21	22	23	24	25
26	27	28				

MARCH
S	M	T	W	T	F	S
			1	2	3	4
5	6	7	8	9	10	11
12	13	14	15	16	17	18
19	20	21	22	23	24	25
26	27	28	29	30	31	

APRIL
S	M	T	W	T	F	S
						1
2	3	4	5	6	7	8
9	10	11	12	13	14	15
16	17	18	19	20	21	22
23	24	25	26	27	28	29
30						

MAY
S	M	T	W	T	F	S
	1	2	3	4	5	6
7	8	9	10	11	12	13
14	15	16	17	18	19	20
21	22	23	24	25	26	27
28	29	30	31			

JUNE
S	M	T	W	T	F	S
				1	2	3
4	5	6	7	8	9	10
11	12	13	14	15	16	17
18	19	20	21	22	23	24
25	26	27	28	29	30	

JULY
S	M	T	W	T	F	S
						1
2	3	4	5	6	7	8
9	10	11	12	13	14	15
16	17	18	19	20	21	22
23	24	25	26	27	28	29
30	31					

AUGUST
S	M	T	W	T	F	S
		1	2	3	4	5
6	7	8	9	10	11	12
13	14	15	16	17	18	19
20	21	22	23	24	25	26
27	28	29	30	31		

SEPTEMBER
S	M	T	W	T	F	S
					1	2
3	4	5	6	7	8	9
10	11	12	13	14	15	16
17	18	19	20	21	22	23
24	25	26	27	28	29	30

OCTOBER
S	M	T	W	T	F	S
1	2	3	4	5	6	7
8	9	10	11	12	13	14
15	16	17	18	19	20	21
22	23	24	25	26	27	28
29	30	31				

NOVEMBER
S	M	T	W	T	F	S
			1	2	3	4
5	6	7	8	9	10	11
12	13	14	15	16	17	18
19	20	21	22	23	24	25
26	27	28	29	30		

DECEMBER
S	M	T	W	T	F	S
					1	2
3	4	5	6	7	8	9
10	11	12	13	14	15	16
17	18	19	20	21	22	23
24	25	26	27	28	29	30
31						

awes8me

Festive Parades

THESE SUPER SPECTACLES WILL PUT YOU IN A PARTY MOOD.

2 **FLOWER POWER**

For more than a century, fantastic flower-covered floats and marching bands have dazzled crowds at the annual Rose Parade in Pasadena, California, U.S.A., on New Year's Day. Not a fan of flowers? Stick around for a college football game that follows the parade.

4 COLORFUL RITUAL

Millions of people of the Hindu faith come together to take a ritual dip in one of four sacred rivers in India as part of the Kumbh Mela festival. The religious procession can include elephants and camels, and festival organizers often provide music and dance performances.

5 BALLOON BONANZA

More than three million people lined the streets of New York City to watch the debut of this Hello Kitty balloon in the Macy's Thanksgiving Day Parade. The parade has been held on the morning of Thanksgiving almost every year since 1924.

3 BLAZING BOAT

The Up Helly Aa festival in Lerwick, Scotland, ends every January in a blaze. Harking back to a Viking ritual, hundreds of torchbearers march through the town's streets before setting a 30-foot (9-m)-long galley—a type of ship—on fire.

DANCE PARTY 6

With fancy headdresses and costumes, dancers perform the samba, an Afro-Brazilian group dance, in front of a crowd at the Carnival parade in Rio de Janeiro, Brazil. Carnival, a festival of merrymaking and feasting, allows people to let loose.

7 FLOATING FESTIVAL

People in Venice, Italy, take their parades to the water. That's because this city is built in a lagoon with canals for streets. Revelers float down the Grand Canal in decorated gondolas and other boats, like this giant mouse gondola, during the annual Carnival festival.

8 CLOWN REVELRY

Giant jesters parade through the streets of the historic French Quarter in New Orleans, Louisiana. During the annual Mardi Gras celebration, nearly a hundred krewes—or festive groups—toss goodies, including toys, stuffed animals, and Mardi Gras beads, to the people who come to watch.

What's Your Chinese Horoscope?
Locate your birth year to find out.

In Chinese astrology, the zodiac runs on a 12-year cycle, based on the lunar calendar. Each year corresponds to one of 12 animals, each representing one of 12 personality types. Read on to find out which animal year you were born in and what that might say about you.

RAT
1972, '84, '96, 2008, '20
Say cheese! You're attractive, charming, and creative. When you get mad, you can have really sharp teeth!

RABBIT
1975, '87, '99, 2011, '23
Your ambition and talent make you jump at opportunity. You also keep your ears open for gossip.

HORSE
1966, '78, '90, 2002, '14
Being happy is your *mane* goal. And though you're smart and hardworking, your teacher may ride you for talking too much.

ROOSTER
1969, '81, '93, 2005, '17
You crow about your adventures, but inside you're really shy. You're thoughtful, capable, brave, and talented.

OX
1973, '85, '97, 2009, '21
You're smart, patient, and as strong as an ... well, you know. Though you're a leader, you never brag.

DRAGON
1988, 2000, '12, '24
You're on fire! Health, energy, honesty, and bravery make you a living legend.

SHEEP
1967, '79, '91, 2003, '15
Gentle as a lamb, you're also artistic, compassionate, and wise. You're often shy.

DOG
1970, '82, '94, 2006, '18
Often the leader of the pack, you're loyal and honest. You can also keep a secret.

TIGER
1974, '86, '98, 2010, '22
You may be a nice person, but no one should ever enter your room without asking—you might attack!

SNAKE
1977, '89, 2001, '13
You may not speak often, but you're very smart. You always seem to have a stash of cash.

MONKEY
1968, '80, '92, 2004, '16
No "monkey see, monkey do" for you. You're a clever problem-solver with an excellent memory.

PIG
1971, '83, '95, 2007, '19
Even though you're courageous, honest, and kind, you never hog all the attention.

6 Spooky Facts for Halloween

1 Cat **urine** can **glow** under **black light.**

2 **Phasmophobia** is the **fear of ghosts.**

3 A man **sculpted a statue** of himself using his own **hair, teeth,** and **nails.**

4 **Vampire bats** don't actually **suck blood—** they **lap it up** with their **tongues.**

5 Mike the **chicken** set a world record by living for **18 months** without a head, from **1945 to 1947.**

6 In ancient Egypt, **a mummy's brain** was removed through the **nose.**

THE WORLD'S LARGEST SANDCASTLE STANDS AS TALL AS A SIX-STORY BUILDING.

The **CASTLE IN DENMARK** beat the previous **RECORD-HOLDING CASTLE,** built in Germany, by about **10 FEET.** (3 m)

IMAGES of **WINDSURFING** and **KITESURFING**—two popular activities in the beach town where it was built— **ARE CARVED INTO THE CASTLE.**

Built in Denmark in 2021 by a squad of 30 sculptors, the sizable sandcastle is solid enough to stand tall through stormy weather. The secret ingredient to get it to stay put? A little bit of clay and a layer of glue.

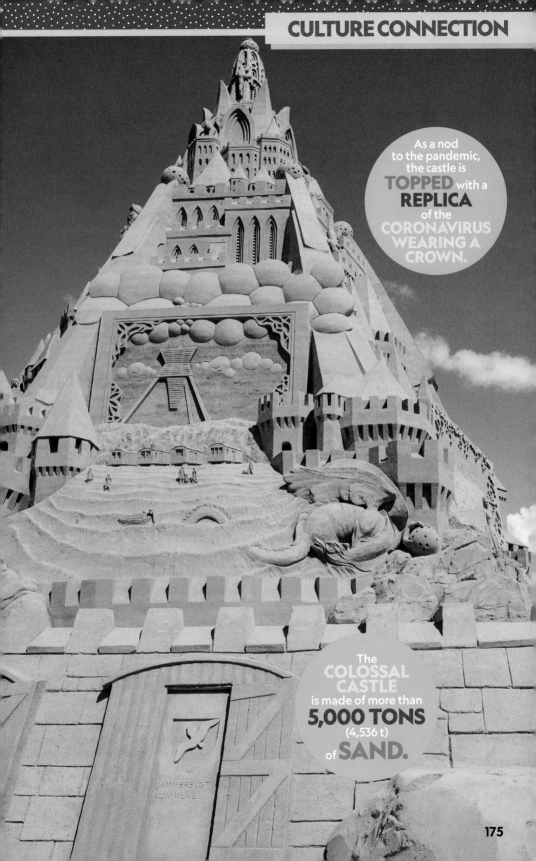

As a nod to the pandemic, the castle is **TOPPED** with a **REPLICA** of the **CORONAVIRUS WEARING A CROWN.**

The **COLOSSAL CASTLE** is made of more than **5,000 TONS** (4,536 t) of **SAND.**

JAMMERBUGT KOMMUNE

Cake Fakes

How bakers cook up these desserts in disguise

According to cake artists, the best thing about baking fancy cakes isn't eating them—it's delivering their awesome creations to customers. "In the 50 years I've been doing this, the thing I most look forward to is someone's reaction when I present them with their cake," cake decorator Serdar Yener says. Cake artists like Yener use some cool tricks to inspire these reactions from customers—and to make their baked goods look extra-realistic. A few of these artists spill their secrets here.

TOILET PAPER ... YUM?

Baker Kate Pritchett knew her toilet-paper-roll cake looked like the real deal when her husband found it in the fridge and tried to take it out. "He thought it was actual toilet paper and didn't know why it was in the refrigerator!" she says. The fake TP is actually a three-layer chocolate cake topped with marshmallow-flavored icing. Pritchett used several tools to scratch patterns on the icing to give it a toilet paper–like appearance.

SWEET TOOTH, ER, TEETH

Makeup artist Molly Robbins decided to try painting cakes instead of people's faces after making desserts that resembled her customers' pets. She eventually moved on to crafting complicated wild animals, such as sloths, giraffes, and, yup, sharks. To give this predator its sharp-looking teeth, Robbins sculpted cubes of sugar into some 30 individual shark teeth—only a 10th as many as the 300 a real great white shark would have.

THE PERFECT PIZZA

Bite into this greasy-looking slice of pepperoni pizza and you'll get a sugary surprise: chocolate cake, vanilla buttercream, and pieces of chocolate painted to look like pepperoni. Baker Ben Cullen drizzled a sugary glaze over the "cheese" to make it look oily, plus he curled up the edges of the chocolate pepperonis with a tweezer for a just-out-of-the-oven appearance. To get the crust color right, he experimented with yellow, red, and brown food dyes for a slightly burnt look.

ONE SCOOP OF CAKE, PLEASE

This sundae actually *is* as sweet as it looks! But the entire treat is made of mostly cake, and not, well, ice cream. Decorator BethAnn Goldberg uses a special icing called fondant that's easy to mold and creates a smooth surface. The cherry on top? A hunk of fondant. The bowl and spoon? Also fondant. "Working with fondant is sort of like playing with edible Play-Doh," Goldberg says. She did include *some* cake in the dish: The "scoops" of ice cream are cake—they're flavored to taste like the ice cream they represent.

TIGER-LICIOUS

This 10-pound (4.5-kg) tiger cake gets its real-life look from colored airbrushing: orange-and-white fur that was airbrushed on, then finished with airbrushed black stripes. Its eyeballs are actually white-sugar spheres that have been painted to look like a real tiger's eyes. To keep the heavy cake head from falling off, Yener stuck chopsticks on both sides of the tiger's neck to hold the head in place.

SNEAKY SNEAKERS

Goldberg scuffed up these kicks on purpose, like new-but-ripped jeans. "That's what makes it look like it's *really* a shoe," she says. Goldberg started with a block of vanilla sponge cake that she carved into a sneaker shape. Then she molded fondant over the sneaker structure. Finally, she brushed powdered edible paint over the fondant to look like fabric and added gray scuff marks with a tiny paintbrush.

EAT THE BEAT

You can strum this guitar cake—but you'd have to lick your fingers afterward. Except for the flexible cords used to mimic real guitar strings, this 2.8-foot (0.9-m)-long instrument is completely edible. Plus, the whole thing is coated in a sweet glaze to make it shine. To make the neck, Yener used a sugar paste that dries superhard; the body of the guitar is made of sponge cake that Yener covered with colored fondant. "The hardest part of making any cake is always delivering it," he says. "You're like an airline pilot that has to land *very* carefully."

THE SECRET HISTORY OF
CHOCOLATE

THESE FACTS WILL MELT IN YOUR MOUTH.

Deep in the South American rainforest is ... a chocolate tree? One-foot (0.3-m)-long bright yellow pods hang from its branches. Inside are small, bitter seeds that give the tree its name: cacao (kuh-KOW). (The first part of the seed's scientific name, *Theobroma cacao*, translates to "food of the gods" in Greek.) These seeds are how we make chocolate.

The seeds—which grow only near the Equator—don't look or taste delicious.

But ancient people figured out how to use them to make tasty treats. Check out this timeline for the sweet scoop on the history of chocolate.

① 3300 B.C.

The earliest people known to have used the cacao plant are the ancient Mayo-Chinchipe people of what's now Ecuador, a country in South America. Experts aren't sure whether these people used the plant for food, drink, or medicine. But they do know the culture used cacao often, because they found traces of theobromine— a natural chemical compound that comes from the plant—in artifacts found at archaeological sites throughout the region.

② ca 1800 B.C.

The ancient Olmec people of Mesoamerica (what's now Mexico and Central America) begin using cacao seeds—also called cocoa beans—to brew warm, flavored drinks. Historians aren't sure how the Olmec figured out that the plant's bitter beans would make tasty beverages. But one guess is that when they ate the fruit surrounding the seeds, they'd spit the seeds into a fire, which gave off a pleasing smell.

CACAO BEANS GROW INSIDE PODS LIKE THESE. THE COLOR OF THE POD CHANGES BASED ON SEVERAL THINGS, LIKE THE PLANT'S LOCATION.

Historians don't always know the exact dates of historical events. That's why you'll see a "ca" next to some of the years on these pages. It stands for "circa," meaning "around."

Chocolate bars have been taken on every American and Russian space voyage.

③ ca EIGHTH CENTURY A.D.

Cha-ching! The Maya, another group of ancient people from Mesoamerica, start using cocoa beans as money. Archaeologists have even found counterfeit beans made of clay that people tried to pass off as the real deal.

4 1500s

Many Aztec—ancient people who lived in what's now central Mexico—are drinking cacao every day, mixing the seeds with chilies to make a spicy, frothy beverage. In 1519, Spanish explorer Hernán Cortés reported that Aztec ruler Montezuma II drank 50 cups a day. Cortés brings the drink back to Spain in 1528, and the Spaniards make one big change—adding sugar.

5 1600s–1700s

Chocolate houses—similar to coffeehouses today—become popular gathering spots for rich Europeans and Americans to meet over a hot chocolate drink. During the Revolutionary War, which lasts from 1775 to 1783, wounded soldiers are given the beverage to warm them and provide an energy boost, and troops are sometimes paid with cocoa beans. In 1785, Thomas Jefferson predicts that hot chocolate will become as popular as tea or coffee.

6 1800s

A company called J. S. Fry & Sons of England adds extra cacao butter to liquid chocolate, turning it solid and creating the first mass-produced chocolate bars. Over the next several decades, chocolate makers add milk powder to their recipes to create milk chocolate.

FRY'S CHOCOLATE CREAM

Chocolate is still kind of ... chewy. So in 1879, Rodolphe Lindt of Switzerland comes up with a process called conching, in which a machine stirs the chocolate until it gets that melt-in-your-mouth texture. Dozens of different brands start making their own chocolate bars with the conching process.

A chemical in cacao releases feel-good chemicals in the brain.

7 EARLY 1900s

At the beginning of the 20th century, the main ingredient in chocolate—cocoa—becomes much cheaper. Chocolate is no longer a treat for just rich people, and stores around the world are stocked with affordable chocolate bars for everyone.

8 2023

Chocolate can now be found in grocery stores, candy shops ... and on the runway. Salon du Chocolat, the world's biggest chocolate festival, features a chocolate fashion show in Paris, France, every year, with clothes made of the sweet treat. The outfits are too fragile to be sold, so after the festival some are put on display in what must be the best-smelling museum exhibit ever.

MONEY AROUND THE WORLD!

The Southern Cross constellation appears on **Brazilian coins.**

ACCORDING to some **PEOPLE, CANADA'S $100 BANKNOTE** gives off the scent of **MAPLE SYRUP.**

A British businessman created his own currency —named the **PUFFIN—** for an island he owned off England.

IN FEBRUARY 2015, SCUBA DIVERS OFF ISRAEL FOUND MORE THAN 2,600 GOLD COINS DATING BACK AS FAR AS THE NINTH CENTURY.

Bank of **BOTSWANA**

400141

This note is legal tender for

Ten Pula

10

Botswana's currency is named **PULA,** meaning **"RAIN,"** which is **VALUABLE** in this **ARID NATION.**

A **JANITOR** at a **GERMAN LIBRARY** found and turned in a **BOX OF RARE COINS** thought to be worth **HUNDREDS OF THOUSANDS OF DOLLARS.**

ANCIENT GREEKS believed that **PLACING A COIN IN A DEAD PERSON'S MOUTH** would pay for the ferry ride to the afterlife.

COINS CREATED IN **1616** FOR WHAT IS NOW **BERMUDA** WERE NICKNAMED **"HOGGIES"** BECAUSE THEY HAD IMAGES OF **HOGS** ON THEM.

More than **$5 TRILLION** in **MONOPOLY MONEY** has been printed since 1935.

KING TUT APPEARS ON THE EGYPTIAN 1-POUND COIN.

IN INDIA, the SLANG TERM for **100,000 RUPEES IS** *PETI*, OR **SUITCASE.** You might need one to carry that much money!

A BRITISH ARTIST MADE A DRESS OUT OF USED **BANKNOTES** FROM AROUND THE **WORLD.**

MONEY TIP! CLIP COUPONS FOR YOUR PARENTS. Ask if they'll put the money they save into your piggy bank.

SAVING
Languages At Risk

Today, there are more than 7,000 languages spoken on Earth. But by 2100, more than half of these may disappear. In fact, some experts say one language dies every two weeks, as a result of the increasing dominance of languages such as English, Spanish, and Mandarin.

So what can be done to keep dialects from disappearing altogether? To start, several National Geographic Explorers have embarked on various projects around the planet. Together, they are part of the race to save some of the world's most threatened languages, as well as to protect and preserve the cultures they belong to. Here are some of the Explorers' stories.

The Explorer: Tam Thi Ton
The Language: Bahnar

The Work: By gathering folklore like riddles and comics, Ton is creating bilingual learning materials for elementary students to teach them Bahnar, the language of an ethnic group living in Vietnam's Central Highlands.

TON IN A BAHNAR CLASSROOM

The Explorer: Sandhya Narayanan
The Languages: Quechua and Aymara

The Work: By immersing herself in the Indigenous languages of the Andean region along the Peru-Bolivia border, Narayanan aims to understand how inter-actions among Indigenous groups affect language over time.

NARAYANAN SHARES STORIES FROM THE FIELD AT NATIONAL GEOGRAPHIC'S HEADQUARTERS IN WASHINGTON, D.C., U.S.A.

HARRISON DOING AN INTERVIEW

The Explorer: K. David Harrison
The Language: Koro-Aka

The Work: Harrison led an expedition to India that identified Koro-Aka, a language which was completely new to science. He is also vice president of the Living Tongues Institute for Endangered Languages, dedicated to raising awareness and revitalizing little-documented languages.

The Explorer: Susan Barfield
The Language: Mapudungun

The Work: Barfield shines a light on the language of the Mapuche people of southern Chile with her trilingual children's book, *El Copihue*. The book is based on a Mapuche folktale and is illustrated by Mapuche students.

BARFIELD PRESENTS AN OFFERING DURING A BOOK BLESSING CEREMONY.

PERLIN INTERVIEWS A VILLAGE LEADER.

The Explorer: Ross Perlin
The Language: Seke

The Work: In an effort to preserve the Seke language of northern Nepal, Perlin has been working closely with speakers both in their villages and in New York, where many now live, including young speakers determined to document their own language.

The Explorer: Lal Rapacha
The Language: Kiranti-Kõits

The Work: As the founder and director of the Research Institute for Kiratology in Kathmandu, Nepal, Rapacha carries out research on the lesser known languages of Indigenous Himalayan people, including Kiranti-Kõits, his endangered mother tongue.

RAPACHA WORKING IN THE FIELD IN NEPAL

MYTHOLOGY

GREEK

EGYPTIAN

The ancient Greeks believed that many gods and goddesses ruled the universe. According to this mythology, the Olympians lived high atop Greece's Mount Olympus. Each of these 12 principal gods and goddesses had a unique personality that corresponded to particular aspects of life, such as love or death.

Egyptian mythology is based on a creation myth that tells of an egg that appeared on the ocean. When the egg hatched, out came Ra, the sun god. As a result, ancient Egyptians became worshippers of the sun and of the nine original deities, most of whom were the children and grandchildren of Ra.

THE OLYMPIANS

Aphrodite was the goddess of love and beauty.

Apollo, Zeus's son, was the god of the sun, music, and healing. Artemis was his twin.

Ares, Zeus's son, was the god of war.

Artemis, Zeus's daughter and Apollo's twin, was the goddess of the hunt and of childbirth.

Athena, born from the forehead of Zeus, was the goddess of wisdom and crafts.

Demeter was the goddess of fertility and nature.

Hades, Zeus's brother, was the god of the underworld and the dead.

Hephaestus, the son of Hera and Zeus, was the god of fire.

Hera, the wife and older sister of Zeus, was the goddess of women and marriage.

Hermes, Zeus's son, was the messenger of the gods.

Poseidon, the brother of Zeus, was the god of the seas and earthquakes.

Zeus was the most powerful of the gods and the top Olympian. He wielded a thunderbolt and was the god of the sky and thunder.

THE NINE DEITIES

Geb, son of Shu and Tefnut, was the god of the earth.

Isis (Ast), daughter of Geb and Nut, was the goddess of fertility and motherhood.

Nephthys (Nebet-Hut), daughter of Geb and Nut, was protector of the dead.

Nut, daughter of Shu and Tefnut, was the goddess of the sky.

Osiris (Usir), son of Geb and Nut, was the god of the afterlife.

Ra (Re), the sun god, is generally viewed as the creator. He represents life and health.

Seth (Set), son of Geb and Nut, was the god of the desert and chaos.

Shu, son of Ra, was the god of air.

Tefnut, daughter of Ra, was the goddess of rain.

All cultures around the world have unique legends and traditions that have been passed down over generations. Many myths refer to gods or supernatural heroes who are responsible for occurrences in the world. For example, Norse mythology tells of the red-bearded Thor, the god of thunder, who is responsible for creating lightning and thunderstorms. And many creation myths, especially those from some of North America's native cultures, tell of an earth-diver represented as an animal that brings a piece of sand or mud up from the deep sea. From this tiny piece of earth, the entire world takes shape.

NORSE

ROMAN

Norse mythology originated in Scandinavia, in northern Europe. It was complete with gods and goddesses who lived in a heavenly place called Asgard that could be reached only by crossing a rainbow bridge.

Although Norse mythology is lesser known, we use it every day. Most days of the week are named after Norse gods, including some of these major deities.

NORSE GODS

Balder was the god of light and beauty.

Freya was the goddess of love, beauty, and fertility.

Frigg, for whom Friday was named, was the queen of Asgard. She was the goddess of marriage, motherhood, and the home.

Heimdall was the watchman of the rainbow bridge and the guardian of the gods.

Hel, the daughter of Loki, was the goddess of death.

Loki, a shape-shifter, was a trickster who helped the gods—and caused them problems.

Skadi was the goddess of winter and of the hunt. She is often represented as the "Snow Queen."

Thor, for whom Thursday was named, was the god of thunder and lightning.

Tyr, for whom Tuesday was named, was the god of the sky and war.

Wodan, for whom Wednesday was named, was the god of war, wisdom, death, and magic.

Much of Roman mythology was adopted from Greek mythology, but the Romans also developed a lot of original myths as well. The gods of Roman mythology lived everywhere, and each had a role to play. There were thousands of Roman gods, but here are a few of the stars of Roman myths.

ANCIENT ROMAN GODS

Ceres was the goddess of the harvest and motherly love.

Diana, daughter of Jupiter, was the goddess of hunting and the moon.

Juno, Jupiter's wife, was the goddess of women and fertility.

Jupiter, the patron of Rome and master of the gods, was the god of the sky.

Mars, the son of Jupiter and Juno, was the god of war.

Mercury, the son of Jupiter, was the messenger of the gods and the god of travelers.

Minerva was the goddess of wisdom, learning, and the arts and crafts.

Neptune, the brother of Jupiter, was the god of the sea.

Venus was the goddess of love and beauty.

Vesta was the goddess of fire and the hearth. She was one of the most important of the Roman deities.

World Religions

Around the world, religion takes many forms. Some belief systems, such as Christianity, Islam, and Judaism, are monotheistic, meaning that followers believe in just one supreme being. Others, like Hinduism, Shintoism, and most native belief systems, are polytheistic, meaning that many of their followers believe in multiple gods.

All of the major religions have their origins in Asia, but they have spread around the world. Christianity, with the largest number of followers, has three divisions—Roman Catholic, Eastern Orthodox, and Protestant. Islam, with about one-quarter of all believers, has two main divisions—Sunni and Shiite. Hinduism and Buddhism account for almost another one-fifth of believers. Judaism, dating back some 4,000 years, has nearly 15 million followers, less than one percent of all believers.

CHRISTIANITY

Based on the teachings of Jesus Christ, a Jew born some 2,000 years ago in the area of modern-day Israel, Christianity has spread worldwide and actively seeks converts. Followers in Switzerland (above) participate in an Easter season procession with lanterns and crosses.

BUDDHISM

Founded about 2,400 years ago in northern India by the Hindu prince Gautama Buddha, Buddhism spread throughout East and Southeast Asia. Buddhist temples have statues, such as the Mihintale Buddha (above) in Sri Lanka.

HINDUISM

Dating back more than 4,000 years, Hinduism is practiced mainly in India. Hindus follow sacred texts known as the Vedas and believe in reincarnation. During the festival of Navratri, which honors the goddess Durga, the Garba dance is performed (above).

Spreading Light

Sisters in traditional Indian clothing celebrate Diwali by placing clay lamps on rangoli—decorative patterns created on the floor with materials such as colored powders or sand. Diwali is a five-day Hindu festival celebrating the triumph of light over darkness.

ISLAM

Muslims believe that the Quran, Islam's sacred book, records the words of Allah (God) as revealed to the Prophet Muhammad beginning around A.D. 610. Believers (above) circle the Kaaba in the Grand Mosque in Mecca, Saudi Arabia, the spiritual center of the faith.

JUDAISM

The traditions, laws, and beliefs of Judaism date back to Abraham (the patriarch) and the Torah (the first five books of the Old Testament). Followers pray before the Western Wall (above), which stands below Islam's Dome of the Rock in Jerusalem.

187

QUIZ WHIZ

How vast is your knowledge about the world around you? Quiz yourself!

Write your answers on a piece of paper. Then check them below.

1 In ancient Egypt, how was a mummy's brain removed?
a. through the mouth
b. through the belly button
c. through the nose
d. It wasn't removed.

2 In which city does an annual Mardi Gras parade with giant jesters take place?
a. New York, New York
b. New Orleans, Louisiana
c. New Delhi, India
d. Lerwick, Scotland

3 In India, the slang term for 100,000 rupees is _____.
a. treasure
b. penny
c. token
d. peti

4 The earliest people known to have used the cacao plant are the _____.
a. Mayo-Chinchipe
b. Chinese
c. Egyptian
d. Olmec

5 True or false? Everything in this sneaker, pictured to the right, is edible—down to the shoelaces!

Not **STUMPED** yet? Check out the *NATIONAL GEOGRAPHIC KIDS QUIZ WHIZ* collection for more crazy **CULTURE** questions!

ANSWERS: 1. c; 2. b; 3. d; 4. a; 5. True

HOMEWORK HELP

Explore a New Culture

STAMPS OF BRAZIL

CURRENCY AND COINS OF BRAZIL

FLAG OF BRAZIL

YOU'RE A STUDENT, but you're also a citizen of the world. Writing a report on another country or your own country is a great way to better understand and appreciate how different people live. Pick the country of your ancestors, one that's been in the news, or one that you'd like to visit someday.

Passport to Success

A country report follows the format of an expository essay because you're "exposing" information about the country you choose.

The following step-by-step tips will help you with this international task.

 RESEARCH. Gathering information is the most important step in writing a good country report. Look to internet sources, encyclopedias, books, magazine and newspaper articles, and other sources to find important and interesting details about your subject.

2 ORGANIZE YOUR NOTES. Put the information you gather into a rough outline. For example, sort everything you found about the country's system of government, climate, etc.

3 WRITE IT UP. Follow the basic structure of good writing: introduction, body, and conclusion. Remember that each paragraph should have a topic sentence that is then supported by facts and details. Incorporate the information from your notes, but make sure it's in your own words. And make your writing flow with good transitions and descriptive language.

4 ADD VISUALS. Include maps, diagrams, photos, and other visual aids.

 PROOFREAD AND REVISE. Correct any mistakes, and polish your language. Do your best!

6 CITE YOUR SOURCES. Be sure to keep a record of your sources.

A gloved scientist holds a petri dish containing a culture of bacteria.

SCIENCE and
TECHNOLOGY

THIS RACE CAR

CAN REACH TOP SPEEDS OF MORE THAN 2OO MILES AN HOUR (322 KM/H)— MORE THAN THREE TIMES THE LEGAL LIMIT ON MOST HIGHWAYS.

HYPERCARS can ACCELERATE from 0 TO 60 MILES AN HOUR (0 to 97 km/h) in less than three seconds, about four seconds faster than a minivan.

Forget flying cars: This is the future of racing. Known as hypercars, these custom-built, super-lightweight vehicles have powerful engines with electric components that can rocket them to breakneck speeds. Top competitions, such as the Le Mans 24 Hours race in France, now have a special division for hypercars.

IN 2021, **TOYOTA'S GR010 HYBRID** raced into the **RECORD BOOKS,** becoming the **FIRST CAR TO WIN** in the new Hypercar category at Le Mans.

The **ELECTRIC MOTORS** used in **HYPERCARS** allow them to **SPEED UP FASTER** than cars powered by gas alone.

A hypercar's body is usually made of **CARBON FIBER**—a material that is up to **10 TIMES STRONGER THAN STEEL,** but five times lighter.

Toyota GR010 Hybrid

6 COOL INVENTIONS

SUPERSMART GADGETS, ACCESSORIES, AND VEHICLES THAT COULD CHANGE YOUR LIFE

① BIKE TAKES FLIGHT

The Speeder has a seat and handlebars just like a motorcycle, but this contraption travels to a place you could never reach on a regular bike—the sky! Just press a button to take off. Four turbojet engines on the bike's front and back launch it off the ground. Steer the handlebars to move the craft through the air. Weighing about 230 pounds (104 kg), the bike won't require a pilot's license to fly. Although still being tested, the Speeder is expected to reach speeds of 60 miles an hour (97 km/h) and climb up to 15,000 feet (4,572 m). Talk about getting a lift!

② SMOKELESS FIREPLACE

Typically, where there's smoke, there's fire—and vice versa. But a neat new gadget called the Le Feu generates the heat and ambiance of a flickering fire ... and that's it. How? The burner inside this sleek, steel orb is heated by bioethanol fuel, which is made from plants like corn and sugarcane, and doesn't produce any smoke. And the Le Feu doesn't just keep you cozy: It's better for the environment, too, since bioethanol emits no harmful or toxic gases, either. Meaning it warms you up without contributing to global warming.

③ VIRTUAL KEYBOARD

Tap out an **email right on** your **kitchen table,** or type up a report on your bedroom floor. With the **Magic Cube,** you can turn any flat, opaque surface into a **keyboard.** Connect the small, cube-shaped device to a smartphone, tablet, or computer. The cube uses a laser beam to **project a keyboard** onto the surface. A **sensor** inside the cube **tracks** where your fingers are tapping and then translates the movements into letters and numbers. The cube even plays **tapping sounds** while you type, just in case you miss the **clickety-clack** of your old-fashioned keyboard.

④ BENDY BIKE

Here's one way to confuse a bike thief: Wrap your bike around a pole! Bendy bikes let you do just that, thanks to a frame that's **flexible enough to wrap around lampposts and street signs.** Hoping to decrease the number of bikes stolen each year, a design student came up with this **clever cycle** that looks like a regular bike when you're riding it. Once you're ready to lock it up, however, loosen a cable below the seat to **split the bike into two segments.** Then **bend the frame** up to 180 degrees. Next, secure it to a pole with a regular bike lock, leaving would-be thieves **scratching their heads.**

⑤ IN-EAR TRANSLATOR

So you're visiting Paris, **but you don't speak** French. No problem! Just pop in the Pilot earpiece and use the **app to understand every word another user says to you.** The earbud device **translates languages** like Spanish and Italian in real time. Simply select which language you want from an **app on your phone,** then let the Pilot do the translating. Voilà!

SMART ⑥ RING

When the lights are too low for you to read on your couch, just tap your thumb to your ring finger three times. And while you're at it, **make a call,** too—all without ever touching your phone. That's what a smart ring called **ORII** can do. Simply slide the ring onto your finger, and a **Bluetooth chip** in the ring will control your smart devices wirelessly. **Sync it to your smart gadget,** then call a friend or **shoot off a text** just by speaking into a pair of microphones on the inside of the device. This ring's not quite the same as having a personal assistant—but it's the **next best thing.**

WHAT IS LIFE?

This seems like such an easy question to answer. Everybody knows that singing birds are alive and rocks are not. But when we start studying bacteria and other microscopic creatures, things get more complicated.

SO WHAT EXACTLY IS LIFE?

Most scientists agree that something is alive if it can reproduce, grow in size to become more complex in structure, take in nutrients to survive, give off waste products, and respond to external stimuli, such as increased sunlight or changes in temperature.

KINDS OF LIFE

Biologists classify living organisms by how they get their energy. Organisms such as algae, green plants, and some bacteria use sunlight as an energy source. Animals (like humans), fungi, and some single-celled microscopic organisms called Archaea use chemicals to provide energy. When we eat food, chemical reactions within our digestive system turn our food into fuel.

Living things inhabit land, sea, and air. In fact, life thrives deep beneath the oceans, embedded in rocks miles below Earth's crust, in ice, and in other extreme environments. The life-forms that thrive in these challenging environments are called extremophiles. Some of these draw directly upon the chemicals surrounding them for energy. Because these are very different forms of life than what we're used to, we may not think of them as alive, but they are.

HOW IT ALL WORKS

To understand how a living organism works, it helps to look at one example of its simplest form—the single-celled bacterium called *Streptococcus*. There are many kinds of these tiny organisms, and some are responsible for human illnesses. What makes us sick or uncomfortable are the toxins the bacteria give off in our bodies.

A single *Streptococcus* bacterium is so small that at least 500 of them could fit on the dot above this letter *i*. These bacteria are some of the simplest forms of life we know. They have no moving parts, no lungs, no brain, no heart, no liver, and no leaves or fruit. Yet this life-form reproduces. It grows in size by producing long-chain structures, takes in nutrients, and gives off waste products. This tiny life-form is alive, just as you are alive.

What makes something alive is a question scientists grapple with when they study viruses, such as the ones that cause the common cold and COVID-19. They can grow and reproduce within host cells, such as those that make up your body. Because viruses lack cells and cannot metabolize nutrients for energy or reproduce without a host, scientists ask if they are indeed alive. And don't go looking for them without a strong microscope—viruses are a hundred times smaller than bacteria.

Scientists think life began on Earth more than four billion years ago, but no fossils exist from that time. The earliest fossils ever found are from the primitive life that existed 3.5 billion years ago. Other life-forms, some of which are shown below, soon followed. Scientists continue to study how life evolved on Earth and whether it is possible that life exists on other planets.

MICROSCOPIC ORGANISMS

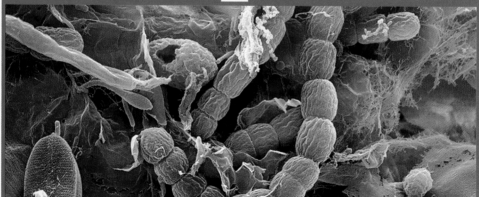

The Three Domains of Life

Biologists divide all living organisms into three domains, or groups: Bacteria, Archaea, and Eukarya. Archaea and Bacteria cells do not have nuclei—cellular parts that are essential to reproduction and other cell functions—but they are different from each other in many ways. Because human cells have a nucleus, we belong to the Eukarya domain.

1 BACTERIA

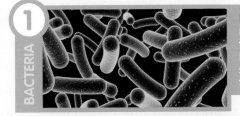

DOMAIN BACTERIA: These single-celled microorganisms are found almost everywhere in the world. Bacteria are small and do not have nuclei. They can be shaped like rods, spirals, or spheres. Some of them are helpful to humans, and some are harmful.

2 ARCHAEA

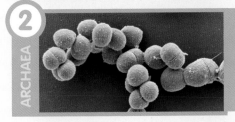

DOMAIN ARCHAEA: These single-celled micro-organisms are often found in extremely hostile environments. Like Bacteria, Archaea do not have nuclei, but they have some genes in common with Eukarya. For this reason, scientists think the Archaea living today most closely resemble the earliest forms of life on Earth.

3 EUKARYA

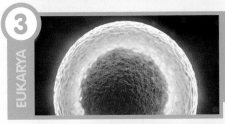

DOMAIN EUKARYA: This diverse group of life-forms is more complicated than Bacteria and Archaea, as Eukarya have one or more cells with nuclei. These are the tiny cells that make up your whole body. Eukarya are divided into four groups: fungi, protists, plants, and animals.

FYI

WHAT IS A DOMAIN? Scientifically speaking, a domain is a major taxonomic division into which natural objects are classified (see page 44 for "What Is Taxonomy?").

FUNGI

KINGDOM FUNGI Mainly multicellular organisms, fungi cannot make their own food. Mushrooms and yeast are fungi.

PROTISTS

PROTISTS Once considered a kingdom, this group is a "grab bag" that includes unicellular and multicellular organisms of great variety.

PLANTS

KINGDOM PLANTAE Plants are multi-cellular, and many can make their own food using photosynthesis (see page 198 for "Photosynthesis").

ANIMALS

KINGDOM ANIMALIA Most animals, which are multicellular, have their own organ systems. Animals do not make their own food.

HOW DOES YOUR GARDEN GROW?

The plant kingdom is about 400,000 species strong, growing all over the world: on top of mountains, in the sea, in frigid temperatures—everywhere. Without plants, life on Earth would not be able to survive. Plants provide food and oxygen for animals, including humans.

Plants have three distinct characteristics:

1. Most have chlorophyll (a green pigment that makes photosynthesis work and turns sunlight into energy), while some are parasitic. Parasitic plants don't make their own food—they take it from other plants.
2. Plants cannot change their location on their own.
3. Their cell walls are made from a stiff material called cellulose.

Photosynthesis

Plants are lucky—most don't have to hunt or shop for food. Most use the sun to produce their own food. In a process called photosynthesis, a plant's chloroplast (the part of the plant where the chemical chlorophyll is located) captures the sun's energy and combines it with carbon dioxide from the air and nutrient-rich water from the ground to produce a sugar called glucose.

Plants burn the glucose for energy to help them grow. As a waste product, plants emit oxygen, which humans and other animals need to breathe. When we breathe, we exhale carbon dioxide, which the plants then use for more photosynthesis—it's all a big, finely tuned system. So the next time you pass a lonely houseplant, give it thanks for helping you live.

Plants That STINK!

Not all plants smell like roses. Here are two of the **STINKIEST** members of the plant kingdom.

Giant Rafflesia

THE RAFFLESIA IS THE LARGEST FLOWER IN THE WORLD.

THE RAFFLESIA'S ODOR ATTRACTS FLIES.

Western Skunk Cabbage

EASTERN SKUNK CABBAGE

If you ever walk by a rafflesia flower or a skunk cabbage, you may be unpleasantly surprised by the not-so-sweet smell wafting from these peculiar plants. The giant rafflesia, which grows in the rainforests of Indonesia and is also the largest flower in the world, is called the "corpse flower" because of its offensive odor. Some people compare it to the smell of rotting meat or fish! And the skunk cabbage, a wildflower that grows in swampy, wet areas in North American forests, gets its name from the pungent scent that its leaves and flowers emit when they're crushed or bruised.

So what's up with these flowers' funky fragrances? The odor is actually the plants' superpower! The stink of the rafflesia attracts flies and beetles, which sometimes even lay their eggs inside the flower and help to pollinate it. And the skunk cabbage's stink does the same for flies, butterflies, wasps, and other pollinators. Both plants also generate heat—a very rare trait among plants—which creates an extra-cozy spot for bugs to hang out and lay eggs.

While humans may, uh, turn their noses up at the stench of stinky plants, insects experience just the opposite effect, and that's a good thing. Why? Pollination is super important. Without it, plants can't make seeds and reproduce. And because all plants play a role in maintaining a healthy ecosystem, we need them around—no matter how bad they smell.

Your Amazing Body!

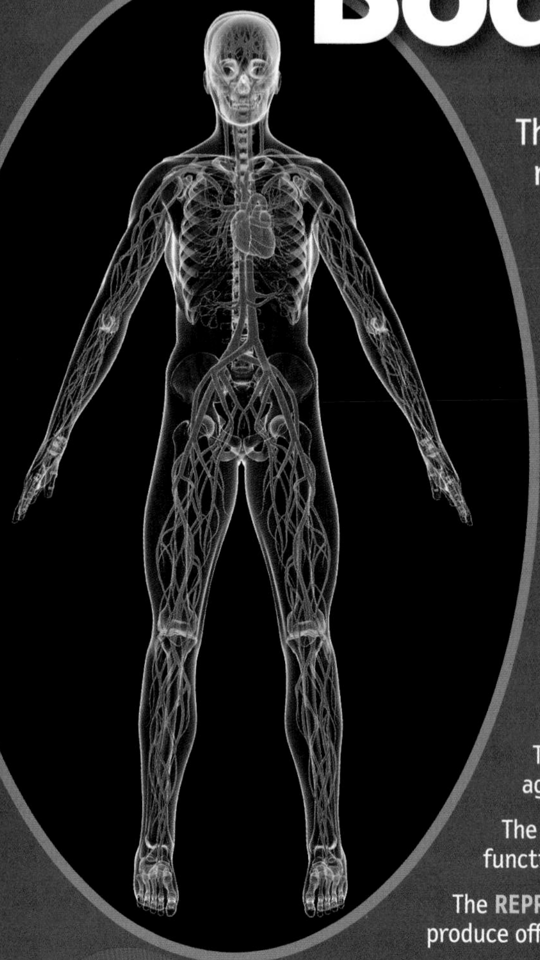

About 10,000 of the CELLS in your body could fit on the head of a PIN.

The human body is a complicated mass of systems—nine systems, to be exact. Each has a unique and critical purpose in the body, and we wouldn't be able to survive without all of them.

The **NERVOUS** system controls the body.

The **MUSCULAR** system makes movement possible.

The **SKELETAL** system supports the body.

The **CIRCULATORY** system moves blood throughout the body.

The **RESPIRATORY** system provides the body with oxygen.

The **DIGESTIVE** system breaks down food into nutrients and gets rid of waste.

The **IMMUNE** system protects the body against disease and infection.

The **ENDOCRINE** system regulates the body's functions.

The **REPRODUCTIVE** system enables people to produce offspring.

Weird but true!

If you **NEVER CUT YOUR HAIR,** it could grow more than **30 FEET** (9 M) in your lifetime.

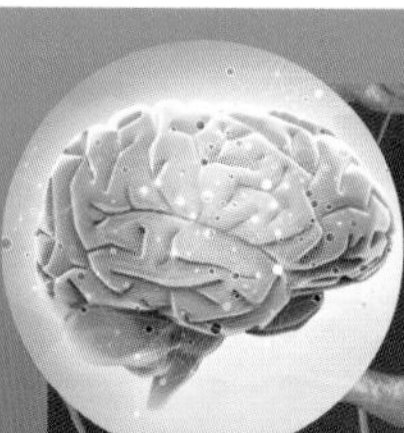

MESSAGES FROM YOUR BRAIN TRAVEL ALONG YOUR NERVES at up to 200 MILES AN HOUR (322 KM/H).

WHAT'S YOUR TYPE?

Everyone's blood is made of the same basic elements, but not all blood is alike. There are four main blood types. If a person needs to use donated blood, the donated blood can react with their body's immune system if it's not the right type. This diagram shows which types of blood are compatible with each other.

GROUP O can donate red blood cells to anybody. It's the universal donor.

GROUP A can donate red blood cells to A's and AB's.

GROUP B can donate red blood cells to B's and AB's.

GROUP AB can donate to other AB's, but can receive from all others.

O+ is the most common blood type:

38%

of people in the U.S. have this type.

Blood types can be positive or negative. Only **18%** of people in the U.S. have a negative blood type.

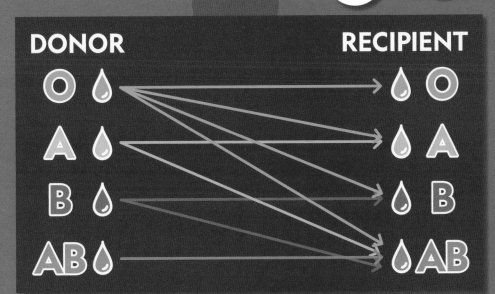

DONOR   RECIPIENT

O → O

A → A

B → B

AB → AB

WHY can't
I eat peanuts or pet a fluffy dog without
FEELING ICKY?

Sounds like you have an allergy, and you're not alone! As many as 30 percent of grown-ups and 40 percent of kids suffer from allergies. Allergic reactions include itching, sneezing, coughing, a runny nose, vomiting, rashes, and shortness of breath. They happen when your body's immune system—which normally fights germs—treats something harmless, like food or a particular medicine, like it's a dangerous invader. Once it detects one of these intruders, called an allergen, your immune system goes into high alert. It creates antibodies to repel the intruder, causing the tissues around the allergen to become inflamed or swollen, which can make it hard for you to breathe. Extreme reactions can even result in a potentially deadly full-body response known as anaphylactic shock.

AWFUL allergens

PEANUTS
One of the most common food allergens, along with shellfish.

PET DANDER
Tiny flakes of shed fur and feathers can make your eyes water and your nose go *ahchoo!*

DUST MITES

Millions of these microscopic arachnids live in your house, feasting on your dead skin cells. Cleaning stirs up clouds of mite shells and their micro-poop.

PENICILLIN

Antibiotics like penicillin kill bacteria that make us sick, but they can do more harm than good for patients allergic to them.

POLLEN

Plants project this fine powdery substance into the breeze to fertilize other plants. It can irritate the nasal passages of allergy sufferers, causing sneezing and watery eyes—a condition commonly called hay fever.

Why do
we have allergies?

Stories of allergies go back to ancient Egypt, yet their causes largely remain a mystery. Not everyone has allergies. Some form in childhood. Some happen later in life. And sometimes they go away as you get older. You may inherit a likelihood of having allergies from your parents but usually not their particular allergies.

Scientists suspect humans evolved with these extreme and mysterious immune reactions to combat genuinely deadly threats, such as parasitic worms or other toxins. And though doctors are doubtful they can ever cure allergies, they've come up with many ways to test for them and provide medications that treat the symptoms.

A majority of food allergies are caused by "the Big 8"— milk, eggs, fish, shellfish, tree nuts, peanuts, wheat, and soy.

WHY can't I USE my left hand as well as my right one (or the other way around)?

About nine out of 10 of you reading this book will turn its pages with your right hand—

the same hand you use to write a note or chuck a fastball. About 90 percent of humans are right-handed, meaning their right hand is their dominant hand. The other 10 percent are left-handed. Activities that feel natural with the dominant hand are awkward or difficult with the other one. Ever try to sign your name with your nondominant hand? Not so easy!

Cave paintings going back more than 5,000 years show humans favoring their right or left hand according to the same nine-to-one ratio we see today. And the same goes for the stone tools our evolutionary ancestors used 1.5 million years ago: Studies show a similar dominance of the right hand long before the human species, *Homo sapiens*, appeared in the fossil record.

ARE YOU A "mixed-hander"?

What about people who can use their nondominant hand almost as well as their dominant? They're called mixed-handers. (Scientists don't like using the term "ambidextrous," which implies neither hand is dominant.) About one percent of people are elite lefties/righties. Are you? Grab a piece of scratch paper and find out!

So why is one hand dominant?

Scientists have discovered a sequence of genes linked to hand dominance, making it a trait that's passed along to children just like hair color or dimples. These traits determine how our brains are wired. How? The brain is split into two symmetrical halves known as hemispheres. In about 90 percent of people, the left side of the brain processes language skills. These people are typically right-handed. People born with genes for left-handedness—about 10 percent of the population—typically have brains that process speech on the right side.

So whichever side of the brain controls speech usually corresponds with a dominant hand on the opposite side. Because the left side of the brain controls the right side of the body and vice versa, scientists suspect that the evolution of our dominant hand is somehow connected to the development of our language capabilities. Humans can have a dominant eye, foot, and ear, too—but scientists aren't quite sure why. That's just one of many reasons the human brain is considered the most complex object in the universe.

15 COOL THINGS ABOUT SLEEP

Ancient Greeks believed that **LETTUCE JUICE** could help them sleep.

A hotel straddling the **border of France and Switzerland** lets you sleep with your **head in one country** and your **feet in the other.**

The position you sleep in may provide clues to **YOUR PERSONALITY.** If you sleep curled up, you might be shy.

Humans spend about **ONE-THIRD** of their lives **ASLEEP.**

ON AVERAGE, a person **PASSES GAS 14 times a day—** mostly while asleep.

People tend to **SLEEP LESS** during a **FULL MOON.**

The **LOUDEST SNORES** can reach more than **100 DECIBELS.** That's as loud as **highway traffic!**

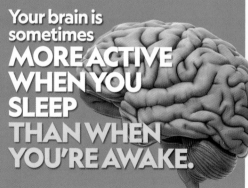

Your brain is sometimes **MORE ACTIVE WHEN YOU SLEEP THAN WHEN YOU'RE AWAKE.**

ASTRONAUTS on spaceships typically **sleep in sleeping bags** that **ARE STRAPPED TO THE WALL.**

You're **more likely to yawn** if **someone near you does,** especially if **you know them.**

PILLOWS have been found in **ANCIENT EGYPTIAN TOMBS.**

Your brain makes memories while you sleep.

To STAY AWAKE on the **FIRST EVER SOLO FLIGHT** over the Atlantic Ocean **in 1927, aviator Charles Lindbergh** held his eyes open with his fingers.

On average, it takes a 10-year-old kid **about 20 minutes** to fall asleep.

MYTH BUSTED: The chemical **tryptophan,** found in turkey, **doesn't actually make you sleepy.**

205

THE SCIENCE OF
SPOOKY

HOW THESE CREEPY THINGS AFFECT YOUR BRAIN

What's that strange noise in the night? Is it the wind? Or something else?

"When you encounter something scary, your brain releases chemicals," psychologist Martin Antony says. "These chemicals make our hearts race, so we breathe faster and sweat. Your nervous system is preparing your body to either fight a threat or run away from it." Scientists call this the "fight-or-flight" response.

So which so-called spookiness makes us feel this way—and why? Discover what puts the eek! in these five freaky things.

THE FEAR: SPIDERS

SCIENTIFIC NAME: Arachnophobia

SPOOKY SCIENCE: Humans have been afraid of spiders since our ancient human ancestors thought they carried deadly diseases. "Today, we know that's not true," psychologist Kyle Rexer says. "But a lot of people still have incorrect ideas about how dangerous spiders are." Although some spiders *can* be deadly, most are not. In fact, humans actually benefit from the existence of spiders. By eating disease-carrying critters such as mosquitoes and cockroaches, these arachnids act as a form of pest control. Plus, scientists are currently studying spider venom in the hope that it can one day be used in medicines to manage pain or cure illnesses.

THE FEAR: CLOWNS

SCIENTIFIC NAME: Coulrophobia

SPOOKY SCIENCE: One way we decide if a person is friend or foe is by evaluating their facial expressions. Clowns—with their makeup, wigs, and fake noses—are hard to read, which is what makes them scary to some people. "It's hard to tell how a clown is feeling," psychology professor Frank McAndrew says. "So we think, If clowns can hide their emotions, what else might they be hiding?"

FIGHT THE FRIGHT

It's natural to avoid things that scare us. "But to get over your fears—whether you're afraid of spiders, clowns, the dark, or, well, anything—you have to *focus* on them instead of avoid them," Rexer says. He shares some useful tips to help you manage your fears.

THE FEAR: HEIGHTS

SCIENTIFIC NAME: Acrophobia

SPOOKY SCIENCE: When you're standing on solid ground, your eyes work with your inner ears to help you stay balanced. But if you're standing, say, at the edge of a cliff, your sense of balance can get out of whack. "Your inner ear is saying you're surrounded by solid ground, but your eyes are saying, 'Nope,'" inner-ear specialist Dennis Fitzgerald says. Your brain is getting mixed signals, which can cause vertigo, or dizziness that makes heights feel scary.

THE FEAR: DARKNESS

SCIENTIFIC NAME: Nyctophobia

SPOOKY SCIENCE: As with other phobias, humans developed a fear of the dark to avoid danger. Our ancestors had to be extra cautious at night to protect themselves against things like animal predators and human invaders. (This was before electric lighting!) "Many people still have that fear of the dark today," Antony says. "It's a fear of the unknown."

THE FEAR: SMALL SPACES

SCIENTIFIC NAME: Claustrophobia

SPOOKY SCIENCE: Maybe you've been stuck in an elevator before and thought it was no big deal. For some people, though, just the fear of being stuck can cause them to take the stairs. "Small spaces might cause some people to worry about running out of oxygen, or never being able to get out—no matter how unlikely that is," Antony says. "To increase our chances of survival, people have evolved to avoid being trapped. For some, that could be anywhere."

- Expose yourself to things that you're afraid of in a way that you feel safe. For example, if you fear public speaking, try practicing in front of a mirror first, and then give the speech to a small group of trusted friends.

- If you feel anxious, place one or both of your hands on your stomach and focus on breathing slowly and deeply. Regulating your breathing will help you feel calmer and can lessen your sense of panic.

- Don't be too hard on yourself! Everyone's afraid of *something*. Just make sure it doesn't stop you from living your life. Talk to an adult if it feels like too much to handle on your own.

FUTURE WORLD:

The year is 2070, and it's time to get dressed for school. You step in front of a large video mirror that projects different clothes on you. After you decide on your favorite T-shirt, a robot fetches your outfit. No time is lost trying to find matching socks! Chores? What chores? Get ready for a whole new homelife.

STAY CONNECTED

Whether your future home is an urban skyscraper or an underwater pod, all buildings will one day be connected via a central communications hub. Want to check out a *T. rex* skeleton at a faraway museum? You can virtually connect to it as though you were checking it out in person. But you're not just seeing something miles away. Connect to a beach house's balcony and smell the salty air and feel the breeze. Buildings might also share information about incoming weather and emergencies to keep you safe.

CUSTOM COMFORT

Soon, your house may give you a personal welcome home. No need for keys—sensors will scan your body and open the door. Walk into the living room, and the lighting adjusts to your preferred setting. Thirsty? A glass of water pops up on the counter. Before bed, you enter the bathroom and say, "Shower, please." The water starts flowing at exactly the temperature you want.

ON LOCATION

Your room has a spectacular view of the ocean ... because your house is suspended above it. New technologies will allow us to build our homes in unusual spots. In the future, "floating" structures elevated by supporting poles above water or other hard-to-access spots (think mountain peaks) will be more common as cities become more crowded. And this won't be limited to dry land on Earth. That means that one day your family could even live in space!

Homes

ON THE GO

Homes of the future will always be on the move. Walls will be capable of expanding and contracting, and houses will rotate with the sun's movements to conserve energy. Buildings will also be capable of changing size depending on who's inside. Grandparents could "move in" by attaching a modular section to the front, back, or top of the house.

BRING ON THE BOTS

While you were outside playing with your friends, your house robot did the laundry, vacuumed, and cleaned the bathroom. Meanwhile, a drone just delivered groceries for the home-bot to put away. Minutes later, lunch is ready. The service is great … but how will you earn your allowance? Instead of taking out the garbage or setting the table, you'll earn money by helping clean and maintain the robots.

FUTURE WORLD:

What will restaurants be like decades from now? "You can expect a lot of changes in terms of using technology to grow and order our meals," says Paul Takhistov, a food scientist at Rutgers University in New Brunswick, New Jersey, U.S.A. "We'll also be able to personalize our food more." Check out what's cooking at this restaurant of the future.

HUNGRY? PRESS PRINT

A quick finger scan at your table shows that you're low on certain nutrients. Just press a button, and a 3D printer uses pureed food cartridges to "print" lasagna that's packed with specific vitamins that your body needs. "Healthy food isn't one size fits all," Takhistov says. "We have different bodies, so we need different nutrients." These printers will also increase efficiency, allowing chefs to quickly print personalized food for large crowds.

FOOD-IN-A-BOX

Some of the lettuce in this kitchen is sad. Or rather, one of the lettuce emojis on the giant computer screens is frowning. That's because the chef didn't use the right recipe of sunlight, water, and nutrients to get the real-life leafy plant inside a box behind the screen to grow. So she taps the touch screen to make the temperature cooler, and the lettuce's frown turns upside down on the fridge-shaped "box farm." Without planting seeds in soil, this restaurant can grow all the fruits and vegetables it needs. "Anybody can be a farmer," says Hildreth England, a senior strategist at the Massachusetts Institute of Technology. "If you live in Iceland, you can grow strawberries that taste as if they're from Mexico."

WASTE NOT

Researchers are currently working on ways to convert human waste into nutrients. Whether you're eating on Earth or during a space vacation, in the future some of your food will likely have recycled ingredients.

Food

GROW UP

What will happen to farms in the future? Some will be *much* taller. Cities will continue to expand as the human population climbs to nine billion people, leaving less land to farm. Agriculture will likely be housed in towering vertical skyscrapers situated in these cities. Luckily, indoor farms typically use less water, and plants seem to grow faster in these environments.

HUNTING FOR HOLOGRAMS

Let's go fishing ... in the kitchen? The catch of the day is a 3D hologram that the chef hooks in midair. One day people will stock their kitchens by gathering ingredients in a virtual world. Simply pick a berry from a digital bush or choose a cut of beef from a cow on a virtual farm. After you're done foraging, the hologram setup sends details to a local market that delivers your order. Scientists working on this program hope to connect people to their food sources and make shopping more fun.

GET SMART

To order with ease and keep germs from spreading at your favorite restaurant, you tap the table to open a digital menu and choose from freshly grown salads and 3D-printed creations. An alarm lets you know when your food is waiting in the cubby at one side of the table—just lift the door and take your meal. Forgot something? A robot server will stop by to see if you need anything else.

QUIZ WHIZ

Test your science and technology smarts by taking this quiz!

Write your answers on a piece of paper. Then check them below.

1. The giant rafflesia flower is called the "corpse flower" because it _____.
   a. blooms on Halloween
   b. has an offensive odor
   c. grows only in graveyards
   d. looks like a dead animal

2. True or false? Peanuts are one of the most common food allergens.

3. A fear of clowns is also called _____.
   a. chionophobia
   b. clownaphobia
   c. claustrophobia
   d. coulrophobia

4. In the near future, you may be able to _____.
   a. project a keyboard onto any flat surface
   b. make a phone call from a ring on your finger
   c. warm yourself by a smokeless fire
   d. all of the above

5. Ancient Greeks believed that lettuce juice could _____.
   a. help them sleep
   b. clean their teeth
   c. build big muscles
   d. give them more energy

Not **STUMPED** yet? Check out the *NATIONAL GEOGRAPHIC KIDS QUIZ WHIZ* collection for more crazy **SCIENCE AND TECHNOLOGY** questions!

ANSWERS: 1. b; 2. True; 3. d; 4. d; 5. a

This Is How It's Done!

Sometimes, the most complicated problems are solved with step-by-step directions. These "how-to" instructions are also known as a process analysis essay. Although scientists and engineers use this tool to program robots and write computer code, you also use process analysis every day, from following a recipe to putting together a new toy or gadget. Here's how to write a basic process analysis essay.

Step 1: Choose Your Topic Sentence

Pick a clear and concise topic sentence that describes what you're writing about. Be sure to explain to the readers why the task is important—and how many steps there are to complete it.

Step 2: List Materials

Do you need specific ingredients or equipment to complete your process? Mention these right away so the readers will have all they need to do the activity.

Step 3: Write Your Directions

Your directions should be clear and easy to follow. Assume that you are explaining the process for the first time, and define any unfamiliar terms. List your steps in the exact order the readers will need to follow to complete the activity. Try to keep your essay limited to no more than six steps.

Step 4: Restate Your Main Idea

Your closing idea should revisit your topic sentence, drawing a conclusion relating to the importance of the subject.

EXAMPLE OF A PROCESS ANALYSIS ESSAY

Downloading an app is a simple way to enhance your tablet. Today, I'd like to show you how to search for and add an app to your tablet. First, you will need a tablet with the ability to access the internet. You'll also want to ask a parent for permission before you download anything onto your tablet. Next, select the specific app you want by going to the app store on your tablet and entering the app's name into the search bar. Once you find the app you're seeking, select "download" and wait for the app to load. When you see that the app has fully loaded, tap on the icon and you will be able to access it. Now you can enjoy your app and have more fun with your tablet.

An aurora borealis glows brightly over Fairbanks, Alaska, U.S.A. This natural light show, also known as the northern lights, happens when solar wind interacts with Earth's magnetic field.

WONDERS of NATURE

Biomes

A BIOME, OFTEN CALLED A MAJOR LIFE ZONE, is one of the natural world's major communities where plants and animals adapt to their specific surroundings. Biomes are classified depending on the predominant vegetation, climate, and geography of a region. They can be divided into six major types: forest, freshwater, marine, desert, grassland, and tundra. Each biome consists of many ecosystems.

Biomes are extremely important. Balanced ecological relationships among biomes help to maintain the environment and life on Earth as we know it. For example, an increase in one species of plant, such as an invasive one, can cause a ripple effect throughout a whole biome.

FOREST

Forests occupy about one-third of Earth's land area. There are three major types of forests: tropical, temperate, and boreal (taiga). Forests are home to a diversity of plants, some of which may hold medicinal qualities for humans, as well as thousands of animal species, some still undiscovered. Forests can also absorb carbon dioxide, a greenhouse gas, and give off oxygen.

In a tropical rainforest, less than 2 percent of the sunlight ever reaches the ground.

FRESHWATER

Most water on Earth is salty, but freshwater ecosystems—including lakes, ponds, wetlands, rivers, and streams—usually contain water with less than one percent salt concentration. The countless animal and plant species that live in freshwater biomes vary from continent to continent, but they include algae, frogs, turtles, fish, and the larvae of many insects.

Covering 1.5 million acres (607,000 ha), Everglades National Park in Florida, U.S.A., is one of the largest freshwater biomes in the world.

MARINE

The marine biome covers almost three-fourths of Earth's surface, making it the largest habitat on our planet. Oceans make up the majority of the saltwater marine biome. Coral reefs are considered to be the most biodiverse of any of the biome habitats. The marine biome is home to more than one million plant and animal species.

Scientists are almost certain that life originated in the ocean.

DESERT

Covering about one-fifth of Earth's surface, deserts are places where precipitation is less than 10 inches (25 cm) a year. Although most deserts are hot, there are other kinds as well. The four major kinds of deserts are hot, semiarid, coastal, and cold. Far from being barren wastelands, deserts are biologically rich habitats.

More than one billion people in the world live in deserts.

GRASSLAND

Biomes called grasslands are characterized by having grasses instead of large shrubs or trees. Grasslands generally have precipitation for only about half to three-fourths of the year. If it were more, they would become forests. Grasslands can be divided into two types: tropical (savannas) and temperate. Some of the world's largest land animals, such as elephants, live there.

Once thought to be extinct, the pygmy hog—the world's smallest pig (it's the size of a kitten)—recently made a return to the grasslands of the Himalayan foothills.

TUNDRA

The coldest of all biomes, a tundra is characterized by an extremely cold climate, simple vegetation, little precipitation, poor nutrients, and a short growing season. There are two types of tundra: Arctic and alpine. A tundra is home to few kinds of vegetation. Surprisingly, though, quite a few animal species can survive the tundra's extremes, such as wolves and caribou, and even mosquitoes.

The word "tundra" comes from the Finnish word *tunturia*, which means "treeless plain."

Sizing up
THE GREAT BARRIER REEF

The Great Barrier Reef is home to both huge whale sharks, which can reach 40 feet (12 m) in length, and tiny one-third-inch (8-mm)-long infantfish.

FISH SWIM AMONG ORANGE COMMON SEA FANS AND COLORFUL CORAL OF THE GREAT BARRIER REEF.

In June 1770, the ship *Endeavour* slammed into a razor-sharp reef somewhere in the middle of the Coral Sea, a part of the southwestern Pacific Ocean. At the helm of the ship? Captain James Cook, a British explorer who had been exploring the Pacific and ultimately mapped the east coast of Australia. What Cook soon realized was that the reef that nearly sank his ship wasn't just any coral formation: It was the Great Barrier Reef, the world's largest coral reef ecosystem. Covering 133,000 square miles (344,400 sq km), the Great Barrier Reef is bigger than the United Kingdom, Switzerland, and Holland combined! It's so big, in fact, that it can be spotted from space.

Experts believe the Great Barrier Reef first formed millions of years ago. Aboriginal Australians and the Torres Strait Islanders are considered the Traditional Owners of the Great Barrier Reef region, as their connection to the reef goes back 60,000 years.

A REEF AT RISK

Today the reef faces threats that are far worse than shipwrecks. Climate change, poor water quality due to pollution, overfishing, and other factors like an invasive, coral-eating starfish are huge threats to the future of the Great Barrier Reef and the marine life that call it home, like sharks, turtles, crocodiles, and thousands of

Great Barrier Reef
By the Numbers

1,625: Species of fish that call the Great Barrier Reef home

3,000: Individual coral reef systems that compose the Great Barrier Reef as a whole

980: Approximate number of islands found along the Great Barrier Reef

1,000: Life span in years of boulder coral colonies—the longest-living coral on the Great Barrier Reef

2.4 million: Average number of visitors who travel to the Great Barrier Reef Marine Park in a typical year

ANTHIAS FISH SWIM AROUND BRANCH CORAL.

A DIVER SCRUBS ALGAE FROM CORAL IN A CORAL NURSERY.

other species. Sadly, the reef has shrunk by more than 50 percent in recent years.

PROTECTING THE FUTURE

The good news? Conservationists are working hard to protect and preserve the Great Barrier Reef, which was declared a marine protected area. They hope that by educating people about global warming, making laws to prevent overfishing, and taking other steps, such as creating "coral nurseries" to rescue and rehabilitate unhealthy coral, the remaining reef may be saved.

NEW REEF DISCOVERED

Scientists in Australia recently discovered a giant coral reef off the coast of Queensland, Australia. The massive detached reef is more than a mile (1,609 m) wide and measures some 1,640 feet (500 m) high. That's taller than the Empire State Building! The reef, detached from the Great Barrier Reef, is the first discovery of its kind in 120 years. The find is a bright light for the marine world, as it means there may be more healthy ecosystems lurking beneath the ocean's surface.

THE OCEANS

PACIFIC OCEAN

STATS

Surface area
65,100,000 sq mi (168,600,000 sq km)

Percentage of all oceans
46 percent

Surface temperatures
Summer high:
90°F (32°C)
Winter low: 28°F (-2°C)

Tides
Highest: 30 ft (9 m)
near Korean Peninsula
Lowest: 1 ft (0.3 m) near Midway Islands

Cool creatures: giant Pacific octopus, bottlenose whale, clownfish, great white shark

Clownfish

ATLANTIC OCEAN

STATS

Surface area
33,100,000 sq mi (85,600,000 sq km)

Percentage of all oceans
24 percent

Surface temperatures
Summer high: 90°F (32°C)
Winter low: 28°F (-2°C)

Tides
Highest: 52 ft (16 m)
Bay of Fundy, Canada
Lowest: 1.5 ft (0.5 m)
Gulf of Mexico and Mediterranean Sea

Cool creatures: blue whale, Atlantic spotted dolphin, sea turtle, bottlenose dolphin

Bottlenose dolphin

INDIAN OCEAN

STATS

Surface area
27,500,000 sq mi (71,200,000 sq km)

Percentage of all oceans
20 percent

Surface temperatures
Summer high: 93°F (34°C)
Winter low: 28°F (-2°C)

Tides
Highest: 36 ft (11 m)
Lowest: 2 ft (0.6 m)
Both along Australia's west coast

Cool creatures: **humpback whale, Portuguese man-of-war, dugong (sea cow), leatherback turtle**

Leatherback turtle

ARCTIC OCEAN

STATS

Surface area
6,100,000 sq mi (15,700,000 sq km)

Percentage of all oceans
4 percent

Surface temperatures
Summer high: 41°F (5°C)
Winter low: 28°F (-2°C)

Tides
Less than 1 ft (0.3 m) variation throughout the ocean

Cool creatures: **beluga whale, orca, harp seal, narwhal**

Narwhal

SOUTHERN OCEAN

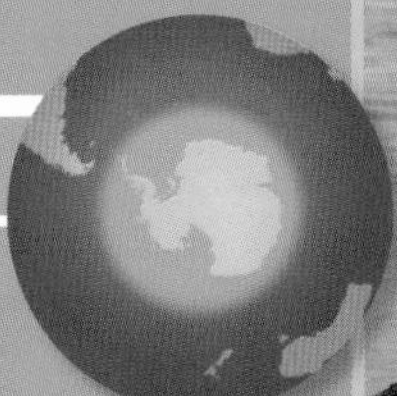

STATS

Surface area
8,500,000 sq mi (21,900,000 sq km)

Percentage of all oceans
6 percent

Surface temperatures
Summer high: 50°F (10°C)
Winter low: 28°F (-2°C)

Tides
Less than 2 ft (0.6 m) variation throughout the ocean

Cool creatures: **emperor penguin, colossal squid, mackerel icefish, Antarctic toothfish**

Emperor penguin

To see the major oceans and bays in relation to landmasses, look at the map on pages 272 and 273.

THE DEEP BLUE SEA

Oceans cover 71 percent of our planet's surface. Some areas in them are so deep that they'd cover the tallest mountains on Earth! Dive in and discover the deepest parts of our oceans.

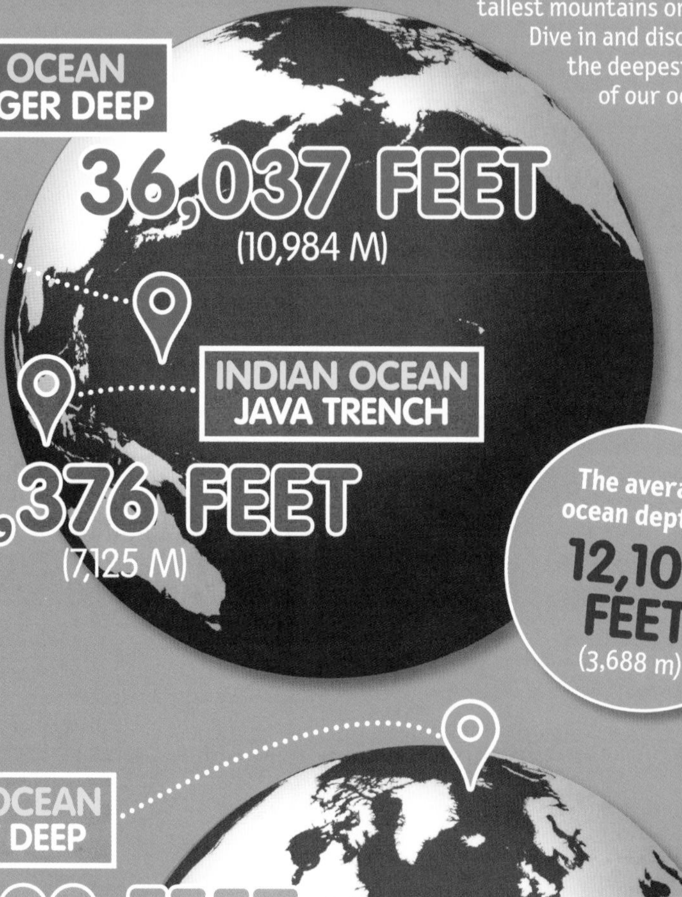

PACIFIC OCEAN
CHALLENGER DEEP

36,037 FEET
(10,984 M)

INDIAN OCEAN
JAVA TRENCH

23,376 FEET
(7,125 M)

The average ocean depth is
12,100 FEET
(3,688 m).

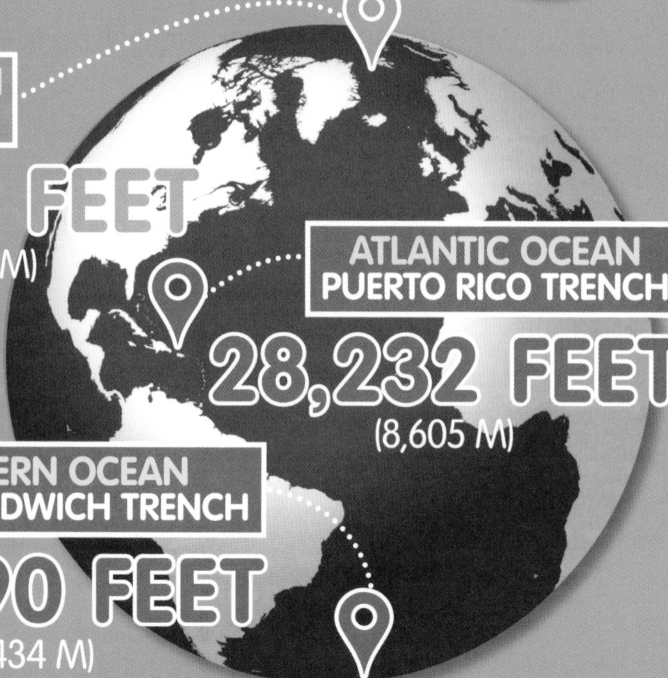

ARCTIC OCEAN
MOLLOY DEEP

18,599 FEET
(5,669 M)

ATLANTIC OCEAN
PUERTO RICO TRENCH

28,232 FEET
(8,605 M)

SOUTHERN OCEAN
SOUTH SANDWICH TRENCH

24,390 FEET
(7,434 M)

WATER CYCLE

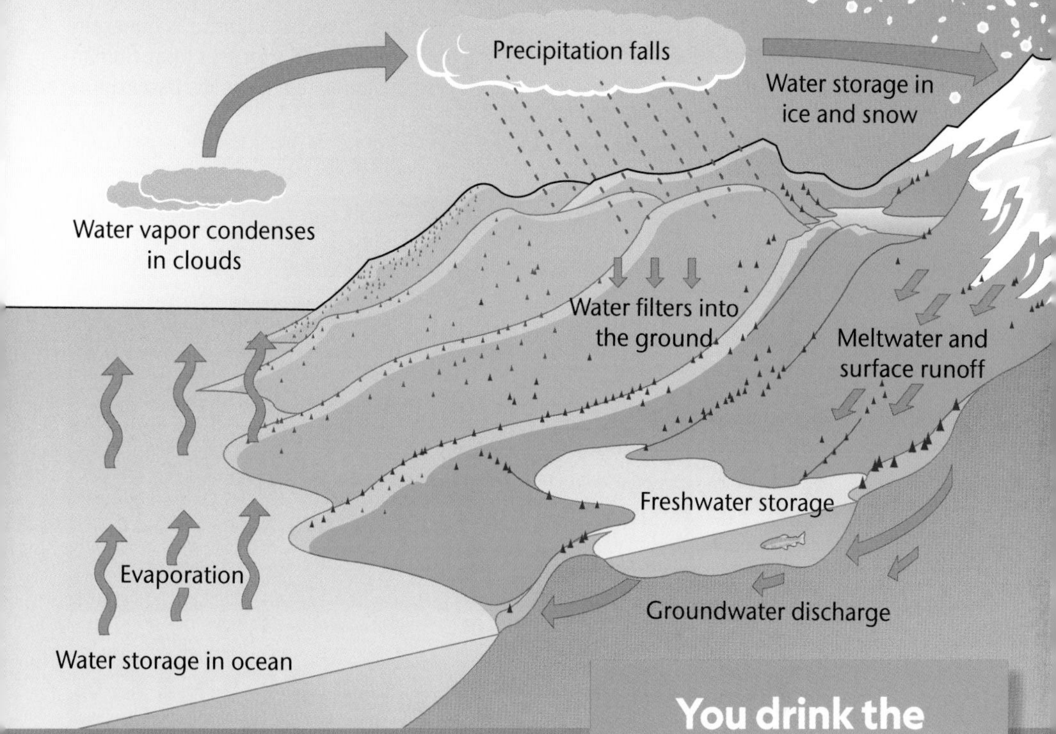

Precipitation falls

Water storage in ice and snow

Water vapor condenses in clouds

Water filters into the ground

Meltwater and surface runoff

Freshwater storage

Evaporation

Groundwater discharge

Water storage in ocean

The amount of water on Earth is more or less constant— only the form changes. As the sun warms Earth's surface, liquid water is changed into water vapor in a process called **evaporation.** Water on the surface of plants' leaves turns into water vapor in a process called **transpiration.** As water vapor rises into the air, it cools and changes form again. This time, it becomes clouds in a process called **condensation.** Water droplets fall from the clouds as **precipitation,** which then travels as groundwater or runoff back to the lakes, rivers, and oceans, where the cycle (shown above) starts all over again.

To a meteorologist— a person who studies the weather—a "light rain" is less than 1/48 inch (0.5 mm). A "heavy rain" is more than 1/6 inch (4 mm).

You drink the same water as the dinosaurs! Earth has been recycling water for more than four billion years.

Weather and Climate

Weather is the condition of the atmosphere—temperature, wind, humidity, and precipitation—at a given place at a given time. Climate, however, is the average weather for a particular place over a long period of time. Different places on Earth have different climates, but climate is not a random occurrence. It is a pattern that is controlled by factors such as latitude, elevation, prevailing winds, the temperature of ocean currents, and location on land relative to water. Climate is generally constant, but evidence indicates that human activity is causing a change in its patterns.

WEATHER EXTREMES

MOST SNOW RECORDED IN ONE SEASON: 1,140 inches (29 m) in Mount Baker, Washington, U.S.A.

FASTEST TEMPERATURE RISE: 49 degrees Fahrenheit (27.2°C) in two minutes, in Rapid City, South Dakota, U.S.A.

HEAVIEST HAILSTONE: 2.25 pounds (1 kg) in Gopalganj, Bangladesh

GLOBAL CLIMATE ZONES

Climatologists, people who study climate, have created different systems for classifying climates. One that is often used is called the Köppen system, which classifies climate zones according to precipitation, temperature, and vegetation. It has five major categories—tropical, dry, temperate, cold, and polar—with a sixth category for locations where high elevations override other factors.

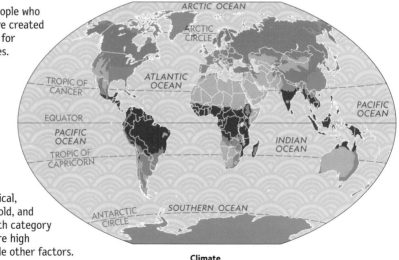

Climate

■ Tropical ■ Dry ■ Temperate ■ Cold ■ Polar

Climate CHANGE

A POLAR BEAR ON A PIECE OF MELTING ICEBERG

Rising Temperatures, Explained

Fact: The world is getting warmer.
Earth's surface temperature has been increasing. In the past 50 years, our planet has warmed twice as fast as in the 50 years before that. This is the direct effect of climate change, which refers not only to the increase in Earth's average temperature (known as global warming), but also to its long-term effects on winds, rain, and ocean currents. Global warming is the reason glaciers and polar ice sheets are melting—resulting in rising sea levels and shrinking habitats. This makes survival for some animals a big challenge. Warming also means more flooding along the coasts and drought for inland areas.

Why are temperatures climbing?
While some of the recent climate changes can be tied to natural causes—such as changes in the sun's intensity, the unusually warm ocean

SCIENTISTS ARE CONCERNED THAT GREENLAND'S ICE SHEET HAS BEGUN TO MELT IN SUMMER. BIRTHDAY CANYON, SHOWN HERE, WAS CARVED BY MELTWATER.

currents of El Niño, and volcanic activity—human activities are the greatest contributor.

Everyday activities that require burning fossil fuels, such as driving gasoline-powered cars, contribute to global warming. These activities produce greenhouse gases, which enter the atmosphere and trap heat. At the current rate, Earth's global average temperature is projected to rise some 5.4°F (3°C) by the year 2100, and it will get even warmer after that. And as the climate continues to warm, it will unfortunately continue to affect the environment and our society in many ways.

225

THERE ARE ABOUT 40 LIGHTNING FLASHES ON EARTH EVERY SECOND.

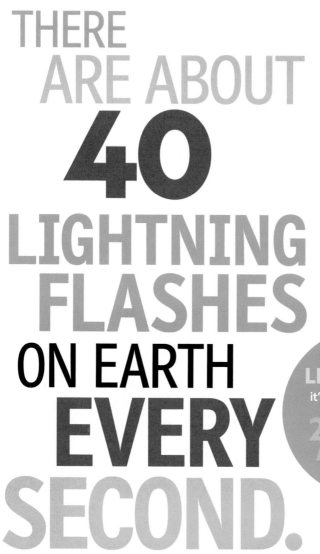

When you see **LIGHTNING,** it's **TRAVELING** at about **227 MILLION** miles an hour. **(365 MILLION KM/H)**

LIGHTNING can produce **HEAT** up to **FIVE TIMES HOTTER** than the sun.

Just how long can a lightning bolt be? Some of these giant electrical sparks can extend five miles (8 km) from top to bottom. One horizontal lightning bolt, spotted in South America, was a whopping 440 miles (708 km) long!

Lightning **STRIKES** the **EIFFEL TOWER** in Paris, France, about **10 TIMES A YEAR.**

ONE LIGHTNING FLASH has enough energy to **LIGHT** a **100-WATT BULB** for three months.

THE SKY IS FALLING

THE SKY CAN'T ACTUALLY FALL, BUT MOISTURE IN THE AIR CAN AND DOES.

"PRECIPITATION" IS A FANCY WORD
FOR THE WET STUFF THAT FALLS FROM THE SKY.

Precipitation is rain, freezing rain, sleet, snow, or hail. It forms when water vapor in the air condenses into clouds, gets heavier, and drops to the ground. Precipitation can ruin a picnic, but life on Earth couldn't exist without it.

Develops when ice crystals fall toward the ground, partly melt, and then refreeze. This happens mainly in winter when air near the ground is below freezing temperatures.

SLEET

RAIN

Formed when ice crystals in high, cold clouds get heavy and fall. Even in summer, falling ice crystals could remain frozen, but warm air near the ground melts them into raindrops.

FREEZING RAIN

Falls during winter, when rain freezes immediately as it hits a surface. Freezing rain creates layers of ice on roads and causes dangerous driving conditions.

Produced when ice crystals in clouds get heavy enough to fall. The air has to be cold enough all the way down for the crystals to stay frozen.

SNOW

HAIL

Formed inside thunderstorms when ice crystals covered in water pass through patches of freezing air in the tops of cumulonimbus clouds. The water on the ice crystals freezes. The crystals become heavy and fall to the ground.

Types of Clouds

If you want a clue about the weather, look up at the clouds. They'll tell a lot about the condition of the air and what weather might be on the way. Clouds are made of both air and water. On fair days, warm air currents rise up and push against the water in clouds, keeping it from falling. But as the raindrops in a cloud get bigger, it's time to set them free. The bigger raindrops become too heavy for the air currents to hold up, and they fall to the ground.

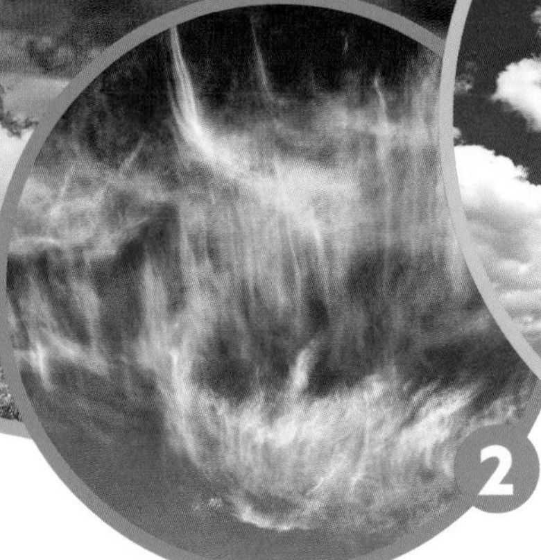

How Much Does a Cloud Weigh?

A light, fluffy cumulus cloud typically weighs about 216,000 pounds (98,000 kg). That's about the weight of 18 elephants. A rain-soaked cumulonimbus cloud typically weighs 105.8 million pounds (48 million kg), or about the same as 9,000 elephants.

1 STRATUS These clouds make the sky look like a bowl of thick gray porridge. They hang low in the sky, blanketing the day in dreary darkness. Stratus clouds form when cold, moist air close to the ground moves over a region.

2 CIRRUS These wispy tufts of clouds are thin and hang high up in the atmosphere where the air is extremely cold. Cirrus clouds are made of tiny ice crystals.

3 CUMULUS These white, fluffy clouds make people sing, "Oh, what a beautiful morning!" They form low in the atmosphere and look like marshmallows. They often mix with large patches of blue sky. Formed when hot air rises, cumulus clouds usually disappear when the air cools at night.

4 CUMULONIMBUS These are the monster clouds. Rising air currents force fluffy cumulus clouds to swell and shoot upward, as much as 70,000 feet (21,000 m). When these clouds bump against the top of the troposphere, known as the tropopause, they flatten out on top like tabletops.

HURRICANE
HAPPENINGS

A storm is brewing—but is this a tropical cyclone, a hurricane, or a typhoon? These weather events go by different names depending on where they form, how fast their winds get, or both. Strong tropical cyclones are called hurricanes in the Atlantic and parts of the Pacific Ocean; in the western Pacific, they are called typhoons. But any way you look at it, these storms pack a punch. And they all form when warm moist air rises from the ocean, causing air from surrounding areas to be "sucked" in. That air then becomes warm and moist, and rises, too, beginning a cycle that forms clouds, which rotate with the spin of Earth. If there is enough warm water to feed the storm, it will result in a hurricane. And the warmer the water, and the more moisture in the air, the more powerful the hurricane.

HURRICANE NAMES FOR 2023

Atlantic hurricane names come from six official international lists. The names alternate between male and female. When a storm becomes a hurricane, a name from the list is used, in alphabetical order. (If the hurricane season is especially active and the list runs out, the World Meteorological Organization will provide extra names to draw from.) Each list is reused every six years. A name is "retired" if that hurricane caused a lot of damage or many deaths.

Arlene	Franklin	Jose	Nigel	Sean
Bret	Gert	Katia	Ophelia	Tammy
Cindy	Harold	Lee	Philippe	Vince
Don	Idalia	Margot	Rina	Whitney
Emily				

SCALE OF HURRICANE INTENSITY

CATEGORY	ONE	TWO	THREE	FOUR	FIVE
DAMAGE	Minimal	Moderate	Extensive	Extreme	Catastrophic
WINDS	74–95 mph (119–153 km/h)	96–110 mph (154–177 km/h)	111–129 mph (178–208 km/h)	130–156 mph (209–251 km/h)	157 mph or higher (252+ km/h)

(DAMAGE refers to wind and water damage combined.)

THE ENHANCED FUJITA SCALE

The Enhanced Fujita (EF) Scale, named after tornado expert T. Theodore Fujita, classifies tornadoes based on wind speed and the intensity of damage that they cause.

What Is a Tornado?

EF0
65–85 mph winds
(105–137 km/h)
Slight damage

EF1
86–110 mph winds
(138–177 km/h)
Moderate damage

EF2
111–135 mph winds
(178–217 km/h)
Substantial damage

EF3
136–165 mph winds
(218–266 km/h)
Severe damage

EF4
166–200 mph winds
(267–322 km/h)
Massive damage

EF5
More than 200 mph winds
(322+ km/h)
Catastrophic damage

TORNADOES, ALSO KNOWN AS TWISTERS, are funnels of rapidly rotating air that are created during a thunderstorm. With wind speeds that can exceed 300 miles an hour (483 km/h), tornadoes have the power to pick up and destroy everything in their path.

THIS ROTATING FUNNEL OF AIR, formed in a cumulus or cumulonimbus cloud, became a tornado when it touched the ground.

TORNADOES HAVE OCCURRED IN ALL 50 U.S. STATES AND ON EVERY CONTINENT EXCEPT ANTARCTICA.

FLOOD

For an entire week in July 2020, torrential rain battered the island of Kyushu, the southernmost of Japan's four main islands. The record-breaking band of storms brought rain that fell at times nearly four inches (10 cm) an hour on the island. That triggered rivers to burst past their banks, unleashing a watery torrent that washed over main streets, neighborhoods, bridges, and businesses. The entire island experienced widespread flooding, with the water level rising to eight feet (2.5 m) in some parts. There were also landslides that caused even more damage. All told, nearly 15,000 homes in Japan were damaged, and, sadly, more than 75 people perished.

To aid the ailing island, Japan's Prime Minister Shinzo Abe dispatched tens of thousands of Japanese troops. Along with firefighters and coast guard sailors, the rescue teams steered boats down the streets to save those stranded in the rising water and help others in need. And as the rains slowed and the water receded, Kyushu was slowly able to begin the recovery process.

FREEZE

When three severe winter storms swept across Texas, U.S.A., in February 2021, residents were hit with an unexpected double disaster. First, as people cranked up the heat in their homes and businesses to warm up in the unusually frigid temps, the sudden electricity spike caused a massive power grid failure that impacted some 4.5 million residences. This left Texans stuck in their homes with no heat as temperatures outside dipped to lows the state hadn't seen in some 70 years. Those who did leave their homes to travel to a safer spot faced icy roads and malfunctioning streetlights, causing car crashes and even more hardship. At least 111 Texans died as a result of the winter weather.

When power was restored days later, another catastrophe: flooded homes. Millions of homes faced water damage as pipes, which had frozen, burst under pressure while thawing. Water treatment plants were also impacted, resulting in a crisis in which millions had no running water or were under orders to boil it before use to kill harmful microorganisms and make it safe to drink.

While the Texas freeze was devastating, those impacted have been able to recover and rebuild. And, perhaps most important, the entire state will be better prepared to avoid a similar catastrophe in the future.

BOBCAT WILDFIRE RESCUE

An injured bobcat searches for prey among blackened tree stumps but finds nothing to eat. It's been three weeks since the Camp Fire destroyed the cat's habitat in northern California, U.S.A. The underweight juvenile won't survive much longer without food.

Luckily, a passerby spots the cat and calls Sallysue Stein, the founder of Gold Country Wildlife Rescue. Stein arranges to have the cat brought to her facility. "When he arrived, we could see that his paws were singed and he was obviously hungry," Stein says. "When we were able to examine him, we saw that the pads of his paws had been burned all the way to the bone."

Although bobcats are rarely seen, they're the most common wild cat in North America.

HIGH-TECH TREATMENT

Medicine helps make the cat comfortable, but his paws need much more care. The cat's rescuers call in veterinarian Jamie Peyton, who specializes in animal burns.

Peyton suggests a new type of treatment to heal the animal's wounds: fish skin. By wrapping the cat's paws in bandages made from tilapia (a type of fish) skin, they can protect his paws from getting infected; plus, the collagen—a kind of protein—found in the tilapia might help the wounds heal faster.

After a week of treatments, the bobcat's appetite increases, and he switches from just gruel to having birds and mice added to his meals. "We knew he was ready to be released when he started trying to escape from his kennel," Stein says.

GOING HOME

After 11 weeks of treatment, the bobcat is taken to Big Chico Creek Ecological Reserve, which hasn't been impacted by the fires. The cage door is opened. The bobcat steps out, sprints up a tall tree, and disappears from view.

"Our goal was to give the bobcat a second chance in the wild," Stein says. "It's where he belongs."

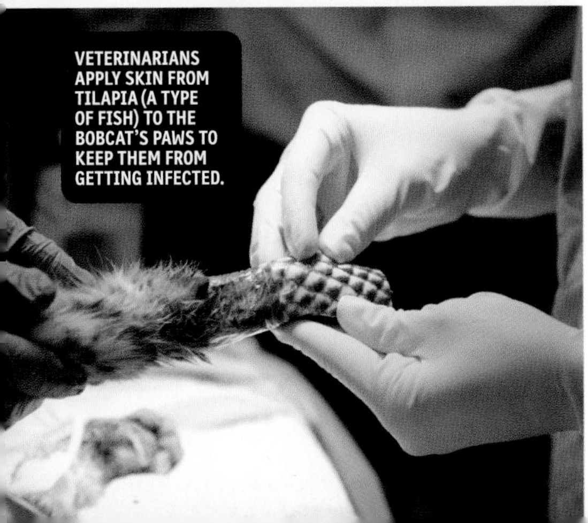

VETERINARIANS APPLY SKIN FROM TILAPIA (A TYPE OF FISH) TO THE BOBCAT'S PAWS TO KEEP THEM FROM GETTING INFECTED.

NEARLY FOUR MONTHS AFTER BEING INJURED IN A FIRE, THE HEALED BOBCAT IS ABLE TO CLIMB TREES AGAIN.

QUIZ WHIZ

Quiz yourself
to find out
if you're a natural
when it comes to
nature knowledge!

Write your answers
on a piece of paper.
Then check them below.

1 **True or false?** A rain-soaked cumulonimbus cloud weighs about the same as 9,000 pandas.

2 **Which is NOT an example of precipitation?**
a. rain
b. sleet
c. hail
d. thunder

3 In February 2021, _____ were an unexpected double disaster in parts of Texas, U.S.A.
a. a widespread power outage and flooded homes
b. a heat wave and wildfires
c. a hailstorm and dented cars
d. a rain deluge and flooded streets

4 **True or false?** The Great Barrier Reef is bigger than the United Kingdom, Switzerland, and Holland combined.

5 At the current rate, Earth's global average temperature is projected to rise some _____ by the year 2100.
a. .54°F (-17.5°C)
b. 5.4°F (3°C)
c. 54°F (12°C)
d. 540°F (282°C)

Not **STUMPED** yet? Check out the *NATIONAL GEOGRAPHIC KIDS QUIZ WHIZ* collection for more crazy **NATURE** questions!

ANSWERS: 1. False: It weighs the same as 9,000 elephants.; 2. d; 3. a; 4. True; 5. b

HOMEWORK HELP

Oral Reports Made Easy

TIP: Make sure you practice your presentation a few times. Stand in front of a mirror or have a parent record you so you can see if you need to work on anything, such as eye contact.

Does the thought of public speaking start your stomach churning like a tornado? Would you rather get caught in an avalanche than give a speech?

Giving an oral report does not have to be a natural disaster. The basic format is very similar to that of a written essay. There are two main elements that make up a good oral report—the writing and the presentation. As you write your oral report, remember that your audience will be hearing the information as opposed to reading it. Follow the guidelines below, and there will be clear skies ahead.

Writing Your Material

Follow the steps in the "How to Write a Perfect Essay" section on page 129, but prepare your report to be spoken rather than written. Try to keep your sentences short and simple. Long, complex sentences are harder to follow. Limit yourself to just a few key points. You don't want to overwhelm your audience with too much information. To be most effective, hit your key points in the introduction, elaborate on them in the body, and then repeat them once again in your conclusion.

AN ORAL REPORT HAS THREE BASIC PARTS:

- Introduction—This is your chance to engage your audience and really capture their interest in the subject you are presenting. Use a funny personal experience or a dramatic story, or start with an intriguing question.

- Body—This is the longest part of your report. Here you elaborate on the facts and ideas you want to convey. Give information that supports your main idea, and expand on it with specific examples or details. In other words, structure your oral report in the same way you would a written essay, so that your thoughts are presented in a clear and organized manner.

- Conclusion—This is the time to summarize the information and emphasize your most important points to the audience one last time.

Preparing Your Delivery

1 Practice makes perfect. Practice! Practice! Practice! Confidence, enthusiasm, and energy are key to delivering an effective oral report, and they can best be achieved through rehearsal. Ask family and friends to be your practice audience and give you feedback when you're done. Were they able to follow your ideas? Did you seem knowledgeable and confident? Did you speak too slowly or too fast, too softly or too loudly? The more times you practice giving your report, the more you'll master the material. Then you won't have to rely so heavily on your notes or papers, and you will be able to give your report in a relaxed and confident manner.

2 Present with everything you've got. Be as creative as you can. Incorporate videos, sound clips, slide presentations, charts, diagrams, and photos. Visual aids help stimulate your audience's senses and keep them intrigued and engaged. They can also help to reinforce your key points. And remember that when you're giving an oral report, you're a performer. Take charge of the spotlight and be as animated and entertaining as you can. Have fun with it.

3 Keep your nerves under control. Everyone gets a little nervous when speaking in front of a group. That's normal. But the more preparation you've done— meaning plenty of researching, organizing, and rehearsing—the more confident you'll be. Preparation is the key. And if you make a mistake or stumble over your words, just regroup and keep going. Nobody's perfect, and nobody expects you to be.

HISTORY HAPPENS

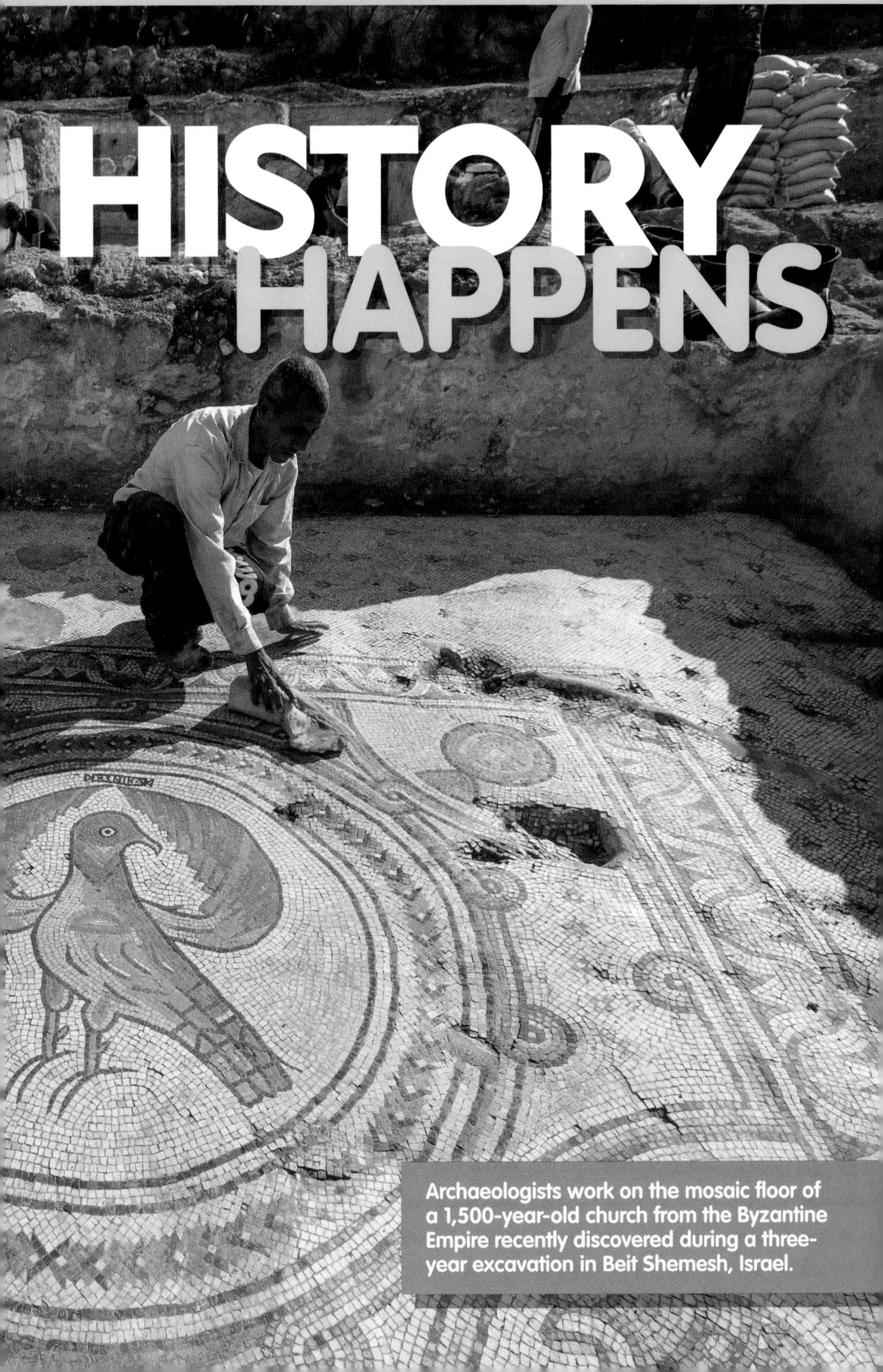

Archaeologists work on the mosaic floor of a 1,500-year-old church from the Byzantine Empire recently discovered during a three-year excavation in Beit Shemesh, Israel.

ANCIENT EGYPT
BY THE NUMBERS

1
Number of major organs left in the body after mummification. The heart was kept inside, but all other organs were removed.

9
Age that King Tut became pharaoh of Egypt, in 1332 B.C.

97
Percentage of ancient Egyptian land that was covered in desert.

130
Number of Egyptian pyramids discovered to date.

2.8 TONS (2.5 t)
Weight of a single stone block used to build a pyramid.

1 MILE (1.6 km)
The average length of the bandages used to wrap an Egyptian mummy.

Brainy Questions

HEY, SMARTY-PANTS!

GOT BIG, WEIRD QUESTIONS?

WE'VE GOT ANSWERS!

Why are ancient statues and buildings always white?

The paint has come off! Ancient Greeks and Romans painted their statues and temples in many different colors, but over the past few thousand years, the paint has worn away. Ancient artists mixed colorful minerals—like crushed-up malachite for green or azurite for blue—with beeswax or egg yolks to create paint. Today, archaeologists are using ultraviolet and infrared lamps, along with chemical analysis to discover the traces of colors and patterns left behind on the statues. We know ancient people would approve: A line in one Greek play implies that wiping color off a statue would make it uglier.

What's inside the Great Pyramid of Giza?

Not much, anymore! The Great Pyramid was built about 4,570 years ago as the final resting place of Khufu, an Egyptian pharaoh. It also stored all the stuff he'd need in the afterlife, like bread, fruit, furniture, clothes, and jewelry. The 481-foot (147-m)-tall stone structure was Khufu's way of telling people that he was super important. But it also screamed, "Hey, stuff to steal inside!" Today, you can walk through a passageway deep into the center of the pyramid until you reach the King's Chamber, which has a granite sarcophagus—but nothing else.

THE LOST CITY OF
POMPEII

When will the volcano that buried this ancient civilization blow again?

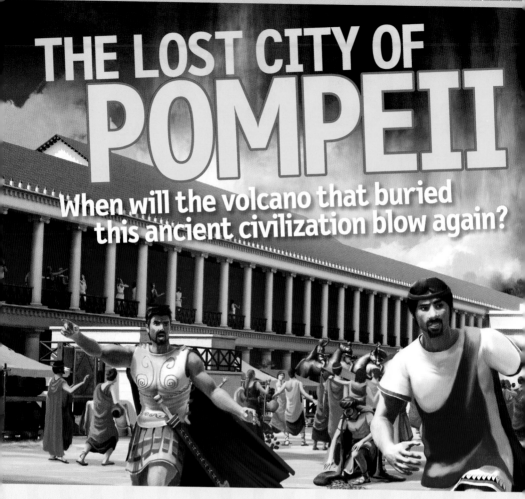

A deafening boom roars through Pompeii's crowded marketplace. The ground shakes violently, throwing the midday shoppers off balance and toppling stands of fish and meat. People start screaming and pointing toward Mount Vesuvius, a massive volcano that rises above the bustling city, located in what is now southern Italy.

Vesuvius has been silent for nearly 2,000 years, but it roars back to life, shooting ash and smoke into the air. Almost overnight, the city and most of its residents vanish under a blanket of ash and lava.

Now, almost 2,000 years later, scientists agree that Vesuvius is overdue for another major eruption—but no one knows when it will happen. Three million people live in the volcano's shadow, in the modern-day city of Naples, Italy. Correctly predicting when the eruption might take place will mean the difference between life and death for many.

THE SKY IS FALLING

Thanks to excavations that started in 1748 and continue to this day, scientists have been able to re-create almost exactly what happened in Pompeii on that terrible day in A.D. 79.

"The thick ash turned everything black," says Pompeii expert Andrew Wallace-Hadrill.

"People couldn't see the sun. All the landmarks disappeared. They didn't have the foggiest idea which way they were going."

Some people ran for their lives, clutching their valuable coins and jewelry. Other people took shelter in their homes. But the debris kept falling. Piles grew as deep as nine feet (2.7 m) in some places, blocking doorways and caving in roofs.

Around midnight, the first of four searing-hot clouds, or surges, of ash, pumice, rock, and toxic gas rushed down the mountainside. Traveling toward Pompeii at up to 180 miles an hour (290 km/h), it scorched everything in its path. Around 7 a.m., 18 hours after the

TODAY, MILLIONS OF TOURISTS VISIT THE RUINS OF POMPEII, INCLUDING THE FORUM, BELOW.

THIS ARTIST'S CONCEPT RE-CREATES THE FORUM AT POMPEII AS IT LOOKED THE DAY OF THE ERUPTION IN A.D. 79. THE FORUM WAS THE CENTER OF PUBLIC LIFE.

eruption, the last fiery surge buried the city.

LOST AND FOUND

Visiting the ruins of Pompeii today is like going back in time. The layers of ash actually helped preserve buildings, artwork, and even the forms of bodies. "It gives you the feeling you can reach out and touch the ancient world," Wallace-Hadrill says.

There are kitchens with pots on the stove and bakeries with loaves of bread—now turned to charcoal—still in the ovens. Narrow corridors lead to magnificent mansions with elaborate gardens and fountains. Mosaics, or designs made out of tiles, decorate the walls and floors.

WARNING SIGNS

Pompeii's destruction may be ancient history, but there's little doubt that disaster will strike again. Luckily, people living near Vesuvius today will likely receive evacuation warnings before the volcano blows.

Scientists are closely monitoring Vesuvius for shifts in the ground, earthquakes, and rising levels of certain gases, which could be signs of an upcoming eruption. The Italian government is also working on a plan to help people flee the area in the event of a natural disaster.

CREEPY CASTS

Volcanic ash settled around many of the victims at the moment of death. When the bodies decayed, holes remained inside the solid ash. Scientists poured plaster into the holes to preserve the shapes of the victims.

THE HAGIA SOPHIA
IN ISTANBUL, TURKEY,
HAS BEEN A CATHEDRAL, A MOSQUE, AND A MUSEUM.

The HAGIA SOPHIA was once the **LARGEST CATHEDRAL** in the **WORLD** (it's now the fourth).

The **ORIGINAL DOME** was **DESTROYED** by an **EARTHQUAKE** around A.D. 550. It was soon **REBUILT** to its current height of **182 FEET** (55 m).

The Hagia Sophia (Greek for "holy wisdom") was built as a cathedral some 1,500 years ago. Later, it was transformed into a mosque under Ottoman rule, which is how it remained until 1934, when it opened as a museum. In 2020, Turkey's president declared the site a mosque once again.

There are
140 COLUMNS
in the Hagia Sophia,
INCLUDING
the partly bronze-covered
"SWEATING COLUMN,"
which is damp
to the touch.

MOSAICS
dating back some
700 YEARS
were recently
UNEARTHED
under layers of
plaster beneath
the dome.

243

ROYAL

Check out what some of history's most

FIT FOR A QUEEN

Though militaries of the past were made up mostly of men, a few notable women—royal and otherwise—rode into battle, leading troops to victory. Not much is known about many of them. Check out what we *do* know about fierce females on the battlefield.

Armor for All

The few historical accounts of royal women in battle say that they likely donned the same gear as men. They're usually described as wearing hauberks: garments made of metal that covered the arms, torso, and upper legs.

Legendary Look

Many images of armor-clad women depict fictional figures like Minerva, the Roman goddess of women and warfare. According to legend, Minerva's father, Jupiter, swallowed her pregnant mother after a prophecy foretold that their unborn child would grow up to defeat him. When Minerva eventually escaped from inside Jupiter, she was wearing full battle armor and ready to fight her father.

MINERVA

Secret Suit

Though some historical paintings depict women in metal armor, no one knows for sure how accurate these illustrations are. That means the exact appearance of women's armor in the past is still a mystery, but historians think it looked similar to what men wore, like the suit above worn by English nobility during the 16th century.

Knight Me

In 1149, when invaders threatened to take over the town of Tortosa, Spain, local women threw on men's clothing and fought off the enemy. Spanish count Ramon Berenguer IV was so impressed that he created the Order of the Hatchet, granting the women rights similar to those of knights, such as not having to pay taxes.

Custom Fit

Joan of Arc is one of history's most famous warriors. During the 15th century, France's King Charles VII presented the military leader with armor tailored to fit her perfectly.

CHECK OUT THE BOOK!

THE BOOK OF **Queens**

RUMBLE

fearsome fighters wore on the battlefield.

So Much Metal

Being a knight sounds exciting, but wearing armor was not. Mail armor, invented around the third century B.C., was made of interlocking metal circles layered over quilted fabric to protect against arrows. Plate armor, invented around the late 1300s, was heavy and hard to see out of. But because it was made of bands of steel over leather, it defended against heavy blows while allowing for movement. The best protection? Probably a combination of both.

MAIL ARMOR

PLATE ARMOR

FIT FOR A KING

On the battlefield, sturdy armor meant the difference between life and death. Good armor protected its wearers against a variety of weapons while still allowing them to move easily. Discover what kings and their soldiers wore throughout history.

Works of Art

Today, Japanese samurai are famous for their long blades known as katanas, but their armor during the Heian period (A.D. 794–1185) was just as well known. Samurai armor, called *o-yoroi* (pronounced oh-YO-roy, above), was made of metal and leather and was designed to deflect blades and arrows. It consisted of multiple pieces laced together, including the *kabuto* (helmet), the *menpo* (face mask), and extra leg and arm guards. Some pieces were decorated so beautifully that today they're regarded as works of art.

Cat Fight

The Aztec Empire, which reigned over central Mexico from 1345 to 1521, was known for a group of warriors called the *ocelotl* (pronounced oh-seh-LO-tl), meaning "jaguars." In addition to wearing regular armor in battle, these jaguar fighters donned symbols of their namesake. One example was a helmet shaped like a jaguar head, with room for the soldier to peek out from below the teeth. And they sometimes wore capes made from real jaguar pelts. These outfits were thought to transfer the fierceness of the jaguar to the wearer.

SIXTH-CENTURY STATUE
OF A JAGUAR WARRIOR

Animal Armor

Throughout history, some animals donned armor along with their soldiers, including battle horses and even elephants. War elephants, first used in what is now India during the 12th century, were sometimes dressed in fancy sets of metal armor weighing more than 350 pounds (159 kg). A few were also adorned with "tusk swords," which were metal weapons mounted on the elephants' tusks. Other elephants were saddled with carriages where archers could sit and fire on their enemies.

THE BOOK OF KINGS

**CHECK OUT
THE BOOK!**

TO HONOR A QUEEN

The Taj Mahal might be the world's grandest tomb.

The Taj Mahal in India might look like a fancy home for important kings and queens. After all, it was likely the inspiration for the palace in *Aladdin*. But no one ever lived here: It's actually a tomb. Who's buried inside? Read on to find out!

A PORTRAIT OF MUMTAZ MAHAL (LEFT) AND SHAH JAHAN

MEET THE MAKER

For more than 200 years, the Mughal Empire ruled over parts of what is today India, Pakistan, Afghanistan, and Nepal. To become emperor, a royal male had to prove himself to be the best choice before being named as heir—but the family could still change its mind.

That's what happened to Shah Jahan, a third-born son who had been named heir but later fell from favor. When his father died, he returned home in 1628 to reclaim the throne. And just in case, he put his rivals—including his brother and a few nephews—to death.

The new emperor loved architecture and art, and he adored his second wife, Mumtaz Mahal. (Shah Jahan had three wives; emperors at this time usually had many spouses to gain power through their families.) Mumtaz Mahal traveled with him everywhere, even on military campaigns. "They had a true partnership and a true love," Mughal art historian Mehreen Chida-Razvi says. The couple was married for nearly 20 years before Mumtaz Mahal died in 1631.

Legend says that after his wife's death, Shah Jahan's black hair turned white from grief. He decided her tomb would be a grand monument to his lost love. "Nothing had ever been built like this to honor a queen before," Chida-Razvi says.

BEST BUILDING

About 20,000 craftsmen baked bricks made of mud to form the building's structure. They then

Mumtaz Mahal means "chosen one of the palace."

In the Persian language, Shah Jahan means "king of the world."

Shah Jahan sat on a throne called the Peacock Throne, which was studded with gems from his treasury.

WORKERS CLEAN THE TAJ MAHAL WITH CLAY, THEN WASH IT OFF WITH DISTILLED WATER.

ASIA
INDIA
INDIAN OCEAN

PAKISTAN
CHINA
New Dehli
BHUTAN
Agra
NEPAL
MYANMAR (BURMA)
I N D I A
BANGLADESH
Arabian Sea
Bay of Bengal

Solving a Mystery

Every few years, the Taj Mahal gets a mud bath to remove mysterious yellow-brown stains from the white marble. Environmental scientist Mike Bergin thought that if he could find the cause of the stains, people could better protect the tomb.

In 2012, he placed marble tiles on the monument for two months, then used a special high-powered microscope to look at the stained tiles. He found tiny particles of pollution from cars and the burning of wood, trash, and dung. The pollution absorbed light instead of reflecting it, which created the stains. As a result, the Indian government restricted burning trash and driving cars near the monument to help decrease the staining pollution.

"Once you know the problem," Bergin says, "you can make policies to fix it."

covered them in white marble for the tomb or red sandstone for nearby buildings. Artisans covered the tomb with designs made from more than 40 types of semiprecious gems. And calligraphers hand-carved poems and scripture all over walls and columns.

What looks like Mumtaz Mahal's sarcophagus was placed in the central room. But it's actually a cenotaph, a false tomb that allows visitors to pay their respects without disturbing her actual remains. Those were laid in a crypt directly underneath.

Nearly 20 years later, the massive, 42-acre (17-ha) complex was complete.

INLAID PIECES OF JADE AND CORAL CREATE ART THROUGHOUT THE TAJ MAHAL.

TOMB TRUTH

Shah Jahan likely would have built his own tomb nearby, Chida-Razvi says. But in 1657, he fell gravely ill. Seizing the chance to become ruler—just like Shah Jahan had done 30 years before—one of his sons imprisoned him in a fort. His only comfort: that he could see the Taj Mahal from a window.

The ex-emperor died eight years later, but his son didn't honor him with a majestic tomb. Instead, his body was brought to the Taj Mahal at night. His sarcophagus was plopped to the side of his wife's, even though the tomb was to honor Mumtaz Mahal—and no one else.

More than 350 years later, people still marvel at the Taj Mahal. Shah Jahan would probably be happy that people continue to honor his beloved wife.

247

PiRATES!

MEET THREE OF HISTORY'S MOST FEARSOME HIGH-SEAS BADDIES.

Yo-ho, yo-ho—*uh-oh!* A mysterious ship on the horizon flying a skull-and-crossbones flag wasn't a welcome sight to sailors in the 18th and 19th centuries. That flag meant one thing: pirates. Faced with faster, cannon-crammed vessels typically crewed by pirates, a ship captain was left with two choices: lower the sails and surrender—or turn and fight.

Life wasn't one big swashbuckling adventure for the pirates, however. Lousy food, cramped quarters, stinky crewmates, and hurricanes were all part of the job. Still, a handful of pirates managed to enjoy success at sea ... and inspired fear in those who were unfortunate enough to meet them face-to-face. Check out some of history's most famous pirates.

RACHEL WALL

REIGN OF TERROR New England coast, U.S.A., late 1700s

Rachel Wall and her husband, George, worked together as pirates, targeting small islands off the coast of present-day Maine in the Atlantic Ocean. After storms, they'd stop their sailboat and raise a distress flag. When passersby responded to Rachel's screams for help, they were robbed—or worse—for their trouble. After just two summers of piracy, Rachel and George killed at least 24 men and raked in about $6,000, plus an unknown amount of valuable goods. They later sold their loot, pretending they'd found it washed up on a beach.

CRIME DOESN'T PAY Eventually the law caught up with Rachel Wall. In 1789, she made history when she was the last woman to be hanged in the state of Massachusetts.

CHENG I SAO

REIGN OF TERROR South China Sea, 1801–1810

Cheng I Sao ruled a pirate fleet of nearly 2,000 ships. Sometimes called Madame Cheng, she turned to crime after she married a famous pirate. More than 80,000 buccaneers—men, women, and even children—reported to Madame Cheng. They seized loot in all sorts of ways: selling "protection" from pirate attacks, raiding ships, and kidnapping for ransom. Madame Cheng was best known for paying her pirates cash for each head they brought back from their assaults. (Yikes!)

CRIME DOESN'T PAY—USUALLY Every government attempt to stop Madame Cheng was a failure. Rumor has it that after she retired from piracy, she started a second career as a smuggler. She died peacefully at age 69.

BLACKBEARD

REIGN OF TERROR North America's East Coast and the Caribbean, 1713–1718

Nobody knows Blackbeard's real name—historians think it might've been Edward Teach—but he's arguably history's most famous pirate. He began his career as a privateer, or a kind of legal pirate, who was hired by the British government to attack enemy fleets and steal their goods.

Blackbeard abandoned privateering in 1713 and went full-pirate when he sailed to the Caribbean on a French ship that was gifted to him by another pirate, adding cannons to the vessel and renaming it *Queen Anne's Revenge*. He terrified his enemies by strapping pistols and knives across his chest and sticking smoking cannon fuses in his beard. According to legend, Blackbeard hid a treasure somewhere ... but it's never been found.

CRIME DOESN'T PAY A few years into Blackbeard's time as a pirate, he was nabbed by the British Navy. He was executed, and his head stuck on the front of a ship as a way to warn wannabe pirates to stay away from seafaring crime.

249

GOING TO WAR

Since the beginning of time, different countries, territories, and cultures have feuded with each other over land, power, and politics. Major military conflicts include the following wars:

1095-1291 THE CRUSADES
Starting late in the 11th century, these wars over religion were fought in the Middle East for nearly 200 years.

1337-1453 HUNDRED YEARS' WAR
France and England battled over rights to land for more than a century before the French eventually drove the English out in 1453.

1754-1763 FRENCH AND INDIAN WAR (part of Europe's Seven Years' War)
A nine-year war between the British and French for control of North America.

1775-1783 AMERICAN REVOLUTION
Thirteen British colonies in America united to reject the rule of the British government and to form the United States of America.

1861-1865 AMERICAN CIVIL WAR
This war occurred when the northern states (the Union) went to war with the southern states, which had seceded, or withdrawn, to form the Confederate States of America. Slavery was one of the key issues in the Civil War.

1910-1920 MEXICAN REVOLUTION
The people of Mexico revolted against the rule of dictator President Porfirio Díaz, leading to his eventual defeat and to a democratic government.

1914-1918 WORLD WAR I
The assassination of Austria's Archduke Ferdinand by a Serbian nationalist sparked this wide-spreading war. The U.S. entered after Germany sank the British ship *Lusitania*, killing more than 120 Americans.

1918-1920 RUSSIAN CIVIL WAR
Following the 1917 Russian Revolution, this conflict pitted the Communist Red Army against the foreign-backed White Army. The Red Army won, leading to the establishment of the Union of Soviet Socialist Republics (U.S.S.R.) in 1922.

1936-1939 SPANISH CIVIL WAR
Aid from Italy and Germany helped Spain's Nationalists gain victory over the Communist-supported Republicans. The war resulted in the loss of more than 300,000 lives and increased tension in Europe leading up to World War II.

1939-1945 WORLD WAR II
This massive conflict in Europe, Asia, and North Africa involved many countries that aligned with the two sides: the Allies and the Axis. After the bombing of Pearl Harbor in Hawaii in 1941, the U.S. entered the war on the side of the Allies. More than 50 million people died during the war.

1946-1949
CHINESE CIVIL WAR
Also known as the "War of Liberation," this war pitted the Communist and Nationalist Parties in China against each other. The Communists won.

1950-1953 KOREAN WAR
Kicked off when the Communist forces of North Korea, with backing from the Soviet Union, invaded their democratic neighbor to the south. A coalition of 16 countries from the United Nations stepped in to support South Korea. An armistice, or temporary truce, ended active fighting in 1953.

1950s-1975 VIETNAM WAR
This war was fought between the Communist North, supported by allies including China, and the government of South Vietnam, supported by the United States and other anticommunist nations.

1967 SIX-DAY WAR
This was a battle for land between Israel and the states of Egypt, Jordan, and Syria. The outcome resulted in Israel's gaining control of coveted territory, including the Gaza Strip and the West Bank.

1991-PRESENT
SOMALI CIVIL WAR
The war began when Somalia's last president, a dictator named Mohamed Siad Barre, was overthrown. This has led to years of fighting and anarchy.

2001-2014
WAR IN AFGHANISTAN
After attacks in the U.S. by the terrorist group al Qaeda, a coalition that eventually included more than 40 countries invaded Afghanistan to find Osama bin Laden and other al Qaeda members and to dismantle the Taliban. Bin Laden was killed in a U.S. covert operation in 2011. The North Atlantic Treaty Organization (NATO) took control of the coalition's combat mission in 2003. That combat mission officially ended in 2014.

2003-2011 WAR IN IRAQ
A coalition led by the U.S., and including Britain, Australia, and Spain, invaded Iraq over suspicions that Iraq had weapons of mass destruction.

WARTIME INVENTIONS

It's said that necessity is the mother of invention. And in wartime, necessity—or at least the need for making life easier—is especially key. So it's not too surprising that some of the more useful things in our world today were created during times of conflict—in particular, during World War I, when industrialization led to innovations across the board.

Take, for example, Kleenex tissues. What we use today to blow our noses was born out of what was first meant to be a thin, cottony liner used in a gas mask. In 1924, the company Kimberly-Clark started selling the same tissue liners as a disposable makeup remover for women. But when an employee with hay fever started blowing his nose in the wipes, Kimberly-Clark saw an opportunity—and sold the Kleenex as an alternative to cloth handkerchiefs.

Then there are zippers: Originally known as "hookless fasteners," they first widely appeared on the flying suits of aviators during World War I. Before then, buttons were the fashionable way to fasten shirts, pants, and boots, but the new invention was much more, well, zippy. In 1923, the B.F. Goodrich Company coined the term zipper, and the name stuck.

And whenever you check the time on your wristwatch, you can thank World War I soldiers for making this type of timepiece trendy. At the time of the war, wristwatches were popular with women, while men mostly kept the time on pocket watches, which they'd have tucked away on a chain. But during the war, male soldiers switched to wristwatches for easier access to the time (and to keep both hands free in the trenches). After the war, the wristwatch became a common look for all genders—and remains so today.

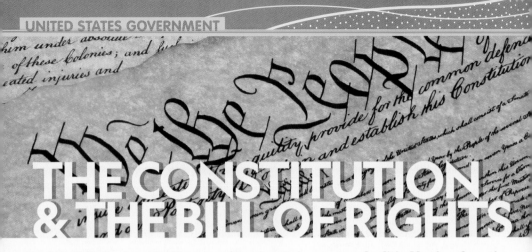

THE CONSTITUTION & THE BILL OF RIGHTS

The United States Constitution was written in 1787 by a group of political leaders from the 13 states that made up the United States at the time. Thirty-nine men, including Benjamin Franklin and James Madison, signed the document to create a national government. While some feared the creation of a strong federal government, all 13 states eventually ratified, or approved, the Constitution, making it the law of the land. The Constitution has three major parts: the preamble, the articles, and the amendments.

Here's a summary of what topics are covered in each part of the Constitution. The Constitution can be found online or at your local library for the full text.

THE PREAMBLE outlines the basic purposes of the government: *We the People of the United States, in order to form a more perfect Union, establish justice, insure domestic tranquility, provide for the common defense, promote the general welfare, and secure the blessings of liberty to ourselves and our posterity, do ordain and establish this Constitution for the United States of America.*

SEVEN ARTICLES outline the powers of Congress, the president, and the court system:

Article I outlines the legislative branch—the Senate and the House of Representatives—and its powers and responsibilities.

Article II outlines the executive branch—the presidency—and its powers and responsibilities.

Article III outlines the judicial branch—the court system—and its powers and responsibilities.

Article IV describes the individual states' rights and powers.

Article V outlines the amendment process.

Article VI establishes the Constitution as the law of the land.

Article VII gives the requirements for the Constitution to be approved.

THE AMENDMENTS, or additions to the Constitution, were put in later as needed. In 1791, the first 10 amendments, known as the **Bill of Rights,** were added. Since then, another 17 amendments have been added. This is the Bill of Rights:

1st Amendment: guarantees freedom of religion, speech, and the press, and the right to assemble and petition. The U.S. may not have a national religion.

2nd Amendment: discusses the militia and the right of people to bear arms

3rd Amendment: prohibits the military or troops from using private homes without consent

4th Amendment: protects people and their homes from search, arrest, or seizure without probable cause or a warrant

5th Amendment: grants people the right to have a trial and prevents punishment before prosecution; protects private property from being taken without compensation

6th Amendment: guarantees the right to a speedy and public trial

7th Amendment: guarantees a trial by jury in certain cases

8th Amendment: forbids "cruel and unusual punishments"

9th Amendment: states that the Constitution is not all-encompassing and does not deny people other, unspecified rights

10th Amendment: grants the powers not covered by the Constitution to the states and the people

Read the full text version of the United States Constitution at constitutioncenter.org/constitution/full-text

White House

BRANCHES OF GOVERNMENT

The **UNITED STATES GOVERNMENT** is divided into three branches: executive, legislative, and judicial. The system of checks and balances is a way to control power and to make sure one branch can't take the reins of government. For example, most of the president's actions require the approval of Congress. Likewise, the laws passed in Congress must be signed by the president before they can take effect.

Executive Branch

The Constitution lists the central powers of the president: to serve as commander in chief of the armed forces; make treaties with other nations; grant pardons; inform Congress on the state of the union; and appoint ambassadors, officials, and judges. The executive branch includes the president and the 15 governmental departments.

Legislative Branch

This branch is made up of Congress—the Senate and the House of Representatives. The Constitution grants Congress the power to make laws. Congress is made up of elected representatives from each state. Each state has two representatives in the Senate, while the number of representatives in the House is determined by the size of the state's population. Washington, D.C., and the territories elect nonvoting representatives to the House of Representatives. The Founding Fathers set up this system as a compromise between big states—which wanted representation based on population—and small states—which wanted all states to have equal representation rights.

The U.S. Capitol in Washington, D.C.

Judicial Branch

The U.S. Supreme Court Building in Washington, D.C.

The judicial branch is composed of the federal court system—the U.S. Supreme Court, the courts of appeals, and the district courts. The Supreme Court is the most powerful court. Its motto is "Equal Justice Under Law." This influential court is responsible for interpreting the Constitution and applying it to the cases that it hears. The decisions of the Supreme Court are absolute—they are the final word on any legal question.

There are nine justices on the Supreme Court. They are appointed by the president of the United States and confirmed by the Senate.

253

The Native American Experience

Native Americans are Indigenous

to North and South America—they are the people who were here before Columbus and other European explorers came to these lands. They live in nations, tribes, and bands across both continents. For decades following the arrival of Europeans in 1492, Native Americans clashed with the newcomers who had ruptured the Indigenous people's ways of living.

Tribal Land

During the 19th century, both United States legislation and military action restricted the movement of Native Americans, forcing them to live on reservations and attempting to dismantle tribal structures. For centuries, Native Americans were displaced or killed, or became assimilated into the general U.S. population. In 1924, the Indian Citizenship Act granted citizenship to all Native Americans. Unfortunately, this was not enough to end the social discrimination and mistreatment that many Indigenous people have faced. Today, Native Americans living in the United States still face many challenges.

Healing the Past

Many members of the 560-plus recognized tribes in the United States live primarily on reservations. Some tribes have more than one reservation, while others have none. Together these reservations make up less than 3 percent of the nation's land area. The tribal governments on reservations have the right to form their own governments and to enforce laws, similar to individual states. Many feel that this sovereignty is still not enough to right the wrongs of the past: They hope for a change in the U.S. government's relationship with Native Americans.

An annual powwow in New Mexico features more than 3,000 dancers from more than 500 North American tribes.

Navajo is the most commonly spoken Native American language in the United States.

Top: A Navajo teenager holds her pet lamb.

Middle: A Monacan girl dances in a traditional jingle dress.

Bottom: Navajo siblings on their horses

The president of the United States is the chief of the executive branch, the commander in chief of the U.S. armed forces, and head of the federal government. Elected every four years, the president is the highest policy-maker in the nation. The 22nd Amendment (1951) says that no person may be elected to the office of president more than twice. There have been 46 presidencies and 45 presidents.

GEORGE WASHINGTON
1st President of the United States ★ 1789–1797
BORN Feb. 22, 1732, in Pope's Creek, Westmoreland County, VA
POLITICAL PARTY Federalist
NO. OF TERMS two
VICE PRESIDENT John Adams
DIED Dec. 14, 1799, at Mount Vernon, VA

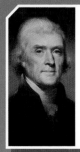

Every U.S. president has a favorite food. **GEORGE WASHINGTON'S WAS ICE CREAM.**

JOHN ADAMS
2nd President of the United States ★ 1797–1801
BORN Oct. 30, 1735, in Braintree (now Quincy), MA
POLITICAL PARTY Federalist
NO. OF TERMS one
VICE PRESIDENT Thomas Jefferson
DIED July 4, 1826, in Quincy, MA

THOMAS JEFFERSON
3rd President of the United States ★ 1801–1809
BORN April 13, 1743, at Shadwell, Goochland (now Albemarle) County, VA
POLITICAL PARTY Democratic-Republican
NO. OF TERMS two
VICE PRESIDENTS 1st term: Aaron Burr
2nd term: George Clinton
DIED July 4, 1826, at Monticello, Charlottesville, VA

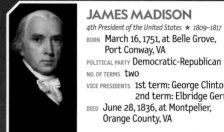

JAMES MADISON
4th President of the United States ★ 1809–1817
BORN March 16, 1751, at Belle Grove, Port Conway, VA
POLITICAL PARTY Democratic-Republican
NO. OF TERMS two
VICE PRESIDENTS 1st term: George Clinton
2nd term: Elbridge Gerry
DIED June 28, 1836, at Montpelier, Orange County, VA

JAMES MONROE
5th President of the United States ★ 1817–1825
BORN April 28, 1758, in Westmoreland County, VA
POLITICAL PARTY Democratic-Republican
NO. OF TERMS two
VICE PRESIDENT Daniel D. Tompkins
DIED July 4, 1831, in New York, NY

JOHN QUINCY ADAMS
6th President of the United States ★ 1825–1829
BORN July 11, 1767, in Braintree (now Quincy), MA
POLITICAL PARTY Democratic-Republican
NO. OF TERMS one
VICE PRESIDENT John Caldwell Calhoun
DIED Feb. 23, 1848, at the U.S. Capitol, Washington, D.C.

ANDREW JACKSON
7th President of the United States ★ 1829–1837
BORN March 15, 1767, in the Waxhaw region, NC and SC
POLITICAL PARTY Democrat
NO. OF TERMS two
VICE PRESIDENTS 1st term: John Caldwell Calhoun
2nd term: Martin Van Buren
DIED June 8, 1845, in Nashville, TN

MARTIN VAN BUREN
8th President of the United States ★ 1837–1841
BORN Dec. 5, 1782, in Kinderhook, NY
POLITICAL PARTY Democrat
NO. OF TERMS one
VICE PRESIDENT Richard M. Johnson
DIED July 24, 1862, in Kinderhook, NY

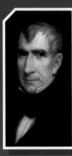

WILLIAM HENRY HARRISON
9th President of the United States ★ *1841*

BORN Feb. 9, 1773, in Charles City County, VA

POLITICAL PARTY Whig

NO. OF TERMS one (died while in office)

VICE PRESIDENT John Tyler

DIED April 4, 1841, in the White House, Washington, D.C.

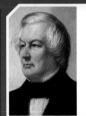

MILLARD FILLMORE
13th President of the United States ★ *1850–1853*

BORN Jan. 7, 1800, in Cayuga County, NY

POLITICAL PARTY Whig

NO. OF TERMS one (partial)

VICE PRESIDENT none

DIED March 8, 1874, in Buffalo, NY

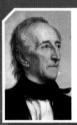

JOHN TYLER
10th President of the United States ★ *1841–1845*

BORN March 29, 1790, in Charles City County, VA

POLITICAL PARTY Whig

NO. OF TERMS one (partial)

VICE PRESIDENT none

DIED Jan. 18, 1862, in Richmond, VA

FRANKLIN PIERCE
14th President of the United States ★ *1853–1857*

BORN Nov. 23, 1804, in Hillsborough (now Hillsboro), NH

POLITICAL PARTY Democrat

NO. OF TERMS one

VICE PRESIDENT William Rufus De Vane King

DIED Oct. 8, 1869, in Concord, NH

JOHN TYLER HAD 15 KIDS— THE MOST OF ANY PRESIDENT!

JAMES BUCHANAN
15th President of the United States ★ *1857–1861*

BORN April 23, 1791, in Cove Gap, PA

POLITICAL PARTY Democrat

NO. OF TERMS one

VICE PRESIDENT John Cabell Breckinridge

DIED June 1, 1868, in Lancaster, PA

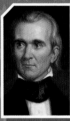

JAMES K. POLK
11th President of the United States ★ *1845–1849*

BORN Nov. 2, 1795, near Pineville, Mecklenburg County, NC

POLITICAL PARTY Democrat

NO. OF TERMS one

VICE PRESIDENT George Mifflin Dallas

DIED June 15, 1849, in Nashville, TN

ABRAHAM LINCOLN
16th President of the United States ★ *1861–1865*

BORN Feb. 12, 1809, near Hodgenville, KY

POLITICAL PARTY Republican (formerly Whig)

NO. OF TERMS two (assassinated)

VICE PRESIDENTS 1st term: Hannibal Hamlin
2nd term: Andrew Johnson

DIED April 15, 1865, in Washington, D.C.

ZACHARY TAYLOR
12th President of the United States ★ *1849–1850*

BORN Nov. 24, 1784, in Orange County, VA

POLITICAL PARTY Whig

NO. OF TERMS one (died while in office)

VICE PRESIDENT Millard Fillmore

DIED July 9, 1850, in the White House, Washington, D.C.

ANDREW JOHNSON
17th President of the United States ★ *1865–1869*

BORN Dec. 29, 1808, in Raleigh, NC

POLITICAL PARTY Democrat

NO. OF TERMS one (partial)

VICE PRESIDENT none

DIED July 31, 1875, in Carter's Station, TN

ULYSSES S. GRANT

18th President of the United States ★ *1869–1877*

BORN April 27, 1822,
in Point Pleasant, OH

POLITICAL PARTY Republican

NO. OF TERMS two

VICE PRESIDENTS 1st term: Schuyler Colfax
2nd term: Henry Wilson

DIED July 23, 1885, in Mount
McGregor, NY

RUTHERFORD B. HAYES

19th President of the United States ★ *1877–1881*

BORN Oct. 4, 1822,
in Delaware, OH

POLITICAL PARTY Republican

NO. OF TERMS one

VICE PRESIDENT William Almon Wheeler

DIED Jan. 17, 1893, in Fremont, OH

JAMES A. GARFIELD

20th President of the United States ★ *1881*

BORN Nov. 19, 1831, near
Orange, OH

POLITICAL PARTY Republican

NO. OF TERMS one (assassinated)

VICE PRESIDENT Chester A. Arthur

DIED Sept. 19, 1881, in Elberon, NJ

CHESTER A. ARTHUR

21st President of the United States ★ *1881–1885*

BORN Oct. 5, 1829, in Fairfield, VT

POLITICAL PARTY Republican

NO. OF TERMS one (partial)

VICE PRESIDENT none

DIED Nov. 18, 1886, in New York, NY

GROVER CLEVELAND

22nd and 24th President of the United States
1885–1889 ★ *1893–1897*

BORN March 18, 1837, in Caldwell, NJ

POLITICAL PARTY Democrat

NO. OF TERMS two (nonconsecutive)

VICE PRESIDENTS 1st administration:
Thomas Andrews Hendricks
2nd administration:
Adlai Ewing Stevenson

DIED June 24, 1908, in Princeton, NJ

BENJAMIN HARRISON

23rd President of the United States ★ *1889–1893*

BORN Aug. 20, 1833, in North Bend, OH

POLITICAL PARTY Republican

NO. OF TERMS one

VICE PRESIDENT Levi Parsons Morton

DIED March 13, 1901, in Indianapolis, IN

WILLIAM MCKINLEY

25th President of the United States ★ *1897–1901*

BORN Jan. 29, 1843, in Niles, OH

POLITICAL PARTY Republican

NO. OF TERMS two (assassinated)

VICE PRESIDENTS 1st term:
Garret Augustus Hobart
2nd term:
Theodore Roosevelt

DIED Sept. 14, 1901, in Buffalo, NY

THEODORE ROOSEVELT

26th President of the United States ★ *1901–1909*

BORN Oct. 27, 1858, in New York, NY

POLITICAL PARTY Republican

NO. OF TERMS one, plus balance of
McKinley's term

VICE PRESIDENTS 1st term: none
2nd term: Charles
Warren Fairbanks

DIED Jan. 6, 1919, in Oyster Bay, NY

WILLIAM HOWARD TAFT

27th President of the United States ★ *1909–1913*

BORN Sept. 15, 1857, in Cincinnati, OH

POLITICAL PARTY Republican

NO. OF TERMS one

VICE PRESIDENT James Schoolcraft
Sherman

DIED March 8, 1930, in Washington, D.C.

WOODROW WILSON

28th President of the United States ★ *1913–1921*

BORN Dec. 29, 1856, in Staunton, VA

POLITICAL PARTY Democrat

NO. OF TERMS two

VICE PRESIDENT Thomas Riley Marshall

DIED Feb. 3, 1924, in Washington, D.C.

WARREN G. HARDING

29th President of the United States ★ 1921–1923

BORN Nov. 2, 1865, in Caledonia
(now Blooming Grove), OH
POLITICAL PARTY Republican
NO. OF TERMS one (died while in office)
VICE PRESIDENT Calvin Coolidge
DIED Aug. 2, 1923, in San Francisco, CA

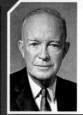

DWIGHT D. EISENHOWER

34th President of the United States ★ 1953–1961

BORN Oct. 14, 1890, in Denison, TX
POLITICAL PARTY Republican
NO. OF TERMS two
VICE PRESIDENT Richard Nixon
DIED March 28, 1969,
in Washington, D.C.

CALVIN COOLIDGE

30th President of the United States ★ 1923–1929

BORN July 4, 1872, in Plymouth, VT
POLITICAL PARTY Republican
NO. OF TERMS one, plus balance of
Harding's term
VICE PRESIDENTS 1st term: none
2nd term:
Charles Gates Dawes
DIED Jan. 5, 1933, in Northampton, MA

JOHN F. KENNEDY

35th President of the United States ★ 1961–1963

BORN May 29, 1917, in Brookline, MA
POLITICAL PARTY Democrat
NO. OF TERMS one (assassinated)
VICE PRESIDENT Lyndon B. Johnson
DIED Nov. 22, 1963, in Dallas, TX

HERBERT HOOVER

31st President of the United States ★ 1929–1933

BORN Aug. 10, 1874,
in West Branch, IA
POLITICAL PARTY Republican
NO. OF TERMS one
VICE PRESIDENT Charles Curtis
DIED Oct. 20, 1964, in New York, NY

DURING STRESSFUL MEETINGS, JOHN F. KENNEDY LIKED TO DOODLE. HIS SPECIALTY? SHAPES AND SAILBOATS.

FRANKLIN D. ROOSEVELT

32nd President of the United States ★ 1933–1945

BORN Jan. 30, 1882, in Hyde Park, NY
POLITICAL PARTY Democrat
NO. OF TERMS four (died while in office)
VICE PRESIDENTS 1st & 2nd terms: John
Nance Garner; 3rd term:
Henry Agard Wallace;
4th term: Harry S. Truman
DIED April 12, 1945,
in Warm Springs, GA

LYNDON B. JOHNSON

36th President of the United States ★ 1963–1969

BORN Aug. 27, 1908, near Stonewall, TX
POLITICAL PARTY Democrat
NO. OF TERMS one, plus balance of
Kennedy's term
VICE PRESIDENTS 1st term: none
2nd term: Hubert
Horatio Humphrey
DIED Jan. 22, 1973, near San Antonio, TX

HARRY S. TRUMAN

33rd President of the United States ★ 1945–1953

BORN May 8, 1884, in Lamar, MO
POLITICAL PARTY Democrat
NO. OF TERMS one, plus balance of
Franklin D. Roosevelt's term
VICE PRESIDENTS 1st term: none
2nd term:
Alben William Barkley
DIED Dec. 26, 1972, in Independence, MO

RICHARD NIXON

37th President of the United States ★ 1969–1974

BORN Jan. 9, 1913, in Yorba Linda, CA
POLITICAL PARTY Republican
NO. OF TERMS two (resigned)
VICE PRESIDENTS 1st term & 2nd term
(partial): Spiro Theodore
Agnew; 2nd term
(balance): Gerald R. Ford
DIED April 22, 1994, in New York, NY

GERALD R. FORD

38th President of the United States ★ 1974–1977

BORN July 14, 1913, in Omaha, NE

POLITICAL PARTY Republican

NO. OF TERMS one (partial)

VICE PRESIDENT Nelson Aldrich Rockefeller

DIED Dec. 26, 2006, in Rancho Mirage, CA

JIMMY CARTER

39th President of the United States ★ 1977–1981

BORN Oct. 1, 1924, in Plains, GA

POLITICAL PARTY Democrat

NO. OF TERMS one

VICE PRESIDENT Walter Frederick (Fritz) Mondale

RONALD REAGAN

40th President of the United States ★ 1981–1989

BORN Feb. 6, 1911, in Tampico, IL

POLITICAL PARTY Republican

NO. OF TERMS two

VICE PRESIDENT George H. W. Bush

DIED June 5, 2004, in Los Angeles, CA

GEORGE H. W. BUSH

41st President of the United States ★ 1989–1993

BORN June 12, 1924, in Milton, MA

POLITICAL PARTY Republican

NO. OF TERMS one

VICE PRESIDENT James Danforth (Dan) Quayle III

DIED Nov. 30, 2018, in Houston, TX

BILL CLINTON

42nd President of the United States ★ 1993–2001

BORN Aug. 19, 1946, in Hope, AR

POLITICAL PARTY Democrat

NO. OF TERMS two

VICE PRESIDENT Albert Arnold Gore, Jr.

GEORGE W. BUSH

43rd President of the United States ★ 2001–2009

BORN July 6, 1946, in New Haven, CT

POLITICAL PARTY Republican

NO. OF TERMS two

VICE PRESIDENT Richard Bruce Cheney

BARACK OBAMA

44th President of the United States ★ 2009–2017

BORN Aug. 4, 1961, in Honolulu, HI

POLITICAL PARTY Democrat

NO. OF TERMS two

VICE PRESIDENT Joe Biden

DONALD TRUMP

45th President of the United States ★ 2017–2021

BORN June 14, 1946, in Queens, NY

POLITICAL PARTY Republican

NO. OF TERMS one

VICE PRESIDENT Mike Pence

JOE BIDEN

46th President of the United States ★ 2021–

BORN November 20, 1942, in Scranton, PA

POLITICAL PARTY Democrat

VICE PRESIDENT Kamala Harris

Check out this book!

OUR COUNTRY'S PRESIDENTS

AS A LAWYER IN DELAWARE, JOE BIDEN ONCE DEFENDED A FISHERMAN WHO STOLE A PRIZE-WINNING COW.

AMAZING ANIMALS

PRESIDENTIAL Pets

BO

U.S. presidents might lead the country, but their pets rule the White House.

COMMANDER PLAYS ON THE SOUTH LAWN OF THE WHITE HOUSE.

The President: Joe Biden
Years in office: 2021 to present
The pet: In December 2021, the Bidens welcomed a **German shepherd** puppy to the White House. The new puppy's name is **Commander.**

FIRST LADY GRACE COOLIDGE HOLDS REBECCA AT THE WHITE HOUSE EASTER EGG ROLL IN 1927.

The president: Calvin Coolidge
Years in office: 1923 to 1929
The pet: A raccoon named **Rebecca** was a gift to President Coolidge. She spent hours splashing around in a partly filled bathtub and even walked on a leash.

The president: Abraham Lincoln
Years in office: 1861 to 1865
The pet: A citizen sent the Lincoln family **a turkey** as a gift for their Christmas feast. The president's youngest son, Tad, quickly bonded with the bird—named **Jack**—and convinced his father to let him keep it as a pet. (Earlier that year, in 1863, President Lincoln had proclaimed the first national Thanksgiving holiday.)

PAULINE WAYNE WALKS ON THE LAWN OF WHAT'S NOW THE EISENHOWER EXECUTIVE OFFICE BUILDING NEXT TO THE WHITE HOUSE.

PRESIDENT KENNEDY STANDS WITH HIS KIDS, JOHN JR. (LEFT) AND CAROLINE, AT THE WHITE HOUSE.

The president: William Howard Taft
Years in office: 1909 to 1913
The pet: President Taft kept **a dairy cow** named **Pauline Wayne** that grazed on the White House lawn.

The president: John F. Kennedy
Years in office: 1961 to 1963
The pet: President Kennedy's daughter, Caroline, had **a pony** called **Macaroni** that she rode around the White House gardens.

BO (LEFT) AND SUNNY SIT AT A TABLE IN THE STATE DINING ROOM OF THE WHITE HOUSE.

PRESIDENT JOHNSON PLAYS WITH YUKI.

The president: Barack Obama
Years in office: 2009 to 2017
The pets: President Obama promised his daughters, Sasha and Malia, that they could adopt a dog after the 2008 election. Eventually the family adopted not one but **two Portuguese water dogs, Bo** and **Sunny**. The pups had a few official duties, such as cheering up patients at hospitals and greeting visiting world leaders. But that didn't stop them from occasionally being naughty: Bo once chewed on the commander in chief's gym shoes.

The president:
Lyndon B. Johnson
Years in office: 1963 to 1969
The pet: President Johnson enjoyed having howling duets in the Oval Office with **Yuki the mutt,** one of his six dogs.

CIVIL RIGHTS

Although the Constitution protects the civil rights of American citizens, it has not always been able to protect all Americans from persecution or discrimination. During the first half of the 20th century, many Americans, particularly Black Americans, were subjected to widespread discrimination and racism. By the mid-1950s, many people were eager to end the barriers caused by racism and bring freedom to all men and women.

The civil rights movement of the 1950s and 1960s sought to end racial discrimination against Black people, especially in the southern states. The movement wanted to give the fundamentals of economic and social equality to those who had been oppressed.

Woolworth Counter Sit-in

On February 1, 1960, four Black college students walked into a Woolworth's "five-and-dime" store in Greensboro, North Carolina. They planned to have lunch there, but were refused service as soon as they sat down at the counter. In a time of heightened racial tension, the Woolworth's manager had a strict whites-only policy. But the students wouldn't take no for an answer. The men—later dubbed the "Greensboro Four"—stayed seated, peacefully and quietly, at the lunch counter until closing. The next day, they returned with 15 additional college students. The following day, even more. By February 5, some 300 students gathered at Woolworth's, forming one of the most famous sit-ins of the civil rights movement. The protest—which sparked similar sit-ins throughout the country—worked: Just six months later, restaurants across the South began to integrate.

Key Events in the Civil Rights Movement

1954	The Supreme Court case *Brown v. Board of Education* declares school segregation illegal.
1955	Rosa Parks refuses to give up her bus seat to a white passenger and spurs a bus boycott.
1957	The Little Rock Nine help to integrate schools.
1960	Four Black college students begin sit-ins at a restaurant in Greensboro, North Carolina.
1961	Freedom Rides to southern states begin as a way to protest segregation in transportation.
1963	Martin Luther King, Jr., leads the famous March on Washington.
1964	The Civil Rights Act, signed by President Lyndon B. Johnson, prohibits discrimination based on race, color, religion, sex, and national origin.
1967	Thurgood Marshall becomes the first Black American to be named to the Supreme Court.
1968	President Lyndon B. Johnson signs the Civil Rights Act of 1968, which prohibits discrimination in the sale, rental, and financing of housing.

STONE OF HOPE:
THE LEGACY OF MARTIN LUTHER KING, JR.

On April 4, 1968, Dr. Martin Luther King, Jr., was shot by James Earl Ray while standing on a hotel balcony in Memphis, Tennessee, U.S.A. The news of his death sent shock waves throughout the world: Dr. King, a Baptist minister and founder of the Southern Christian Leadership Conference, was the most prominent civil rights leader of his time. His nonviolent protests and marches against segregation, as well as his powerful speeches—including his famous "I Have a Dream" speech—motivated people to fight for justice for all.

More than 50 years after his death, Dr. King's dream lives on through a memorial on the National Mall in Washington, D.C. Built in 2011, the memorial features a 30-foot (9-m) statue of Dr. King carved into a granite boulder named the "Stone of Hope."

Today, Dr. King continues to inspire people around the world with his words and his vision for a peaceful world without racism. He will forever be remembered as one of the most prominent leaders of the civil rights movement.

"The time is always right to do what is right."

Martin Luther King, Jr., Memorial in Washington, D.C.

JOHN LEWIS: GETTING IN GOOD TROUBLE

John Lewis joins hands with President Barack Obama as they lead a commemorative march across the Edmund Pettus Bridge in Selma, Alabama, in 2015.

On March 7, 1965, a 25-year-old man linked arms with five other people, including Dr. Martin Luther King, Jr., as they led hundreds in a march across the Edmund Pettus Bridge in Selma, Alabama, U.S.A. It was a simple act, but it carried a very loud message: Those marching along the bridge were marching for racial justice and equality during a time when Black people were treated unjustly by many and were denied the same basic rights as white people, including the right to vote.

That young man was John Lewis. And, after crossing the bridge, Lewis was attacked by state troopers and beaten badly. The scene was so shocking that it made national news and created a public outcry. An act that prevented Black people from being denied the right to vote was passed just five months later. From then on, Lewis, who survived the attack, became a legend in the civil rights movement for his quiet yet powerful ability to create change. He called it getting in "good trouble": Standing up for what you believe is right and just, even if it means ruffling feathers along the way.

Lewis went on to serve in the U.S. House of Representatives for 33 years until his death in 2020. Before he passed, he was able to speak about the Black Lives Matter movement, once again encouraging people to fight for justice. "We must use our time and our space on this little planet that we call Earth to make a lasting contribution, to leave it a little better than we found it," said Lewis. "And now that need is greater than ever before."

263

WOMEN
FIGHTING FOR EQUALITY

Women in New York City cast their votes for the first time in November 1920.

Today, women make up about half of the workforce in the United States. But a little over a century ago, less than 20 percent worked outside the home. In fact, they didn't even have the right to vote!

That began to change in the mid-1800s when women, led by pioneers like Elizabeth Cady Stanton and Susan B. Anthony, started speaking up about inequality. They organized public demonstrations, gave speeches, published documents, and wrote newspaper articles to express their ideas. In 1848, about 300 people attended the Seneca Falls Convention in New York State to address the need for equal rights. By the late 1800s, the National American Woman Suffrage Association had made great strides toward giving women the freedom to vote. One by one, states began allowing women to vote. By 1920, the U.S. Constitution was amended, giving women across the country the ability to cast a vote during any election.

But the fight for equality did not end there. In the 1960s and 1970s, the women's rights movement experienced a rebirth, as feminists protested against injustices in areas such as the workplace and in education.

While these efforts enabled women to make great strides in our society, the efforts to even the playing field among men and women continue today.

New Zealand gave women the right to vote in 1893, becoming the world's first country to do so.

In 2020, Katie Sowers became the first female football coach in Super Bowl history.

KAMALA HARRIS IS SWORN IN AS VICE PRESIDENT ON JANUARY 20, 2021.

Key Events in U.S. Women's History

1848: **Elizabeth Cady Stanton** and **Lucretia Mott** organize the Seneca Falls Convention in New York. Attendees rally for equitable laws, equal educational and job opportunities, and the right to vote.

1920: **The 19th Amendment,** guaranteeing women the right to vote, is ratified.

1964: **Title VII of the Civil Rights Act of 1964,** which prohibits employment discrimination on the basis of sex, is successfully amended.

1971: **Gloria Steinem** heads up the National Women's Political Caucus, which encourages women to be active in government. She also launches *Ms.,* a magazine about women's issues.

1972: Congress approves **the Equal Rights Amendment** (ERA), proposing that women and men have equal rights under the law. It is ratified by 35 of the necessary 38 states, and is still not part of the U.S. Constitution.

1981: President Ronald Reagan appoints **Sandra Day O'Connor** as the first female Supreme Court justice.

2009: President Obama signs **the Lilly Ledbetter Fair Pay Act** to protect against pay discrimination among men and women.

2013: The **ban against women in military combat positions** is removed, overturning a 1994 Pentagon decision restricting women from combat roles.

2016: Democratic presidential nominee **Hillary Rodham Clinton** becomes the first woman to lead the ticket of a major U.S. party.

2021: **Kamala Harris** is sworn in as vice president of the United States, becoming the first woman to hold that office.

Ava DuVernay
Lived: 1972–

WHY SHE'S MEMORABLE: A history-making director, writer, and producer, DuVernay is the first Black woman to win Best Director at the Sundance Film Festival, be nominated as Best Director at the Golden Globes, and to direct a film nominated for Best Picture at the Academy Awards. Getting her start as a director at the age of 32 after a career in marketing and publicity, DuVernay went on to become an innovator behind the camera—and the highest-grossing Black female director in American box office history. Through her films, which include *Selma* and *A Wrinkle in Time,* DuVernay is known for telling powerful stories that focus on the lives and times of Black Americans.

Patsy Takemoto Mink
Lived: 1927–2002

WHY SHE'S MEMORABLE: Not only was Mink the first woman of color in Congress, but she played an important role in the passing of Title IX, which guaranteed equal opportunity in education for all students regardless of their gender. An Asian-American, Mink was born in Hawaii and faced both gender and racial discrimination herself as a student, even being rejected from medical school, likely because she was a woman. This sparked her desire to advocate for equal rights for future generations, and she worked tirelessly to earn the nickname of "The Mother of Title IX." Mink is also known for becoming the first Asian-American woman to run for president, which she did unsuccessfully in 1972.

265

QUIZ WHIZ

Go back in time to seek the answers to this history quiz!

Write your answers on a piece of paper. Then check them below.

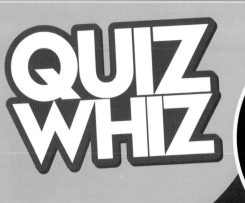

1 **True or false?** Kleenex tissues were first used as liners in gas masks during World War I.

2 At the ruins of Pompeii, layers of ash have helped to preserve what kinds of artifacts?
a. artwork
b. loaves of bread
c. kitchen pots
d. all of the above

3 **The Taj Mahal was originally built for which purpose?**
a. a place of worship
b. an event space for grand parties
c. a shopping mall
d. an elaborate tomb for a queen

4 **True or false?** Japanese Samurai armor was made of metal and leather to deflect blades and arrows.

5 **What was the name of Blackbeard's famous pirate ship?**
a. *The Caribbean Conqueror*
b. *Queen Anne's Revenge*
c. *Blackbeard's Boat*
d. *The Treasure Hunter*

Not **STUMPED** yet? Check out the *NATIONAL GEOGRAPHIC KIDS QUIZ WHIZ* collection for more crazy **HISTORY** questions!

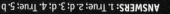
ANSWERS: 1. True; 2. d; 3. d; 4. True; 5. b

HOMEWORK HELP

Brilliant Biographies

Malala Yousafzai

A biography is the story of a person's life. It can be a brief summary or a long book. Biographers—those who write biographies—use many different sources to learn about their subjects. You can write your own biography of a famous person you find inspiring.

How to Get Started

Choose a subject you find interesting. If you think Cleopatra is cool, you have a good chance of getting your readers interested, too. If you're bored by ancient Egypt, your readers will be snoring after your first paragraph.

Your subject can be almost anyone: an author, an inventor, a celebrity, a politician, or a member of your family. To find someone to write about, ask yourself these simple questions:

1. Who do I want to know more about?
2. What did this person do that was special?
3. How did this person change the world?

Do Your Research

- Find out as much about your subject as possible. Read books, news articles, and encyclopedia entries. Watch video clips and movies. Conduct interviews, if possible.
- Take notes, writing down important facts and interesting stories about your subject.

Write the Biography

- Come up with a title. Include the person's name.
- Write an introduction. Consider asking a probing question about your subject.
- Include information about the person's childhood. When was this person born? Where did he or she grow up? Who did he or she admire?
- Highlight the person's talents, accomplishments, and personal attributes.
- Describe the specific events that helped to shape this person's life. Did this person ever have a problem and overcome it?
- Write a conclusion. Include your thoughts about why it is important to learn about this person.
- Once you have finished your first draft, revise and then proofread your work.

Here's a SAMPLE BIOGRAPHY of Malala Yousafzai, a human rights advocate and the youngest ever recipient of the Nobel Peace Prize. Of course, there is so much more for you to discover and write about on your own!

Malala Yousafzai

Malala Yousafzai was born in Pakistan on July 12, 1997. Malala's father, Ziauddin, a teacher, made it a priority for his daughter to receive a proper education. Malala loved school. She learned to speak three languages and even wrote a blog about her experiences as a student.

Around the time Malala turned 10, the Taliban—a group of strict Muslims who believe women should stay at home— took over the region where she lived. The Taliban did not approve of Malala's outspoken love of learning. One day, on her way home from school, Malala was shot in the head by a Taliban gunman. Very badly injured, she was sent to a hospital in England.

Not only did Malala survive the shooting—she thrived. She used her experience as a platform to fight for girls' education worldwide. She began speaking out about educational opportunities for all. Her efforts gained worldwide attention, and she was eventually awarded the Nobel Peace Prize in 2014 at the age of 17. She is the youngest person to earn the prestigious prize.

Each year on July 12, World Malala Day honors her heroic efforts to bring attention to human rights issues.

267

GEOGRAPHY
ROCKS

Acid ponds and hot springs create an alien-looking landscape in the Danakil Depression in Ethiopia—one of the hottest and driest places on Earth.

THE POLITICAL WORLD

Earth's land area is made up of seven continents, but people have divided much of the land into smaller political units called countries. Australia is a continent made up of a single country, and Antarctica is used for scientific research. But the other five continents include almost 200 independent countries. The political map shown here depicts boundaries—imaginary lines created by treaties—that separate countries. Some boundaries, such as the one between the United States and Canada, are very stable and have been recognized for many years.

ARCTIC

Queen Elizabeth Is.

Chukchi Sea
Beaufort Sea
Greenland (Kalaallit Nunaat) (Denmark)
Greenland Sea

RUSSIA

Alaska (U.S.)

Baffin Bay

ARCTIC CIRCLE
ICELAND

Bering Sea

Gulf of Alaska

Great Bear Lake
Great Slave Lake

Hudson Bay

Labrador Sea

UNITED KINGDOM

CANADA

Lake Winnipeg
Great Lakes

IRELAND (ÉIRE)

FRANCE

Great Salt Lake

UNITED STATES

PORT. SPAIN

See Europe map for more detail.

MOROCCO

TROPIC OF CANCER

Hawai'i (U.S.)

Gulf of Mexico

WESTERN SAHARA (Morocco)

MEXICO

THE BAHAMAS
CUBA
DOMINICAN REP.
Puerto Rico (U.S.)

CABO VERDE
MAURITANIA
MALI

BELIZE
JAMAICA
HAITI
ST. KITTS & NEVIS
ANTIGUA & BARBUDA
Guadeloupe (France)
DOMINICA

BURKINA FASO

GUATEMALA
HONDURAS
EL SALVADOR
NICARAGUA
Caribbean Sea
ST. LUCIA
Martinique (France)
BARBADOS

THE GAMBIA
SENEGAL

COSTA RICA
GRENADA
ST. VINCENT & THE GRENADINES
TRINIDAD AND TOBAGO

GUINEA-BISSAU

PANAMA
VENEZUELA
GUYANA

GUINEA
SIERRA LEONE
LIBERIA

EQUATOR
150°
120°
90°
30°
0°

COLOMBIA
French Guiana (France)

KIRIBATI

PACIFIC

Galápagos Islands (Ecuador)
ECUADOR

SURINAME

CÔTE D'IVOIRE (IVORY COAST)

OCEAN

Marquesas Islands (France)

PERU

BRAZIL

EQ. GUINEA

SAO TOME AND PRINCIPE

SAMOA
American Samoa (U.S.)

French Polynesia (France)

BOLIVIA

ATLANTIC

TONGA

PARAGUAY

TROPIC OF CAPRICORN

OCEAN

30°

CHILE

URUGUAY

ARGENTINA

0   miles   2000
0   kilometers   3000

Winkel Tripel Projection

Falkland Islands (Islas Malvinas) (U.K.)

Meridian of Greenwich (London)

Chatham Is. (N.Z.)

Tierra del Fuego

Strait of Magellan

Drake Passage

SOUTHERN

ANTARCTIC

60°

Weddell Sea

Ross Sea

A N T

Other boundaries, such as the one between Sudan and South Sudan in northeast Africa, are relatively new and still disputed. Countries come in all shapes and sizes. Russia and Canada are giants; others, such as El Salvador and Qatar, are small. Some countries are long and skinny—look at Chile in South America! Still other countries—such as Indonesia and Japan in Asia—are made up of groups of islands. The political map is a clue to the diversity that makes Earth so fascinating.

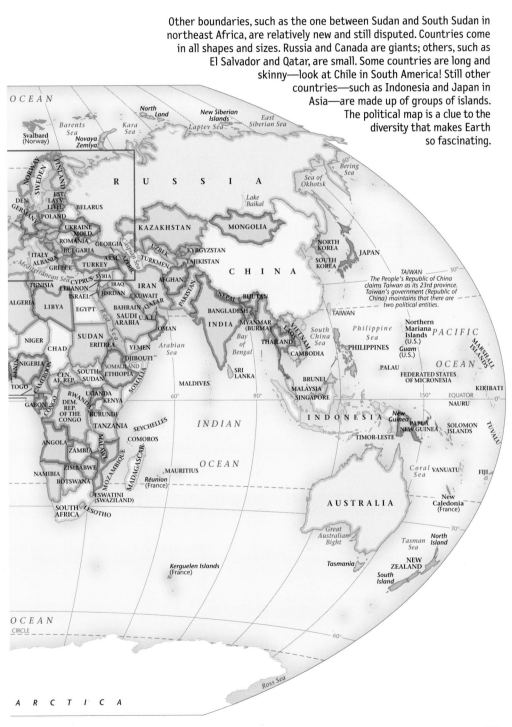

OCEAN

Barents Sea
Kara Sea
North Land
New Siberian Islands
Laptev Sea
East Siberian Sea
Svalbard (Norway)
Novaya Zemlya

NORWAY
SWEDEN
FINLAND
DEN.
GERMANY
EST.
LATV.
LITH.
BELARUS
POLAND
UKRAINE
MOLD.
ROMANIA
BULGARIA
GEORGIA
ITALY
ALBANIA
GREECE
TURKEY
ARM.
AZERB.
CYPRUS
SYRIA
TUNISIA
LEBANON
IRAQ
ISRAEL
JORDAN
ALGERIA
LIBYA
EGYPT

R U S S I A

Sea of Okhotsk
Bering Sea
Lake Baikal

KAZAKHSTAN
MONGOLIA
UZBEK.
KYRGYZSTAN
TURKMEN.
TAJIKISTAN
AFGHAN.
IRAN
BAHRAIN
QATAR
SAUDI ARABIA
U.A.E.
OMAN
PAKISTAN

C H I N A

NORTH KOREA
SOUTH KOREA
JAPAN

TAIWAN
The People's Republic of China claims Taiwan as its 23rd province. Taiwan's government (Republic of China) maintains that there are two political entities.

TAIWAN

NIGER
CHAD
SUDAN
ERITREA
YEMEN
NIGERIA
CEN. AF. REP.
SOUTH SUDAN
ETHIOPIA
SOMALILAND
DJIBOUTI
SOMALIA
TOGO
CAMEROON
GABON
CONGO
DEM. REP. OF THE CONGO
RWANDA
BURUNDI
UGANDA
KENYA
TANZANIA
SEYCHELLES
COMOROS
ANGOLA
ZAMBIA
MALAWI
ZIMBABWE
MOZAMBIQUE
MADAGASCAR
NAMIBIA
BOTSWANA
RÉUNION (France)
MAURITIUS
ESWATINI (SWAZILAND)
SOUTH AFRICA
LESOTHO

Red Sea
Arabian Sea
NEPAL
BHUTAN
BANGLADESH
INDIA
MYANMAR (BURMA)
Bay of Bengal
THAILAND
LAOS
VIETNAM
CAMBODIA
South China Sea
Philippine Sea
Northern Mariana Islands (U.S.)
PACIFIC
MARSHALL ISLANDS
PHILIPPINES
Guam (U.S.)
PALAU
FEDERATED STATES OF MICRONESIA
OCEAN
KIRIBATI

SRI LANKA
MALDIVES
BRUNEI
MALAYSIA
SINGAPORE
EQUATOR
NAURU

INDIAN
OCEAN

INDONESIA
New Guinea
PAPUA NEW GUINEA
SOLOMON ISLANDS
TUVALU
TIMOR-LESTE

Coral Sea
VANUATU
FIJI

AUSTRALIA
New Caledonia (France)

Kerguelen Islands (France)

Great Australian Bight
Tasman Sea
North Island
Tasmania
South Island
NEW ZEALAND

OCEAN
CIRCLE

Ross Sea

A R C T I C A

THE PHYSICAL WORLD

Earth is dominated by large landmasses called continents—seven in all—and by an interconnected global ocean that is divided into five parts by the continents. More than 70 percent of Earth's surface is covered by oceans, and the rest is made up of land areas.

Different landforms give variety to the surface of the continents. The Rocky Mountains divide North America, the Andes mark the western edge of South America, and the Himalaya tower above South Asia. The Plateau of Tibet forms the rugged core of Asia,

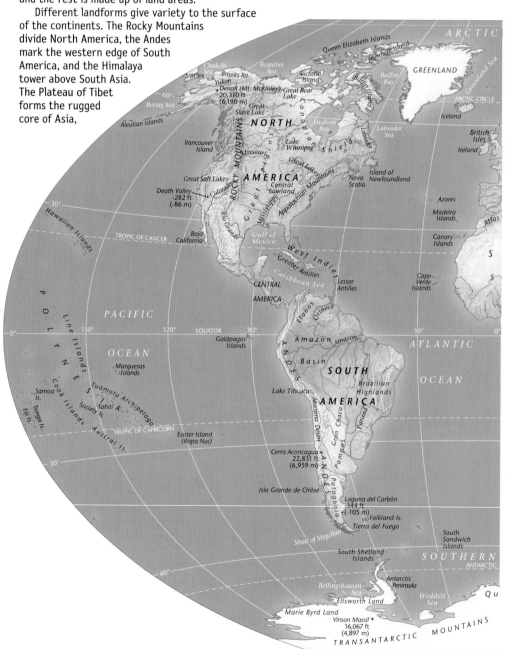

272

while the Northern European Plain extends from the North Sea to the Ural Mountains. Much of Africa is a plateau, and dry plains cover large areas of Australia. Mountains rise more than 16,000 feet (4,877 m) above Antarctica's massive ice sheets. Mountains and trenches make the ocean floors as varied as any continent. A mountain chain called the Mid-Atlantic Ridge runs the length of the Atlantic Ocean. In the western Pacific, trenches drop deep into the ocean floor.

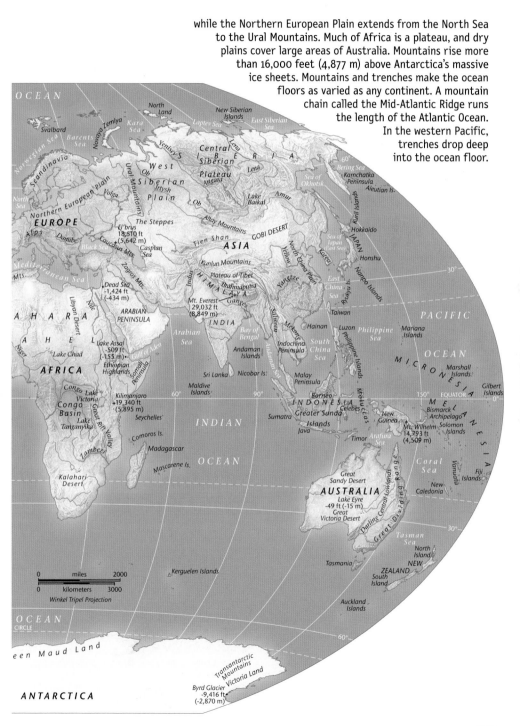

KINDS OF MAPS

Maps are special tools that geographers use to tell a story about Earth. Maps can be used to show just about anything related to places. Some maps show physical features, such as mountains or vegetation. Maps can also show climates or natural hazards and other things we cannot easily see. Other maps illustrate different features on Earth—political boundaries, urban centers, and economic systems.

AN IMPERFECT TOOL

Maps are not perfect. A globe is a scale model of Earth with accurate relative sizes and locations. Because maps are flat, they involve distortions of size, shape, and direction. Also, cartographers—people who create maps—make choices about what information to include. Because of this, it is important to study many different types of maps to learn the complete story of Earth. Three commonly found kinds of maps are shown on this page.

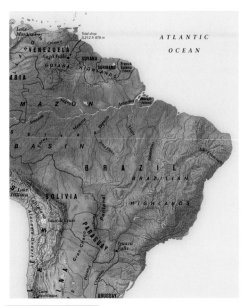

PHYSICAL MAPS. Earth's natural features—landforms, water bodies, and vegetation—are shown on physical maps. The map above uses color and shading to illustrate mountains, lakes, rivers, and deserts of central South America. Country names and borders are added for reference, but they are not natural features.

POLITICAL MAPS. These maps represent characteristics of the landscape created by humans, such as boundaries, cities, and place-names. Natural features are added only for reference. On the map above, capital cities are represented with a star inside a circle, while other cities are shown with black dots.

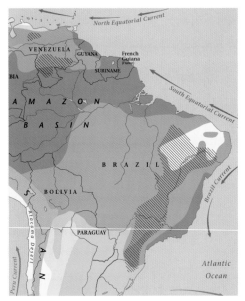

THEMATIC MAPS. Patterns related to a particular topic or theme, such as population distribution, appear on these maps. The map above displays the region's climate zones, which range from tropical wet (bright green) to tropical wet and dry (light green) to semiarid (dark yellow) to arid or desert (light yellow).

MAKING MAPS

Meet a Cartographer!

As a National Geographic cartographer, **Mike McNey** works with maps every day. Here, he shares more about his cool career.

National Geographic staff cartographers Mike McNey and Rosemary Wardley review a map of Africa for the *National Geographic Kids World Atlas.*

What exactly does a cartographer do?

I create maps specifically for books and atlases to help the text tell the story on the page. The maps need to fit into the size and the style of the book, with the final goal being that it's accurate and appealing for the reader.

What kinds of stories have you told with your maps?

Once, I created a map that showed the spread of the Burmese python population in Florida around the Everglades National Park. I've also made maps that show data like farmland, food production, cattle density, and fish catch in a particular location, like the United States.

How do you rely on technology in your job?

All aspects of mapmaking are on the computer. This makes it much quicker to make a map. It also makes it easier to change anything on the map. If you want to change the color of the rivers on the map, you just have to hit one button on the mouse.

How do you create your maps?

I work with geographic information systems (GIS), a computer software that allows us to represent any data on a specific location of the world, or even the entire world. Data can be anything from endangered species, animal ranges, and population of a particular place. We also use remote systems, like satellites and aerial imagery, to analyze Earth's surface.

Satellites in orbit around Earth act as eyes in the sky, recording data about the planet's land and ocean areas. The data are converted to numbers transmitted back to computers that are specially programmed to interpret the data. They record the information in a form that cartographers can use to create maps.

What will maps of the future look like?

In the future, you'll see more and more data on maps. I also think more online maps are going to be made in a way that you can switch from a world view to a local view to see data at any scale.

What's the best part of your job?

I love the combination of science and design involved in it. It's also fun to make maps interesting for kids.

275

UNDERSTANDING
MAPS

MAKING A PROJECTION

Globes present a model of Earth as it is—a sphere— but they are bulky and can be difficult to use and store. Flat maps are much more convenient, but certain problems can result from transferring Earth's curved surface to a flat piece of paper, a process called projection. Imagine a globe that has been cut in half, like the one to the right. If a light is shined into it, the lines of latitude and longitude and the shapes of the continent will cast shadows that can be "projected" onto a piece of paper, as shown here. Depending on how the paper is positioned, the shadows will be distorted in different ways.

KNOW THE CODE

Every map has a story to tell, but first you have to know how to read one. Maps represent information by using a language of symbols. When you know how to read these symbols, you can access a wide range of information. Look at the scale and compass rose or arrow to understand distance and direction (see box below).

To find out what each symbol on a map means, you must use the key. It's your secret decoder— identifying information by each symbol on the map.

There are three main types of map symbols: points, lines, and areas. Points, which can be either dots or small icons, represent the location or the number of things, such as schools, cities, or landmarks. Lines are used to show boundaries, roads, or rivers and can vary in color or thickness. Area symbols use pattern or color to show regions, such as a sandy area or a neighborhood.

SCALE AND DIRECTION

The scale on a map can be shown as a fraction, as words, or as a line or bar. It relates distance on the map to distance in the real world. Sometimes the scale identifies the type of map projection. Maps may include an arrow to indicate north on the map or a compass rose to show all principal directions.

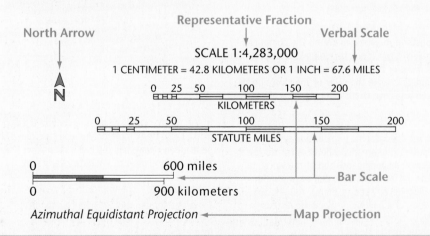

North Arrow

Representative Fraction

Verbal Scale

SCALE 1:4,283,000

1 CENTIMETER = 42.8 KILOMETERS OR 1 INCH = 67.6 MILES

0 25 50 100 150 200
KILOMETERS

0 25 50 100 150 200
STATUTE MILES

0   600 miles
0   900 kilometers

Bar Scale

Azimuthal Equidistant Projection ← Map Projection

GEOGRAPHIC FEATURES

From roaring rivers to parched deserts, from underwater canyons to jagged mountains, Earth is covered with beautiful and diverse environments. Here are examples of the most common types of geographic features found around the world.

WATERFALL

Waterfalls form when a river reaches an abrupt change in elevation. At left, the Iguazú waterfall system—on the border of Brazil and Argentina—is made up of 275 falls.

VALLEY

Valleys, cut by running water or moving ice, may be broad and flat or narrow and steep, such as the Indus River Valley (above)in Ladakh, India.

RIVER

As a river moves through flatlands, it twists and turns. Above, the Rio Los Amigos winds through a rainforest in Peru.

MOUNTAIN

Mountains are Earth's tallest landforms, and Mount Everest (above) rises highest of all, at 29,031.69 feet (8,848.86 m) above sea level.

GLACIER

Glaciers—"rivers" of ice—such as Hubbard Glacier (above) in Alaska, U.S.A., move slowly from mountains to the sea. Global warming is shrinking them.

CANYON

Steep-sided valleys called canyons are created mainly by running water. Buckskin Gulch (above) in Utah, U.S.A., is the deepest "slot" canyon in the American Southwest.

DESERT

Deserts are land features created by climate, specifically by a lack of water. Here, a camel caravan crosses the Sahara in North Africa.

MOUNT EVEREST,
THE WORLD'S TALLEST MOUNTAIN,
NOW MEASURES
2.8 FEET (.86 M)
HIGHER
THAN NEPALI OFFICIALS PREVIOUSLY CALCULATED.

Experts used high-tech **GPS SATELLITES** and **LASER-EQUIPPED TOOLS** to get an **ACCURATE MEASUREMENT** of Mount Everest.

What's up with the mega mountain's growth spurt? It happened when Nepal and China, which both share the mountain, agreed to measure the snowcap on top, a point under debate until recently. Their new official measurement is 29,031.69 feet (8,848.86 m).

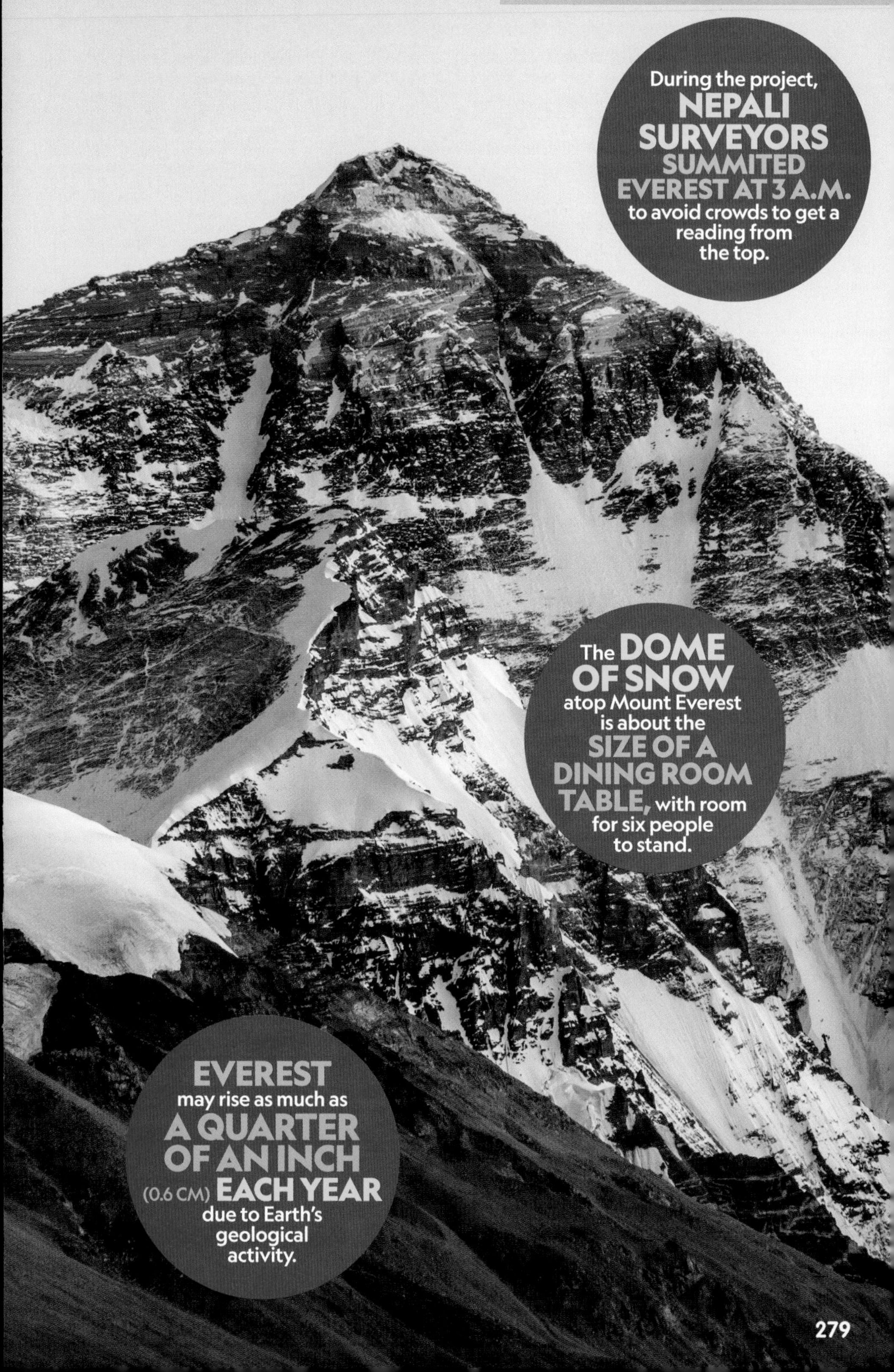

During the project, **NEPALI SURVEYORS SUMMITED EVEREST AT 3 A.M.** to avoid crowds to get a reading from the top.

The **DOME OF SNOW** atop Mount Everest is about the **SIZE OF A DINING ROOM TABLE,** with room for six people to stand.

EVEREST may rise as much as **A QUARTER OF AN INCH** (0.6 CM) **EACH YEAR** due to Earth's geological activity.

279

AFRICA

In 1979, 2016, 2018, and 2021, snow fell on parts of the Sahara.

Leopards are able to hear five times as many sounds as humans can hear.

A leopard in South Africa

The massive continent of Africa, where humankind began millions of years ago, is second only to Asia in size. Stretching nearly as far from west to east as it does from north to south, Africa is home to both the longest river in the world (the Nile) and the largest hot desert on Earth (the Sahara).

Luanda, Angola

NANO-CHAMELEON

Talk about a little lizard! What may be the world's smallest chameleon was recently discovered in the mountains of Madagascar. Male nano-chameleons are less than an inch long (25 mm), tiny enough to fit on the fingertip of an adult human.

COOL CANYON

Local legend says that Namibia's Fish River Canyon—the largest canyon in Africa—was carved by a giant serpent when it burrowed deep into the ground while hiding from hunters.

Great Pyramid, Great Numbers
How do the numbers for Earth's biggest pyramid stack up?

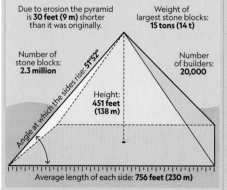

Due to erosion the pyramid is **30 feet (9 m)** shorter than it was originally.

Weight of largest stone blocks: **15 tons (14 t)**

Number of stone blocks: **2.3 million**

Number of builders: **20,000**

Angle at which the sides rise: **51°52'**

Height: **451 feet (138 m)**

Average length of each side: **756 feet (230 m)**

MASSIVE DESERT

When it comes to deserts, the Sahara surely stands out! The massive stretch of sand is the largest hot desert in the world, reaching an area of 3.475 million square miles (9 million sq km)—slightly smaller than the area of the United States.

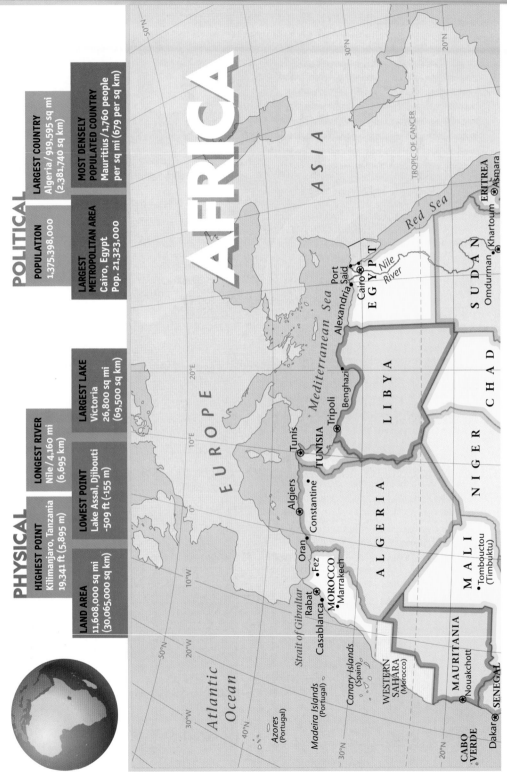

AFRICA

PHYSICAL

HIGHEST POINT	LOWEST POINT	LONGEST RIVER	LARGEST LAKE
Kilimanjaro, Tanzania 19,341 ft (5,895 m)	Lake Assal, Djibouti -509 ft (-155 m)	Nile / 4,160 mi (6,695 km)	Victoria 26,800 sq mi (69,500 sq km)

LAND AREA
11,608,000 sq mi (30,065,000 sq km)

POLITICAL

POPULATION	LARGEST COUNTRY
1,375,398,000	Algeria / 919,595 sq mi (2,381,740 sq km)

LARGEST METROPOLITAN AREA	MOST DENSELY POPULATED COUNTRY
Cairo, Egypt Pop. 21,323,000	Mauritius / 1,760 people per sq mi (679 per sq km)

Atlantic Ocean

EUROPE

ASIA

Mediterranean Sea

Red Sea

Strait of Gibraltar

Azores (Portugal)

Madeira Islands (Portugal)

Canary Islands (Spain)

Rabat
Casablanca
Marrakech
MOROCCO
Fez
Oran
Constantine
Algiers
Tunis
TUNISIA
Tripoli
Benghazi

ALGERIA

LIBYA

EGYPT
Alexandria
Cairo
Port Said

Nile River

SUDAN
Omdurman Khartoum
Asmara
ERITREA

WESTERN SAHARA (Morocco)

MAURITANIA
Nouakchott

MALI
Tombouctou (Timbuktu)

NIGER

CHAD

SENEGAL
Dakar

CABO VERDE

TROPIC OF CANCER

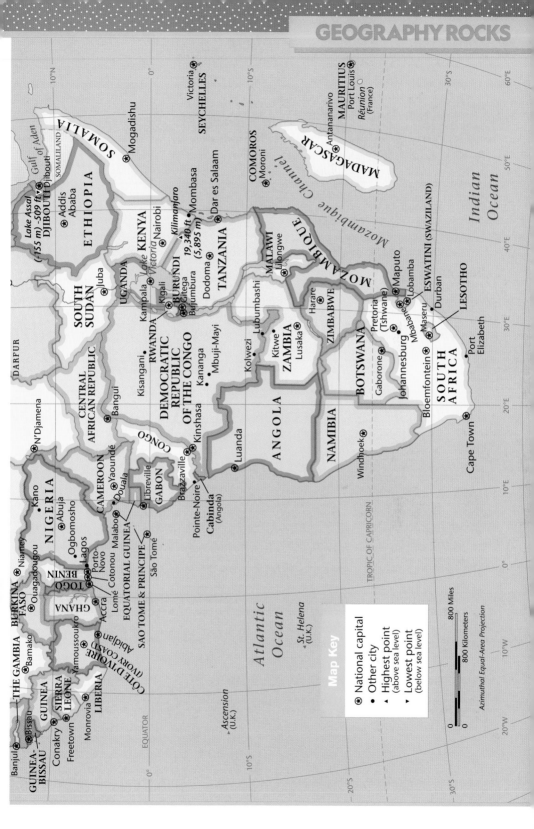

Map Key

⊛ National capital
• Other city
▲ Highest point (above sea level)
▼ Lowest point (below sea level)

0   800 Miles
0   800 Kilometers

Azimuthal Equal-Area Projection

283

ANTARCTICA

Chinstrap penguin

No dogs are allowed in Antarctica.

Some penguins can spend up to 75 percent of their lives in the water.

This frozen continent may be a cool place to visit, but unless you're a penguin, you probably wouldn't want to hang out in Antarctica for long. The fact that it's the coldest, windiest, and driest continent helps explain why humans never colonized this ice-covered land surrounding the South Pole.

Weddell seal

GOING THE DISTANCE

Each year, a few dozen runners from around the world compete in the Antarctic Ice Marathon, during which participants face an average temperature with windchill of minus 4°F (-20°C).

WARMER THAN EVER

With Antarctica experiencing record-breaking high temperatures, the continent as a whole is getting warmer. Temperatures reached a record high of nearly 70°F (21°C) in February 2020, making the area one of the fastest warming regions on Earth.

50 — 50
40 — 40
30 — 30
20 — 20
10 — 10
0 — 0
10 — 10
20 — 20
30 — 30
40 — 40
50 — 50

Annual Average Snowfall

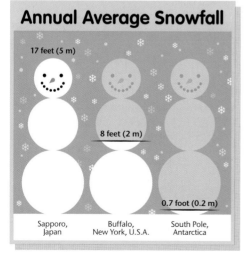

17 feet (5 m)

8 feet (2 m)

0.7 foot (0.2 m)

Sapporo, Japan

Buffalo, New York, U.S.A.

South Pole, Antarctica

SEEING GREEN

Green snow? Yes, it's in Antarctica! Swaths of the colorful snow can be seen spreading across the continent. Scientists say that the snow gets its odd hue from a type of algae that, because of climate change, is now growing faster than ever.

285

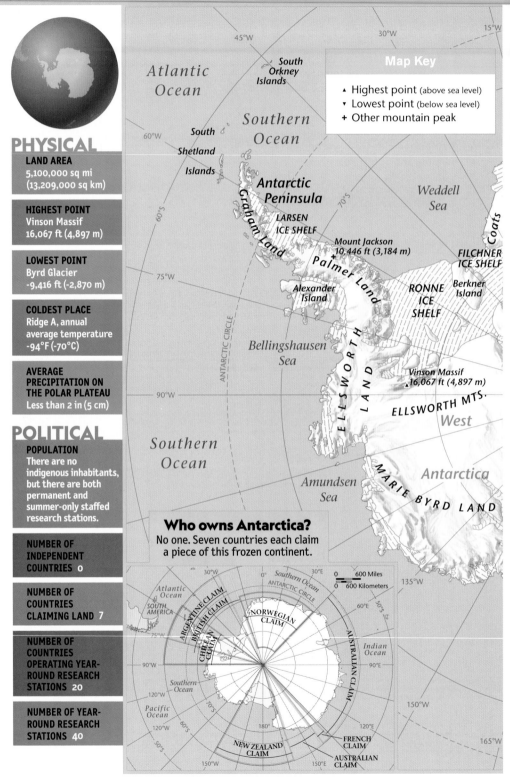

PHYSICAL

LAND AREA
5,100,000 sq mi
(13,209,000 sq km)

HIGHEST POINT
Vinson Massif
16,067 ft (4,897 m)

LOWEST POINT
Byrd Glacier
-9,416 ft (-2,870 m)

COLDEST PLACE
Ridge A, annual
average temperature
-94°F (-70°C)

**AVERAGE
PRECIPITATION ON
THE POLAR PLATEAU**
Less than 2 in (5 cm)

POLITICAL

POPULATION
There are no
indigenous inhabitants,
but there are both
permanent and
summer-only staffed
research stations.

**NUMBER OF
INDEPENDENT
COUNTRIES** 0

**NUMBER OF
COUNTRIES
CLAIMING LAND** 7

**NUMBER OF
COUNTRIES
OPERATING YEAR-
ROUND RESEARCH
STATIONS** 20

**NUMBER OF YEAR-
ROUND RESEARCH
STATIONS** 40

Map Key

▲ Highest point (above sea level)
▼ Lowest point (below sea level)
+ Other mountain peak

Atlantic
Ocean

South
Orkney
Islands

Southern
Ocean

South
Shetland
Islands

Weddell
Sea

**Antarctic
Peninsula**

Graham Land

LARSEN
ICE SHELF

Mount Jackson
10,446 ft (3,184 m)

FILCHNER
ICE SHELF

Palmer Land

Coats

Alexander
Island

RONNE
ICE
SHELF

Berkner
Island

Bellingshausen
Sea

Vinson Massif
▲16,067 ft (4,897 m)

ELLSWORTH MTS.

ELLSWORTH LAND

West

Southern
Ocean

Amundsen
Sea

Antarctica

MARIE BYRD LAND

ANTARCTIC CIRCLE

Who owns Antarctica?
No one. Seven countries each claim
a piece of this frozen continent.

Atlantic
Ocean

SOUTH
AMERICA

ARGENTINE CLAIM

BRITISH CLAIM

CHILEAN CLAIM

NORWEGIAN
CLAIM

Southern Ocean
ANTARCTIC CIRCLE

0   600 Miles
0   600 Kilometers

Indian
Ocean

AUSTRALIAN CLAIM

Southern
Ocean

Pacific
Ocean

NEW ZEALAND
CLAIM

FRENCH
CLAIM

AUSTRALIAN
CLAIM

ANTARCTICA

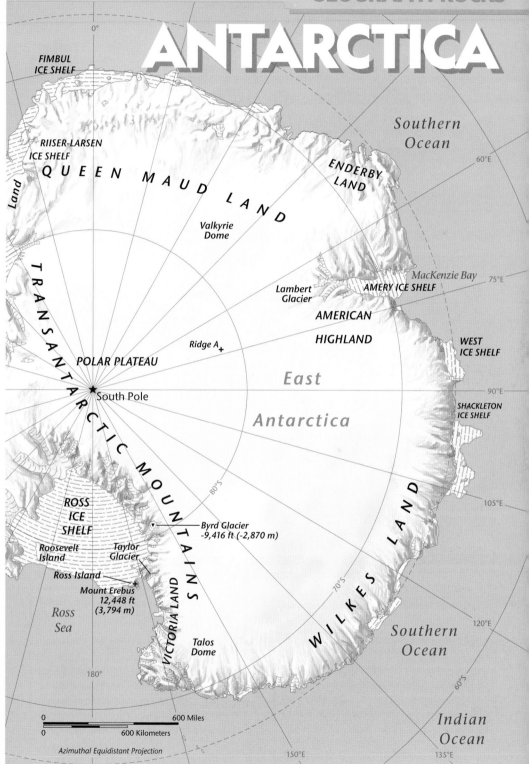

FIMBUL
ICE SHELF

RIISER-LARSEN
ICE SHELF

QUEEN MAUD LAND

Land

Valkyrie
Dome

ENDERBY
LAND

Southern
Ocean

60°E

MacKenzie Bay

AMERY ICE SHELF

75°E

Lambert
Glacier

AMERICAN

HIGHLAND

WEST
ICE SHELF

Ridge A

POLAR PLATEAU

TRANSANTARCTIC MOUNTAINS

South Pole

East

Antarctica

90°E

SHACKLETON
ICE SHELF

105°E

80°S

ROSS
ICE
SHELF

Byrd Glacier
-9,416 ft (-2,870 m)

Roosevelt
Island

Taylor
Glacier

Ross Island

Mount Erebus
12,448 ft
(3,794 m)

VICTORIA LAND

Ross
Sea

WILKES LAND

70°S

Southern
Ocean

120°E

Talos
Dome

180°

60°S

0   600 Miles
0   600 Kilometers

135°E

150°E

Indian
Ocean

Azimuthal Equidistant Projection

0°

ASIA

A whirling dervish performs in Istanbul, Turkey.

You can cross from Asia to Europe on an underwater railway in Turkey.

In Japan you can buy octopus-flavored ice cream.

Made up of 46 countries, Asia is the world's largest continent. Just how big is it? From western Turkey to the eastern tip of Russia, Asia spans nearly half the globe! Home to more than four billion citizens—that's three out of five people on the planet—Asia's population is bigger than that of all the other continents combined.

Women bicycling in Jakarta, Indonesia

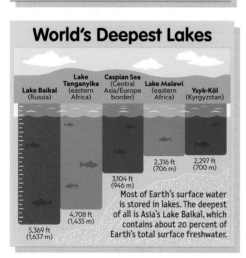

CITY SCENTS

The name Hong Kong translates to "fragrant harbor" in Cantonese, the main language of the bustling city. Researchers think the name comes from Hong Kong's past as a trading post for oil and incense.

TREES, PLEASE

Plans are underway for one million trees to be planted throughout Singapore by 2030. The hope? To improve air quality and add more parks, so that everyone in the city will one day be within a 10-minute walk to a green space.

SAVING THE SNOW LEOPARDS

Countries with political tensions in Central and South Asia have found something to agree upon. "Peace parks"—protected stretches of the snow leopard's native habitat—will soon appear in border areas shared by countries that have a history of disputes.

World's Deepest Lakes

Lake Baikal (Russia)	Lake Tanganyika (eastern Africa)	Caspian Sea (Central Asia/Europe border)	Lake Malawi (eastern Africa)	Ysyk-Köl (Kyrgyzstan)
			2,316 ft (706 m)	2,297 ft (700 m)
		3,104 ft (946 m)		
	4,708 ft (1,435 m)			
5,369 ft (1,637 m)				

Most of Earth's surface water is stored in lakes. The deepest of all is Asia's Lake Baikal, which contains about 20 percent of Earth's total surface freshwater.

PHYSICAL

LAND AREA
17,208,000 sq mi
(44,570,000 sq km)

HIGHEST POINT
Mount Everest,
China–Nepal
29,032 ft (8,849 m)

LOWEST POINT
Dead Sea,
Israel–Jordan
-1,424 ft (-434 m)

LONGEST RIVER
Yangtze, China
3,880 mi (6,244 km)

**LARGEST LAKE
ENTIRELY IN ASIA**
Lake Baikal, Russia
12,200 sq mi
(31,500 sq km)

POLITICAL

POPULATION
4,582,970,000

**LARGEST
METROPOLITAN AREA**
Tokyo, Japan
Pop. 37,340,000

**LARGEST COUNTRY
ENTIRELY IN ASIA**
China
3,705,405 sq mi
(9,596,960 sq km)

**MOST DENSELY
POPULATED COUNTRY**
Singapore
21,101 people
per sq mi
(8,159 per sq km)

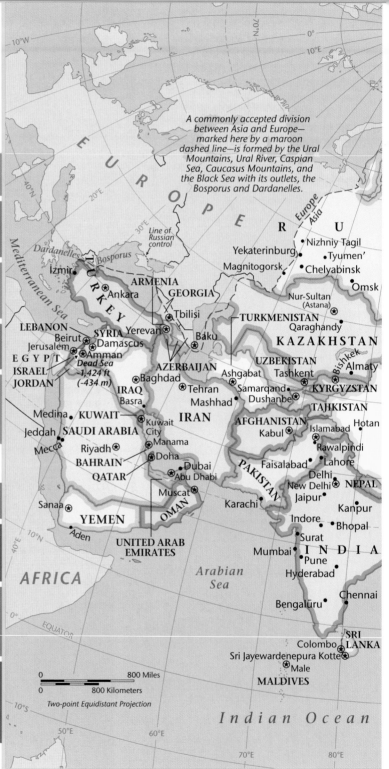

A commonly accepted division between Asia and Europe—marked here by a maroon dashed line—is formed by the Ural Mountains, Ural River, Caspian Sea, Caucasus Mountains, and the Black Sea with its outlets, the Bosporus and Dardanelles.

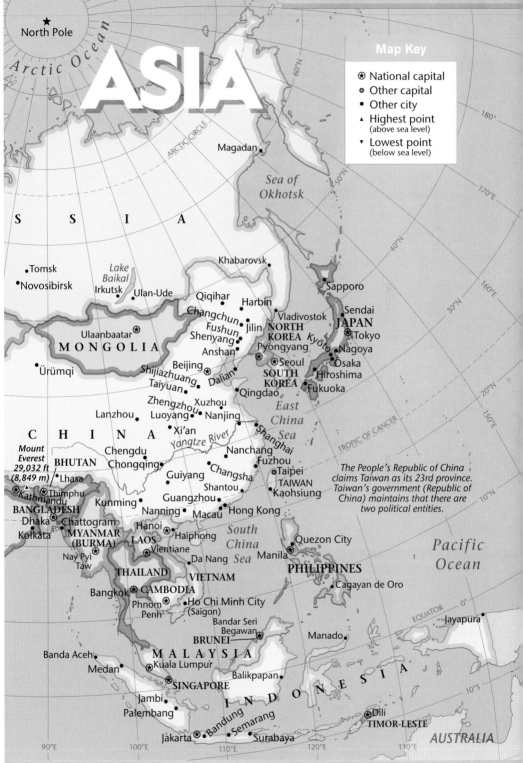

North Pole

Arctic Ocean

ASIA

Map Key
⊛ National capital
⊚ Other capital
• Other city
▲ Highest point
(above sea level)
▼ Lowest point
(below sea level)

ARCTIC CIRCLE

Magadan

Sea of
Okhotsk

R S S I A

Tomsk
Novosibirsk
Lake Baikal
Irkutsk Ulan-Ude

Khabarovsk

Sapporo

Qiqihar Harbin
Changchun Vladivostok Sendai
Fushun Jilin NORTH JAPAN
Ulaanbaatar Shenyang KOREA Kyōto Tokyo
MONGOLIA Anshan Pyongyang Nagoya
Ürümqi Beijing Seoul Osaka
Shijiazhuang Dalian SOUTH Hiroshima
Taiyuan Qingdao KOREA Fukuoka
Zhengzhou Xuzhou East
Lanzhou Luoyang Nanjing China
Xi'an Sea
C H I N A Yangtze River Shanghai
Mount Chengdu Nanchang
Everest BHUTAN Chongqing Fuzhou
29,032 ft Guiyang Changsha Taipei TROPIC OF CANCER
(8,849 m) Lhasa Shantou TAIWAN The People's Republic of China
Kathmandu Kunming Guangzhou Kaohsiung claims Taiwan as its 23rd province.
Thimphu Taiwan's government (Republic of
BANGLADESH Nanning Macau Hong Kong China) maintains that there are
Dhaka Chattogram Hanoi two political entities.
Kolkata MYANMAR Haiphong South
(BURMA) LAOS China Quezon City
Nay Pyi Vientiane Da Nang Sea Manila Pacific
Taw THAILAND VIETNAM PHILIPPINES Ocean
Bangkok CAMBODIA Cagayan de Oro
Phnom Ho Chi Minh City
Penh (Saigon)
Bandar Seri EQUATOR Jayapura
Begawan Manado
BRUNEI
Banda Aceh MALAYSIA
Medan Kuala Lumpur Balikpapan
SINGAPORE I N D O N E S I A
Jambi Dili
Palembang Bandung Semarang TIMOR-LESTE
Jakarta Surabaya AUSTRALIA

AUSTRALIA, NEW ZEALAND, AND OCEANIA

It is considered rude to wear a hat in villages in Fiji.

Koalas eat so much eucalyptus, they often smell like it.

A koala munches on a eucalyptus leaf in Australia.

G'day, mate! This vast region, covering almost 3.3 million square miles (8.5 million sq km), includes Australia—the world's smallest and flattest continent—and New Zealand, as well as a fleet of mostly tiny islands scattered across the Pacific Ocean. Also known as "down under," most of the countries in this region are in the Southern Hemisphere, below the Equator.

Maori children of New Zealand in ceremonial clothing

WANGARRUS BOUNCE BACK

Good news for the wangarru: After a deluge of rain in Australia's outback, the species—also known as the yellow-footed rock wallaby—saw some growth in its dwindling numbers. It's a promising sign for the wild wangarru population, which had been shrinking due to drought.

ROCK ON

Western Australia's Mount Augustus—also called Burringurrah by the local Aboriginal people—is the world's largest rock. Actually made up of several different types of rocks, the reddish brown formation stands out against its barren desert surroundings, rising 2,346 feet (715 m) above the plain and stretching for five miles (8 km).

RAD RUINS

On a tiny island in the middle of the Pacific Ocean, you'll find Nan Madol, the only ancient city ever built atop a coral reef. What's left today—stone walls and columns—are the ruins of a once thriving civilization known as the Saudeleur, a dynasty that ruled the island of Pohnpei.

More Animals Than People

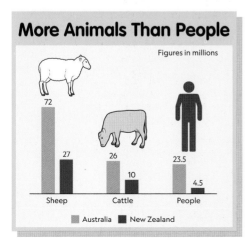

Figures in millions

Sheep: Australia 72, New Zealand 27
Cattle: Australia 26, New Zealand 10
People: Australia 23.5, New Zealand 4.5

Australia   New Zealand

PHYSICAL

LAND AREA
3,297,000 sq mi
(8,538,000 sq km)

HIGHEST POINT*
Mount Wilhelm,
Papua New Guinea
14,793 ft (4,509 m)
*Includes Oceania

LOWEST POINT
Lake Eyre, Australia
-49 ft (-15 m)

LONGEST RIVER
Murray,
Australia
1,558 mi (2,508 km)

LARGEST LAKE
Lake Eyre, Australia
3,741 sq mi
(9,690 sq km)

POLITICAL

POPULATION
41,668,000

**LARGEST
METROPOLITAN AREA**
Melbourne, Australia
Pop. 5,061,000

LARGEST COUNTRY
Australia
2,988,902 sq mi
(7,741,220 sq km)

**MOST DENSELY
POPULATED COUNTRY**
Nauru
1,221 people per sq mi
(465 per sq km)

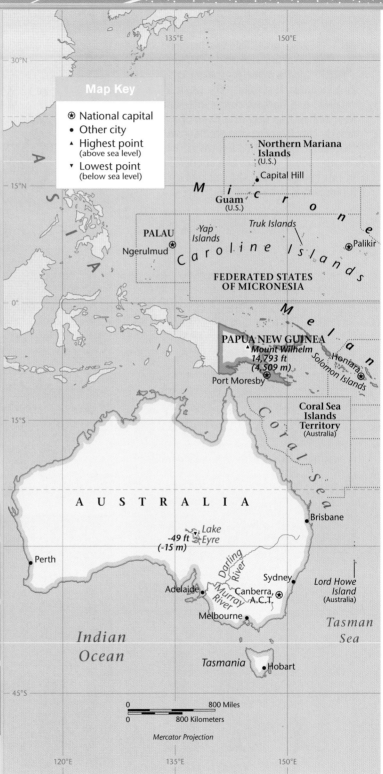

Map Key

⊛ National capital
• Other city
▲ Highest point
(above sea level)
▼ Lowest point
(below sea level)

A S I A

M i c r o n e s i a

Northern Mariana
Islands
(U.S.)
• Capital Hill

Guam
(U.S.)

Yap
Islands

Truk Islands

PALAU
Ngerulmud ⊛

C a r o l i n e   I s l a n d s

⊛ Palikir

FEDERATED STATES
OF MICRONESIA

M e l a n e s i a

PAPUA NEW GUINEA
▲ Mount Wilhelm
14,793 ft
(4,509 m)
Port Moresby ⊛

Honiara
⊛
Solomon Islands

Coral Sea
Islands
Territory
(Australia)

C o r a l   S e a

A U S T R A L I A

Brisbane •

• Perth

-49 ft
(-15 m)
Lake
Eyre ▼

Darling
River

Murray
River

Adelaide •

Canberra, ⊛
A.C.T.

Sydney •

Lord Howe
Island
(Australia)

Melbourne •

Indian
Ocean

Tasmania

Tasman
Sea

• Hobart

0   800 Miles
0   800 Kilometers

Mercator Projection

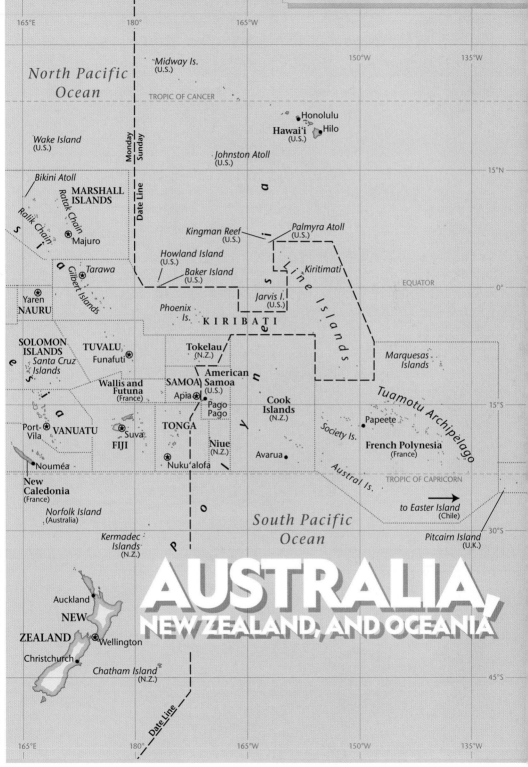

165°E · 180° · 165°W · 150°W · 135°W

North Pacific
Ocean

Midway Is.
(U.S.)

TROPIC OF CANCER

Honolulu
Hawai'i Hilo
(U.S.)

Wake Island
(U.S.)

Monday Sunday

Johnston Atoll
(U.S.)

15°N

Bikini Atoll

**MARSHALL
ISLANDS**

Ratak Chain

Date Line

Ralik Chain

Majuro

Kingman Reef
(U.S.)

Palmyra Atoll
(U.S.)

Howland Island
(U.S.)

Kiritimati

Tarawa

Baker Island
(U.S.)

Gilbert Islands

Line Islands

EQUATOR · 0°

Yaren
NAURU

Jarvis I.
(U.S.)

Phoenix
Is.

K I R I B A T I

**SOLOMON
ISLANDS**

*Santa Cruz
Islands*

TUVALU

Funafuti

Tokelau
(N.Z.)

*Marquesas
Islands*

Phoenix

15°S

**Wallis and
Futuna**
(France)

SAMOA

**American
Samoa**
(U.S.)

Apia

Pago
Pago

**Cook
Islands**
(N.Z.)

Papeete

Society Is.

Tuamotu Archipelago

Port-
Vila **VANUATU**

Suva

TONGA

FIJI

Niue
(N.Z.)

Avarua

French Polynesia
(France)

Nouméa

Nuku'alofa

Austral Is.

TROPIC OF CAPRICORN

**New
Caledonia**
(France)

Norfolk Island
(Australia)

to Easter Island
(Chile)

30°S

*Kermadec
Islands*
(N.Z.)

**South Pacific
Ocean**

Pitcairn Island
(U.K.)

AUSTRALIA,
NEW ZEALAND, AND OCEANIA

Auckland

NEW

ZEALAND Wellington

Christchurch

Chatham Island
(N.Z.)

45°S

Date Line

165°E · 180° · 165°W · 150°W · 135°W

EUROPE

A dachshund parade is held each September in Kraków, Poland.

There are no snakes in Ireland—except for those kept as pets.

Wawel Castle overlooks the Vistula River in Kraków, Poland.

A cluster of peninsulas and islands jutting west from Asia, Europe is bordered by the Atlantic and Arctic Oceans and more than a dozen seas. Here you'll find a variety of scenery, from mountains to countryside to coastlines. Europe is also known for its rich culture and fascinating history, which make it one of the most visited continents on Earth.

Traditional dance performed in Greece

BUG OFF

One place you'll never have to worry about mosquito bites? Iceland! The country is totally mosquito free, likely because of its unique weather patterns that disrupt the life cycle from egg to pesky bug.

COOL COMEBACK

Bring back the bison! The European bison's numbers are increasing across the continent, thanks to recent conservation efforts. At one point, the animals' population was about 50, but now it is up to around 7,000 in the wild and in captivity.

CHOCOLATE, CHOCOLATE EVERYWHERE

Attention chocolate lovers! Switzerland is now home to a museum all about the sweet stuff. The Lindt Home of Chocolate offers a deep dive into the rich history of chocolate and features what may be the world's tallest chocolate fountain at a soaring three stories high.

Europe's Longest Rivers

Volga	2,290 mi (3,685 km)
Danube	1,770 mi (2,848 km)
Dnieper	1,420 mi (2,285 km)
Rhine	765 mi (1,230 km)
Elbe	724 mi (1,165 km)

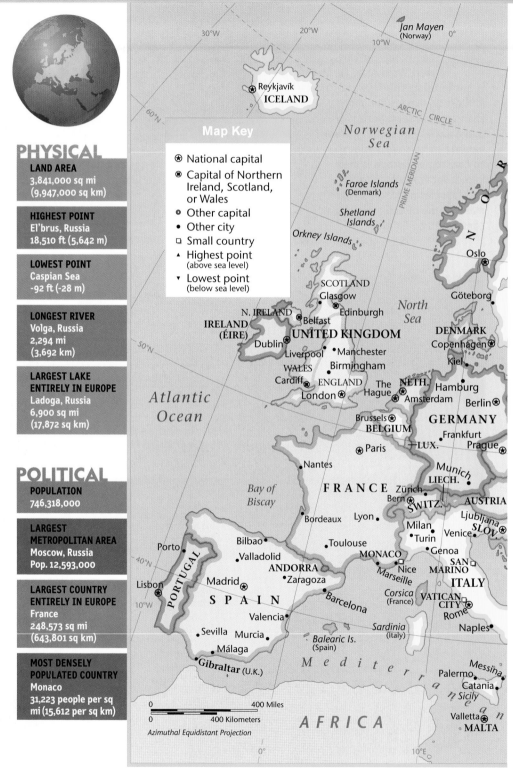

PHYSICAL

LAND AREA
3,841,000 sq mi
(9,947,000 sq km)

HIGHEST POINT
El'brus, Russia
18,510 ft (5,642 m)

LOWEST POINT
Caspian Sea
-92 ft (-28 m)

LONGEST RIVER
Volga, Russia
2,294 mi
(3,692 km)

**LARGEST LAKE
ENTIRELY IN EUROPE**
Ladoga, Russia
6,900 sq mi
(17,872 sq km)

POLITICAL

POPULATION
746,318,000

**LARGEST
METROPOLITAN AREA**
Moscow, Russia
Pop. 12,593,000

**LARGEST COUNTRY
ENTIRELY IN EUROPE**
France
248,573 sq mi
(643,801 sq km)

**MOST DENSELY
POPULATED COUNTRY**
Monaco
31,223 people per sq
mi (15,612 per sq km)

Map Key

⊛ National capital
◉ Capital of Northern Ireland, Scotland, or Wales
◉ Other capital
• Other city
▫ Small country
▲ Highest point (above sea level)
▼ Lowest point (below sea level)

Jan Mayen (Norway)

30°W   20°W   10°W   0°

Reykjavík
ICELAND

ARCTIC CIRCLE

60°N

Norwegian Sea

Faroe Islands (Denmark)

Shetland Islands

Orkney Islands

PRIME MERIDIAN

Oslo ⊛

Göteborg

SCOTLAND
Glasgow
Edinburgh

North Sea

DENMARK
Copenhagen ⊛

N. IRELAND
IRELAND (ÉIRE)
Belfast
Dublin ◉
UNITED KINGDOM
Liverpool • Manchester
WALES Birmingham
Cardiff ◉ **ENGLAND**
London ⊛   The Hague ◉
Kiel •

50°N

Atlantic Ocean

NETH.
Amsterdam ⊛
Hamburg •
Berlin ⊛

Brussels ⊛
BELGIUM
GERMANY
Frankfurt •

⊛ Paris
—LUX.
Prague ◉

• Nantes

Munich •
LIECH.

Bay of Biscay
F R A N C E Zürich •
Bern ◉
SWITZ.
AUSTRIA
Ljubljana ◉
SLOV.

Bordeaux • Lyon •
Milan •
Turin •
Venice •

40°N

Porto •
Bilbao •
Valladolid •
ANDORRA
Zaragoza •
• Toulouse
MONACO
• Nice
Genoa •
SAN MARINO ▫
Marseille

Lisbon •
Madrid ⊛
S P A I N
Barcelona •
Corsica (France)
VATICAN CITY ⊛
ITALY
Rome •
Naples •

10°W
Valencia •
Sevilla •
Murcia •
Málaga •
Sardinia (Italy)
Balearic Is. (Spain)

Gibraltar (U.K.)

M e d i t e r r a n e a n

Palermo •
Messina •
Catania •
Sicily

Valletta ◉
MALTA

0   400 Miles
0   400 Kilometers
Azimuthal Equidistant Projection

A F R I C A

0°   10°E

298

A commonly accepted division between Asia and Europe—marked here by a maroon dashed line—is formed by the Ural Mountains, Ural River, Caspian Sea, Caucasus Mountains, and the Black Sea with its outlets, the Bosporus and Dardanelles.

Asia / Europe

Barents Sea

10°E 20°E 30°E 40°E 50°E 60°E

Murmansk

Arkhangel'sk

R U S S I A

EUROPE

60°N

S W E D E N

N O R W A Y

F I N L A N D

Lake Ladoga

St. Petersburg

Helsinki

Tallinn
⊛ Stockholm
ESTONIA

Baltic Sea

Rīga
LATVIA

LITHUANIA
Vitsyebsk
Vilnius ⊛
Kaunas
Russia
Gdańsk

⊛ Minsk

BELARUS
Homyel'

Volga River Kazan'

•Ufa

Yaroslavl'
Tver'   Nizhniy
⊛ Moscow   Novgorod

Ryazan'

Samara Orenburg

Smolensk

•Penza

Bryansk

Saratov

KAZAKHSTAN

Kursk

POLAND
⊛Warsaw
Bydgoszcz
•Łódź
•Wrocław Kraków

⊛ Kyiv   •Kharkiv
Poltava•
U K R A I N E
L'viv   Donets'k
Vinnytsya   Dnipro

Volgograd

50°N

**CZECHIA
(CZECH REP.)**
Vienna
⊛ **SLOVAKIA**
⊛ Bratislava
⊛ Budapest
HUNGARY
⊛ Zagreb
CROATIA
**BOSNIA &
HERZEGOVINA**
Sarajevo •⊛
MONTENEGRO
Podgorica ⊛
Tirana ⊛

MOLDOVA
⊛Chisinau

Line of
Russian
control

Rostov
na Donu

Astrakhan'

Boundary claimed
by Ukraine

-92 ft ▾
(-28 m)

Caspian Sea

ROMANIA

⊛ Belgrade   Bucharest
SERBIA
KOSOVO
⊛Prishtinë **BULGARIA**
⊛ Skopje   ⊛Sofia
N. MAC.

Odesa
CRIMEA
Simferopol'⊛
Sevastopol'

El'brus
(5,642 m) 18,510 ft

Groznyy

B l a c k   S e a

Sochi

GEORGIA

Baku
⊛

AZERBAIJAN

40°N

ALBANIA   •Thessaloniki

Varna

Bosporus

Istanbul

GREECE

Dardanelles

T U R K E Y

⊛ Athens

S e a

Crete

NORTHERN CYPRUS
Nicosia ⊛
CYPRUS

CRIMEA
Russia invaded Crimea in 2014 and, after secession from Ukraine was approved in a disputed and boycotted referendum held in Crimea, the Russian parliament voted to annex Crimea into the Russian Federation. The United Nations General Assembly subsequently adopted a nonbinding resolution declaring the annexation invalid and affirming Ukraine's territorial jurisdiction. Russia administers and controls the peninsula, while Ukraine continues to maintain that Crimea is its sovereign territory.

20°E   30°E   40°E

299

NORTH AMERICA

Flamingos are the national bird of the Bahamas.

Canada has more doughnut shops per person than any other country.

American flamingos

From the Great Plains of the United States and Canada to the rainforests of Panama, North America stretches 5,500 miles (8,850 km) from north to south. The third largest continent, North America can be divided into five regions: the mountainous west (including parts of Mexico and Central America's western coast), the Great Plains, the Canadian Shield, the varied eastern region (including Central America's lowlands and coastal plains), and the Caribbean.

A Day of the Dead (Día de los Muertos) parade in Mexico City, Mexico

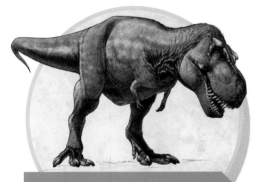

BIG BONES

Canada was once a hotbed of activity for dinosaurs. In fact, the skeleton of the largest *Tyrannosaurus rex* found to date was recently uncovered by researchers at a site in Saskatchewan, Canada. Estimated to weigh more than an elephant, the giant dino—nicknamed "Scotty"—stomped around some 68 million years ago.

BRING BACK THE BEES

Efforts to boost honeybee numbers in the United States appear to be working. A recent study showed an increase in colonies across the country, which is good news for the buzzing pollinators, which have been threatened by climate change, habitat loss, and the use of harmful pesticides.

World's Longest Coastlines

Canada	151,023 miles (243,048 km)
Indonesia	33,998 miles (54,716 km)
Russia	23,397 miles (37,653 km)
Philippines	22,549 miles (36,289 km)
Japan	18,486 miles (29,751 km)

BLOW ON

For the first time in history, wind recently surpassed hydroelectricity as the top source of renewable energy in the United States. Currently, more than 60,000 wind turbines in the country can power at least 32 million homes across more than 40 states.

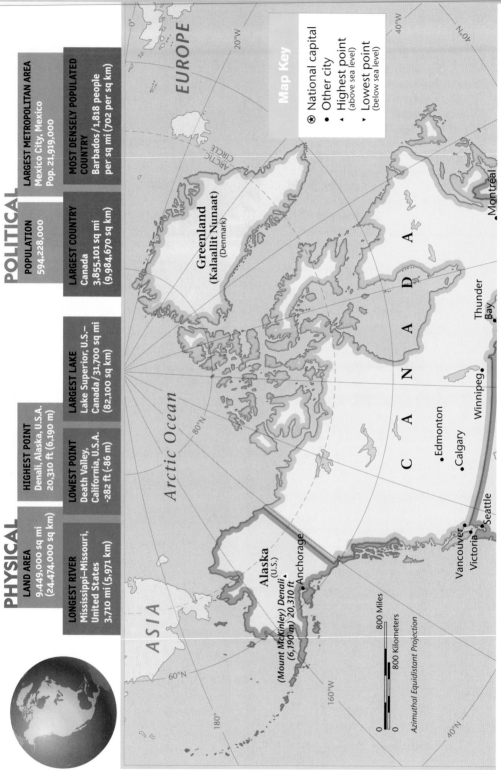

PHYSICAL

LAND AREA
9,449,000 sq mi
(24,474,000 sq km)

LONGEST RIVER
Mississippi–Missouri,
United States
3,710 mi (5,971 km)

HIGHEST POINT
Denali, Alaska, U.S.A.
20,310 ft (6,190 m)

LOWEST POINT
Death Valley,
California, U.S.A.
-282 ft (-86 m)

LARGEST LAKE
Lake Superior, U.S.–
Canada / 31,700 sq mi
(82,100 sq km)

POLITICAL

POPULATION
594,228,000

LARGEST COUNTRY
Canada
3,855,101 sq mi
(9,984,670 sq km)

LARGEST METROPOLITAN AREA
Mexico City, Mexico
Pop. 21,919,000

MOST DENSELY POPULATED COUNTRY
Barbados / 1,818 people
per sq mi (702 per sq km)

Map Key

⊛ National capital
• Other city
▲ Highest point
(above sea level)
▼ Lowest point
(below sea level)

EUROPE

ASIA

Arctic Ocean

Greenland
(Kalaallit Nunaat)
(Denmark)

C A N A D A

Alaska
(U.S.)
(Mount McKinley) Denali ▲
(6,190 m) 20,310 ft
Anchorage

Edmonton
Calgary
Winnipeg
Thunder
Bay
Montréal

Vancouver
Victoria
Seattle

ARCTIC CIRCLE

800 Miles
800 Kilometers

Azimuthal Equidistant Projection

180°
160°W
80°N
60°N
40°N
40°W
20°W
40°N

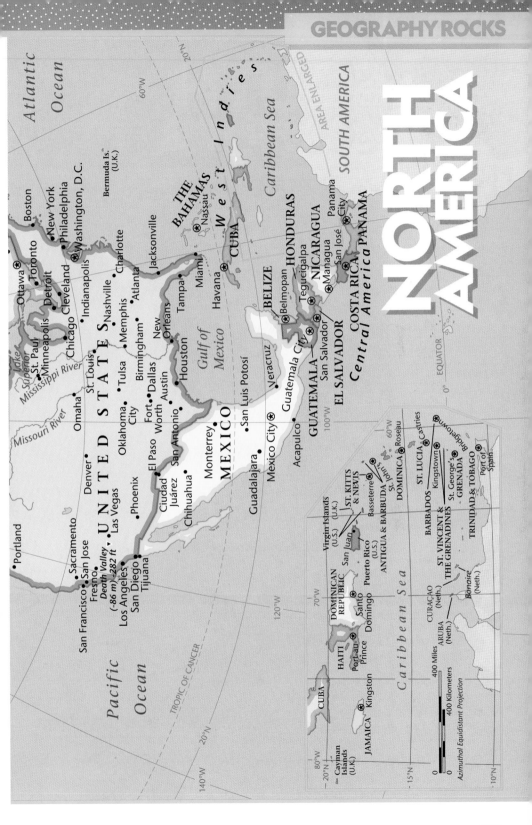

NORTH AMERICA

AREA ENLARGED

SOUTH AMERICA

Atlantic Ocean

Pacific Ocean

Caribbean Sea

UNITED STATES

MEXICO

Gulf of Mexico

Portland
San Francisco
Sacramento
San Jose
Fresno
Las Vegas
Los Angeles
San Diego
Tijuana
Death Valley (-86 m) -282 ft ▼
Phoenix
Denver
Omaha
St. Paul
Minneapolis
St. Louis
Oklahoma City
Tulsa
Fort Worth
Dallas
Austin
San Antonio
El Paso
Ciudad Juárez
Chihuahua
Guadalajara
Monterrey
San Luis Potosí
Mexico City ✪
Acapulco
Veracruz
Houston
New Orleans
Birmingham
Memphis
Nashville
Atlanta
Indianapolis
Chicago
Detroit
Cleveland
Charlotte
Jacksonville
Tampa
Miami
Havana
Washington, D.C. ✪
Philadelphia
New York
Boston
Toronto
Ottawa ✪
Portland

Lake Superior
Mississippi River
Missouri River

Bermuda Is. (U.K.)

THE BAHAMAS
Nassau ✪

W e s t   I n d i e s

CUBA

Caribbean Sea

BELIZE
Belmopan ✪
GUATEMALA
Guatemala City ✪
San Salvador ✪
EL SALVADOR
HONDURAS
Tegucigalpa ✪
NICARAGUA
Managua ✪
San José ✪
COSTA RICA
PANAMA
Panama City ✪

Central America

EQUATOR

20°N
60°W
20°N
20°N
0°
80°W
70°W
60°W
100°W
120°W
140°W
TROPIC OF CANCER
15°N
10°N

(Inset — Caribbean)

CUBA
Kingston
JAMAICA
Cayman Islands (U.K.)
HAITI
Port-au-Prince
DOMINICAN REPUBLIC
Santo Domingo
Virgin Islands (U.S.) (U.K.)
San Juan
Puerto Rico (U.S.)
ST. KITTS & NEVIS
Basseterre
ANTIGUA & BARBUDA
St. John's
DOMINICA
Roseau
ST. LUCIA
Castries
BARBADOS
Bridgetown
ST. VINCENT & THE GRENADINES
Kingstown
GRENADA
St. George's
CURAÇAO (Neth.)
ARUBA (Neth.)
Bonaire (Neth.)
TRINIDAD & TOBAGO
Port of Spain

Caribbean Sea

400 Miles
400 Kilometers
0
0
Azimuthal Equidistant Projection

SOUTH AMERICA

Cuy, or guinea pig, is a traditional dish in Peru.

Argentina's name comes from *argentum*—the Latin word for "silver."

A woman sells fruit in Chivay, Peru.

South America is bordered by three major bodies of water—the Caribbean Sea, Atlantic Ocean, and Pacific Ocean. The world's fourth largest continent extends over a range of climates, from tropical in the north to subarctic in the south. South America produces a rich diversity of natural resources, including nuts, fruits, sugar, grains, coffee, and chocolate.

Santiago Cathedral in Santiago, Chile

RUNNING WILD

Guanacos, wild relatives of camels that look like small llamas with longer necks, are native to the grasslands of the Andes. Super-speedy animals that can run as fast as 35 miles an hour (56 km/h), guanacos are a protected species in Chile and Peru.

CHECKMATE

Chess has a long history in Montevideo, Uruguay. The game has been part of the cultural heritage for decades, and the capital city even hosted the World Youth Chess Championship in 2017. Today, you can usually spot people playing in parks or on the sidewalks of Montevideo.

Vast Watershed

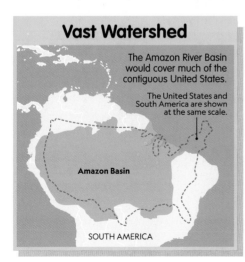

The Amazon River Basin would cover much of the contiguous United States.

The United States and South America are shown at the same scale.

Amazon Basin

SOUTH AMERICA

ANCIENT BRIDGE

Deep in the Peruvian Andes, a suspension bridge made of handwoven grass stretches more than 100 feet (30 m) over a rushing river. Once used to connect two villages on either side of the river, the bridge, which dates back more than 500 years, is now more of a symbolic nod to the past. Each June, the suspension bridge is rebuilt and replaced by the local Indigenous community.

305

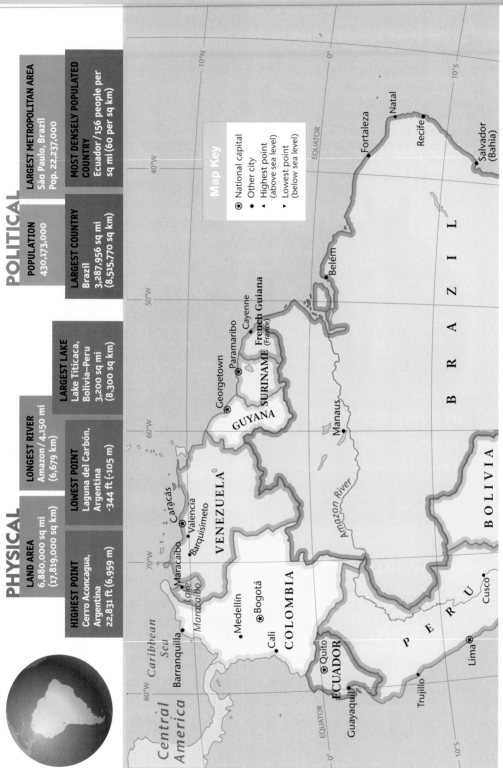

PHYSICAL

HIGHEST POINT
Cerro Aconcagua, Argentina
22,831 ft (6,959 m)

LAND AREA
6,880,000 sq mi
(17,819,000 sq km)

LOWEST POINT
Laguna del Carbón, Argentina
-344 ft (-105 m)

LONGEST RIVER
Amazon / 4,150 mi
(6,679 km)

LARGEST LAKE
Lake Titicaca, Bolivia–Peru
3,200 sq mi
(8,300 sq km)

POLITICAL

POPULATION
430,173,000

LARGEST COUNTRY
Brazil
3,287,956 sq mi
(8,515,770 sq km)

LARGEST METROPOLITAN AREA
São Paulo, Brazil
Pop. 22,237,000

MOST DENSELY POPULATED COUNTRY
Ecuador / 156 people per sq mi (60 per sq km)

Map Key
⊛ National capital
• Other city
▲ Highest point (above sea level)
▼ Lowest point (below sea level)

Central America

Caribbean Sea

Barranquilla
Maracaibo
Lake Maracaibo
Medellín
Cali
⊛ Bogotá

COLOMBIA

Caracas ⊛
Valencia
Barquisimeto

VENEZUELA

Georgetown ⊛

GUYANA

Paramaribo ⊛
SURINAME

Cayenne
French Guiana (France)

ECUADOR
⊛ Quito
Guayaquil

Manaus

Amazon River

PERU

Lima ⊛
Trujillo
Cusco

BOLIVIA

BRAZIL

Belém
Fortaleza
Natal
Recife
Salvador (Bahia)

EQUATOR

10°N
0°
10°S
40°W
50°W
60°W
70°W
80°W

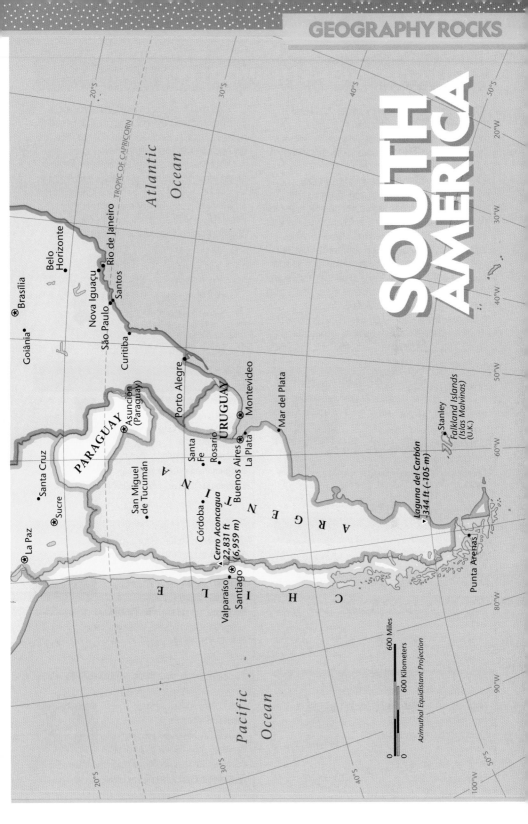

SOUTH AMERICA

Atlantic Ocean

Pacific Ocean

Brasília

Belo Horizonte

Goiânia

Rio de Janeiro

Nova Iguaçu

Santos

São Paulo

Curitiba

Porto Alegre

PARAGUAY

Asunción (Paraguay)

URUGUAY

Montevideo

Mar del Plata

Santa Cruz

Sucre

La Paz

San Miguel de Tucumán

Santa Fe

Rosario

Buenos Aires

La Plata

ARGENTINA

Córdoba

Cerro Aconcagua 22,831 ft (6,959 m)

Valparaíso

Santiago

CHILE

Laguna del Carbón 344 ft (-105 m)

Stanley

Falkland Islands (Islas Malvinas) (U.K.)

Punta Arenas

TROPIC OF CAPRICORN

20°S

30°S

40°S

50°S

20°W

30°W

40°W

50°W

60°W

70°W

80°W

90°W

100°W

600 Miles

600 Kilometers

Azimuthal Equidistant Projection

307

COUNTRIES OF THE WORLD

The following pages present a general overview of all 195 independent countries recognized by the National Geographic Society, including the newest nation, South Sudan, which gained independence in 2011.

The flags of each independent country symbolize diverse cultures and histories. The statistical data cover highlights of geography and demography and provide a brief overview of each country. They present general characteristics and are not intended to be comprehensive. For example, not every language spoken in a specific country can be listed. Thus, languages shown are the most representative of that area. This is also true of the religions mentioned.

A country is defined as a political body with its own independent government, geographical space, and, in most cases, laws, military, and taxes.

Disputed areas such as Northern Cyprus and Taiwan, and dependencies of independent nations, such as Bermuda and Puerto Rico, are not included in this listing.

Note the color key at the bottom of the pages and the locator map below, which assign a color to each country based on the continent on which it is located. Some capital city populations include that city's metro area. All information is accurate as of press time.

Color Key by Continent

Afghanistan

Area: 251,827 sq mi (652,230 sq km)
Population: 37,466,000
Capital: Kabul, pop. 4,336,000
Currency: afghani (AFN)
Religion: Muslim
Languages: Afghan Persian (Dari), Pashto, Uzbek, English

Albania

Area: 11,100 sq mi (28,748 sq km)
Population: 3,088,000
Capital: Tirana, pop. 503,000
Currency: lek (ALL)
Religions: Muslim, Roman Catholic, Eastern Orthodox
Language: Albanian

Algeria

Area: 919,595 sq mi (2,381,740 sq km)
Population: 43,577,000
Capital: Algiers, pop. 2,809,000
Currency: Algerian dinar (DZD)
Religion: Muslim
Languages: Arabic, French, Berber (Tamazight)

Andorra

Area: 181 sq mi (468 sq km)
Population: 86,000
Capital: Andorra la Vella, pop. 23,000
Currency: euro (EUR)
Religion: Roman Catholic
Languages: Catalan, French, Castilian, Portuguese

Angola

Area: 481,353 sq mi (1,246,700 sq km)
Population: 33,643,000
Capital: Luanda, pop. 8,632,000
Currency: kwanza (AOA)
Religions: Roman Catholic, Protestant
Languages: Portuguese, Umbundu, other African languages

Antigua and Barbuda

Area: 171 sq mi (443 sq km)
Population: 99,000
Capital: St. John's, pop. 21,000
Currency: East Caribbean dollar (XCD)
Religions: Protestant, Roman Catholic, other Christian
Languages: English, Antiguan creole

Argentina

Area: 1,073,518 sq mi
(2,780,400 sq km)
Population: 45,865,000
Capital: Buenos Aires,
pop. 15,258,000
Currency: Argentine peso (ARS)
Religion: Roman Catholic
Languages: Spanish, Italian, English, German, French

Austria

Area: 32,383 sq mi (83,871 sq km)
Population: 8,885,000
Capital: Vienna, pop. 1,945,000
Currency: euro (EUR)
Religions: Roman Catholic, Eastern Orthodox, Muslim
Languages: German, Croatian

Armenia

Area: 11,484 sq mi
(29,743 sq km)
Population: 3,012,000
Capital: Yerevan,
pop. 1,089,000
Currency: dram (AMD)
Religion: Oriental Orthodox
Languages: Armenian, Russian

Azerbaijan

Area: 33,436 sq mi
(86,600 sq km)
Population: 10,282,000
Capital: Baku, pop. 2,371,000
Currency: Azerbaijani manat (AZN)
Religion: Muslim
Languages: Azerbaijani (Azeri), Russian

Australia

Area: 2,988,902 sq mi
(7,741,220 sq km)
Population: 25,810,000
Capital: Canberra, A.C.T.,
pop. 462,000
Currency: Australian dollar (AUD)
Religions: Protestant, Roman Catholic
Language: English

Bahamas, The

Area: 5,359 sq mi
(13,880 sq km)
Population: 353,000
Capital: Nassau, pop. 280,000
Currency: Bahamian dollar (BSD)
Religions: Protestant, Roman Catholic, other Christian
Languages: English, Creole

3 cool things about AUSTRALIA

1. Australia is the only continent without an active volcano.

2. Australia was called New Holland by early Dutch settlers. It got its current name, which means "southern" in Latin, in 1803.

3. The main island of Australia is surrounded by some 8,000 smaller and secluded islands—all of which are part of the continent.

Bahrain

Area: 293 sq mi (760 sq km)
Population: 1,527,000
Capital: Manama, pop. 664,000
Currency: Bahraini dinar (BHD)
Religions: Muslim, Christian
Languages: Arabic, English, Farsi, Urdu

Bangladesh

Area: 57,321 sq mi
(148,460 sq km)
Population: 164,099,000
Capital: Dhaka, pop. 21,741,000
Currency: taka (BDT)
Religions: Muslim, Hindu
Language: Bangla (Bengali)

Barbados

Area: 166 sq mi (430 sq km)
Population: 302,000
Capital: Bridgetown, pop. 89,000
Currency: Barbadian dollar (BBD)
Religions: Protestant, other Christian
Languages: English, Bajan

Belgium

Area: 11,787 sq mi (30,528 sq km)
Population: 11,779,000
Capital: Brussels, pop. 2,096,000
Currency: euro (EUR)
Religions: Roman Catholic, Muslim
Languages: Dutch, French, German

Belarus

Area: 80,155 sq mi (207,600 sq km)
Population: 9,442,000
Capital: Minsk, pop. 2,039,000
Currency: Belarusian ruble (BYN)
Religions: Eastern Orthodox, Roman Catholic
Languages: Russian, Belarusian

Belize

Area: 8,867 sq mi (22,966 sq km)
Population: 406,000
Capital: Belmopan, pop. 23,000
Currency: Belizean dollar (BZD)
Religions: Roman Catholic, Protestant
Languages: English, Spanish, Creole, Maya

SNAPSH⊙T
Botswana

A male African elephant faces the camera in Botswana, home to more elephants than any other country in the world.

COLOR KEY ● Africa ● Australia, New Zealand, and Oceania

Benin

Area: 43,484 sq mi (112,622 sq km)
Population: 13,302,000
Capitals: Porto-Novo, pop. 285,000; Cotonou, pop. 699,000
Currency: CFA franc BCEAO (XOF)
Religions: Muslim, Roman Catholic, Protestant, Vodoun, other Christian
Languages: French, Fon, Yoruba, tribal languages

Bhutan

Area: 14,824 sq mi (38,394 sq km)
Population: 857,000
Capital: Thimphu, pop. 203,000
Currency: ngultrum (BTN)
Religions: Buddhist, Hindu
Languages: Sharchhopka, Dzongkha, Lhotshamkha

Bolivia

Area: 424,164 sq mi (1,098,581 sq km)
Population: 11,759,000
Capitals: La Paz, pop. 1,882,000; Sucre, pop. 278,000
Currency: boliviano (BOB)
Religions: Roman Catholic, Protestant
Languages: Spanish, Quechua, Aymara, Guarani

Bosnia and Herzegovina

Area: 19,767 sq mi (51,197 sq km)
Population: 3,825,000
Capital: Sarajevo, pop. 344,000
Currency: convertible mark (BAM)
Religions: Muslim, Eastern Orthodox, Roman Catholic
Languages: Bosnian, Serbian, Croatian

Botswana

Area: 224,607 sq mi (581,730 sq km)
Population: 2,351,000
Capital: Gaborone, pop. 269,000
Currency: pula (BWP)
Religion: Christian
Languages: Setswana, Sekalanga, Shekgalagadi, English

Brazil

Area: 3,287,956 sq mi (8,515,770 sq km)
Population: 213,445,000
Capital: Brasília, pop. 4,728,000
Currency: real (BRL)
Religions: Roman Catholic, Protestant
Language: Portuguese

Brunei

Area: 2,226 sq mi (5,765 sq km)
Population: 471,000
Capital: Bandar Seri Begawan, pop. 241,000
Currency: Bruneian dollar (BND)
Religions: Muslim, Christian, Buddhist, Indigenous beliefs
Languages: Malay, English, Chinese

Bulgaria

Area: 42,811 sq mi (110,879 sq km)
Population: 6,919,000
Capital: Sofia, pop. 1,284,000
Currency: lev (BGN)
Religions: Eastern Orthodox, Muslim
Language: Bulgarian

Burkina Faso

Area: 105,869 sq mi (274,200 sq km)
Population: 21,383,000
Capital: Ouagadougou, pop. 2,915,000
Currency: CFA franc BCEAO (XOF)
Religions: Muslim, Roman Catholic, traditional or animist, Protestant
Languages: French, African languages

Burundi

Area: 10,745 sq mi (27,830 sq km)
Population: 12,241,000
Capitals: Bujumbura, pop. 1,075,000; Gitega, pop. 135,000
Currency: Burundi franc (BIF)
Religions: Roman Catholic, Protestant
Languages: Kirundi, French, English, Swahili

Cabo Verde

Area: 1,557 sq mi (4,033 sq km)
Population: 589,000
Capital: Praia, pop. 168,000
Currency: Cabo Verdean escudo (CVE)
Religions: Roman Catholic, Protestant
Languages: Portuguese, Krioulo

Cambodia

Area: 69,898 sq mi (181,035 sq km)
Population: 17,304,000
Capital: Phnom Penh, pop. 2,144,000
Currency: riel (KHR)
Religion: Buddhist
Language: Khmer

Cameroon

Area: 183,568 sq mi (475,440 sq km)
Population: 28,524,000
Capital: Yaoundé, pop. 4,164,000
Currency: CFA franc BEAC (XAF)
Religions: Roman Catholic, Protestant, other Christian, Muslim
Languages: African languages, English, French

Canada

Area: 3,855,101 sq mi (9,984,670 sq km)
Population: 37,943,000
Capital: Ottawa, pop. 1,408,000
Currency: Canadian dollar (CAD)
Religions: Roman Catholic, Protestant, other Christian
Languages: English, French

Central African Republic

Area: 240,535 sq mi (622,984 sq km)
Population: 5,358,000
Capital: Bangui, pop. 910,000
Currency: CFA franc BEAC (XAF)
Religions: Christian, Muslim
Languages: French, Sangho, tribal languages

Chad

Area: 495,755 sq mi (1,284,000 sq km)
Population: 17,414,000
Capital: N'Djamena, pop. 1,476,000
Currency: CFA franc BEAC (XAF)
Religions: Muslim, Protestant, Roman Catholic
Languages: French, Arabic, Sara, Indigenous languages

Chile

Area: 291,932 sq mi (756,102 sq km)
Population: 18,308,000
Capital: Santiago, pop. 6,812,000
Currency: Chilean peso (CLP)
Religions: Roman Catholic, Protestant
Languages: Spanish, English

China

Area: 3,705,405 sq mi (9,596,960 sq km)
Population: 1,397,898,000
Capital: Beijing, pop. 20,897,000
Currency: Renminbi yuan (RMB)
Religions: folk religion, Buddhist, Christian
Languages: Standard Chinese (Mandarin), Yue (Cantonese), Wu, Minbei, Minnan, Xiang, Gan, regional official languages

Colombia

Area: 439,735 sq mi (1,138,910 sq km)
Population: 50,356,000
Capital: Bogotá, pop. 11,167,000
Currency: Colombian peso (COP)
Religions: Roman Catholic, Protestant
Language: Spanish

Comoros

Area: 863 sq mi (2,235 sq km)
Population: 864,000
Capital: Moroni, pop. 62,000
Currency: Comoran franc (KMF)
Religion: Muslim
Languages: Arabic, French, Shikomoro (Comorian)

Congo

Area: 132,047 sq mi (342,000 sq km)
Population: 5,417,000
Capital: Brazzaville, pop. 2,470,000
Currency: CFA franc BEAC (XAF)
Religions: Roman Catholic, other Christian, Protestant
Languages: French, Lingala, Monokutuba, Kikongo, local languages

Côte d'Ivoire (Ivory Coast)

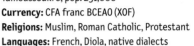

Area: 124,504 sq mi (322,463 sq km)
Population: 28,088,000
Capitals: Abidjan, pop. 5,355,000; Yamoussoukro, pop. 231,000
Currency: CFA franc BCEAO (XOF)
Religions: Muslim, Roman Catholic, Protestant
Languages: French, Diola, native dialects

Costa Rica

Area: 19,730 sq mi (51,100 sq km)
Population: 5,151,000
Capital: San José, pop. 1,421,000
Currency: Costa Rican colón (CRC)
Religions: Roman Catholic, Protestant
Languages: Spanish, English

Croatia

Area: 21,851 sq mi (56,594 sq km)
Population: 4,209,000
Capital: Zagreb, pop. 685,000
Currency: kuna (HRK)
Religion: Roman Catholic
Languages: Croatian, Serbian

SNAPSHOT
Chile

A visitor gazes at the massive "Mano del Desierto" ("Hand of the Desert") sculpture in Antofagasta, Chile.

Cuba

Area: 42,803 sq mi
(110,860 sq km)
Population: 11,032,000
Capital: Havana, pop. 2,143,000
Currency: Cuban peso (CUP)
Religions: Christian, folk religion
Language: Spanish

Democratic Republic of the Congo

Area: 905,354 sq mi
(2,344,858 sq km)
Population: 105,045,000
Capital: Kinshasa, pop. 14,970,000
Currency: Congolese franc (CDF)
Religions: Roman Catholic, Protestant, other Christian
Languages: French, Lingala, Kingwana, Kikongo, Tshiluba

Cyprus

Area: 3,572 sq mi (9,251 sq km)
Population: 1,282,000
Capital: Nicosia, pop. 269,000
Currency: euro (EUR)
Religion: Eastern Orthodox
Languages: Greek, Turkish, English

Denmark

Area: 16,639 sq mi
(43,094 sq km)
Population: 5,895,000
Capital: Copenhagen, pop. 1,359,000
Currency: Danish krone (DKK)
Religions: Protestant, Muslim
Languages: Danish, Faroese, Greenlandic, English

Czechia (Czech Republic)

Area: 30,451 sq mi (78,867 sq km)
Population: 10,703,000
Capital: Prague, pop. 1,312,000
Currency: koruna (CZK)
Religion: Roman Catholic
Languages: Czech, Slovak

Djibouti

Area: 8,958 sq mi
(23,200 sq km)
Population: 938,000
Capital: Djibouti, pop. 584,000
Currency: Djiboutian franc (DJF)
Religions: Muslim, Christian
Languages: French, Arabic, Somali, Afar

3 cool things about CZECHIA

1. Built in the ninth century, Prague Castle is the world's largest ancient castle and the official residence of Czechia's president.

2. Foraging for mushrooms in the forest is a popular pastime in Czechia.

3. Czech author Karel Čapek is credited for first using the word "robot" in his 1920 play *R.U.R.* about humanlike machines.

Dominica

Area: 290 sq mi (751 sq km)
Population: 75,000
Capital: Roseau, pop. 15,000
Currency: East Caribbean dollar (XCD)
Religions: Roman Catholic, Protestant
Languages: English, French patois

Dominican Republic

Area: 18,792 sq mi
(48,670 sq km)
Population: 10,597,000
Capital: Santo Domingo, pop. 3,389,000
Currency: Dominican peso (DOP)
Religions: Roman Catholic, Protestant
Language: Spanish

Ecuador

Area: 109,483 sq mi
(283,561 sq km)
Population: 17,093,000
Capital: Quito, pop. 1,901,000
Currency: U.S. dollar (USD)
Religions: Roman Catholic, Protestant
Languages: Spanish, Amerindian languages

The PEAK of Ecuador's MOUNT CHIMBORAZO is CLOSER TO THE SUN than ANYWHERE ELSE on Earth.

Egypt

Area: 386,662 sq mi
(1,001,450 sq km)
Population: 106,437,000
Capital: Cairo, pop. 21,323,000
Currency: Egyptian pound (EGP)
Religions: Muslim, Oriental Orthodox
Languages: Arabic, English, French

El Salvador

Area: 8,124 sq mi
(21,041 sq km)
Population: 6,528,000
Capital: San Salvador,
pop. 1,107,000
Currency: U.S. dollar (USD)
Religions: Roman Catholic, Protestant
Language: Spanish

Equatorial Guinea

Area: 10,831 sq mi (28,051 sq km)
Population: 857,000
Capital: Malabo, pop. 297,000
Currency: CFA franc BEAC (XAF)
Religions: Roman Catholic, Muslim, Baha'i, animist, Indigenous beliefs
Languages: Spanish, Portuguese, French, Fang, Bubi

Eritrea

Area: 45,406 sq mi (117,600 sq km)
Population: 6,147,000
Capital: Asmara, pop. 998,000
Currency: nakfa (ERN)
Religions: Muslim, Oriental Orthodox, Roman Catholic, Protestant
Languages: Tigrinya, Arabic, English, Tigre, Kunama, Afar, other Cushitic languages

Estonia

Area: 17,463 sq mi (45,228 sq km)
Population: 1,220,000
Capital: Tallinn, pop. 449,000
Currency: euro (EUR)
Religions: Eastern Orthodox, Protestant
Languages: Estonian, Russian

Eswatini (Swaziland)

Area: 6,704 sq mi (17,364 sq km)
Population: 1,113,000
Capitals: Mbabane, pop. 68,000;
Lobamba, pop. 11,000
Currency: lilangeni (SZL)
Religions: Roman Catholic, other Christian
Languages: English, siSwati

Ethiopia

Area: 426,372 sq mi
(1,104,300 sq km)
Population: 110,871,000
Capital: Addis Ababa,
pop. 5,006,000
Currency: birr (ETB)
Religions: Oriental Orthodox, Muslim, Protestant
Languages: Oromo, Amharic, Somali, Tigrinya, Afar

Fiji

Area: 7,056 sq mi
(18,274 sq km)
Population: 940,000
Capital: Suva, pop. 178,000
Currency: Fijian dollar (FJD)
Religions: Protestant, Roman Catholic, other Christian, Hindu, Muslim
Languages: English, Fijian, Hindustani

Finland

Area: 130,558 sq mi
(338,145 sq km)
Population: 5,587,000
Capital: Helsinki, pop. 1,317,000
Currency: euro (EUR)
Religion: Protestant
Languages: Finnish, Swedish

France

Area: 248,573 sq mi
(643,801 sq km)
Population: 68,084,000
Capital: Paris, pop. 11,079,000
Currency: euro (EUR)
Religions: Roman Catholic, Muslim
Language: French

Gabon

Area: 103,347 sq mi (267,667 sq km)
Population: 2,285,000
Capital: Libreville, pop. 845,000
Currency: CFA franc BEAC (XAF)
Religions: Roman Catholic, Protestant, other Christian, Muslim
Languages: French, Fang, Myene, Nzebi, Bapounou/Eschira, Bandjabi

Gambia, The

Area: 4,363 sq mi (11,300 sq km)
Population: 2,221,000
Capital: Banjul, pop. 459,000
Currency: dalasi (GMD)
Religion: Muslim
Languages: English, Mandinka, Wolof, Fula

Georgia

Area: 26,911 sq mi (69,700 sq km)
Population: 4,934,000
Capital: Tbilisi, pop. 1,079,000
Currency: lari (GEL)
Religions: Eastern Orthodox, Muslim
Language: Georgian

Germany

Area: 137,847 sq mi
(357,022 sq km)
Population: 79,903,000
Capital: Berlin, pop. 3,567,000
Currency: euro (EUR)
Religions: Roman Catholic, Protestant, Muslim
Language: German

Ghana

Area: 92,098 sq mi (238,533 sq km)
Population: 32,373,000
Capital: Accra, pop. 2,557,000
Currency: cedi (GHC)
Religions: Protestant, Roman Catholic, other Christian, Muslim, traditional
Languages: Assanta, Ewe, Fante, English

Greece

Area: 50,949 sq mi (131,957 sq km)
Population: 10,570,000
Capital: Athens, pop. 3,153,000
Currency: euro (EUR)
Religion: Eastern Orthodox
Language: Greek

Grenada

Area: 133 sq mi (344 sq km)
Population: 114,000
Capital: St. George's, pop. 39,000
Currency: East Caribbean dollar (XCD)
Religions: Protestant, Roman Catholic
Languages: English, French patois

Guatemala

Area: 42,042 sq mi (108,889 sq km)
Population: 17,423,000
Capital: Guatemala City, pop. 2,983,000
Currency: quetzal (GTQ)
Religions: Roman Catholic, Protestant, Indigenous beliefs
Languages: Spanish, Maya languages

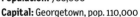
Guinea

Area: 94,926 sq mi (245,857 sq km)
Population: 12,878,000
Capital: Conakry, pop. 1,991,000
Currency: Guinean franc (GNF)
Religions: Muslim, Christian
Languages: French, African languages

Guyana

Area: 83,000 sq mi (214,969 sq km)
Population: 788,000
Capital: Georgetown, pop. 110,000
Currency: Guyanese dollar (GYD)
Religions: Hindu, Protestant, Roman Catholic, other Christian, Muslim
Languages: English, Guyanese Creole, Amerindian languages, Indian languages, Chinese

Guinea-Bissau

Area: 13,948 sq mi (36,125 sq km)
Population: 1,976,000
Capital: Bissau, pop. 621,000
Currency: CFA franc BCEAO (XOF)
Religions: Muslim, Christian, animist
Languages: Crioulu, Portuguese, Pular, Mandingo

Haiti

Area: 10,714 sq mi (27,750 sq km)
Population: 11,198,000
Capital: Port-au-Prince, pop. 2,844,000
Currency: gourde (HTG)
Religions: Roman Catholic, Protestant, voodoo
Languages: French, Creole

SNAPSHOT
Guatemala

Two brightly decorated modified buses, called chicken buses, in Antigua, Guatemala

Honduras

Area: 43,278 sq mi
(112,090 sq km)
Population: 9,346,000
Capital: Tegucigalpa,
pop. 1,485,000
Currency: lempira (HNL)
Religions: Roman Catholic, Protestant
Languages: Spanish, Amerindian dialects

Iceland

Area: 39,769 sq mi
(103,000 sq km)
Population: 354,000
Capital: Reykjavík, pop. 216,000
Currency: Icelandic krona (ISK)
Religion: Protestant
Languages: Icelandic, English, Nordic
languages, German

Hungary

Area: 35,918 sq mi (93,028 sq km)
Population: 9,728,000
Capital: Budapest, pop. 1,772,000
Currency: forint (HUF)
Religions: Roman Catholic, Protestant
Languages: Hungarian, English, German

India

Area: 1,269,219 sq mi (3,287,263 sq km)
Population: 1,339,331,000
Capital: New Delhi, pop. 31,181,000
Currency: Indian rupee (INR)
Religions: Hindu, Muslim
Languages: Hindi, English

SNAPSHOT India

Doused in colorful powder and water, friends celebrate Holi, an annual festival in India commemorating spring.

COLOR KEY ● Africa ● Australia, New Zealand, and Oceania

Indonesia

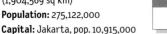

Area: 735,358 sq mi
(1,904,569 sq km)
Population: 275,122,000
Capital: Jakarta, pop. 10,915,000
Currency: Indonesian rupiah (IDR)
Religions: Muslim, Protestant
Languages: Bahasa Indonesia, English, Dutch, local dialects

Iran

Area: 636,371 sq mi
(1,648,195 sq km)
Population: 85,889,000
Capital: Tehran, pop. 9,259,000
Currency: Iranian rial (IRR)
Religion: Muslim
Languages: Persian (Farsi), Turkic dialects, Kurdish

Iraq

Area: 169,235 sq mi
(438,317 sq km)
Population: 39,650,000
Capital: Baghdad, pop. 7,323,000
Currency: Iraqi dinar (IQD)
Religion: Muslim
Languages: Arabic, Kurdish, Turkmen, Syriac, Armenian

Ireland (Éire)

Area: 27,133 sq mi
(70,273 sq km)
Population: 5,225,000
Capital: Dublin
(Baile Átha Cliath), pop. 1,242,000
Currency: euro (EUR)
Religion: Roman Catholic
Languages: English, Irish (Gaelic)

Israel

Area: 8,970 sq mi (23,232 sq km)
Population: 8,787,000
Capital: Jerusalem, pop. 944,000
Currency: new Israeli shekel (ILS)
Religions: Jewish, Muslim
Languages: Hebrew, Arabic, English

Italy

Area: 116,348 sq mi
(301,340 sq km)
Population: 62,390,000
Capital: Rome, pop. 4,278,000
Currency: euro (EUR)
Religion: Roman Catholic
Languages: Italian, German, French, Slovene

Jamaica

Area: 4,244 sq mi
(10,991 sq km)
Population: 2,817,000
Capital: Kingston, pop. 592,000
Currency: Jamaican dollar (JMD)
Religion: Protestant
Languages: English, English patois

Japan

Area: 145,914 sq mi (377,915 sq km)
Population: 124,687,000
Capital: Tokyo, pop. 37,340,000
Currency: yen (JPY)
Religions: Shinto, Buddhist
Language: Japanese

Jordan

Area: 34,495 sq mi
(89,342 sq km)
Population: 10,910,000
Capital: Amman, pop. 2,182,000
Currency: Jordanian dinar (JOD)
Religion: Muslim
Languages: Arabic, English

Kazakhstan

Area: 1,052,089 sq mi
(2,724,900 sq km)
Population: 19,246,000
Capital: Nur-Sultan (Astana),
pop. 1,212,000
Currency: tenge (KZT)
Religions: Muslim, Eastern Orthodox
Languages: Kazakh (Qazaq), Russian, English

● Asia ● Europe ● North America ● South America

Kenya

Area: 224,081 sq mi (580,367 sq km)
Population: 54,685,000
Capital: Nairobi, pop. 4,922,000
Currency: Kenyan shilling (KES)
Religions: Protestant, Roman Catholic, other Christian, Muslim
Languages: English, Kiswahili, Indigenous languages

Laos

Area: 91,429 sq mi (236,800 sq km)
Population: 7,574,000
Capital: Vientiane, pop. 694,000
Currency: kip (LAK)
Religion: Buddhist
Languages: Lao, French, English, ethnic languages

Kiribati

Area: 313 sq mi (811 sq km)
Population: 113,000
Capital: Tarawa, pop. 64,000
Currency: Australian dollar (AUD)
Religions: Roman Catholic, Protestant, Mormon
Languages: I-Kiribati, English

Latvia

Area: 24,938 sq mi (64,589 sq km)
Population: 1,863,000
Capital: Riga, pop. 628,000
Currency: euro (EUR)
Religions: Protestant, Roman Catholic, Eastern Orthodox, Druze
Languages: Latvian, Russian

Kosovo

Area: 4,203 sq mi (10,887 sq km)
Population: 1,935,000
Capital: Pristina, pop. 217,000
Currency: euro (EUR)
Religion: Muslim
Languages: Albanian, Serbian, Bosnian

Lebanon

Area: 4,015 sq mi (10,400 sq km)
Population: 5,261,000
Capital: Beirut, pop. 2,435,000
Currency: Lebanese pound (LBP)
Religions: Muslim, Eastern Catholic
Languages: Arabic, French, English, Armenian

Kuwait

Area: 6,880 sq mi (17,818 sq km)
Population: 3,032,000
Capital: Kuwait City, pop. 3,177,000
Currency: Kuwaiti dinar (KWD)
Religions: Muslim, Christian
Languages: Arabic, English

Lesotho

Area: 11,720 sq mi (30,355 sq km)
Population: 2,178,000
Capital: Maseru, pop. 202,000
Currency: loti (LSL)
Religions: Protestant, Roman Catholic, other Christian
Languages: Sesotho, English, Zulu, Xhosa

Kyrgyzstan

Area: 77,201 sq mi (199,951 sq km)
Population: 6,019,000
Capital: Bishkek, pop. 1,060,000
Currency: Som (KGS)
Religions: Muslim, Eastern Orthodox
Languages: Kyrgyz, Uzbek, Russian

Liberia

Area: 43,000 sq mi (111,369 sq km)
Population: 5,214,000
Capital: Monrovia, pop. 1,569,000
Currency: Liberian dollar (LRD)
Religions: Christian, Muslim
Languages: English, Indigenous languages

Libya

Area: 679,362 sq mi
(1,759,540 sq km)
Population: 7,017,000
Capital: Tripoli, pop. 1,170,000
Currency: Libyan dinar (LYD)
Religion: Muslim
Languages: Arabic, Italian, English, Berber

Lithuania

Area: 25,212 sq mi
(65,300 sq km)
Population: 2,712,000
Capital: Vilnius, pop. 540,000
Currency: euro (EUR)
Religion: Roman Catholic
Language: Lithuanian

Liechtenstein

Area: 62 sq mi (160 sq km)
Population: 39,000
Capital: Vaduz, pop. 5,000
Currency: Swiss franc (CHF)
Religions: Roman Catholic, Protestant, Muslim
Language: German

Luxembourg

Area: 998 sq mi (2,586 sq km)
Population: 640,000
Capital: Luxembourg,
pop. 120,000
Currency: euro (EUR)
Religion: Roman Catholic
Languages: Luxembourgish, Portuguese,
French, German

SNAPSHOT
Kosovo

Kosovo's Old Stone Bridge, in the small
town of Prizren, is more than 500 years old.

● Asia ● Europe ● North America ● South America

Madagascar

Area: 226,658 sq mi
(587,041 sq km)
Population: 27,534,000
Capital: Antananarivo,
pop. 3,532,000
Currency: Malagasy ariary (MGA)
Religions: Christian, Indigenous beliefs, Muslim
Languages: French, Malagasy, English

Malawi

Area: 45,747 sq mi
(118,484 sq km)
Population: 20,309,000
Capital: Lilongwe, pop. 1,171,000
Currency: Malawian kwacha (MWK)
Religions: Protestant, Roman Catholic, other
Christian, Muslim
Languages: English, Chewa, other Bantu languages

Malaysia

Area: 127,355 sq mi (329,847 sq km)
Population: 33,519,000
Capital: Kuala Lumpur,
pop. 8,211,000
Currency: ringgit (MYR)
Religions: Muslim, Buddhist, Christian, Hindu
Languages: Bahasa Malaysia (Malay), English, Chinese,
Tamil, Telugu, Malayalam, Panjabi, Thai

Maldives

Area: 115 sq mi (298 sq km)
Population: 391,000
Capital: Male, pop. 177,000
Currency: rufiyaa (MVR)
Religion: Muslim
Languages: Dhivehi, English

Mali

Area: 478,841 sq mi (1,240,192 sq km)
Population: 20,138,000
Capital: Bamako, pop. 2,713,000
Currency: CFA franc BCEAO (XOF)
Religion: Muslim
Languages: French, Bambara, African languages

Malta

Area: 122 sq mi (316 sq km)
Population: 461,000
Capital: Valletta, pop. 213,000
Currency: euro (EUR)
Religion: Roman Catholic
Languages: Maltese, English

You can EXPLORE a 6,000-year-old UNDERGROUND BURIAL CHAMBER in Malta.

Marshall Islands

Area: 70 sq mi (181 sq km)
Population: 79,000
Capital: Majuro, pop. 31,000
Currency: U.S. dollar (USD)
Religions: Protestant, Roman Catholic, Mormon
Languages: Marshallese, English

Mauritania

Area: 397,955 sq mi
(1,030,700 sq km)
Population: 4,079,000
Capital: Nouakchott, pop. 1,372,000
Currency: ouguiya (MRU)
Religion: Muslim
Languages: Arabic, Pulaar, Soninke, Wolof, French

Mauritius

Area: 788 sq mi (2,040 sq km)
Population: 1,386,000
Capital: Port Louis, pop. 149,000
Currency: Mauritian rupee (MUR)
Religions: Hindu, Muslim,
Roman Catholic, other Christian
Languages: Creole, English

Mexico

Area: 758,449 sq mi
(1,964,375 sq km)
Population: 130,207,000
Capital: Mexico City,
pop. 21,919,000
Currency: Mexican peso (MXN)
Religions: Roman Catholic, Protestant
Language: Spanish

Micronesia, Federated States of

Area: 271 sq mi (702 sq km)
Population: 102,000
Capital: Palikir, pop. 7,000
Currency: U.S. dollar (USD)
Religions: Roman Catholic, Protestant
Languages: English, Chuukese, Kosrean, Pohnpeian,
other Indigenous languages

Moldova

Area: 13,070 sq mi
(33,851 sq km)
Population: 3,324,000
Capital: Chişinău,
pop. 494,000
Currency: Moldovan leu (MDL)
Religion: Eastern Orthodox
Languages: Moldovan, Romanian

Monaco

Area: 1 sq mi (2 sq km)
Population: 31,000
Capital: Monaco, pop. 31,000
Currency: euro (EUR)
Religion: Roman Catholic
Languages: French, English, Italian, Monegasque

Mongolia

Area: 603,908 sq mi
(1,564,116 sq km)
Population: 3,199,000
Capital: Ulaanbaatar,
pop. 1,615,000
Currency: tugrik (MNT)
Religion: Buddhist
Languages: Mongolian, Turkic, Russian

Montenegro

Area: 5,333 sq mi
(13,812 sq km)
Population: 607,000
Capital: Podgorica, pop. 177,000
Currency: euro (EUR)
Religions: Eastern Orthodox, Muslim
Languages: Serbian, Montenegrin

Morocco

Area: 276,662 sq mi
(716,550 sq km)
Population: 36,562,000
Capital: Rabat, pop. 1,907,000
Currency: Moroccan dirham (MAD)
Religion: Muslim
Languages: Arabic, Tamazight, other Berber
languages, French

3 cool things about MOROCCO

1. Morocco is the only African country to border both the Atlantic Ocean and the Mediterranean Sea.

2. Mint tea is the traditional drink of Morocco, served at meals and sipped throughout the day.

3. Morocco is one of just three kingdoms on the continent of Africa. (Eswatini and Lesotho are the others.)

Mozambique

Area: 308,642 sq mi
(799,380 sq km)
Population: 30,888,000
Capital: Maputo, pop. 1,122,000
Currency: metical (MZN)
Religions: Roman Catholic, Protestant, other Christian,
Muslim
Languages: Makhuwa, Portuguese, local languages

Myanmar (Burma)

Area: 261,228 sq mi
(676,578 sq km)
Population: 57,069,000
Capital: Nay Pyi Taw,
pop. 640,000
Currency: kyat (MMK)
Religions: Buddhist, Christian
Language: Burmese

Nauru

Area: 8 sq mi (21 sq km)
Population: 10,000
Capital: Yaren, pop. 1,000
Currency: Australian
dollar (AUD)
Religions: Protestant, Roman Catholic
Languages: Nauruan, English

Namibia

Area: 318,261 sq mi
(824,292 sq km)
Population: 2,678,000
Capital: Windhoek, pop. 446,000
Currency: Namibian dollar (NAD)
Religions: Protestant, Indigenous beliefs
Languages: Indigenous languages, Afrikaans, English

Nepal

Area: 56,827 sq mi
(147,181 sq km)
Population: 30,425,000
Capital: Kathmandu, pop. 1,472,000
Currency: Nepalese rupee (NPR)
Religions: Hindu, Buddhist
Languages: Nepali, Maithali

SNAPSHOT North Korea

North Koreans participate in a
mass dance in a Pyongyang square.

COLOR KEY ● Africa ● Australia, New Zealand, and Oceania

Netherlands

Area: 16,040 sq mi
(41,543 sq km)
Population: 17,337,000
Capitals: Amsterdam, pop. 1,158,000;
The Hague, pop. 704,000
Currency: euro (EUR)
Religions: Roman Catholic, Protestant, Muslim
Language: Dutch

New Zealand

Area: 103,799 sq mi
(268,838 sq km)
Population: 4,991,000
Capital: Wellington, pop. 417,000
Currency: New Zealand dollar (NZD)
Religions: Roman Catholic, Protestant
Languages: English, Maori

Nicaragua

Area: 50,336 sq mi
(130,370 sq km)
Population: 6,244,000
Capital: Managua, pop. 1,073,000
Currency: cordoba oro (NIO)
Religions: Roman Catholic, Protestant
Language: Spanish

Niger

Area: 489,191 sq mi (1,267,000 sq km)
Population: 23,606,000
Capital: Niamey, pop. 1,336,000
Currency: CFA franc BCEAO (XOF)
Religion: Muslim
Languages: French, Hausa, Djerma

Nigeria

Area: 356,669 sq mi
(923,768 sq km)
Population: 219,464,000
Capital: Abuja, pop. 3,464,000
Currency: naira (NGN)
Religions: Muslim, Roman Catholic, other Christian
Languages: English, Indigenous languages

North Korea

Area: 46,540 sq mi
(120,538 sq km)
Population: 25,831,000
Capital: Pyongyang,
pop. 3,108,000
Currency: North Korean won (KPW)
Religions: Buddhist, Confucianist, Christian,
syncretic Chondogyo
Language: Korean

North Macedonia

Area: 9,928 sq mi
(25,713 sq km)
Population: 2,128,000
Capital: Skopje, pop. 601,000
Currency: Macedonian denar (MKD)
Religions: Macedonian Orthodox, Muslim
Languages: Macedonian, Albanian

Norway

Area: 125,021 sq mi
(323,802 sq km)
Population: 5,510,000
Capital: Oslo, pop. 1,056,000
Currency: Norwegian krone (NOK)
Religion: Protestant
Languages: Bokmal Norwegian, Nynorsk Norwegian

Oman

Area: 119,499 sq mi
(309,500 sq km)
Population: 3,695,000
Capital: Muscat, pop. 1,590,000
Currency: Omani rial (OMR)
Religions: Muslim, Christian, Hindu
Languages: Arabic, English, Baluchi, Swahili, Urdu,
Indian dialects

Pakistan

Area: 307,374 sq mi
(796,095 sq km)
Population: 238,181,000
Capital: Islamabad, pop. 1,164,000
Currency: Pakistan rupee (PKR)
Religion: Muslim
Languages: Punjabi, Sindhi, Saraiki, Urdu, English

● Asia ● Europe ● North America ● South America

Palau

Area: 177 sq mi (459 sq km)
Population: 22,000
Capital: Ngerulmud, pop. 277
Currency: U.S. dollar (USD)
Religions: Roman Catholic, Protestant, Modekngei
Languages: Palauan, English, Filipino

Philippines

Area: 115,831 sq mi (300,000 sq km)
Population: 110,818,000
Capital: Manila, pop. 14,159,000
Currency: Philippine peso (PHP)
Religions: Roman Catholic, Protestant, Muslim
Languages: Filipino (Tagalog), English, Indigenous languages

Panama

Area: 29,120 sq mi (75,420 sq km)
Population: 3,929,000
Capital: Panama City, pop. 1,899,000
Currency: balboa (PAB)
Religions: Roman Catholic, Protestant
Languages: Spanish, Indigenous languages, English

Poland

Area: 120,728 sq mi (312,685 sq km)
Population: 38,186,000
Capital: Warsaw, pop. 1,790,000
Currency: zloty (PLN)
Religion: Roman Catholic
Language: Polish

Papua New Guinea

Area: 178,703 sq mi (462,840 sq km)
Population: 7,400,000
Capital: Port Moresby, pop. 391,000
Currency: kina (PGK)
Religions: Protestant, Roman Catholic, other Christian
Languages: Tok Pisin, English, Hiri Motu, other Indigenous languages

Portugal

Area: 35,556 sq mi (92,090 sq km)
Population: 10,264,000
Capital: Lisbon, pop. 2,972,000
Currency: euro (EUR)
Religion: Roman Catholic
Languages: Portuguese, Mirandese

Paraguay

Area: 157,048 sq mi (406,752 sq km)
Population: 7,273,000
Capital: Asunción (Paraguay), pop. 3,394,000
Currency: Guarani (PYG)
Religions: Roman Catholic, Protestant
Languages: Spanish, Guarani

Qatar

Area: 4,473 sq mi (11,586 sq km)
Population: 2,480,000
Capital: Doha, pop. 646,000
Currency: Qatari rial (QAR)
Religions: Muslim, Christian, Hindu
Languages: Arabic, English

Peru

Area: 496,224 sq mi (1,285,216 sq km)
Population: 32,201,000
Capital: Lima, pop. 10,883,000
Currency: nuevo sol (PEN)
Religions: Roman Catholic, Protestant
Languages: Spanish, Quechua, Aymara

Romania

Area: 92,043 sq mi (238,391 sq km)
Population: 21,230,000
Capital: Bucharest, pop. 1,794,000
Currency: leu (RON)
Religions: Eastern Orthodox, Protestant
Language: Romanian

Russia

Area: 6,601,665 sq mi
(17,098,242 sq km)
Population: 142,321,000
Capital: Moscow, pop. 12,593,000
Currency: Russian ruble (RUB)
Religions: Eastern Orthodox, Muslim
Language: Russian
*Note: Russia is in both Europe and Asia, but its capital is in Europe,
so it is classified here as a European country.*

Samoa

Area: 1,093 sq mi
(2,831 sq km)
Population: 205,000
Capital: Apia, pop. 36,000
Currency: tala (SAT)
Religions: Protestant, Roman Catholic, Mormon
Languages: Samoan (Polynesian), English

Rwanda

Area: 10,169 sq mi
(26,338 sq km)
Population: 12,943,000
Capital: Kigali, pop. 1,170,000
Currency: Rwandan franc (RWF)
Religions: Protestant, Roman Catholic
Languages: Kinyarwanda, French, English,
Kiswahili (Swahili)

San Marino

Area: 24 sq mi (61 sq km)
Population: 34,000
Capital: San Marino, pop. 4,000
Currency: euro (EUR)
Religion: Roman Catholic
Language: Italian

SNAPSHOT
Samoa

A wooden ladder leads down
to the To Sua Ocean Trench
swimming hole in Upolu, Samoa.

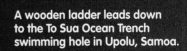

Sao Tome and Principe

Area: 372 sq mi (964 sq km)
Population: 214,000
Capital: São Tomé, pop. 80,000
Currency: dobra (STN)
Religion: Roman Catholic
Languages: Portuguese, Forro

Saudi Arabia

Area: 830,000 sq mi (2,149,690 sq km)
Population: 34,784,000
Capital: Riyadh, pop. 7,388,000
Currency: Saudi riyal (SAR)
Religion: Muslim
Language: Arabic

Senegal

Area: 75,955 sq mi (196,722 sq km)
Population: 16,082,000
Capital: Dakar, pop. 3,230,000
Currency: CFA franc BCEAO (XOF)
Religion: Muslim
Languages: French, Wolof, other Indigenous languages

Serbia

Area: 29,913 sq mi (77,474 sq km)
Population: 6,974,000
Capital: Belgrade, pop. 1,402,000
Currency: Serbian dinar (RSD)
Religions: Eastern Orthodox, Roman Catholic
Language: Serbian

Seychelles

Area: 176 sq mi (455 sq km)
Population: 96,000
Capital: Victoria, pop. 28,000
Currency: Seychelles rupee (SCR)
Religions: Roman Catholic, Protestant
Languages: Seychellois Creole, English, French

Sierra Leone

Area: 27,699 sq mi (71,740 sq km)
Population: 6,807,000
Capital: Freetown, pop. 1,236,000
Currency: leone (SLL)
Religions: Muslim, Christian
Languages: English, Mende, Temne, Krio

Singapore

Area: 278 sq mi (719 sq km)
Population: 5,866,000
Capital: Singapore, pop. 5,866,000
Currency: Singapore dollar (SGD)
Religions: Buddhist, Christian, Muslim, Taoist, Hindu
Languages: English, Mandarin, other Chinese dialects, Malay, Tamil

3 cool things about SINGAPORE

1. Singapore's mascot is the merlion, a half-fish, half-lion mythical creature said to represent Singapore's name in Malay—Singapura—which means "Lion City."

2. The country's Changi Airport features a butterfly garden, an indoor waterfall, a movie theater, and Singapore's tallest slide at four stories high.

3. Singapore's Night Safari, the world's first nighttime zoo, welcomes guests to check out animals in the dark.

Slovakia

Area: 18,933 sq mi (49,035 sq km)
Population: 5,436,000
Capital: Bratislava, pop. 437,000
Currency: euro (EUR)
Religions: Roman Catholic, Protestant
Language: Slovak

Slovenia

Area: 7,827 sq mi
(20,273 sq km)
Population: 2,102,000
Capital: Ljubljana,
pop. 286,000
Currency: euro (EUR)
Religion: Roman Catholic
Language: Slovenian

Solomon Islands

Area: 11,157 sq mi
(28,896 sq km)
Population: 691,000
Capital: Honiara, pop. 82,000
Currency: Solomon Islands dollar (SBD)
Religions: Protestant, Roman Catholic
Languages: Melanesian pidgin, English,
Indigenous languages

Somalia

Area: 246,201 sq mi
(637,657 sq km)
Population: 12,095,000
Capital: Mogadishu, pop. 2,388,000
Currency: Somali shilling (SOS)
Religion: Muslim
Languages: Somali, Arabic, Italian, English

South Africa

Area: 470,693 sq mi (1,219,090 sq km)
Population: 56,979,000
Capitals: Pretoria (Tshwane),
pop. 2,655,000; Cape Town, pop.
4,710,000; Bloemfontein, pop. 578,000
Currency: rand (ZAR)
Religions: Christian, traditional or animist
Languages: isiZulu, isiXhosa, other Indigenous languages,
Afrikaans, English

South Korea

Area: 38,502 sq mi
(99,720 sq km)
Population: 51,715,000
Capital: Seoul, pop. 9,968,000
Currency: South Korean won (KRW)
Religions: Protestant, Buddhist, Roman Catholic
Languages: Korean, English

South Sudan

Area: 248,777 sq mi
(644,329 sq km)
Population: 10,984,000
Capital: Juba, pop. 421,000
Currency: South Sudanese pound (SSP)
Religions: animist, Christian, Muslim
Languages: English, Arabic, Dinka, Nuer, Bari,
Zande, Shilluk

Spain

Area: 195,124 sq mi (505,370 sq km)
Population: 47,261,000
Capital: Madrid, pop. 6,669,000
Currency: euro (EUR)
Religion: Roman Catholic
Languages: Castilian Spanish, Catalan,
Galician, Basque

Sri Lanka

Area: 25,332 sq mi
(65,610 sq km)
Population: 23,044,000
Capitals: Colombo, pop. 619,000;
Sri Jayewardenepura Kotte, pop. 103,000
Currency: Sri Lankan rupee (LKR)
Religions: Buddhist, Hindu, Muslim, Roman Catholic
Languages: Sinhala, Tamil, English

St. Kitts and Nevis

Area: 101 sq mi (261 sq km)
Population: 54,000
Capital: Basseterre, pop. 14,000
Currency: East Caribbean
dollar (XCD)
Religions: Protestant, Roman Catholic
Language: English

St. Lucia

Area: 238 sq mi (616 sq km)
Population: 167,000
Capital: Castries,
pop. 22,000
Currency: East Caribbean dollar (XCD)
Religions: Roman Catholic, Protestant
Languages: English, French patois

St. Vincent and the Grenadines

Area: 150 sq mi (389 sq km)
Population: 101,000
Capital: Kingstown, pop. 27,000
Currency: East Caribbean dollar (XCD)
Religions: Protestant, Roman Catholic
Languages: English, Vincentian Creole English, French patois

Switzerland

Area: 15,937 sq mi (41,277 sq km)
Population: 8,454,000
Capital: Bern, pop. 434,000
Currency: Swiss franc (CHF)
Religions: Roman Catholic, Protestant, other Christian, Muslim
Languages: German (Swiss German), French, Italian, Romansch

Sudan

Area: 718,723 sq mi (1,861,484 sq km)
Population: 46,751,000
Capital: Khartoum, pop. 5,989,000
Currency: Sudanese pound (SDG)
Religion: Muslim
Languages: Arabic, English, Nubian, Ta Bedawie, Fur

Syria

Area: 71,870 sq mi (186,142 sq km)
Population: 20,384,000
Capital: Damascus, pop. 2,440,000
Currency: Syrian pound (SYP)
Religions: Muslim, Eastern Orthodox, Oriental Orthodox, Eastern Catholic, other Christian
Languages: Arabic, Kurdish, Armenian, Aramaic, Circassian, French, English

SUDAN is home to MORE PYRAMIDS than EGYPT.

Tajikistan

Area: 55,637 sq mi (144,100 sq km)
Population: 8,991,000
Capital: Dushanbe, pop. 938,000
Currency: Tajikistani somoni (TJS)
Religion: Muslim
Languages: Tajik, Uzbek

Suriname

Area: 63,251 sq mi (163,820 sq km)
Population: 615,000
Capital: Paramaribo, pop. 239,000
Currency: Surinamese dollar (SRD)
Religions: Protestant, Hindu, Roman Catholic, Muslim
Languages: Dutch, English, Sranang Tongo, Caribbean Hindustani, Javanese

Tanzania

Area: 365,754 sq mi (947,300 sq km)
Population: 62,093,000
Capitals: Dar es Salaam, pop. 7,047,000; Dodoma, pop. 262,000
Currency: Tanzanian shilling (TZS)
Religions: Christian, Muslim
Languages: Kiswahili (Swahili), Kiunguja, English, Arabic, local languages

Sweden

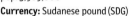

Area: 173,860 sq mi (450,295 sq km)
Population: 10,262,000
Capital: Stockholm, pop. 1,657,000
Currency: Swedish krona (SEK)
Religion: Protestant
Language: Swedish

Thailand

Area: 198,117 sq mi (513,120 sq km)
Population: 69,481,000
Capital: Bangkok, pop. 10,723,000
Currency: baht (THB)
Religion: Buddhist
Languages: Thai, English

Timor-Leste

Area: 5,743 sq mi
(14,874 sq km)
Population: 1,414,000
Capital: Dili, pop. 281,000
Currency: U.S. dollar (USD)
Religion: Roman Catholic
Languages: Tetun, Mambai, Makasai, Portuguese, Indonesian, English

A record-setting average of 253 REEF FISH SPECIES swim off the shores of TIMOR-LESTE'S ATAURO ISLAND.

Togo

Area: 21,925 sq mi (56,785 sq km)
Population: 8,283,000
Capital: Lomé, pop. 1,874,000
Currency: CFA franc BCEAO (XOF)
Religions: Christian, folk religion, Muslim
Languages: French, Ewe, Mina, Kabye, Dagomba

Tonga

Area: 288 sq mi (747 sq km)
Population: 106,000
Capital: Nuku'alofa,
pop. 23,000
Currency: pa'anga (TOP)
Religions: Protestant, Mormon, Roman Catholic
Languages: Tongan, English

Trinidad and Tobago

Area: 1,980 sq mi (5,128 sq km)
Population: 1,221,000
Capital: Port of Spain,
pop. 544,000
Currency: Trinidad and Tobago dollar (TTD)
Religions: Protestant, Roman Catholic, Hindu, Muslim
Languages: English, Creole, Caribbean Hindustani, Spanish, Chinese

Tunisia

Area: 63,170 sq mi
(163,610 sq km)
Population: 11,811,000
Capital: Tunis, pop. 2,403,000
Currency: Tunisian dinar (TND)
Religion: Muslim
Languages: Arabic, French, Berber

Turkey

Area: 302,535 sq mi
(783,562 sq km)
Population: 82,482,000
Capital: Ankara, pop. 5,216,000
Currency: Turkish lira (TRY)
Religion: Muslim
Languages: Turkish, Kurdish

Turkmenistan

Area: 188,456 sq mi
(488,100 sq km)
Population: 5,580,000
Capital: Ashgabat, pop. 865,000
Currency: Turkmenistani manat (TMT)
Religions: Muslim, Eastern Orthodox
Languages: Turkmen, Russian

Tuvalu

Area: 10 sq mi (26 sq km)
Population: 11,000
Capital: Funafuti,
pop. 7,000
Currency: Australian dollar (AUD)
Religion: Protestant
Languages: Tuvaluan, English, Samoan, Kiribati

Uganda

Area: 93,065 sq mi
(241,038 sq km)
Population: 44,712,000
Capital: Kampala, pop. 3,470,000
Currency: Ugandan shilling (UGX)
Religions: Protestant, Roman Catholic, Muslim
Languages: English, Ganda (Luganda), local languages, Swahili, Arabic

Ukraine

Area: 233,032 sq mi
(603,550 sq km)
Population: 43,746,000
Capital: Kyiv, pop. 3,001,000
Currency: hryvnia (UAH)
Religions: Eastern Orthodox, Eastern Catholic, Roman Catholic, Protestant
Languages: Ukrainian, Russian

United Kingdom

Area: 94,058 sq mi
(243,610 sq km)
Population: 66,052,000
Capital: London, pop. 9,426,000
Currency: pound sterling (GBP)
Religions: Protestant, Roman Catholic
Languages: English, Scots, Scottish Gaelic, Welsh, Irish, Cornish

United Arab Emirates

Area: 32,278 sq mi (83,600 sq km)
Population: 9,857,000
Capital: Abu Dhabi,
pop. 1,512,000
Currency: UAE dirham (AED)
Religions: Muslim, Christian
Languages: Arabic, English, Hindi, Malayam, Urdu, Pashto, Tagalog, Persian

United States

Area: 3,796,741 sq mi
(9,833,517 sq km)
Population: 334,998,000
Capital: Washington, D.C.,
pop. 5,378,000
Currency: U.S. dollar (USD)
Religions: Protestant, Roman Catholic
Languages: English, Spanish, Native American languages

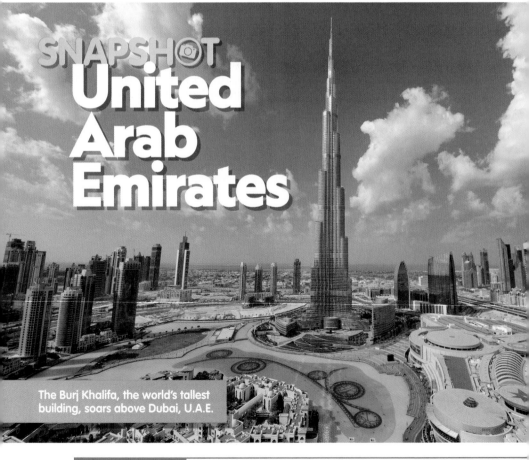

SNAPSHOT
United Arab Emirates

The Burj Khalifa, the world's tallest building, soars above Dubai, U.A.E.

COLOR KEY ● Africa ● Australia, New Zealand, and Oceania

Uruguay

Area: 68,037 sq mi
(176,215 sq km)
Population: 3,398,000
Capital: Montevideo, pop. 1,760,000
Currency: Uruguayan peso (UYU)
Religions: Roman Catholic, other Christian
Language: Spanish

Uzbekistan

Area: 172,742 sq mi
(447,400 sq km)
Population: 30,843,000
Capital: Tashkent,
pop. 2,545,000
Currency: Uzbekistan sum (UZS)
Religions: Muslim, Eastern Orthodox
Languages: Uzbek, Russian, Tajik

Vanuatu

Area: 4,706 sq mi (12,189 sq km)
Population: 303,000
Capital: Port-Vila, pop. 53,000
Currency: Vatu (VUV)
Religions: Protestant, Roman Catholic
Languages: Local languages, Bislama, English, French

Vatican City

Area: 0.2 sq mi (0.4 sq km)
Population: 1,000
Capital: Vatican City, pop. 1,000
Currency: euro (EUR)
Religion: Roman Catholic
Languages: Italian, Latin, French

Venezuela

Area: 352,144 sq mi
(912,050 sq km)
Population: 29,069,000
Capital: Caracas, pop. 2,946,000
Currency: bolivar soberano (VES)
Religion: Roman Catholic
Languages: Spanish, Indigenous languages

Vietnam

Area: 127,881 sq mi
(331,210 sq km)
Population: 102,790,000
Capital: Hanoi, pop. 4,875,000
Currency: dong (VND)
Religions: Buddhist, Roman Catholic
Languages: Vietnamese, English, French, Chinese, Khmer, Mon-Khmer, Malayo-Polynesian

Yemen

Area: 203,850 sq mi
(527,968 sq km)
Population: 30,399,000
Capital: Sanaa, pop. 3,075,000
Currency: Yemeni rial (YER)
Religion: Muslim
Language: Arabic

Zambia

Area: 290,587 sq mi
(752,618 sq km)
Population: 19,078,000
Capital: Lusaka, pop. 2,906,000
Currency: Zambian kwacha (ZMW)
Religions: Protestant, Roman Catholic
Languages: Bembe, Nyanja, Tonga, other Indigenous languages, English

You can spot
TERMITE HILLS
as **TALL** as a
HOUSE in ZAMBIA.

Zimbabwe

Area: 150,872 sq mi
(390,757 sq km)
Population: 14,830,000
Capital: Harare, pop. 1,542,000
Currency: Zimbabwean dollar (ZWL)
Religions: Protestant, Roman Catholic, other Christian
Languages: Shona, Ndebele, English, Indigenous languages

THE POLITICAL UNITED STATES

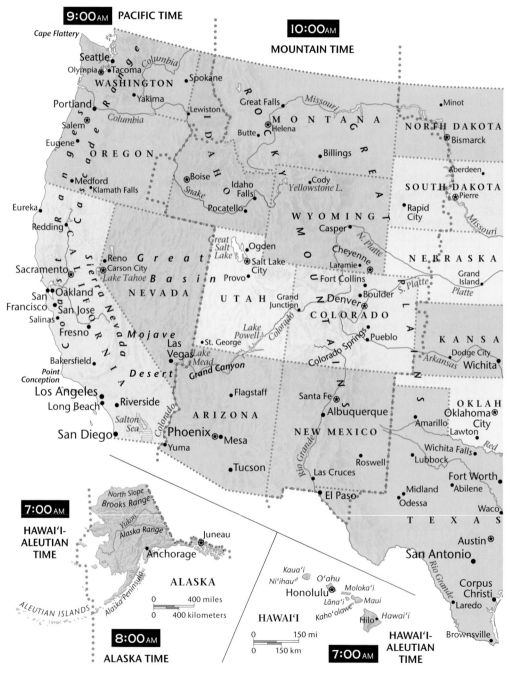

9:00AM PACIFIC TIME

10:00AM MOUNTAIN TIME

Cape Flattery

Seattle
Olympia · Tacoma
WASHINGTON · Spokane
Portland · Yakima
Salem
Eugene
OREGON

Columbia
Columbia

Lewiston
Great Falls
Missouri
MONTANA
Butte Helena
Billings
Minot
NORTH DAKOTA
Bismarck
Aberdeen
SOUTH DAKOTA
Pierre

Medford
Klamath Falls
IDAHO
Boise
Idaho Falls
Snake
Pocatello
Cody
Yellowstone L.
WYOMING
Casper
N. Platte
Cheyenne
Laramie
Fort Collins
Rapid City
Missouri
NEBRASKA
Grand Island
Platte

Eureka
Redding
CALIFORNIA
Sacramento
San Francisco
Oakland
San Jose
Salinas
Fresno
Bakersfield
Point Conception

Reno Great
Carson City
Lake Tahoe Basin
NEVADA
Sierra Nevada
Mojave
Desert

Great Salt Lake
Ogden
Salt Lake City
Provo
UTAH
Grand Junction
Lake Powell
St. George
Las Vegas
Lake Mead
Grand Canyon
Colorado

Denver
Boulder
COLORADO
Colorado Springs
Pueblo
S. Platte
Arkansas
KANSAS
Dodge City
Wichita
Red

Los Angeles
Long Beach · Riverside
San Diego
Salton Sea
Colorado

Flagstaff
ARIZONA
Phoenix · Mesa
Yuma
Tucson

Santa Fe
Albuquerque
NEW MEXICO
Rio Grande
Las Cruces
Roswell
El Paso

Amarillo
Lawton
Wichita Falls
Lubbock
OKLAH
Oklahoma City
Fort Worth
Midland Abilene
Odessa
Waco
TEXAS
Austin
San Antonio
Corpus Christi
Laredo
Brownsville

7:00AM HAWAI'I-ALEUTIAN TIME

North Slope
Brooks Range
Yukon
Alaska Range
Juneau
Anchorage
ALASKA
Alaska Peninsula
ALEUTIAN ISLANDS

0 400 miles
0 400 kilometers

8:00AM ALASKA TIME

Kaua'i
Ni'ihau
O'ahu
Moloka'i
Honolulu
Lāna'i Maui
HAWAI'I
Kaho'olawe Hawai'i
Hilo

0 150 mi
0 150 km

7:00AM HAWAI'I-ALEUTIAN TIME

The United States is made up of 50 states joined like a giant quilt. Each is unique, but together they make a national fabric held together by a constitution and a federal government. State boundaries, outlined in dotted lines on the map, set apart internal political units within the country. The national capital—Washington, D.C.—is marked by a star in a double circle. The capital of each state is marked by a star in a single circle.

11:00AM
CENTRAL TIME

12:00NOON
EASTERN TIME

0   300 miles
0   300 kilometers
Albers Conic Equal-Area Projection

TIME ZONES: Earth is divided into 24 time zones, each about 15 degrees of longitude wide, reflecting the distance Earth turns from west to east each hour. The U.S. is divided into six time zones, indicated by red dotted lines on the map.

THE PHYSICAL UNITED STATES

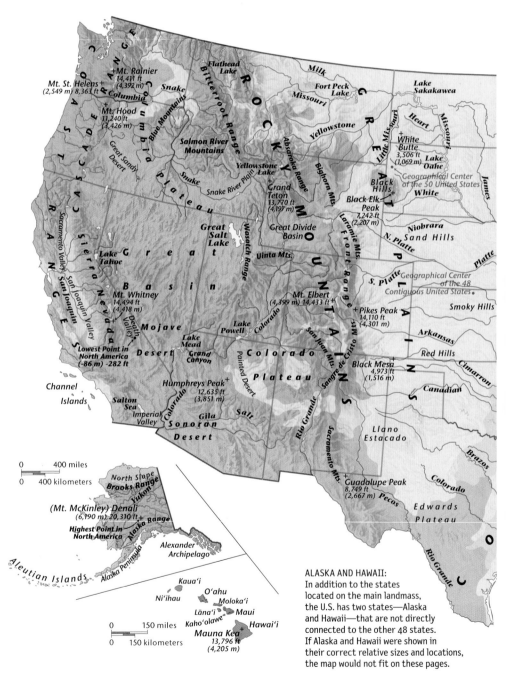

Mt. Rainier
14,411 ft
(4,392 m)
Mt. St. Helens +
(2,549 m) 8,363 ft
Columbia

Mt. Hood
11,240 ft
(3,426 m)

CASCADE RANGE

Columbia Plateau

Columbia

Snake

Blue Mountains

Great Sandy Desert

Snake

BITTERROOT RANGE

Flathead Lake

Salmon River Mountains

Snake River Plain

Yellowstone Lake

Grand Teton
13,770 ft
(4,197 m)

ROCKY

Absaroka Range

Bighorn Mts.

Milk

Missouri

Fort Peck Lake

Yellowstone

Little Missouri

Lake Sakakawea

Heart

Missouri

White Butte
3,506 ft
(1,069 m)

Lake Oahe

Geographical Center of the 50 United States

White

James

Great Salt Lake

Wasatch Range

Uinta Mts.

Great Divide Basin

M O U N T A I N S

Black Hills

Black Elk Peak
7,242 ft
(2,207 m)

Niobrara

Sand Hills

N. Platte

GREAT PLAINS

Platte

Lake Tahoe

Sierra Nevada

G r e a t   B a s i n

Mt. Whitney
14,494 ft
(4,418 m)

Death Valley

Mojave

Lake Powell

Mt. Elbert
(4,399 m) 14,433 ft +

Colorado

San Juan Mts.

Laramie Mts.

Front Range

S. Platte

Geographical Center of the 48 Contiguous United States

Pikes Peak
14,110 ft
(4,301 m)

Smoky Hills

Arkansas

Red Hills

Sacramento Valley

San Joaquin

San Joaquin Valley

Lowest Point in North America
(-86 m) -282 ft

Death Valley

Desert

Lake Mead

Grand Canyon

C o l o r a d o   P l a t e a u

Painted Desert

Colorado

Sangre de Cristo Mts.

Black Mesa
4,973 ft
(1,516 m)

Canadian

Cimarron

Channel

Islands

Salton Sea

Imperial Valley

Humphreys Peak +
12,635 ft
(3,851 m)

Colorado

Gila

S o n o r a n   D e s e r t

Salt

Rio Grande

Llano Estacado

Brazos

0   400 miles

0   400 kilometers

North Slope

Brooks Range

Yukon

(Mt. McKinley) Denali
(6,190 m), 20,310 ft +

Highest Point in North America

Alaska Range

Sacramento Mts.

Guadalupe Peak
8,749 ft
(2,667 m)

Pecos

Colorado

Edwards Plateau

Aleutian Islands

Alaska Peninsula

Alexander Archipelago

Kaua'i

Ni'ihau

O'ahu

Moloka'i

Lāna'i   Maui

Kaho'olawe   Hawai'i

Mauna Kea
13,796 ft
(4,205 m)

0   150 miles

0   150 kilometers

Rio Grande

ALASKA AND HAWAII:
In addition to the states located on the main landmass, the U.S. has two states—Alaska and Hawaii—that are not directly connected to the other 48 states. If Alaska and Hawaii were shown in their correct relative sizes and locations, the map would not fit on these pages.

Stretching from the Atlantic Ocean in the east to the Pacific Ocean in the west, the United States is the third largest country (by area) in the world. Its physical diversity ranges from mountains to fertile plains to dry deserts. Shading on the map indicates changes in elevation, while colors show different vegetation patterns.

0   400 miles

0   400 kilometers

Albers Conic Equal-Area Projection

NATURAL VEGETATION

- NEEDLELEAF FOREST
- BROADLEAF FOREST
- MIXED FOREST
- GRASSLAND
- TROPICAL VEGETATION
- DESERT
- TUNDRA

Lake of the Woods

Isle Royale

Eagle Mt.+ 2,301 ft (701 m)

Lake Superior

Upper Peninsula

Source of the Mississippi (Lake Itasca)

Red River of the North

Minnesota

Mississippi

Wisconsin

Lake Winnebago

Lake Michigan

Lower Peninsula

Lake Huron

Lake St. Clair

Lake Erie

Lake Ontario

Niagara Falls

Lake Champlain

+Mt. Washington 6,288 ft (1,917 m)

Cape Cod

Adirondack Mts.

Green Mts.

Connecticut

Catskill Mts.

Hudson

Allegheny

Delaware

Long Island

Cedar

C E N T R A L

L O W L A N D

Des Moines

Illinois

Wabash

Ohio

Allegheny Plateau

Susquehanna

Potomac

Delaware Bay

Missouri

James

Chesapeake Bay

Lake of the Ozarks

Harry S. Truman Res.

Ozark Plateau

Kentucky Lake

Lake Barkley

Ohio

Tennessee

Cumberland

Cumberland Plateau

Appalachian

A P P A L A C H I A N   M O U N T A I N S

Roanoke

Cape Hatteras

Magazine Mt. 2,753 ft (839 m) +

Arkansas

Ouachita Mts.

+Mt. Mitchell 6,684 ft (2,037 m)

Cape Fear

Great Pee Dee

Red

Ouachita

Mississippi

Black Belt

Cape Fear

Trinity

Sabine

Red

Savannah

Altamaha

C O A S T A L   P L A I N

Chattahoochee

Okefenokee Swamp

Lake Pontchartrain

Mississippi River Delta

Cape Canaveral

Lake Okeechobee

The Everglades

Florida Keys

THE STATES

From sea to shining sea, the United States of America is a nation of diversity. In the 244 years since its creation, the nation has grown to become home to a wide range of peoples, industries, and cultures. The following pages present a general overview of all 50 states in the United States.

The country is generally divided into five large regions: the Northeast, the Southeast, the Midwest, the Southwest, and the West. Though loosely defined, these zones tend to share important similarities, including climate, history, and geography. The color key below provides a guide to which states are in each region.

The flag of each state and highlights of demography and industry are also included. These details offer a brief overview of each state.

In addition, each state's official flower and bird are identified.

Color Key by Region

Alabama

Nickname: Heart of Dixie
Area: 52,420 sq mi (135,767 sq km)
Population: 4,922,000
Capital: Montgomery; population 360,000
Statehood: December 14, 1819; 22nd state
State flower/bird: Camellia/yellowhammer (northern flicker)

Residents of **MAGNOLIA SPRINGS, ALABAMA,** get their **MAIL DELIVERED BY BOAT.**

Alaska

Nickname: Last Frontier
Area: 665,384 sq mi (1,723,337 sq km)
Population: 731,000
Capital: Juneau; population 32,000
Statehood: January 3, 1959; 49th state
State flower/bird: Forget-me-not/ willow ptarmigan

Arizona

Nickname: Grand Canyon State
Area: 113,990 sq mi (295,234 sq km)
Population: 7,421,000
Capital: Phoenix; population 4,584,000
Statehood: February 14, 1912; 48th state
State flower/bird: Saguaro cactus blossom/ cactus wren

Arkansas

Nickname: Natural State
Area: 53,179 sq mi (137,732 sq km)
Population: 3,031,000
Capital: Little Rock; population 521,000
Statehood: June 15, 1836; 25th state
State flower/bird: Apple blossom/ mockingbird

California

Nickname: Golden State
Area: 163,695 sq mi (423,967 sq km)
Population: 39,368,000
Capital: Sacramento; population 2,155,000
Statehood: September 9, 1850; 31st state
State flower/bird: California poppy/ California quail

Colorado

Nickname: Centennial State
Area: 104,094 sq mi (269,601 sq km)
Population: 5,808,000
Capital: Denver; population 2,862,000
Statehood: August 1, 1876; 38th state
State flower/bird: Rocky Mountain columbine/ lark bunting

COLOR KEY ● Northeast ● Southeast

Connecticut

Nickname: Constitution State
Area: 5,543 sq mi (14,357 sq km)
Population: 3,557,000
Capital: Hartford; population 1,004,000
Statehood: January 9, 1788; 5th state
State flower/bird: Mountain laurel/
American robin

Delaware

Nickname: First State
Area: 2,489 sq mi (6,446 sq km)
Population: 987,000
Capital: Dover; population 38,000
Statehood: December 7, 1787; 1st state
State flower/bird: Peach blossom/
blue hen chicken

> **DELAWARE's state colors, blue and buff, were inspired by George Washington's military UNIFORM.**

Florida

Nickname: Sunshine State
Area: 65,758 sq mi (170,312 sq km)
Population: 21,733,000
Capital: Tallahassee; population 195,000
Statehood: March 3, 1845; 27th state
State flower/bird: Orange blossom/
mockingbird

Georgia

Nickname: Peach State
Area: 59,425 sq mi
(153,910 sq km)
Population: 10,710,000
Capital: Atlanta; population 5,911,000
Statehood: January 2, 1788; 4th state
State flower/bird: Cherokee rose/brown thrasher

Hawaii

Nickname: Aloha State
Area: 10,932 sq mi
(28,313 sq km)
Population: 1,407,000
Capital: Honolulu; population 898,000
Statehood: August 21, 1959; 50th state
State flower/bird: Pua aloalo/
Nene (Hawaiian goose)

Idaho

Nickname: Gem State
Area: 83,569 sq mi (216,443 sq km)
Population: 1,827,000
Capital: Boise; population 455,000
Statehood: July 3, 1890; 43rd state
State flower/bird: Syringa/
mountain bluebird

Illinois

Nickname: Prairie State
Area: 57,914 sq mi (149,995 sq km)
Population: 12,588,000
Capital: Springfield; population 114,000
Statehood: December 3, 1818; 21st state
State flower/bird: Violet/northern cardinal

Indiana

Nickname: Hoosier State
Area: 36,420 sq mi
(94,326 sq km)
Population: 6,755,000
Capital: Indianapolis; population 1,833,000
Statehood: December 11, 1816; 19th state
State flower/bird: Peony/northern cardinal

Iowa

Nickname: Hawkeye State
Area: 56,273 sq mi (145,746 sq km)
Population: 3,164,000
Capital: Des Moines; population 552,000
Statehood: December 28, 1846; 29th state
State flower/bird: Wild prairie rose/
American goldfinch

Kansas

Nickname: Sunflower State
Area: 82,278 sq mi (213,100 sq km)
Population: 2,914,000
Capital: Topeka; population 125,000
Statehood: January 29, 1861; 34th state
State flower/bird: Wild native sunflower/
western meadowlark

Kentucky

Nickname: Bluegrass State
Area: 40,408 sq mi
(104,656 sq km)
Population: 4,477,000
Capital: Frankfort; population 28,000
Statehood: June 1, 1792; 15th state
State flower/bird: Goldenrod/northern cardinal

Louisiana

Nickname: Pelican State
Area: 52,378 sq mi
(135,659 sq km)
Population: 4,645,000
Capital: Baton Rouge; population 746,000
Statehood: April 30, 1812; 18th state
State flower/bird: Magnolia/brown pelican

Maine

Nickname: Pine Tree State
Area: 35,380 sq mi (91,633 sq km)
Population: 1,350,000
Capital: Augusta; population 19,000
Statehood: March 15, 1820; 23rd state
State flower/bird: White pine cone and tassel/
black-capped chickadee

Maryland

Nickname: Old Line State
Area: 12,406 sq mi (32,131 sq km)
Population: 6,056,000
Capital: Annapolis; population 39,000
Statehood: April 28, 1788; 7th state
State flower/bird: Black-eyed Susan/
Baltimore oriole

Massachusetts

Nickname: Bay State
Area: 10,554 sq mi (27,336 sq km)
Population: 6,894,000
Capital: Boston; population 4,315,000
Statehood: February 6, 1788; 6th state
State flower/bird: Mayflower/
black-capped chickadee

Michigan

Nickname: Wolverine State
Area: 96,714 sq mi (250,487 sq km)
Population: 9,967,000
Capital: Lansing; population 326,000
Statehood: January 26, 1837; 26th state
State flower/bird: Apple blossom/
American robin

You're never more than 85 miles (137 km) away from a GREAT LAKE IN MICHIGAN.

Minnesota

Nickname: North Star State
Area: 86,936 sq mi (225,163 sq km)
Population: 5,657,000
Capital: St. Paul; population 2,946,000
Statehood: May 11, 1858; 32nd state
State flower/bird: Pink and white lady slipper/
common loon

Mississippi

Nickname: Magnolia State
Area: 48,432 sq mi (125,438 sq km)
Population: 2,967,000
Capital: Jackson; population 426,000
Statehood: December 10, 1817; 20th state
State flower/bird: Magnolia/mockingbird

COLOR KEY ● Northeast ● Southeast

Missouri

Nickname: Show-Me State
Area: 69,707 sq mi (180,540 sq km)
Population: 6,152,000
Capital: Jefferson City; population 43,000
Statehood: August 10, 1821; 24th state
State flower/bird: Hawthorn blossom/
eastern bluebird

Montana

Nickname: Treasure State
Area: 147,040 sq mi (380,831 sq km)
Population: 1,081,000
Capital: Helena; population 33,000
Statehood: November 8, 1889; 41st state
State flower/bird: Bitterroot/
western meadowlark

A 1959 EARTHQUAKE in MONTANA created a lake five miles (8 km) long.

Nebraska

Nickname: Cornhusker State
Area: 77,348 sq mi (200,330 sq km)
Population: 1,938,000
Capital: Lincoln; population 289,000
Statehood: March 1, 1867; 37th state
State flower/bird: Goldenrod/
western meadowlark

Nevada

Nickname: Silver State
Area: 110,572 sq mi (286,380 sq km)
Population: 3,138,000
Capital: Carson City; population 56,000
Statehood: October 31, 1864; 36th state
State flower/bird: Sagebrush/
mountain bluebird

New Hampshire

Nickname: Granite State
Area: 9,349 sq mi (24,214 sq km)
Population: 1,366,000
Capital: Concord; population 44,000
Statehood: June 21, 1788; 9th state
State flower/bird: Purple lilac/purple finch

New Jersey

Nickname: Garden State
Area: 8,723 sq mi (22,591 sq km)
Population: 8,882,000
Capital: Trenton; population 331,000
Statehood: December 18, 1787; 3rd state
State flower/bird: Violet/Eastern goldfinch

New Mexico

Nickname: Land of Enchantment
Area: 121,590 sq mi
(314,917 sq km)
Population: 2,106,000
Capital: Santa Fe; population 85,000
Statehood: January 6, 1912; 47th state
State flower/bird: Yucca/greater roadrunner

New York

Nickname: Empire State
Area: 54,555 sq mi
(141,297 sq km)
Population: 19,337,000
Capital: Albany; population 632,000
Statehood: July 26, 1788; 11th state
State flower/bird: Rose/eastern bluebird

North Carolina

Nickname: Tar Heel State
Area: 53,819 sq mi (139,391 sq km)
Population: 10,601,000
Capital: Raleigh; population 1,498,000
Statehood: November 21, 1789; 12th state
State flower/bird: Flowering dogwood/
northern cardinal

● Midwest ● Southwest ● West

North Dakota

Nickname: Peace Garden State
Area: 70,698 sq mi (183,108 sq km)
Population: 765,000
Capital: Bismarck; population 74,000
Statehood: November 2, 1889; 39th state
State flower/bird: Wild prairie rose/
western meadowlark

Oregon

Nickname: Beaver State
Area: 98,379 sq mi (254,799 sq km)
Population: 4,242,000
Capital: Salem; population 174,000
Statehood: February 14, 1859; 33rd state
State flower/bird: Oregon grape/
western meadowlark

Ohio

Nickname: Buckeye State
Area: 44,826 sq mi (116,098 sq km)
Population: 11,693,000
Capital: Columbus; population 1,666,000
Statehood: February 19, 1803; 17th state
State flower/bird: Scarlet carnation/
northern cardinal

Pennsylvania

Nickname: Keystone State
Area: 46,054 sq mi (119,280 sq km)
Population: 12,783,000
Capital: Harrisburg; population 550,000
Statehood: December 12, 1787; 2nd state
State flower/bird: Mountain laurel/
ruffed grouse

Oklahoma

Nickname: Sooner State
Area: 69,899 sq mi (181,037 sq km)
Population: 3,981,000
Capital: Oklahoma City; population 998,000
Statehood: November 16, 1907; 46th state
State flower/bird: Oklahoma rose/
scissor-tailed flycatcher

Rhode Island

Nickname: Ocean State
Area: 1,545 sq mi (4,001 sq km)
Population: 1,057,000
Capital: Providence; population 1,200,000
Statehood: May 29, 1790; 13th state
State flower/bird: Violet/
Rhode Island red

3 cool things about OKLAHOMA

1. The world's first parking meter, known as Park-O-Meter No. 1, was installed in Oklahoma City in 1935.

2. Oklahoma's Cimarron County is the only county in the U.S. that touches four states: Colorado, New Mexico, Texas, and Kansas.

3. The swimming pool in the backyard of the governor's mansion is shaped like the state of Oklahoma.

South Carolina

Nickname: Palmetto State
Area: 32,020 sq mi (82,933 sq km)
Population: 5,218,000
Capital: Columbia; population 730,000
Statehood: May 23, 1788; 8th state
State flower/bird: Yellow jessamine/
Carolina wren

South Dakota

Nickname: Mount Rushmore State
Area: 77,116 sq mi (199,729 sq km)
Population: 893,000
Capital: Pierre; population 14,000
Statehood: November 2, 1889; 40th state
State flower/bird: American pasque/
ring-necked pheasant

COLOR KEY ● Northeast ● Southeast

Tennessee

Nickname: Volunteer State
Area: 42,144 sq mi (109,153 sq km)
Population: 6,887,000
Capital: Nashville; population 1,272,000
Statehood: June 1, 1796; 16th state
State flower/bird: Iris/mockingbird

Texas

Nickname: Lone Star State
Area: 268,596 sq mi (695,662 sq km)
Population: 29,361,000
Capital: Austin; population 2,117,000
Statehood: December 29, 1845; 28th state
State flower/bird: Bluebonnet/mockingbird

Utah

Nickname: Beehive State
Area: 84,897 sq mi (219,882 sq km)
Population: 3,250,000
Capital: Salt Lake City; population 1,180,000
Statehood: January 4, 1896; 45th state
State flower/bird: Sego lily/California gull

Vermont

Nickname: Green Mountain State
Area: 9,616 sq mi (24,906 sq km)
Population: 623,000
Capital: Montpelier; population 7,000
Statehood: March 4, 1791; 14th state
State flower/bird: Red clover/hermit thrush

Virginia
Nickname: Old Dominion
Area: 42,775 sq mi (110,787 sq km)
Population: 8,591,000
Capital: Richmond; population 1,117,000
Statehood: June 25, 1788; 10th state
State flower/bird: American dogwood/northern cardinal

Washington

Nickname: Evergreen State
Area: 71,298 sq mi (184,661 sq km)
Population: 7,694,000
Capital: Olympia; population 53,000
Statehood: November 11, 1889; 42nd state
State flower/bird: Coast rhododendron/American goldfinch

West Virginia

Nickname: Mountain State
Area: 24,230 sq mi (62,756 sq km)
Population: 1,785,000
Capital: Charleston; population 47,000
Statehood: June 20, 1863; 35th state
State flower/bird: Rhododendron/northern cardinal

In the late 1950s, the U.S. government built a **TOP SECRET BUNKER BENEATH A HOTEL** in **WHITE SULPHUR SPRINGS, WEST VIRGINIA.**

Wisconsin

Nickname: Badger State
Area: 65,496 sq mi (169,635 sq km)
Population: 5,833,000
Capital: Madison; population 494,000
Statehood: May 29, 1848; 30th state
State flower/bird: Wood violet/American robin

Wyoming

Nickname: Equality State
Area: 97,813 sq mi (253,335 sq km)
Population: 582,000
Capital: Cheyenne; population 64,000
Statehood: July 10, 1890; 44th state
State flower/bird: Indian paintbrush/western meadowlark

● Midwest ● Southwest ● West

THE TERRITORIES

The United States has 14 territories— political divisions that are not states. Three of these are in the Caribbean Sea, and the other 11 are in the Pacific Ocean.

St. John, U.S. Virgin Islands

Convention Center, San Juan, Puerto Rico

Talofofo Falls, Guam

U.S. CARIBBEAN TERRITORIES

Puerto Rico

Area: 5,325 sq mi (13,791 sq km)
Population: 3,143,000
Capital: San Juan; population 2,445,000
Languages: Spanish, English

U.S. Virgin Islands

Area: 733 sq mi (1,898 sq km)
Population: 106,000
Capital: Charlotte Amalie; population 52,000
Languages: English, Spanish, French

U.S. PACIFIC TERRITORIES

American Samoa

Area: 581 sq mi (1,505 sq km)
Population: 46,000
Capital: Pago Pago; population 49,000
Language: Samoan, English

Guam
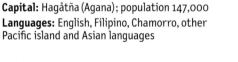
Area: 571 sq mi (1,478 sq km)
Population: 169,000
Capital: Hagåtña (Agana); population 147,000
Languages: English, Filipino, Chamorro, other Pacific island and Asian languages

Northern Mariana Islands

Area: 1,976 sq mi (5,117 sq km)
Population: 52,000
Capital: Capital Hill; population 51,000
Languages: Philippine languages, Chinese, Chamorro, English

Other U.S. Territories
Baker Island, Howland Island, Jarvis Island, Johnston Atoll, Kingman Reef, Midway Islands, Palmyra Atoll, Wake Island, Navassa Island (in the Caribbean)

Figures for capital cities vary widely between sources because of differences in the way areas are defined and other projection methods.

THE U.S. CAPITAL

District of Columbia
Area: 68 sq mi (177 sq km)
Population: 5,378,000

The Lincoln Memorial celebrated its 100th anniversary in 2022.

Abraham Lincoln, who was president during the Civil War and an opponent of slavery, is remembered in the Lincoln Memorial, located at the opposite end of the National Mall from the U.S. Capitol Building.

COLOR KEY ● Territories ● Northeast

weird but true!

Check out these outrageous U.S.A. facts.

Ghost fireflies of the southeastern United States **glow blue.**

So many peeps!

THERE ARE **600 TIMES MORE CHICKENS** THAN HUMANS IN DELAWARE.

JELL-O is the **official state snack** of **UTAH.**

The trunk of the **LARGEST TREE** located in California, weighs as much as **200 AFRICAN ELEPHANTS.**

It's tree-rific!

GENERAL SHERMAN

ACCORDING TO NEW JERSEY FOLKLORE, the **JERSEY DEVIL** is a creature with the head of a goat, bat wings, and a forked tail.

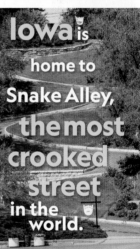

Iowa is home to **Snake Alley,** the most crooked street in the world.

At the Georgia State Fair, the **winning pig** in the pig races gets an **Oreo cookie.**

THE **INK** USED TO PRINT U.S. PAPER MONEY IS **MAGNETIC.**

NUTTY NARROWS BRIDGE in Longview, Washington, was built so **SQUIRRELS CAN SAFELY CROSS A BUSY ROAD.**

WHAT WEIRD DESTINATION IS RIGHT FOR YOU?

Do you like your weirdness from a distance?

Lake Hillier, Middle Island, western Australia
Researchers think that bacteria in this pink lake give it its rosy color. But because the island is used only for research, your visit will be from the air.

Spotted Lake, British Columbia, Canada
The water of this lake evaporates in summer, leaving behind small mineral pools of varying color. They're best viewed from far enough away that you can see all the quirky circles at once.

Skylodge Adventure Suites, Cusco, Peru
Get cozy in your transparent bedroom capsule 1,000 feet (305 m) up—hanging from the side of a cliff in Peru's Sacred Valley.

Or do you prefer your weirdness up close?

Bonne Terre Mine, Missouri, U.S.A.
Scuba dive to your heart's content in this flooded underground lead mine—now the world's largest freshwater dive resort.

RACING ROLLER COASTER

Get ready for a supercharged ride!
Kingda Ka at Six Flags Great Adventure in New Jersey, U.S.A., is not only the world's tallest roller coaster—it's the world's second fastest, too! Hang on tight and check out these heart-pumping facts about the ride.

DROP
418 FEET
(127 M)

PEAK
129- (39-M)
FEET-TALL
CAMEL HUMP

HEIGHT
456 FEET
(142 M)
THAT'S AS TALL AS A
45-STORY BUILDING!

SPEED
128 (206 KM/H)
MILES AN HOUR
HAVE A NEED FOR SPEED? RIDERS REACH TOP SPEED IN JUST **3.5 SECONDS!**

RIDE DURATION
50.6 SECONDS

CLIMB ANGLE
90°

LENGTH **3,118 FEET** (950 M)

347

15 AMAZING FACTS ABOUT THE WORLD

CHINA'S MOUNTAINOUS **BAMBOO FORESTS** can rise sharply—but **GIANT PANDAS** can easily **CLIMB AS HIGH AS 13,000 FEET** (3,962 m) up the slopes.

Earth **ROTATES** on its **AXIS 1.5 MILLISECONDS SLOWER EVERY CENTURY.**

About **12,000 years ago,** the **Sahara** was covered with **millions of trees.**

In Jordan's **ANCIENT CITY OF PETRA,** buildings were carved directly into cliff walls.

The **SURFACE** of the **PACIFIC OCEAN is LARGER** than all of **EARTH'S CONTINENTS** combined.

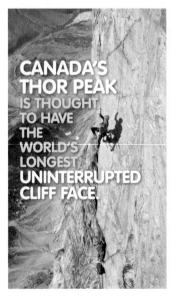

CANADA'S THOR PEAK IS THOUGHT TO HAVE THE WORLD'S LONGEST **UNINTERRUPTED CLIFF FACE.**

More people live in **TAMPA, FLORIDA, U.S.A.,** than in all of **ICELAND.**

Greetings from **TAMPA** FLORIDA

CARTOGRAPHERS used to ride in **HOT-AIR BALLOONS** to view and map land.

When forests **FLOOD ALONG SOUTH AMERICA'S AMAZON RIVER,** river dolphins sometimes swim around trees.

The **Dead Sea's water level drops** more than **3 FEET (0.9 M) EACH YEAR.**

One CAVE in MALAYSIA is big enough to hold eight **JUMBO JETS.**

INDONESIA'S REMOTE FOJA MOUNTAINS ARE HOME TO BIZARRE SPECIES SUCH AS THE PINOCCHIO FROG.

The **CHOCOLATE HILLS** in the **PHILIPPINES** are shaped like giant **Hershey's KISSES.**

KISSES®

The United Arab Emirates has two artificial islands SHAPED LIKE PALM TREES.

The SCORCHING DESERTS of NORTH AFRICA don't hurt the SAND CAT—the animal's PAW PADS ARE COVERED IN FUR to protect its feet from heat.

Bizarre Beaches

THE WORLD'S COOLEST COASTLINES OFFER SO MUCH MORE THAN SANDY SHORES.

BLACK-OUT

WHAT: Punaluʻu Black Sand Beach
WHERE: Big Island, Hawaii, U.S.A.
WHY IT'S BIZARRE: The jet-black sand on this skinny stretch of beach is made up of tiny bits of hardened lava, produced over centuries by the nearby (and still active) Kilauea volcano. This cool spot is also a popular nesting place for hawksbill and green sea turtles.

GLASS FROM THE PAST

WHAT: Glass Beach
WHERE: Fort Bragg, California, U.S.A.
WHY IT'S BIZARRE: Decades ago, the water along this beach was a dumping ground for glass bottles and other debris. Now what was once tossed in the ocean has washed up as a rainbow of shimmering sea glass covering the coves.

FOR THE BIRDS

WHAT: Boulders Beach
WHERE: Harbour Island, Bahamas
WHY IT'S BIZARRE: You might expect to see penguins on an icy coast. But these birds like it hot! African penguins splash in the warm waters of this national park next to 540-million-year-old granite boulders.

TIP-OFF

WHAT: Zlatni Rat
WHERE: Bol, Croatia
WHY IT'S BIZARRE: This narrow beach is a real shape-shifter. Its tip—which sticks out as much as 1,640 feet (500 m) into the crystal blue water—shifts in different directions as a result of wind, waves, and currents.

THE ORIGINAL 7 WONDERS of the WORLD

More than 2,000 years ago, many travelers wrote about sights they had seen on their journeys. Over time, seven of those places made history as the "wonders of the ancient world." There are seven because the Greeks, who made the list, believed the number seven to be magical.

THE NEW 7 WONDERS of the WORLD

Why name new wonders of the world? Most of the original ancient wonders no longer exist. To be eligible for the new list, the wonders had to be human-made before the year 2000 and in preservation. They were selected through a poll of more than 100 million voters!

THE PYRAMIDS OF GIZA, EGYPT
BUILT: ABOUT 2600 B.C.
MASSIVE TOMBS OF EGYPTIAN PHARAOHS LIE INSIDE THIS ANCIENT WONDER—THE ONLY ONE STILL STANDING TODAY.

HANGING GARDENS OF BABYLON, IRAQ
BUILT: DATE UNKNOWN
LEGEND HAS IT THAT THIS GARDEN PARADISE WAS PLANTED ON AN ARTIFICIAL MOUNTAIN, BUT MANY EXPERTS SAY IT NEVER REALLY EXISTED.

TEMPLE OF ARTEMIS AT EPHESUS, TURKEY
BUILT: SIXTH CENTURY B.C.
THIS TOWERING TEMPLE WAS BUILT TO HONOR ARTEMIS, THE GREEK GODDESS OF THE HUNT.

STATUE OF ZEUS, GREECE
BUILT: FIFTH CENTURY B.C.
THIS 40-FOOT (12-M) STATUE DEPICTED THE KING OF THE GREEK GODS.

MAUSOLEUM AT HALICARNASSUS, TURKEY
BUILT: FOURTH CENTURY B.C.
THIS ELABORATE TOMB WAS BUILT FOR KING MAUSOLUS.

COLOSSUS OF RHODES, RHODES (AN ISLAND IN THE AEGEAN SEA)
BUILT: FOURTH CENTURY B.C.
A 110-FOOT (34-M) STATUE HONORING THE GREEK SUN GOD HELIOS.

LIGHTHOUSE OF ALEXANDRIA, EGYPT
BUILT: THIRD CENTURY B.C.
THE WORLD'S FIRST LIGHTHOUSE, IT USED MIRRORS TO REFLECT SUNLIGHT FOR MILES OUT TO SEA.

TAJ MAHAL, INDIA
COMPLETED: 1648
THIS LAVISH TOMB WAS BUILT AS A FINAL RESTING PLACE FOR THE BELOVED WIFE OF EMPEROR SHAH JAHAN.

PETRA, SOUTHWEST JORDAN
COMPLETED: ABOUT 200 B.C.
SOME 30,000 PEOPLE ONCE LIVED IN THIS ROCK CITY CARVED INTO CLIFF WALLS.

MACHU PICCHU, PERU
COMPLETED: ABOUT 1450
OFTEN CALLED THE "LOST CITY IN THE CLOUDS," MACHU PICCHU IS PERCHED 7,710 FEET (2,350 M) HIGH IN THE ANDES.

THE COLOSSEUM, ITALY
COMPLETED: A.D. 80
WILD ANIMALS—AND HUMANS—FOUGHT EACH OTHER TO THE DEATH BEFORE 50,000 SPECTATORS IN THIS ARENA.

CHRIST THE REDEEMER STATUE, BRAZIL
COMPLETED: 1931
TOWERING ATOP CORCOVADO MOUNTAIN, THIS STATUE IS TALLER THAN A 12-STORY BUILDING AND WEIGHS ABOUT 2.5 MILLION POUNDS (1.1 MILLION KG).

CHICHÉN ITZÁ, MEXICO
COMPLETED: 10TH CENTURY
ONCE THE CAPITAL CITY OF THE ANCIENT MAYA EMPIRE, CHICHÉN ITZÁ IS HOME TO THE FAMOUS PYRAMID OF KUKULCÁN.

GREAT WALL OF CHINA, CHINA
COMPLETED: 1644
THE LONGEST HUMAN-MADE STRUCTURE EVER BUILT, IT WINDS OVER AN ESTIMATED 4,500 MILES (7,200 KM).

QUIZ WHIZ

Is your geography knowledge off the map? Quiz yourself to find out!

Write your answers on a piece of paper. Then check them below.

1 Where in the world is Glass Beach?

a. Koh Samui, Thailand
b. Fort Bragg, California, U.S.A.
c. St. George, Bermuda
d. Fort Fisher, North Carolina, U.S.A.

2 What stands out about Lake Hillier in western Australia?

a. its depth
b. its abundance of fish
c. its pink water
d. its heart shape

3 What caused Australia's wangarru population to dwindle?

a. drought
b. poaching
c. cold weather
d. They hopped away to New Zealand.

4 **True or false?** The United Arab Emirates has two artificial islands shaped like pine trees.

5 In Singapore, there are plans underway to plant _____ new trees by 2030.

a. 100
b. 1,000
c. 100,000
d. 1,000,000

Not STUMPED yet? Check out the *NATIONAL GEOGRAPHIC KIDS QUIZ WHIZ* collection for more crazy GEOGRAPHY questions!

ANSWERS: 1. b; 2. c; 3. a; 4. False: They're shaped like palm trees.; 5. d

HOMEWORK HELP

Finding Your Way Around

LATITUDE AND LONGITUDE lines help us determine locations on Earth. Every place on Earth has a special address called absolute location. Imaginary lines called lines of latitude run west to east, parallel to the Equator. These lines measure distance in degrees north or south from the Equator (0° latitude) to the North Pole (90° N) or to the South Pole (90° S). One degree of latitude is approximately 70 miles (113 km).

Lines of longitude run north to south, meeting at the poles. These lines measure distance in degrees east or west from 0° longitude (prime meridian) to 180° longitude. The prime meridian runs through Greenwich, England.

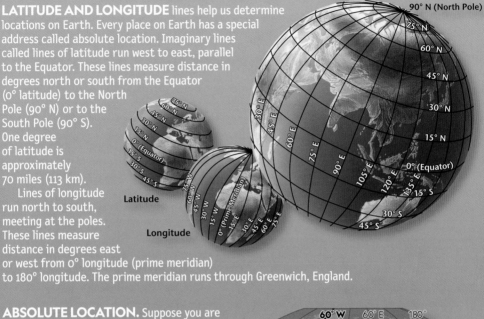

ABSOLUTE LOCATION. Suppose you are using latitude and longitude to play a game of global scavenger hunt. The clue says the prize is hidden at absolute location 30° S, 60° W. You know that the first number is south of the Equator, and the second is west of the prime meridian. On the map at right, find the line of latitude labeled 30° S. Now find the line of longitude labeled 60° W. Trace these lines with your fingers until they meet. Identify this spot. The prize must be located in northern Argentina (see arrow, right).

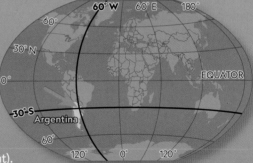

CHALLENGE!

1. Look at the map of Africa on pp. 282–283. Which country can you find at 10° S, 20° E?

2. Look at the map of Asia on pp. 290–291. Which country can you find at 20° N, 80° E?

3. On the map of Europe on pp. 298–299, which country is found at 50° N, 30° E?

4. Look at the map of North America on pp. 302–303. Which country can you find at 20° N, 100° W?

ANSWERS: 1. Angola; 2. India; 3. Ukraine; 4. Mexico

GAME

What in the World?
page 133

Top row: spider, scorpion, beetle
Middle row: termites, centipede,
cockroach
Bottom row: worms, salamander, slug

Signs of the Times
page 134

Signs 3 and 6 are fake.

Noun Town
page 136

The 12 compound nouns are:
1. sleeping bag, 2. eggplant, 3. catfish,
4. bellhop, 5. ladybug, 6. housework,
7. butterfly, 8. limelight, 9. arrowhead,
10. full moon, 11. tree house,
12. coffee table

Find the Hidden Animals
page 137

1. A, 2. E, 3. C, 4. D, 5. B, 6. F

What in the World?
page 138

Top row: surfboards, Great Barrier Reef,
kangaroo
Middle row: cassowary, boomerang, Uluru
Bottom row: flag, koala, Sydney Opera
House

Stump Your Parents
page 139

1. D, 2. B, 3. A, 4. A, 5. B, 6. C, 7. A, 8. C, 9. D,
10. A-3; B-4 ; C-5; D-2; E-1

What in the World?
page 142

Top row: palm tree, sandcastle, snorkel
and mask
Middle row: swimsuit, beach ball, seaweed
Bottom row: seashell, beach towel,
umbrella

Find the Hidden Animals
page 143

1. E, 2. F, 3. D, 4. B, 5. A, 6. C

Stump Your Parents
page 145

1. C, 2. D, 3. B, 4. A, 5. D, 6. C, 7. B, 8. C, 9. A, 10. C

What in the World?
page 146

Top row: raspberries, bicycle, ruby
Middle row: gloves, red fox, peppers
Bottom row: sneaker, pomegranate,
cardinal

Want to Learn More?

Find more information about topics in this book in these National Geographic Kids resources.

Brain Candy series

Weird But True! series

Just Joking series

5,000 Awesome Facts (About Everything!) series

Beastly Bionics
Jennifer Swanson
June 2020

Ultimate U.S. Road Trip Atlas, 2nd edition
Crispin Boyer
April 2020

Fetch! A How to Speak Dog Training Guide
Aubre Andrus
August 2020

Girls Can!
Marissa Sebastian,
Tora Shae Pruden,
Paige Towler
October 2020

Breaking the News
Robin Terry Brown
October 2020

Cutest Animals on the Planet
National Geographic Kids
March 2021

Top Secret
Crispin Boyer
April 2021

Ultimate Rockopedia
Steve Tomecek
December 2020

Your World 2023 (8–17)

p. 11 "Welcome to Otter Island" by Claire Turrell; p. 17 "New Superhero: Ratman" by Kitson Jazynka; all other articles in section by Sarah Wassner Flynn

Kids vs. Plastic (18–33)

pp. 20–23 "What Is Plastic?" & "Deadly Debris" by Julie Beer; pp. 24–25 "There are Some 5.25 Trillion ..." by Sarah Wassner Flynn; p. 27–29 "Your Plastic-Free Guide to Snacks" & "Granola Bar Goodies" by Ella Schwartz; pp. 30–31 "Sea Turtle Rescue" by Julie Beer

Amazing Animals (34–85)

pp. 36–39 "Extraordinary Animals" by Brandon McIntyre (seal), Deborah Kay Underwood (ape), and Amanda Pressner (dingo); p. 38 "Hippo Kisses Hyena" by Katie Stacey; p. 39 "Animal Myths Busted" by C.M. Tomlin; pp. 40–43 "Cute Animal Superlatives" by Sarah Wassner Flynn; pp. 44–45 "What Is Taxonomy?" & "Vertebrates"/"Invertebrates" by Susan K. Donnelly; pp. 46–52 "Comeback Critter: Golden Lion Tamarin" & "Sun Bear Rescue" & "Shark Fest" & "Unicorns of the Sea" by Allyson Shaw; p. 53 "Gnarly Nudibranches" by Sarah Wassner Flynn and Brittany Moya Del Pino; pp. 54–55 "Humpback Whales ..." by Sarah Wassner Flynn; p. 56 "Sit! Stay! Swim!" by Scott Elder; p. 58 "Foxes on Ice" by Karen De Seve; p. 59 "Ninja Giraffes" by David Brown; pp. 60–61 "Frog Squad" by Rose Davidson; p. 62 "Super Snakes" by Chana Stiefel; p. 63 "Deadly Cuties" by Jamie Kiffel-Alcheh; pp. 64–65 "Surf Pups" by Allyson Shaw; p. 66 "7 Bee Facts to Buzz About" by Jeannette Swain; pp. 68–69 "Big Cats" by Elizabeth Carney; p. 70 "Weirdest. Cat. Ever." by Scott Elder; p. 71 "Journey of the Jaguar" by Jamie Kiffel-Alcheh; pp. 72–73 "Tigers in the Snow" by Karen de Seve; p. 75 (left) "Dog Protects Piglet" by Sarah Wassner Flynn; p. 75 (right) "Do Pets Know Their Names?" by Allyson Shaw; pp. 76–77 "How to Speak Cat" by Aline Alexander Newman and Gary Weitzman, D.V.M.; pp. 78–80 "Prehistoric Timeline" & "Dino Classification" by Susan K. Donnelly; p. 78 "What Killed the Dinosaurs?" by Sarah Wassner Flynn; pp. 82–83 "Dino Secrets Revealed" by Michael Greshko

Space and Earth (86–107)

pp. 88–89 "15 Cool Things About Planets" by Kay Boatner; p. 92 "Dwarf Planets" by Sarah Wassner Flynn; p. 93 "What's the Farthest ...?" by Allyson Shaw; p. 94 "Destination Space: Alien Sea" by Stephanie Warren Drimmer; p. 96 "A Look Inside" by Kathy Furgang; p. 96 "What If You Could ...?" by Crispin Boyer; p. 97 "Rock Stars" by Steve Tomecek; pp. 98–99 "Identifying Minerals" by Nancy Honovich; pp. 101–102 "A New Type of Rock..." by Sarah Wassner Flynn; pp. 102–103 "A Hot Topic" by Kathy Furgang; pp. 104–105 "Blue Volcano" by Renee Skelton

Awesome Exploration (108–129)

pp. 110–111 "This Cliff ..." by Sarah Wassner Flynn; pp. 114–115 "Dare to Explore" by Kitson Jazynka; pp. 118–121 "Epic Science Fails" & "Keep Earth Wild" by Allyson Shaw; pp. 122–123 "Getting the Shot" by April Capochino Myers; p. 125 "Extreme Job!" by Jen Agresta and Sarah Wassner Flynn; pp. 126–127 "Soaring Sports" by Julie Beer and Michelle Harris

20 Things to Make You Happy (150–165)

All articles in section by Lisa Gerry

Culture Connection (166–189)

pp. 170–171 "Festive Parades" by Julie Beer and Michelle Harris; p. 172 "What's Your Chinese Horoscope?" by Geoff Williams; p. 173 "6 Spooky Facts for Halloween" by Erin Whitmer; pp. 174–175 "The World's Largest Sandcastle ..." by Sarah Wassner Flynn; pp. 176–177 "Cake Fakes" by Kitson Jazynka; pp. 178–179 "The Secret History of Chocolate" by Jamie Kiffel-Alcheh; pp. 180–181 "Money Around the World!" by Kristin Baird Rattini and C.M. Tomlin; pp. 182–183 "Saving Languages at Risk" by Sarah Wassner Flynn; pp. 184–185 "Mythology" by Susan K. Donnelly; pp. 186–187 "World Religions" by Mark Bockenhauer

Science and Technology (190–213)

pp. 192–193 "This Race Car ..." by Sarah Wassner Flynn; p. 194 "Cool Inventions" by Sarah Wassner Flynn (fireplace); p. 197 "The Three Domains of Life" by Susan K. Donnelly; p. 198 "How Does Your Garden Grow?" by Susan K. Donnelly; p. 199 "Plants That Stink!" by Sarah Wassner Flynn; p. 200 "Weird But True!" by Jeffrey Wandell; pp. 202–203 "Why Can't I ...?" by Crispin Boyer; pp. 204–205 "15 Cool Things About Sleep" by Kay Boatner; pp. 206–207 "The Science of Spooky" by Aaron Sidder; pp. 208–211 "Future World: Homes" & "Future World: Food" by Karen De Seve

Wonders of Nature (214–235)

pp. 216–217 "Biomes" by Susan K. Donnelly; pp. 218–219 "Sizing Up the Great Barrier Reef" by Sarah Wassner Flynn; p. 224 "Weather and Climate" by Mark Bockenhauer; p. 225 "Climate Change" by Sarah Wassner Flynn; pp. 226–227 "Lightning Flashes ..." by Sarah Wassner Flynn; pp. 228–229 "The Sky Is Falling" & "Types of Clouds" by Kathy Furgang; p. 230 "Hurricane Happenings" by Sarah Wassner Flynn; p. 231 "What Is a Tornado?" by Kathy Furgang; p. 232 "Flood" & "Freeze" by Sarah Wassner Flynn; p. 233 "Bobcat Wildfire Rescue" by Jamie Kiffel-Alcheh

History Happens (236–267)

p. 238 "Ancient Egypt by the Numbers" by Sarah Wassner Flynn; p. 239 "Brainy Questions" by Allyson Shaw; pp. 240–241 "The Lost City of Pompeii" by Kristin Baird Rattini; pp. 242–243 "The Hagia Sophia ..." by Sarah Wassner Flynn; pp. 244–245 "Royal Rumble" by Stephanie Warren Drimmer and Caleb Magyar; pp. 246–247 "To Honor a Queen" by Allyson Shaw; pp. 248–249 "Pirates!" by Sara Lorimer and Jamie Kiffel-Alcheh; pp. 250–251 "Going to War" by Susan K. Donnelly and Sarah Wassner Flynn; p. 251 "Wartime Inventions" by Sarah Wassner Flynn; pp. 252–253 "The Constitution & the Bill of Rights" & "Branches of Government" by Susan K. Donnelly; p. 254 "The Native American Experience" by Martha B. Sharma; pp. 260–261 "Presidential Pets" by Allyson Shaw and Sarah Wassner Flynn (Biden); pp. 262 "Civil Rights" by Susan K. Donnelly; pp. 262–263 "Woolworth Counter Sit-in" & "Stone of Hope" & "John Lewis" by Sarah Wassner Flynn; pp. 264–265 "Women Fighting for Equality" by Sarah Wassner Flynn

Geography Rocks (268–353)

pp. 270–274 & pp. 276–277 by Mark Bockenhauer; pp. 278–279 "Mount Everest ..." by Sarah Wassner Flynn; pp. 280–307 by Sarah Wassner Flynn, Mark Bockenhauer, and Susan K. Donnelly; pp. 308–317 "Snapshot" by Sarah Wassner Flynn; p. 346 "What Weird Destination ...?" by Julie Beer and Michelle Harris; p. 347 "Racing Roller Coaster" by Jennifer Adrion and Omar Noory; pp. 348–349 "Amazing Facts About the World" by Zachary Petit; p. 350 "Bizarre Beaches" by Julie Beer and Michelle Harris; p. 351 "7 Wonders" by Elisabeth Deffner

All "Homework Help" by Vicki Ariyasu, except p. 213 "This Is How It's Done!" by Sarah Wassner Flynn

Abbreviations:

AL: Alamy Stock Photo
AS: Adobe Stock
DS: Dreamstime
GI: Getty Images
IS: iStockphoto
MP: Minden Pictures
NGIC: National Geographic Image Collection
SS: Shutterstock

All Maps

By National Geographic

All Illustrations & Charts

By Stuart Armstrong unless otherwise noted

Front Cover

(tiger) Tom and Pat Leeson; (smiley face), pixelliebe/SS; (pyramids), Merydolla/SS; (dinosaur), Luis V. Rey

Spine

(tiger), Tom and Pat Leeson

Back Cover

(Earth), ixpert/SS; (climber), Westend61/AL; (koala), Gary Bell/oceanwideimages; (Taj Mahal), Jim Zuckerman/GI; (giraffe), prapass/SS; (northern lights), Stuart Westmorland/Danita Delimont/AS; (butterfly), Steven Russell Smith/AL

Front Matter (2-7)

2-3, Tony Heald/Nature Picture Library; 5 (UP), Kuttig - Travel/AL; 5 (UP CTR), Hilary Andrews/NG Staff; 5 (LO CTR), Tomatito26/DS; 5 (LO LE), Anton Brink/Anadolu Agency via GI; 5 (LO RT), Exp 351 Science Team/Leeds University; 6 (UP LE), Westend61/AL; 6 (UP RT), Arctic Images/AL; 6 (UP CTR LE), Thichaa/SS; 6 (UP CTR RT), dan sipple; 6 (CTR LE), Chendongshan/SS; 6 (CTR RT), Hello World/GI; 6 (LO CTR LE), Prisma by Dukas Presseagentur GmbH/AL; 6 (LO CTR RT), SylvainB/SS; 6 (LO LE), AndreasReh/GI; 6 (LO RT), Eric Isselee/SS; 7 (UP LE), Stuart Westmorland/Danita Delimont/AS; 7 (UP RT), Jim Reed; 7 (UP CTR LE), Menahem Kahana/afp/AFP via GI; 7 (LO CTR LE), Roberto Moiola/Sysaworld/GI

Your World 2023 (8-17)

8-9, Kuttig - Travel/AL; 10 (UP), Andrej Cukic/EPA-EFE/SS; 10 (LO), Cheryl Ramalho/AS; 11 (UP), Stefano Unterthiner; 11 (LO), Bradley Smith; 12 (UP LE), Jason Mendez/Everett Collection; 12 (UP CTR), Sarah J. Mock; 12 (LO), Busch Wildlife Sanctuary; 13 (UP), Xinhua/AL; 13 (UP RT), Xinhua/AL; 13 (CTR), Chris Walker/Chicago Tribune/TNS/Alamy Live News; 13 (LO), Xinhua/AL; 14 (UP), Lars Gustavsen/NIKU; 14 (INSETS), Martin Tangen Schmidt/The Museum of Cultural History; 14 (LO), Milan Ingegneria SpA, Labics, Arch, Fabio Fumagalli, CROMA, Consilium di Ingegneria; 15 (UP LE), Saule/AS; 15 (UP RT), Paul Rushton/AS; 15 (LO RT), Reuters/List Niesner; 15 (LO LE), Reuters/Kim Hong-Ji; 16 (bicycle), Monkey Business/AS; 16 (chocolate), Constantine Pankin/SS; 16 (elephant), Linettesimoesphotography/DS; 16 (cat), Ermolaev Alexander/SS; 16 (LO LE), Carola G./AS; 16 (LO LE), Anatolii/AS; 16 (clock), Sorapop Udomsri/SS; 16 (women), Svitlana Sokolova/SS; 16 (sweats), serbogachuk/AS; 17 (UP), Kennedy News/Mike Bowers; 17 (CTR), PDSA/Cover

Images via AP Images; 17 (LO), Michel Keck and Harbour North

Kids vs. Plastic (18-33)

18-19, Hilary Andrews/NG Staff; 20-21 (BACKGROUND), trialartinf/AS; 21 (UP), Jacobs Stock Photography Ltd/GI; 21 (CTR RT), SeeCee/SS; 21 (CTR LE), Norbert Pouchain/EyeEm/GI; 21 (Graph Background), Chones/SS 22-23 (BACKGROUND), STEVE DE NEEF/NGIC; 22 (LE), Pete Atkinson/GI; 22 (RT), Aflo/SS; 23 (UP RT), photka/SS; 25, Alexandre Rotenberg/SS; 26 (UP LE), Fascinadora/IS/GI; 26 (UP RT), Steven Cukrov/DS; 26 (CTR LE), Paul Quayle/AL; 26 (1), Cristian M. Vela/AL; 26 (2), Katerina Solovyeva/AL; 26 (3), nalinratphi/SS; 26 (4), nalinratphi/SS; 27 (UP LE), Elena Veselova/SS; 27 (UP RT), Maks Narodenko/SS; 27 (LO), Melica/SS; 28-29 (ALL), Hilary Andrews/NG Staff; 30-31 (BACKGROUND), Luis Javier Sandoval Alvarado/SuperStock; 30 (LE), Clearwater Marine Aquarium; 30 (RT), Clearwater Marine Aquarium; 31 (LE), Clearwater Marine Aquarium; 31 (RT), Norbert Wu/MP; 32 (UP LE), Jacobs Stock Photography Ltd/GI; 32 (UP RT), photka/SS; 32 (CTR RT), Norbert Wu/MP; 32 (LO LE), Elena Veselova/SS; 33, Alboo03/SS

Amazing Animals (34-85)

34-35, Tomatito26/DS; 36, Brittany Dolan/NOAA Fisheries; 37 (UP), BBC Natural History/GI; 37 (LO), Barry Skipsey; 38, Shenton Safaris; 39 (ALL), Dean MacAdam; 40 (UP LE), Steven Kazlowski/Nature Picture Library; 40 (CTR RT), Piotr Naskrecki/MP; 40 (LO LE), Marie Hickman/GI; 41 (UP LE), Wijnand vT/SS; 41 (CTR RT), Cyril Ruoso/MP; 41 (UP RT), YAY Media AS/AL; 41 (LO RT), Ryan M. Bolton/AL; 42 (UP LE), Karl Ammann/npl/MP; 42 (UP RT), Masatsugu Ohashi/SS; 42 (LO RT), Heather Burditt/GI; 42 (LO LE), Randy Kokesch; 43 (UP RT), Ryan Korpi/IS/GI; 43 (CTR LE), Samuel Blanc/Biosphoto; 43 (CTR RT), Dirk Ercken/SS; 43 (LO LE), John Shaw/Nature Picture Library; 44 (UP RT), Shin Yoshino/MP; 44 (CTR LE), DioGen/SS; 44 (LO RT), Nick Garbutt; 45 (UP CTR), Kant Liang/EyeEm/GI; 45 (UP RT), reptiles4all/SS; 45 (CTR), Hiroya Minakuchi/MP; 45 (CTR RT), FP media/SS; 45 (LO), Ziva_K/IS/GI; 46, Eric Gevaert/AL; 47 (UP), AP Photo/Martin Meissner; 47 (LO), Haroldo Palo Jr./Avalon; 48-49, Bornean Sun Bear Conservation Centre; 49 (UP), Siew te Wong/Bornean Sun Bear Conservation Centre; 49 (LO), Bornean Sun Bear Conservation Centre; 50 (UP), WaterFrame/AL; 50 (CTR), Andy Murch/Blue Planet Archive; 50 (LO), David Gruber; 51 (UP), Masa Ushioda/Blue Planet Archive; 51 (CTR), Saul Gonor/Blue Planet Archive; 51 (LO), Richard Carey/AS; 52 (BACKGROUND), Paul Nicklen/NGIC; 52 (UP LE), Paul Nicklen/NGIC; 52 (UP RT), Paul Nicklen/NGIC; 52 (LO RT), Russ Kinne/age fotostock; 52 (LO CTR), Flip Nicklin/MP; 53 (UP), Mauricio Handler/NGIC; 53 (CTR LE), S. Rohrlach/GI; 53 (CTR RT), WaterFrame/AL; 53 (LO), WaterFrame/AL; 55, Paul Souders/Worldfoto/MP; 56 (UP), mbolenski/GI; 56 (LO), ktmoffitt/GI; 57 (UP), Tui De Roy/MP; 57 (CTR RT), Alex Mustard/Nature Picture Library; 57 (LO RT), Tui De Roy/MP; 57 (LO LE), WaterFrame_fur/AL; 58 (UP), Yva Momatiuk and John Eastcott/MP; 58 (CTR RT), Steven Kazlowski/Nature Picture Library; 58 (LO), Michio Hoshino/MP; 59 (illustrations), Stuart Armstrong; 59 (UP

CTR), Richard du Toit/GI; 59 (UP RT), Richard Du Toit/MP; 59 (CTR LE), Mitsuaki Iwago/MP; 59 (LO LE), Will Burrard-Lucas/MP; 59 (LO RT), Richard Du Toit/MP; 60 (UP), Martin van Lokven/MP; 60 (eyes), Ingo Arndt/MP; 60 (LO), Chien Lee/MP; 61 (UP), Stu Porter/SS; 61 (CTR), Stephen Dalton/MP; 61 (LO), reptiles4all/GI; 62 (UP), Michael D. Kern; 62 (CTR), Hitendra Sinkar Photography/Alamy; 62 (CTR LE), Stephen Dalton/MP; 62 (CTR RT), AtSkwongPhoto/SS; 62 (LO), Heidi & Hans-Juergen Koch/MP; 63 (UP), Andrew Walmsley/Nature Picture Library; 63 (LO), Andrew Walmsley/Nature Picture Library/AL; 64 (UP), Ian McAllister/NGIC; 64 (LO), Bertie Gregory/MP; 65 (UP), Paul Nicklen/NGIC; 65 (CTR), Ian McAllister/Pacific Wild; 65 (LO RT), Paul Nicklen/NGIC; 65 (LO LE), Paul Nicklen/NGIC; 66, Michael Durham/MP; 67, Mircea Costina/SS; 68, Beverly Joubert/NGIC; 69 (snow leopard fur), Eric Isselee/SS; 69 (jaguar fur), worldswildlifewonders/SS; 69 (tiger fur), Kesu/SS; 69 (leopard fur), WitR/SS; 69 (lion fur), Eric Isselee/SS; 69 (jaguar), DLILLC/Corbis/GI; 69 (lion), Eric Isselee/SS; 69 (tiger), Eric Isselee/SS; 69 (snow leopard), Eric Isselee/SS; 69 (leopard), Eric Isselee/SS; 70 (LE), GERARD LACZ/Science Source; 70 (CTR), FionaAyerst/GI; 70 (RT), Suzi Eszterhas/MP; 71 (UP), Henner Damke/AS; 71 (CTR LE), Nick Garbutt/MP; 71 (LO LE), Kris Wiktor/SS; 71 (LO RT), Jak Wonderly/NGIC; 72 (UP), Image Source/Corbis/GI; 72 (LO), Juniors/SuperStock; 73 (UP), Tom & Pat Leeson/ARDEA; 73 (LO), Lisa & Mike Husar/Team Husar; 74 (UP LE), Design Pics/AL; 74 (UP RT), Alexa Miller/Workbook Stock/GI; 74 (LO RT), Arnaud Martinez/AL; 74 (LO LE), Giel, O./juniors@wildlife/AL; 75 (UP), courtesy Roland Adam; 75 (LO LE), courtesy Roland Adam; 75 (LO RT), Alice Brereton; 76 (UP), Shawna and Damien Richard/SS; 76 (LO), kurhan/SS; 77 (UP), SJ Duran/SS; 77 (LO), Hulya Ozkok/GI; 78 (UP), Chris Butler/Science Photo Library/Photo Researchers, Inc.; 78 (CTR), Publiphoto/Photo Researchers, Inc.; 78 (LO), Pixeldust Studios/NGIC; 79 (A), Publiphoto/Photo Researchers, Inc.; 79 (B), Laurie O'Keefe/Photo Researchers, Inc.; 79 (C), Chris Butler/Photo Researchers, Inc.; 79 (D), Publiphoto/Photo Researchers, Inc.; 79 (E), image courtesy of Project Exploration; 80 (ALL), Franco Tempesta; 81 (UP LE), Jorge L. Blanco; 81 (UP RT), Masato Hattori; 81 (LO RT), Mauricio Alvarez Abel; 81 (LO LE), Luis V. Rey; 82-83, Davide Bonadonna; 84 (UP RT), AP Photo/Martin Meissner; 84 (CTR RT), Shawna and Damien Richard/SS; 84 (CTR LE), PAUL NICKLEN/NGIC; 84 (LO LE), Ziva_K/IS/GI; 85, GOLFX/SS

Space and Earth (86-107)

86-87, Anton Brink/Anadolu Agency via GI; 88 (UP LE), Tristan3D/SS; 88 (CTR), NASA/JSC/Stanford University/Science Source; 88 (CTR RT), MarcelClemens/SS; 88 (CTR LE), Tomas Ragina/AS; 88 (LO), nasidastudio/SS; 89 (UP LE), CGiHeart/AS; 89 (UP RT), NASA, ESA, A. Simon (Goddard Space Flight Center) and M.H. Wong (University of California, Berkeley); 89 (sun), Ed Connor/SS; 89 (snow), Kichigin/SS; 89 (CTR RT), NASA/JPL/Space Science Institute; 89 (LO RT), parameter/GI; 89 (LO LE), NASA/JPL/USGS; 90-91, David Aguilar; 92 (haumea), David Aguilar; 92 (eris), David Aguilar; 92 (pluto), NASA/JHUAPL/SwRI 93 (UP), EHT Collaboration/

NASA; 93 (LO), Alice Brereton; 94, Mondolithic Studios; 95 (UP), Allexxandar/IS/GI; 95 (Jupiter), rtype/AS; 95 (eclipse), Igor Kovalchuk/SS; 95 (supermoon), JSirlin/AS; 96 (UP), NGIC; 96 (LO), Joe Rocco; 97 (UP), Ralph Lee Hopkins/NGIC; 97 (andesite), losmandarinas/SS; 97 (porphyry), MarekPhotoDesign/AS; 97 (schist), Yes058 Montree Nanta/SS; 97 (gneiss), Dirk Wiersma/Science Source; 97 (limestone), Charles D. Winters/Photo Researchers, Inc.; 97 (halite), Theodore Clutter/Science Source; 98 (UP LE), raiwa/IS; 98 (UP RT), MarcelC/IS; 98 (CTR RT), Anatoly Maslennikov/SS; 98 (LO RT), IS; 98 (LO LE), Albert Russ/SS; 99 (UP RT), Mark A. Schneider/Science Source; 99 (UP LE), didyk/IS; 99 (Talc), Ben Johnson/Science Source; 99 (Gypsum), Meetchum/DS; 99 (Calcite), Kazakovmaksim/DS; 99 (Fluorite), Albertruss/DS; 99 (Apatite), Ingemar Magnusson/DS; 99 (Orthoclase), Joel Arem/Science Source; 99 (Topaz), Igorkali/DS; 99 (Corundum), oldeez/DS; 99 (Diamond), 123dartist/DS; 101, Exp 351 Science Team/Leeds University; 102, Frank Ippolito; 103 (UP LE), Gary Fiegehen/All Canada Photos/Alamy; 103 (UP RT), Salvatore Gebbia/NGIC; 103 (CTR LE), NASA; 103 (CTR RT), Diane Cook & Len Jenshel/NGIC; 104-105, Nicolas Marino/mauritius images GmbH/AL; 105 (UP), Chris Philpot; 105 (CTR LE), Taiga/AS; 105 (LO RT), Mazur Travel/AS; 106 (UP RT), Charles D. Winters/Photo Researchers, Inc.; 106 (CTR LE), Igor Kovalchuk/SS; 106 (LO RT), CGiHeart/AS; 107, pixhook/E+/GI

Awesome Exploration (108–129)

108-109, Westend61/AL; 111, Diego Camilo Carranza Jimenez/Anadolu Agency/GI; 112 (CTR LE), Roger Winstead; 112 (CTR RT), Michael Nolan/robertharding/GI; 112 (LO), Meg Lowman; 113 (UP), Smileus/AS; 113 (UP RT), AVTG/AS; 113 (binoculars), Nataliya Hora/DS; 113 (paper), Photo_SS/SS; 113 (pencil), photastic/SS; 113 (LO), Aditi Sundar; 114 (UP), Thomas Marent/MP; 114 (CTR RT), Jonathan Byers; 114 (CTR LE), Robert Liddell; 115 (UP), Sora Devore/NGIC; 115 (CTR), Carsten Peter/NGIC; 115 (CTR RT), Carsten Peter/NGIC; 116-117(ALL), Gab Mejia; 118-119 (UP), Aga Nowack; 118 (Jungblut), Arwyn Edwards; 118 (Wynn-Grant), Christine Jean Chambers; 118 (LO), Tibor Bognar/GI; 119 (Somaweera), Ruchira Somaweera 119 (UP RT), Nilu Gunarathne; 119 (Medici), Liana John; 119 (LO RT), Marina Klink; 119 (Daniel Dick), Max Chipman; 119 (CTR LE), Daniel Dick; 120-121 (ALL), Joel Sartore, National Geographic Photo Ark/NGIC; 122, Mattias Klum/NGIC; 123 (UP), Brian J. Skerry/NGIC; 123 (LO), Michael Nichols/NGIC; 124 (LE), Gabby Wild; 124 (UP RT), Rebecca Hale/NG Staff; 124 (LO RT), Theo Allofs/MP; 125 (BACKGROUND), Arctic-Images/Corbis/GI; 125 (UP RT), ARCTIC IMAGES/AL; 125 (LO LE), ARCTIC IMAGES/AL; 126 (UP), Daniel Milchev/GI; 126 (LO), Laurence Griffiths/GI; 127 (UP LE), Robert Mora/GI; 127 (UP RT), Zapata Racing; 127 (CTR RT), Don Bartletti/Los Angeles Times via GI; 127 (LO RT), ohrim/SS; 127 (LO LE), Mathieu Belanger/The New York Times/Redux Pictures; 127 (CTR LE), JVT/GI; 128 (UP RT), Zapata Racing; 128 (CTR LE), Thomas Marent/MP; 128 (CTR RT), Diego Camilo Carranza Jimenez/Anadolu Agency/GI; 128 (LO LE), Theo Allofs/MP; 129, Grady Reese/IS

130-131, Thichaa/SS; 132 (UP), Sean Crane/MP; 132 (moose), Scott Suriano/GI; 132 (grouse), pchoui/iStock/GI; 132 (lynx), Michael Quinton/MP; 132 (hare), Jim Cumming/GI; 132 (profile), Mark Raycroft/MP; 132 (male grouse), Wayne Lynch/All Canada Photos/AL; 132 (tufts), Michael Quinton/MP; 132 (swimming), Ron Sanford/GI; 132 (snow), Diana Robinson Photography/GI; 132 (fur), Jurgen and Christine Sohns/MP; 133 (UP LE), Antonio Veraldi/DS; 133 (UP CTR), Ghm Meuffels/DS; 133 (UP RT), Sweetcrisis/DS; 133 (CTR LE), Sydeen/DS; 133 (CTR), Antonio Veraldi/DS; 133 (CTR RT), Unteroffizier/DS; 133 (LO LE), Mikhail Kokhanchikov/DS; 133 (LO CTR), Fotosutra/DS; 133 (LO RT), Derrick Neill/DS; 134 (UP LE), Travel Pictures/AL; 134 (UP RT), Thomas Winz/GI; 134 (CTR RT), Richard Newstead/GI; 134 (LO RT), MyLoupe/Universal Images Group via GI; 134 (LO CTR), Andrew Holt/GI; 134 (LO LE), Owaki/Kulla/GI; 134 (CTR RT), Charles Gullung/GI; 135, Jason Tharp; 136, Joren Cull; 137 (UP CTR), Fabio Liverani/Nature Picture Library; 137 (UP RT), John Cancalosi/Nature Picture Library; 137 (CTR LE), atese/GI; 137 (CTR RT), Jurgen Freund/Nature Picture Library; 137 (LO LE), Terry Andrewartha/Nature Picture Library; 137 (LO RT), Jose B. Ruiz/Nature Picture Library; 138 (UP LE), surflover/SS; 138 (UP CTR), Felix Martinez/GI; 138 (UP RT), age fotostock/Superstock; 138 (CTR LE), Andy Gehrig/GI; 138 (CTR), Kharidehal Abhirama Ashwin/SS; 138 (CTR RT), lkpro/SS; 138 (LO LE), Nils Versemann/SS; 138 (LO CTR), Gary Bell/oceanwideimages; 138 (LO RT), age fotostock/Stuperstock; 139 (UP), Pltphotography/DS; 139 (CTR RT), Charles Krebs/GI; 139 (LO RT), Ryan McVay/GI; 139 (LO LE), Markstout/GI; 139 (tree), Cornelia Doerr/GI; 139 (compass), Kisan/SS; 139 (CTR LE), Kevin Kelley/GI; 140, Dan Sipple; 141, Chris Ware; 142 (UP LE), image100/AL; 142 (UP CTR), Subbotina Anna/AS; 142 (UP RT), Kletr/SS; 142 (CTR LE), Ron Levine/Photodisc Red/GI; 142 (CTR), koosen/SS; 142 (CTR RT), Gary Bell/GI; 142 (LO LE), Alexander Raths/SS; 142 (LO CTR), Wendy Carrig/GI; 142 (LO RT), Kalabi Yau/SS; 143 (UP CTR), Brandon Cole; 143 (UP RT), Kevin Schafer/GI; 143 (CTR LE), Chris Mattison/FLPA/MP; 143 (CTR RT), Andy Mann/GI; 143 (LO LE), Thomas Marent/MP; 143 (LO RT), David Fleetham/Nature Picture Library; 144, Jason Tharp; 145 (UP), Eric Isselee/SS; 145 (CTR LE), J.-J. Klein & M.-L. Hubert/MP; 145 (CTR RT), godrick/SS; 145 (LO RT), Smit/SS; 145 (LO LE), Suzi Eszterhas/MP; 146 (UP LE), Sergii Kolesnyk/DS; 146 (UP CTR), Sorachar Tangjitjaroen/DS; 146 (UP RT), Andrii Mykhailov/DS; 146 (CTR LE), Aleksandr Bryliaev/SS; 146 (CTR), Brian Sedgbeer/DS; 146 (CTR RT), Saltcityphotography/DS; 146 (LO LE), matka_Wariatka/SS; 146 (LO CTR), Katerina Kovaleva/DS; 146 (LO RT), Brian Kushner/DS; 147 (UP), imageBROKER/Jurgen & Christine Sohns/GI; 147 (kangaroo), D. Parer and E. Parer-Cook/MP; 147 (platypus), Tom McHugh/Science Source; 147 (spider), ©Jürgen Otto; 147 (skink), Gerry Ellis/MP; 147 (pouch), Yva Momatiuk and John Eastcott/MP; 147 (swimming), Dave Watts/MP; 147 (dancing), ©Jürgen Otto; 147 (mob), Malcolm Schuyl/MP; 148-149, Strika Entertainment

150-151, Chendongshan/SS; 152, Pete Pahham/SS; 153 (UP), Peter Augustin/GI; 153 (LO), Voronin76/SS; 154 (UP), Gts/SS; 154 (LO), Krakenimages/SS; 155, Zaretska Olga/SS; 156, Daniel Milchev/GI; 157, Flashpop/GI; 158 (fishing), Jupiterimages/SuperStock; 158 (planting), Sofiaworld/SS; 158 (baking), Bashutskyy/SS; 158 (photography), Marian Stanca/AL; 158 (golf), vm/GI; 158-159 (LO), Image Source Plus/AL; 160, Ivory27/SS; 161 (UP), Yury Zap/AL; 161 (LO), SuperStock; 162 (UP), Ariel Skelley/GI; 162 (LO), Potapov Alexander/SS; 163 (UP), MM Productions/GI; 163 (LO), Vinko93/SS; 164, Beskova Ekaterina/SS; 165, Hello World/GI

Culture Connection (166–189)

166-167, Prisma by Dukas Presseagentur GmbH/AL; 168 (UP LE), CreativeNature.nl/SS; 168 (UP RT), Roka/SS; 168 (CTR LE), Phoenix Tenebra/SS; 168 (CTR RT), Orchid photho/SS; 168 (LO LE), Tubol Evgeniya/SS; 169 (UP), SylvainB/SS; 169 (CTR RT), Dinodia Photos; 169 (CTR LE), Zee/Alamy; 169 (LO), wacpan/SS; 170 (UP), Scott Keeler/Tampa Bay Times/ZUMA Wire/AL; 170 (LO), Marie1969/SS; 171 (UP LE), VisitBritain/John Coutts/GI; 171 (UP RT), lev radin/SS; 171 (CTR RT), Viviane Ponti/GI; 171 (CTR LE), CR Shelare/GI; 171 (LO RT), Carol M. Highsmith/Library of Congress Prints and Photographs Division; 171 (LO LE), epa european pressphoto agency b.v./AL; 172, Chonnanit/SS; 173, Eric Isselee/SS; 175, Claus Bjoern Larsen/Ritzau Scanpix/AFP via GI; 176 (UP), Kate Pritchett; 176 (CTR RT), the_bakeking/Cover Images/Newscom; 176 (LO LE), Molly Robbins; 177 (UP), Serdar Yener of Yeners Way, Online Cake Tutorials; 177 (CTR LE), Studio Cake; 177 (LO CTR), Serdar Yener of Yeners Way, Online Cake Tutorials; 177 (LO RT), Studio Cake; 178-179 (BACKGROUND), Subbotina Anna/SS; 178-179 (cartoons), JOE ROCCO; 178 (CTR RT), adit_ajie/SS; 179 (CTR RT), Retro AdArchives/Alamy; 180 (UP LE), Radomir Tarasov/SS; 180 (UP CTR), maogg/GI; 180 (UP RT), Paul Poplis/GI; 180 (CTR LE), Mlenny/iStock/GI ; 180 (CTR RT), JACK GUEZ/AFP/GI; 180 (LO LE), Glyn Thomas/Alamy; 180 (LO RT), Brian Hagiwara/GI; 181 (UP LE), Georgios Kollidas/Alamy; 181 (UP RT), Joe Pepler/Rex USA/SS; 181 (pig), Igor Stramyk/SS; 181 (CTR LE), Mohamed Osama/DS; 181 (CTR RT), Daniel Krylov/DS; 181 (LO LE), Colin Hampden-White 2010; 181 (LO RT), Kelley Miller/NGS Staff; 182 (Ton), Nguyen Dai Duong; 182 (CTR RT), Ho Trung Lam; 182 (LO LE), Mark Thiessen/NGP; 182 (Narayanan), RANDALL SCOTT/NGIC; 183 (UP LE), Jeremy Fahringer; 183 (Harrison), Mark Thiessen/NGIC; 183 (Barfield), Robert Massee; 183 (CTR RT), Catherine Cofré; 183 (CTR LE), K. Bista; 183 (Perlin), Mark Thiessen/NG Staff; 183 (Rapacha), Jeevan Sunuwar Kirat; 183 (LO RT), Jeevan Sunuwar Kirat; 184 (UP RT), Jose Ignacio Soto/SS; 184 (UP LE), liquidlibrary/GI Plu/GI; 184 (LO), Photosani/SS; 185 (LE), Corey Ford/DS; 185 (RT), IS; 186 (UP), Randy Olson; 186 (LO RT), Sam Panthaky/AFP/GI; 186 (LO LE), Martin Gray/NGIC; 187 (UP), Mayur Kakade/GI; 187 (LO RT), Richard Nowitz/NGIC; 187 (LO LE), Reza/NGIC; 188 (UP LE), Carol M. Highsmith/

360

NATIONAL GEOGRAPHIC and Yellow Border Design are trademarks of the
National Geographic Society, used under license.

Since 1888, the National Geographic Society has funded more than
14,000 research, conservation, education, and storytelling projects around
the world. National Geographic Partners distributes a portion of the funds
it receives from your purchase to National Geographic Society to support
programs including the conservation of animals and their habitats.
To learn more, visit natgeo.com/info.

For more information, visit nationalgeographic.com,
call 1-877-873-6846, or write to the following address:

National Geographic Partners, LLC
1145 17th Street N.W.
Washington, DC 20036-4688 U.S.A.

For librarians and teachers:
nationalgeographic.com/books/librarians-and-educators

More for kids from National Geographic: natgeokids.com

National Geographic Kids magazine inspires children to explore their world
with fun yet educational articles on animals, science, nature, and more.
Using fresh storytelling and amazing photography, *Nat Geo Kids* shows kids
ages 6 to 14 the fascinating truth about the world—and why they should care.
natgeo.com/subscribe

For rights or permissions inquiries, please contact National Geographic
Books Subsidiary Rights: bookrights@natgeo.com

Designed by Kathryn Robbins and Ruthie Thompson

The publisher would like to thank everyone who worked to make this book
come together: Mary Jones, project editor; Angela Modany, editor;
Sarah Wassner Flynn, writer; Michelle Harris, researcher; Sarah J. Mock,
senior photo editor; Mike McNey, map production; Anne LeongSon and Gus Tello,
design production assistants; Joan Gossett, editorial production manager;
and Molly Reid, production editor.

Trade paperback ISBN: 978-1-4263-7283-4
Trade hardcover ISBN: 978-1-4263-7336-7

Printed in the United States of America
22/WOR/1

Sightseeing Key

0 km   1
0 miles   0.5

Museum of London

St Paul's Cathedral

THE CITY AND THE EAST END

Shakespeare's Globe

HMS Belfast

Tower of London

Thames

SOUTHWARK AND THE SOUTH BANK

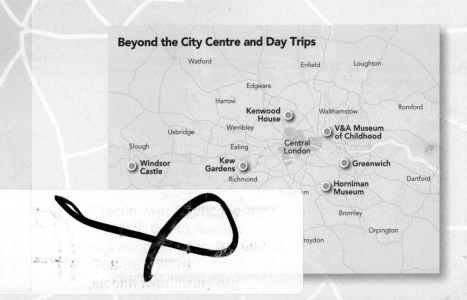

Beyond the City Centre and Day Trips

Watford
Enfield
Loughton
Edgware
Harrow
Kenwood House
Walthamstow
Romford
Uxbridge
Wembley
V&A Museum of Childhood
Slough
Ealing
Central London
Windsor Castle
Kew Gardens
Greenwich
Dartford
Richmond
Horniman Museum
Bromley
Orpington
Croydon

EYEWITNESS TRAVEL
FAMILY GUIDE
LONDON

EYEWITNESS TRAVEL

FAMILY GUIDE

LONDON

DK

PUBLISHER
Vivien Antwi

LIST MANAGER
Christine Stroyan

MANAGING ART EDITOR
Mabel Chan

SENIOR EDITOR
Michelle Crane

EDITORS
Vicki Allen, Hugh Thompson,
Alexandra Whittleton

DESIGNERS
Louise Dick, Marisa Renzullo

PICTURE RESEARCH
Ellen Root

SENIOR DTP DESIGNER
Jason Little

SENIOR CARTOGRAPHIC MANAGER
Uma Bhattacharya

CARTOGRAPHER Schchida Nand
Pradhan

SENIOR CARTOGRAPHIC EDITOR
Casper Morris

PRODUCTION CONTROLLER
Rebecca Short

PHOTOGRAPHY
Max Alexander

CARTOONS
Tom Morgan-Jones

OTHER ILLUSTRATIONS
Arun Pottirayil, Brian Delf, Trevor
Hill, Robbie Polley

DESIGN CONCEPT Keith Hagan at
www.greenwichdesign.co.uk

Printed and bound in China

First published in the United States in
2012 by Dorling Kindersley Limited,
80 Strand, London WC2R 0RL, UK.
A Penguin Random House Company

15 16 17 18 10 9 8 7 6 5 4 3 2 1

Reprinted with revisions 2016

Copyright 2012, 2016 © Dorling
Kindersley Limited, London

A CIP catalogue record is available from
the Library of Congress.

ISBN 978-1-4654-3965-9

MIX
Paper from
responsible sources
FSC
www.fsc.org   FSC™ C018179

Contents

*Colourful soft toys in Eric Snook's toy
shop, Covent Garden*

Getting hands-on in a helicopter cockpit at the Royal Air Force Museum, Hendon

How to Use this Guide

This guide is designed to help families to get the most from a visit to London, providing expert recommendations for sightseeing with kids along with detailed practical information.

The opening section contains an introduction to London and its highlights, as well as all the essentials required to plan a family holiday (including how to get there, getting around, health, insurance, money and communications), a guide to family-friendly festivals and a brief historical overview.

The main sightseeing section is divided into areas. A "best of" feature is followed by the key sights and other attractions in the area, as well as options for where to eat, drink and play and have more fun. At the back of the book are detailed maps of London.

INTRODUCING THE AREA
Each area chapter is opened by a double-page spread setting it in context, with a short introduction, locator map and a selection of highlights.

Locator map locates the region.

Brief highlights give a flavour of what to see in the area.

THE BEST OF...
A planner to show at a glance the best things for families to see and do in each area, with themed suggestions ranging from history, art and culture to gardens and games.

Themed suggestions for the best things to see and do with kids.

WHERE TO STAY
Our expert authors have compiled a wide range of recommendations for places to stay with families, from hotels and B&Bs that welcome children to self-catering apartments.

Easy-to-use symbols show the key family-friendly features of places to stay.

Price Guide box gives details of the price categories for a family of four.

SIGHTSEEING IN LONDON

Each area features a number of "hub" sights (see below): pragmatic and enjoyable plans for a morning, afternoon or day's visit. These give adults and children a real insight into the destination, focusing on the key sights and what makes them interesting to kids. The sights are balanced by places to let off steam, "take cover" options for rainy days, suggestions for where to eat, drink and shop with kids, ideas for where to continue sightseeing, and all the practicalities, including transport.

Introductory text focuses on the practical aspects of the area, from the best time of day to visit to how to get around using public transport.

The hub map identifies the sights featured in the chapter, as well as restaurants, shops, places to stay, transport, and the nearest playgrounds, supermarkets and pharmacies.

The Lowdown gives all the practical information you need to visit the area. The key to the symbols is on the back jacket flap.

The hub sights are the best places to visit in each area, and use lively and informative text to engage and entertain both adults and children.

Kids' Corner is featured on all sightseeing pages (see below).

Find out more gives suggestions for downloads, games, apps or films to enthuse children about a place and help them to learn more about it.

Key Features uses illustrated artworks to show the most interesting features of each sight, highlighting elements likely to appeal to children.

Eat and drink lists recommendations for family-friendly places to eat and drink, from picnic options and snacks to proper meals and gourmet dining.

The Lowdown provides comprehensive practical information, including transport, opening times, costs, activities, age range suitability and how long to allow for a visit.

Letting off steam suggests a place to take children to play freely following a cultural visit.

Next stop... suggests other places to visit, either near the key sight, thematically linked to the sight or a complete change of pace for the rest of the day.

Further sights around each hub, selected to appeal to both adults and children, are given on the following pages.

Kids' Corners are designed to involve children with the sight, with things to look out for, games to play, cartoons and fun facts. Answers to quizzes are given at the bottom of the panel.

Places of interest are recommended, with an emphasis on the aspects most likely to attract children, and incorporating quirky stories and unusual facts. Each one includes a suggestion for letting off steam or taking cover.

The Lowdown provides the usual comprehensive practical and transport information for each sight.

*Colourful Union Jack balloons
floating in front of Big Ben*

Introducing
LONDON

The Best of London

A city with a rich history, impressive architecture, world-class museums, lush parks, superb shops and incomparable theatre, London is a treasure chest for visitors and has a wide choice of family-friendly activities. Explore famous monuments, then relax on a river cruise or in a park. Attend an art workshop, take part in an exciting sport, then find time to witness the spectacle of one of London's traditional ceremonies, full of heritage, pomp and colour.

For culture vultures

Start the day at **Tate Britain** *(see p68–9)* and try out the Art Trolley. Continue to **Westminster Abbey** *(see pp66–7)*, where you can follow the Children's Trail, and then dress up as monks in the museum. Spend the afternoon with exciting games, map-making and clue-matching in **Tate Modern** *(see p148)*.

Another day, take a family tour at the **National Portrait Gallery** *(see pp82–3)*. Break for lunch in Chinatown, near Leicester Square, then follow one of the children's audio tours or printed trails at the **National Gallery** *(see pp80–81)*.

Alternatively, climb up to the Whispering Gallery at **St Paul's Cathedral** *(see pp130–31)*, and then explore the fascinating **Museum of**

Right Toys from the past on display at the Museum of London
Below Soldiers taking part in the Changing the Guard

Children in colourful costumes taking part in the annual celebrations of the Notting Hill Carnival

London *(see pp136–7)*. Hop on the Tube to the **V&A Museum of Childhood** *(see pp208–9)* and spend the afternoon doing a gallery trail.

In three days

Take an open-top bus tour *(see p22)* and hop off at the Queen's London residence, **Buckingham Palace** *(see pp74-5)*, to watch the Changing the Guard. Spend the afternoon in the **Science** and **Natural History museums** *(see pp180–83)*, then let off steam in the **Diana Princess of Wales Memorial Playground** *(see p174)*.

Next day, arrive early for a morning at that castle of castles, the **Tower of London** *(see pp122–3)*, followed by lunch in picturesque **St Katharine's Dock** *(see pp126–7)*. Go by river bus to the South Bank for a trip on the **London Eye** *(see pp160–61)* and a 3D movie at the Imax.

On the last day, spend the morning at **Madame Tussauds** *(see pp114–15)*. Enjoy lunch in Marylebone High Street, then visit a classic attraction – **London Zoo** *(see pp110–11)* or the **British Museum** *(see pp102–3)*.

By season

In spring, visit **Kew Gardens** *(see pp228–9)* to see spectacular carpets of bluebells and yellow daffodils, and stunning blossom. Take part in free, fun activities, such as the chocolate workshop and Easter egg hunt.

Book tickets in advance for a summer concert at glorious **Kenwood House** *(see pp216–17)*; pack a rug and delicious picnic (or pre-order one). Dress up in something colourful for the lively, late August Notting Hill Carnival.

Go for an autumnal walk on **Hampstead Heath** *(see pp216–17)* to see the glorious leaf colours, and, if it's one of those clear, sunny, autumn days, take a trip on the London Eye.

Do some Christmas shopping in **Harrods** *(see p185)* and visit Santa's Grotto. Go skating on the large outdoor rink at Hyde Park's Winter Wonderland *(see p16)*, then warm up afterwards with traditional tea at Brown's Hotel *(see p248)*.

Outdoors

After a morning at **Battersea Park Children's Zoo** *(see pp188–9)*, hire bikes and cycle round the park. Take a train to Waterloo and have lunch in Gabriel's Wharf, before visiting **Shakespeare's Globe** *(see pp146–7)*.

Let the kids loose in **Coram's Fields** *(see p52)*, then explore the canals from Little Venice to **London Zoo** *(see pp110–11)*. After visiting the zoo, go for a row on the boating lake in **Regent's Park** *(see pp112)* and finish with a play at Regent's Park Open Air Theatre.

Visit **Kew Gardens** *(see pp228–9)* to clamber inside a giant badger sett and along the Xstrata Treetop Walkway. Or take a river cruise to **Hampton Court Palace** *(see pp236–7)* and get lost in the 300-year-old maze.

Left *Costumed chefs rustle up historical delicacies in the Tudor kitchens at Hampton Court Palace*

Above *Youngsters having fun in one of London's many free playgrounds* **Above right** *Running around and letting off steam in the grounds outside the British Museum*

On a budget

Entry is free to the permanent collections of London's major museums and galleries. Many also offer complimentary or inexpensive children's tours, trails, storytelling and workshops. The capital's parks *(see pp52–3)* also provide plenty of free family entertainment, including some playgrounds. And the city's excellent urban farms, such as **Vauxhall** *(www.vauxhallcityfarm. org)* and **Mudchute** *(www.mudchute.org)*, do not charge for admission – although a donation of some kind is appreciated.

A great way to get to know the city is on foot, as London and its fascinating, historic architecture is like a living walk-through museum. **Transport for London** *(www.tfl.gov.uk/ gettingaround/walking/default.aspx)* suggests routes, or simply follow the river and watch the boats as you walk. A stroll around **Covent Garden** *(see pp88–9)* guarantees hours of amusement from the street performers.

For discount theatre tickets, visit the **tkts** booth in Leicester Square *(www.tkts.co.uk)*, or one of the internet sites: **www. discounttheatre.com** or **www.lastminute. com**. The cheapest places to eat *(see pp36–9)*, apart from a do-it-yourself picnic in a park, are often local cafés or ethnic restaurants outside of the central touristy areas – sometimes only a few streets away from the main drag.

Stage and screen

A number of London theatres are dedicated to performances for children *(see pp46–7)*. Other theatres stage plays for younger audiences,

particularly during school holidays, among them, the **Tricycle** *(www.tricycle.co.uk)*, **Chickenshed** *(www.chickenshed.org.uk)*, **Rose Theatre** *(www.rosetheatrekingston.org)*, **New Wimbledon Theatre and Studio** *(www. ambassadortickets.com/Wimbledon)* and **Hackney Empire** *(www.hackneyempire.co.uk)*.

A pantomime is a Christmas holiday highlight – for adults as well as children: among the best are those at the **Old Vic** *(www.oldvictheatre.com)* and **Richmond Theatre** *(www.atgtickets.com/venue/ Richmond-Theatre)*. Also at Christmas, there are ballets for children at the **Coliseum** *(www.ballet.org.uk)* and the **Royal Opera House** *(see p90)*, and throughout the year at Sadler's Wells' **Peacock Theatre** and **Lilian Baylis Studio** *(www.sadlerswells.com)*.

London's principal cinemas are **Odeon** *(www.odeon.co.uk)*, **Vue** *(www.myvue.com)* and **Cineworld** *(www.cineworld.co.uk)*. These and the independent **Clapham Picture House** *(www.picturehouses.co.uk/cinema/Clapham_ Picturehouse)* and **Electric Cinema** *(www. electriccinema.co.uk)*, have regular kids' clubs.

Active London

Sports-mad families will find plenty going on in London to keep their heart rates up, whether they want to be participants or spectators *(see pp50–51)*. Other activities that should appeal to energetic kids are climbing, go-karting, bowling, inline skating and even dry skiing.

Westway Sports Centre has a terrific beginners' climbing wall and a junior programme that includes family sessions (www.westwaysportscentre.org.uk/climbing). The best places for budding racing drivers (aged 8+) to go-karting are **Playscape** (www.playscape.co.uk) and **Daytona** (www.daytona.co.uk), while children's bowling is offered at **Hollywood Bowl** (www.hollywoodbowl.co.uk), with special lightweight bowls, and **Bloomsbury Bowling** (www.bloomsburybowling.com). There are inline skating programmes for children in Kensington Gardens, run by **Kids Rollerblading Lessons** (www.kidsrollerbladinglessons.co.uk), **LondonSkaters** (www.londonskaters.com) and **Citiskate** (www.citiskate.co.uk), which also operates elsewhere. For dry skiing within the M25, try **Sandown Ski Centre** (www.sandownsports.co.uk) and **Bromley Ski & Snow Board Centre** (www.bromleyski.co.uk).

Above Children trying their hands at the arts and crafts on offer at Somerset House

Behind the scenes

London museums – big and small – often host highly imaginative workshops for families. Some of the best are at the **Geffrye Museum** (see p210), where the creative emphasis is on making or decorating objects. Workshops at the **Imperial War Museum** (see p166) can introduce children to storytelling through art and handle the difficult subject of war in a sensitive and involving way. At the small and slightly eccentric **Horniman Museum** (see pp222–3), children can find their imagination fired by being able to handle some of the extraordinary objects from the collection. As you would imagine, the **British Museum** (see pp102–3) puts on some excellent workshops, using technology to create fun, sometimes gruesome animations about mummification, fantastical creatures or the Aztec gods.

Going behind the scenes at a theatre can be fascinating for children, offering a glimpse into the hidden worlds of costumes, lighting, scenery shifting and even technical wizardry. Of all London's backstage tours, the most impressive are those organised by the **National Theatre** (see p162), **Royal Opera House** (see p90), **Shakespeare's Globe** (see pp144–7) and **Theatre Royal Drury Lane** (see pp91).

Below Enjoying a rollerblading lesson from a member of the Kids Rollerblading Lessons team in leafy Kensington Gardens

London Through the Year

The best time for a trip to London depends on what your family likes to do. The late spring, summer and early autumn will appeal to families who like being outdoors, while those who are happiest visiting museums and galleries might prefer to come in the winter, when the city is quieter and activities are not so dependent on the weather. Regardless of the elements, every season in London has plenty to recommend it.

Spring

Springtime in London, when the blossom is out, can be wonderful for a visit. Although London is among the most temperate parts of the UK and spring is often pleasant, the weather can be unpredictable, chilly and wet, so warm clothes and waterproofs are sensible precautions. From March onwards, outdoor sporting (see p50–51) and social events are fun for all the family and there is plenty in the calendar around Easter, especially for children.

A charming **Oranges and Lemons Service** is usually held on the third Thursday in March in St Clement Danes church. Pupils from the local primary school recite the well-known nursery rhyme, and each child is given an orange and a lemon after the service. On 21 March, the **Spring Equinox**, the first day of the solar New Year, is celebrated at Tower Hill in a historic pagan ceremony with contemporary druids dressed in long white robes.

On Good Friday, after an 11am service held at St Bartholomew the Great, Smithfield, hot-cross buns and coins are distributed to local children by the **Butterworth Charity**. Over the Easter weekend, there are **Easter egg hunts** at Battersea Park Zoo, Kenwood House, Fenton House, Handel House Museum and Kew Gardens. There is egg painting and rolling at Ham House, and, suitable for older children, the **London Bridge Experience** stages a gruesome treasure hunt for missing severed heads. There are traditional Easter **funfairs** on Hampstead Heath and the green opposite Hampton Court, and **London Friday Night Skate & Sunday Stroll** is a weekly family street-skating event in Hyde Park, aimed at skaters of all levels. Over the May Day bank holiday weekend, **Canalway Cavalcade** is a colourful occasion in Little Venice, featuring a boat rally, puppet shows and street entertainers. May is traditionally the month of fairs, and on the first Saturday in May, the **Punch and Judy Festival** is staged in Covent Garden Piazza, with shows from 10:30am–5:30pm. The **Covent Garden May Fayre and Puppet Festival** is celebrated on the Sunday nearest Punch's birthday on 9 May. A morning procession is followed by a service in St Paul's Church, and until 5:30pm there are performances of Punch and Judy shows on the site where, in 1662, Samuel Pepys watched the first ever show staged in England. Over four days at the end of May, gardeners can enjoy the gardens at the **Chelsea Flower Show** at the Royal Hospital Chelsea.

Below left Children taking part in the Easter egg hunt at Fenton House in Hampstead. *Below right* A colourful and energetic performance of Crazy for You at Regent's Park Open Air Theatre

Summer

Although never entirely reliable, the weather in summer is usually fine and sunny, with long days and light evenings. People picnic in the parks; restaurants and cafés move their tables outside; and the city takes on an almost Mediterranean feel. There is always plenty to entertain families, from ceremonies (see pp18–19) and sporting events (see p50–51) to open-air theatre and concerts. The downside is that London can be very hot and crowded during July and August.

Summer has arrived when the **Royal Academy Summer Exhibition** opens in early June. It continues until mid-August and has a reputation as the art world's most eclectic show. Also on throughout the summer is the **City of London Festival**, an extensive programme of music, art, films and talks all over the city, and there are open-air plays (some specifically for children) at the **Regent's Park Open Air Theatre** and **Shakespeare's Globe**, operas (some for children) in **Holland Park**, and picnic concerts at **Kenwood House**. One of the first outdoor events of the summer is the **London Green Fair** in Regent's Park, with eco-friendly attractions such as a mini farm, willow weaving, sewing classes and wigwam building.

Osterley Weekend, in July, is a village fête featuring a host of activities, including a funfair, a mini farm, and archery as well as dance and music workshops. There are also a number of stalls to eat and drink at. From mid- to late June, the streets of East London are filled with classical, jazz and contemporary music at the **Spitalfields Festival**, which includes toddlers' concerts, guided walks and musical picnics. There is more lively outdoor music, plus dancing and processions at the week-long **Greenwich & Docklands International Festival**.

In early July, the five-day **Hampton Court Palace Flower Show** rivals Chelsea for its colour and variety, but is not as crowded. Mid-July sees the start of the ever-popular, two-month-long **BBC Promenade Concerts** (the "Proms") at the Royal Albert Hall, founded to bring both classical and modern music to a wider audience. Also in mid-July, **Doggett's Coat and Badge Race** dates from 1714 and sees apprentice Watermen of the River Thames in bright costumes rowing single sculls from London Bridge to Chelsea Pier. The summer season culminates with the Caribbean **Notting Hill Carnival** over August bank-holiday weekend. Europe's largest carnival, it is musical, vibrant

and colourful, with a procession of eye-catching floats and costumes, steel bands and food stalls. Sunday is children's day.

Autumn

Once the summer crowds have gone, new shows open in the theatres, the shops restock and autumn days can still be blue-skied and sunny. In early September the **Mayor's Thames Festival** combines carnival, street art, music and river events between Westminster and Tower bridges. The highlight is **Sunday's Night Carnival**, when performers take to the streets, followed by fireworks on the river. The next Saturday, spectators return to the river to watch as some 300 boats, ranging from Hawaiian canoes to Viking longboats, row the **Great River Race**. Also in early September is **On Blackheath**, a family-friendly festival with music, arts and crafts and a village fête vibe.

In late September, the **Pearly Kings & Queens Harvest Festival** at St Martin-in-the-Fields church is the flagship event of the Pearly calendar, attended by Cockney pearly kings and queens.

Visit London between the end of October and the beginning of November for the festivals of Halloween and Bonfire Night.

Below left Vibrant costumes and floats take centre stage at the Notting Hill Carnival *Below right* Tucking into a feast on Southwark Bridge, part of the Mayor's Thames Festival

October Plenty, the autumn harvest festival held in Southwark, has a mix of fun-filled activities on its agenda, ranging from seasonal customs such as apple bobbing and conker fights to festive theatre and delicious food. For **Halloween**, there are always hair-raising shows at the London Dungeon and London Bridge Experience, and a spine-tingling tunnel ride on a narrowboat, courtesy of the London Canal Museum. Wrap up warm to watch the fireworks celebrating **Bonfire Night** on or near 5 November. Among the best are those in Bishop's Park, Ravenscourt Park, Battersea Park and on Blackheath.

If yours is a family of early birds, between sunrise and 8:30am on the first Sunday in November, a splendid collection of vintage, pre-1905 cars leaves Hyde Park on the **London to Brighton Veteran Car Run**. Sleepy heads might prefer to catch the cars as they parade down Regent's Street the day before, from 1–4pm.

As evidence that winter is on its way, mid-November sees the switching on of the **Regent Street Christmas Lights** and the arrival of **Winter Wonderland** in Hyde Park (until early Jan), with the city's largest outdoor ice rink, a circus, toboggan slide and a host of other rides.

Winter

From early December, Christmas lights twinkle in the streets, decorations transform shops and public places, and Santa mans his grottoes. Skaters flock to outdoor rinks (see p50–1) and carol singing and the scent of roasting chestnuts spread through the streets. For families who enjoy culture, there are exhibitions, plays and ballets, and for those who prefer to shop, there are the sales. When it snows, children gather in the parks to toboggan and make snowmen. The downside is that transport tends to grind to a halt, and the snow quickly turns to slush.

If your children are aching for a glimpse of Father Christmas, take them to visit him in one of **Santa's Grottoes** in Harrods, Selfridges, Hamleys, Kew Gardens or Canary Wharf. On the first Thursday in December, there is a **Christmas Tree Lighting ceremony** to switch on the 500 lights that decorate the gigantic Norwegian spruce in Trafalgar Square. The event kicks off at 6pm with carol singing, and the lights are switched on at 6:30pm. Carols are sung beneath the tree most evenings in the run-up to Christmas, and there are also **carol concerts** at the Royal Albert Hall and the Horniman Museum and

carol services at many London churches. Magical candlelit services are held at St Mary-at-Hill, Southwark Cathedral and All Hallows-by-the-Tower.

A pre-Christmas treat for horse and dog lovers, the week-long **London International Horse Show** is held at Olympia in mid-December. Highlights include show jumping and dressage competitions, a Shetland pony race and dog agility and jumping events. Christmas Day is quiet in London, but there is a tremendous celebration on **New Year's Eve** with midnight fireworks at the London Eye (shown on giant screens in Trafalgar and Parliament Squares). The following day, more than 10,000 performers take part in the **New Year's Day Parade** from Piccadilly to Parliament Square from noon–3pm. There is a carnival atmosphere, with steel and marching bands, clowns, jugglers and classic cars and motorbikes.

Gasp at the impressive speed and skills of the sculptors at the **London Ice Sculpting Festival** in Canada Square Park in mid-January. In late January or early February, **Chinese New Year** is a wonderfully colourful and noisy Chinatown event, accompanied by dancing dragons, lanterns, flags, torches, food and firecrackers.

Below left A horse and rider taking part in an event at the Olympia London International Horse Show *Below right* One of the sculptors at work on his ice sculpture at the London Ice Sculpting Festival, held at Canary Wharf

The Lowdown

Spring

Battersea Park Zoo www.batterseaparkzoo.co.uk

Butterworth Charity www.greatstbarts.com

Canalway Cavalcade www.waterways.org.uk/events_festivals

Chelsea Flower Show www.rhs.org.uk

Covent Garden May Fayre & Puppet Festival www.alternativearts.co.uk

Fenton House www.nationaltrust.org.uk

Ham House www.nationaltrust.org.uk

Hampstead Heath funfair www.hampsteadheath.org.uk

Hampton Court funfair www.hamptoncourtfunfair.co.uk

Handel House Museum www.handelhouse.org

Kenwood House www.englishheritage.org.uk/daysout/properties/kenwood

Kew Gardens www.kew.org

London Bridge Experience www.thelondonbridgeexperience.com

London Friday Night Skate & Sunday Stroll www.lfns.co.uk

Oranges and Lemons Service www.raf.mod.uk/stclementdanes

Punch & Judy Festival www.thepjf.com

Summer

BBC Promenade Concerts www.bbc.co.uk/proms

City of London Festival www.colf.org

Doggett's Coat and Badge Race www.watermenshall.org

Greenwich & Docklands International Festival www.festival.org

Hampton Court Palace Flower Show www.rhs.org.uk

Kenwood House www.englishheritage.org.uk/daysout/properties/kenwood-house

London Green Fair www.londongreenfair.org

Notting Hill Carnival www.thenottinghillcarnival.com

On Blackheath www.onblackheath.com

Osterley Weekend www.nationaltrust.org.uk

Regent's Park Open Air Theatre www.openairtheatre.org

Royal Academy Summer Exhibition www.royalacademy.org.uk

Shakespeare's Globe www.shakespearesglobe.com

Spitalfields Festival www.spitalfieldsfestival.org.uk

Autumn

Battersea Park www.wandsworth.gov.uk

Bishop's Park & Ravenscourt Park www.lbhf.gov.uk

Blackheath www.lewisham.gov.uk/NewsAndEvents/Events/Fireworks

Great River Race www.greatriverrace.co.uk

London Bridge Experience www.thelondonbridgeexperience.com

London Canal Museum www.canalmuseum.org.uk

London Dungeon www.thedungeons.com/london/en

London to Brighton Veteran Car Run www.veterancarrun.com

Mayor's Thames Festival www.thamesfestival.org

October Plenty www.thelionspart.co.uk/octoberplenty

Pearly Kings & Queens Harvest Festival www.pearlysociety.co.uk

Regent's Street Christmas Lights www.regentstreetonline.com

Winter Wonderland www.hydeparkwinterwonderland.com

Winter

Carol services: All Hallows-by-the-Tower www.ahbtt.org.uk; Horniman Museum www.horniman.ac.uk; Royal Albert Hall www.royalalberthall.com; St Mary-at-Hill www.stmary-at-hill.org; Southwark Cathedral cathedral.southwark.anglican.org

Chinese New Year www.chinatownlondon.org

London Ice Sculpting Festival www.londonicesculptingfestival.co.uk

London International Horse Show www.olympiahorseshow.com

New Year's Day Parade www.londonparade.co.uk

Santa's Grottoes: Canary Wharf www.mycanarywharf.com; Hamleys www.hamleys.com; Harrods www.harrods.com; Kew Gardens www.kew.org; Selfridges www.selfridges.com; Christmas Tree Lighting www.london.gov.uk/priorities/art-culture/trafalgar-square/events

Public holidays

New Year's Day 1 Jan

Good Friday Mar/Apr

Easter Monday Mar/Apr

May Day first Mon in May

Spring Bank Holiday last Mon in May

August Bank Holiday last Mon in Aug

Christmas Day 25 Dec

Boxing Day 26 Dec

Below left Performers in lion costumes dance on podiums in Trafalgar Square to celebrate Chinese New Year *Below right* A young enthusiast inspects a display of vintage cars; part of the London to Brighton Veteran Car Run

London's Ceremonies

London has a full calendar of ceremonial events, occasions and customs, most of them connected with the royal family and many dating back to the Middle Ages or beyond. Not only are these colourful ceremonies historically important, but they are also bursting with spectacular costumes and pageantry, making them thrilling to watch for the whole family.

Trooping the Colour

Combining pageantry, military precision and music, this splendid ceremony in Horse Guards Parade honours the Queen's official birthday on a Saturday in mid-June. The Queen inspects a Guards' regiment from the Household Division, resplendent in their scarlet tunics and bearskins or plumed helmets and carrying the "colour" (their regimental flag). Afterwards, the Queen is escorted to Buckingham Palace to appear on the balcony.

Changing the Guard

Troops from the Household Division have been guarding the monarch since 1660, and a colourful ceremony marks the handover of duty from the old guard to a new one, usually with the Foot Guards in their full-dress uniform. Accompanied by a Guards' band, it takes place at Buckingham Palace daily from May–July and on alternate days throughout the rest of the year, starting soon after 11am. Children will enjoy the colour and spectacle.

State Opening of Parliament

The Queen opens the new session of Parliament each year, usually in November or December, with this historic ceremony. Although the actual ceremony – in which the Queen announces a programme of proposed legislation on behalf of her government – is closed to the public, it is televised and the royal procession from Buckingham Palace to Westminster can be seen along The Mall and Whitehall. The Queen travels in a state coach, while the Imperial State Crown has its own carriage.

Remembrance Day

Through this solemn ceremony in Whitehall on the second Sunday in November, the nation commemorates those who died in the two world wars and other more recent conflicts. The Queen and the royal family, political leaders and representatives of the armed forces observe a two-minute silence at 11am and, after the sounding of the last post, lay wreaths of poppies at the foot of the Cenotaph. Once the Queen has left, war veterans march past the Cenotaph to pay their respects.

Gun Salutes

The custom of firing a cannon was once a sign of respect or welcome, an unloaded gun indicating friendly intent. Today, gun salutes at the Tower of London and in Hyde Park mark royal occasions, such as

Below left *The magnificent state coach taking part in the celebrations and pageantry of the Lord Mayor's Show*
Below right *Wreaths of poppies laid at the foot of the Cenotaph as part of the Remembrance Day ceremonies*

birthdays or anniversaries, and in Green Park, state visits, the State Opening of Parliament and the Queen's birthday parade. The basic royal salute is 21 rounds, but 20 extra rounds are included if it is fired in a royal park, palace or fortress. Salutes usually take place at 11am or noon.

Ceremony of the Keys

Yeoman Warders, or "Beefeaters", have performed this ceremony, which is open to the public, to secure the Tower of London every night for 700 years. The gates are locked at exactly 9:53pm by the Chief Yeoman Warder, escorted by four armed guards. He is challenged by a sentry, who then allows him to pass, acknowledging that he is the bearer of the Queen's keys. The ceremony ends with the Chief Warder taking the keys to safety while a trumpeter sounds the last post.

Lord Mayor's Show

This procession occurs on the second Saturday in November, taking the newly elected Lord Mayor in a state coach from the Guildhall to the Royal Courts of Justice, where he/she pledges allegiance to the Crown, and then comes back again. The custom,

The Lowdown

Beating Retreat *www.royal.gov.uk/ royaleventsandceremonies/ beatingretreat/beatingre treat.aspx*
Beating the Bounds *www.allhallows bythetower.org.uk/history/ beating-the-bounds*
Ceremony of the Keys *www.hrp.org. uk/toweroflondon/whatson/ ceremonyofthekeys*

Lord Mayor's Show *www.lordmayorsshow.org*
Oak Apple Day *www.chelsea-pensioners.co.uk/founders-day*
Royal Ceremonies (Trooping the Colour; Changing the Guard; State Opening of Parliament; Remembrance Day; Gun Salutes) *www.royal.gov.uk/ RoyalEventsandCeremonies/ Overview.aspx*

which is almost 800 years old, starts at 11am, includes floats, military bands and City guildsmen, and culminates in fireworks at 5pm.

Beating Retreat

In a spectacular show, the massed bands of the Household Division perform this ceremony on two consecutive June evenings. It dates back to the time when a drum was used to communicate on the battlefield. Beating a retreat signalled the soldiers to stop fighting and return to camp. Rousing tunes are played by 300 musicians and the Queen usually takes the salute.

Oak Apple Day

Celebrated on 29 May, Oak Apple Day commemorates the lucky escape of the future Charles II from

Parliamentary forces by hiding in a hollow oak tree. The date was both Charles's birthday and the day in 1660 when he returned to London to claim the throne. Today, it is celebrated by Chelsea Pensioners, who decorate the statue of Charles II, their founder, at the Royal Hospital, and parade before royalty.

Beating the Bounds

Dating back to a time when there were few maps and boundaries were constantly in dispute, this custom involves walking around parish boundaries, whacking them with a stick and praying for protection. It is still observed on Ascension Day at All-Hallows-by-the-Tower, where the parish's southern boundary is in the middle of the Thames. Members of the party must board a boat to beat the boundary mark in the water.

Below left The Queen making her speech in the House of Lords during the State Opening of Parliament *Below right* Gun salute outside the Tower of London, marking a Royal occasion or celebration

Getting to London

London is a major European transport hub, and there are many ways to reach it. By air, there is a huge choice of carriers from all over the world, and competition and budget airlines have driven down prices. Eurostar links the UK to Europe, and ferries, jetfoils and catamarans cross the English Channel and North Sea. Coaches to London from Europe are often the cheapest option.

Arriving by air

Five airports serve London: Heathrow, Gatwick, Stansted, Luton and City.

FROM HEATHROW

Heathrow is 24 km (15 miles) west of Central London. The quickest way in is by the **Heathrow Express**, a 15–20-minute non-stop train to Paddington Station. Trains depart every 15 minutes 5am–11:40pm. **Heathrow Connect**'s 25–35-minute stopping trains to Paddington depart every 30 minutes 5am–11pm. Three stations link Heathrow to **London Underground**'s Piccadilly line, which takes around 50 minutes to reach the West End. At night, the N9 bus runs to Aldwych, Central London, leaving every 10–20 minutes.

    National Express runs a coach service to Victoria from Heathrow's bus station from 5:20am–9:40pm, as well as the Heathrow Hoppa Service buses at £4. A shuttle bus service to various London hotels is run by **Heathrow Shuttle** and **SkyShuttle**, a cheaper alternative to taxis, which cost £45–75. The journey into London by road takes around 1 hour.

FROM GATWICK

London's second airport is 50 km (31 miles) south of the city and has two terminals. **Gatwick Express** trains leave the South Terminal every 15 minutes from 4:35am–1:35am and take 30–35 minutes to get to Victoria Station. Cheaper Southern services also run to Victoria and **Thameslink** connects Gatwick with St Pancras International and London Bridge. National Express coaches leave for Victoria every 30–60 minutes from 5:15am–9:45pm. Departing every 15 minutes round the clock, **easyBus** runs coaches to Earl's Court/ West Brompton. There are coach pick-up points in both terminals and the journey takes 65 minutes. Taxis to central London cost £50–60.

FROM STANSTED

The quickest way to travel the 56 km (35 miles) southwest to London from Stansted is on the **Stansted Express**. Trains run to Liverpool Street every 15 minutes from 5:30–1am, and take about 45 minutes. National Express provides 24-hour coaches to Victoria (every 20–30 minutes) and Stratford (every 30 minutes). **Terravision** coaches leave every 30 minutes for Victoria (7:15–1am) and Liverpool Street (6–1am). The 24-hour easyBus runs coaches to Baker Street and Stratford every 20–30 minutes. Coaches to East London take 45–55 minutes and to the centre, 60–90 minutes. Taxis to the centre of town cost £70–80.

FROM LUTON

From Luton, 50 km (31 miles) north of London, a 5–10-minute shuttle bus runs from 5am–midnight to Luton Airport Parkway station

Below left Ferry leaving the port of Dover, heading for France *Below centre* The Docklands Light Railway station at London City Airport, from where the DLR takes passengers directly into Central London

(price included in rail tickets). From there, trains to St Pancras International are run by Thameslink (5am–midnight, every 15 minutes, taking 20–30 minutes) and **East Midlands Trains** (6am–10:30pm, every hour, taking 25–35 minutes). **Green Line 757** and easyBus both have a 24-hour coach link to Victoria. The journey takes just over an hour. Green Line coaches leave every 20 minutes–1 hour; easyBus ones leave every 15–30 minutes.

FROM LONDON CITY

London City Airport is in Docklands, 14 km (9 miles) east from the centre. From the **Docklands Light Railway** (DLR) station, trains leave every 8–15 minutes to Canning Town and Bank, both also on the Underground with connections to major rail stations. Bus number 473 goes to Stratford and the 474 goes to Canning Town. Taxis cost from £25 to the City and from £30 to the West End.

Arriving by train

St Pancras International is the London terminus for the **Eurostar**, the high-speed train linking the UK and Europe. From King's Cross St Pancras Underground station, it is possible to travel almost anywhere in the city via six Underground lines.

The city's other main stations and the areas they serve are **Liverpool Street**, East Anglia; **King's Cross**, the northeast; **Euston**, the northwest; **Paddington**, the west; **Waterloo**, the southwest; **Charing Cross** and **Victoria**, the southeast. All have Underground stations. Buy tickets in advance from **National Rail**.

Arriving by sea

The UK's ferry ports all have good rail links. Trains arrive at St Pancras International from **Dover**, which serves Calais and Ostend, and **Folkestone** (Calais and Boulogne), which is also the terminus for the **Eurotunnel**, the drive-on-drive-off rail service for cars. From **Newhaven**, which serves Dieppe, trains arrive at Victoria. Trains from **Portsmouth**, which serve the northern French ports, arrive at Waterloo, and from **Harwich**, which serves the Hook of Holland, they stop at Liverpool Street.

Arriving by coach

Coaches from European and UK destinations arrive at **Victoria Coach Station**, often stopping at other London drop-off points. The biggest operator within the UK is National Express, with **Eurolines** serving as its European arm.

The Lowdown

Airports

Heathrow www.heathrowairport. com; **Gatwick** www.gatwickairport. com; **Luton** www.london-luton.co. uk; **London City** www. londoncityairport.com; **Stansted** www.stanstedairport.com

Underground/Buses/DLR

Transport for London www.tfl.gov.uk

Buses/Shuttle buses

easyBus www.easybus.co.uk; **Green Line 757** www.greenline.co.uk; **Heathrow Shuttle** www. heathrowshuttle.com; **National Express** www.nationalexpress.com; **SkyShuttle** www.skyshuttle.co.uk; **Terravision** www.terravision.eu

Trains/Stations

Charing Cross www.networkrail.co. uk/aspx/795.aspx; **East Midlands Trains** www.eastmidlandstrains.co. uk; **Eurostar** www.eurostar.com; **Euston** www.networkrail.co.uk/ aspx/819.aspx; **Gatwick Express** www.gatwickexpress.com; **Heathrow Connect** www. heathrowconnect.com; **Heathrow Express** www.heathrowexpress.com; **King's Cross** www.networkrail.co.uk/ aspx/867.aspx; **Liverpool Street** www.networkrail.co.uk/aspx/897. aspx; **National Rail** www.nationalrail. co.uk; **Paddington** www.networkrail. co.uk/aspx/935.aspx; **Stansted Express** www.stanstedexpress.com; **St Pancras International** www. stpancras.com; **Thameslink** www. thameslinkrailway.com; **Victoria** www.networkrail.co.uk/aspx/947. aspx; **Waterloo** www.networkrail. co.uk/aspx/959.aspx

Ports

Dover www.doverport.co.uk; **Eurotunnel** www.eurotunnel.com; **Folkestone** www.directferries.co.uk/ folkestone.htm; **Harwich** www. harwich.co.uk; **Newhaven** www. newhavenferryport.co.uk; **Portsmouth** www.portsmouth-port. co.uk

Coach

Eurolines www.eurolines.com; **Victoria Coach Station** www.tfl.gov. uk/gettingaround/1210.aspx

Below left A British Airways plane on the tarmac at London City Airport *Below right* One of Eurolines' fleet of coaches, which serve the rest of the UK and much of Europe

Getting Around London

London has an excellent, comprehensive and busy public transport system. Transport for London (TfL) is responsible for buses, the Underground, Docklands Light Railway (DLR), London Overground, Barclays Cycle Hire and River Buses. The worst times to travel are during the morning and afternoon rush hours – 8–9:30am and 4:30–6:30pm from Monday to Friday. Possibly the most pleasant way to travel in London is by river bus.

By bus

London buses generally run from 5am to 12:30am (7:30am–11:30pm Sun), with night buses, recognizable by the prefix N before the number, providing a less frequent service on many popular routes. Sometimes slow, particularly during rush hours, buses have dedicated lanes on most main roads and cover parts of the city that the Underground does not.

The traditional double-decker Routemaster, now only in service on two heritage routes, has been replaced by modern double-decker and single-decker buses. A line of eye-catching buses, promoted as the 21st–century version of the Routemaster, called The New Bus for London has been introduced. By 2016, there will be more than 600 of these buses running in the capital. Routes are displayed at bus stops and on the **Transport for London** (TfL) website. The destination is indicated on the front of the bus. Make sure you are heading in the right direction.

Although there are technically still two types of bus stop, compulsory and request, current TfL practice means you should always signal if you want to board a bus and, when on the bus, ring the bell if you want to disembark. Night buses only stop on request.

Routemaster heritage buses Nos 9 and 15 are great for sight seeing, but if the weather is fine, an even better way to see the city is from an open-topped double-decker. Guided bus tours are offer ed by **Big Bus Tours** and **Original London Sightseeing Tours**, which provide commentaries specially designed for children. Tickets are valid for 24 hours, and routes include most major landmarks, the service is hop-on-hop-off. The London Tramlink is a useful alternative to buses in some areas like Croydon. It is linked to Wimbledon Town Centre and connects the southernmost points of the Tube and London Overground as well.

By Underground, DLR and train

The London Underground (the "Tube") is the fastest and easiest way to get around the city. It operates daily, except for 25 December, from approximately 5am to 12:30am and from 7:30am to 11:30pm Sun. If planning a journey late at night with several connections, be sure to set off in good time. Trains can be very crowded during rush hours.

Stations are easily recognized by the TfL logo – a blue horizontal line across a red circle. There are 11 colour-coded lines, making it

Below left An iconic red double-decker London bus travelling through Central London Below right London Underground sign showing where to pick up the different lines

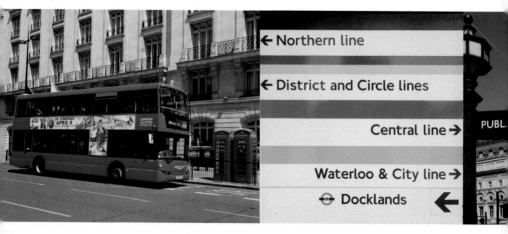

simple to plan journeys and changes. Maps are displayed in Tube stations and on trains. Some lines are straightforward single routes; others have branches. The Circle Line operates from Hammersmith to Edgware Road clockwise, and then back again.

Once you are through the ticket barrier (see Tickets below), follow the signs to the platform for the line and direction you need. Check the front of the train and the platform's electronic indicator for the final destination to make sure it's not branching off or terminating early. On leaving the train, there are well-signed exits, as well as connections to other lines.

The **Docklands Light Railway** (DLR) is an automated, driver-less light rail system linking the City of London with the redeveloped Docklands area, including City Airport, and **London Overground**, a rail overground network serving suburban boroughs. The suburbs are also served by **National Rail** (visit its website). DLR trains run from 5:30am to 12:30am Mon–Sat and 6:30am to 11:30pm Sun. Overground train timetables are available on the TfL website.

With the exception of new stations, few Underground stations have a lift. In all, there are 66 stations with step-free access. The TfL website has a map marked with wheelchair symbols indicating Tube stations that have disabled access. Travelling on the Underground with a pram or pushchair can be awkward, particularly during the rush hours.

Tickets

TfL divides the city into six charging zones for Tube, DLR, London Overground and National Rail services, radiating out from the most central Zone 1 to Zone 6, which includes the outer suburbs. Zones 7–9 extend beyond Greater London. The most economical tickets that can be used on all forms of transport, including National Rail to Zone 9, are **Travelcards** – paper tickets available for one or seven days and in various combinations of zones – and **Visitor Oyster cards** – "smartcards" that store credit to pay for journeys. Both are available from the TfL website, Tube stations and **Travel Information Centres**. Oyster cards are also available from the many **Oyster Ticket Stops** (mostly newsagents) across London and can be charged up here, at Travel Information Centres and at Tube stations – but not National Rail stations. A small returnable deposit is charged for the card, but the card never expires so you can keep it for your next visit. Oyster cards are valid across all zones and automatically calculate the cheapest fare for the journeys you make in a day. To use your Oyster card, touch it on the yellow reader when you enter a bus and at the start and end of every Tube or train journey. Travelcards must be shown to the bus driver and placed into the ticket machine at the start and end of Tube or train journeys.

Children under 11 travel free on buses and up to four under-11s travel free on the Tube, DLR, London Overground and National Rail services when accompanied by an adult. Under-16s are also eligible for free bus and discounted Tube travel provided they have an 11–15 Oyster photocard, which must be ordered for a fee from the TfL website at least three weeks in advance. A simpler option, the child Travelcard gives 11–15–year-olds half-price travel on all Tube and rail networks.

Cash fares are not accepted on any buses anywhere in London. You must use a Travelcard, Oyster card or contactless bank card to pay your fare. Contactless cards are touched on the yellow reader in the same way as Oyster cards are. They also calculate the discounted fare and daily price cap.

Below left The red, blue and white London Underground logo, which can be found at every Tube station throughout the city
Below right Platform in one of London's bustling overground stations

By taxi

London's distinctive "black" cabs (although some now sport different colours) have drivers who must pass a tough test to prove their familiarity with the city before being licensed. Cabs can be hailed in the street if their yellow "taxi" light is illuminated. They can also be found at ranks outside airports, stations and some major hotels and stores, as well as various other locations throughout the capital. Once they have stopped, taxis are obliged to take you to your destination, provided it is within 9.6 km (6 miles) of the pick-up point and inside the Metropolitan area. The fare is shown on the meter, which will start ticking as soon as the driver accepts your custom. There are three fare tariffs: between 6am and 8pm, and 8pm and 10pm on weekdays; and between 6am to 10pm on weekends. For public holidays, it is between 10pm and 6am. Tip the driver 10–15 per cent of the fare. Cabs can also be ordered online or by phone from **Radio Taxis** and **Dial-a-Cab**.

By mini-cab

Mini-cabs are not governed by the same strict regulations as black cabs and the drivers are not as well qualified, but they are quite professional. Order a mini-cab by phone, or email or by visiting a mini-cab office, and agree the fare in advance. Do not hail one in the street as it is illegal for mini-cab drivers to take customers without a booking. For names of local mini-cab firms, enter your location into **Cabwise** on the TfL website. **Lady Minicabs** only employs women drivers.

By car

Expensive parking and congestion charging are designed to deter people from driving in Central London, and traffic, particularly on arterial roads outside the congestion zone, can be very heavy during rush hours. The charge for driving in the congestion zone, which covers the area to the east of Park Lane, south of Marylebone/Euston Road, west of Tower Hamlets and north of Elephant and Castle, is £11.50 per day (7am–6pm, Mon–Fri), payable on the day, or £14 if paid by midnight the following day. It costs £10.50 if you register online for **Congestion Charging Auto Pay**. Payments can be made online, by phone, by text. If you fail to pay in time, you will be fined £130, reduced to £65 if you then pay within 14 days.

Parking in Central London, usually in pay-and-display bays with payment by mobile or text, can be scarce and restrictions need to be observed. Be careful not to park in a residents-only bay during the designated hours. There is also no parking on red routes or on double yellow lines. You can park on single yellow lines in the evenings and on Sundays. Parking illegally or overstaying the time limit in a pay-and-display bay can result in a fine and/or your car being wheel-clamped or towed away. A notice should be displayed informing drivers of where to go to pay their fine and collect their vehicle.

There are plenty of car-hire firms in London, including **Avis**, **Budget**, **Europcar**, **Hertz** and **Thrifty**, which have offices at airports and other locations throughout the city, but the best rates are through comparison websites such as **travelsupermarket. com**. For large families, **5th Gear** has 7- and 9-seaters, plus child and booster seats to rent. Most firms offer a car delivery and collection service. All drivers need to study the UK **Highway Code** and familiarize themselves with the traffic signs used in London.

By river

Regular river services are operated by TfL's **River Bus**, which operates

Below left A London "black" cab travelling through the streets of Central London *Below right* The many Santander Cycle Hire bikes at one of the ranks located throughout the city

four lines between Putney in the west and Woolwich Arsenal in the east. Timetables, which change according to the season, and maps are available on the TfL website. For river tours and cruises, see p28.

By bicycle

Santander Cycle Hire is a public bicycle-sharing scheme launched in 2010 and originally sponsored by Barclays. Its red-and-grey bikes are available from docking stations throughout central and eastern London (shown on a map on the TfL website). Register online, or pay at the terminals, borrow a bike and drop it off at any docking station in the scheme. The bikes have three gears and adjustable seats. They are quite heavy though, so maybe not ideal for long rides. Bikes suitable for all the family can be rented from the **London Bicycle Tour Company**, which also arranges cycle tours, and **Go Pedal**, which offers child seats and trailers. If you are cycling with children, TfL promotes **Greenways** – safe, family-friendly routes running through parks, forests, and quiet streets and along waterways. It is always advisable to wear reflective clothing and a helmet when cycling and to use a strong lock to deter thieves.

The Lowdown

By bus
Big Bus Tours www.bigbustours.com
Original London Sightseeing Tours www.theoriginaltour.com
Transport for London www.tfl.gov.uk

By Underground, DLR & train
Docklands Light Railway www.tfl.gov.uk/dlr/timetable/dlr
London Overground www.tfl.gov.uk/modes/london-overground
National Rail Enquiries www.nationalrail.co.uk
Oyster Ticket Stops ticketstoplocator.tfl.gov.uk
Travel Information Centres www.tfl.gov.uk/fares-and-payments/buying-tickets/

By taxi and mini-cab
Dial-a-Cab www.dialacab.co.uk
Cabwise www.tfl.gov.uk/cabwise
Lady Minicabs www.ladyminicabs.co.uk
Radio Taxis www.radiotaxis.co.uk

By car
5th Gear www.5th-gear.net
Avis www.avis.co.uk

Budget www.budget.co.uk
Congestion Charging Auto Pay www.tfl.gov.uk/modes/driving/congestion-charge?cid=pp020
Europcar www.europcar.co.uk
Hertz www.hertz.co.uk
Highway Code www.gov.uk/browse/driving/highway-code
Thrifty www.thrifty.com
travelsupermarket.com www.travelsupermarket.com

By river
River Bus www.tfl.gov.uk/modes/river/about-river-bus

By bicycle
Santander Cycle Hire http://www.tfl.gov.uk/modes/cycling/
Go Pedal www.gopedal.co.uk
Greenways www.tfl.gov.uk/cdn/static/cms/documents/greenways-final-annual-monitoring-report.pdf
London Bicycle Tour Company www.londonbicycle.com

On foot
London Walks www.walks.com
Transport for London www.tfl.gov.uk/gettingaround/walking

On foot

Although it is large, London is still a great city to explore on foot, whether it's a stroll around the back streets of Covent Garden or the City or a more serious ramble through the green spaces of Richmond Park or over Hampstead Heath. The TfL website has a walking route planner. A number of companies arrange themed walks, from Ghosts of the Old City to Harry Potter Film Locations. The most established operator is **London Walks**.

Below left A river bus cruising along the Thames, past Cleopatra's Needle on the Embankment Below right A family walking across Westminster Bridge, leaving the Houses of Parliament and Big Ben behind them

London by River
Westminster Bridge to Blackfriars Bridge

The Thames has always been at the heart of London life. Today, its banks are lined with important, historic buildings and monuments, from the medieval Tower to the Houses of Parliament. Although commercial ships no longer ply the Thames as they did until the 1950s, the river now has a role as an attraction. Whether you take a river cruise or a commuter shuttle, a boat trip is a fascinating way to see the city. For most cruises, children must be at least 5 years old.

Westminster Bridge
to Blackfriars Bridge

see next page

South
Bank

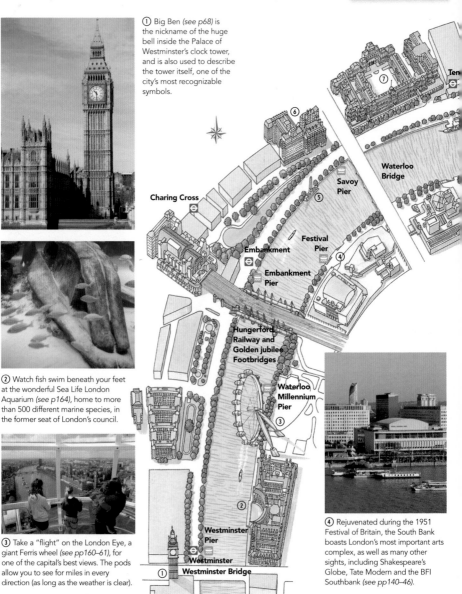

① Big Ben (see p68) is the nickname of the huge bell inside the Palace of Westminster's clock tower, and is also used to describe the tower itself, one of the city's most recognizable symbols.

② Watch fish swim beneath your feet at the wonderful Sea Life London Aquarium (see p164), home to more than 500 different marine species, in the former seat of London's council.

③ Take a "flight" on the London Eye, a giant Ferris wheel (see pp160–61), for one of the capital's best views. The pods allow you to see for miles in every direction (as long as the weather is clear).

④ Rejuvenated during the 1951 Festival of Britain, the South Bank boasts London's most important arts complex, as well as many other sights, including Shakespeare's Globe, Tate Modern and the BFI Southbank (see pp140–46).

Charing Cross

Embankment

Embankment
Pier

Festival
Pier

Savoy
Pier

Waterloo
Bridge

Ten

Hungerford
Railway and
Golden Jubilee
Footbridges

Waterloo
Millennium
Pier

Westminster
Pier

Westminster

Westminster Bridge

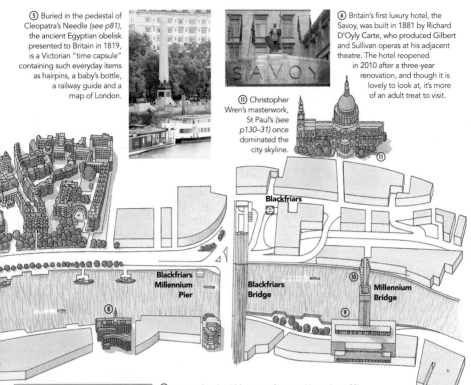

⑤ Buried in the pedestal of Cleopatra's Needle (see p81), the ancient Egyptian obelisk presented to Britain in 1819, is a Victorian "time capsule" containing such everyday items as hairpins, a baby's bottle, a railway guide and a map of London.

⑥ Britain's first luxury hotel, the Savoy, was built in 1881 by Richard D'Oyly Carte, who produced Gilbert and Sullivan operas at his adjacent theatre. The hotel reopened in 2010 after a three-year renovation, and though it is lovely to look at, it's more of an adult treat to visit.

⑪ Christopher Wren's masterwork, St Paul's (see p130–31) once dominated the city skyline.

Blackfriars

Blackfriars Millennium Pier

Blackfriars Bridge

⑩

Millennium Bridge

⑧ ⑨

⑦ In winter, head to 18th-century Somerset House (see p93) to skate on its central courtyard's open-air ice rink; in summer enjoy one of the concerts or outdoor movies held there. Inside is the superb Courtauld Gallery art collection.

⑧ A landmark building, the OXO Tower was owned by a company that makes beef stock. As advertisements were banned, the windows were designed to spell out the name of the famous brand. The top-floor restaurant and public gallery have terrific views.

⑨ The capital's showcase for significant international modern art, Tate Modern has 88 light and airy galleries in the former Bankside power station.

⑩ When the Millennium Bridge opened in 2000, pedestrians were unnerved to feel it swaying. The "Wobbly Bridge", closed for two years while the wobble was eliminated, connects Tate Modern (see p148) to St Paul's (see pp130– 31).

The Lowdown

🌐 **Big Ben** www.parliament.uk/about/living-heritage/building/palace/big-ben

London Eye www.londoneye.com

OXO Tower Barge House Street, SE1 9PH; www.harveynichols.com/oxo-tower-london

Savoy Hotel Strand, WC2R 0EU; www.fairmont.com/savoy

Sea Life London Aquarium www.visitsealife.com/London

Somerset House Strand, WC2R 1LA; www.somersethouse.org.uk

South Bank www.southbanklondon.com & www.southbankcentre.co.uk

Tate Modern Bankside, SE1 9TG; www.tate.org.uk/modern

London by River (continued)
Southwark Bridge to St Katharine's Dock

Southwark Bridge
to St Katharine's Dock

see previous page

City

Southwark

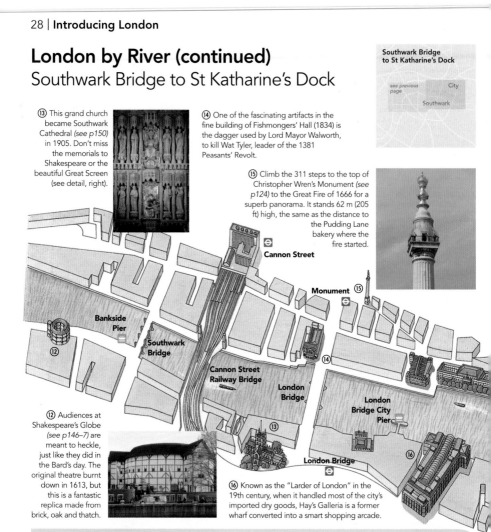

⑬ This grand church became Southwark Cathedral (see p150) in 1905. Don't miss the memorials to Shakespeare or the beautiful Great Screen (see detail, right).

⑭ One of the fascinating artifacts in the fine building of Fishmongers' Hall (1834) is the dagger used by Lord Mayor Walworth, to kill Wat Tyler, leader of the 1381 Peasants' Revolt.

⑮ Climb the 311 steps to the top of Christopher Wren's Monument (see p124) to the Great Fire of 1666 for a superb panorama. It stands 62 m (205 ft) high, the same as the distance to the Pudding Lane bakery where the fire started.

Cannon Street

Monument ⑮

Bankside Pier

Southwark Bridge

Cannon Street Railway Bridge

London Bridge

London Bridge City Pier

⑫

⑭

⑬

⑯

⑫ Audiences at Shakespeare's Globe (see p146–7) are meant to heckle, just like they did in the Bard's day. The original theatre burnt down in 1613, but this is a fantastic replica made from brick, oak and thatch.

London Bridge

⑯ Known as the "Larder of London" in the 19th century, when it handled most of the city's imported dry goods, Hay's Galleria is a former wharf converted into a smart shopping arcade.

The Lowdown

Design Museum Shad Thames, SE1 2YD; www. designmuseum.org

Fishmongers' Hall London Bridge, EC4R 9EL; www.fishhall.org.uk

Hay's Galleria London Bridge City, Tooley Street, SE1 2HD; www.haysgalleria.co.uk

HMS *Belfast* Morgan's Lane, Tooley Street, SE1 2JH; hmsbelfast.iwm.org.uk

The Monument www. themonument.info

St Katharine's Dock www. skdocks.co.uk

Shakespeare's Globe 21 New Globe Walk, Bankside, SE1 9DT; www.shakespearesglobe.com

Southwark Cathedral London Bridge, SE1 9DA; cathedral. southwark.anglican.org

Tower Bridge www.towerbridge. org.uk

Tower of London www.hrp.org. uk/toweroflondon

Thames Cruises, Taxi Services and River Buses **Bateaux London** 020 7695 1800; www.bateauxlondon.com

City Cruises (Westminster to Greenwich) 020 7740 0400; www.citycruises.com

Thames Clippers (London Eye to Greenwich) 0870 781 5049; www.thamesclippers.com

Thames Executive Private Charters & River Taxi 01342 820600; www. thamesexecutivecharters.com

Thames River Services (Greenwich, Thames Barrier) 020 7930 4097; www. thamesriverservices.co.uk

Transport for London River Bus and River Tours Information www.tfl.gov.uk/river

Turks (Kingston, Richmond & Hampton Court) 020 8546 2434; www.turks.co.uk

Westminster Passenger Services Association (Kew, Richmond & Hampton Court) 020 7930 2062; www.wpsa.co.uk

⑰ Kids can clamber up ladders, duck through hatches and let their imagination run riot on the navigation deck of HMS *Belfast (see pp154–5)*, a World War II warship that played a crucial role in the Normandy landings of 1944.

⑱ Britain's most famous medieval fortress, the Tower of London *(see pp122–3)* is steeped in gory history. Prisoners were brought by boat through the notorious Traitors' Gate for execution. The Tower contains a superb collection of arms and armour as well as the priceless Crown Jewels.

Fishy fact: Jaws!

In February 2004, a recently dead red-bellied piranha, a native of the Amazon, was discovered on the deck of a boat in the Thames. The mystery was that this razor-toothed killer fish with short powerful jaws, which, in a group, can devour large prey in seconds, is unable to survive in cold temperatures. It appeared to have been dropped by a seagull onto the deck. But how had the seagull got hold of it? It is likely that it was a pet that grew too big and was set free by its owner. It died in the cold water and floated to the surface, where it was picked up by a gull, but the bird must have decided it had bitten off more than it could chew!

⑲ A London icon, Tower Bridge is still raised to let ships pass, but not as often as it was in the days of tall-masted cargo vessels. Visit the exhibition to see the hydraulic machinery that operated the bridge before electrification in the 1970s.

Tower Millennium Pier

⑰

⑱

Tower Bridge

⑲

St Katharine's Pier

⑳

㉑

⑳ Now a lively marina, St Katharine's Dock *(see pp126–7)* was built on a site with over 1,000 years of history. This was London's first and most successful Docklands' redevelopment in the 1970s.

㉑ Play vintage video games or glimpse the styles of the future at the Design Museum *(see p157)*, which opened in this white 1930s-style building in 1989.

Practical Information

London has an impressive range of useful facilities for visitors, many of which are available 24 hours a day. Among them are cashpoint machines (ATM), bureaux de change, pharmacies and the health advice and information service, NHS Direct. To make the most of a visit – and to ensure everything goes as smoothly as possible – it is essential to have some inside knowledge of the city.

Passports, visas and customs

Visitors from outside the European Economic Area (EEA) and Switzerland need a valid passport to enter the UK; EEA and Swiss nationals can use identity cards instead. Most countries now require children (under the age of 18) to have individual passports, and children travelling to the UK must have their own passport.

Visitors from European Union (EU) states do not need a visa. Neither do visitors from the USA, Canada, South Africa, Australia and New Zealand who are in the UK for less than six months. Visitors from other countries should visit the **Home Office UK Border Agency** website to check whether a visa is required and, if so, how to apply. Visitors from EU states can bring unlimited quantities of most goods into the UK for personal use without paying duty. For information about allowances from outside the EU, visit the **HM Revenue & Customs** website.

Insurance

It is advisable to take out travel insurance to cover the cancellation or curtailment of your trip, the theft or loss of money and other personal property, and any necessary medical treatment. If you are planning to drive in London, take out fully comprehensive driving insurance and carry a valid driver's licence. Keep all car receipts and police reports in case of an insurance claim.

The UK has reciprocal health care agreements with all EEA states, Australia, New Zealand and a number of other countries listed on the **National Health Service** (NHS) website. Visitors from these countries, are entitled to free treatment under the NHS. However, there are exceptions for certain kinds of treatment, which is why taking out medical insurance is always advisable. Ensure you bring all documentation with you, such as the **European Health Insurance Card** (EHIC).

Visitors from a country without a reciprocal health agreement, such as the US, are only covered for treatment received in a hospital Accident and Emergency (A&E) department, so insurance is particularly important.

Health

In a medical emergency, dial 999 for an ambulance. They are on call 24 hours a day. There are a number of London hospitals with 24-hour A&E

Below left Some of the coins currently in circulation in the UK *Below right* London police officers on duty in the busy area surrounding Piccadilly Circus

departments, but not all treat children. **Chelsea and Westminster**, the **Royal London** and **St Mary's** have specialist paediatric departments. To find a General Practitioner (GP), or to check out symptoms online or by phone, use **NHS Direct**, which has a website and a 24-hour telephone advice line staffed by nurses.

For minor injuries or ailments, consult a pharmacist. Search for your nearest pharmacy on the NHS Direct website. Most have the same opening hours as other shops, although some stay open later. **Zafash** is open 24 hours daily; pharmacies that open till midnight include **Pharmacentre, Bliss, Boots Victoria Station** (9pm Sun) and **Boots Piccadilly Circus** (6pm Sun). Although it is possible to buy many medicines over the counter, some are only available on prescription. Pack any prescription drugs your family is likely to need, including allergy medication. There is now a keen awareness of serious food allergies and intolerances and items in shops are usually clearly labelled. If you have an intolerance, check the ingredients of dishes served in hotels and restaurants. The UK sun can be surprisingly hot and burning, especially for young children, so it is wise to use a good sunscreen.

Personal safety

Crowded shopping areas such as Oxford Street, busy markets, and Tube stations and bus stops are popular with thieves, who sometimes work in teams. Carry a handbag that closes effectively and keep it near you. Don't carry large amounts of money, or valuables, around with you, and avoid badly lit areas at night.

Never leave a bag or suitcase unattended on the Tube, at a station or in any other public place. It may be treated as a suspect package and cause a security alert.

In an emergency, dial 999 or 112. Report serious crimes at a Police Station (the **Metropolitan Police** website lists station addresses). For non-emergency crimes you can complete a form (available on the website) or dial 101. If you lose something on public transport, report it via the TfL website or visit the **TfL Lost Property Office**.

When out, arrange a safe meeting place with your children in case you become separated. Make sure they know where you are staying and the best people to ask for help (a police officer or security guard) if they get lost. Remind your children that cars in the UK drive on the left, and to always use pedestrian crossings or underpasses to cross the road.

Money

The unit of currency in the UK is the pound sterling (£), divided into 100 pence (p). There are coins in circulation for 1p, 2p, 5p, 10p, 20p, 50p, £1 and £2, and notes for £5, £10, £20 and £50. There is no limit to the amount of cash you can bring into the UK, but a pre-paid cash passport, used like a debit card, or traveller's cheques are more secure alternatives. Keep a separate note of the cheques' serial numbers. Visa and MasterCard are the most widely accepted, followed by American Express, Diners Club and JCB.

High street banks, such as **HSBC, Barclays** and **NatWest**, and post offices will change money and traveller's cheques at better rates than bureaux de change, whose advantage is longer opening hours. **Thomas Cook** and **Chequepoint** have numerous London offices, and Chequepoint in Gloucester Road is open 24 hours. **Travelex** and **American Express** cash traveller's cheques (remember your passport). Cashpoint machines (ATMs) are also widely available, but beware of ATM crime. Only use an ATM where and when you feel comfortable. Never accept help from strangers while using the ATM, don't be distracted and always cover your hand when you enter your PIN.

Below left The Boots pharmacy in Piccadilly Circus *Below right* London officers patrolling a busy platform in one of London's many Tube stations

Communications

The UK telephone country code is +44 and the area code for London is 020. To phone abroad, dial 00, followed by the country code. If you have problems with a number, call the operator on 100 or the international operator on 155. The main mobile phone network providers are **Orange, O2, T-Mobile** and **Vodafone**. To save money, consider buying a UK SIM card. Most public phones are operated by coins, credit cards and **British Telecom Calling Cards**, available through the BT website. Some are Internet phones, from which you can send emails and texts.

Wi-Fi is available in most hotels, often for a fee, and for free in many cafés, parks and other public places. Public libraries offer free Internet access on their computers, although you might have to queue. **Visit London** features a list of Internet cafés.

Apart from numerous satellite and cable channels, UK television has a number of digital stations, of which two, BBC1 and BBC2, are public service; the rest, including ITV1, Channel 4 and Channel 5, are commercial. Check BBC News or Sky News for regular weather updates. London's radio stations, BBC London Live (94.9FM), Capital FM (98.4FM) and LBC (97.3FM), have regular news and travel bulletins. For news plus entertainment listings, the daily *Evening Standard* newspaper is free. The magazine *Time Out* is also excellent for listings. The *International Herald Tribune* is available on the day of issue, and European publications usually appear a day or so later. **Gray's Inn News** in Theobald's Road stocks a range of foreign newspapers and magazines.

Opening hours

Shops are generally open 9:30am–6pm Mon–Sat and 11am–5pm Sun, with late-night shopping until 8pm on Wed or Thu in central areas. Official banking hours are 9:30am–3:30pm Mon–Fri, although most banks stay open until 5pm and many are open 9:30am–noon Sat. In general, museums and galleries open daily 10am–5:30pm or 6pm; some stay open later one night a week, usually Friday. Tourist attractions often open at 9am or 9:30am; last admission is 30 minutes before closing time. Always check times before setting out.

Visitor information

The Visit London website provides information on popular attractions and places to stay and lists what's on. Another website, **Young London**, suggests events for kids. The main Tourist Information Centre is **The City of London Information Centre**. Other tourist information centres can be found at railway stations including **King's Cross St Pancras**.

Disabled facilities

Most of London's major sights are wheelchair accessible. Before a visit, phone to check that your needs can be met. Websites for accessible attractions are **Artsline, Disability Now** and Visit London (which also features hotels). For accessibility on public transport, visit the **TfL** website. There are an increasing number of adapted toilets; many are part of the National Key Scheme (NKS), unlocked by a key from the **Royal Association for Disability and Rehabilitation** (RADAR), which also produces a guide to their locations.

Time

London operates on Greenwich Mean Time (GMT) in winter, 5 hours ahead of Eastern Standard Time, and from late March to late October, changes to British Summer Time, 1 hour ahead of GMT. You can check the exact time by phoning the BT Speaking Clock on 123.

Below left The Internet café area of The Hoxton hotel **Below right** *Child playing with a Nintendo DS – be sure to pack a variety of games and activities to keep youngsters occupied*

Electricity

UK voltage is 240V AC, and plugs have three square pins and take 3-, 5- or 13-amp fuses. Visitors will need an adaptor for appliances.

What to pack

If you forget something, don't worry unless it is your child's much-loved toy or blanket. You can buy almost anything else in London, but bring particular brands if your children have strong preferences. Let the children choose some of their favourite clothes and toys. Be super-organized and order nappies and wipes through **Amazon** to be delivered to your hotel or apartment.

Be prepared for changeable weather: raincoats and umbrellas are essential, even in summer, when you may also need sunscreen. In winter, bring warm clothes and shoes with non-slip soles. Always pack comfy shoes. For young children, a compact buggy might be handy.

Bring toys for the journey that will keep the kids occupied but won't disturb other passengers. If it's a long flight, buy a few new toys and hand them out at intervals. Include books, puzzles, crayons, paper, colouring and sticker books and cards.

The Lowdown

Visas and customs

Home Office UK Border Agency www.gov.uk/government/organisations/uk-visas-and-immigration

HM Revenue & Customs www.hmrc.gov.uk

Insurance

European Health Insurance Card ec.europa.eu

NHS www.nhs.uk/NHSEngland/Healthcareabroad/Pages/Healthcareabroad.aspx

Health

Bliss 5–6 Marble Arch, W1H 7EL; 020 7723 6116

Boots Victoria Station; 44–6 Regent St, W1B 5RA; 020 7834 0676; www.boots.com

Chelsea and Westminster Hospital 369 Fulham Rd, SW10 9NH; 020 8746 8000; www.chelwest.nhs.uk

NHS Direct www.nhsdirect.nhs.uk

Pharmacentre 149 Edgware Rd, W2 2HU; 0207 7723 2336; www.pharmacentre.com

Royal London Hospital Whitechapel Rd, E1 1BB; 020 7377 7000; www.bartsandthelondon.nhs.uk/about-us/how-to-find-us/the-royal-london

St Mary's Hospital Praed St, W2 1NY; 020 3312 6666; www.imperial.nhs.uk/stmarys

Zafash 233–235 Old Brompton Rd, SW5 0EA; 020 7373 2798; www.zafashpharmacy.co.uk

Personal safety

Metropolitan Police 101

TfL Lost Property Office 200 Baker Street, NW1 5RZ; 0343 222 1234; www.tfl.gov.uk/corporate/useful-contacts/lost-property

Money

American Express www.americanexpress.com/uk

Barclays www.barclays.co.uk

Chequepoint www.chequepoint.com

HSBC www.hsbc.co.uk

NatWest www.natwest.com

Post Office www.postoffice.co.uk

Thomas Cook www.thomascookmoney.com

Travelex www.travelex.com

Communications

British Telecom Calling Cards www.payphones.bt.com

Gray's Inn News graysinnnews.com

O2 www.o2.co.uk

Orange www.orange.co.uk

T-Mobile www.t-mobile.co.uk

Vodafone www.vodafone.co.uk

Visitor information

King's Cross St Pancras Travel Information Centre Western Ticket Hall N1 9AL; www.visitlondon.com

The City of London Information Centre Guildhall, EC2P 2EJ; 020 7606 3030; www.cityoflondon.gov.uk

Young London www.london.gov.uk/young-london/kids/index.jsp

Disabled Facilities

Artsline www.artsline.org.uk

Disability Now www.disabilitynow.org.uk

RADAR www.radar.org.uk

TfL www.tfl.gov.uk/gettingaround/transportaccessibility/1167.aspx

What to pack

Amazon www.amazon.com

Below left A huge selection of tourist brochures and leaflets on display at Allen House apartments *Below right* The main desk at the City of London Information Centre

Where to Stay

Staying in London is expensive, but there are plenty of family options among the hotels, B&Bs and apartments. Some hotels and B&Bs provide rooms for four, or suites of connected rooms. Some can provide camp beds or sofa beds, but typical rooms are not large and will be a squeeze for four. Apartments can be more flexible. The best family accommodation provides cots, high-chairs and even babysitting services. Check what is on offer before you book. For information on accommodation options, go to the Visit London website.

Hotels

London hotels once had a reputation for being unfriendly places for families, where children were rarely seen, and if they were, they should certainly not be heard. But times have changed and most welcome children now. Many have special children's rates or allow kids to stay free in their parents' room and provide them with complimentary or half-price breakfast. Some also have flexible meal times. Expensive West End hotels are now among the most child-friendly. Many employ kids' concierges, who can suggest fun outings and make reservations for shows and attractions. They also keep collections of story books, toys and suitable DVDs, arrange special meals, and provide a host of things to tempt tinies, from fun bed linen to cookery sessions.

Hip designer hotels are not often so family-friendly, but in the same price bracket there is a core of charming, family-run establishments with genial staff prepared to go the extra mile for their younger guests.

Chain hotels can be an excellent choice for families. What they lack in character and location, they make up for in value for money and children's facilities. Among the family-friendliest chains are **Apex**, **Crowne Plaza**, **Marriott** and **Park Plaza** at the upper end of the market, and **Ibis Styles**, **Novotel** and **Premier Inn** at the budget end.

Bed & breakfast

There are two types of B&B: a simple hotel with no restaurant, and a private home where bedrooms are let out to guests. At their best clean, comfortable and friendly, the former offer a less expensive alternative to hotels and a base from which to explore the city (most have limited public areas and are not generally places in which to hang out). The breakfast is usually a full English and included in the price.

If the owners are welcoming and amenable, staying in a home can be remarkably successful, and you might even make friends for life. But success is not guaranteed: most private houses only have a few rooms to let and it can be tricky to find one with suitable family accommodation. Using a specialist homestay agency is advisable (see p242), or try the **Bed & Breakfast and Homestay Association**, an affiliation of several reputable agencies whose properties are inspected regularly.

Below left Stylish bedroom at The Hoxton hotel in Shoreditch *Below right* The kitchen and living area of one of the self-catering SACO – Holborn apartments located in Central London

Self-catering

Staying in an apartment is probably the most relaxing option for families, especially if you are in London for more than a few days. Most apartments have a minimum stay of two nights to one week. Jet-lagged children, on the go from dawn, can have the run of the apartment without disturbing others. It also means you don't always have to eat out. You can cook your children's favourite meals (particularly useful for fussy eaters) and save money. Another alternative, is a home swap. This is best arranged through an established agency such as **Home Base Holidays**, **Home Link**, **Intervac** or the US-based **Home Exchange**.

The choice of apartments is between serviced and privately owned. Most London apartments are serviced, with a concierge and a cleaner. **BridgeStreet**, **Cheval Residences**, **Citadines**, **Fraser Place** and **SACO** all have several buildings in good locations for families. Other apartments are attached to a hotel, where guests can still have breakfast and use the facilities. Privately owned apartments are less expensive, but harder to find. Some agencies have them on their books (see p242). Most are in the suburbs.

The Lowdown

Apex www.apexhotels.co.uk
Bed & Breakfast and Homestay Association www.bbha.org.uk
BridgeStreet www.bridgestreet.com
Cheval Residences www.chevalresidences.com
Citadines www.citadines.com
Crowne Plaza www.ichotelsgroup.com/crowneplaza
Expedia www.expedia.co.uk
Fraser Place www.frasershospitality.com
Home Base Holidays www.homebase-hols.com
Home Exchange www.homeexchange.com

Home Link www.homelink.org
Ibis Styles www.ibis.com
Intervac www.intervac.co.uk
lastminute.com www.lastminute.com
Late Rooms www.laterooms.com
Marriott www.marriott.co.uk
Novotel www.novotel.com
Park Plaza www.parkplaza.com
Premier Inn www.premierinn.com
SACO www.sacoapartments.com
Travelocity www.travelocity.co.uk
Visit London www.visitlondon.com

Rates

London hotels usually quote room rates rather than prices per person and include VAT, but not always breakfast (double check before booking). Rates tend to remain high throughout the year, although it is possible to find reductions through special offers and weekend breaks, often on a minimum two-night stay. Generally, the longer you stay, the better the rate, and the best-value deals are available by booking in advance online. If they are not fully booked, some hotels offer last-minute discounts on their published "rack rates". Some of the best deals are available through websites such as **Late Rooms** and, for city breaks as well as accommodation, **Expedia**, **lastminute.com** and **Travelocity**.

Price categories

The three price categories in this guide are based on accommodation for a family of four for one night during high season, inclusive of service charges and any additional taxes. The inexpensive category is under £150; moderate is £150–250; and expensive is over £250. Inexpensive accommodation is extremely hard to find in London, where hotels are notoriously costly.

Below left The elegant exterior of the Arosfa B&B near Regent's Park **Below right** The smart lobby of the Grange City hotel, located minutes from the Tower of London

Where to Eat

Once hushed and barely tolerant of children, London's restaurants have become more accommodating towards families, and dining has grown more informal. Noisy children will not be welcome in any restaurant, but even upmarket establishments will be happy to see well-behaved ones, and often provide high chairs, colouring books and crayons. The choice of cuisines is enormous, offering dishes from all over the world. Prices given in this guide allow for a two-course lunch for a family of four, excluding wine but including soft drinks.

Chinese

The obvious place to go for Chinese food is Chinatown in the West End. Its pulsing heart, pedestrian-only Gerrard Street, is lined with exotic aroma-filled supermarkets and restaurants that range from plain eateries with bare tables and rows of glazed ducks in the windows to elegant places with wide-ranging menus. Chinese families eat out regularly and the restaurants are all geared to cater for children. Many have high chairs, and all will provide small portions – try dim sum, which only comes in small servings. Most children love the delicate flavours, from rice, noodles and dim sum dumplings to spring rolls and crispy aromatic duck (a fun dish for children as they can construct their own pancake parcels).

Indian

Indian curries are among the UK's favourite dishes. For truly authentic dishes, head to the Indian communities of Southall in West London or Brick Lane and Bethnal Green in the east, where you will also find Bangladeshi and Pakistani restaurants. Although many dishes are likely to be too hot and spicy for young taste buds, there are many gentle versions that older children might relish, such as tandoori, tikka masala, korma and pasanda. Mild curries are often made with coconut milk. If the dish is too hot, a little yogurt will calm it down (water provides only temporary relief). Curries are served with rice or flat breads, such as naan or chapati, and crisp poppadoms. Vindaloo, madras and jalfrezi are among the spiciest. Two family-friendly Indian restaurants with kids' menus are **Imli**, which has a vibrant dining room, and the Covent Garden **Masala Zone**, with many Rajasthani puppets suspended from the ceiling.

Thai

Kensington and Fulham have a choice of Thai restaurants, including the well-established **Blue Elephant**, with its interior inspired by the atmosphere of the historical Saranrom Palace of Bangkok. There are also plenty of modest local restaurants and pubs and cafés that serve Thai food. Although some dishes are incredibly fiery (ask the waiter if unsure), Thai menus always contain milder ones, often inspired by Chinese cuisine. Satay (made with peanuts), noodle recipes

*Below left Indian restaurants and curry houses line Brick Lane in East London **Below right** The interior of a Chinese restaurant in Chinatown, in the heart of the West End*

such as pad Thai, sweet and sour dishes and spare ribs usually appeal to children.

Greek and Turkish

The food is very similar to that of the Middle East, with mezze (small bites and dips) being an integral part of the meal. Greek specialities include tzatziki (yogurt, garlic and cucumber dip), dolmadakia (vine leaves stuffed with rice, herbs and sometimes meat), spanakotyropita (filo pastry parcels filled with spinach and feta cheese), keftedes (meatballs with mint and shallots), moussaka (layers of potatoes, aubergines, courgettes and minced lamb topped with béchamel sauce and cheese), lamb and chicken kebabs and simply grilled meat and fish.

Similar Turkish dishes have slightly different names: for instance, cacik is a version of tzatziki and dolma of dolmadakia. It is traditional to start a meal with soup, and then children might enjoy kuzu tandir (oven cooked-lamb), eksili köfte (meatballs in a lemon sauce) or iskender (mixed grill with yogurt and tomato sauce served over pitta bread). In both cuisines, desserts such as baklava are very sweet and syrupy. The restaurants are concentrated in Central and North London, and dinner is often accompanied by music and dancing, and sometimes plate smashing in Greek restaurants. For Greek food, try the traditional tavernas **The Four Lanterns** and **Konaki**, and for Turkish, try **Sofra**.

Indonesian and Malaysian

If your children have adventurous tastes, seek out London's Indonesian and Malaysian restaurants: most are in the centre, including **Penag** and **Bali Bali**, which serve dishes from both countries. They don't have children's menus, but obliging staff will be happy to bring children's portions. Both cuisines have been influenced by Thailand, China, India and the Middle East. Rice and noodles are staples, and satay chicken and beef kebabs appear regularly on menus. Some dishes contain hot chilli peppers, but Indonesian specialities that might tempt children include gado-gado, (vegetable salad with peanut dressing) and nasi uduk (rice in coconut milk). Milder Malaysian dishes include Hainanese chicken and noodle dishes such as hokkien mee and konloh mee. Finish with fragrant purple mangosteen (fruit) or goreng pisang (banana fritters).

The Lowdown

Al Waha 75 Westbourne Grove, W2 4UL; 020 7229 0806; www.alwaharestaurant.com

Ask www.askitalian.co.uk

Bali Bali 150 Shaftesbury Avenue, WC2H 8HL; 020 7836 2644; www.balibalirestaurant.com

Benihana www.benihana.com

Blue Elephant The Boulevard, Imperial Wharf, Townmead Rd, SW6 2UB; 020 7751 3111; www.blueelephant.com

Café Rouge www.caferouge.co.uk

Carluccio's www.carluccios.com

Chicago Rib Shack 145 Knightsbridge, SW1X 7PA; 020 7591 4664; www.thechicagoribshack.co.uk

The Diner www.goodlifediner.com
Ed's Easy Diner www.edseasydiner.com

The Four Lanterns 96 Cleveland St, W1T 6NP; 020 7387 0704; www.the4lanterns.com

Giraffe www.giraffe.net

Gourmet Burger Kitchen www.gbk.co.uk

Hard Rock Café 150 Old Park Lane, W1K 1QZ; 020 7514 1700; www.hardrock.com

Imli 167–9 Wardour St, W1F 8WR; 020 7287 4243; www.imli.co.uk

Konaki 5 Coptic St, WC1A 1NH; 020 7580 9730; www.konaki.co.uk

Leon www.leonrestaurants.co.uk

Maroush www.maroush.com

Masala Zone 48 Floral St, WC2E 9DA; 020 7379 0101; www.masalazone.com

Nando's www.nandos.co.uk

Noura www.noura.co.uk

Penag Southern Terrace, Westfield, W12 7GA; 020 8811 1474; www.eatpenang.co.uk

Ping Pong www.pingpongdimsum.com

Pizza Express www.pizzaexpress.com

Roast The Floral Hall, Stoney St, SE1 1TL; 0845 034 7300; www.roast-restaurant.com

The Real Greek www.therealgreek.com

Sofra 36 Tavistock St, WC2E 7PB; 020 7240 3773; www.sofra.co.uk/sofra_coventgarden.htm

Spaghetti House www.spaghettihouse.co.uk

Strada www.strada.co.uk

Tas www.tasrestaurant.com

Wagamama www.wagamama.com

Wahaca www.wahaca.co.uk

Zizzi www.zizzi.co.uk

Below left The outside seating area of The Real Greek restaurant on the South Bank
Below right The buffet at Young Cheng, Chinatown

Middle Eastern

It is easy to overlook Middle Eastern food as a family option, but the selections of little hot and cold dishes – mezze – particularly suit children. Most kids are familiar with hummus (a smooth, mild chickpea dip), but there are plenty of new dishes to try: samboussek (a pastry triangle filled with meat, cheese or vegetables), tabbouleh (a salad of bulgur wheat, chopped mint, parsley, tomato and spring onion, with lemon juice and olive oil) and fatoush (a lemon-flavoured salad with parsley, mint and thin, crisp pieces of toasted flatbread), as well as larger dishes of marinated chicken and lamb. At their best, these dishes are bursting with fragrant flavours without being too spicy. There is a cluster of Middle Eastern restaurants in and around Edgware Road, most of which specialize in Lebanese food, among them are several in the **Maroush** chain and, slightly further west, **Al Waha**.

British

Once burdened with a reputation for being tasteless and stodgy, British cuisine was unpopular with other nationalities. But times have changed and a clutch of high-profile chefs, such as Jamie Oliver, Heston Blumenthal and Gordon Ramsay, have transformed it, borrowing from other nations while never forgetting their roots.

Some British restaurants make a great effort to appeal to families: one such is **Roast** in the foodie paradise of Borough Market. Here, you will find high chairs, colouring books and a children's menu, as well as excellent traditional British cooking using locally sourced, free range and organic ingredients. Excellent food is also available in a number of the city's gastropubs – pub-restaurants that opened in the 1990s and serve good-quality food in pleasant surroundings, most of which welcome children.

Italian

Of all the world's cuisines, Italian food has to be the most child-friendly, at least in the form of pizza, pasta and ice cream. Children will also be welcomed and fussed over by the friendly staff in Italian restaurants, trattorie and pizzerias. The best places tend to be family-run and unpretentious, serving classic, reasonably priced dishes, with a special menu for children, perhaps including pasta with a simple sauce such as pesto (basil and cheese), pomodoro (tomato), bolognese (meat) or carbonara (eggs, cheese and ham or bacon), home-made pizza or simply cooked meat. There will usually be a choice of different flavoured ice creams to follow.

Spanish

The growing popularity of tapas restaurants and bars has raised the profile of Spanish cuisine in London. Like the Italians, the Spanish are well-disposed to children, and their tapas meals (small portions of different dishes) allow kids to try out new flavours and ingredients without having to order a whole course. The restaurants are usually informal and meals relaxed. Some have children's menus, but tapas such as jamón Serrano and jamón Ibérico (both dry-cured hams), calamares fritos (fried squid), gambas al ajillo (garlic prawns), tortilla (Spanish omelette) and croquetas (croquettes) are tasty without being too sophisticated.

French

The French, whose cuisine is considered one of the finest in the world, have been influencing British cooking ever since the Norman Conquest, and in London today

Below left A branch of the popular Italian chain Carluccio's *Below right* A serving of the classic British dish, fish and chips, best eaten straight from the paper wrapping it comes in

there are plenty of good French restaurants serving high-grade food. As people have become more health-conscious, the once typical rich cream- and butter-based sauces have been replaced by lighter, more delicate dishes. Brasseries and bistros are more likely to have children's menus than upmarket restaurants, and feature such favourites as steak or steak haché (burger) and frites (fries), chicken, omelettes and salade Niçoise, with plenty of choice for dessert, from apple or lemon tart to chocolate mousse and ice cream.

North American

Londoners have had a love affair with North American food since the **Hard Rock Café** opened in 1971. With its juicy burgers and fries, hot dogs, barbecued chicken and ribs, creamy milkshakes, American-style decor and rock'n'roll music, the Hard Rock Cafe is a piece of the States transported to Old Park Lane. Other restaurants appeared in its wake, including the authentic and child-friendly **Chicago Rib Shack** in Knightsbridge, and a number of replica diners. The food is hearty, the setting is fun and children couldn't be better catered for.

Chain restaurants

They may not be the most imaginative choice, but chain restaurants are guaranteed to be a safe option for families, with high chairs, easy-wipe surfaces, suitable, good-value food, and no complicated dishes, pristine linen, snooty staff or exorbitant prices. For North American food, try **Ed's Easy Diner** and **The Diner**, replicas of a 1950s original; for good-quality burgers, try the **Gourmet Burger Kitchen**. Another popular chain, **Nando's**, specializes in chicken dishes with Portuguese flavours. For Chinese food, the **Ping Pong** chain serves up dim sum-style dumplings, and Pan-Asian dishes are staples at **Wagamama**. Although Japanese food is not usually popular with children, at **Benihana**, meals are theatre, with all the ingredients cooked sizzlingly before your eyes. **Maroush** and **Noura** are Lebanese chains; the **Real Greek** really is Greek; **Tas** is Turkish; **Wahaca** is Mexican and **Café Rouge** is French. Among the most family-friendly Italian chains are **Ask**, **Carluccio's**, **Pizza Express**, **Spaghetti House**, **Strada** and **Zizzi**. And for good-value international food that kids all love, there's **Giraffe** and restaurant chain **Leon**, with its delicious fast food.

Below left Tucking into a meal at Giraffe *Below right* A delicious selection of cakes and pastries on display at Paul

Shopping

Whether it's in a shiny modern mall, a famous traditional department store, a distinctive independent shop or a lively street market, shopping in London is an exciting experience. It is one of the world's great commercial cities, with thousands of stores selling everything anyone in the family could want. Although luxury items are expensive here, dedicated hunters can find bargains in year-round sales, street markets and cut-price shops.

Shopping streets

OXFORD STREET, W1

London's main shopping street is lined with more than 500 shops, from major department stores such as **Selfridges, John Lewis** (see *Department stores and shopping malls for both*) and **Debenhams** (Nos. 334–348), to the flagship stores of world-famous brands, including **Nike** (No. 236) and **Topshop** (No. 216) and **Gap** (Nos. 223–225), along with a generous smattering of tacky tourist shops. At the western end, the Marble Arch **Marks & Spencer** (No. 458) is the company's largest and best-stocked store. Busy and brash, Oxford Street heaves with crowds at weekends, during the January and June sales and before Christmas, when it is decked with festive lights. When it's busy, using Oxford Street Tube station can be a disconcerting experience for anyone with children. It's easier to use Bond Street Tube station, which is a little further west along Oxford Street, close to John Lewis and Selfridges.

KING'S ROAD, SW3

Chelsea's King's Road had its heyday in the "Swinging Sixties", when it was at the heart of bohemian London. Though not so trendsetting today, it remains popular for its upmarket High Street clothes, jewellery and accessories shops. On Sloane Square, **Peter Jones** is the department store West Londoners find indispensable. Other useful shops include **Trotters** (no. 34) and **Igloo** (no. 227) for children's clothes and a few toys; **Paperchase** (no. 289) for stationery, art supplies and gifts; and **Bluebird** (No. 350), a smart restaurant, chilled café with courtyard and food store rolled into one.

KENSINGTON HIGH STREET, W8

Favoured by fashion-conscious hippies in the 1960s and 1970s, "High Street Ken", as it is affectionately known, is not as crowded as Oxford Street and is possibly more functional than the King's Road. As for shops, it has all the usual suspects: **Trotters** (No. 127), **Topshop** (Nos. 42–44), for fashion-conscious children's clothes, **Russell & Bromley** (No. 151) for good-quality shoes, **Waterstone's** (No. 193) for books and magazines, and **TK Maxx** (Nos. 26–40), which sells designer clothes at knock-down prices. There is also a huge branch of the American organic grocery store, **Whole Foods Market** (Nos. 63–97). The best thing is that it's easy to escape to nearby Hyde Park or Kensington Gardens (see pp172–75) when the children start to droop and need an energizing runaround.

Below left The children's clothing store Trotters, on the King's Road in Chelsea *Below right* Meeting a shop's mascot outside one of the many gift shops located on Oxford Street

Department stores and shopping malls

HARRODS see p85

The UK's biggest shop will wow children and adults alike. It sells high-end clothes, beauty products, electronic goods, sports equipment, toys and has a fabulous food hall.

SELFRIDGES

One of London's most popular stores, Selfridges opened in 1909 in the Oxford Street building it still occupies today. It was founded by American magnate Harry Gordon Selfridge, who wanted to transform shopping from a chore into something fun. More recently it has become known for its bold window displays, which are almost as much of an attraction as the award-winning store itself. It has an excellent range of adult and kids' fashion, a superb food hall and a new toy department.

JOHN LEWIS

"Never knowingly undersold" is the motto of the John Lewis Partnership, which has a chain of practical, upmarket department stores in the UK, including Peter Jones. Its Oxford Street branch, opened in 1864 as a draper's shop, is the flagship store. It still has a particularly good range of fabrics, and holds a Royal Warrant as a supplier of haberdashery and household goods to the Queen. You'll also find everything you could possibly need for a baby, from rattles to a pushchair. Shoppers love the store's no-quibble returns policy and two-year guarantee on electrical goods.

WESTFIELD

This West London shopping mall, which opened in 2008, is so huge that it could comfortably hold 30 football pitches. It has plenty to occupy families who are happy to shop till they drop, with more than 250 shops over several levels, 50 restaurants and cafés, a "soft" play space and a multiplex cinema. Among the most child-oriented shops are the **Early Learning Centre**, **Mamas & Papas**, **LEGO**, **Build-A-Bear Workshop** and the **Disney Store**. "The Village" is an area devoted to the most sought-after designers, including **Versace**, **Miu Miu** and **Tiffany & Co**.

Clothing

RACHEL RILEY

Located in the heart of Marylebone, this stylishly decorated shop offers smart clothes for babies, children and ladies – all made in-house from beautiful fabrics. Launched in 1998, designer Rachel Riley's creations have become so popular that she has opened a store in New York. She designs custom-made outfits for special occasions on request. Also loved are her hand-made slippers, which are produced in France.

LA STUPENDERIA

If you're looking for something special for your children to wear, try the Italian label La Stupenderia, which has a swanky Knightsbridge store. The collection caters for boys and girls from newborn to 12 years old. The superb quality of the fabrics is typically Italian, and the look is classic and elegant: tweed jackets combined with shorts and waistcoats for boys; full skirts and dresses for girls. There are also plenty of well-cut casual styles, though even these come with a high price tag.

OH BABY LONDON

New Zealand-born designer Hannah McHalick was so uninspired by the choice of dull, pastel-coloured baby clothes on the market when she was pregnant, that she started creating her own fun, original designs. She sells her cool clothes for kids aged 0–8, including T-shirts and playsuits with clever captions, from her shop in buzzing, fashionable Brick Lane.

Below left Main concourse of the vast Westfield Centre in White City *Below right* Playtime in the Toy Kingdom area of the enormous Harrods department store in Knightsbridge

Books

TALES ON MOON LANE

This award-winning, independent children's bookshop is committed to making books and reading fun. The family-centred environment is the setting for regular public events, including book fairs and visits by popular children's authors, and the knowledgeable staff are always on hand to help identify a book that is right for your child.

CHILDREN'S BOOKSHOP

This family-run children's bookshop is one of the oldest in the UK and has delighted several generations of young customers. The shop stocks over 25,000 books, suitable for anyone from babies to teenagers, and hosts author signings as well as Thursday morning story time. The enthusiastic staff are always happy to offer guidance, and they actively encourage browsing.

Toys and games

BENJAMIN POLLOCK'S TOYSHOP

If you think toys were better in the past than they are today, this is the place to confirm your belief. Pollock's sells all kinds of traditional toys, from spinning tops and music boxes to rag dolls and tiny tea sets. The original shop in Shoreditch was run by Benjamin Pollock, who produced toy theatres. The Covent Garden shop still stocks a wonderful array of these, along with puppets – finger, glove and on strings.

DAVENPORT'S MAGIC SHOP

Tucked away in an arcade, this shop is a must for all aspiring members of the Magic Circle. It was established in 1898 by Lewis Davenport, a magician and music hall entertainer, and is the oldest family-run magic shop in the world. Whether you're a novice or a pro, it's a treasure trove of ingenious tricks and illusions, some simple, others sophisticated. There are cards, books, DVDs and accessories, including handkerchiefs, miracle rings, balls and beakers.

DISNEY STORE

For children besotted with Jack Sparrow or Hannah Montana, this US import will be a hit. The Covent Garden store is one of two in Central London. Kids might be tempted by a *Toy Story* Zurg's Blaster or 3-D puzzle, a pair of pink cowboy boots just like Hannah Montana's or an iconic Mickey Mouse T-shirt.

EARLY LEARNING CENTRE

A British chain specializing in toys for very young children, the Early Learning Centre has six London stores, with the most central in Kensington High Street *(see p40)*. Colourful and well-made, the indoor and outdoor toys are designed not only for play, but also to encourage mental and physical development. Tough, hard-wearing materials range from wood to plastic, and toys include puzzles and activity centres. The stores are child-friendly, with toys to try out.

HAMLEYS *see p181*

This is the kind of shop that Santa Claus shops at – floor after floor of every type of toy and game.

MYSTICAL FAIRIES

A dream come true for little girls, this pink, fairy-themed shop has everything with glitter and sparkle. There are clothes, fancy-dress costumes, bags, jewellery and accessories, as well as craft kits, games, stationery and a host of other affordable toys guaranteed to enchant your little ones. The fairy dust only completes the magical experience. There is also a wizard section for the boys who may feel left out.

HONEYJAM

Honeyjam was inspired by childhood memories of toyshops bursting to the brim with the most

Below left A stall selling freshly baked bread, pastries and savoury treats at Borough Market *Below right* A member of staff welcoming customers to the jam-packed Hamleys toy shop

enchanting and desirable toys, hanging from ceilings and filling table tops. With seven children between them, the two owners are passionate about toys and cater to all tastes and budgets. The selection here is a glorious blend of traditional and modern, silly and educational. A delight for children and adults alike.

Markets

BOROUGH see p146

see p146

Open Monday to Saturday, Borough Market is foodie heaven, with top-quality (and top-dollar) global treats as well as the best of British produce.

CAMDEN LOCK MARKET

This rambling weekend market has a fun mix of junk and wonderful finds, including antiques, books, music, crafts and new and second-hand street fashion. It started in a small way in 1974, since when it has spread along Chalk Farm Road. With a hippie-punk vibe, the main market is down beside Regent's Canal and makes a great family outing on a Saturday; Sundays can be a crush.

PETTICOAT LANE

An East End institution, this Sunday street market spills over from Petticoat Lane (whose real location is Middlesex Street) into the maze of roads that surrounds it, and is where you might catch traders chatting in Cockney rhyming slang. If your children are extremely early risers, come with the serious bargain hunters at 4am. The more touristy part isn't in full swing till 9am, although it gets very crowded by 11am. Bargains are likely to be elusive, but there's an impressive range of leather goods, clothes, jewellery and toys, plus fast food.

PORTOBELLO ROAD

Follow the Saturday crowd from Notting Hill Gate Tube station swarming to this vibrant street, lined with stalls, arcades and funky shops. Several markets rolled into one, it has more than 1,000 stalls, from upmarket antiques, jewellery and silverware as it heads north, to bric-a-brac, crafts, food, clothes and music. Dodge into Portobello Green covered market, just north of the Westway, for original youth fashion.

The Lowdown

Benjamin Pollock's Toyshop 44 The Market, Covent Garden, WC2E 8RF; 020 7379 7866; www.pollockscoventgarden.co.uk

Camden Lock Market www.camdenlockmarket.com

Children's Bookshop 29 Fortis Green Road, Muswell Hill, N10 3HP; 020 8444 5500; www.childrensbookshoplondon.com

Davenport's Magic Shop 7 Charing Cross Underground Arcade, The Strand, WC2N 4HZ; 020 7836 0408; www.davenportsmagic.co.uk

Disney Store 10 The Piazza, Covent Garden, WC2E 8HD; 020 7836 5037; www.disneystore.co.uk

Early Learning Centre Westfield Shopping Centre, W12 7GB; 020 8746 0885; www.elc.co.uk

Honeyjam 2 Blenheim Crescent, W11 1NN; 020 7243 03393; www.honeyjam.co.uk

John Lewis 300 Oxford Street, W1A 1EX; www.johnlewis.com

King's Road kingsroad.co.uk

Mystical Fairies 12 Flask Walk, Hampstead, NW3 1HE; 020 7431 1888; www.mysticalfairies.co.uk

Oh Baby London 162 Brick Lane, E1 6RU; 020 7247 4949; www.ohbabylondon.com

Oxford Street www.oxfordstreet.co.uk

Petticoat Lane petticoatlanemarket.net

Portobello Road www.portobelloroad.co.uk

Rachel Riley 82 Marylebone High Street, W1U 4QW; 020 7935 8345; www.rachelriley.co.uk

Selfridges 400 Oxford Street, W1A 1AB; www.selfridges.com

La Stupenderia 16 Motcomb Street, SW1X 8LB; www.lastupenderia.com

Tales on Moon Lane 25 Half Moon Lane Herne Hill, SE24 9JU; 020 7274 5759; www.talesonmoonlane.co.uk

Westfield uk.westfield.com/london

Below left Storytime at one of London's popular children's bookshops *Below right* A second-hand stall at Camden Lock Market, bursting with collectibles – books, magazines, toys and much more

Entertainment

London's theatre (see pp46–7), music and cinema scene is one of the very best in the world – and there's plenty for families to enjoy. There are children's festivals, notably LolliBop for under-10s, in Regent's Park in August; and Imagine, on the South Bank in February. To find out what's coming up, register for a free bulletin at www.officiallondontheatre.co.uk, and check the listings on www.timeout.com/london/kids or www.visitlondon.com/attractions/family.

Music

London's smartest music venues are keen to woo families: the **Royal Opera House** (see p90–91) puts on Christmas shows, Sounding Out workshops and a Summer Screens season, which beams live opera and ballet from Covent Garden onto big screens in Trafalgar Square and Canary Wharf. Nearby, at the London Coliseum, the **English National Opera's** kids' music-making sessions are pitched at ages six months and up – while the grown-ups get to sneak off and enjoy a matinee. There are Saturday afternoon classical concerts for families at **St Martin-in-the-Fields Church** on Trafalgar Square, and regular Discovery Concerts for ages 7–12 from the **London Symphony Orchestra**. There are also strong children's programmes at **Wigmore Hall** in the West End (mostly chamber music) and the **Southbank Centre's** (see p164) Royal Festival Hall (jazz, world and classical). Summer brings free outdoor music and theatre to **The Scoop**, beside Tower Bridge.

A popular outdoor concert venue is Hampstead's **Kenwood House** (see pp216–17). London's grandest alfresco venue, however, must be **Somerset House** (see p93), which invites pop stars to its courtyard in August. The **Underage** rock festival – for 13–17-year-olds only – blasts into Hackney's Victoria Park in August.

Cinema

London's West End cinemas, such as the **Odeon Leicester Square**, show mostly mainstream Hollywood fare. For more eclectic movies, try the **Barbican Centre's** (see p138) Framed Film Club or its London Children's Film Festival week, in November, when kids get to make films as well as watch them. The Southbank Centre's **British Film Institute's (BFI)** (see p162) programme of children's film focuses on the BFI IMAX – book ahead for its Film Funday gatherings. Family clubs run at cinemas across the city, including **Clapham Picture House**, the **Electric Cinema** in Portobello Road and the **Renoir** in Bloomsbury; while summer heralds 12 days of screenings in the courtyard at Somerset House.

Arts and crafts

There is always something creative afoot for families at the city's art goliaths, such as the **National Gallery** (see pp80–81), **Tate Modern** (see p148), the **British Museum**

Below left Children watching the interactive "bubbles bubbles bubbles" show at the Science Museum *Below right* A child learning how to weave with characters dressed in Tudor costume at Sutton House

(see pp102–3) and the **National Portrait Gallery** (see pp82–3). Family days at **Sutton House** (see p212) offer fancy dress, activities and more.

The **Whitechapel Gallery** (see p127), in the East End, boasts family workshops in its dedicated children's studio; and the distinctly more traditional **Dulwich Picture Gallery** (see p224), whose twice-monthly "Artplay" sessions spill out into the grounds on Wednesdays in summer: bring a picnic. Bloomsbury's **Cartoon Museum** has a permanent art room for kids, and monthly doodling drop-ins for families. In summer, don't miss the outdoor season at the **Serpentine Galleries** (see pp176–7), set in its landmark pavilion on the lawns of Kensington Gardens. An art-themed "playscape" is in the offing at the Serpentine's new satellite gallery nearby.

The **V&A Museum** (see p184) offers "Drop-in Design" sessions on Sundays and Saturday workshops in applied arts for older children, and masterminds the **London Design Festival** every September.

The best of the rest

Little bookworms are well looked after in London, with free family

The Lowdown

Cartoon Museum 35 Little Russell Street, WC1A 2HH; 020 7580 8155; www.cartoonmuseum.org

Clapham Picture House 76 Venn Street, SW4 0AT; 0871 902 5727; www.picturehouses.co.uk

Electric Cinema 191 Portobello Road, W11 2ED; 020 7908 9696; www.electriccinema.co.uk

English National Opera London Coliseum, St. Martin's Lane, WC2N 4ES; 020 7845 9300; www.eno.org

Imagine Children's Festival Southbank Centre, Belvedere Road, London, SE1 8XX; 020 7960 4200; www.southbankcentre.co.uk/whatson/festivals-series/imagine-childrens-festival

LolliBop Festival 020 8365 9695; www.lollibopfestival.co.uk

London Symphony Orchestra Barbican Centre, Silk Street, EC2Y 8DS; 020 7588 1116; www.lso.co.uk

London Design Festival 020 7734 6444; www.londondesignfestival.com

Odeon Leicester Square 0871 224 4007; www.odeon.co.uk

Renoir Cinema Brunswick Square, WC1N 1AW; 033 0500 1331; www.curzoncinemas.com

Royal Observatory Blackheath Avenue, SE10 8XJ; www.rmg.co.uk

St Martin-in-the-Fields Church Trafalgar Square, WC2N 4JJ; 020 7766 1100; www.smitf.org

The Scoop 2a More London Riverside, SE1 2DB; 020 7403 4866; www.morelondon.co.uk/scoop.html

Underage Festival www.underagefestivals.com

Wigmore Hall 36 Wigmore Street, W1U 2BP; 020 7935 2141; www.wigmore-hall.org.uk

storytelling events at nearly all the major museums across the city (covered in the sightseeing part of this guide). So, too, are budding scientists, with the plethora of live science demonstrations, shows and hands-on sessions that take place regularly: kids can get to grips with rocket-launching at the **Science Museum** (see pp180–81) and "speed surgery" at the **Old**

Operating Theatre (see p151). Entertaining "Nature Live" shows run more or less daily at the **Natural History Museum** (pp182-83) , while there are dedicated space shows for children at the **Royal Observatory**'s (see pp201) planetarium in Greenwich. Finally, no family should miss the world-class clowning, magic and pop-opera on the streets of Covent Garden.

Below left Getting creative during the Framed Film Club at the Barbican Centre *Below right* Enthralled children at a Sounding Out workshop at the Royal Opera House

Best Theatres and Shows

One of the major centres of theatre in the world, London offers a remarkable range of superb, high-quality drama. Across the different categories of theatre – subsidized, West End and fringe – there is always a choice of plays to entertain and engage children of all ages, as well as their parents. Alongside new productions, there are also plenty of old favourites to choose from.

Best theatres

HALF MOON YOUNG PEOPLE'S THEATRE

Founded in the 1980s in East London, Half Moon produces theatre for and with young people. The company uses drama to teach, inspire and engage children from all backgrounds and with all abilities. Plays are often by promising new playwrights. The London season runs from October to April.

LITTLE ANGEL THEATRE

This 100-seat puppet theatre, in a former Temperance Hall in Islington, puts on plays and runs workshops, during which a production is developed and the puppets are made. The Little Angel Theatre tours worldwide and showcases performances by visiting companies. Various cultures inspire productions, which include firm favourites *The Secret Garden* and *The Sleeping Beauty*.

The theatre also runs creative family Fun Days to coincide with shows.

LYRIC THEATRE HAMMERSMITH

It is not specifically a children's theatre, but the Lyric often puts on wonderful shows for children in its two superb performance spaces. The theatre also offers a lively pantomime at Christmas, as well as imaginative hands-on activities, usually geared to under-7s, such as "Messy Play" workshops.

NATIONAL THEATRE

Each year, London's main publicly funded theatre stages a number of productions for children, mostly during the holidays. It has three auditoriums, ranging from the grand Olivier to the tiny Cottesloe (renamed the Dorfman in 2013). The summer Watch this Space Festival, which celebrates outdoor theatre, offers children's performance classes.

POLKA THEATRE

More than 100,000 children visit this Wimbledon theatre every year. Its aim is to entertain, inspire and stimulate, both with brand-new plays and adaptations of much-loved classics. The plays, shown in two auditoriums, are chosen not only to spark kids' imaginations, but to be accessible and relevant. Its Early Years programme embraces simple, visual stories for children between ages 6 months and 6 years.

PUPPET BARGE

A unique concept, this floating puppet theatre makes a terrific family outing. The 55-seat barge has a regular mooring in Little Venice from April–July, but tours each summer, with a mooring in Richmond August–September. The company, Movingstage, is known for its inventive productions and traditional stories with a modern twist.

Below left A performance of The Tempest by puppets at the Puppet Barge, moored in Little Venice *Below right* Actors and puppets take to the stage in a vibrant performance of The Lion King

UNICORN THEATRE

From a mobile theatre operating out of an old truck, the Unicorn has grown into one of the UK's flagship children's companies, with an airy, purpose-built South Bank building. Here, it stages more than 600 performances a year. Family workshops complement the shows by exploring their various themes.

Best family shows

THE LION KING

Since 1999, this joyful screen-to-stage musical has been delighting audiences at the Lyceum Theatre with its magical evocation of the Serengeti Plain, re-created through movement and puppetry. Visually, it is spectacular: the stage is packed with dancers sporting fabulous costumes and masks, and there is rousing African-inspired music.

STOMP

With no speech, dialogue or plot it may seem like an odd choice, but Stomp will enthrall kids with the creativity, movement and music achieved from everyday objects. The dancers and musicians use bins, plastic bags and even Zippo lighters to create a rhythmically enchanting spectacle.

WICKED

The stage prequel to *The Wizard of Oz*, *Wicked* delves into the past of two Oz witches reinvented as university students – the good Glinda and the Wicked Witch of the West, Elphaba. It premiered in London at the Apollo Victoria Theatre in 2006, and has been showing there ever since. It can be appreciated on different levels by adults and children alike.

Tickets

London's West End theatreland is the place for blockbusting shows. Visit *www.thisistheatre.com* for the latest listings. Calls to a theatre box office will usually be redirected to ticketing giant **Ticketmaster**, which has an online family section (*www.ticketmaster.co.uk*). For discounted seats, visit **Tkts** (Leicester Square; open 10am–7pm Mon–Fri, 11am–4pm Sun); the website lists bargains (*www.tkts.co.uk*), but does not sell tickets. Prime time for theatre-loving families is **Kids Week**, a fortnight of shows and workshops in August. Watch out for the Child's Play sessions at **Shakespeare's Globe** (*see pp146–7*), timed so that kids act up while their parents take in a play. The **Theatre Royal Drury Lane** has London's child-friendliest

The Lowdown

Half Moon Young People's Theatre 43 White Horse Road, E1 0ND; 020 7709 8900; *www.halfmoon.org.uk*

Kids Week *www.kidsweek.co.uk*

Little Angel Theatre 14 Dagmar Passage, N1 2DN; 020 7226 1787; *www.littleangeltheatre.com*

Lyric Theatre Hammersmith Lyric Square, King Street, W6 0QL; 020 8741 6843; *www.lyric.co.uk*

National Theatre South Bank, SE1 9PX; 020 7452 3000; *www.nationaltheatre.org.uk*

Polka Theatre 240 The Broadway, SW19 1SB; 0202 8543 4888; *www.polkatheatre.com*

Puppet Barge opposite 35 Blomfield Road, W9 2PF; 020 7249 6876; *www.puppetbarge.com*

Stomp *www.stomplondon.com*

Theatre Royal Drury Lane Catherine Street, WC2B; 0844 412 2955; *www.reallyuseful.com/theatres*

The Lion King *www.thelionking.co.uk*

Unicorn Theatre 147 Tooley Street, SE1 2HZ; 020 7645 0560; *www.unicorntheatre.com*

Wicked *www.wickedthemusical.co.uk*

backstage tour (book the costumed version) and those at the **National Theatre** and **Regent's Park Open-Air Theatre** (*see p112*) are fun, too.

Below left The interior of the Unicorn Theatre near London's South Bank *Below right* Actors performing in All Join in and Other Stories at Wimbledon's renowned Polka Theatre

London at Play

A visit to a theme park, playground or fun zone can be the highlight of a family holiday, but it's always best to plan ahead. Buy tickets in advance online and try to go on a weekday to avoid the biggest queues. Check with theme parks and fun zones for height restrictions – minimum and maximum – so if your children are too small or tall, they won't be disappointed. Fun zones can close to the public when hired for private parties, so check they're open before setting out.

Best theme parks

CHESSINGTON WORLD OF ADVENTURES

A mix of amusement park and zoo, Chessington and its themed lands will keep everyone entertained for the day. Older kids will be keen to try white-knuckle rides, such as Dragon's Fury, a spinning roller coaster, and Runaway Train, which careers along at speed, while the tamer Bubbleworks and Toytown rides are perfect for little ones. Take the Safari Skyway to spy the zoo's big cats, gorillas and sea lions.

THORPE PARK

Smaller than Chessington, Thorpe Park nevertheless features record-breaking rides including Stealth, Europe's fastest roller coaster and Tidal Wave, a terrifyingly high water ride, as well as the Colossus and Nemesis Inferno roller coasters. There are calmer alternatives exclusively for families with young children, such as the scenic Canada Creek Railway and the Wet Wet Wet water slide.

Best playgrounds

BATTERSEA PARK ADVENTURE PLAYGROUND

A host of fun things to climb up, slide down, swing on, scramble over and explore make this wooden adventure playground a great place for 5–16 year-olds. The nearby toddlers' playground is full of colourful structures to play on.

CORAM'S FIELDS

This Bloomsbury playground was built on the site of a children's hospital. There are grassy areas and equipment for all ages, including climbing frames, slides and a zip wire. The big draw for toddlers, apart from the sandpits and paddling pool, is pets' corner, with its sheep, goats, rabbits and other animals.

DIANA, PRINCESS OF WALES MEMORIAL PLAYGROUND see p174

HOLLAND PARK ADVENTURE PLAYGROUND

For any would-be Tarzan aged 5 plus, this playground is perfect. It contains swinging ropes, an aerial runway, a zip wire, climbing frames and a tower, as well as swings, a giant tyre and slides. Conveniently placed next door, is an enclosed play area for tots, with swings, slides and a seesaw.

Best fun zones

BRAMLEY'S BIG ADVENTURE

Kids up to age 11 play happily and safely in this indoor playground. It consists of a colourful three-level frame, a maze of slides, ball pools,

Below left Riding the excellent bowl at Camden's Cantelowe Skate Park **Below centre** All the fun of the fair on a carousel at Gambado Chelsea **Below right** Feeding time at the squirrel monkey enclosure, Chessington World of Adventures

Above *The exciting Colossus roller coaster at Thorpe Park* **Left** *Imaginative adventure park, Coram's Fields*

swings, ladders and a "spook den" complete with sound effects. It is all designed to build confidence by challenging children physically and intellectually as they work out their routes. There are separate areas for under-5s and babies, and a café for parents if the noise gets too much.

CLOWNTOWN

North London's version of Bramley's, ClownTown has a similar activity frame with slides, runways, rope climbs and "spook room" to keep young adventurers entertained. It has an area for crawlers and one for toddlers, with a ball pool, bouncy castle and climbing zone. On some weekdays, craft sessions are held and there is also an on-site café.

GAMBADO, CHELSEA

This large indoor adventure play centre holds dodgems, a "Tiger Pots" ride and a huge multi-level play frame. Kids will spend all day on the fairground rides, sliding, climbing and squeezing through tunnels, or having their faces painted. There's a junior climbing wall for budding mountaineers; a sensory play area for tots; and free Wi-Fi access for adults, while friendly staff are on hand. Birthday parties are

catered for, and there is another Gambado in Watford for those staying in north London.

Best BMX & skate parks

BAY SIXTY6

Tucked under the Westway in Notting Hill, this concrete street park is practical, well equipped and under cover if it rains. It has a bowl, jump and fun boxes, a handrail, transitions, ramps and pipes. The park suits beginners as well as experienced BMX riders and skate boarders. There are sessions for novice boarders on Saturday and Sunday mornings, and set times for BMXers.

CANTELOWES SKATEPARK

One of the best BMX/skateparks in London, this has a cradle, concrete bowl, mini and vertical ramps, skid rails, practice pavements, a fun box and performance platform. There are separate areas for beginners and experts. The park is supervised and floodlit after dark.

The Lowdown

Battersea Park Adventure Playground *www.batterseapark.org/html/playgrounds.html*
Bay Sixty6 66 Acklam Rd, W10 5YU; 020 8969 4669; *www.baysixty6.com*
Bramley's Big Adventure 136 Bramley Rd, W10 6TJ; 020 8960 1515; *www.bramleysbigadventure.co.uk*
Cantelowes Skatepark Cantelowes Gardens, 212 Camden Rd, NW1 9HG; *www.skatesandladders.com/skate-parks*
Chessington World of Adventures Leatherhead Rd, Chessington, Surrey KT9 2NE; 0871 663 4477; *www.chessington.com*
ClownTown The Coppetts Centre, N12 0SH; 020 8361 6600; *clowntown.co.uk*
Coram's Fields *www.coramsfields.org*
Gambado, Chelsea 7 Station Court, Townmead Rd, SW6 2PY; 020 7384 1635; *www.gambado.com/clubs/chelsea*
Holland Park Adventure Playground *www.rbkc.gov.uk/leisureandlibraries/parksandgardens/yourlocalpark/hollandpark.aspx*
Thorpe Park Staines Rd, Chertsey, Surrey KT16 8PN; 0871 663 1673; *www.thorpepark.com*

Sporting London

London has an impressive variety of sports on offer, to be enjoyed both as a spectator and a player – below are some of the most popular. Enthusiastic young fans might enjoy a behind-the-scenes glimpse of their favourite sports stadium. Most of these, including Wembley (football), Twickenham (rugby) and Lord's (cricket), organize regular tours.

Athletics

Most major track and field events are held at **Crystal Palace National Sports Centre**, but one of the most fun events of the year is the **Virgin London Marathon**, with a course from Blackheath to the Mall through Central London. Runners will find tracks at **Battersea Park Millennium Arena** and **Linford Christie Sports Centre**. For more casual running, there's a track in **Regent's Park**.

Cricket

An integral part of an English summer, amateur cricket matches are played throughout London at the weekends. Among the more central are those in **Regent's Park** and on **Barnes Common**. To watch first-class professional cricket, try **Lord's**, home of the famous MCC (Marylebone Cricket Club) and Middlesex, or Surrey's **Kia Oval**.

Football

Football is the UK's most popular spectator sport. The season runs from Aug–May, and fans flock to cup finals and international games at **Wembley Stadium**. London's top clubs are **Arsenal** and **Tottenham Hotspur** in north London and **Chelsea** in west London. However, it is easier to come by tickets to see less high-profile teams, such as west London's **Queens Park Rangers**, and **Crystal Palace** in south London.

Horse Riding

Stables are located near a number of London parks. **Ross Nye** and **Hyde Park Stables** are on Hyde Park's doorstep. **Stag Lodge Stables** are just outside Richmond Park's Robin Hood Gate, and **Ridgway** and **Wimbledon Village Stables** are both within easy reach of Richmond Park and Wimbledon Common.

Ice-skating

London's major permanent covered rinks are **Queen's Ice and Bowl**, and **Streatham Ice Arena**. During winter months, outdoor temporary ice rinks crop up across the city. Popular ones are at **Broadgate**, **Hampton Court**, **Hyde Park**, the **Natural History Museum**, **Somerset House** and the **Tower of London**. All are floodlit, many run until 10pm.

Rowing

Of the regular races on the Thames, the highlight is the **Oxford and Cambridge Boat Race** from Putney to Mortlake. Supporters line the river to watch the "eights" of these rival universities battle it out on the river in April. Rowing is also a fun family activity, and there are boats for hire on the **Serpentine** (Easter–Oct) and the lakes in **Greenwich** (Feb–Oct) and **Regent's parks** (Apr–Sep).

Below left Skating on the outdoor ice rink at the Natural History Museum *Below centre* Enjoying a riding lesson at Hyde Park Stables *Below right* Fans celebrating in the stands at Wembley Stadium

Rugby

A 15-a-side sport, rugby union has certain similarities to American Football. International and major matches are played at **Twickenham Stadium**, the sport's headquarters. London-based clubs include **Harlequins, London Welsh, London Scottish** and **Rosslyn Park**. Matches can be watched most Saturday afternoons (Sep–Apr).

Swimming

Although there are many pools in London, surprisingly few are geared towards children. For kid's pools, try **Brentford Fountain, Newham** and **Woolwich Waterfront Leisure Centres**, which all have water slides. **Finchley Lido Leisure Centre** has indoor and outdoor pools and is popular with families. **Chelsea Sports Centre** and **Oasis** are not so family-friendly, but are more central. For outdoor pools, try **Oasis** or the **Parliament Hill** or **Serpentine lidos**.

Tennis

There are quite a few municipal tennis courts around London, and these can usually be booked on the day. Bring your own tennis racket and balls. Good local courts include **Holland Park** and **Battersea Park**. When it comes to watching tennis, June–July brings the grass court **AEGON Championships** at Queens and, of course, **Wimbledon**, the home of the sport – a must for any tennis or strawberry enthusiast.

Water sports

Sailing, canoeing and kayaking courses and more are on offer for kids aged 8+ at **Thames Young Mariners, Docklands Sailing and Watersports Centre, Surrey Docks Watersports Centre** and **Royal Victoria Dock Watersports Centre**. For less complicated water sports, there is a children's pond in Regent's Park with mini pedal boats (over-5s).

The Lowdown

Athletics

Battersea Park Millennium Arena www.wandsworth.gov.uk

Crystal Palace National Sports Centre www.bettervenues.org.uk/venues/crystal-palace

Linford Christie Sports Centre www.lbhf.gov.uk/Directory/Leisure_and_Culture/Sports_and_leisure/Leisure_centres/37548_Linford_Christie_Outdoor_Sports_Centre.asp

Regent's Park www.royalparks.org.uk/parks/the-regents-park

Virgin London Marathon www.virginlondonmarathon.com

Cricket

Barnes Common Cricket Club www.barnescommoncc.co.uk

Kia Oval www.kiaoval.com

Lord's www.lords.org

Regent's Park Cricket Club www.regentspark.play-cricket.com

Football

Arsenal www.arsenal.com

Chelsea www.chelseafc.com

Crystal Palace www.cpfc.co.uk

Queens Park Rangers www.qpr.co.uk

Tottenham Hotspur www.tottenhamhotspur.com

Wembley www.wembleystadium.com

Horse Riding

Hyde Park Stables www.hydeparkstables.com

Ross Nye Stables www.rossnyestables.co.uk

Ridgway Stables www.ridgwaystables.co.uk

Stag Lodge Stables www.ridinginlondon.com

Wimbledon Village Stables www.wvstables.com

Ice-skating

Broadgate www.broadgate.co.uk

Hampton Court www.thehamptoncourticerink.co.uk

Hyde Park www.hydeparkwinterwonderland.com/rink.html

Natural History Museum www.nhm.ac.uk/visit-us/whats-on/ice-rink/index.html

Queen's Ice and Bowl www.queensiceandbowl.co.uk

Somerset House www.somersethouse.org.uk/ice_rink/default.asp

Streatham Ice Arena streathamicearena.co.uk

Tower of London www.toweroflondonicerink.com

Rowing

Greenwich www.solarshuttle.co.uk/greenwich.html

Oxford and Cambridge Boat Race www.theboatrace.org

Regent's Park www.royalparks.org.uk/parks/the-regents-park/things-to-see-and-do/sports-and-leisure/boat-and-pedalo-hire

Serpentine www.solarshuttle.co.uk/hydepark.html

Rugby

Harlequins www.quins.co.uk

London Scottish www.londonscottish.com

London Welsh www.london-welsh.co.uk

Rosslyn Park www.rosslynpark.co.uk

Twickenham Stadium www.englandrugby.com/twickenham

Swimming

Brentford Fountain Leisure Centre www.fusion-lifestyle.com/centres/Brentford_Fountain_Leisure_Centre

Chelsea Sports Centre www.better.org.uk/chelsea-sports-centre#/

Finchley Lido Leisure Centre www.better.org.uk/finchley-lido-leisure-centre#/

Newham Leisure Centre www.activenewham.org.uk/newham

Oasis www.better.org.uk/leisure/oasis-sports-centre#/

Parliament Hill Lido www.camden.gov.uk/ccm/content/contacts/categories/contacts-for-open-air-swimming.en

Serpentine Lido www.serpentinelido.com

Woolwich Waterfront Leisure Centre www.better.org.uk/leisure/waterfront-leisure-centre#/

Tennis

AEGON Championships www.lta.org.uk/major-events/aegon-championships/

Battersea Park www.batterseapark.org/info/what-to-do/sports/tennis/

Holland Park www.rbkc.gov.uk/leisureandlibraries/sportsandleisure/sportsfacilitiesinparks/tennis.aspx

Wimbledon www.wimbledon.com

Water sports

Docklands Sailing and Watersports Centre www.dswc.org

Royal Victoria Dock Watersports Centre www.royaldockstrust.org.uk/summerwatersports.htm

Surrey Docks Watersports Centre www.fusion-lifestyle.com/centres/Surrey_Docks_Watersports_Centre

Thames Young Mariners www.surreycc.gov.uk/outdoorlearning

Outdoor London

Celebrated for its many beautiful parks, London even manages to cram green spaces into its bustling centre. Most of these larger expanses – and some of the small ones – date from the Middle Ages: some were always common land, others were preserved for the exclusive use of royalty as hunting grounds, and only later opened to the public. As a result, wherever you are in London, you are only minutes away from historic open spaces.

Battersea Park

With a boating lake, a small zoo and an adventure playground, this is an all-action destination (see pp186–9).

Blackheath

Once covered by thick gorse, which made it popular with highwaymen, Blackheath has long been a rallying point, from Wat Tyler's rebellious peasants in 1381 to suffragette marches in the early 20th century. It also has a sporting heritage: James I introduced the Scottish game of golf to England here, and it is the start of the London Marathon (see p50). The most popular pastime here is kite-flying.

Enjoying a pedalo session in the glorious surroundings of Regent's Park boating lake

Coram's Fields

This space has enough to keep kids happy: a paddling pool, a farmyard, a playground, sports pitches and play sessions (see p48 and p106).

Green Park

With mature trees and grassy lawns, Green Park (see p73) is perfect for walks and picnics. In spring, carpets of daffodils turn the grass yellow. A royal hunting ground until Charles II enclosed it in 1668, it was turned into a pleasure garden in the early 18th century, with temples and pools (now long gone). Later, it became a favourite spot for duels.

Greenwich Park

You can see most of London on a clear day from this park. On its eastern side, excavations have unearthed evidence of a Roman temple. On one of the hills that crown it, stands the Royal Observatory, where east meets west at the Meridian Line (see p196).

Hampstead Heath

"The Heath", as locals call it, is a stunning area of hills, ponds, woods and glades. There is plenty for families, from outdoor swimming, model boating or the adventure playground. Nearby, Golders Hill Park has a children's zoo and putting green, and there's a great view from Parliament Hill (see p214).

Holland Park

Although bombs destroyed most of the Jacobean Holland House in 1941, its glorious park survived, with paths that wind through woods, and a wildlife enclosure that is home to peacocks and other exotic birds. A peaceful Japanese and formal flower garden, an adventure playground and play area, and space to kick a football, make it a park for all ages.

Hyde Park and Kensington Gardens

One of the finest royal parks in London, this is also close to many must-see sights (see pp174–5).

Primrose Hill

A good place to come when it snows, this 78-m (256-ft) hill (see p113), just north of Regent's Park, is perfect for tobogganing. In the 16th century, Henry VIII appropriated it for hunting, and was not until 1841

Above Panoramic view over London from Primrose Hill *Below* A fine 12-pointer red deer stag and small female in Richmond Park

that the public were allowed in. It can be very windy at the top, which makes it popular with kite-flyers. From here, the view includes the O2 Arena and the Post Office Tower.

Regent's Park

Run around in open spaces to the sound of lions from nearby London Zoo, walk along the canal or enjoy the boating lake (*see p112*).

Richmond Park

Charles I's personal hunting ground, Richmond (*see p232*) is the largest and most wild of the royal parks. Its heath and woods are home to a large variety of native plants, birds and animals, including herds of red and fallow deer that roam freely.

Royal Botanic Gardens, Kew

No longer a stuffy Victorian botany collection, there are lots of exciting things for kids at the Royal Botanic Gardens (*see pp228–9*).

St James's Park

The oldest of the royal parks, this is close to Buckingham Palace and boasts lovely flower beds (*see p72*).

Wimbledon and Putney Commons

Once popular for duels, these commons form London's largest expanse of heath and woodland. They are used for activities ranging from golf and horse riding to model boating and blackberry picking. Don't miss the 1817 windmill, now the Windmill Museum (*open Apr–Oct: 2–5pm Sat, 11am–5pm Sun & public hols*), with displays of models, machinery and tools, and a nearby Nature Trail.

WWT London Wetland Centre

More than 180 species of birds and animals shelter in this lovely nature reserve (*see p230*).

The Lowdown

Blackheath *www.lewisham.gov.uk/ inmyarea/openspaces/parks/ blackheath/pages/default.aspx*

Green Park *www.royalparks.org.uk/ parks/green-park*

Greenwich Park *www.royalparks. org.uk/parks/greenwich-park*

Hampstead Heath *www. cityoflondon.gov.uk/things-to-do/ green-spaces/hampstead-heath/ pages/default.aspx*

Holland Park *www.rbkc.gov.uk/ leisureandlibraries/parksandgardens/ yourlocalpark/hollandpark.aspx*

Primrose Hill *www.royalparks.org. uk/parks/the-regents-park/ things-to-see-and-do/primrose-hill*

Richmond Park *www.royalparks.org. uk/parks/richmond-park*

St James's Park *www.royalparks.org. uk/parks/st-Jamess-park*

Wimbledon and Putney Commons *www.wpcc.org.uk*

The History of London

Although there was only a small collection of huts beside the River Thames at the time of the first Roman invasion in 55 BC, some 100 years later, a small port and trading community had been established, which the Romans called "Londinium". Growing rapidly, London was the obvious choice for the capital by the time of the Norman Conquest in 1066. Over the next 1,000 years, the city grew in size and importance, becoming one of the major cities of the world.

The Romans

In AD 43, rampaging Romans under the Emperor Claudius defeated the unruly Celtic tribes of southeastern Britain and, in AD 50, founded "Londinium", building a bridge across the River Thames close to the site of the later London Bridge.

Early Roman London became a flourishing port and settlement at the centre of the network of straight roads that the Romans were so fond of building. In AD 60–61, a revolt by the Iceni tribe from Norfolk, led by the fierce warrior Queen Boudicca, ended with London being burnt to the ground. Like a phoenix, the city rose from the ashes to become capital of England, a prosperous financial and trading centre, and headquarters of Britain's Roman governor, with a market and its own mint. By AD 200, the Romans had fortified the city with a defensive wall, but the Roman Empire was already in decline. At the end of the 3rd century, the Romans had to use ferocious Germanic mercenaries to help them repel Saxon raiders. Roman rule ended in AD 410.

The Anglo-Saxons

The Romans' fine houses were left to decline, and the city remained mostly uninhabited for some 400 years. When the Anglo-Saxon warrior kings eventually arrived, they settled an area just to the west of the old Roman city. Anglo-Saxon London was not as developed as Roman London had been, becoming instead a simple farming town. During the early 9th century, however, London's importance grew as a market town. England reunited under the Kings of Wessex from Winchester (including King Alfred), Christianity was reintroduced and with it came education.

The Vikings

In 836 London was sacked by the Vikings, who continued their attacks throughout the 9th century. After Alfred the Great's victory over the Vikings in 878, London was returned to the Anglo-Saxons and there was a brief period of calm, during which the inhabitants moved east, back to the more secure area within the

A 10th-century vellum depicting Vikings arriving in England

rebuilt Roman walls. The raids started again in 994, until a final battle in 1014. Legend has it that in a fine strategic move, Olaf, an ally of the Anglo-Saxons, tied his boats to London Bridge and pulled it down – possibly the basis for the song, *London Bridge is Falling Down*.

The Normans

The year 1066 saw the Norman invasion of England. After the death of the Anglo-Saxon king, Edward

Timeline

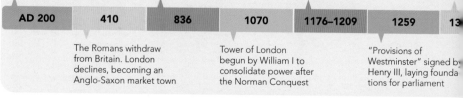

| AD 200 | 410 | 836 | 1070 | 1176–1209 | 1259 | 13 |

Roman invaders build a bridge across the Thames and found "Londinium", fortifying it with a defensive wall

London sacked by Vikings; later the Anglo-Saxons regain control under Alfred the Great

First stone London Bridge constructed. Lined with houses and shops, it survives for more than 600 years

The Black De ravages the c wiping out ha of all Londor

The Romans withdraw from Britain. London declines, becoming an Anglo-Saxon market town

Tower of London begun by William I to consolidate power after the Norman Conquest

"Provisions of Westminster" signed by Henry III, laying founda tions for parliament

the Confessor, his warlike cousin, William of Normandy, claimed the throne, but found that Edward's brother-in-law Harold had been crowned in his place. William defeated Harold at Hastings, but didn't want to attack well-fortified London. Instead, he razed the fields around it and the city swiftly accepted William the Conqueror as king. He was crowned in Westminster Abbey on Christmas Day 1066.

Under the Normans, London thrived and in 1070 William started work on the Tower of London, where he lived until he moved to the Palace of Westminster, built alongside Westminster Abbey by Edward the Confessor in the mid-11th century.

The Middle Ages

In 1215, angered by heavy taxes, London supported the barons in drafting the Magna Carta to limit the powers of King John. The 13th century saw a building boom in the city, with the construction of Henry III's abbey at Westminster (1269) and the first St Paul's Cathedral (1280) – half as tall as the current version.

In 1338 Edward III made Westminster the place for regular Parliamentary sessions, but there was trouble ahead. In 1348, the Black Death struck the city, killing half its 60,000 inhabitants. In 1381, the peasants revolted: an army of serfs led by Wat Tyler took over London for two days, but the revolt ended when Tyler was killed by the mayor. The early 15th century saw

the rise of a wealthy class of former soldiers and tradesmen, threatening the feudal aristocracy. By 1461 London's support was crucial to Edward IV, who won the Wars of the Roses, to restore stability to England.

The Tudors

During the 16th-century rule of the Tudors, England was transformed from a minor state into a major world power, London's economy boomed and its population quadrupled. The downside was that slums developed on its outskirts. In Henry VIII's Reformation of 1533, the new gentry acquired the land freed by the dissolution of the monasteries (half of the city was occupied by religious buildings). After Henry's death, "Bloody Mary" reinstated Catholicism and martyred hundreds of Protestants at Smithfield from 1553–8. On Mary's death, Protestant Elizabeth I came to the throne. She was supported by the people of London for her 45-year reign, during which the city flourished as a centre of European trade, exploration and discovery.

A painting of Henry VIII with his third wife, Jane Seymour, and their son, Prince Edward, circa 1545

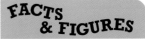

FACTS & FIGURES

Two-in-one
London contains two cities, not one: the ancient City of London and the neighbouring City of Westminster, created in 1965, and containing Buckingham Palace and Big Ben. Home to nearly 8 million people, London is the biggest city in Europe.

Trojan origins
Legend claims that London was founded 1,000 years before the Romans arrived by the Trojan warrior Brutus. He slew two giants, Gog and Magog, and to this day, their fearsome statues are paraded at the Lord Mayor's Show every November.

No entry, Ma'am!
The only place in London that the Queen is forbidden to enter is the House of Commons, because she is not a "commoner". The rule was introduced when the monarchy was restored in 1661, after the English Civil War.

City centre
The official centre of London is the statue of Charles I on horseback just south of Trafalgar Square: all distances from the city are measured from here.

Fire escape
The Great Fire of 1666 devastated London, but according to official figures, no more than eight people died.

London firsts
The very first "television show" was demonstrated in 1926 by inventor John Logie Baird in a room at 22 Frith Street, Soho. Various other London inventions include the first daily newspaper (1702), roller skates (1760), Christmas cards (1843), traffic lights (1863) and penicillin (1928).

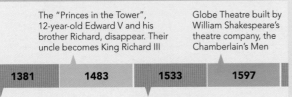

The "Princes in the Tower", 12-year-old Edward V and his brother Richard, disappear. Their uncle becomes King Richard III

Globe Theatre built by William Shakespeare's theatre company, the Chamberlain's Men

| 1381 | 1483 | 1533 | 1597 |

Rebels storm the Tower of London to demand an end to serfdom, in the failed Peasants' Revolt

Henry VIII breaks with the Vatican and forms the Church of England

The Stuarts

In the 17th century a new generation of moneyed gentry expanded the city's boundaries westwards by building on land in Piccadilly and Leicester Square. Puritanism increased as a reaction against the high-handed Stuart kings, James I and Charles I, and in the ensuing English Civil War (1642–9), London merchants put their finances behind Parliament. The war ended when Charles I was beheaded in London in 1649 and England became a Commonwealth republic under Oliver Cromwell. After Cromwell's death, there were numerous quick-fire changes of government and, fed up with the Puritan restrictions on simple pleasures such as dancing and theatre, Londoners vigorously supported the restoration of Charles II to the throne in 1660.

Plague and fire

The Black Death broke out in 1665. Although there had been earlier outbreaks, this was the last and the worst, in which nearly 100,000 people died. Pits were dug and cartloads of bodies thrown into them. The following year, the Great Fire of London swept through the medieval city, after a blaze that started in a bakery in Pudding Lane spread to the surrounding streets. The fire destroyed 60 per cent of London, including St Paul's Cathedral. Reconstruction in the late 17th century saw stone buildings replace wooden ones and narrow

Illustration showing residents fleeing the Great Fire of London in1666

streets swapped for broad ones. Sir Christopher Wren built 52 churches, including his masterpiece, the new St Paul's. The fire also cleansed the city of the plague and led to the dispersal of the population over a wider area.

Georgian London

In the early 18th century, the population exploded again, with an increase in the poor as well as the rich. By 1750 London had 675,000 inhabitants. The villages of Kensington, Knightsbridge and Marylebone were incorporated into the city, building started in Greenwich, and stylish St James's and Mayfair were developed for the elite. There were also slums to the east and south, where the poor drank too much gin and only one child in four lived beyond the age of five. In 1750 Westminster Bridge

was opened – only the second over the Thames. The 1780 Gordon Riots, a violent Protestant uprising against Roman Catholic freedoms, led eventually to the establishment of the Metropolitan Police force in 1829. The policemen were known as "Bobbies" or "Peelers" after their founder, Robert Peel. Between 1820 and 1838, the foppish Prince Regent (later George IV) and architect John Nash developed Regent Street, Regent's Park, Buckingham Palace and The Mall.

The Victorian era

During the 19th century, London became the largest city in the world and the rich, powerful capital of the British Empire. But as its wealth increased, so did its poverty. The overcrowding and foul, insanitary conditions of London's slums preoccupied Charles Dickens and

Timeline

Guy Fawkes and his Catholic conspirators make an abortive attempt to blow up Parliament in the Gunpowder Plot	The Great Fire destroys the city, clearing the way for Sir Christopher Wren's city of stone, including St Paul's		Queen Victoria ascends the throne, and Buckingham Palace becomes the monarch's official residence		The Representation of ▸ People Act grants vote all men over 21 and sor women over 30	
1605	**1649**	**1666**	**1721**	**1837**	**1863**	19
	Charles I beheaded at the Banqueting House, as Oliver Cromwell's Parliamentarians triumph in the English Civil War		Robert Walpole is named First Lord of the Treasury, effectively Britain's first prime minister		The first line opens on London Underground; comprehensive sewera network follows later	

other writers. In 1832–66 cholera killed thousands, and in the summer of 1858, the smell in London grew so bad it was called the "Great Stink" and Parliament had to stop work. But not everything was bad, Victorian successes included Crystal Palace's 1851 Great Exhibition, celebrating British dominance in trade, science and industry; Charles Barry's Gothic Palace of Westminster (1840); the UK's railway network; London's first Underground line (1863); and Joseph Bazalgette's sewage system (1875). The quality of life improved with more mobility and progress in public health and education. In 1897, the normally rather reserved Victorians joyfully celebrated Queen Victoria's Diamond Jubilee with street parties.

Model Twiggy on the King's Road during the "Swinging"1960s

The 20th century

In the early years of the 20th century, public transport expanded and so did the sprawling suburbs. During World War I (1914–18), women took over many of London's public services, and in 1918 the suffragettes won the vote for some women. In 1920–30 immigration increased and the capital quadrupled in size, reaching an all-time population peak

in 1939. In World War II, London was bombed heavily during the 1940–41 Blitz. The post-war years saw the Olympics at Wembley in 1948, the Festival of Britain (1951) and a property boom from 1955–65. After the Great Smog of 1952, the 1956 Clean Air Act put a stop to London's famous "pea-soupers" and marked the end of industrial London.

In the 1960s, the city became known as "Swinging London", a centre of fashionable youth culture. There was conflict in the 1970s, when "The Troubles" in Northern Ireland made London a target of terrorist attacks by the Provisional IRA, and again in the mid-1980s when racial tension surfaced in the Brixton Riots. A boom in the 1980s was followed by bust in the 1990s.

The 21st century…

In 2000, Tony Blair's government created the Greater London Authority, led by an elected mayor. On 6 July 2005 London won the bid for the 2012 Olympics, but celebrations were short lived; terrorists bombed the London Underground and a bus the next day. As a global recession loomed, the first coalition government since World War II was formed in May 2010. In April 2011, London held jubilant celebrations in honour of the wedding of Prince William and Kate Middleton and in 2012 it celebrated the Queen's Diamond Jubilee marking her 60-year reign, followed by the Olympics.

HEROES & VILLAINS

Boudicca
She burnt London to the ground in AD 60, but this warrior queen is a heroine to many because she almost beat the Roman invaders. Look for her on Westminster Bridge (see p69) and at All Hallows by the Tower (see p125).

Dick Whittington
This 14th-century merchant became Lord Mayor of London four times. He was much loved – but nobody knows if he really owned a cat! Look for him at Westminster Abbey (see pp66–7) and The Guildhall (see p133).

Guy Fawkes
In 1605 Fawkes tried to wipe out King James I by stacking gunpowder under the Houses of Parliament. He is remembered on Bonfire Night (5 Nov). Look for him at the Museum of London (see pp136–7).

Christopher Wren
London's greatest architect helped the city rise from the ashes after the Great Fire of 1666, building 51 churches and St Paul's Cathedral. Look for him there (see pp130–31), and at The Monument (see p124).

Colonel Thomas Blood

This Irishman is famous for plotting to steal the Crown Jewels in 1671, disguised as a priest. His gang stuffed some of the gems down their trousers – but were captured while fleeing. Look for him at the Tower of London (see pp122–3).

Charles Dickens
This famous writer created Oliver Twist and Mr Scrooge, and campaigned against the cruel treatment of poor children and orphans in London. Look for him at the Charles Dickens Museum (see pp106–7).

1940–41	1965	1991	2012
	"Swinging London" is the world's trendiest city; stars include singer Mick Jagger and actor Michael Caine		The Olympic Games come to London for the third time
The Blitz destroys or damages 1 million London homes, and kills more than 20,000 civilians		Canary Wharf, Britain's tallest building, spearheads the regeneration of the Docklands as a business quarter	

The Queen's Household Cavalry
Mounted Regiment outside
Buckingham Palace

Exploring
LONDON

Westminster
and the West End

Only two things stand still in the thumping heart of Central London: the "living statues" in their fabulous costumes in Covent Garden, and the stony-faced sentries standing like toy soldiers outside Buckingham Palace. Everything else seems in perpetual motion, and there is enough to keep families fulfilled for weeks, including 40 theatres, a dozen cinemas and some of the world's greatest museums and galleries.

Bloomsbury and Regent's Park

The City and the East End

Westminster and the West End

Southwark and the South Bank

Kensington, Chelsea and Battersea

Highlights

Guards Museum
Watch the Foot Guards leave Wellington Barracks, then don a bearskin in the museum and take home a soldier or two from the shop *(see p76)*.

St James's Park
Say hello to squirrels and see the famous pelicans near Duck Island in this lush green wedge between Westminster and the West End. It's picnic paradise *(see p74)*.

London Transport Museum
Step back in time in this giant "play barn" full of classic buses to board and vintage trains to ride. All aboard! *(see p92)*.

Royal Opera House
Peeking into a rehearsal on a backstage tour of the opera house feels like a great privilege, while the family Christmas shows are amazing spectacles *(see p90–91)*.

Somerset House
Pack your beachwear and brave the water jets in the Neo-Classical Fountain Court. In winter, it hosts one of the most glamorous ice rinks in London *(see p93)*.

The National Gallery
This place cleverly brings painting alive with "Teach Your Grown-ups About Art" trails, where the kids lead the tour *(see pp80–81)*.

Left *Panoramic view of Westminster showing part of the London Eye, Big Ben and Westminster Abbey*
Above *The Young Dancer (1988), by Enzo Plazzotta, is a fitting statue for the theatrical area of Covent Garden*

The Best of
Westminster & the West End

From Big Ben to Buckingham Palace, Nelson's Column to the National Gallery, this is picture-postcard London, squeezing scores of museums and monuments into 5 square kilometres (2 square miles) on the north bank of the Thames. Visiting families can be in the House of Commons one minute, pretending to be the prime minister, and wander through the Queen's throne room the next – but please don't sit on Her Majesty's chair!

Pomp and circumstance

Soaking up the full majesty of royal London takes careful planning. The State Rooms at **Buckingham Palace** (see pp74–5) are open in summer only: book ahead online for the first tour of the day at 9:45am. There's just enough time to tour the palace and get to Wellington Barracks by 11am, when the troops line up for the **Changing the Guard** (see p76) – it gets less crowded here than on the Palace forecourt.

Visit the tombs of former monarchs at **Westminster Abbey** (see pp66–7) – resting place of 16 kings and queens – and be sure to follow the engaging children's trail. Admire, too, Big Ben and the impressive **Houses of Parliament** (see p68). After lunch by the lake in **St James's Park** (see p74), watch the pelicans get theirs – the daily feed takes place at 2:30pm. Finish the day with a horsey treat: either a tour of The Royal Mews (Mar–Dec – see p76) or a close-up look at the sentries at **Horse Guards Parade** (see p70), where kids can dress up as guardsmen at the museum.

Seasonal festivities

Spring makes a colourful splash here, from the St Patrick's Day Parade that musters in Green Park in March to the London Marathon on The Mall in April. Children will love the twirling ribbons and dancing strings of the Covent Garden May Fayre & Puppet Festival (May).

In summer, Trooping the Colour at **Horse Guards Parade** celebrates the Queen's official birthday in June. It's a great time to take a riverboat cruise along the Thames. In the West End meanwhile, children can get free theatre tickets to a host of shows during Kids' Week (see p46), which runs for a fortnight in August.

London puts on a good Christmas, too. Enjoy carols round the Norwegian Christmas tree in

Above right Covent Garden May Fayre & Puppet Festival
Right Spectacular New Year's Eve fireworks display

Above Crowds gathered outside Buckingham Palace on The Mall, the finishing line for the London Marathon

Trafalgar Square *(see p82)*, the bright lights of **Hamleys** toy shop in Regent Street *(see p85)*, or the fairy-tale ice rink at **Somerset House** *(see p93)*. There are two New Year celebrations to choose from: the fireworks show along the Thames on 31 December, or the dragons dancing through Chinatown for Chinese New Year about a month later.

Backstage West End

Begin a starry day out in Theatreland at the **Royal Opera House** *(see p90)* in Covent Garden. If it's Monday, be at the box office for 10am to get tickets for the free lunchtime recital. Failing that, sign up for the 10:30am backstage tour – a glimpse behind the scenes at the Royal Ballet, to see where the principal dancers practise their *pas de deux*. Next, explore the smart boutiques and busy lunch spots around **Covent Garden** *(see pp88–9)*, where there's always a mix of performers to see on the streets.

If it's Wednesday or Saturday, take in a matinée of a musical at Britain's oldest working playhouse, the **Theatre Royal Drury Lane** *(see p91)*. For star-struck youngsters, the stage door is in Russell Street. This theatre, too, offers family-friendly daily tours. As night falls, head for **Leicester Square** *(see p84)* and hunt for film-star handprints in the pavement, grab cut-price tickets for a show, or choose from dozens of films at the cinemas on every corner.

Art versus Science

It may be best known for shows and shopping, but the West End offers plenty to stimulate young minds, too. The galleries beside Trafalgar Square are the perfect introduction to fine art: the **National Gallery** *(see pp80–81)* has three audio-trails just for families, plus drawing and daubing workshops. Next door, the **National Portrait Gallery** *(see p82)* has artist-led "tour and draw" events. Tiny geniuses may prefer **Tate Britain** *(see pp68-9)*, which dispenses free build-it-yourself art boxes to children.

For children unmoved by Van Gogh and Van Eyck, how about the fascinating Faraday and Franklin? Both men have museums dedicated to them here. **The Royal Institution** *(see p77)* has restored the lab where Michael Faraday tamed electricity, and kids get to explore using a cool console packed with puzzles and games. The **Benjamin Franklin House** *(see p83)* uses a sound and light show to tell the great statesman's story.

Right Buckingham Palace guards in traditional red tunics and bearskin hats during the Changing the Guard

Westminster Abbey and around

Ever since Christmas Day 1066, when William the Conqueror was crowned here, Westminster Abbey has been the coronation site of monarchs – and the resting place of many too, including Henry V and Elizabeth I. Outside, the pomp of Parliament Square is dented a little by traffic, so save the surrounding sights for a Sunday, when it's quieter. St James's Park and the attractions along Whitehall can be comfortably tackled on foot, but hop on a bus (number 87 or 88) to visit the Tate Britain gallery.

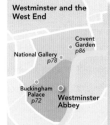

Westminster and the West End

River bus – a fun way to see many of the sights of Central London

The Lowdown

🚗 **Train** Charing Cross. **Tube** Westminster or St James's Park; Pimlico for Tate Britain. **Bus** Parliament Square: route numbers 3, 11, 12, 24, 53, 87, 88, 148, 159, 211 or 453; Tate Britain: 87, 88, C10, 185, 360, 436. **River bus** Westminster Pier to St Katharine's Dock daily, May–Sep; to Bankside on weekends and public holidays in winter. Seasonal services to Hampton Court, Kew Gardens to the west; Tower of London, Greenwich to the east

ℹ️ **Visitor information** Victoria Railway station, SW1E 5NE

🛒 **Supermarkets** Tesco Express, 8 Bridge St, SW1A 2JR (opposite Big Ben). Costcutter, 31 Horseferry Rd, SW1P 2AY **Markets** Strutton Ground (St James's Park tube), 9am–2:30pm Mon–Fri; and Tachbrook St (Pimlico tube) 8am–6pm Mon–Sat

🎉 **Festivals** New Year's Day Parade (1 Jan); Trooping the Colour, Horse Guards Parade (Jun); Mayor's Thames Festival (Sep); Festival of Remembrance, Whitehall (11 Nov); State Opening of Parliament (Nov); Christmas Carol Service, Westminster Abbey (23 & 24 Dec)

➕ **Pharmacies** Boots, 11 Bridge St, SW1A 2JR (across from Big Ben), open daily. Or search at www.nhs.uk/servicedirectories

🛝 **Nearest playgrounds** Victoria Tower Gardens (Lambeth Bridge end); Causton St playground; and playground in St James's Park

The Houses of Parliament, seen from across the River Thames

Trying on a uniform at the Household Cavalry Museum on Horse Guards Parade

Places of Interest

SIGHTS

1. Westminster Abbey
2. Houses of Parliament
3. Tate Britain
4. Churchill War Rooms
5. Horse Guards Parade
6. Banqueting House

EAT AND DRINK

1. Le Pain du Jour
2. Wesley's Café
3. The Clarence
4. The Rex Whistler Restaurant
5. Wagamama
6. Inn the Park
7. Pret A Manger

See also Houses of Parliament (p68), Tate Britain (p68) and Churchill War Rooms (p70).

WHERE TO STAY

1. The Goring
2. Luna Simone
3. Taj 51 Buckingham Gate

Replica of St Edward's Crown at the Westminster Abbey Museum

The shelter in the Churchill War Rooms, from where the prime minister conducted Britain's World War II campaign

① Westminster Abbey
Poets, princes and some rather smelly monks

Henry VIII ejected the Benedictine monks in 1540 when he dissolved the monasteries and founded the Church of England, but Westminster Abbey has retained its importance down the centuries. As well as witnessing the coronations of 39 kings and queens, the atmospheric building is also the final resting place of many world-famous writers, musicians and scientists. It is packed full of spooky tombs, sleeping knights and secret gardens, and there is even a creepy wax museum.

Gargoyle over the door of Westminster Abbey

Key Features

Dick Whittington Window This shows London's most famous lord mayor – his cat is hiding at his feet in the stained glass.

Dick Whittington Window

High Altar Queen Elizabeth II was crowned here in 1953, in front of 8,251 packed-in people. The gilded Coronation Chair is 700 years old – and has been carved with graffiti by naughty Westminster schoolboys.

Lady Chapel This 16th-century chapel has a stone ceiling as delicate as a cobweb, and there are cheeky carvings under the choir stalls. Look for a wife thrashing her husband's bottom with a birch rod!

Poets' Corner The first great writer buried here was Geoffrey Chaucer, 600 years ago. The novelist Thomas Hardy's ashes are here, but not his heart, which is buried alongside his first wife in his beloved Dorset.

Cloisters These contain the earliest parts of the abbey, including the Pyx Chamber, a strong room where kings kept some of their treasure. The monks lived around the cloisters, and they even bathed here – though only four times a year.

Queen Elizabeth I's Tomb (above) is shared with Queen Mary Tudor.
Grave of the Unknown Warrior (left) This tribute to all who have lost their lives in war was unveiled in 1920.

The Lowdown

🌐 **Map reference** 16 G1
Address 20 Dean's Yard, SW1P 3PA; 020 7222 5152; *www. westminster-abbey.org*

🚌 **Tube** Westminster. **Bus stop** Westminster Abbey or Victoria St. **River bus** Westminster Pier

🕐 **Open** 9:30am–3:30pm Mon–Fri (11am–6pm Wed); 9:30am–1:30pm Sat. Last admission 1 hour before closing. On Sun and religious holidays, the abbey is open for worship only – all are welcome

💲 **Price** £45; under-5s free

👥 **Skipping the queue** Tickets can't be pre-booked. Attending church services is free: the choir sings Evensong daily except Wed (5pm weekdays; 3pm weekends)

🚩 **Guided tours** Free audio tour; there are verger-led guided tours up to five times daily (£5)

👫 **Age range** 5 plus

🏃 **Activities** Children's trail (ages 5–12) in English, French, German, Spanish, Italian; kids aged 5–12 can dress up as a monk in the museum (free). Art, dancing and drama workshops

on summer afternoons in College Garden (ages 5 plus, free)

🕐 **Allow** Up to 2 hours

♿ **Wheelchair access** Yes, via North Door; some areas inaccessible

☕ **Café** Cellarium Café in the cloisters offers afternoon tea

🛍 **Shop** Outside the West Door

🚻 **Toilets** Near Poets' Corner

Good family value?
Plenty to dazzle here, though adult admission is expensive.

College Garden, Westminster Abbey, once used by monks for growing herbs

Letting off steam

The tidy lawns and paths of **College Garden**, in the grounds of Westminster Abbey, are open Tuesday to Thursday only: concerts and children's events are held here in July and August. However, for a proper run-around, head for **St James's Park** with its lake and playground, at the Buckingham Palace end *(see p74)*. If it rains, get even wetter at the **Queen Mother Sports Centre** *(223 Vauxhall Bridge Road, SW1V 1EL; open daily)*, where the children's swimming pool has a great flume.

Eat and drink

Picnic: under £22; Snacks: £23; Real meal: £44; Family treat: £60 or more (based on a family of four)

PICNIC Le Pain du Jour *(10 Strutton Ground, SW1P 2HP; 020 7222 3722; 7:30am–4pm Mon–Fri)* is the pick of a parade of sandwich places along Strutton Ground, near St James's Park tube. Eat by the lake in St James's Park.
SNACKS Wesley's Café *(Central Hall Westminster, Storey's Gate, SW1H 9NH; 020 7222 8010; 8am–4pm Mon–Fri, 9am–4pm Sat & Sun)* is located downstairs at the Methodist Central Hall and serves hot and cold meals, as well as paninis, salads and sandwiches. It also offers a wide range of cakes, scones and biscuits in the afternoon.

Enjoying lunch at Wesley's Café, Methodist Central Hall

REAL MEAL There are limited options near Parliament Square so try **The Clarence** *(53 Whitehall, SW1A 2HP; 020 7930 4808; 11am–11pm Mon–Sat; noon–10:30pm Sun)*, a scrubbed-up gastropub with half-price children's dishes, including beef stew and gammon and eggs.
FAMILY TREAT The Rex Whistler Restaurant at Tate Britain *(020 7887 8825; noon–5pm daily)* is a posh pillared dining room with food to match. One child under 13 can lunch for free with an adult eating a main and a dessert à la carte *(£25–35)*. The murals, painted by Whistler in 1927, when he was still a student, make a jolly talking point.

Find out more

DIGITAL Create your own colourful coat of arms like those of the knights of Westminster Abbey at *www.makeyourcoatofarms.com*. Test your knowledge about Guy Fawkes and the Gunpowder Plot – and answer as quick as you can, to stop the fizzing fuse, at: *www.bbc. co.uk/history/british/civil_war_ revolution/launch_gms_ gunpowder_plot.shtml.*

The famous front door at No. 10 Downing Street

Next stop...

NO. 10 DOWNING STREET Stroll along Whitehall to peek through the railings into Downing Street, home of prime ministers since 1730. Until 1982 tourists could walk up and take photos of No. 10.
WESTMINSTER CATHEDRAL Near Victoria station is this impressive cathedral, which is the Catholic Church's headquarters in Britain *(42 Francis Street, SW1P 1QW; www.westminstercathedral.org.uk; 8am–7pm Mon–Fri; 10am–1pm Sat & Sun)*. The 83-m (272-ft) tower is closed for engineering works.

The Neo-Gothic Houses of Parliament, rebuilt in the 19th century after a massive fire

② Houses of Parliament

Home of UK democracy and those famous bongs

Officially called the Palace of Westminster, the Houses of Parliament began with Westminster Hall, built in 1097 by the son of William the Conqueror and little changed since. Guy Fawkes was tried here after trying to blow the building up in 1605, Sir Winston Churchill lay in state in 1965, and Henry VIII's tennis ball was found in the rafters, nearly 400 years after it got stuck there. Today, the hall is a pretty grand visitors' lobby – with its lofty timber roof, it feels like being inside an upturned Viking longship.

Free guided tours begin here and run all year for British residents, plus every Saturday and on weekdays in summer for paying visitors. When MPs are in session, or "sitting", it's also possible to attend a debate by queuing down the ramp on Cromwell Green. The tour passes through Westminster Hall and the shop, set inside St Stephen's Hall, where Spencer Perceval was shot dead in 1812 – Britain's only assassinated prime minister.

Where Guy Fawkes failed, a cleaner succeeded, accidentally burning down Parliament in 1834. Most of the building visible today was designed by Charles Barry in Victorian Gothic style and built in 1840–60 with sumptuous interiors by Augustus Pugin. The 75-minute tour is unstuffy and full of anecdotes and follows the same route as the Queen when she attends the State Opening of Parliament each November. The tour reveals why Her Majesty arrives on a blue carpet, the location of her secret toilet, and why the statues of past prime ministers have shiny shoes. It doesn't visit Big Ben, though – that tour is only available to British residents (age 11 plus) who apply to their MP. The tower's iconic clock first ticked on 31 May 1859 and its famous "bongs" have heralded some BBC radio news bulletins since 1923.

The standard tour climaxes in the Commons Chamber, a surprisingly snug space just 20 m (66 ft) long – it can seat only 427 of Britain's 650 MPs. Visitors are able to stand where the prime minister does, but sitting down on any of the seats is not allowed – only MPs can do that. Parliament Square, just outside, is home to several large statues of leaders and politicians.

Letting off steam

Victoria Tower Gardens (*Abingdon Street, SW1P 3*) has a grassy riverside, plus a small swing park.

③ Tate Britain

A masterpiece in every room

This site once stored prisoners, not paintings: in Victorian times the Millbank Penitentiary held convicts about to be shipped off to Australia as punishment. In 1897 Henry Tate, the sugar tycoon, paid for a national gallery, and it became the world's biggest collection of British art.

Prices given are for a family of four

The Lowdown

🌐 **Map reference** 16 G3
Address Millbank, SW1P; 020 7887 8888; www.tate.org.uk/visit/tate-britain

🚇 **Tube** Pimlico, Vauxhall
Bus stop Millbank, Vauxhall Bridge Road, John Islip Street
River bus Tate Boat (www.tate.org.uk/visit/tate-boat) shuttles every 40 minutes to Tate Modern (see p148) during opening hours

🕐 **Open** 10am–6pm (last admission 5:15pm); till 10pm Fri

💲 **Price** Free; special temporary exhibitions individually priced

👫 **Skipping the queue** Tickets for temporary exhibitions can be booked ahead online

🚩 **Guided tours** Free tours four times daily, plus multimedia guide £4

👫 **Age range** 3 plus

🏃 **Activities** Children's activity packs; Art Trolley on weekends and school holidays (free); occasional family workshops

⏱ **Allow** 1–2 hours

♿ **Wheelchair access** Yes, Manton entrance, Atterbury Street

🍽 **Eat and drink** Snacks The Café has a kids' menu. Family treat The Rex Whistler Restaurant offers a free meal for one child under 13 when an adult orders two courses à la carte

🛍 **Shops** Millbank and Manton entrances

🚻 **Toilets** Manton entrance

The 30-room collection spans 500 years and includes everything from Hogarth to Hockney, Gainsborough to Gilbert and George. What's actually on display varies, but there are always plenty of works to capture young imaginations: story pictures (perhaps *The Lady of Shalott* by John Waterhouse); scary pictures (try Bacon's *Figures at the Base of a Crucifixion*); pictures of animals (Stubbs's *Horse Devoured by a Lion*) and of children (Sargent's *Carnation, Lily, Lily, Rose*). The Pre-Raphaelites, with their fairytale lushness, go down especially well, and in the Modern and Contemporary galleries, children will be heartened to learn that bold stripes of colour (Bridget Riley) or splodges of paint (Gillian Ayres) can also qualify as genius. Beware, though: Damien Hirst's pickled sheep is lurking.

The gallery also encourages kids to scribble their way around. Begin at the Manton entrance and ask for a themed activity pack. Give your age to ensure you get the right one. At weekends, the Tate, in partnership with a regularly changing programme of artists, runs a session called Liminal, in which younger visitors are invited to physically and socially interact with sculpture. The dedicated Tate Kids website (http://kids.tate.org.uk) is brimming with craft ideas and interactive games.

Letting off steam

Tucked away in a back street 5 minutes from the Tate, the terrific **Causton Street Playground** has a ball court, sandpit, paddling pool and play kit for ages 3–7.

The façade of Tate Britain

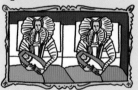

④ Churchill War Rooms

Hidden passages, secret messages

Everyone loves a secret labyrinth, and here's one right under the heart of London. The Churchill War Rooms are where Winston Churchill ran Britain's campaign against the Axis powers during World War II. This warren of chambers was designed to resist enemy bombs – just as well, as the House of Commons took a direct hit during the Blitz. The rooms became the nerve centre for picking up secret messages from the front, with some staff living like moles almost full time, even using sun-lamps to prevent Vitamin D deficiency.

What is enthralling is that along with a few shop-dummy typists and military men poised over maps, the rooms remain frozen in time, filled with original clutter and musty smells. Churchill's bedroom looks like he's just popped out for a quick cigar – which he liked to do, often climbing to the roof during Luftwaffe raids to watch.

The children's audio tour extends into the adjoining Churchill Museum,

Plotting the course of World War II in Churchill's Cabinet War Rooms

a 21st-century space that uses audio, film and touch-screen wizardry to canter through Churchill's career. Despite all the gizmos, this area will mainly interest older children.

Letting off steam

Cross the road into **St James's Park** (see p74), which has refreshment kiosks and plump ducks to feed.

The Lowdown

🌐 **Map reference** 10 F6
Address Clive Steps, King Charles Street, SW1A; 020 7930 6961; http://cwr.iwm.org.uk

🚗 **Tube** Westminster, St James's Park **Bus stop** Parliament Street, Parliament Square **River bus** Westminster Pier

🕐 **Open** 9:30am–6pm daily (last admission 5pm)

💲 **Price** £42.95, under-5s free

🚩 **Guided tours** No. Free audio guide

🚻 **Age range** 8 plus

🎨 **Activities** Children's audio guide (English only), plus War Rooms family trail. Kids' activity sheets for Churchill Museum downloadable from website. Occasional school holiday workshops for families

⏱ **Allow** Up to 2 hours

♿ **Wheelchair access** Yes, use Great George Street entrance

🍽 **Eat and drink** *Snacks* The Switch Room Café, halfway though the tour, sells main dishes and snacks

🛍 **Shop** At the end of the tour

🚻 **Toilets** In ticket lobby

⑤ Horse Guards Parade

A polished performance

In Tudor times, the royal palace was at Whitehall, and Horse Guards Parade started life as Henry VIII's jousting yard. That's why Her Majesty's Life Guard stand sentry on the pavement here to this day. Every morning, the new guard trots in on horseback along The Mall from Hyde Park Barracks, silver helmets glinting, heading for the changing ceremony – a 15-minute silent stand-off followed by lots of bellowing as the old guard departs. Beside the parade ground is the Household Cavalry Museum, displaying historic regimental memorabilia. The main attraction, though, is the cobbled stables – a glass wall in the museum looks right in on the troops as they groom their horses and prepare their kit. Most of the action happens at the guard-change time, and at 4pm, when the troops dismount. The smells are authentic, too! There is real armour

The Lowdown

🌐 **Map reference** 10 F6
Address Horse Guards, Whitehall, SW1A; 020 7930 3070; www.householdcavalrymuseum.co.uk

🚗 **Tube** Westminster, Embankment, Charing Cross **Bus stop** Whitehall **River bus** Westminster Pier

🕐 **Open** Changing the Guard, 11am daily (10am Sun); museum open 10am–6pm daily (Apr–Oct); till 5pm (Nov–Mar)

💲 **Price** £18–24

🚻 **Skipping the queue** To guarantee a good view of the guard change, arrive by 10:45am

🚩 **Guided tour** No

🚻 **Age range** 4 plus

🎨 **Activities** Dressing-up uniforms and good age-specific museum quizzes. Pre-bookable school-holiday craft activities (free with an admission-paying adult)

⏱ **Allow** 1 hour

♿ **Wheelchair access** Yes

🍽 **Eat and drink** *Real meal* Inn the Park, nearby (see p74).

🛍 **Shop** Gifts and souvenirs

🚻 **Toilets** In the museum

Filling in a quiz-sheet kit inspection at the Household Cavalry Museum

Mounted sentries on Horse Guards Parade

for kids to try on, quiz sheets to complete and touch-screen TVs with footage of the guards talking about their work. Young recruits spend up to 12 hours a day buffing their uniforms, and each morning the smartest one gets to be a mounted "boxman" or sentry, while the least polished is saddled with foot duty. So, is it acceptable for visitors to pull faces and make them smile? Permission denied!

Letting off steam

The spacious and well-tended lawns and lakes of **St James's Park** *(see p74)* are right opposite.

⑥ Banqueting House

Where a king lost his head

Four hundred years ago, English kings believed they were agents of God. James I threw dazzling courtly entertainments, or masques, in which actors cavorted as devils and beasts with the monarch restoring order at the end. Banqueting House was built in 1622 to stage them and designed by Inigo Jones, who excited London with the Neo-Classical architecture he had brought back from Italy.

Today, a visit begins with a film history in the Undercroft, moodily lit by candelabras. Then, head upstairs into the white-and-gold hall with its double-decker columns and painted ceiling. This was commissioned from Baroque master Peter Paul Rubens by Charles I and shows his father, King James I, rising gloriously into Heaven. Children are encouraged to lie on their backs and ogle the closest thing in the UK to the Sistine Chapel in Rome.

The lively audio guide tells the building's stories, such as the "touching the king's evil" ceremony, where sufferers of the hideous skin disease scrofula gathered to be "cured" by the monarch's touch.

Charles I inherited his father's belief in the superiority of kings over the common man. However, in 1649, just 11 years after his ceiling was finished, Charles was marched out of Banqueting House and had his head chopped off for treason.

Letting off steam

St James's Park *(see p74)* is across the road, via Horse Guards Parade, with activities for kids of all ages.

The Lowdown

- 🌐 **Map reference 10 G6 Address** Whitehall, SW1A; 0844 482 7777; www.hrp.org.uk/ banquetinghouse
- 🚗 **Tube** Westminster, Charing Cross, Embankment **Bus stop** Whitehall **River bus** Westminster Pier
- 🕐 **Open** 10am–5pm daily (last admission 4:30pm, call in advance as can close ahead of functions)
- 💲 **Price** £14–25, under-16s free. Free audio guide
- 🎫 **Skipping the queue** Rarely busy
- 👣 **Guided tour** No
- 🧍 **Age range** 9 plus
- 🕐 **Allow** Up to 1 hour
- ♿ **Wheelchair access** Limited. Call 020 3166 6155/6152 for details
- 🍴 **Eat and drink** *Picnic* Pret A Manger *(1 Whitehall, SW1A 2DD; 020 7932 5216)* offers eat in or out sandwiches and salads *Snacks* The Portrait Café serves light meals *(see p82)*
- 🛍 **Shop** On the main stairwell
- 🚻 **Toilets** In the Undercroft

Picnic under £20; **Snacks** £20–40; **Real meal** £40–60; **Family treat** £60 or more (based on a family of four)

Buckingham Palace and around

Each year, thousands press their noses to the gilded railings of Buckingham Palace, the headquarters of the royal family since 1837. The Palace has been open for pre-booked tours (August and September only) since 1993, but check the calendar to ensure your visit coincides with the Changing the Guard ceremony. Approach along Birdcage Walk from St James's Park Tube Station, and explore the children's playground en route. Then while away the afternoon around the lake in St James's Park, or wander across Green Park to window shop in the swish arcades along Piccadilly. It's all within walking distance.

Westminster and the West End

0 metres 200

0 yards 200

The small but compelling Guards Museum, filled with military kit from historic battles to modern-day wars

One of the Queen's garden parties at Buckingham Palace

The Lowdown

🚆 **Train** Victoria (five-minute walk) or Charing Cross (10–15 minutes) **Tube** Victoria, St James's Park or Green Park **Bus** Grosvenor Place: route numbers 2, 16, 36, 38, 52, 73, 82, 148, 436 or C2; or Buckingham Palace Rd: 11, 211, C1 or C10

ℹ️ **Visitor information** Victoria Railway Station (opposite platform 8) or Piccadilly Circus Underground Station, W1D 7DH

🛒 **Supermarkets** Sainsbury's, 150 Victoria St, SW1E 5LB; Marks & Spencer, 78 Piccadilly, W1J 8AQ **Markets** Arts & crafts market, St James's Churchyard, Piccadilly W1J 9LL; 10am–6pm Wed–Sat

🎊 **Festivals** St Patrick's Day Parade, Green Park (Sun nearest Mar 17); Trooping the Colour, Horse Guards Parade (any Sat in Jun); Virgin London Marathon, ends in The Mall (Apr); Royal Academy Summer Exhibition (Jun–Aug)

➕ **Pharmacies** Boots, 13 Cathedral Walk (8:30am–7pm Mon–Sat, 9am–4pm Sun). For 24-hour pharmacies, search at www.nhs.uk/servicedirectories

🛝 **Nearest playground** St James's Park (Buckingham Palace end of Birdcage Walk)

Places of Interest

SIGHTS

1. Buckingham Palace
2. The Royal Mews
3. Guards Museum
4. Royal Institution

● EAT AND DRINK

1. Inn the Park
2. The Parlour Restaurant at Fortnum & Mason
3. The Café at the Institute of Contemporary Arts
4. Benihana
5. Crumpets
6. Le Signore
7. Picnic Kiosk
8. Caffe Grana
9. Laduree

See also Royal Institution (p77) and Shopping (below)

● SHOPPING

1. Prestat
2. Burlington Arcade
3. Fortnum & Mason

● WHERE TO STAY

1. Brown's
2. Duke's
3. The Goring
4. Taj 51 Buckingham Gate
5. Athenaeum Apartments
6. Flemings Apartments
7. 44 Curzon Street Apartments

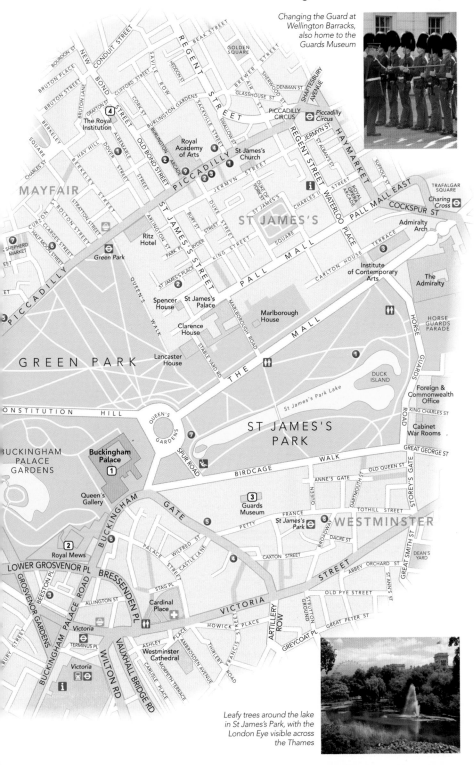

Changing the Guard at
Wellington Barracks,
also home to the
Guards Museum

BEAK STREET

GOLDEN
SQUARE

BOURDON ST

NEW BOND STREET

CONDUIT STREET

SAVILE ROW

BRUTON PLACE

BRUTON STREET

BRUTON LANE

REGENT STREET

BREWER ST

SHERWOOD ST

DENMAN ST

SHAFTESBURY AVENUE

HEDDON ST

AIR ST

GLASSHOUSE ST

CLIFFORD STREET

GRAFTON ST

4

CORK ST

BURLINGTON GARDENS

SACKVILLE STREET

SWALLOW ST

BURLINGTON ARCADE

**The Royal
Institution**

BERKELEY SQUARE

HAY HILL

BERKELEY STREET

CHARLES ST

STRATTON STREET

DOVER STREET

ALBEMARLE STREET

OLD BOND STREET

2

**Royal
Academy
of Arts** **4**

**St James's
Church** **1**

PICCADILLY CIRCUS

PICCADILLY
CIRCUS

**Piccadilly
Circus**

REGENT STREET

JERMYN ST

ST ALBAN'S ST

HAYMARKET

MAYFAIR

CURZON STREET

CLARGES STREET

BOLTON STREET

HALF MOON STREET

7

**SHEPHERD
MARKET**

PICCADILLY **2** **3** **4**

JERMYN STREET

PICCADILLY ARCADE

DUKE OF YORK ST

ST JAMES'S
SQUARE

CHARLES II STREET

ROYAL OPERA ARCADE

WATERLOO PLACE

PALL MALL EAST

SUFFOLK ST

TRAFALGAR
SQUARE

Charing
Cross

COCKSPUR ST

i

ST JAMES'S

RITZ
Hotel

ARLINGTON STREET

ST JAMES'S STREET

DUKE STREET

BURY STREET

KING STREET

RYDER STREET

PARK PL

ST JAMES'S PLACE

2

QUEEN'S WALK

Green Park

7

PALL MALL

CARLTON HOUSE TERRACE

**Admiralty
Arch**

**Institute
of Contemporary
Arts**

**The
Admiralty**

**Spencer
House**

**St James's
Palace**

**Marlborough
House**

MARLBOROUGH ROAD

**Clarence
House**

**Lancaster
House**

STABLE YARD RD

GREEN PARK

THE MALL

St James's Park Lake

DUCK
ISLAND

i

HORSE GUARDS

**Foreign &
Commonwealth
Office**

HORSE
GUARDS
PARADE

KING CHARLES ST

**Cabinet
War Rooms**

GREAT GEORGE ST

CONSTITUTION HILL

QUEEN'S
GARDENS

SPUR ROAD

7

**ST JAMES'S
PARK**

WALK

**BUCKINGHAM
PALACE
GARDENS**

**Buckingham
Palace**

1

BIRDCAGE

ANNE'S GATE

OLD QUEEN ST

QUEEN STREET

DARTMOUTH ST

TOTHILL STREET

STOREY'S GATE

**Queen's
Gallery**

BUCKINGHAM GATE

3

**Guards
Museum**

PETTY FRANCE

**St James's
Park**

BROADWAY

DACRE ST

WESTMINSTER

5

PALACE STREET

WILFRED ST

CASTLE LANE

4

CAXTON STREET

GREAT SMITH STREET

DEAN'S
YARD

2

Royal Mews

6

STAG PL

ALLINGTON ST

ABBEY ORCHARD ST

OLD PYE STREET

GREAT PETER ST

ST ANN'S ST

LOWER GROSVENOR PL

BRESSENDEN PL

**Cardinal
Place**

VICTORIA

STREET

GROSVENOR GARDENS

BEESTON PL

3

BURY STREET

WILTON RD

Victoria

TERMINUS PL

i

Victoria

**Westminster
Cathedral**

ASHLEY PLACE

AMBROSDEN AVENUE

MORETH TERRACE

CARLISLE PLACE

HOWICK PLACE

FRANCIS STREET

THIRLEBY ROAD

ARTILLERY ROW

GREYCOAT PL

GREAT PETER ST

VAUXHALL BRIDGE RD

WILTON RD

OLD PYE STREET

STRUTTON GROUND

Leafy trees around the lake
in St James's Park, with the
London Eye visible across
the Thames

① Buckingham Palace
When the Queen's away, there are visits to pay

Full of priceless porcelain, jewelled cabinets and gold leaf, Buckingham Palace owes its splendour to George IV, who came to the throne in 1820 and lavished a fortune on it – but never lived here. Queen Elizabeth II first moved in as a 10-year-old princess, and now shares the palace with 350 staff, from cleaners to courtiers. Visitor tours operate in summer, when Her Majesty is at her holiday home, Balmoral Castle in Scotland. Only 19 state rooms are open to the public – just as well, as there are 775 rooms in all.

Sentry guard

Key Features

Grand Staircase

State Ballroom The French-style ballroom is used for state banquets and conferring awards.

White Drawing Room This has a secret panel that swings back to allow the royals to appear as if by magic.

Grand Staircase This was the centrepiece of George IV's extravagant conversion of the old "Buckingham House". The ornate bronze cast balustrade alone cost £200,000 in today's money.

State Dining Room

Throne room

State Dining Room The dining table seats 46 guests, and the footmen carry special rulers to make sure cutlery and glassware are positioned correctly. The Queen always makes a final check!

Throne Room The two thrones here are embroidered with "ER" and "P" and were used by Elizabeth II and the Duke of Edinburgh at the Coronation in 1953.

Letting off steam

St James's Park *(0300 061 2350; www.royalparks.org.uk)* is nearby, with a great playground for children aged up to 11 at the Palace end – it has a sandpit, kids-only toilets, a refreshment kiosk and picnic tables. Admire the geese and swans as they glide across the lake, but the kings of the park are the pelicans, fed at 2:30pm near Duck Island. The first pelicans were a gift from the Russian ambassador in 1664. There's a smart conservatory restaurant nearby *(see right)* and deck chairs for hire, band concerts on summer weekends, occasional guided walks… and no "keep off the grass" signs.

Prices given are for a family of four

Eat and drink

Picnic: under £20–40; Snacks: £28–40; Real meal: £25–40; Family treat: £45–60 (based on a family of four)

PICNIC Inn the Park *(St James's Park; 020 7451 9999; www.innthepark.com; 8am–11am, noon–5pm Mon–Fri, 9am–11am, noon–5pm Sat–Sun)* is a lakeside eatery in the park, with wide windows and an eco-friendly turf roof. The children's menu is pricey but there are tasty "grab and go" sandwiches and luscious cakes that are perfect for eating on the surrounding lawns.

SNACKS The Parlour Restaurant at Fortnum & Mason *(181 Piccadilly, W1A 1ER; 020 7734*

Clambering over boulders in St James's Park sandpit

8040; www.fortnumandmason.com; 10am–7:30pm Mon–Sat; 11:30am–5:30pm Sun) does superb ice-cream sundaes and hot chocolate, and has a handy toasted sandwich menu for under-8s.

The Lowdown

- 🌐 **Map reference** 15 D1
  Address Buckingham Palace Road, SW1A; 020 7766 7300; *www.royalcollection.org.uk*
- 🚗 **Tube** Victoria, St James's Park.
  Bus stop Buckingham Palace Rd
- 🕐 **Open** State Rooms Aug: 9:30am–7:30pm (last admission 3:45pm). Changing the Guard May–Jul: 11:30am daily; Aug–Apr: alternate days; cancelled in heavy rain
- 💲 **Price** £52.80, under-5s free
- 👪 **Skipping the queue** Book tickets in advance online. The palace forecourt gets squeezed during the Changing the Guard – children will get a better view on nearby Friary Court, outside St James's Palace. Aim to be there before 11am
- 🚩 **Guided tours** Free audio guide in eight languages

- 👫 **Age range** 5 plus
- 🎨 **Activities** Children's audio guide (ages 7–11), plus garden nature trail on request (or downloadable online). Family room with free activities during summer holiday: design a hat for a garden party
- ⏱ **Allow** 2 hours
- ♿ **Wheelchair access** Yes, but must be booked in advance: 020 7766 7324
- ☕ **Café** On the garden terrace
- 🛍 **Shop** Large shop at the end of the Palace gardens, at the end of the visit
- 🚻 **Toilets** In the garden at the end of visit

Good family value?
The palace tour is far from cheap, though the children's audio guide and sparky summer activities make it just about worth the money.

REAL MEAL The Café at the Institute of Contemporary Arts *(020 7930 8619; 11am–11pm Tue–Sun)*, on The Mall, is a cool alternative to the chain restaurants on nearby Haymarket. No children's menu, but smaller portions of pasta and burgers on request. High chairs and baby-changing facilities, too.
FAMILY TREAT Benihana *(37 Sackville Street, W1S 3DQ; 020 7494 2525; www.benihana.co.uk; noon–3pm daily; 5:30–10:30pm Mon–Sat; 5–10pm Sun)* is cooking as theatre: the Japanese dishes sizzle up spectacularly on a teppan hot-plate at your table.

Shopping

After visiting the Queen, head for the aristocratic shops of St James's. **Prestat** *(14 Princes Arcade, SW1Y 6DS; www.prestat.co.uk)* purveys deluxe chocolates and truffles, while in the exclusive **Burlington Arcade** *(Mayfair, W1; www.burlington-arcade. co.uk)*, which claims to be the world's first mall, the top-hatted security guards – Beadles – have been keeping the peace since 1819. **Fortnum & Mason** *(181 Piccadilly, W1A 1ER; www.fortnumandmason. london)* has elegant frock-coated assistants who look like escaped palace footmen. See if the kids will try the chocolate-covered scorpions.

The confectionery counter inside Fortnum & Mason

Find out more

DIGITAL Take one of Buckingham Palace's most famous inhabitants, Queen Victoria, to the seaside, then help her to write a postcard, at *www.museumnetworkuk.org/ portraits/activities/activities.html*.
FILM At the start of the 1996 film *101 Dalmatians*, Anita and Roger fall into the lake (and in love) in St James's Park thanks to their dogs.

Next stop...

QUEEN'S GALLERY Just around the corner on Buckingham Gate, the Queen's Gallery *(www.royal collection.org.uk)* shows off art, jewels and family heirlooms from the royal collections. There's also a good children's trail.

② The Royal Mews
A coach fit for Cinderella

This must be the most picturesque garage in London: a 200-year-old Georgian stable yard, complete with an ornate clock tower and surrounded by the cottage-like quarters of the Queen's coachmen and their families. It looks enchanting at Christmas, when Santa slides in on his regal sleigh to the Queen's annual children's party.

Up to 30 horses are stabled here – they go to school for two years before they are qualified to pull a coach. The trainers wave flags, blow trumpets and play the sound of cannon fire to prepare them for the London crowds. The horses even learn to stop at red traffic lights.

As well as Santa's sleigh, a visit takes in the Glass Coach that Lady Diana Spencer rode in to her wedding to Prince Charles in 1981, and the little donkey carriage (or barouche) once driven by Queen Victoria's children. Apparently, the latter came in handy to get to the bathrooms in the vast royal palaces. The biggest gasp of all is reserved for the Gold State Coach used for coronation parades, presented in full harness and looking every bit like it's been borrowed from Cinderella. It is so big they have to remove a wall to get it out of the building.

The magic of the Mews for most children, though, springs from being among the sounds and smells of a working stable in the heart of London – and, if they're lucky, there might be a horse or two to meet and greet at the exit.

Helping a guardsman with his job (and getting a photo) at Horse Guards Parade

Letting off steam

A few minutes along Buckingham Gate lies **St James's Park** (*see p74*), with its excellent children's playground, just off Birdcage Walk.

③ Guards Museum
Royal sentries and toy soldiers

Part of Wellington Barracks, this modest museum fills a handful of basement rooms with the bloody exploits of the five British Guards regiments (and Household Cavalry). Learn the stories behind Charles II's musketeers, Wellington's overcoat and Florence Nightingale's medicine cup. Most compelling, perhaps, is the display of kit and mementos from the conflict in Afghanistan.

A quiz sheet for youngsters is usually available, and the kids can

The Lowdown

- 🌐 **Map reference** 16 E1
  Address Wellington Barracks, Birdcage Walk, SW1E; 020 7414 3271; www. theguardsmuseum.com
- 🚇 **Tube** St James's Park **Bus stop** Victoria Street
- 🕐 **Open** 10am–4pm (last admission 3:30pm)
- 💷 **Price** £8–12, under-16s free
- 🚶 **Skipping the queue** Rarely busy
- 🚩 **Guided tours** No
- 👪 **Age range** Museum, 8 plus; shop, 5 plus
- 🎨 **Activities** Dressing-up, £6; ask about the children's quiz sheet
- ⏱ **Allow** Up to 1 hour
- ♿ **Wheelchair access** Yes, via lift
- 🍴 **Eat and drink** *Picnic* A kiosk by St James's Park lake (*Palace end*) sells snacks and ices *Snacks* Caffè Grana (*St James's Park tube station*) sells snacks and hot food
- 🛍 **Shop** On the right, just after the gates on Birdcage Walk, selling armies of toy soldiers
- 🚻 **Toilets** No

don a guard's tunic and bearskin for a photo, though there's an extra charge. If short of time, head for the toy soldier shop on the forecourt, which has shelf after shelf of brilliant thumb-sized battle scenes.

Outside, on the parade ground, troops line up at 11am ready to march to Buckingham Palace for the Changing the Guard ceremony (*see p75*), and viewpoints here are usually less congested than the more famous observation points at the Palace. There are often drills at other times too: listen out for the military drum beat booming out across St James's Park.

Letting off steam

The excellent **St James's Park** playground, complete with sandpit, is just across the road (*see p74*).

Toy soldiers at the Guards Museum – perfect for children of all ages

The Lowdown

- 🌐 **Map reference** 15 D1
  Address Buckingham Palace, SW1W; 020 7766 7302; www.royalcollection.org.uk
- 🚇 **Tube** Victoria, Green Park or Hyde Park corner **Bus stop** Buckingham Palace Road
- 🕐 **Open** Feb, Mar, Nov & Dec: 10am–4pm Mon–Sat; Apr–Oct: 10am–5pm daily (last admission 45 minutes before closing); check website for dates when closed
- 💷 **Price** £24–35, under-5s free
- 🚶 **Skipping the queue** Buy tickets online before visiting
- 🚩 **Guided tours** Hourly; free
- 👪 **Age range** 5 plus
- 🎨 **Activities** Children's audio guide; unsupervised art room for ages 5–11 at weekends (free); occasional school holiday workshops
- ⏱ **Allow** 1 hour
- ♿ **Wheelchair access** Yes, for more information, call 020 7766 7324
- 🍴 **Eat and drink** *Picnic* Crumpets (*82 Buckingham Gate, SW1E 6PD*) offers good sandwiches, toasted sandwiches and, of course, crumpets. *Snacks* Le Signore (*4 Palace Street, SW1E 5HY*) is a reliable Italian café
- 🛍 **Shop** On Buckingham Palace Rd
- 🚻 **Toilets** Near the entrance, with baby-changing facilities

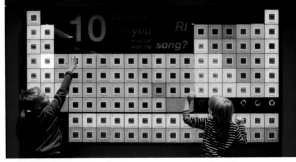

Exploring the elements, Royal Institution

④ Royal Institution

A genius introduction to ground-breaking science

Smash glass, electrocute a frog and blow up a laboratory assistant. That's the irresistible promise of a visit to the "Science in the Making" exhibition at the Royal Institution. Luckily, the glass-smashing and frog-frazzling are achieved virtually, using the museum's ingenious eGuide – a hand-held console which plays interactive cartoons of historic experiments at regular points around the museum. Even so, it's a great way to get budding geniuses interested in the mysteries of science.

Fourteen Nobel Prize winners have worked at the Royal Institution,

so there are fascinating artifacts to see – Alessandro Volta's prototype battery, James Dewar's first vacuum flask and Michael Faraday's original transformer. The laboratory where Faraday first harnessed electricity survives just as it was in the 1850s. In a clever touch, the Institution has a laboratory right opposite, where scientists can sometimes be seen working on special projects, such as developing tiny nanomagnets that can find and zap cancer cells.

Most children will be more engaged by the eGuide and its amusing clips and games. The handy device also brings to life some of the most popular bits of the Royal Institution's celebrated Christmas lectures, which have been enthralling children since 1825. For example, learn how a toy kangaroo can unlock the secrets of gravity, and how to turn a bicycle wheel into a gyroscope.

Letting off steam

A 10-minute walk away along Piccadilly lie the grassy expanses of **Green Park** (see p73), perfect for a run around, with deck-chair hire and refreshment kiosks.

The Lowdown

🌐 **Map reference** 9 D4
Address 21 Albemarle St, W1S 4BS; 020 7409 2992; *www.rigb.org*

🚗 **Tube** Green Park or Piccadilly Circus. **Bus stop** Berkeley St or Piccadilly

🕐 **Open** 9am–6pm Mon–Fri

💲 **Price** Free

👣 **Guided tours** No; free eGuide

👫 **Age range** 7 plus

🏃 **Activities** Hands-on science sessions six times a year (ages 5–12): £16–20

⏱ **Allow** Up to 2 hours

♿ **Wheelchair access** Yes

🍴 **Eat and drink** *Snacks* Laduree (71 Burlington Arcade, W1J 0QX; www.laduree.com/en_gb/) was established in Paris in 1862 and is a temple to French macaroons *Family treat* Ri Bar + Kitchen at the museum has good-value set lunches. There is a less formal cafe too

🚻 **Toilets** In the lobby

Michael Faraday glass egg, used to test theories about electricity

National Gallery and around

In one room, St George spears the dragon straight through the eye. In another, a teenaged queen is led blindfolded to the chopping block. Who said art galleries are boring? The National unlocks the stories behind every canvas, with kids' trails and workshops. Its Sainsbury Wing is the best way in for families – aim left when approaching across Trafalgar Square. The cinemas and street life of the West End are a short stroll up Charing Cross Road – and best explored by day. To see Piccadilly Circus and Hamleys toy shop, take the Bakerloo Line from Charing Cross.

Westminster and the West End

Covent Garden *p86*

National Gallery

Buckingham Palace *p72*

Westminster Abbey *p64*

Above The grand porticoed entrance of the National Gallery, completed in 1838
Below Holbein's The Ambassadors (1533) shows two stately men with symbols of power

Below The metal in the brass lions in Trafalgar Square reputedly came from French guns captured at the Battle of Trafalgar (1805)

Inside the National Portrait Gallery

The Lowdown

🚗 **Train** Charing Cross **Tube** Charing Cross, Embankment or Leicester Square **Bus** Trafalgar Square: routes 3, 6, 9, 11, 12, 13, 15, 23, 24, 29, 53, 87, 88, 91, 139, 159, 176, 453; Piccadilly Circus: 3, 6, 9, 12, 13, 15, 22, 23, 88, 94, 139, 159, 453; Shaftesbury Avenue: 14, 19, 38 **River bus** Embankment Pier, services to Westminster and St Katharine's Dock (Crown River Cruises: 020 7936 2033; www.crownriver.com)

ℹ️ **Visitor information** Leicester Square; Britain & London Visitor Centre, 1 Regent St; or at Piccadilly Circus Tube Station

🍜 **Supermarkets** New Loon Moon Chinese supermarket, 9a Gerrard St, W1D 5PL; Tesco Metro, 17–25 Regent St, SW1Y 4LR **Markets** Berwick Street (food, fish, flowers) and Rupert Street (books, jewellery, hot food), both in Soho: 9am–6pm Mon–Sat

🎆 **Festivals** New Year's Day Parade, Trafalgar Square (1 Jan); Chinese New Year, Soho (Feb); St George's Day, Trafalgar Square (Apr); Kids' Week Theatre Festival, West End theatres (Aug); Regent Street Festival (Sep); Trafalgar Day Parade (Oct); London Film Festival, Leicester Square cinemas (Oct); Christmas Lights, Regent Street (Nov–Dec)

➕ **Pharmacies** Boots, 5–7 Strand, WC2N 5HR (7:30am–9pm Mon–Fri, 9am–8pm Sat, 11am–5pm Sun). For 24-hour pharmacies search at www.nhs.uk/servicedirectories

🛝 **Nearest playgrounds** Phoenix Garden in St Giles-in-the-Fields churchyard, or in St James's Park (see p73)

0 metres 200
0 yards 200

Places of Interest

SIGHTS

1. National Gallery
2. Trafalgar Square
3. National Portrait Gallery
4. Benjamin Franklin House
5. Leicester Square
6. Piccadilly Circus
7. Hamleys

● EAT AND DRINK

1. Tesco Metro
2. The Café in the Crypt
3. Ed's Easy Diner
4. Portrait Restaurant
5. Leon
6. Patisserie Pompidou
7. Lupita
8. Häagen-Dazs Café
9. Little Lamb
10. Millies
11. The Rainforest Café
12. Refectory

See also Trafalgar Square (p82), National Portrait Gallery (p82–3) and Hamleys (p85)

● SHOPPING

1. Marchpane
2. Mamas & Papas
3. TokyoToys

William Hamley's toy shop has been bewitching children since 1760 and is now a major tourist attraction

① National Gallery

Heroes and angels, monsters and murderers

Britain's richest art collection began life in 1824 with just 38 paintings. Now it has 2,300, from the vivid saints and serpents in the medieval galleries, to the iconic sunflowers and waterlilies in the 19th-century rooms. With school groups sitting cross-legged in front of assorted canvases, there is plenty of happy hubbub throughout. Start at the audio guide desk, where family trails include Teach Your Grown-Ups About Art, a genius idea that turns children into instant experts.

National Gallery main entrance

Key Features

Main Gallery Building
Paintings from 1500 to 1900 are displayed here.

Sainsbury Wing This houses the early Renaissance Collection of paintings from 1250 to 1500.

Main entrance
on ground floor

③ Perseus Turning Phineas and his Followers to Stone (1680s) An attacking army is petrified by the face of the snake-haired Medusa, a mythological event brilliantly captured by Luca Giordano. (Room 32)

④ The Execution of Lady Jane Grey (1833) Paul Delaroche's painting shows the doomed, blindfolded 17-year-old queen groping towards the chopping block. Gallery-goers wept when it was first exhibited in 1834. (Room 41)

⑤ Bathers at Asnières (1884) Georges Seurat used his new technique – tiny dots of contrasting colour called pointillism – to make his paintings glow. (Room 44)

① St George and the Dragon (1470) Paolo Uccello illustrates two episodes from the story of St George in one picture: the knight's victory, and the rescued princess bringing the fearsome prey to heel. (Room 54)

② Peepshow (1655–60) A mind-boggling "perspective box" by Samuel Von Hoogstraten. Through the main window it all looks skewed, but have a look through the eyeholes for a surprise. (Room 25)

⑥ Sunflowers (1888) Vincent van Gogh sold only one painting, for about £50, during his lifetime. His famous *Sunflowers* is now worth a million times that sum. The flowers symbolized happiness for him. (Room 45)

The Lowdown

Map ref 10 F4
Address Trafalgar Square, WC2N 5DN; 020 7747 2885; *www.nationalgallery.org.uk*

Train Charing Cross
Tube Charing Cross or Leicester Square.
Bus stop Trafalgar Square **River bus** Embankment Pier

Open 10am–6pm daily; until 9pm Fri. Closed 1 Jan, 24–26 Dec

Price Permanent collection free; temporary exhibitions individually priced

Skipping the queue The Sainsbury Wing entrance (corner of Trafalgar Square) is less busy Arrive early for kids' workshops

Guided tours "Taster tours" of the collection twice daily, plus Fridays at 7pm

Age range 5 plus

Activities Family audio tours (under-12s free), plus themed workbook trails: download these at *www.nationalgallery.org.uk/ families*. Family Sunday sessions for under-5s and for 5–11s (2 hours; free). There are school holiday workshops, too

Allow Up to 3 hours

Wheelchair access Yes

Café National Café (Level 0) for brunch, lunch and afternoon tea; National Dining Rooms (Level 1) for more formal dining

Shop Sainsbury Wing and main building, selling art-themed books, cards, prints, jewellery and gifts

Toilets All floors main building; Level 1, Sainsbury Wing

Good family value?
Excellent, thanks to the inventive kids' stuff. Visit the Art Start room (Sainsbury Wing) to find out what's happening on the day.

Letting off steam

Outside the gallery, in **Trafalgar Square** (see p82), there is fun to be had chasing pigeons, dodging spray from the fountains and scampering around Nelson's Column – though riding his famous lions is fraught with slippery danger. For softer landings, stroll 2 minutes through Admiralty Arch onto the well-kept lawns of **St James's Park** (see p74).

Chasing pigeons outside The National Gallery on Trafalgar Square

Eat and drink

Picnic: under £20; Snacks: £20–40; Real meal: £40–60; Family treat: £60 or more (based on a family of four)

PICNIC Buy supplies from the **Tesco Metro** supermarket behind St Martin's Lane (22–25 Bedford Street, WC2E 9EQ; 0845 677 9173; 7am–8pm Mon–Tues, noon–6pm Sun) and walk down to Victoria Embankment Gardens for a picnic.
SNACKS The Café in the Crypt (Trafalgar Square, WC2N 4JJ; 020 7766 1158; www.smitf.org; 8am–8pm Mon–Tues; 8am–10.30pm Wed (jazz night ticket holders only after 7:30pm); 8am–9pm Thu–Sat; 11am–6pm Sun) serves super-fresh canteen-style dishes in the crypt of St Martin-in-the-Fields church.
REAL MEAL Ed's Easy Diner (London Trocadero, 19 Rupert Street, W1D 7PA; 020 7287 1951; www.edseasydiner.com; 11am–10pm Mon–Thu & Sun, till 11:30pm Fri & Sat) is a temple to 1950s Americana, with hot dogs, shakes and retro jukeboxes at every table.
FAMILY TREAT Portrait Restaurant (National Portrait Gallery; 020 7312 2490; www.npg.org.uk; 10am–6pm

The magnificent Cleopatra's Needle, situated on the Embankment

daily; till 9pm Thu & Fri) offers half-size portions of its dishes for kids, with fantastic views of Admiral Nelson in Trafalgar Square, Big Ben, and the London Eye. Book well in advance for Saturday night dining.

Shopping

West End shopping heaven is close by, dominated by the seven storeys of hyperactive play at **Hamleys** (see p85). For vintage children's books, there is **Marchpane** (16 Cecil Court, WC2N 4HE), while designer toddlers enjoy **Mamas & Papas** (256–8 Regent Street, W1B 3AF), which also has a good café. Teenage anime fiends will love **TokyoToys**, in the Trocadero Centre (13 Coventry Street, W1D 7DH).

Find out more

DIGITAL Make a 3D perspective box like Samuel Van Hoogstraten's at http://kids.tate.org.uk/create/sunsets_box.shtm.

Next stop…

ROYAL ACADEMY OF ARTS On nearby Piccadilly, the **Royal Academy** (www.royalacademy.org.uk) is another treasure house of British painting, with Art Detective family trails, downloadable guides and occasional free workshops for families. In summer, its café spills into the courtyard, and kids are even able to frolic in the fountains.
CLEOPATRA'S NEEDLE Stroll down to the Embankment and investigate this 3,500-year-old Egyptian obelisk, raised beside the river in 1878. Its guardian (19th-century) sphinxes are at child-friendly height for a photo.

The entrance courtyard of the Royal Academy of Arts, Piccadilly

② Trafalgar Square

Lions and fountains

As monumental playgrounds go, Trafalgar Square, with its splashing mermaids and watchful lions, is as grand as it gets. This has been the official centre of London for 800 years – ever since Edward I erected the original "Charing Cross" here to remember his queen, Eleanor. The square was completed by Nelson's Column in 1840, and Britain's most famous naval commander gazes off towards Portsmouth, home of his flagship HMS *Victory*, from a 46-m (151-ft) plinth above the crowds.

At times of national celebration or mourning, people gather here: the square has seen anti-apartheid rallies, World Cup victory parades and a record-breaking performance by "the world's largest coconut orchestra". A big talking point has been the Fourth Plinth, vacant for decades because nobody could agree on what to erect there. It is now a yearly changing showcase for contemporary art, including (in 2009) Antony Gormley's *One and Other*, which invited 2,400 ordinary people to occupy the podium for 1 hour each – with eccentric results.

Visitors have always flocked here, but today more do so than ever before, thanks to a 2003 redevelopment, which pedestrianized the National Gallery side of the square, installed a café

Nelson's 5.5-m (18-ft) statue atop his column made of Dartmoor granite

and toilets, and drove out most of the 35,000 pigeons with falcons. Uniformed "heritage wardens" are now on 24-hour duty to help visitors.

Take cover

St Martin-in-the-Fields Church (020 7766 1100; www.smitf.org), beside the square, is home to the London Brass Rubbing Centre, where indoor fun can be had waxing William Shakespeare or King Arthur. Prices vary, instruction given. There's a good café and Saturday afternoon concerts most months (ages 5 plus). The church itself is worth a look, too.

③ National Portrait Gallery

Famous faces and much more

"The world's biggest collection of faces" numbers a jaw-dropping 160,000 portraits in all, and crams 1,000 of them onto the walls of its three gallery levels, from King Henry

VII (Room 1) to actor Ian McKellen, perhaps recognisable to youngsters as "Gandalf the Grey" (Room 37).

Begin with those schoolbook favourites, the Tudors, on Floor 2, where there are plenty of extravagantly dressed children to catch the eye: the future King Charles II, for example, painted by Anthony Van Dyck in full armour at the age of eight. It's an exaggeration of history, though: Charles didn't fight seriously until the Battle of Edgehill (1642)… when he was 12!

Floor 1 spans the Victorians to the 20th century, showcasing many names that kids may know: Beatrix Potter, LS Lowry, Paul McCartney, Princess Diana and Winston Churchill. A multimedia guide just for children reveals historical nuggets along the way: find out the grisly truth about Walter Raleigh's head, and meet the strange pet that Florence Nightingale kept in her pocket.

For celeb-spotting, though, the ground floor galleries win every time: the contemporary cast here might include JK Rowling, Lily Allen or

The Lowdown

- 🌐 **Map reference** 10 F4
  Address St Martin's Place, WC2H; 020 7306 0055; www.npg.org.uk
- 🚆 **Train** Charing Cross **Tube** Charing Cross, Leicester Square or Embankment **Bus stop** Trafalgar Square
- 🕐 **Open** 10am–6pm Sat–Wed; 10am–9pm Thu–Fri
- 💷 **Price** Permanent collection free; temporary exhibitions individually priced
- 👪 **Skipping the queue** Tickets for the free family art workshops are put on sale 1hr before the event
- 👫 **Guided tours** No. Audio guide £3
- 👫 **Age range** 6 plus
- 👫 **Activities** Free storytelling sessions (age 3 plus) at 10:30am & 1:30pm and art workshops (age 5 plus) at 11:30am & 2:30pm on 3rd Sat of every month; artist-led sessions in school holidays. Activity cards and audio tours for kids from front desk.
- 🕐 **Allow** 2 hours
- ♿ **Wheelchair access** Yes
- 🍴 **Eat and drink** *Snacks* Portrait Café (*Floor 2*) offers light snacks and meals. *Real meal* Portrait Restaurant (*Floor 3*) is a great option for à la carte with a view.
- 🛍 **Shop** Ground floor
- 🚻 **Toilets** On Floor 0 and Floor 3

The Lowdown

- 🌐 **Map reference** 10 F5
  Address WC2H; www.london. gov.uk/priorities/arts-culture/ trafalgar-square
- 🚆 **Train** Charing Cross **Tube** Charing Cross, Embankment or Leicester Square **Bus stop** Trafalgar Square
- 👫 **Activities** Annual events include St Patrick's Day (Mar), St George's Day (Apr), Eid (Sep), the Diwali Festival (Oct or Nov), and Christmas carols in Dec; check website.
- 🕐 **Allow** 1 hour
- 🍴 **Eat and drink** *Snacks* The Café on the Square (*10am–6pm daily*), under the central staircase, is a good lunch option. *Real meal* Leon (73–76 Strand), part of a chain of burgeoning "healthy fast food" restaurants, is in striking range.
- 🚻 **Toilets** Under the central staircase

Exterior of the National Portrait Gallery

A peaceful promenade with pretty flower displays in Victoria Embankment Gardens

David Beckham – though it pays to check online beforehand, because the faces change regularly. Kids can search for favourites using the computers in the mezzanine lounge.

Letting off steam

The fountains and lions – perfect for running around – are mere strides away in **Trafalgar Square**.

④ Benjamin Franklin House

Lightning flashes of inspiration and voices from the past

The tall-windowed townhouse at 36 Craven Street looks unremarkable at first, but its walls once contained a human whirlwind. Benjamin Franklin, American Founding Father, inventor, diplomat, and all-round Enlightenment hero, lived here for 16 years, working as deputy postmaster to the Colonies, inventing the lightning rod, measuring the Gulf Stream and calming unrest between England and America. The latter was unsuccessful – and by 1775, as the War of Independence loomed, Franklin had to flee or be arrested.

The house itself is an experiment in "museum as theatre" – visitors are whisked through its apartments by "Polly Hewson", Franklin's surrogate daughter, while being assailed by the smells of a Georgian kitchen, flashes of lightning from the laboratory, and the echoing voices of Franklin and his landlady. It's a

state-of-the-art effects show that older kids will find especially engaging. Franklin, ever the innovator, would have approved.

Letting off steam

It's a 2-minute walk to **Victoria Embankment Gardens**, which offers lunchtime concerts (May to August), and the Embankment Café (*www.embankmentcafe.co.uk*).

The Lowdown

🌐 **Map reference** 10 G5
Address 36 Craven St, WC2N; 020 7925 1405; www.benjaminfranklinhouse.org

🚆 **Train** Charing Cross **Tube** Charing Cross or Embankment **Bus stop** Trafalgar Square or Strand

🕐 **Open** noon–5pm Wed–Mon. The Historical Experience runs at noon, 1pm, 2pm, 3:15pm, 4:15pm Wed–Sun

💷 **Price** £14–19, under-16s free

🎫 **Guided tours** Yes. Mon only (times as above): adults £7, under-16s free

🚹 **Age range** 8 plus

🏃 **Activities** School holiday art and science workshops; period-dress Christmas party for kids

⏱ **Allow** 1 hour

♿ **Wheelchair access** No

🍴 **Eat and drink** *Snacks* Patisserie Pompidou (*35 Villiers St, WC2N 6ND; 020 7839 6010*), sells salads and sandwiches. *Real meal* Lupita (*13 Villiers St, WC2N 6ND; 020 7930 5355*) dishes up Mexican fare in kid-friendly tasting portions.

🚻 **Toilets** In the basement

Picnic under £20; **Snacks** £20–40; **Real meal** £40–60; **Family treat** £60 or more (based on a family of four)

⑤ Leicester Square

Blockbusters and buzz

Every autumn a gaudy funfair sets up in Leicester Square Gardens – which seems like overkill. This is already London's most garish entertainment zone, ringed by blockbuster cinemas (often host to starry premieres), fast-food palaces and souvenir stores manned by giant bears in guards' uniforms. There is also a squad of street artists scribbling caricatures of passers-by and usually a choice of buskers.

The square once had more illustrious residents, among them scientist Isaac Newton (1643–1727) and artists Joshua Reynolds (1723–92) and William Hogarth (1697–1764) – look for their statues here.

Although the atmosphere can be a bit grown-up at night, by day it's a buzzy place for all; traffic-free and with benches for lunch, it's a good spot to check out the evening's theatre bargains. The best ticket booth is TKTS on the south side of Leicester Square Gardens (10am–7pm Mon–Sat, 11am–4:30pm Sun).

A 2-minute walk away, around Gerrard Street, lies the lively and aromatic Chinatown (www.chinatownlondon.org), with its colourful pagoda gateways and authentic Chinese grocery stores, barbers and beauty parlours. Again, it's perhaps best explored by day.

The Lowdown

- 🌐 **Map reference** 10 F4
- 🚗 **Tube** Leicester Square or Piccadilly Circus **Bus stop** Shaftesbury Avenue or Charing Cross Road
- 🧍 **Activities** There are about 50 film premieres annually, mostly at the Odeon Leicester Square (0871 224 4007; www.odeon.co.uk). There's also a Christmas fair, occasional funfairs and music events. For Chinese New Year (late Jan or Feb; www.chinatownlondon.org), Chinatown comes alive with lion dances, acrobatics and music
- ⏱ **Allow** 1 hour
- ☕ **Eat and drink** Snacks Häagen-Dazs Café (14 Leicester Square WC2H 7NG; 020 7287 9577) has sumptuous ice cream Real meal Little Lamb (72 Shaftesbury Ave, W1D 6NA; 020 7287 8078) offers the chance to cook your own meal – dip titbits into communal hot and spicy broth (messy fun, best for older kids)
- 🚻 **Toilets** Underground on the north side, with changing facilities

Take cover

With 20 screens and more than 6,000 seats to choose from, it has to be the cinema if it rains. Check which of the latest films are showing at Odeon Leicester Square (0871 224 4007; www.odeon.co.uk), Vue (0871 224 0240; www.myvue.com) and the Empire (0871 471 4714; www.empirecinemas.co.uk).

The main thoroughfare in bustling Chinatown

Prices given are for a family of four

Bustling with people and traffic, colourful Piccadilly Circus

⑥ Piccadilly Circus

Bright lights and amusement arcades

Piccadilly Circus is often used in books, film and television to signify London – children might know it as the scene of a horseback chase in Anthony Horowitz's Alex Rider novels, for example; it also starred as Dr Evil's lair in the first Austin Powers movie. Basically a traffic intersection, thanks to its power as a geographical signifier (and the Trocadero Centre), it's a focal point for visitors. Sit on the steps of the famous fountain (installed to honour philanthropist Lord Shaftesbury in 1893, and one of the first statues cast in aluminium) and take in the famous giant neon billboards, first erected in 1923.

The tube station is a good starting point for exploring London's Theatreland district – it has a Visitor Information desk and toilets. Right on the junction stands the **Ripley's Believe It Or Not** attraction (1 Piccadilly Circus, W1J 0DA;

The Lowdown

- 🌐 **Map reference** 10 E4
- 🚗 **Tube** Piccadilly Circus. **Bus stop** Piccadilly Circus
- ⏱ **Allow** 1 hour
- ☕ **Eat and drink** Picnic Millies (Trocadero Centre, W1D 7DH) sells freshly baked cookies and ice cream Real meal The Rainforest Café (20 Shaftesbury Ave, W1D 7EU) is an extraordinary themed restaurant, set in an animatronic jungle with monsoon soundtrack. Queues at weekends
- 🚻 **Toilets** In the subway to Piccadilly Circus tube station

Enjoying a freaky exhibit at Ripley's Believe It or Not

www.ripleyslondon.com), part fun-park, part freak-show. It brings together bizarre curiosities from across the globe, from Maori cannibal forks to cars coated in crystals. Beware, though: it's implausibly expensive.

Take cover

Located inside London's famous Trocadero Centre, **Star Command** (3–10pm Mon–Fri, 11am–10pm Sat & Sun) is the latest in laser tag combat. Surreal lighting and full surround sound help players immerse themselves in the game. Pricey for just 20 minutes play; discounts can be found online (www.londontrocadero.com).

⑦ Hamleys

Toys, toys, toys

This emporium is considered by some to be "the world's finest toy shop". Kids certainly think so, and entering the seven-storey store on Regent Street feels like plunging headlong into a children's play heaven. Wandering jesters blow bubbles, conjurors make things magically disappear and tots gather, giggling, around the puppet theatre, while remote-control planes whizz overhead: it's undeniably fun.

And that's just the ground floor. Other levels are themed: working up from the basement, they feature computer games and Lego; then board games and jigsaws; pre-school books and toys; dolls and dressing-up; hobbies, train sets and remote-control cars; and finally action figures. If it all gets a little too

The Lowdown

🌐 **Map reference** 9 D3
Address 188–196 Regent St, W1B; www.hamleys.com

🚗 **Tube** Piccadilly Circus or Oxford Circus. **Bus stop** Regent Street

🕐 **Open** 10am–8pm Mon–Wed & Sat; 10am–9pm Thu & Fri; noon–6pm Sun

🧑‍🤝‍🧑 **Activities** Lots of hands-on play tables in store, plus storytime sessions and costumed events, often linked to promotions. Real reindeer visit at Christmas.

⏱ **Allow** Up to 1 hour

🍴 **Eat and drink** Picnic Refectory (74 Broadwick Street) has cakes and pastries. Snacks Crumbs and Doilies (1 Kingly Court, W1B) has great cupcakes and other sweet delights.

🚻 **Toilets** Top floor

manic, head to the princess-themed café on the top floor.

The equivalent of Hamleys for grown-ups is close by. **Carnaby Street** (www.carnaby.co.uk), somewhat changed since its 1960s heyday as the epicentre of Swinging London, is a pedestrianized precinct of mostly chain boutiques of casual wear, along with gift shops and cafés. Shop for children's gear at **David & Goliath** (15 Carnaby Street) and **Carry Me Home** (Kingly Court).

Letting off steam

It is only 5 minutes around the corner to grassy **Hanover Square** (Mayfair, W1): stop off along the way at **Sunflower Café** (3 Pollen Street, W1S 1NA) for picnic supplies.

Absorbed in a doll's house at Hamleys toy shop

Covent Garden and around

From the high art at the Royal Opera House to the low comedy of the street-corner clowns, children love the buzz of London's original public square. The pedestrianized piazza is safe for kids, and surrounded by the city's oldest theatre, its quirkiest church and the London Transport Museum. On summer weekends, the sheer volume of the crowds can overwhelm Covent Garden's charms: instead, consider visiting on a Monday, when the markets are quieter and the Opera House stages free lunchtime recitals.

Westminster and the West End

Covent Garden

National Gallery
p78

Buckingham Palace *p72*

Westminster Abbey *p64*

Places of Interest

SIGHTS

1. Covent Garden
2. St Paul's Church
3. Royal Opera House
4. Theatre Royal Drury Lane
5. London Transport Museum
6. Somerset House
7. Sir John Soane's Museum
8. Hunterian Museum
9. St Clement Danes

● EAT AND DRINK

1. Kastner and Ovens
2. Lola's
3. Masala Zone
4. Wahaca
5. Paul (29 Bedford Street, WC2E 9ED)
6. Gourmet Burger Kitchen
7. Zizzi
8. Hope and Greenwood
9. Benito's Hat
10. Rules
11. Paul (296–98 High Holborn, WC1V 7JH)
12. Strada
13. Caffè Nero (Kingsway)
14. Fleet River Bakery
15. Caffè Nero (Strand)
See also Royal Opera House (p90), London Transport Museum (p92) and Somerset House (p93)

● SHOPPING

1. Build-A-Bear Workshop
2. Games Workshop
3. Disney Store
4. Tintin Shop
5. Eric Snook's
6. Benjamin Pollock's Toyshop

● WHERE TO STAY

1. Rosewood London Hotel
2. Strand Palace Hotel
3. Citadines Prestige Holborn-Covent Garden

0 metres 100

0 yards 100

A personal performance, given in the streets around Covent Garden

Street performers in front of the grand portico of St Paul's Church, in Covent Garden's West Piazza

Skeleton of a "giant" at the Hunterian Museum, one of the fascinating, varied and sometimes a little gory exhibits at the Royal College of Surgeons

The Lowdown

🚗 **Train** Charing Cross (5-minute walk away)
Tube Covent Garden, Leicester Square or Holborn
Bus Nearest stops at Aldwych, route numbers RV1, 9, 13, 15, 23, 139 or 153; Strand: 6, 9, 11, 13, 15, 23, 87, 91, 139, 176 **River bus** Embankment Pier, beside Charing Cross – services to Westminster and St Katharine's Dock (Crown River Cruises: 020 7936 2033; www.crownriver.com)

🛒 **Supermarkets** Supersave Express, 158 Drury Lane, WC2B 5QG; Tesco Metro, 22–25 Bedford St, WC2 5RF; Marks & Spencer, 107–111 Long Acre, WC2 3RG.
Markets Antiques market, Mon; craft markets daily plus "Real Food" market on the East Piazza, Apr–Dec, 11am–7pm Thu (becomes Christmas market in Dec)

🎏 **Festivals** Covent Garden May Fayre and Puppet Festival, St Paul's Church Gardens (2nd Sun in May); Summer Fair, St Paul's Church (Jul)

➕ **Pharmacies** Boots, 4 James St, WC2E 8BH: 8:30am–9pm Mon–Fri; 9am–9pm Sat; 10am–7pm Sun. For 24-hour pharmacies, visit www.nhs.ukservicedirectories.com

🛝 **Nearest playground** Drury Lane Gardens, WC2N 5TH, 8am–dusk (see p91) and Phoenix Garden, WC2H 8DG

Wonderful taxis, buses and trains from a bygone era at the London Transport Museum

① Covent Garden

Fire-eaters, opera singers and lots and lots of cupcakes

From the Apple Market to the Apple Store, Covent Garden is London's best location for shopping as entertainment and an irresistible visitor attraction. It is scary to think it was almost bulldozed in the 1970s – locals fought to save it. The square was built by Inigo Jones in 1632, based on a Palladian piazza he had seen in Livorno, Italy. Today, it's full of child-pleasing fun, from the "living statues" along James Street to the street performers who dice with death daily outside St Paul's Church.

London Transport Museum poster

Key Sights

Apple Store
The world's largest Apple Store is a temple to technology, with classical columns, glass stairways and three storeys of hi-tech wizardry.

Jubilee Market
Squashed into the South Piazza, the souk-like passageways here are full of stalls selling trinkets and T-shirts – perfect pocket-money fodder. Monday is antiques day.

Apple Market
Once home to London's main produce market, this glass-roofed arcade now has craft stalls, fashion boutiques and West End divas singing arias al fresco in the South Courtyard.

Apple Store

Royal Opera House

The Young Dancer

London Transport Museum

JAMES STREET

COVENT GARDEN

RUSSELL STREET

KING STREET

HENRIETTA STREET

SOUTHAMPTON ST

Street shows In 1662, Samuel Pepys saw England's first recorded Punch and Judy show outside St Paul's Church. Today, you can watch a mix of music, acrobatics and magic.

St Paul's Church

The Young Dancer (1988) by Enzo Plazzotta, is said to portray Ninette de Valois, who founded the Royal Ballet in 1931.

Letting off steam

The piazza is cobbled and car-free, but for more room to race about, head for **Somerset House** (see p93). For a weatherproof option, walk north along Endell Street to the **Oasis Sports Centre** (020 7831 1804; www. better.org.uk/leisure/oasis-sports-centre#/), with indoor and outdoor pools, a sun deck and towel hire.

Eat and drink

Picnic: under £20; Snacks: £20–40; Real meal: £40–60; Family treat: £60 or more (based on a family of four)

Prices given are for a family of four

PICNIC Kastner & Ovens (52 Floral St, WC2E 9DA; 8am–5pm weekdays) does fabulous quiches, pies, salads and mouth-watering cakes to take away. Pick up some treats for a picnic on the jaunty benches in **Neal's Yard** (see opposite).
SNACKS Who does Covent Garden's best cupcakes? The classic choice is **Lola's** (14–18 Neal Street, WC2H 9LY; 8am–8pm Mon–Fri; 9:30am–8pm Sat, 10am–7pm Sun), with its display cabinet filled with delicious sugary treats. Two types of cupcake frostings are available – butter cream and cream cheese.

REAL MEAL Masala Zone (48 Floral St, WC2E 9DA; 020 7379 0101; noon–11pm Mon–Sat; 12:30–10:30pm Sun) is a great option for Indian fare. The restaurant is super-friendly, its ceiling all a-dangle with Rajasthani puppets, and serves an authentic thali platter for kids.
FAMILY TREAT Wahaca (66 Chandos Place, WC2N 4HG; 020 7240 1883; noon–11pm Mon–Sat; noon–10:30pm Sun) offers a zingy take on Mexican cuisine, serving up authentic street food. There are child-size portions, high chairs and baby-changing facilities.

The Lowdown

🌐 **Map ref** 10 G3
Address Covent Garden Piazza, WC2E 8HD; 0870 780 5001; *www.coventgardenlondonuk.com*

🚗 **Tube** Covent Garden
Bus stop Aldwych **River bus** Embankment Pier

🕐 **Open** Apple Market: 10:30am–6pm daily (till 7:30pm Thu). Jubilee Market: 10:30am–7pm Tue–Fri; 10am–6pm Sat & Sun. Apple Store (1 The Piazza, WC2E 8HA): 10am–8pm Mon–Sat; noon–6pm Sun

👫 **Skipping the queue** Covent Garden tube can be a scrum at rush hour and lunchtime; consider walking from Holborn, Temple, Leicester Square or Charing Cross (10–15 mins)

👫 **Age range** All

🤹 **Activities** Check website for family street events – circus workshops in summer holidays, reindeer-petting at Christmas

⏱ **Allow** 2 hours for shopping and street entertainment

👫 **Toilets** West Piazza, beside St Paul's Church; Tavistock Place (with baby-changing facilities), right of the Transport Museum

Good family value?
Hours of free fun just window-shopping and busker-watching – but do put a pound in the hat if the show is any good!

Benjamin Pollock's Toyshop, a jewel of a place selling creative and theatrical toys

Shopping

Plenty for all ages, from bear-making at the **Build-A-Bear Workshop** (9 The Piazza, WC2H 9HP) to table warfare at the **Games Workshop** (33 The Market, WC2E 8BE). There's also a **Disney Store** (The Piazza, WC2E 8HD) and the **Tintin Shop** (34 Floral Street, WC2E 9DJ). Best of all are the area's historic toy emporia: **Eric Snook's** (32 The Market, WC2E 8RE) – open since 1980 – and **Benjamin Pollock's Toyshop** (44 The Market, WC2E 8RF), selling paper theatres since 1880.

Find out more

DIGITAL Download a 19th-century toy theatre to build and colour, at the Victoria & Albert Museum site: *www.vam.ac.uk/content/articles/m/make-your-own-toy-theatre/*
FILM The movie musical *My Fair Lady* begins at the Royal Opera House, where Henry Higgins sees flower-seller Eliza Dolittle and vows to turn her into "a proper lady".

Take cover

The **London Transport Museum** (see p92) is a strong wet-weather standby: its shop and café alone should while away an hour.

Next stop...

NEAL'S YARD It's a short stroll north to this cluster of healthfood shops and New Age cafés painted in bright colours. There is picnic space, a magic mirror, and infinite I-spy potential.
ENGLISH NATIONAL OPERA Kids who enjoyed their blast of street opera can book a workshop here (St Martin's Lane, WC2N 4ES; 020 7632 8484; www.eno.org). Scheduled so that parents can take in a matinée, Opera Tots is for ages 6 months to 4 years, and Opera Stars ages for 7–12.

The shop and café in the fascinating London Transport Museum

The Lowdown

- 🌐 **Map reference** 10 G4
  Address Bedford St, WC2E; 020 7836 5221; www.actorschurch.org
- 🚗 **Tube** Covent Garden or Leicester Square **Bus stop** Aldwych
- 🕐 **Open** 8:30am–5pm Mon–Fri; times vary Sat; 9am–1pm Sun
- 💲 **Price** Donations
- 👫 **Activities** Services Tue, Wed & Sun; plus regular concerts
- ⏱ **Allow** 30 minutes
- ☕ **Eat and drink** *Snacks* Paul (29 Bedford Street, WC2E 9ED) offers sumptuous pastries and cakes *Real meal* Gourmet Burger Kitchen (13–14 Maiden Lane, WC2E 7NE) has fine tasty burgers
- 👫 **Toilets** Next door, on the West Piazza

② St Paul's Church

The actors' church

Where's the door? That's the mystery of St Paul's portico, with its soaring marble columns. The answer is: around the back. After Inigo Jones designed the church as the centrepiece of his new piazza in 1631, the Bishop of London insisted the altar must be at the eastern end, so that worshippers faced Jerusalem – which means this grand gateway was never used.

Today, it makes a perfect stage for Covent Garden's acrobats and clowns, which is fitting, since St Paul's has long been the "actors' church", and inside there are inscriptions remembering Charlie Chaplin,

Vivien Leigh and more. Children can hunt for the actor who first played Frankenstein's monster, Boris Karloff, and Percy Press, "King of Punch and Judy", whose memorial depicts the puppet pair.

Look out, too, for the church's vintage model theatre, which was once shown off in village halls to raise money for a London hostel where actors could lodge their children while they went on tour.

The first victim of the Great Plague of 1665–66, Margaret Porteous, is buried here. It went on to claim one in five Londoners.

Letting off steam

Escape the Covent Garden crowds in the church garden – but get there early to bag a bench for lunchtime.

③ Royal Opera House

Tenors, sopranos and pirouetting ballerinas

Home to both the Royal Opera and Royal Ballet companies, this showpiece theatre was begun in 1732 by John Rich, a famous harlequin who staged Britain's first pantomime. George Frideric Handel (1685–1759) was its musical director: he gave his *Messiah* its UK premiere here and also introduced the risqué dancing of Marie Sallé.

Following a makeover in the 1990s, the theatre has endeavoured to lessen opera's elitist image. Ticket prices have been reduced, there's a free recital most Mondays and

Drury Lane Gardens, a small playground for little ones in the backstreets

guided backstage tours daily. Tours start in the jaw-dropping auditorium, built in 1858, with its 15-m- (50-ft-) high stage and balconies dripping with gilt. Tours usually visit the Model Room, too, where doll's-house-size sets are delicately

The Lowdown

- 🌐 **Map reference** 10 G3
  Address Covent Garden, WC2E; 020 7304 4000; www.roh.org.uk
- 🚗 **Tube** Covent Garden **Bus stop** Aldwych
- 🕐 **Open** 10am–3:30pm Mon–Sat and for performances
- 💲 **Price** Show tickets start from £40
- 👫 **Skipping the queue** Tickets for free Monday recitals are released online nine days ahead, but most are held back till the day – 10am at the box office
- 🚩 **Guided tours** Mon–Sat (£39–42)
- 👫 **Activities** A free children's activity trail explores the public areas; creative workshops in May half-term; Christmas productions suit kids aged 6 and up
- 👫 **Age range** 8 plus (guided tours); 7 plus (workshops)
- ⏱ **Allow** 75 minutes for the tour
- ♿ **Wheelchair access** Yes, lifts give access to most of the auditoria
- ☕ **Eat and drink** *Snacks* The rooftop terrace at the Amphitheatre Bar serves light lunches 10am–3pm *Real meal* Zizzi (20 Bow St, WC2E 7AW) serves up scrumptious pizzas
- 🛍 **Shop** Covent Garden entrance and in Amphitheatre Bar before a show
- 👫 **Toilets** In the lobby

The green spaces of St Paul's Church garden, an oasis of calm in Covent Garden

Prices given are for a family of four

Royal Ballet dancers performing Swan Lake at the Royal Opera House

constructed for every new show. But the highlight is peering into a Royal Ballet rehearsal studio, where the dancers might be pirouetting away.

Letting off steam

The tiny playground in **Drury Lane Gardens** (along Broad Court, then right on Drury Lane) used to be a graveyard! Today it has swings and slides for ages 3–7.

④ Theatre Royal Drury Lane

Theatrical magic and spooks

London's oldest working playhouse started life in 1663, when Charles II lifted the 11-year theatre ban imposed by Oliver Cromwell. The entire building would fit on the stage today: it was roofless and featured Britain's first ever female actors and the first proscenium arch or "picture box stage".

Today, the oak-lined lobby is worth a peek, or take a backstage tour run by actors in costume. Nell

An entertaining backstage tour at the historic Theatre Royal Drury Lane

Gwynne, actress and mistress of Charles II, reveals the royal retiring room where George V knighted the actor Frank Benson with his own prop sword, then it's down under the stage to see the trap doors.

Shows at "the Lane" have been famous for their spectacular special effects, including an earthquake and a horse race with 12 real horses running on a treadmill. *Miss Saigon*, which ran for 10 years and 4,263 performances, "landed" a real helicopter on the stage every time!

Letting off steam

To reach **Drury Lane Gardens** playground (*see left*), head along Russell Street and turn left.

The Lowdown

- 🌐 **Map reference** 10 H3
  Address Catherine St, WC2B; *www.reallyuseful.com/theatres*
- 🚗 **Tube** Covent Garden or Holborn. **Bus stop** Aldwych
- 🕐 **Open** Box office 10am–8pm
- 💲 **Price** Show tickets from £80
- 🚩 **Guided tours** Twice daily, Mon–Sat (£32–6)
- 👫 **Age range** Tours suit ages 6 plus
- 🕐 **Allow** 1 hour for the tour
- ♿ **Wheelchair access** Limited. Call 08444 124648 for information
- 🍴 **Eat and drink** *Picnic* Hope and Greenwood (*1 Russell St, WC2B 5JD*) sells old-fashioned sweets. *Real meal* Boswell's (*8 Russell St, WC2B 5HZ*) offers sandwiches, salads, pastries and more.
- 🚻 **Toilets** On request

Picnic under £20; **Snacks** £20–40; **Real meal** £40–60; **Family treat** £60 or more (based on a family of four)

⑤ London Transport Museum

This really is travelling back in time

Don't be put off by the subject matter – this is one of the most hooting, tooting museums in London. It crams 20 vintage buses, trams and trains into a steel-and-glass cavern once occupied by the Covent Garden flower market, and visitors get to climb aboard many of them to "take a drive". It's a hands-on experience, so hold tight!

Start on Level 2, up in the rafters, with its full-size sedan chair and London's earliest horse-drawn omnibus. Jump in and sit beside a top-hatted gent as he reels off the rules of the road, 1829-style. There are sound clips of crossing-sweepers (who cleared a path through the horse muck) and bus conductors, and cartoon quizzes to answer.

Level 1 has the first underground steam train from the 1860s, occupied by lifelike passengers, while vintage posters recall how the expansion of the tube sent London sprawling out into the suburbs. On a balcony is the Interchange, a push-button zone for children (age 7–11), where they can dress up as engine drivers and try their hand at driving the latest eco-friendly bus.

Younger kids will want to sprint straight to the open-plan and neon-lit ground floor (Level 0), with

Above One of the many vintage trains at the London Transport Museum
Below right Enjoying a hands-on experience – driving a bus

a dozen or so vehicles to explore, plus sit-in simulators where they can manoeuvre the "dead man's handle" that drives a modern-day tube train (once the adults get out of the way). There is a themed play corner for under-7s, with picnic tables alongside. Finally, it's out into the shop and café, with retro-cool posters for parents, die-cast models for kids, and Circle Line smoothies for all.

Letting off steam
The museum is comfortable about kids careering around. For outdoor frolics, head along Russell Street to **Drury Lane Gardens**, with slides and seesaws for ages 3–7; or across Strand into Somerset House (see opposite).

On board a horse-drawn double-decker "London Omnibus", phased out in 1911

The Lowdown

- 🌐 **Map ref** 10 H3
  Address Covent Garden Piazza, WC2E 7BB; 020 7565 7299; www.ltmuseum.co.uk
- 🚗 **Tube** Covent Garden
  Bus stop Aldwych
- 🕐 **Open** 10am–6pm Sat–Thu; 11am–6pm Fri
- 💲 **Price** £27–32, under-7s free
- 👫 **Skipping the queue** Tickets give free entry for a whole year
- 🚩 **Guided tours** No
- 👫 **Age range** 3 plus
- 🎨 **Activities** Collect cards from the ticket desk for kids to stamp as they go around the museum. Download trails from the website beforehand. There are free drop-in activities in school holidays
- ⏱ **Allow** Up to 3 hours
- ♿ **Wheelchair access** Yes, but some vehicles are inaccessible
- 🍴 **Eat and drink** Snacks Upper Deck café-bar in lobby serves quick bites Family treat Rules (35 Maiden Lane, WC2E 7LB; 020 7836 5314) serves classic British dishes
- 🛍 **Shop** Gifts and memorabilia
- 👫 **Toilets** Ground floor gallery

Splashing around in the Fountain Court, Somerset House

⑥ Somerset House

Enjoy a great day at the office

Somerset House looks like a palace, and originally there was one here, the scene of 17th-century royal masques (see p71). But the Palladian quadrangle we see today was actually the first ever purpose-built office block, for decades the home of tax inspectors and the register of births, deaths and marriages.

It is now open to the public, and the Embankment Galleries, by the riverside, house temporary shows on 20th-century fashion, design and photography, usually incorporating lots of interactive gizmos and family workshops. The Courtauld Gallery, by Strand, is a modest collection with several paintings that even little ones might know: Van Gogh with his ear bandaged, Manet's staring barmaid at the Folies-Bergère and Degas's graceful ballet dancers.

The big draw for families, though, is the spectacular Fountain Court in the centre, now a pleasure space where 55 water jets dance from Easter till October, just begging for youngsters to chase and splash. There are big-name pop concerts and family film matinées here in summer; while from November to January it becomes London's most glamorous ice rink, with cocktails, DJs and a giant Christmas tree.

Letting off steam

Fountain Court takes on a seaside feel in summer, with café tables at the edges and families spreading out towels and donning swimsuits.

The Lowdown

🌐 **Map ref** 10 H4
Address Strand, WC2R 1LA; 020 7845 4600; www.somersethouse.org.uk; 020 7848 2526; www.courtauld.ac.uk

🚇 **Tube** Temple **Bus stop** Strand **River bus** Embankment pier

🕐 **Open** Embankment Galleries and Courtauld Gallery 10am–6pm daily; Fountain Court 7:30am–11pm

💰 **Price** Embankment Galleries Adult admission fee varies, under 12s free; Courtauld Gallery £14–19, under-18s free

🚶 **Skipping the queue** Tickets for Saturday workshops are released at 1pm sharp. Book ahead for the popular ice rink (www.somersethouse.org.uk/ice-rink)

🚩 **Guided tours** Thu and Sat (free)

👫 **Age range** All

🤸 **Activities** Family fact-finding sheets for most temporary shows. Free art and fashion workshops on school-holiday weekends, plus every Sat for ages 6–12, and 1st Sun of the month for under-5s. There are studio days for teens in the school holidays

🕐 **Allow** 1 hour

♿ **Wheelchair access** Yes

☕ **Eat and drink** Snacks The Café at the Courtauld is cosy, with a patio garden, funky teapots and yummy cakes Real Meal Tom's Kitchen, in the Embankment wing, serves brasserie food in a refectory-style area, run by Michelin-starred chef Tom Aikens

🛍 **Shop** Rizzoli Bookshop sells art books; Courtauld Shop offers items inspired by the artworks

🚻 **Toilets** Downstairs, on the Embankment side

Picnic: under £20; Snacks: £20–40; Real meal: £40–60; Family treat: £60 or more (based on a family of four)

⑦ Sir John Soane's Museum

3,000 years of history packed into one house

This townhouse museum comprises a warren of poky passages filled with wonders: a magic picture gallery, a monk's cell, even a real mummy's coffin from ancient Egypt.

Sir John Soane was a bricklayer's son who became a top architect: he designed the Bank of England in 1788. He brought his young family to the house in 1792, and spent the next 45 years filling every nook and cranny with his bizarre collection of gargoyles, statues, busts and bric-à-brac from the ancient world. Luckily, before he died Soane insisted everything was left exactly as it was, for visitors to enjoy.

This means the house is one big time capsule. Audio guides lead the way, but watch out for Soane's tricks: mirrors where you can't see your feet; secret panels that reveal hidden paintings; even a writing desk hidden inside a statue. Best of all is the

Inside the fascinating Sir John Soane's Museum

mummy's sarcophagus down in "the Crypt", which belonged to Pharaoh Seti I. It is 3,300 years old and covered in hieroglyphics. Soane paid £2,000 for it, and threw a three-night candlelit party to celebrate.

Letting off steam

Lincoln's Inn Fields, opposite, was laid out in the 17th century by Inigo Jones. The lawns, once popular for duels, are green and wide. There are tennis courts (*£11.15 per hour, seniors and under-16s £4.25; 07525 278647*).

The Lowdown

- 🌐 **Map reference** 10 H2
  Address 13 Lincoln's Inn Fields, WC2A 3BP; 020 7405 2107; www.soane.org
- 🚗 **Tube** Holborn **Bus stop** High Holborn, Aldwych or Kingsway
- 🕐 **Open** 10am–5pm Tue–Sat (last entry 4:30pm). Candlelit opening 6–9pm 1st Tue of each month
- 💷 **Price** Free
- 🚶 **Skipping the queue** No pre-booking, so there are often large queues. Get there by 10am
- 🚩 **Guided tours** 11:30am Tue–Fri (also 3:30pm Wed & Thu); 11am Sat (£10 per person)
- 👫 **Age range** 7 plus
- 🧒 **Activities** Children's audio tour must be downloaded before visiting. Imaginative holiday workshops for ages 7 plus (£20 full day, £12 half day)
- ⏱ **Allow** 1–2 hours
- ♿ **Wheelchair access** Limited, due to stairs. Contact 020 7405 2107
- 🍽 **Eat and drink** *Snacks* Paul (296–298 High Holborn, WC1V 7JH) offers filled baguettes and patisserie *Real Meal* Strada (6 Great Queen Street, WC2B 5DH) does pizzas and classic Italian food
- 🚻 **Toilets** In the basement

⑧ Hunterian Museum

Bones and body parts

The Hunterian might be the most stomach-turning museum in London – its website even has a "parental advisory" section – but most children are gripped by its sparkling cut-glass receptacles full of bits and pieces of bodies, weird wildlife and gruesome gadgets, all collected in

The Lowdown

- 🌐 **Map reference** 10 H2
  Address 35–43 Lincoln's Inn Fields, WC2A 3PE; 020 7869 6560; www.hunterianmuseum.org
- 🚗 **Tube** Holborn or Temple **Bus stop** High Holborn, Aldwych or Kingsway
- 🕐 **Open** 10am–5pm Tue–Sat
- 💷 **Price** Free
- 🚶 **Skipping the queue** Download the audio guide from the website for free before visiting; at the museum it costs £4
- 🚩 **Guided tours** Wed, 1pm (free)
- 👫 **Age range** 6 plus, though parental guidance advisable
- 🧒 **Activities** Half-term holiday sessions for families
- ⏱ **Allow** 1–2 hours
- ♿ **Wheelchair access** Yes, via Nuffield College entrance
- 🍽 **Eat and drink** *Picnic* Caffè Nero (77d Kingsway, WC2B 6ST) serves sandwiches and snacks *Snacks* Fleet River Bakery (71 Lincoln's Inn Fields, WC2A 3JF) does sandwiches, salads and soup
- 🚻 **Toilets** In the basement

the 18th century by John Hunter, the pioneer of modern surgery.

Hunter is not very well-known these days, but he's the man who insisted surgery should be based on evidence – which meant cutting things up to show what they look like inside. He performed public dissections for his students at a time when only the bodies of hanged criminals could be used for medical science: don't miss the display about the notorious

Lincoln's Inn Fields, London's largest public square, a great place to stretch the legs

Items from the early days of anatomical discovery at the Hunterian Museum

bodysnatchers who raided local graveyards to supply Hunter with corpses. These were bumped upstairs at his grand house in Leicester Square – a house big enough to hold his stuffed giraffe, the first ever seen in England.

The museum has an audio guide suitable for older children and adults, plus quiz sheets for ages 5–7 and 8–11. The upstairs gallery has gory TV clips of modern operations and there are art materials, moveable skeletons and tunics stuck with Velcro organs in a side room, which is usually open for kids (phone ahead to check).

Letting off steam

The well-tended lawns of **Lincoln's Inn Fields** are right opposite *(see left)*, perfect for running around.

⑨ St Clement Danes

Home of a nursery rhyme?

The strange name of this church is said to come from the Vikings, who murdered and pillaged their way along what is now the River Thames in the 9th century. Finally defeated by King Alfred the Great, those with English wives were allowed to settle in this part of London.

St Clement's has been rebuilt twice: by Christopher Wren after the Great Fire of London (1666) and again after being blasted by German bombers in the Blitz (1941) – which is why it became the central church of the Royal Air Force. Aim to visit at 9am, noon, 3pm or 6pm, when

the church bells peal out the tune to the nursery rhyme *Oranges and Lemons*. First written down in 1744, some say it refers to local children who helped smugglers unload their cargo from the Thames, and were given fruit as a reward. Oranges and lemons are still handed out to children here today, as part of a service in March.

The church's creepiest treasure is in the crypt a chain that was used to clamp shut coffins to protect the recently deceased from the bodysnatchers who raided graveyards to steal corpses for medical research.

Letting off steam

Temple Gardens, at the bottom of Arundel Street, has slivers of grass, but for more space, head along the Strand to **Somerset House** *(see p93)*.

The Lowdown

🌐 **Map reference** 11 A3
Address Strand, WC2 1DH; 020 7242 8282; www.raf.mod.uk/ stclementdanes/

🚇 **Tube** Temple **Bus stop** Strand

🕐 **Open** 9am–4pm (except bank holidays); services Wed, Fri & Sun

🎫 **Price** Donations

⏱ **Allow** 30 minutes

☕ **Eat and drink** *Snacks* Caffè Nero *(181 Strand, WC2R 1EA)*, opposite, serves sandwiches and snacks *Real Meal* The Courtauld Gallery Café *(150 Somerset House, WC2R 0NR; daily 10am-5:30pm)* is cooler, with quirky crockery and big cakes

🚻 **Toilets** No

Picnic under £20; **Snacks** £20–40; **Real meal** £40–60; **Family treat** £60 or more (based on a family of four)

Bloomsbury
and Regent's Park

It's hard to beat this part of London for sheer spectacle: it has mummies and movie stars, lions and labyrinths. It's possible to go a full weekend without setting foot outside Regent's Park, thanks to its zoo, open-air theatre, canals and lakes, while the busy Madame Tussauds is nearby. If the vast treasures of the British Museum don't attract, then fascinating smaller museums cover canal boats, toys, medicine and more.

Highlights

British Museum
Among this museum's many marvels, the mummy galleries will always be the star attraction. Plan ahead and kids can even have a sleepover (see p102–3).

Coram's Fields
Possibly London's top playground, Coram's Fields has an adventure play area, zipwire and sandpits, plus a farmyard (see p106).

Wellcome Collection
Children get a cardboard moustache to wear during their visit here. Why? Who knows! It is part of the zaniest – and best – children's museum pack in London (see p104).

ZSL London Zoo
Yes, there are lions and tigers, gorillas and giraffes, but George the scarlet macaw upstages them all in the daily Animals in Action live show (see p110–11).

Puppet Theatre Barge
This red-and-yellow narrowboat at Little Venice is home to London's most delightful family theatre experience. Glide there along the canal from Camden (see p111).

Camden Market
It's about as close as London gets to a souk. Older children especially love exploring the market's labyrinth of exotic stalls and shops (see p112–13).

Left Clambering on one of the boats on display in the London Canal Museum
Above Getting up close to a tarantula at London Zoo

The Best of
Bloomsbury & Regent's Park

This well-to-do part of London divides neatly in two – one half cerebral, the other sensory. Both are walkable for even the littlest legs and filled with literary and artistic connections. To the east, stately Bloomsbury offers a day or two of family-friendly brainwork, its mix of unusual museums providing all manner of kids' activities. For more active fun or some relaxation, head west to the great green playground of Regent's Park.

A Year in Regent's Park

With or without a trip to London Zoo, little ones will adore **Regent's Park** *(see p112)*. In spring, guided walks show off the blooms of the wildlife garden near York Bridge; or venture out on the boating pond. June is prime time for the roses in Queen Mary's Gardens, where the rock garden is perfect for hide-and-seek. The school summer holiday heralds playground sessions and sports coaching at The Hub, and there are matinée performances at the Open Air Theatre.

Come autumn, the tree-lined towpath along Regent's Canal is very colourful, and October's Frieze Art Fair dots eye-catching artworks around the park. By November, over-wintering wildfowl are swooping onto the lake from colder climes: Long Bridge is the best viewing spot. If it really freezes, warm up in the indoor rainforest pavilion at **ZSL London Zoo** *(see pp110–11)*, or take in the Christmas show at the **Puppet Theatre Barge** *(see p111)*. Whatever the season, the friendly Garden Café has a menu to match *(see p111)*.

Storybook London

Pooh and Potter, Peter Pan and Paddington – many favourites from children's literature have links with this part of London. The original Winnie the Pooh lived at London Zoo *(see pp110–11)* in the 1920s: author AA Milne and his son Christopher Robin loved visiting the bear, and a statue now remembers Winnie in the zoo's Animal Adventure zone. Just across the fence in Regent's Park stood the home of Pongo and Missis, heroes of *The Hundred and One Dalmatians*; while over in Bloomsbury, a statue of Peter Pan and Tinkerbell stands outside Great Ormond Street children's hospital; Peter's creator JM Barrie donated the royalties from his play to hospital funds.

Above right Playing on the forecourt of the British Museum
Below right Gorillas lounging at ZSL London Zoo

Above *Admiring the spring flowers in Regent's Park, one of London's most beautiful green spaces*

It's a short walk from there to the **Charles Dickens Museum** (see p106–07), where the great Victorian novelist wrote *Oliver Twist* – see the window that Oliver scrambled through on his burgling mission with Bill Sikes. Wander up to the **British Library** (see p105) and flick through a digital version of Lewis Carroll's original manuscript for *Alice in Wonderland*, before heading home – preferably via platform 9¾ at King's Cross Station, Harry Potter's departure point for Hogwarts School of Witchcraft and Wizardry.

A Bloomsbury sketch

There's nowhere better in London for families to travel armed with sketchbook and pencils. An inspiring place to start is the **Cartoon Museum** (see p103), with its art room and monthly family workshops. Just up the road, **Pollock's Toy Museum** (see p104) devotes a gallery to the exquisite paper theatres stencilled and coloured by Benjamin Pollock and his family in Victorian times, and sells kits to construct at home. The **Wellcome Collection** (see p104–05) also encourages budding artists – its children's pack includes modelling clay and a mask-making kit – while the nearby **Foundling Museum** (see p106) invites young visitors to design a postcard inspired by its exhibition, and hosts family craft sessions each month.

Running out of paper? Never fear: the **British Museum** (see pp102–03) has the mother of all children's activity programmes – and hands out free art materials to every junior visitor.

A fun-filled weekend

There is always something afoot for families at the British Museum (see pp102–103), but especially on Saturdays. Arrive by 10am, check out the day's programme, then head for the Paul Hamlyn Library, which hands out children's packs and trails. Organized kids' activities get going at around 11am, usually in the magnificent Great Court. For lunch, escape to nearby Russell Square for a splash in the fountain, and pizza and ice cream from the terrace café. Just around the corner is **Coram's Fields** (see p106), one of London's very best playgrounds.

Sunday is all about **Camden Market** (see p112–13), a maze of stalls selling everything from musky smelling patchouli oil to vintage clothing. Younger children will especially like Camden Lock, with its jaunty narrowboat rides, and Yumchaa teashop is nice for elevenses. Escape before 1pm, when busy Camden Town tube station becomes exit-only, and hop two tube stops south to Euston, where the weird and wonderful **Wellcome Collection** (see p104) will amaze young and old alike with its array of curiosities. Don't miss the free tour at 2:30pm.

Left *Toys for sale at Stables Market, Camden Lock, a great place to browse, with 700 stalls and shops*

British Museum and around

With Sir Norman Foster's splendid Great Court, a cavernous igloo of white space, the British Museum has one of the grandest entrance lobbies in the world. All-action art workshops take place here every weekend, and there is a dedicated children's shop and two cafés. The museum is free to visit and picnicking is permitted: throw in the marvellous playground at nearby Coram's Fields, and this must be London's best budget day out for families. Bloomsbury has a clutch of smaller museums too, devoted to toys, cartoons, canal boats and more.

Bloomsbury and Regent's Park

ZSL London Zoo p108

British Museum

The British Museum, packed with interesting and exotic exhibits from around the world

Exploring Pollock's Toy Museum, filled to bursting with toys, both past and present

Places of Interest

SIGHTS
1. British Museum
2. Pollock's Toy Museum
3. Wellcome Collection
4. British Library
5. Foundling Museum
6. Charles Dickens Museum
7. London Canal Museum

🔴 EAT AND DRINK
1. Little Waitrose
2. My Old Dutch
3. Heal's Gourmet Kitchen
4. Hakkasan
5. Planet Organic
6. Patisserie Valerie
7. Giraffe
8. Kipferl
9. Simmons
10. Oz Café
See also British Museum

(p102–03), Wellcome Collection (p104), British Library (p105), Foundling Museum (p106) and Charles Dickens Museum (p106)

🔴 WHERE TO STAY
1. Bedford
2. Alhambra
3. Arosfa
4. Arran House
5. Euro
6. Jesmond Dene
7. SACO-Holborn

0 metres   200
0 yards   200

Bronze statue of Sir Isaac Newton outside the British Library

The Lowdown

🚇 **Tube** Tottenham Court Road or Holborn **Bus** New Oxford Street: 8, 25, 55, 98; Great Russell Street: 8, 10, 14, 24, 25, 29, 55, 73, 98, 134, 390

ℹ️ **Visitor information** Holborn Information Kiosk, Kingsway, WC2B 6BG; Euston Travel Information Centre, Euston Rail Centre, NW1 2HS

🛒 **Supermarkets** Hannells Food & Wine, 52–56 New Oxford Street, WC1A 1ES; Sainsbury's Central, 129 Kingsway, WC2B 6NH; Waitrose, 23–39 The Brunswick Centre, WC1N 1AF **Markets** Chapel Market (food and household goods) Penton Street, N1 9PX, 9am–5pm Tue–Sat; 10am–4pm Sun (including farmers' market); Camden Passage antiques market, N1 8EA, 9am–5:30pm Wed & Sat. Both are near Angel tube. Covent Garden's markets are also within (30-min) walking range *(see pp86–7)*

🎏 **Festivals** Bloomsbury Festival, music and arts (Oct)

➕ **Pharmacies** Clockwork Pharmacy, 150 Southampton Row, WC1B 5AN (9am–7pm Mon–Fri; 9am–6pm Sat). For 24-hour pharmacies, search at *www.nhs.uk/ servicedirectories*

🤸 **Nearest playgrounds** Alf Barrett Playground *(see p102)*, Coram's Fields *(see p106)* and Crabtree Fields *(see p104)*.

Exploring the fascinating Wellcome Collection

Enjoying one of the many attractions at the popular Coram's Fields playground and park

The Lowdown

Map ref 10 G1
Address British Museum, Great Russell Street, WC1B 3DG; 020 7323 8000; *www.britishmuseum.org*

Tube Tottenham Court Road or Holborn **Bus stop** New Oxford Street, Great Russell Street

Open Galleries 10am–5:30pm daily; selected rooms till 8:30pm Fri. Great Court 9am–6pm Sun–Thu; till 8:30pm Fri

Price Free. Special exhibitions charge entrance fees

Guided tours Free 30-min tours daily in selected galleries; multimedia guide £17

Age range 3 plus

Activities Children's audio tour with a choice of themes. Family workbook trails (ages 3–5 and 6–11) plus activity backpacks available until 3pm at weekends and daily during school holidays from the Great Court. Object-handling in galleries 1, 2, 24, 33, 49 and 68 (11am–4pm). Free family activities and workshops on weekends and school holidays. Free digital workshops every Wed (age 7 plus). Young Friends club (annual membership £20) arranges six sleepovers a year; *www.britishmuseum.org/membership/young_friends.aspx*

Allow At least 3 hours

Wheelchair access Yes

Café Court Cafés (Great Court, Ground Floor) serve snacks and sandwiches. Gallery Café (Ground Floor) has family-friendly hot dishes. Court Restaurant (Great Court, Upper Floor) serves an à la carte menu. Ford Centre for Young Visitors (Lower Floor) has a baby-feeding room and allows picnicking

Shops Several – in the foyer and the Great Court

Toilets On all floors

Good family value?
Unbeatable, with lots of free stuff to hold children's interest, from activity backpacks to object-handling tables and weekend workshops. It's even permissible to bring your own sandwiches.

① British Museum

Heaps of human history under one roof

Pirate gold, a crystal skull, fanged demons – the British Museum is jammed full of wonders. Three floors of galleries chart two million years of human civilization across the globe, so it pays to be choosy. The Egyptian Collection (Rooms 61–66) and Living and Dying (Room 24) are impressive, with their mummies and skulls. Start in the Families Centre in the Great Court, for free kids' trails and backpacks.

Key Features

Levels 4 & 5 Special exhibitions and Asia: China and Korea

Level 3 Ancient Egypt, Greece and Rome; Middle East and Europe

Levels 1 & 2 Asia: China, India, Japan, Southeast Asia

Ground floor America: North America and Mexico; Ancient Greece and Rome, Middle East and Egypt

Level –1 Africa, Greek and Roman architecture

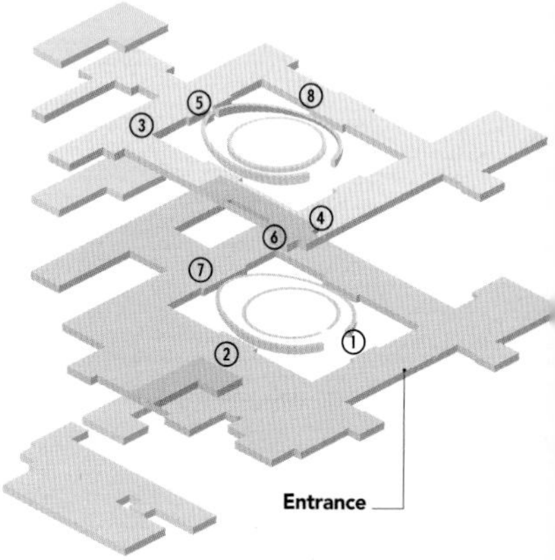

Letting off steam

Alf Barrett Playground *(Old Gloucester Street, WC1B 4DA)*, 10 minutes east of the museum on the corner of Old Gloucester Street and Gage Street, caters for kids up to age 13. Behind the museum, **Russell Square**, remodelled to its original 200-year-old Humphry Repton design, has the perfect fountain for splashing through, plus ice creams to enjoy from the terrace café.

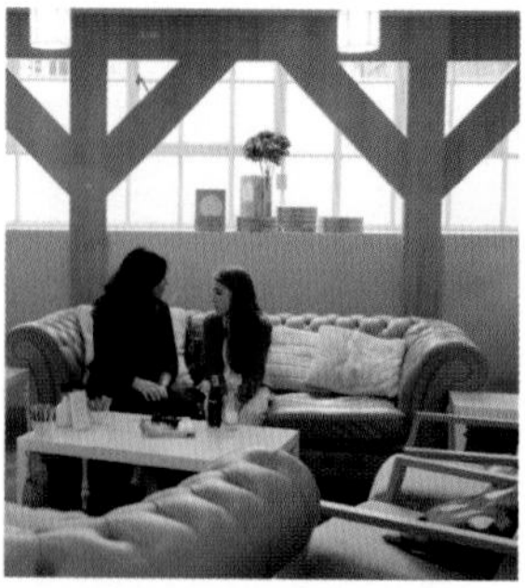

Taking a break in the comfortable surroundings of Meals at Heals

Eat and drink

Picnic: under £20; Snacks: £20–40; Real meal: £40–60; Family treat: £60 or more (based on a family of four)

PICNIC Little Waitrose *(227–233 Tottenham Court Road W1T 7QF; 0800 184 884)* is a smaller version of the British supermarket chain. Pick up a picnic here and eat in nearby Bloomsbury Square.
SNACKS My Old Dutch *(131 High Holborn, WC1V 6PS; 020 7242 5200; www.myolddutch.com)* lets kids build their own crêpes – anyone for a pineapple and red chilli pancake? It also does good smoothies and shakes.
REAL MEAL Heal's Gourmet Kitchen *(196 Tottenham Court Road, W1T 7LQ; 020 7636 1666; www.heals.co.uk)*, on the first floor of Heals, has child-friendly fare.
FAMILY TREAT Hakkasan *(8 Hanway Place, W1T 1HD; 020 7927 7000; www.hakkasan.com)* is at the forefront of contemporary Chinese cuisine and has a Michelin star. The "small eat" dishes are ideal for kids.

Prices given are for a family of four

① Great Court Once an outside courtyard, this is now the largest covered public space in Europe.

② Rosetta Stone Carved with a pharaoh's decree from 196 BC, this is the museum's most visited treasure. It is written in three languages, which enabled experts to decode Egyptian hieroglyphs for the first time. (Room 4)

③ Abydos cat mummy The ancient Egyptians worshipped cats, mummifying thousands as offerings to the cat-goddess Bastet. (Room 62)

④ Pirate treasure Long John Silver's parrot squawked "pieces of eight" – and here they are. In Tudor times (c.1500–1600), these Spanish coins were worth about £50. (Room 68)

⑤ The Royal Game of Ur This Ludo-like dice game was played 4,500 years ago in Mesopotamia. Players raced across the board, trying to land on the lucky rosettes. (Room 56)

⑥ Ball game belt This toad-shaped belt featured in the world's oldest team sport, a type of volleyball played in ancient Mexico. Defeat could be dangerous – the losers were sacrificed to the gods! (Room 27)

⑦ Camera coffin The Ga people of Ghana have been fashioning these fantastical coffins since the 1950s to represent the dead person's interests – such as photography, eagles or planes. (Room 24)

⑧ Mold Cape Discovered in a Welsh burial mound, this Bronze Age cape was a pile of gold fragments, leaving curators with a giant jigsaw puzzle to tackle. (Room 51)

Find out more

DIGITAL The museum's website has a great zone just for children: skip through the centuries in the Time Explorer adventure game: www.britishmuseum.org/explore/young_explorers1.aspx.

Take out the internal organs, then pull the brain out via the nostrils! Make your own mummy at www.bbc.co.uk/history/ancient/egyptians/launch_gms_mummy_maker.shtml.

In the BBC Radio 4 series *A History of the World in 100 Objects*, British Museum director Neil MacGregor chose his world-changing artifacts. Download the series at www.bbc.co.uk/ahistoryoftheworld.

Next stop...

THE PETRIE MUSEUM Part of the University College of London, this museum *(Malet Place, WC1E 6BT; Tue–Sat 1–5pm; www.ucl.ac.uk/museums/petrie)* is stacked high with Egyptian items – and has an art table and Roman togas for children to model.

THE CARTOON MUSEUM This fun place *(35 Little Russell Street, WC1A 2HH; 020 7580 8155; 10:30am–5:30pm Tue–Sat; noon–5:30pm Sun; www.cartoonmuseum.org)* has an art room where kids can doodle their own masterpiece. British cartoons and comic art from the 18th century to the present day are on display. It also offers drop-in family cartooning on the second Saturday of the month and terrific school-holiday workshops for ages 8 plus.

Aspiring young cartoonists getting instruction at the Cartoon Museum

② Pollock's Toy Museum

Playtimes from the past

Winding your way around the snaking stairways and attic rooms of this rickety old house feels like going back in time – which is appropriate, since they are filled with a treasure trove of toys spanning two centuries. Don't tell the children, but it's an irresistible nostalgia trip for parents, too.

The charming, idiosyncratic collection includes Schoenhut's Humpty Dumpty Circus from 1903, and a reconstructed early 20th-century boy's den, complete with dangerous-looking chemistry set and blow football. One room is devoted to the delicate but magical paper theatres of the Pollock family, whose renowned Victorian toy emporium spawned the museum in 1956. Other rooms concentrate on early teddy bears, toy soldiers and slightly spooky wax dolls.

The labels are yellowing and there's little to touch or play with, so give thanks for the toyshop at the end of the visit, stacked with superannuated treats – spinning tops, kaleidoscopes and classic card games such as Happy Families. Pollock's Toy Shop in Covent Garden (see p89) also sells great toys.

Letting off steam

One minute's walk south, **Crabtree Fields** (*Whitfield Street, W1T 2BJ*) has a fun-filled playground and an attractive pergola walkway.

Browsing among the exciting toys in the toyshop of Pollock's Toy Museum

The Lowdown

🌐 **Map ref** 10 E1
Address 1 Scala Street, W1T 2HL; 020 7636 3452; www.pollocksmuseum.co.uk

🚇 **Tube** Goodge Street
Bus stop Tottenham Court Road

🕐 **Open** 10am–5pm Mon–Sat (last admission 4:30pm)

💲 **Price** £16–20

🚩 **Guided tours** No

🎎 **Activities** Occasional toy theatre or puppet shows during school holidays (call to check)

👫 **Age range** 5 plus

⏱ **Allow** 1 hour

♿ **Wheelchair access** Only to ground floor shop due to stairs

🍽 **Eat and drink** *Picnic* Planet Organic (*22 Torrington Place, WC1E 7HJ*) is a healthy grocery-cum-café – picnic on Bedford Square *Snacks* Patisserie Valerie (*24 Torrington Place, WC1E 7HJ*) sells less virtuous, delicious cakes

🛍 **Shop** Toys and gifts

🚻 **Toilets** Ground floor

③ Wellcome Collection

Shrunken heads and massive moustaches

On a par with Ripley's Believe It or Not (*see p84*) is the Wellcome Collection. This giant store of curiosities was collected by an eccentric adventurer called Henry Wellcome, who made his fortune as a medicine salesman, grew Victorian England's bushiest moustache, then travelled the world hunting for medical marvels. He returned with

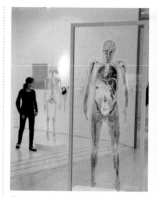
Examining the curious medical exhibits in the Wellcome Collection

some very bizarre booty indeed: prepare to be amazed by a torturer's mask, a Peruvian mummy (minus bandages) and a peculiar device for blowing tobacco smoke up a drowning person's bottom.

The historical gallery is beautifully arranged: slide open drawers to hear sound clips about key objects or to reveal artifacts to touch. The curators are oddly ambivalent about younger visitors: they stress that some of the material has adult themes, yet the museum has produced one of the best children's explorer kits in London, with modelling clay, a false moustache and a guide to making a shrunken head. Parental discretion is needed – steer sensitive souls away from the birth and death cabinets, and focus instead on the exotic masks, votive amulets and celebrity ephemera (Napoleon's toothbrush, George III's hair).

The Wellcome's second gallery, Medicine Now, feels very different:

The Lowdown

🌐 **Map ref** 4 E6
Address 183 Euston Road, NW1 2BE; 020 7611 2222; www.wellcomecollection.org

🚆 **Train** Euston, King's Cross or St Pancras **Tube** Euston Square; Warren Street **Bus stop** Euston Road, Euston Bus Station, Upper Woburn Place

🕐 **Open** 10am–6pm Tue–Sat, 11am–6pm Sun; 10am–10pm Thu

💲 **Price** Free

🚩 **Guided tours** Free 30-min tours of the Medicine Now and Medicine Man galleries at 2:30pm on Sat and Sun respectively

👫 **Age range** 6 plus, though parental guidance advisable

🎎 **Activities** Young Explorers Pack for under-14s. Events programme tends to be adult-focused

⏱ **Allow** 2 hours

♿ **Wheelchair access** Yes

🍽 **Eat and drink** *Snacks* Wellcome Café offers light lunches, muffins and pies *Real meal* The British Library Restaurant & Terrace offers a more substantial feed (*see right*)

🛍 **Shop** Books, gifts and collection-based souvenirs

🚻 **Toilets** On all floors

The spacious courtyard of the British Library

starkly lit and stylish, and devoted to modern wonders such as Dolly the cloned sheep and the human genome. Downstairs in the lobby there are temporary exhibitions on health and well being, plus a cool café with free Wi-Fi and screens for browsing the museum's collection.

Letting off steam
Nearby **Gordon Square Garden** (*Gordon Square, WC1H 0AR*) has a full 100-m (330-ft) lawn, and there's a toddler play-park in adjacent **Woburn Square** (*WC1H 0AB*).

④ British Library
Sshhh! – a temple for books and the printed word

Fourteen million books, three million sound recordings, almost a million journals and newspapers… and just one permanent public gallery. For such a vast institution, the British Library offers thin pickings for the general visitor, especially for families – guided tours are pitched at adults and under-18s are barred from accessing the sound archives.

However, the Treasures Gallery offers a changing collection of important tomes, from England's first printed book, the *Gutenberg Bible* (c.1455), to Leonardo's da Vinci's notebooks, a draft score of Handel's *Messiah*, and Captain Scott's South Pole diaries. For children, the displays are saved from dryness by sound stations where they can listen to bursts of Brahms or the Beatles, and especially by the Turning the Pages interactive displays with touch-screen browsing. Flick through Lewis Carroll's original *Alice's Adventures Under Ground,*

with the author's own pictures; or novelist Jane Austen's *History of England*, written when she was 15 – she had very neat handwriting, too.

Letting off steam
There is a small swing park along Judd Street, across the Euston Road, or walk south for about 15 mintues to **Coram's Fields** (*see p106*).

The Lowdown

🌐 **Map ref** 4 F4
Address 96 Euston Road, NW1 2DB; 0843 208 1144; www.bl.uk

🚗 **Train** King's Cross or St Pancras
Tube King's Cross St Pancras
Bus stop Euston Road

🕙 **Open** 9:30am–8pm Mon, Thu; 9:30am–5pm Fri–Sat; 11am–5pm Sun

💷 **Price** Free

🚩 **Guided Tours** Free Viewing Gallery tours at 1am & 3pm Mon–Sat, 11:30am & 3pm Sun & Public Holidays; Library Tour (*£29; call 01937 546546 to book*) 3pm Mon–Sat, plus 10:30am Sat. Free conservation tour 2pm first Thu of month (over-12s); audio tours are downloadable online

👫 **Age range** 7 plus

👫 **Activities** Occasional free family workshops during school holidays, linked to temporary exhibitions

⏱ **Allow** 1 hour

♿ **Wheelchair access** Yes, via lifts and ramps

☕ **Eat and drink** *Snacks* Peyton & Byrne Café (open daily), upper ground floor, has quality snacks and free Wi-Fi; *Real meal* The British Library Restaurant & Terrace (*9:30am–5pm Mon–Fri; 9:30am–4pm Sat*) offers stir-fries and salads

🛍 **Shop** Ground floor near the entrance

🚻 **Toilets** On all levels

⑤ Foundling Museum

A poignant tale of children lost and found

No single room in any London museum tells a more moving story than the main gallery here. In the early 18th century, before orphanages were established, a thousand babies were abandoned in London's backstreets each year – most of them reluctantly – by their destitute mothers. Pioneering shipwright Thomas Coram (1668–1751) led a heroic 20-year campaign to launch a Foundling Hospital to take them in.

The story has all the ingredients of a blockbuster, from the hospital's celebrity patrons (George Frideric Handel performed his *Messiah* to raise funds; William Hogarth donated paintings, which still hang upstairs) to anguished mothers drawing lots to discover whether their tiny bundles would be saved by the orphanage. Today, visitors get to experience the lottery too – if

Dressing up in a rich child's costume at the Foundling Museum

they draw out a black ball, their "baby" is rejected. There are recordings of interviews with former foundlings (the hospital finally closed in 1953), and most heart-rending of all, a collection of tokens left behind by mothers who hoped one day to reclaim their child.

Themed activity packs help to focus young minds on the story, while in the immaculate Georgian picture gallery, kids can dress up, or browse in the reading corner – which includes *Hetty Feather*, a tale about a Victorian inmate by Jacqueline Wilson. Better still, the book is a perfect way to whet the appetite before a visit.

Letting off steam

Just across the square, **Coram's Fields** (*93 Guildford Street, WC1N 1CN; www.coramsfields.org*) is not so much a playground as a kids' kingdom, with its Olympic-sized paddling pool, mini-farmyard, toddler play sessions, zipwire and sports pitches.

The Lowdown

- 🌐 **Map ref** 4 G6
  Address 40 Brunswick Square, WC1N 1AZ; 020 7841 3600; *www.foundlingmuseum.org.uk*
- 🚌 **Train** King's Cross, St Pancras **Tube** Russell Square **Bus stop** Russell Square, Gray's Inn Road
- 🕐 **Open** 10am–5pm Tue–Sat; 11am–5pm Sun
- 💲 **Price** £15–25, under-16s free
- 🚩 **Guided tours** Yes. Download group booking form
- 👫 **Age range** 3 plus
- 🎨 **Activities** Free treasure-hunt trails (ages 3–12) and activity backpacks (ages 3–5 and 5–8). Drop-in family workshops 1st Sat of each month, plus Thu–Fri in school holidays
- 🕐 **Allow** Up to two hours
- ♿ **Wheelchair access** Yes
- ☕ **Eat and drink** *Snacks* The Foundling Museum Café does light lunches and cream teas and has a children's menu *Real meal* Giraffe (*19–21 Brunswick Centre, WC1N 1AF; 020 7812 1336*) serves burgers, sausages and pizzas and has a kids' menu
- 🛍️ **Shop** In reception, selling toys and collection-inspired gifts
- 🚻 **Toilets** Lower ground, ground and first floor

⑥ Charles Dickens Museum

Oliver Twist's birthplace

The creator of Oliver, Tiny Tim and Little Nell loved children – he had 10 of his own after all. A leading proponent of child welfare in poverty-stricken Victorian London, Dickens lived at this smart Holborn townhouse from 1837–1839, and wrote *Oliver Twist* and *Nicholas Nickleby* here.

The building has been preserved as Dickens knew it, and original furniture, manuscripts and interesting memorabilia such as the

The Lowdown

- 🌐 **Map ref** 4 H6
  Address 48 Doughty Street, WC1N 2LX; 020 7405 2127; *www.dickensmuseum.com*
- 🚗 **Tube** Russell Square, Chancery Lane or Holborn **Bus stop** Gray's Inn Place Theobald's Road
- 🕐 **Open** Daily 10am–5pm (last admission 4pm)
- 💲 **Price** £24–34, under-6s free
- 🚩 **Guided tours** Group bookings
- 👫 **Age range** 8 plus
- 🎨 **Activities** Free children's trail; occasional family activities
- 🕐 **Allow** 1 hour
- ♿ **Wheelchair access** Yes, via ramp but some limitations due to age of building
- ☕ **Eat and drink** *Picnic* Buy sandwiches at the small onsite café. Eat in the courtyard garden *Snacks* Kipferl (*www.kipferl.co.uk*), at Coram's Fields playground, is a kiosk café with an Austrian flavour
- 🛍️ **Shop** Sells memorabilia
- 🚻 **Toilets** Basement floor

Having fun in the exciting Coram's Fields playground and park

quills he used are on display. There are Victorian cookery demonstrations and the house is animated by sound clips of Dickens' words. After a major refurbishment, the museum is more child-friendly, with regular family activities and a kids' trail.

Letting off steam

Coram's Fields (see left), with its playground, pool and other exciting attractions, is just around the corner.

7 London Canal Museum

Horse dung and ice cream

Britain's canal age endured for longer than one might imagine – barges carrying cargo were still moving through Battlebridge Basin on the Regent's Canal in the 1960s. That's good news for the museum that now sits here, because lots of fascinating oral history survives – pick up the antique-style telephones and listen to William Tarbit describe what it was like to live and work on the canals: how he had to crawl into his narrowboat's coal box to clean it – aged three! – and how he snared rabbits and pheasants for his mother's poacher's pie.

The museum has a traditional feel, with an authentic 1850s warehouse setting. It is half filled by the vintage barge *Coronis*, on which younger children can play. The cramped cabin might once have accommodated a family of six. Step out onto the wharf for a look at some modern narrowboats, and

visit the re-created blacksmith's workshop and stable upstairs.

The museum's other theme is guaranteed to get kids' taste buds tingling: the Victorian ice cream trade. The underground chasm in the downstairs gallery once stored vast blocks of ice, imported on barges from Norway by the pioneering pudding-maker Carlo Gatti in the days before refrigeration. And never fear – there is ice cream for sale at the museum shop.

Letting off steam

A 10-minute walk via York Way and Goods Way leads to **Camley Street Natural Park** (12 Camley Street, NW1 0PW; www.wildlondon.org. uk), a canalside wildlife oasis set in a former coalyard amid the bustle of King's Cross. The visitor centre offers activities from 10am–5pm daily (to 4pm in winter). April to August is the best time to visit.

Interactive display showing how a lock's mitre gate works

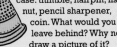

The Lowdown

🌐 **Map ref** 4 H3
Address 12–13 New Wharf Road, N1 9RT; 020 7713 0836; www. canalmuseum.org.uk

🚂 **Train** King's Cross, St Pancras. **Tube** King's Cross **Bus stop** Caledonian Road, Pentonville

🕐 **Open** 10am–4:30pm Tue–Sun (last admission 4pm); till 7:30pm on 1st Thu of the month

💲 **Price** £10, under-4s free

Guided tours There is an audio tour, which must be downloaded beforehand from the website to an MP3 player

🧍 **Age range** 6 plus

🧍 **Activities** Small play corner with books and building blocks; family trails, guided boat trips on some

summer Sun, plus children's activity days every Tue in Aug. Website has kids' pages and a downloadable walk from Camden

⏱ **Allow** 1–2 hours

♿ **Wheelchair access** Yes

☕ **Eat and drink** Snacks Simmons (32 Caledonian Road, N1 9DT) is a tiny, trendy teahouse. Drop in for a pot of tea and a cupcake in the afternoon, or a fruit beer in the evening Real meal Oz Café (53 Caledonian Road, N1 9BU) is a cheery lunchtime diner serving pasta and paninis

🛍 **Shop** Sells books, pottery and model barges

🚻 **Toilets** Ground floor

Picnic: under £20; **Snacks:** £20–40; **Real meal:** £40–60; **Family treat:** £60 or more (based on a family of four)

ZSL London Zoo and around

There are gorillas and tigers to see of course, but these days London Zoo gives centre stage to its smaller creatures, devoting walk-through enclosures to monkeys and meerkats, penguins and sloths. Wait for some sunshine, and dedicate a full day to get the best value for the entrance fee. The nearest Tube station is Camden Town, but it gets congested on Sundays, when the area's manic markets are in full swing. Consider travelling to Baker Street or Regent's Park station, and walking across Regent's Park, with a game of hide-and-seek along the way. Another great option is a canal tour from Camden Lock.

Bloomsbury and Regent's Park

ZSL London Zoo

British Museum p100

An "Animals in Action" demonstration at ZSL London Zoo

Far left
Youngsters enjoying a costumed talk at the Wallace Collection
Left Elegant bandstand in Regent's Park

Places of Interest

SIGHTS
1. ZSL London Zoo
2. Regent's Park
3. Camden Market
4. Jewish Museum
5. Madame Tussauds
6. Sherlock Holmes Museum
7. The Wallace Collection

EAT AND DRINK
1. Whole Foods Market
2. Gelato Mio

3. Strada
4. The Regent's Bar & Kitchen
5. The Cow and Coffee Bean
6. Smokehouse
7. Yumchaa
8. The Ice Wharf
9. Banner's
10. Caffè Nero
11. The Boathouse Cafe
12. Caffè Saporito
13. Nando's

14. Caffè Fratelli
See also Jewish Museum (p113) and Wallace Collection (p115)

PLACES TO STAY
1. The Landmark
2. Blandford
3. Hart House
4. Lincoln House
5. New Inn
6. 23 Greengarden House

Below Browsing at Camden Lock Crafts Market

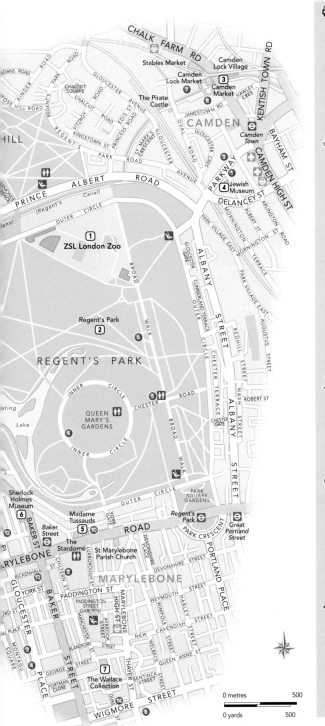

ZSL London Zoo
Regent's Park
REGENT'S PARK
QUEEN MARY'S GARDENS
Sherlock Holmes Museum
Madame Tussauds
The Stardome
Baker Street
St Marylebone Parish Church
MARYLEBONE
The Wallace Collection

0 metres 500
0 yards 500

The Lowdown

🚗 **Train** Camden Road or Marylebone **Tube** Camden Town, St John's Wood **Bus** Prince Albert Road: route number 274; Parkway: C2 **Canal** Services from Camden Lock to Little Venice, daily in summer, weekends in winter (www.londonwaterbus.com; www.jasons.co.uk)

ℹ️ **Visitor information** See pp100–101

🍽️ **Supermarkets** Somerfield, 131–133 Camden High Street, NW1 7JR; Morrisons, Chalk Farm Road, NW1 8AA; Waitrose, 98–101 Marylebone High Street, W1U 4SD **Markets** Camden Markets (fashion, crafts, antiques, gifts) 10am–6pm daily. Marylebone Farmers' Market (mainly produce, Cramer Street Car Park, W1U 4EW) 10am–2pm Sun. Cabbages & Frocks Market (food, fashion, crafts), St Marylebone Parish Church, NW1 5LT, 11am–5pm Sat. Church Street Market (food, clothes, bric-a-brac), 13–25 Church Street, NW8 8DT, 8:30am–4pm Mon–Thu (to 5pm Fri & Sat). Alfies Antique Market, 13–25 Church St NW8 8DT, 10am–6pm Tue–Sat

🎪 **Festivals** Taste of London (food/restaurant festival), Regent's Park (Jun); London Green Fair, Regent's Park (Jun); Pride London (diversity and equality festival) – parade begins Baker Street (Jun–Jul); Frieze Art Fair, Regent's Park (Oct)

➕ **Pharmacies** JP Pharmacy, 139 Camden High Street, NW1 7JR (9am–6:30pm Mon–Fri, 9am–6pm Sat, 10am–4pm Sun). Boots, 173–175 Camden High Street, NW1 7JY (8:30am–8pm Mon–Fri, 9am–7pm Sat, noon–6pm Sun). For 24-hour pharmacies, visit www.nhs.uk/servicedirectories

🛝 **Nearest playgrounds** Regent's Park, NW1 4NR; Marylebone Green, Gloucester Gate, Hanover Gate; Primrose Hill, Prince Albert Road, NW1 4NR; Paddington Street Gardens W1U

The Lowdown

🌐 **Map reference** 3 B3
Address Regent's Park, NW1 4RY; 020 7722 3333 and 0344 225 1826; www.zsl.org

🚗 **Train** Camden Road Station
Tube Camden Town, St John's Wood **Bus stop** Prince Albert Road; **Parkway Canal** Scheduled service along Regent's Canal between Camden Lock and Little Venice, daily April–September, plus winter weekends (www.londonwaterbus.com)

🕐 **Open** 10am–4pm daily (check website for longer summer opening hours); animal houses close 30 minutes earlier

💲 **Price** £60–80, under-3s free (optional 10% surcharge supports conservation work); online saver offers 10% reduction for families (2+2 or 1+3)

👬 **Skipping the queue** Online tickets allow fast-track admission. Head straight for Gorilla Kingdom, before the queues build

🚩 **Guided tours** No

👫 **Age range** All

👪 **Activities** Daily programme might include watching the otters being fed, seeing the llamas on their daily walk and watching penguins waddle on the Penguin Beach. Plus storytelling in the Animal Adventure teepee and brass-rubbing in the Activity Den

⏱️ **Allow** At least half a day

♿ **Wheelchair access**
Yes – however, there are two steep ramps that need caution

☕ **Eat and drink** The Terrace Restaurant offers hot lunches, including children's portions, baby food and a pick-and-mix picnic counter. Also Animal Adventure Café, seasonal pancake and hot dog stands, and picnic lawns

🛍️ **Shops** Near entrance and in Barclay Court

🚻 **Toilets** Near entrance, in Oasis Restaurant and around zoo

Good family value?
It's wildly expensive, though cut-price deals can sometimes be found online. To get value for money, arrive early, pick up the "Dayplanner" events leaflet, and plot the day carefully.

Prices given are for a family of four

① ZSL London Zoo
Face to fang with the world's wildlife

An architectural oddity, ZSL London Zoo is full of strange 1930s buildings, but it also has a gorilla compound, an interactive children's zoo, a tiger territory and a "penguin beach". Kids will be kept busy tiptoeing along the balancing bars in the monkey enclosure, crawling into an aardvark's burrow, or smiling at sloths in the walk-through rainforest. The zoo's watchword is "immersive", and it brings visitors closer to the animals than ever before.

Key Features

① **Butterfly Paradise**
A walk-through butterfly house set in a giant inflatable caterpillar. The fluttering insects sometimes mistake brightly dressed visitors for flowers, so watch out for hitchhikers!

② **Blackburn Pavilion**
Home to jewel-coloured hummingbirds and splendid sunbirds, this steamy tropical bird-house is themed on Victorian explorers. Get ready to take flight!

③ **Rainforest Life** This hothouse takes visitors right in among snoozing sloths and scurrying tamarin monkeys, which chase along the creepers overhead.

Reptile House

Exit

Aquarium

Animal Adventure — **Entrance** — **Snowdon Aviary**

④ **Gorilla Kingdom**
This luxury island enclosure is home to a troop of western lowland gorillas. Watch these impressive apes show off their skills on a climbing wall and swing ropes.

⑤ **B.U.G.S!** There are handling sessions here and views of bird-eating spiders, naked mole rats and the zoo's bug experts in their laboratory.

⑥ **Animals in Action** The zoo's captivating live show runs daily in the amphitheatre. Kids watch wide-eyed as George the Macaw and Archie the Owl swoop on the stage.

Letting off steam

If crawling among porcupines and knuckle-walking with gorillas doesn't tire out your flock, there is formal play equipment at the zoo, next to Butterfly Paradise and in the Animal Adventure zone. Beyond the zoo, head for the Gloucester Gate entrance to **Regent's Park**, which has a spacious playground and (just south of its enclosure) an exciting tangle of tree trunks arranged for scrambling, where children really can make like monkeys.

Climbing in the Animal Adventure zone playground

Eat and drink

Picnic: under £20; Snacks: £20–40; Real meal: £40–60; Family treat: £60 or more (based on a family of four)

PICNIC Whole Foods Market (49 Parkway, NW1 7PN; 020 7428 7575; www.wholefoods market. com/stores/camden; 8am–9pm Mon–Sat; 9am–9pm Sun) is on the way from Camden Town Tube station to the zoo, with healthy, high-class picnic food. Throw a rug down in Regent's Park to eat it.

SNACKS Gelato Mio (138 St John's Wood High Street, NW8 7SE; 020 0011 3889; www.gelatomio.co.uk; 9am–10pm Mon–Thu (to 11pm Fri); 10am–11pm Sat & Sun) serves possibly the tastiest authentic Italian ice creams and sorbets in London. Choose from a wide range of classic flavours.

REAL MEAL Part of a chain, the Italian restaurant **Strada** (40–42 Parkway, NW1 7AH; 020 7428 9653;

www.strada.co.uk; 11:30am–11pm Mon–Sat; to 10:30pm Sun) is a welcoming spot for lunch, with a kids' menu and activity pack.

FAMILY TREAT The Regent's Bar & Kitchen (Inner Circle, Regent's Park, NW1 4NU; 020 7935 5729; 8am–4pm daily), is set in an idyllic location in Regent's Park and offers seasonal English cooking – including a set two-course menu for children.

Find out more

DIGITAL ZSL London Zoo's interactive website has kids' pages that mix animal fact-finding with games. Learn how to weigh a meerkat, make your own colourful animal mask or catch up with the babies born recently at the zoo: www.zsl.org/kids.

Dramatic performance for children on the Puppet Theatre Barge

Next stop...

TOWPATH TRAIL Regent's Canal runs right through the zoo. Escape the excitement with a tranquil walk along the towpath to Camden, with its chaotic, exotic markets (see pp112–13). Head west, perhaps by waterbus, and you'll reach Little Venice, a genteel canal quarter with flower-festooned narrowboats and the delightful **Puppet Theatre Barge**, which puts on seasonal shows for children (nearest tube station Warwick Avenue; 020 7249 6876, www.puppetbarge.com).

Choosing between the many mouthwatering flavours of ice cream at Gelato Mio

② Regent's Park
Playgrounds and playhouses

On a sunny day, few stretches of ground in London lift the spirits quite like Regent's Park. There is just so much to do here: hide-and-seek and ducks to feed for toddlers; football coaching and adventure playgrounds for older children; an open-air theatre and smart dining for mum and dad; even rose gardens and band concerts for granny and grandad.

The park looks wonderful, too: first laid out in 1811 by John Nash, the Buckingham Palace architect, for his great patron the Prince Regent, it was opened to the public 30 years later. There are four excellent playgrounds here (each with attendants and toilets), which often stage activities during school holidays. The elegant Inner Circle has a labyrinthine tangle of snaking pathways, Chinese bridges and cascades, plus the celebrated open-air theatre, which usually includes a family-friendly Shakespeare play in its summer season.

To the west, the pretty boating lake attracts grey herons and has rowing boats and pedalos for hire. Nearby, the Holme Green bandstand stages sedate jazz on Sunday evenings from June to August, when deckchairs can be

Messing about on the water, always a fun option for children in Regent's Park

rented too. There are a number of wildlife walks and allotment workshops in season, including Get Growing family sessions; while to the north of the park, what looks like a crashed flying saucer among the football pitches is actually The Hub *(0207 935 2458; open daily)*, offering a wide range of sports for all ages and holiday sports camps for kids.

Take cover

If it rains, it's a short stroll to the Odeon Camden *(14 Parkway, NW1 7AA; 0871 224 4007; www.odeon. co.uk)*, which offers several film screenings every afternoon.

③ Camden Market
London's most bizarre bazaar

For a first-time visitor, plunging into Camden's maelstrom of markets can feel a little like tumbling down Alice in Wonderland's rabbit hole. It is a passport to an incense-scented alternative universe where the tattooed and pierced buy and sell jewellery, clothes, music, novelties, furniture and food from right across London's vivid cultural spectrum. Take a deep breath, hold on tight to little hands, and go with the flow.

The gentlest introduction is Camden Lock, a cute courtyard right beside Regent's Canal, where prettily painted narrowboats chug out to Little Venice past ZSL London Zoo. The market hall next door majors in sparkly crafts and accessories, from earrings and scarves to candles and carvings, and there's a tasty parade of multi-ethnic food stands. Behind here, things get more chaotic: the labyrinthine Stables Market occupies the site of the stables, horse hospital, warehouses and vaults connected with the canal trade in Victorian times – hence the bronze carthorses that spring out from assorted corners. Teenagers love the groovy goth-punk vibe, while the characterful Horse Tunnel area has more grown-up bric-à-brac.

Just across Chalk Farm Road is Camden Lock Village, another zone of mostly street-fashion stalls set in wooden cabins – look out for the food stands with mopeds as seating.

Prices given are for a family of four

The Lowdown

🌐 **Map ref** 3 C1
Address Camden High Street, NW1; 020 7284 2084; www.camdenlock.net

🚇 **Tube** Camden Town, Chalk Farm **Bus stop** Chalk Farm Road, Camden Town Station **Canal** London Waterbus (www.londonwaterbus.com) and Jason's Trip (www.jasons.co.uk) run daily in spring and summer; London Waterbus runs winter weekends

🕐 **Open** 10am–6pm daily

💷 **Price** Free

🚶 **Skipping the queue** The market heaves at weekends: 1–5:30pm Sun, Camden Town tube station is exit only. Weekdays are quieter.

👫 **Age range** 7 plus

🤸 **Activities** Canal trips (see above)

⏱ **Allow** Up to 2 hours

♿ **Wheelchair access** Yes, via lifts (disabled toilet in Unit 23 on the Stables street level).

🍽 **Eat and drink** Snacks Yumchaa (91–92 Camden Lock Place, NW1 8AF; www.yumchaa.com) offers a huge variety of teas and cakes. Real meal The Ice Wharf (28 Jamestown Road, NW1 7BY; www.jdwetherspoon.co.uk/home/pubs/the-ice-wharf) overlooks the lock and has a good kids' menu

🚻 **Toilets** Various; basement of Stable Market, bridge of Middle Yard

Letting off steam

Primrose Hill, a 10-minute walk via the canal towpath, is a lofty northern satellite of Regent's Park popular with kite fliers. The Pirate Castle (020 7267 6605; www.thepiratecastle.org), a canalside youth club offering kayaking sessions for ages 8–17 on Tue, Thu and Sat, plus most weekdays in summer holidays, is on the way.

Exploring the bustling Camden Lock crafts market

④ Jewish Museum

A poignant 1,000-year immigrant odyssey

From the life of the Victorian prime minister Benjamin Disraeli to that of Auschwitz survivor Leon Greenman, the Jewish Museum puts an emphasis on personal stories. You can get a free taste of the museum from the ground-floor gallery, but the history hall is the highlight, tracing the 1,000-year story of Britain's Jewish community, from their arrival with William the Conqueror in 1066. The senses are engaged: smell the chicken soup in a re-created East End street, play a board game based on the Jewish diaspora or try Yiddish karaoke. Especially poignant for kids are the keepsakes from the Kindertransport, carried by the 10,000 Jewish children who fled Nazi Germany in 1939.

Letting off steam

It's a 5-minute walk along Parkway to Gloucester Gate playground, in **Regent's Park**.

The Lowdown

🌐 **Map ref** 3 D2
Address 129–131 Albert Street, NW1 7NB; 020 7284 7384; www.jewishmuseum.org.uk

🚇 **Tube** Camden Town, Mornington Crescent **Bus stop** Delancey Street, Camden High Street **Canal** Camden Lock (www.londonwaterbus.com; www.jasons.co.uk)

🕐 **Open** 10am–5pm Sun–Thu; 10am–2pm Fri (last admission 30 minutes earlier)

💷 **Price** £18

🚩 **Guided tours** No

👫 **Age range** 7 plus

🤸 **Activities** Family workshops on occasional Sundays and in school holidays, include glass-painting, candle-making and drumming

⏱ **Allow** 1–2 hours

♿ **Wheelchair access** Yes

🍽 **Eat and drink** Snack Banner's (21 Park Road, N8 8TE; 020 8348 2930) serves breakfast apart from other meals. Children's menu features unprocessed food. Real meal The museum's Kosher Café (10am–4pm Sun–Thu; till 2pm Fri) has salt beef, bagels and a kids' menu

🛍 **Shop** Ground floor

🚻 **Toilets** All floors

Iconic red telephone boxes outside the world-famous Madame Tussauds

⑤ Madame Tussauds

Schmooze with the stars

No attraction in the capital divides opinion quite like Marie Tussaud's 175-year-old waxwork show. Despite the pricey admission, visitors queue around the block – and that's really the problem. The galleries can get crowded, defeating the main purpose of a visit – to have your photograph taken with Lady Gaga, Rihanna or Johnny Depp. Small children may even struggle to see

The Lowdown

- 🌐 **Map ref** 3 B6
  Address Marylebone Road, NW1 5LR; 0871 894 3000; *www. madametussauds.com/london*
- 🚗 **Train** Marylebone **Tube** Baker Street **Bus stop** Marylebone Road, Baker Street
- 🕐 **Open** 9:30am–5:30pm Mon–Fri; 9am–6pm Sat–Sun
- 💲 **Price** £120–216. Half-price tickets after 5pm, online only
- 👫 **Skipping the queue** Book online for fast-track entry; online tickets are about 10 per cent cheaper.
- 👫 **Age range** 5 plus
- 👫 **Activities** Free family activity pack, available online only: *www. madametussauds.com/London/ BuyTickets/Families.aspx*
- 🕐 **Allow** 2 hours
- ♿ **Wheelchair access** Yes, apart from the Spirit of London moving ride. No prams allowed in attractions
- 🍽 **Eat and drink** *Snacks* Caffè Nero *(Marylebone Road, NW1 5LR; 8am–6:30pm Mon–Fri, 8:30am–7:30pm Sat–Sun)* serves small eats. *Real meal* The Boathouse Cafe *(Boating Lake, Hanover Gate, Regent's Park, NW1 4NR; 020 7724 4069)* sells pizzas, pastas and salads.
- 🛍 **Shop** In the exit lobby
- 👫 **Toilet** A-list Party and Sports zones

Waxwork of British Olympic diving medal winner Tom Daley

their heroes in the melee. But go when it's quieter, ideally on a weekday morning, and there's no denying the glamour of walking into the first hall – a celebrity party where the likes of Kate Winslet, Robert Pattinson and Emma Watson are waiting for their close-up. Most of the models are spookily lifelike, and there are no ropes to segregate visitors from "VIPs", so you really can rub shoulders with the stars. Younger children may prefer the Hollywood hall, with its rampaging dinosaur and giant Shrek, while downstairs they can play simulated tennis and football (queues permitting), as Nadal and Beckham look on.

In the basement, the Scream horror attraction has live serial killers jumping out of shadowy corners – not for the under-13s. Younger kids can head straight for the two attractions at the end; a ride through London's history in a black cab and a 4D film in which Spider Man, the Hulk and Wolverine battle baddies in modern London.

Letting off steam

Regent's Park is very close – from York Gate, turn right to find the Marylebone Green playground.

⑥ Sherlock Holmes Museum

Home of the world's most famous detective

It's hard to think of many museums devoted to fictional characters – and indeed, some fans refuse to believe that Sir Arthur Conan Doyle's great detective didn't exist. There is a file of genuine letters

The Lowdown

- 🌐 **Map ref** 3 A6
  Address 221b Baker Street, NW1 6XE; 020 7224 3688; *www.sherlock-holmes.co.uk*
- 🚗 **Train** Marylebone **Tube** Baker Street **Bus stop** Baker Street, Marylebone Road
- 🕐 **Open** 9:30am–6pm daily
- 💲 **Price** £20–40
- 👫 **Guided tours** None
- 👫 **Age range** 8 plus
- 🕐 **Allow** Up to 1 hour
- ♿ **Wheelchair access** No
- 🍽 **Eat and drink** *Snacks* Caffè Saporito *(14 Melcombe Street, NW1 6AH)* is great for breakfasts, pizza or dessert. *Real meal* Nando's *(113 Baker Street, W1U 6RS)* serves Afro-Portuguese flame-grilled chicken, plus a Nandino's menu for under 10s.
- 🛍 **Shop** Next door
- 👫 **Toilet** In basement

here, from people around the world, asking for Sherlock Holmes's help with solving their own personal mysteries.

Holmes the sleuth, repeatedly revived by Hollywood, lives on in this moody Victorian townhouse, though kids unfamiliar with the tales will feel a little clueless. The first mystery is the address: why is 221b Baker Street between numbers 237 and 241? Inside, staircases creak, gas-lamps splutter and Dr Watson lurks on the landing, ushering visitors into Holmes's study to sit in his chair, or even puff on his pipe.

Youngsters in period hats, outside the front door of 221b Baker Street

The other five rooms are filled with clues and murder weapons from his famous cases. It is atmospheric, if rather kitschy, and there's not much on more recent screen adaptations. One puzzle remains: why isn't the cleaner dressed up as Mrs Hudson?

Letting off steam

Regent's Park is 2 minutes away, with pedaloes and a playground at nearby Hanover Gate.

⑦ The Wallace Collection

No Gromit, but lots of armour and The Laughing Cavalier

First impressions can be deceptive. The Wallace Collection looks like a typical hushed and highbrow museum of old, a marbled mansion dripping with weighty chandeliers and gilt-framed Old Masters. Even its splendid restaurant has bibbed waiters and pricey food.

However, the Wallace is very keen to woo families: it has teamed up with pupils from a nearby school to create a children's "acoustiguide" and I-Spy trails, and has published a kids' art book based on key exhibits, for sale in the shop.

The collection was mostly put together by the Francophile Fourth Marquess of Hertford in the 1800s and is especially strong on French furniture and Sèvres porcelain – look out for Catherine the Great's tea set. Children will be most excited by the rooms full of gleaming armour displays, which include Rajput warrior regalia and medieval knights on horseback. Upstairs, a series of stuccoed salons are lined with fine art, including Titians, Rembrandts, 22 Canalettos and a certain very famous jovial horseman.

Letting off steam

There is an excellent playground at **Paddington Street Gardens** *(Paddington Street, W1U 4EF; ages 3–11)*, just north of the museum.

The Lowdown

- 🌐 **Map ref** 9 B2
- **Address** Hertford House, Manchester Square, W1U 3BN; 020 7563 9500; www. wallacecollection.org
- 🚆 **Train** Marylebone **Tube** Bond Street, Baker Street **Bus stop** Baker Street, Oxford Street
- 🕙 **Open** 10am–5pm daily
- 💲 **Price** Free
- 🚩 **Guided tours** General tours Wed, Sat, Sun 11:30am and 3pm; themed tour daily 1pm
- 👫 **Age range** 5 plus
- 🎨 **Activities** Two free children's trails plus multimedia guide with touch-screen games (£4). There is armour to try on in the Conservation Gallery. Little Draw art workshops 1st Sun of the month (1:30–4:30pm), plus family events in school holidays
- ⏱ **Allow** 2 hours
- ♿ **Wheelchair access** Yes
- 🍴 **Eat and drink** Snacks Caffè Fratelli *(108 Wigmore Street, W1U 3RW; 020 7487 3100)* sells solid Italian staples and tasty light bites *Real meal* Wallace Restaurant offers an all day menu with European dishes, afternoon teas and dinner (Fri and Sat only)
- 🛍 **Shop** Ground floor
- 🚻 **Toilets** Lower ground floor

A "Meet Marie Antoinette" costumed talk at the Wallace Collection

Picnic under £20; **Snacks** £20–40; **Real meal** £40–60; **Family treat** £60 or more (based on a family of four)

The City
and the East End

Now synonymous with global money markets and the Bank of England, the City of London (or Square Mile) is also where London began – the Romans built a wall around it in AD 200, parts of which still survive. The area is brimful of brilliant buildings and history. The vibrant East End has undergone a radical transformation since Jack the Ripper's time and is now filled with a host of stylish galleries and fun Sunday markets.

Highlights

The Monument
Climbing this memorial comes with a deep sense of occasion – 311 steps to the top, then out onto a blustery balcony 50 m (164 ft) above the City (see p124).

Tower of London
The Tower's famous Beefeaters deliver the most entertaining tour in London. Ask them what happened to the luckless Duke of Monmouth (see pp122–3).

St Paul's Cathedral
It is polite to whisper in church – but high inside the dome here, a whisper travels further than most. The curious acoustics are captivating for kids (see pp130–1).

Postman's Park
This picnic-friendly spot houses a most touching memorial – hand-painted tiles recall people who gave their lives to save others. Bring a hankie (see p136).

Bank of England Museum
This museum is surprisingly welcoming to families – no sign of a pinstripe suit – and where else can you lift up a gold ingot worth more than a house (see p132)?

Here be dragons
Dragons are the City's legendary guardians, and there's great fun to be had tracking them down on statues and street signs. Start hunting at the Guildhall (see p133).

Left Stately and magnificent, St Paul's Cathedral is one of London's most famous landmarks **Above** The fascinating engine room at Tower Bridge

The Best of
The City and the East End

With 300,000 workers and only 10,000 residents, the City is best tackled at the weekend. The focus of the area is a triangle of top attractions: the Tower of London, St Paul's Cathedral and the Museum of London, one of the capital's most exciting museums for families. Meanwhile, beyond the shiny towers of the financial quarter, a lively young arts community has blossomed around Old Spitalfields Market and the Whitechapel Gallery.

A City weekend

For families, the ideal City weekend begins on Saturday morning with Framed Film Club at the **Barbican** (see p138), where curators wheel out activities on trolleys before the movie. There's a great foodhall for lunch and also a deli, so if the weather's kind, walk to **Postman's Park** (see p137) for a picnic. Next, head for **St Paul's Cathedral** (see pp128–9) (it's closed to visitors on Sundays). It offers a family multimedia guide with hidden facts especially for younger visitors.

On Sunday, begin with brunch and a browse at **Old Spitalfields Market** (see p138). Don't linger too long, though, because the **Tower of London** (see pp122–3) is waiting. A tour with a Beefeater is a great introduction, while children get to meet medieval damsels and fire crossbows in the armoury display. Round off the weekend with a bite to eat at nearby **St Katharine's Dock** (see p126).

Roaming with Romans

The City of London was first established by the Romans in the 1st century and many traces of them can still be seen. Start at the **Museum of London** (see pp136–7), which has a mock 2,000-year-old street and offers young visitors an activity pack full of Roman fun and games.

Around the corner on Noble Street stands the best surviving part of Roman London's defensive wall, which once stretched all the way from modern-day Tower Bridge to Blackfriars. Next,

Below Looking down at the intricate floor of St Paul's Cathedral from the Whispering Gallery

stroll east along Gresham Street to the **Guildhall Art Gallery** (see p133) to see the remains of a Roman amphitheatre. A sound and light show brings gladiatorial combat back to life.

Head south to Queen Victoria Street to see the remains of the 3rd-century Temple of Mithras, then hit **Leadenhall Market** (see p124), once the site of London's original Roman forum, to eat.

Nursery-rhyme London

It's amazing how many children's nursery rhymes have their roots in London's history. Begin tracing them at **St Olave's Church** (see p125), where a plaque recalls the burial of Old Mother Goose in 1586. St Olave was an 11th-century Norwegian king who saved London from invading Vikings by towing away London Bridge with his ships – which probably inspired *London Bridge is Falling Down*. The spooky skulls on the church's gateway remember the plague victims buried here, so why not play a game of *Ring-a-Ring-o-Roses* in nearby Seething Lane Gardens? "We all fall down" is thought to refer to people dying of the plague.

Next, head for **The Monument** (see p124), built after the Great Fire of 1666, for a rousing chorus of *London's Burning*.

Finish at **St Mary-le-Bow Church** (see p131) whose great bell is mentioned in *Oranges and Lemons*, and also tolled to call back Dick Whittington to become Lord Mayor of London: Dick's statue presides over nearby Guildhall Yard (see p133).

Money, money, money

From pirate treasure to gold bars, there's no escaping money in the world's second-biggest banking centre. Goldsmiths first gathered here

Above View of the Tower of London from the River Thames
Below Guildhall Art Gallery bringing the gladiator combat of London's Roman amphitheatre to life

in the 15th century and a walk along Lombard Street takes in London's earliest finance houses, with their curious banking signs. After gazing at some modern temples of Mammon (the Lloyd's Building, the "Gherkin"), visit the **Bank of England Museum** (see p132), where children can see a £1,000,000 note.

Nearby, 100 years ago, workmen dug up the world's finest cache of Tudor gems: the Cheapside Hoard. These may originally have been plundered by pirates, and some now glitter at the **Museum of London** (see pp136–7). Even they are outshone, of course, by the Crown Jewels at the **Tower of London** (see pp122–3).

Tower of London and around

Begun in 1078 by William the Conqueror to subdue his new Anglo-Saxon citizens, the Tower of London has extended its special brand of hospitality to the likes of Anne Boleyn, Guy Fawkes and Captain Blood. There's a full day of family fun here, so book online to skip the queues, and try to avoid weekends. The Tower, the Monument and St Katharine's Dock all have an outdoor dimension, so this area is good to visit on a sunny day.

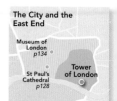

The City and the East End

Museum of London p134

St Paul's Cathedral p128

Tower of London

Places of Interest

SIGHTS
1. Tower of London
2. The Monument
3. Leadenhall Market
4. All Hallows by the Tower
5. Tower Bridge
6. St Katharine's Dock
7. Whitechapel Gallery

● **EAT AND DRINK**
1. Apostrophe
2. Ebb
3. Bodean's
4. The Perkin Reveller
5. Jonathan's Sandwiches
6. Pod
7. Pret A Manger
8. Pizza Express
9. Eat
10. Café Rouge
11. Kilikya's
12. Ping Pong
See also Tower of London (p122), Leadenhall Market (p124) and Whitechapel Gallery (p127)

● **WHERE TO STAY**
1. Apex City of London
2. Grange City
3. Hamlet (UK)

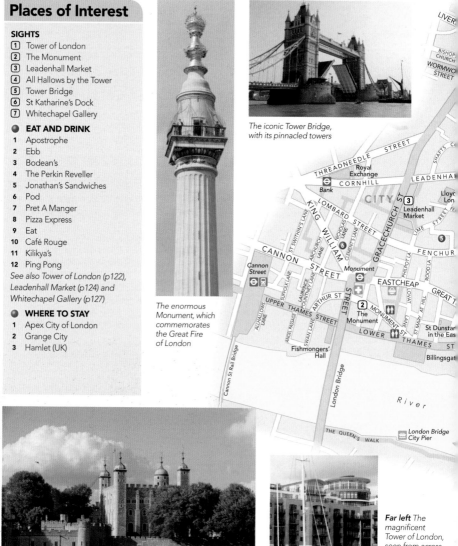

The iconic Tower Bridge, with its pinnacled towers

The enormous Monument, which commemorates the Great Fire of London

Far left The magnificent Tower of London, seen from across the River Thames **Left** The attractive and vibrant marina at St Katharine's Dock

Enjoying an arts and crafts workshop at the cutting-edge Whitechapel Gallery

The Lowdown

🚗 **Train** Fenchurch Street, Cannon Street or Tower Gateway (Docklands Light Railway) **Tube** Tower Hill, Monument, Aldgate or Aldgate East **Bus** Tower Bridge Approach: route numbers 42, 78, RV1; Tower Hill: 15, 25, 100; Gracechurch Street (for the Monument): 35, 40, 47, 48, 149, 344 **River bus** Tower Pier, to Embankment and Woolwich Arsenal via London Eye, Greenwich (0870 781 5049, www.thamesclippers.com); to Greenwich and Westminster via London Eye (020 7740 0400; www.citycruises.com). St Katharine's Pier, circular to Westminster via Embankment, Festival Pier, Bankside Pier (020 7936 2033; www.crownriver.com); to Westminster and Thames Barrier via Greenwich (020 7930 4097; www.thamesriverservices.co.uk)

ℹ️ **Visitor information** See pp128–29

🧺 **Supermarkets** Tesco Metro, 6 Eastcheap, EC3M 1AE; or (much larger) Waitrose at 41 Thomas More Street, St Katharine's Dock, E1W 1YY **Markets** St Katharine's Dock (food), 11am–2pm Fri. Leadenhall Market (general), 11am–4pm Mon–Fri. Petticoat Lane Market (clothing), Middlesex Street, E1 10am–2:30pm Mon–Fri; 9am–2pm Sun

🎊 **Festivals** City of London Festival, music and arts (Jun–Jul); The Mayor's Thames Festival, Tower Bridge (Sep); City Life Family Festival, Leadenhall Market (Sep); Leadenhall Market Winter Festival and Christmas lights (from mid-Nov)

➕ **Pharmacies** Boots, 54 King William St, EC4R 9AA (7:30am–7:30pm Mon–Fri, 10am–4pm Sat). For 24-hour pharmacies, visit www.nhs.uk/servicedirectories

👟 **Nearest playground** Tower Hill Gardens, corner of Tower Hill and Minories Hill

① Tower of London
A pop-up-book castle in modern London

With its stories of beheadings, child-slayings and torture, the Tower has a gory appeal for kids. There are ramparts to patrol, spiralling staircases, execution sites and chambers full of treasure. The interiors are interactive, too: meet a minstrel in Henry III's medieval palace, try on a helmet in the Peasants' Revolt exhibit and fire a crossbow in the White Tower. Touching the Crown Jewels is still banned, however – the last time the guards allowed that, in 1671, Colonel Blood tried to stuff them down his breeches.

A Beefeater standing guard

Key Features

Jewel House The Crown Jewels, including the royal sceptre, which holds one of the largest diamonds in the world, are stored here.

White Tower This houses Henry VIII's armoury – visitors can handle the replica weapons.

Wakefield Tower This has a rack for stretching, manacles for dangling and the "scavenger's daughter", for crushing people to a pulp.

Traitors' Gate Prisoners, many on their way to die, entered the Tower by boat through these gates.

Entrance

Traitor's Gate

Bloody Tower Known as such after the strange disappearance here of 12-year-old Edward V and his 9-year-old brother in 1483. Their uncle, Richard III, was next in line to the throne and is the prime suspect.

Beauchamp Tower The walls are etched with prisoners' graffiti. The inscription "Jane" recalls Lady Jane Grey, who was executed at the age of 17.

Tower Green Queen Anne Boleyn, one of Henry VIII's wives, was beheaded here. She expected a late pardon, so no coffin was made. They buried her in an arrow box.

The ravens Housed at night, the six ravens are now the only prisoners here. Legend says that if they ever leave, the tower and the kingdom will fall.

The Lowdown

🌐 **Map ref 12 G4**
Address Tower of London, EC3N 4AB; 0844 482 7777; www.hrp.org.uk/toweroflondon

🚗 **Train** London Bridge, Fenchurch Street, Tower Gateway (Docklands Light Railway – DLR) **Tube** Tower Hill. **Bus stop** Tower Bridge Approach, Tower Hill **River bus** Tower Pier and St Katharine's Pier

🕐 **Open** Mar–Oct: 9am–5:30pm Tue–Sat; 10am–5:30pm Sun–Mon; Nov–Feb: till 4:30pm (last admission 30 minutes earlier)

💲 **Price** £55–59

👥 **Skipping the queue** Book online beforehand (prices are lower,

too); or the day before your visit from ticket office on Tower Hill

🚩 **Guided tours** Free 45-minute tours every 30 minutes; themed audio tours (extra charge)

👫 **Age range** 5 plus, although torture exhibition and Yeoman Warder tour can be scary

🎭 **Activities** Activity books available free from the Welcome Centre. Downloadable family trails, and an Explore Kit that also covers HMS *Belfast* and Tower Bridge. Costumed interpreters daily in St Thomas's Tower, plus free family fun days on 1st Sat of the month and regular school-holiday children's events.

Tower Moat ice rink, Nov–Jan (extra charge; www.toweroflondonicerink.com)

⏱ **Allow** At least half a day

♿ **Wheelchair access** Limited – there's a downloadable map of accessible areas on the website

☕ **Café** The Armouries Café offers children's meal deals, high-chairs and a microwave for baby food

🛍 **Shops** Five shops selling play armour, books and sweets

👫 **Toilets** Behind Waterloo Block

Good family value?
London's most popular visitor attraction – and it deserves to be.

Enjoying a picnic in the sunshine in the Tower of London's grounds

Letting off steam

There's plenty of running-about room inside the Tower, along the ramparts and on the grass, while riverside **Tower Wharf** is traffic-free, and boasts picnic benches and cannons for youngsters to clamber over. Alternatively, cross Tower Hill to the corner of **Minories Hill**, where you'll find a new playground with swings and slides.

Eat and drink

Picnic: under £20; Snacks: £20–40; Real meal: £40–60; Family treat: £60 or more (based on a family of four)

PICNIC Picnicking is encouraged at the Tower. Try the moat (in summers), the benches around the White Tower, or the riverside at Tower Wharf, where award-winning café **Apostrophe** (8am–6pm Mon–Fri, from 9am Sat & Sun) sells super sandwiches.

SNACKS Head for St Katharine's Dock, and **Ebb** *(Ivory House, E1W 1AT; 020 7702 9792)*, a cute coffee house by the water that sells good milkshakes and boasts comfortable seats and a vibrant atmosphere.
REAL MEAL Bodean's *(16 Byward Street, EC3R 5BA; 020 7488 3883; www.bodeansbbq.com; noon–11pm; till 10:30pm Sun)* offers sizzling barbecue dishes, as well as delicious salads and vegetarian options. One child eats free with an adult between noon and 5pm daily.
FAMILY TREAT The Perkin Reveller *(The Wharf, EC3N 4AB; 020 3166 6949; www.perkinreveller. co.uk; 10am–9:30pm Mon–Sat, till 4pm Sun)*, a modern-day dining hall with views across the Thames, serves delicious meals using seasonal British ingredients.

Find out more

DIGITAL See if you have what it takes to don some armour, grab a weapon and challenge King Henry VIII, at *henryviiidressedtokill. viral-game.co.uk/*. For more kid-friendly information with fun trivia, games and photos, visit *www.hrp.org.uk/palacekids*.

Next stop...

TRINITY SQUARE GARDENS Across Tower Hill in this park *(Tower Hill, EC3N)*, a plaque marks the site of the Scaffold, where 125 churchmen and nobles were publicly beheaded while jugglers and acrobats entertained the crowd. Their heads were placed on spikes along London Bridge.

Youngsters sword-fighting against the impressive backdrop of the Tower

② The Monument

Climb up among the rooftops for views over London

Three centuries before the London Eye, it was possible to admire the city's skyline from 50 m (164 ft) aloft. The view is hard earned: there are 311 corkscrewing steps to reach the caged platform atop The Monument, erected by Sir Christopher Wren in the 1670s to remember the Great Fire of London.

The fire broke out in September 1666, in a bakery in nearby Pudding Lane, and within three days it had reduced 13,000 homes, 87 churches and St Paul's Cathedral to ashes. The good news: it also saw off the Great Plague, which had wiped out 100,000 people the year before.

The Monument is still the world's tallest free-standing column and must have been a marvel in its day. Wren built a laboratory in the basement for conducting his experiments, but soon it was open for visitors. The climb is a challenge for little legs, but well worth it to emerge among the spires and skyscrapers of modern London. The telescope commentaries are hardly worth bothering with; instead, just savour the fabulous views. There is a certificate for everyone who makes it down again intact.

Letting off steam

Still got some puff left after the big climb? A few minutes east, via Lower Thames Street, is the bombed-out shell of the church of St Dunstan in the East (Dunstan's Hill, EC3R), now a garden and perfect for a picnic.

The viewing deck at the top of Wren's grand Monument

Prices given are for a family of four

The Lowdown

- 🌐 **Map ref** 12 F4
  Address Monument Street, EC3R 8AH; 020 7626 2717; *www.themonument.info*
- 🚆 **Train** London Bridge or Fenchurch Street **Tube** Monument **Bus stop** Gracechurch Street
- 🕐 **Open** 9:30am–6pm daily (to 5:30pm Oct–Mar); last admission 30 mins before closing
- 💷 **Price** £12; combined ticket with Tower Bridge Exhibition £32
- 🧍 **Skipping the queue** At weekends, arrive before 11am to avoid waiting
- 👫 **Age range** 5 plus
- ⏱ **Allow** 30 minutes
- ♿ **Wheelchair access** No
- ☕ **Eat and drink** *Picnic* Jonathan's Sandwiches (*17 Cullum St, EC3M 7JJ*), sells excellent salt beef sandwiches *Snacks* Pod (*75 King William St, EC4N 7BE; 020 7283 7460*) serves good salads, noodles and wraps
- 🚻 **Toilets** In nearby Monument Street

③ Leadenhall Market

From Dick Whittington to Harry Potter

This area has a fascinating 600-year history – and it really looks the part. The warren of cobbled arcades is encased in fancy ironwork and lit by quaint lanterns, while pillars gleam in bold carousel colours – cream, claret and green. Snarling dragons guard every corner and there are topsy-turvy taverns and streetwise shoeshine stands. It's like looking into a Victorian kaleidoscope.

The centre of Roman London was here – the ruins of its 1st-century basilica, the same length as St Paul's Cathedral, lie buried beneath the Lamb Tavern. In 1411, the merchant Richard (Dick) Whittington, of pantomime fame, donated Leadenhall to the City of London, and by 1800 it was Europe's best-supplied market, specialising in beef and game.

The arcades were designed in 1881, and now host gourmet butchers and cheesemongers, slick brasseries and bars, plus Pandora's Box and Ben's Cookies for sweet treats. As a family lunch spot, Leadenhall has genuine wow factor – especially when you reveal the Harry

The interior of historic Leadenhall Market, with its bustling cafés

Potter connection. Bull's Head Passage was transformed into Diagon Alley, where our hero buys his wand in *Harry Potter and the Philosopher's Stone*.

Letting off steam

Head towards the Tower of London, to the excellent playground on the corner of Minories (*see p123*).

The Lowdown

- 🌐 **Map ref** 12 F3
  Address Gracechurch Street, EC3V 1LR; *www.leadenhall market.co.uk*
- 🚆 **Train** Fenchurch Street, Bank (DLR) **Tube** Bank or Monument. **Bus stop** Gracechurch Street
- 🕐 **Open** 10am–6pm Mon–Fri; market stalls 11am–4pm
- 💷 **Price** Free
- 🧍 **Skipping the queue** Aim to be there before 1pm, when the eateries fill up with City workers
- 🏃 **Activities** Winter Festival with lunchtime concerts (mid-Nov); City Lights Family Festival, Sep
- ♿ **Wheelchair access** Yes
- ☕ **Eat and drink** *Snacks* Chop'd (*1 Leadenhall Mkt, EC3V 1LR*), serves hearty but healthy stews, broths and sandwiches *Real meal* Ortega (*27 Leadenhall Mkt, EC3R 5AS*) gets busy at lunchtime but the tapas are good
- 🚻 **Toilets** In Monument Street

Grim skull and bone reliefs above the entrance to St Olave's church

④ All Hallows by the Tower

Boudicca, beheadings… and brass-rubbing

London's oldest church is packed to the tower-top with quirky history, from the battles of Boudicca to beheaded bodies and the glowing embers of the Great Fire of 1666.

Begin in the crypt, where a pristine chunk of 2nd-century pavement was uncovered in 1926, along with a layer of ash dating from Queen Boudicca's burning of the city in AD 60. There's also an intricate model of Roman London to look at and scraps of salvaged pottery from imperial days.

Fast forward to Saxon times – an archway survives from the original 7th-century church, revealed suddenly when a bomb blasted the building during World War II. In the 16th century, All Hallows took in the headless corpses from Henry VIII's execution scaffold (*see p123*), including that of Sir Thomas More. The church survived the Great Fire of London thanks to the quick wits of Admiral William Penn (father of Penn of Pennsylvania fame), who blew up nearby buildings to create a fire-break. Meanwhile, Penn's next-door neighbour, Samuel Pepys, climbed the steeple to watch the blaze – having first buried his prized truckle of Parmesan in his garden.

If that doesn't impress the kids, they can take home their very own medieval knight – the church's visitor centre offers brass-rubbing sessions most weekday afternoons.

Letting off steam

Cross Byward Street into Seething Lane Gardens to St Olave's Church – worth a peek for its spooky skulls and crowded plague graves. The woman thought to be responsible for bringing the plague to London is buried here, along with nursery-rhyme character Mother Goose.

Above *The Saxon archway from the original 7th-century All Hallows*
Below *Exposed Roman pavement inside All Hallows*

The Lowdown

- 🌐 **Map ref** 12 G4
  Address Byward Street, EC3R 5BJ; 020 7481 2928; www.ahbtt.org.uk

- 🚆 **Train** Fenchurch Street, Tower Gateway (DLR) **Tube** Tower Hill, Monument **Bus stop** Tower Hill

- 🕐 **Open** 8am–5pm Mon–Fri; 10am–4pm Sat; Sung Eucharist service takes place at 11am on Sundays

- 💷 **Price** Free

- 👫 **Activities** Free guided tours are available most weekdays from 2–4pm Apr–Oct. Occasional themed walking tours in the City (£8 per person) take between 90 minutes to 2 hrs. Check website for dates and times

- ♿ **Wheelchair access** Yes

- 🍴 **Eat and drink** *Picnic* Pret A Manger (12 Byward Street, EC3R 5AS; 6am–7pm Mon–Fri, 8:30am–5:30pm Sat–Sun; www. pret.com) offers sandwiches and salads *Real meal* Pizza Express (1 Byward Street, EC3R 7QN; 11:30am–11pm Mon–Sat, 11:30am–10pm Sun; 020 7626 5025; www.pizzaexpress.com) is a perennial favourite with families

- 🚻 **Toilets** In Tower Place, next door

Tower Bridge opening to allow a high-masted boat through

5 Tower Bridge

The legend of the flying bus driver

"Tawdry … pretentious … absurd". When Tower Bridge opened in 1894, the architecture critics didn't think much of Horace Jones's flamboyant Gothic design. Today, it is London's number-one icon, and its drawbridge-style bascules (the "see-saw" parts) are still raised 1,000 times a year to allow ships to pass. The patriotic paint scheme, first added in 1977 to mark the 25th anniversary of the accession of Queen Elizabeth II, used 22,000 litres (4,840 gallons) of red, white and blue paint.

The bridge's high walkways were designed for pedestrians – but nobody wanted to climb the 300 stairs to use them. Today, an elevator whisks visitors 42 m (138 ft) up onto the twin gantries, for breathtaking views along the river. Little ones may need lifting up to get the full impact, though there's an Explore Kit to keep them occupied, and stickers to collect en route.

Displays focus on bridge trivia, including stories about straying whales, cheeky fighter pilots and Albert Gunter, the "flying bus-driver", who found himself airborne in 1952 when the bascules opened while his No. 78 bus was still crossing the bridge.

The exhibition continues in the Victorian engine rooms, showing off the shiny steam turbines that powered the bridge until 1976, when oil, electricity and hydraulics took over. Here, kids can get to grips with interactive models: for example, sit an unsuspecting sibling in a chair, turn a handle, and watch them suddenly lurch skywards.

Letting off steam

At the southern end of the bridge, on the right as you cross north to south, lies **Potters Fields** *(www. pottersfields.co.uk)*. It is possibly the most panoramic picnic spot in London.

6 St Katharine's Dock

London's floating treasure trove

Hidden behind a phalanx of high buildings, St Katharine's Dock is one of London's loveliest backwaters, where a powerhouse of the Industrial Revolution has been transformed into a jaunty marina lined with yachts and waterside cafés. It's a great place to kick back after tramping around the Tower of London.

The dock's roots as a shipping hub date back to the 10th century, when King Edgar granted 5 ha (13 acres) to 13 knights, with permission to trade. It grew into a prosperous and important mercantile area over the centuries. In the 1820s, the great civil engineer Thomas Telford built the basins we see today, and their warehouses were stacked high with treasure from across the British Empire – marble, ivory, wine, spices and perfume. As late as the 1930s, St Katharine's was reckoned to hold the world's largest concentration of portable wealth.

These days, the warehouses have been turned into office blocks and the money is not in the cargoes, it's in the boats themselves. For children, a wander among the yachts and pleasure cruisers is a glorious glimpse into life afloat.

The Lowdown

- 🌐 **Map ref** 12 H5
  Address Tower Bridge Road, SE1; 020 7403 3761; *www.towerbridge. org.uk*
- 🚆 **Train** Fenchurch Street, London Bridge, Tower Gateway (DLR) **Tube** Tower Hill **Bus stop** Tower Bridge Approach **River bus** Tower Pier, St Katharine's Pier
- 🕐 **Open** Apr–Sep: 10am–5:30pm; Oct–Mar: 9:30am–5pm (last admission one hour earlier)
- 💲 **Price** £21–36, under-5s free; combined ticket with The Monument £31–42
- 🚶 **Skipping the queue** Buy tickets online to avoid queuing
- 🔫 **Guided tours** Available for groups of 10 or more only (extra charge)
- 👫 **Age range** 5 plus
- 🏃 **Activities** A kids' passport, from the ticket desk, has stickers to collect. Separate Explore Kit must

be downloaded beforehand (also covers Tower of London, HMS *Belfast* and All Hallows by the Tower). School-holiday activities might include Victorian games and storytelling

- ⏱ **Allow** 1 hour
- ♿ **Wheelchair access** Yes, via lifts and an alternative ramped route
- 🍴 **Eat and drink** *Picnic* Eat (2 Tower Hill Terrace, EC3N 4EE; 020 7488 1526) is a chain of sandwich bars selling freshly prepared wraps, salads, sandwiches and juices. *Real meal* Café Rouge (50 St Katharine's Way, St Katharine's Dock, E1W 1AA; 020 7702 0195; *www.cafer-ouge.co.uk*) is a chain French bistro set in a pretty spot beside St Katharine's Dock
- 🛍 **Shop** At end of visit
- 👫 **Toilets** In South Tower and Engine Rooms

Boats in the pretty marina at St Katharine's Dock

The Lowdown

🌐 **Map ref** 12 H5
Address St Katharine's Way, E1W 1LA; 020 7488 0555; www.skdocks.co.uk

🚆 **Train** Fenchurch Street, Tower Gateway (DLR) **Tube** Tower Hill. **Bus stop** Tower Hill Approach, East Smithfield **River bus** St Katharine's Pier, Tower Pier

🏃 **Activities** Fine food market on Fri outside Dickens Inn (11am–3pm). Check website for lock opening times – a good time to see boats enter and exit the dock

👫 **Age range** All

⏱ **Allow** Up to 1 hour

♿ **Wheelchair access** Yes

🍴 **Eat and drink** Picnic Kilikya's (St Katharine's Dock, E1W 12 AT) serves delicious pastries, mezes, smoothies and freshly squeezed juices Real meal Ping Pong (Tower Bridge House, E1W 1BA) sells tasty, reliable Chinese food

🚻 **Toilets** Near Starbucks coffee shop (Cloister Walk, E1W 1LA)

Letting off steam

The Tower Hill/Minories playground (see p123) is reached via the underpass to Tower Hill tube station.

⑦ Whitechapel Gallery

Art on the edge

Little Miss Muffet is menaced by a malevolent tarantula. A cute teddy bear suffers an extremely grisly disembowelling. When commissioning artists to mastermind a new exhibition for children, Jake and Dinos Chapman may not seem like an obvious

Creating a masterpiece in one of the Whitechapel Gallery's workshops

choice. But the Whitechapel Gallery likes to push boundaries.

The gallery has been at the cutting edge of contemporary art since 1901, introducing the likes of Frida Kahlo, Jackson Pollock and Gilbert & George to British audiences. In 2009 a £13 million revamp doubled the exhibition space and added a dedicated children's studio on the top floor. The Chapman Brothers' 2010 summer show typified the Whitechapel's thought-provoking approach to art for kids.

The gallery offers free workshops and family days most weekends, and 1–2 day courses (cost varies), inspired and often led by artists. Available all the time is the Make It Yours art detective kit, loaded with scrapbook, stickers and drawing materials.

Letting off steam

Head past Aldgate tube station to find the playground overlooking the Tower of London (see p123).

(see p123)

KIDS' CORNER

Which bridge?

1 Which of London's bridges, opened in 2000, was nicknamed the "Wobbly Bridge" because it swayed when people first walked across it?
2 Which famous bridge over the Thames was sold to an American businessman and rebuilt stone by stone in Arizona?
3 Which bridge is nicknamed "Ladies Bridge", because it was built by women while the men were away fighting in World War II?

Answers at the bottom of the page.

Flying high

The most spectacular Tower Bridge crossing ever was by Robbie Maddison, who did a back-flip as he flew across the open drawbridge on his motorbike, 30 m (98 ft) above the river, in 2009. Watch a film of the feat at the Tower exhibition. But that's nothing. Robbie holds the world record for the longest motorbike jump, at 106.9 m (351 ft) – longer than ten buses!

Sculpture trail

The sculptures scattered around St Katharine's Dock hark back to some of the riches that were once traded there. See if you can find a pair of elephants, a peacock and a turtle. Which precious goods do you think these creatures provided?

jewellery
feathers; turtles for tortoiseshell
ivory; peacocks for hat and fan
Bridge **Sculpture trail** Elephants for
Bridge **2** London Bridge **3** Waterloo
Millennium
Answers: Bridges 1

The Lowdown

🌐 **Map ref** 12 H2
Address 77–82 Whitechapel High Street, E1 7QX; 020 7522 7888; www.whitechapelgallery.org

🚆 **Train** Liverpool Street, Tower Gateway (DLR) **Tube** Aldgate East. **Bus stop** Whitechapel High Street, route numbers 15, 25, 115, 135

⏰ **Open** 11am–6pm Tue–Sun; till 9pm Thu

💲 **Price** Free; charge for special temporary exhibitions

👫 **Age range** 4 plus

🏃 **Activities** Free children's trail suits ages 4–12; weekend and school-holiday children's workshops (check website)

⏱ **Allow** 1 hour

♿ **Wheelchair access** Yes

🍴 **Eat and drink** Snacks The gallery's café-bar claims to make London's best brownies Family treat For something more upscale, try the Gallery Dining Room

🛍 **Shop** Selling art books and cards

🚻 **Toilets** Ground, basement and 2nd floor

Picnic under £20; Snacks £20–40; Real meal £40–60; Family treat £60 or more (based on a family of four)

St Paul's Cathedral and around

Left smouldering by the Great Fire of London in 1666, London's grandest church owes its modern-day magnificence to the great Renaissance architect Christopher Wren, who spent almost 40 years on his masterpiece. Best visited at the weekend, its most dramatic approach with children is on foot via the pedestrianized promenade from Millennium Bridge. Join a guided walk (free for under-12s) from the nearby City of London Information Centre, then climb the cathedral's famous dome and enjoy the fantastic views of the city's skyline.

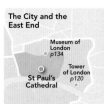

The City and the East End

Museum of London p134

St Paul's Cathedral

Tower of London p120

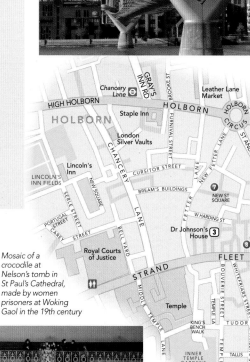

The Millennium Bridge, linking the Tate Modern on Bankside with St Paul's Cathedral and the City

Places of Interest

SIGHTS
1. St Paul's Cathedral
2. Bank of England Museum
3. Dr Johnson's House
4. Guildhall Art Gallery

● **EAT AND DRINK**
1. Starbucks
2. The Café at St Paul's
3. Byron
4. Barbecoa
5. Chop'd
6. Tortilla
7. The Natural Kitchen
8. Ye Olde Cheshire Cheese
9. Hummus Bros
10. The Café Below

● **WHERE TO STAY**
1. Cheval Calico House

Mosaic of a crocodile at Nelson's tomb in St Paul's Cathedral, made by women prisoners at Woking Gaol in the 19th century

The Whispering Gallery in St Paul's Cathedral – a whisper against its walls is audible on the opposite side

The Lowdown

🚗 **Train** Blackfriars, Cannon Street, City Thameslink **Tube** St Paul's, Mansion House **Bus** Fleet Street/Cannon Street: route numbers 4, 11, 15, 23, 26, 76, 172; Threadneedle Street (for Bank of England): 8, 11, 23, 26, 242, 388; Cheapside (for Guildhall): 8 and 25 **River bus** Blackfriars Pier, weekday-only services between London Eye and Woolwich or Blackfriars Pier to Putney via Chelsea (0870 781 5049; www.thamesclippers.com).

ℹ️ **Visitor information** City of London Information Centre, St Paul's Churchyard, EC4M 8BX;

www.cityoflondon.gov.uk/things-to-do/visiting-the-city/pages/default.aspx

🛒 **Supermarkets** M&S Simply Food, 3a One New Change, EC4M 9AF; Sainsbury's Local, 10 Paternoster Square, EC4M 7DX; Tesco Metro, 80b Cheapside, EC2V 6EE **Markets** Leadenhall Market (mostly fine food), 11am–4pm Mon–Fri; Leather Lane Market (North of Holborn Circus; mixed stalls), 10:30am–3pm Mon–Fri

🎡 **Festivals** London Maze history festival, Guildhall (Apr); City of London Festival, music and arts

(Jun–Jul); Pearly Kings and Queens Harvest Festival, St Mary-le-Bow (Sep); The Lord Mayor's Show, procession from Mansion House and fireworks (2nd Sat in Nov); Christmas at St Paul's, carols and services (Dec)

➕ **Pharmacies** Boots, 104 Cheapside, EC2V 6DN (7am–7pm weekdays; 9am–6pm Sat; closed Sun). For 24-hour pharmacies, visit www.nhs.uk/servicedirectories

🛝 **Nearest playground** Fortune Street Park, Fortune Street, EC1 0RY (north of the Barbican)

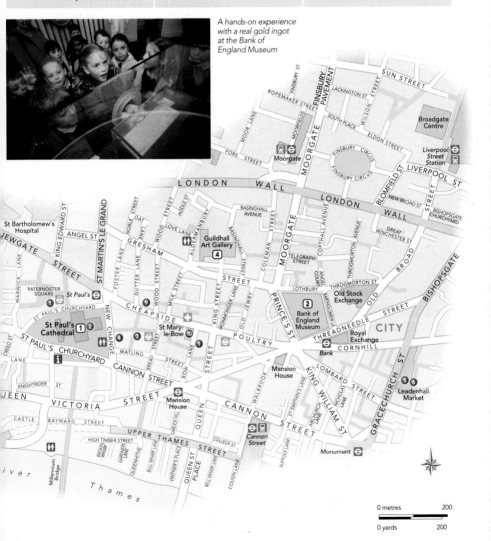

A hands-on experience with a real gold ingot at the Bank of England Museum

0 metres 200

0 yards 200

① St Paul's Cathedral

Possibly the most spectacular church in Christendom

Boasting Britain's biggest bell, Europe's largest crypt and a dome weighing 64,000 tonnes, St Paul's is a superlative building. Its shadowy crypt is full of famous memorials, including those of the Duke of Wellington, Florence Nightingale and Admiral Nelson, but what children will adore is counting the steps to the Whispering Gallery, and the magical sound effects they can create there. The family audio guide keeps things fun, with cartoons, quizzes and nuggets of trivia designed to dazzle even grown-ups.

Wellington Monument

The Lowdown

🌐 **Map ref** 11 D3
Address The Chapter House, St Paul's Churchyard, EC4M 8AD; 020 7246 8350 or 020 7246 8357; www.stpauls.co.uk

🚗 **Train** Cannon Street, Blackfriars **Tube** St Paul's, Mansion House **Bus stop** St Paul's Churchyard **River bus** Blackfriars Pier

🕐 **Open** 8:30am–4:30pm Mon–Sat (last admission 4pm); cathedral galleries 9:30am–4:15pm. Attending services is free, including Evensong, 5pm Tue–Sat and 3:15pm Sun

💲 **Price** £36.50–41.50, under-6s free

👫 **Skipping the queue** Buy tickets online beforehand – it's cheaper and allows use of the new fast-track entrance

🔫 **Guided tours** Free 90-minute tours four times daily, plus multimedia guide

👫 **Age range** 6 plus

🏃 **Activities** Family multimedia guide (English only); or download self-guided children's tours before visiting

⏱ **Allow** Up to 2 hours

♿ **Wheelchair access** Yes, except for the Whispering, Stone and Golden galleries, and the Triforium, which are reached via many steps

☕ **Café** The café in the crypt (see opposite), plus the more formal restaurant alongside

🛍 **Shop** In the crypt, selling books and souvenirs

👫 **Toilets** Beside the café

Good family value?
Cheaper than Westminster Abbey – and a visit includes a free workout to reach one of the most spectacular views in London.

Key Features

The Dome It's as heavy as 50,000 elephants, so Wren cleverly designed a dome within a dome, to bear the weight. As it was built, he was hauled up in a basket twice a week to inspect it.

Old St Paul's The old cathedral, at 149 m (489 ft), was taller than the new one (111 m/ 364 ft), as a model in the crypt shows.

① **Golden Gallery** Lying at the highest point of the dome, it's a pull up all those steps. It's worth the effort – visitors are rewarded with a spellbinding view across London at the top.

② **Whispering Gallery** The quirky acoustics inside the spectacular dome throw a whisper all the way around the walkway, making this an atmospheric echo chamber kids will love.

Oculus This exciting multimedia show, in the former Treasury in the crypt, brings the cathedral's 1,400 years of history to life.

Florence Nightingale's Memorial The hospital reformer first came to prominence as a nurse during the Crimean War (1853–6). She was the first woman to receive the Order of Merit.

Florence Nightingale's Memorial

Oculus

Wellington Monument This tribute to one of Britain's most famous soldiers is in the North Aisle. He died in 1852 – his tomb is in the crypt.

Nelson's Tomb Buried in a coffin hollowed out of the mast of a defeated French flagship, Horatio Nelson gets star billing in the centre of the crypt. Look for seafaring symbols in the mosaic floor.

A quiet spot under the shade of the trees in the gardens at St Paul's Cathedral

Letting off steam

The cathedral's churchyard has small lawns to loll on, or there are the **Festival Gardens** right next door, with a sunken lawn, cooling wall fountain and a great view back to the Dome. Alternatively, how about a romp on the panoramic rooftop of **One New Change** (*www.onenewchange.com*), the sleek shopping centre just east of the cathedral? Six floors high, it claims to be London's loftiest public terrace, and there's a café, too.

Eat and drink

Picnic: under £20; Snacks: £20–40; Real meal: £40–60; Family treat: £60 or more (based on a family of four)

PICNIC Starbucks (*1 Paternoster House, Unit 7, EC4M 7DX; 010 7236 3014*) serves teas, coffees, sandwiches, salads and pastries to eat in or take away – perhaps into neighbouring Paternoster Square, whose stone benches are broad enough for a full family picnic.
SNACKS Located in the crypt of the cathedral, **The Café at St Paul's** (*9am–5pm Mon–Sat, 10am–4pm Sun*), is open to all and specializes in classic British food. Pick a ploughman's lunch from the "Barrow in the Crypt", with ingredients sourced from Borough Market (*see p146*).
REAL MEAL Lots of options in the One New Change centre, including **Byron** (*17 Upper Cheapside Passage, EC2V 6AG; 020 7236 1855; www.byronhamburgers.com*). Serving classy burgers (and knickerbocker glories!), Byron has a dedicated children's menu that includes all the usual favourites.
FAMILY TREAT Barbecoa (*20 New Change Passage, EC4M 9AG; 020 3005 8555; www.barbecoa.com; 11:30am–11pm Mon–Fri; noon–11pm Sat; to 10pm Sun*)

is the hot ticket here, co-owned by celebrity chef Jamie Oliver and majoring in chargrilled meats. There's a selection of seafood starters as well as fish of the day. There is no children's menu but the chef will happily adapt dishes to suit children's tastes.

Find out more

DIGITAL Family trails are available to download from the St Paul's website: *www.stpauls.co.uk*
FILM The children's classic *Mary Poppins* has lovely dreamlike sequences featuring St Paul's, including the "Feed the Birds" scene on the cathedral's steps.

Next stop. . .

ST MARY-LE-BOW CHURCH
Walk along to St Mary-le-Bow church (*Cheapside, EC2V 6AU*), another Christopher Wren gem, with an extravagant tower and a golden dragon atop its steeple. It's said you must be born within the sound of Bow Bells to be a true Cockney. There's a very cosy café in the crypt (*see p133*).
GUIDED WALKS AND TOURS
Opposite St Paul's, the City Information Centre (*Cannon Street, EC4M 8BX*) is the starting point for walks exploring the oldest part of London: discover more Wren churches or learn about Samuel Pepys every Wed & Sun at 2pm (*adults £7, under-12s free*).

The "feed the birds" scene from the 1964 film Mary Poppins, set outside St Paul's

② Bank of England Museum

Crack a safe, grab some gold

Walking into the grand hall of this museum is one of the more surprising experiences in London. There are kids everywhere: piloting hot-air balloons, designing bank notes, cracking safes. This playroom approach strives to make simple economics palatable to young minds – never an easy task.

The hot-air balloon works as an effective metaphor for the nation's finances and kids can get their hands on the controls. Nearby, there's a safe to unlock with the help of quiz answers gathered from around the room.

The rest of the museum is more sober and includes a £1 million note and a gold ingot worth more than £300,000, which children can try their hand at lifting. Look out for the showcase featuring Ratty and

The Lowdown

- **Map ref** 12 E3
  Address Bartholomew Lane, EC2R 8AH; 020 7601 5545; www. bankofengland.co.uk/museum
- **Train** Cannon Street or Bank (DLR) **Tube** Bank **Bus stop** Threadneedle Street
- **Open** Weekdays only 10am–5pm (last admission 4:45pm)
- **Price** Free
- **Skipping the queue** Queues rare
- **Guided tours** None, but free audio tour
- **Age range** 5 plus
- **Activities** Five different children's trails, graded from pre-school to ages 15–17. School holiday events
- **Allow** 1 hour
- **Wheelchair access** Yes, via ramps, please call in advance
- **Eat and drink** Snacks Chop'd (1 Leadenhall Market, EC3V 1LR; 0207 626 3706; www. chopd.co.uk; 7am–3pm Mon–Fri) offers all-natural healthy food Real meal Tortilla (28 Leadenhall Market, EC3V 1LR; 020 7929 7837; www.tortilla.co.uk; 11am–7pm Mon–Fri) does finger-licking Mexican fast food
- **Shop** Souvenirs and gifts
- **Toilets** At the rear of museum

The Sir John Soane-designed building housing the Bank of England Museum

Mole, creations of Wind in the Willows author Kenneth Grahame (1859–1932), who was secretary to the bank from 1879 to 1908.

Letting off steam

The skyscrapers of the **Broadgate Centre** (Eldon Street, EC2M 2QT) enclose traffic-free squares, including grassy **Exchange Square**, with its train-set view down into Liverpool Street Station, and **Broadgate Circle**, whose ice rink is open daily Nov–Feb (www.broadgateinfo.net).

③ Dr Johnson's House

The home of an English eccentric

He collected orange peel, wore the same clothes for weeks, and liked to start every journey with the same foot. But the eccentric Samuel Johnson was a London legend, and

Dressing up in period costume in Dr Johnson's House

The Lowdown

- **Map ref** 11 B3
  Address 17 Gough Square, EC4A 3DE; 020 7353 3745; www. drjohnsonshouse.org
- **Tube** Chancery Lane **Bus stop** Fleet Street
- **Open** Mon–Sat 11am–5:30pm; Oct–Apr till 5pm
- **Price** £10, under-5s free
- **Skipping the queue** Queues rare
- **Guided tours** None; Johnson's London walks, 1st Wed of the month (see website)
- **Age range** 9 plus
- **Activities** Free kids' guide. Occasional concerts and jazz evenings. Activities and trails are organised during school holidays
- **Allow** Up to 1 hour
- **Wheelchair access** No, there are some unavoidable steps
- **Eat and drink** Picnic The Natural Kitchen (15–17 New Street Square, Fetter Lane, EC4A 3AP; 020 7353 5787; www.thenaturalkitchen. com; 7am–6pm Mon–Fri) has a fresh feel to its take-away food. Real meal Ye Olde Cheshire Cheese (145 Fleet Street, EC4A 2BU; 020 7353 6170; 11am–11pm daily) is a 17th-century pub.
- **Shop** Selling books, booklets, posters and souvenirs
- **Toilets** Basement

the great and the good gathered at his house off Fleet Street to enjoy his witty conversation. Today, Dr Johnson is remembered mainly for his English dictionary, compiled here in the 1750s, with a team of scribes who copied literary snippets to illustrate 42,000 definitions. It took nine years to write, during which the debt-ridden Johnson once had to barricade the door with his bed to fend off bailiffs.

Johnson's jokes will fly over the heads of most children, but there is a film telling his story and a dressing-up rack of Georgian frockcoats to try on. Point out the spiked window above the door, to deter burglars from smuggling boy accomplices inside; and challenge kids to track down Hodge, Johnson's spoilt cat. Clue: he's out on the tiles.

Letting off steam

Head west across Fetter Lane to **Lincoln's Inn Fields** (WC2A) with its picnic-perfect lawns and public tennis courts (see p94).

④ Guildhall Art Gallery

Where gladiators fought

Dragons, Dick Whittington, Britain's biggest painting and a ruined Roman amphitheatre – these are just some of the unlikely attractions at the Guildhall Gallery. It stands beside the 15th-century Guildhall, seat of City government since medieval times, whose courtyard has a statue of Dick Whittington, every child's favourite Lord Mayor. The yard is menaced on all sides by dragons, the City's armorial emblem – ideal for a game of I-Spy.

The gallery itself is dominated by John Singleton Copley's eye-popping painting *The Siege of Gibraltar* (1791) – so big that it occupies two floors. Youngsters may prefer the Undercroft Galleries downstairs, lined with sentimental Victorian pictures of children, including John Everett Millais' funny portraits of his daughter dozing off in church.

The main reason to come here, though, lurks in a dark cavern in the basement – the ruins of London's 2,000-year-old Roman amphitheatre, stumbled upon by archaeologists in 1988. In Roman times, up to 6,000 people sat here to watch bloody animal fights, public executions and gladiatorial combat – to the death. Scant foundations survive, but children won't notice that, because spotlights and sound effects do a brilliant job of bringing the arena to life. Stride in through the eastern entrance, as gladiators once did long ago, past the pens used to hold wild beasts, and listen to the deafening roar of the crowd.

The Lowdown

- 🗺 **Map ref** 12 E2
- **Address** Guildhall Yard, Gresham Street, EC2V 5AE; 020 7332 3700; www.cityoflondon.gov.uk/things-to-do/visiting-the-city/attractions-museums-and-galleries/
- 🚇 **Tube** St Paul's, Bank, Moorgate **Bus stop** Cheapside
- 🕐 **Open** 10am–5pm Mon–Sat; noon–4pm Sun (last admission 30 minutes earlier)
- 💷 **Price** Free (fee charged for some exhibitions); under-16s free
- 🚶 **Skipping the queue** Queues rare; go after 3:30pm (or any time on Fri) for free admission
- 🪧 **Guided tours** Fri pm only (free)
- 👫 **Age range** 5 plus
- 🎨 **Activities** Sketching tables in the Undercroft Galleries
- ⏱ **Allow** Up to 1 hour
- ♿ **Wheelchair access** Yes
- 🍴 **Eat and drink** *Snacks* Hummus Bros (128 Cheapside, EC2V 6BT; 020 7726 8011; 7:30am–9pm Mon–Thu, 7:30am–5pm Fri, 11am–5pm Sat) offers hummus and pitta breads with tasty toppings *Real meal* The Café Below (Cheapside, EC2V 6AU; 020 7329 0789; 7:30am–2:30pm Mon & Tue, to 9:15pm Wed–Fri) serves rustic European dishes in the crypt of St Mary-le-Bow Church
- 🛍 **Shop** Near reception
- 🚻 **Toilets** Floor C by cloakroom

Letting off steam

St Mary Aldermanbury Garden (EC2 2EJ), behind the Guildhall, has picnic benches and a majestic bust of William Shakespeare. The master playwright's contemporaries, John Hemynge and Henry Condell, are commemorated in the gardens; it is to them that we owe the printing of Shakespeare's *First Folio* of work.

The Siege of Gibraltar, *one of the UK's biggest paintings at the Guildhall Art Gallery*

Picnic under £20; **Snacks** £20–40; **Real meal** £40–60; **Family treat** £60 or more (based on a family of four)

Museum of London and around

A £20 million revamp has made the Museum of London a supremely welcoming place for families, from the pink-shirted "hosts" to the hands-on exhibits that animate London's story. Arrive on foot along Aldersgate Street from St Paul's tube station, and take the escalator on the right-hand pavement. Weekends are the prime time to visit, when there are fewer school parties, free family events on Sundays and children's films every Saturday at the nearby Barbican. To combine the museum with Old Spitalfields Market, take the Hammersmith & City line from Barbican to Aldgate East.

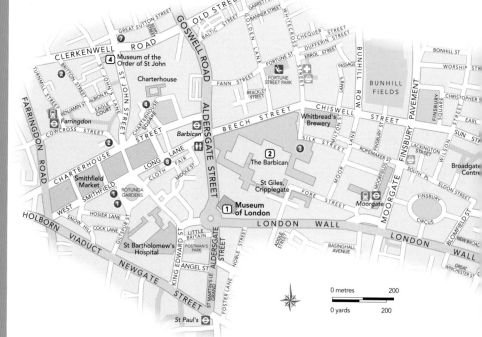

Prisoners' elegant graffiti in an 18th-century cell at the Museum of London

Built in 1757, the Lord Mayor's state coach in the Museum of London is beautifully crafted and still used for the Lord Mayor's Parade

Places of Interest

SIGHTS

1. Museum of London
2. The Barbican
3. Old Spitalfields Market
4. Museum of the Order of St John

● EAT AND DRINK

1. Carluccio's
2. Farm
3. Barbican Foodhall
4. Malmaison Brasserie
5. Patisserie Valerie
6. The Breakfast Club
7. Benugo
8. Dose

See also The Museum of London (pp137) and the Barbican (p138)

● WHERE TO STAY

1. Market View by Bridge Street
2. Eagle Court

The Lowdown

🚇 **Train** Moorgate (5-minute walk), Liverpool Street, Farringdon (10-minute walk); Shoreditch High Street (for Spitalfields Market) **Tube** Barbican, Moorgate, St Paul's **Bus** Moorgate; route numbers 4, 56; London Wall: 100; Barbican tube station: 153; King Edward Street: 8, 25, 242, 521

ℹ️ **Visitor information** See pp128–29

🛒 **Supermarkets** Waitrose, 6L Cherry Tree Walk, EC1Y 8NX. Marks & Spencer, 70 Finsbury Pavement, EC2A 1SA
Markets Leather Lane Market (mixed stalls), 10am–3pm Mon–Fri. Petticoat Lane Market (clothing), Middlesex Street, E1, 10am–2:30pm Mon–Fri; 9am–2pm Sun. Spitalfields Market (antiques, fashion and art), 10am–5pm Mon–Wed; 9am–5pm Thu & Sun; 11am–5pm Sat

🎪 **Festivals** East Festival, arts (Jun). Blaze Festival, music and dance, Barbican Centre (Jun–Jul). City of London Festival, music and arts (Jun–Jul). Story of London Festival, history (Aug). London Children's Film Festival, Barbican Centre (Nov); Spitalfields Music Festivals (Jun–Jul; Dec–Jan)

➕ **Pharmacies** Portman's Pharmacy, Cherry Tree Walk, 5 Whitecross Street, EC1Y 8NX (9am–8:30pm Mon; 9am–6:30 Tue–Fri; 9am–5pm Sat). For 24-hour pharmacies, visit www.nhs.uk/servicedirectories

🛝 **Nearest playgrounds** Christ Church play area (Commercial Street, E1 6LY); Fortune Street Park (Fortune Street, EC1Y 8)

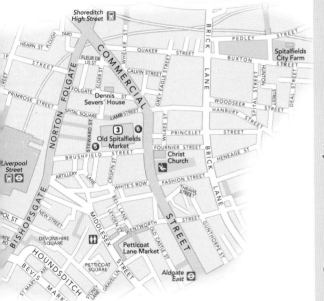

Face to face with a goat at the popular Spitalfields City Farm

① Museum of London
Don't touch? Don't be so old-fashioned!

It's not easy to bring 450,000 years of history to life for children, but the Museum of London does just that, using a mix of interactive gadgetry and eye-catching presentation. The upstairs rooms are arranged chronologically and are packed with prehistoric skulls and Roman treasures, while the Galleries of Modern London resemble a series of spectacular stage sets – including a shadowy Georgian prison cell and a Victorian high street. The excellent activity trails and backpacks encourage kids to explore.

Bronze age shield and helmet c.350–50 BC

Key Features

Entrance

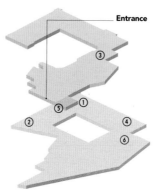

① Victorian Walk Window-shop along a lively Victorian high street, complete with toy shop, pub, bank and barber's shop. The fixtures and fittings are all original.

② Wellclose Prison Cell Enter the dark, claustrophobic cell from a 1750 debtors' prison, its walls scratched with the names of desperate inmates and echoing with their pleas for mercy.

③ Archaeology in Action Get to grips with ancient pottery and other precious booty found in London at the artifact-handling sessions.

■ **Entrance level** History of London from 450,000 BC to the 1660s: Roman London; Medieval London; War, Plague and Fire

■ **Lower Galleries** History of London from 1670s to Today: Expanding City; Victorian Walk; People's City; Modern London

④ Evacuees' Trunks Lift the lids to read real-life letters from schoolchildren on the eve of World War II – and discover what they packed for their flight from London.

⑤ Georgian Pleasure Gardens Explore this re-creation of an 18th-century park, with its harlequins, acrobats and elegant ladies in fancy hats. Children were expected to behave like miniature adults.

⑥ Bill and Ben Find out what children's TV was like in the 1950s, by exploring the wall of toys and TV screens in the museum's Playtime Zone.

The Lowdown

🌐 **Map ref** 11 D2
Address 150 London Wall, EC2Y 5HN; 020 7001 9844; www.museumoflondon.org.uk

🚗 **Tube** Barbican, Moorgate, St Paul's **Bus stop** Moorgate Street, Barbican Station, London Wall

🕐 **Open** 10am–6pm daily

💷 **Price** Free

🧍 **Skipping the queue** Grab a ticket on arrival for the guided tours – they are free, but numbers are limited

🚩 **Guided tours** Free tours of specific galleries four times a day; plus guided walks around the City monthly

🧍 **Age range** 4 plus

🤸 **Activities** Free activity sheets and packs from the welcome desk for ages 4–7 and 7–11. Interactive quizzes and costumes to try on throughout the galleries. There are also regular free family events at the weekends and in school holidays that are constantly updated, and for under-5s there is a rolling programme (www.museumoflondon.org.uk/London-Wall/Visiting-us/Families)

⏱ **Allow** At least 2 hours

♿ **Wheelchair access** Yes

🍽 **Cafés** The museum's Benugo café sells good sandwiches and salads, and has a kids' lunch deal and high-chairs. The Sackler Hall café does lighter bites. Plus, there's an indoor picnic area in the Clore Learning Centre, across the forecourt

🛍 **Shop** In the entrance lobby, selling books, cards and posters related to the exhibitions

🚻 **Toilets** Behind lobby area

Good family value?
Absolutely crawling with children, and with all the hands-on activities and trails, it's easy to see why.

Prices given are for a family of four

Nursery Garden at the Museum of London – one of two small gardens

Letting off steam

The nearest playground is 10 to 15 minutes away, at Rotunda Gardens (5-minute walk) and Fortune Street (10–15 minute walk). **Postman's Park** is much closer, just across Aldersgate Street beside St Botolph's church. It doesn't have climbing apparatus, but there is a small spread of lawns and benches, plus the moving George Frederic Watts Memorial, which honours ordinary folk who sacrificed their lives saving others. Each is remembered on a painted tile, and there are several poignant tales of childhood bravery to discover.

Eat and drink

Picnic: under £20; Snacks: £20–40; Real meal: £40–60; Family treat: £60 or more (based on a family of four)

PICNIC Carluccio's *(12 West Smithfield, EC1A 9JR; 020 7329 5904; www.carluccios.com/caffes/ smithfield; 8am–11pm Mon–Fri, 9am–11pm Sat, to 10:30pm Sun),* just up the road, beside the splendid Victorian halls of Smithfield meat market, offers deli-style delights. Opposite, the shady benches of West Smithfield Park make ideal picnic territory. Postman's Park (see above) is also a good picnic spot.

The Sackler Hall coffee shop in the Museum of London

SNACKS Head towards Smithfield Market, where **Farm** *(91 Cowcross Street, EC1M 6BH; 020 7253 2142; www.eetapp.com/restaurants/farm-collective-restaurant-london-uk-1491; 11:30am–11pm daily)* offers delicious, carefully sourced pies and fishcakes at reasonable prices. **REAL MEAL** The **Barbican Foodhall** *(Barbican Centre, Silk Street, EC2Y 8DS; www.barbican. org.uk/restaurants-bars/barbican-foodhall; 9am–8pm Mon–Sat, 12:30–8pm Sun & bank holidays)* serves up a variety of no-nonsense main courses and salads in its buffet overlooking the arts centre's courtyard. There are even a few board games available to keep the kids entertained. **FAMILY TREAT** The plush burgundy-and-black **Malmaison Brasserie** *(18–21 Charterhouse Square, EC1M 6AH; 0844 693 0656; www.malmaison.com; 7am–10pm Mon–Fri; 8am–11pm Sat & Sun)* has a serious commitment to sourcing seasonal and local ingredients. It is also a very family-friendly place, offering smaller portions for children on request.

Find out more

DIGITAL The museum's website has history-themed games and challenges for kids: survive life as a medieval apprentice, or help aliens dig up household objects from the past. Lots more at *www. museumoflondon.org.uk/Explore-online/Games/.* Play "Roman snakes and ladders", and discover more about real historic artifacts on the way, at *http://romans.tulliehouse. co.uk/flash/snakes/index.htm.*

Next stop...

DENNIS SEVERS' HOUSE After breezing through London's entire history in half a day, try a different kind of museum: Dennis Severs' House *(5–9pm Mon; check website for additional times: bookings required for eve session; 18 Folgate St, E1 6BX; 020 7257 4013; www. dennissevershouse.co.uk)* is a unique time capsule created by a Canadian designer. He furnished his home as a series of still-life tableaux spanning two centuries, as though the occupants have just stepped outside. It's not for younger children, though.

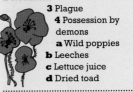

KIDS' CORNER

Kill or cure

Medieval doctors had strange ideas about how to cure the sick, even tasting patients' wee to find out what was wrong with them! Match these ailments with their medieval medicines:
1 Bad eyesight
2 Headache
3 Plague
4 Possession by demons
a Wild poppies
b Leeches
c Lettuce juice
d Dried toad

Answers at the bottom of the page.

In the closet

The museum's collection has some amazing things – from 17,000 skeletons to 1,000 penny toys that belonged to a man called Ernest King when he was a boy. Some are in the toy shop in the Victorian Walk. Do you have any toys the museum might want one day?

Toy trail

Find more historic toys in the downstairs galleries, and answer the questions below:
1 What's for dinner at the Blackett's Dolls' House?
2 What colour are Daisy the Fashion Doll's boots?
3 What is the name of Bill and Ben's friend in the children's TV programme?

Answers at the bottom of the page.

On the tiles

Make your own mosaic like the one in the Roman dining room. Take five sheets of coloured paper and cut them into small triangles and squares. Now make your own pattern from the pieces and glue it down. Can you make a bird, a love-heart or a flower?

Answers: Kill or Cure 1-c 2-a 3-d 4-b
Toy trail 1 Fish 2 Red 3 Little Weed

② The Barbican
Cartoons and crazy art

If you're looking for somewhere to lose the children, the Barbican might just be it. With its innumerable entrances and tangles of stairways and courtyards, Europe's biggest multi-arts complex is a little difficult to navigate. Never fear – head for the main entrance round the back on Silk Street, which curves down into the heart of things.

Inside is a vast black-and-orange bunker packing in two theatres, two art galleries, a music and dance space, a library, three restaurants and three cinemas.

Bustling Old Spitalfields Market filled with a variety of stalls

Ensconced in the Saturday Film Club at the Barbican

There is always something happening and it's often for kids, from the Family Film Club every Saturday morning to a fistful of annual festivals, including the London Children's Film Festival in November and Animate the World in May. The Curve Gallery on Level 0 showcases the kind of conceptual art that's guaranteed to excite the imagination of children, and the library on Level 2 also has a great children's section.

Check the website to find out what's on, or just drop in and enjoy the food hall, overlooking an urban lake with lily-pads and a waterfall.

Letting off steam
Walk north along Whitecross Street to **Fortune Street Park** (see p136), where swings and scrambling nets will keep the kids happy.

③ Old Spitalfields Market
London's liveliest and coolest marketplace

The first market at "Spittle Fields" was licensed to sell flesh, fowl and roots by King Charles I in 1638, but the area's wholesale green-grocers outgrew the site in 1991, paving the way for an inventive community of craftspeople and designers to move in.

Today, Spitalfields Market is cutting-edge cool and on a busy Sunday up to 1,000 traders specializing in vintage fashion, bespoke jewellery and gifts set up stalls. The vibe is youthful and positive – a winner with fashion-conscious kids. Stalls operate every day except Monday and Saturday, but Sunday is when things really get going.

Don't miss a browse among the offbeat boutiques that have popped up in adjoining streets, too – including Wood 'n' Things (57 Brushfield Street, E1 6AA), for high-quality toys and dolls, traditional wooden toys, well-crafted doll's houses, train sets, as well as sit-and-ride toys. The market's "food village" serves aromatic dishes from the world over, while a fine foods market runs on Thursday, Friday and Sunday in nearby Crispin Place.

Just south of Old Spitalfields, along Middlesex Street, lies historic Petticoat Lane Market, a more down-to-earth affair where traders have been shouting their wares since the 1750s – mostly street clothing, leather goods and shoes.

The Lowdown

🌐 **Map ref** 11 D1
Address Silk Street, EC2Y 8DS; 020 7638 4141, Box Office 020 7638 8891; www.barbican.org.uk

🚗 **Train** Liverpool Street, Farringdon, Blackfriars **Tube** Barbican **Bus stop** Barbican tube station, London Wall

🕐 **Open** 9am–11pm Mon–Sat; noon–11pm Sun

💷 **Price** Shows and exhibitions individually priced. Access to Curve Gallery, library, restaurants and courtyard is free

👪 **Skipping the queue** Online booking available for most events

🚩 **Guided tours** Architecture tours Wed, Sat and Sun; £38

👫 **Age range** All

👫 **Activities** Framed Film Club (Sat 11am) lays on art activities before

the film on the last Saturday of each month. Special teenager tickets for London Symphony Orchestra concerts and talks are also available. Do Something Different weekends (Mar & Jul) offer activities for all. Check website for full programme

♿ **Wheelchair access** Yes, via Silk Street entrance

🍴 **Eat and drink** Snacks Barbican Foodhall (see p137) offers deli fare, which can be eaten on its courtyard tables. Family treat The Barbican Lounge (Level 1) and Searcy's (Level 2) are more formal

🛍 **Shops** Foyer Shop (Level G) selling CDs and books; Art Gallery Shop (Level 3) selling souvenir books and posters

🚻 **Toilets** On most levels

The Lowdown

- 🌐 **Map ref** 12 G1
- **Address** 105a Commercial Street, E1 6BG; 020 7247 8556; www.oldspitalfieldsmarket.com
- 🚃 **Train** Liverpool Street **Tube** Liverpool Street, Aldgate East **Bus stop** Commercial Street, Bishopsgate
- 🕐 **Open** Spitalfields: 10am–5pm Mon–Wed & Sat–Sun; 9am–5pm Thu; 10am–4pm Fri. Petticoat Lane: 10am–2:30pm Mon–Fri; 9am–2pm Sun
- 💲 **Price** Free
- 🚻 **Age range** All
- 🏃 **Activities** Spitalfields Music Festival, biannually in Jun–Jul and Dec–Jan (www.spitalfieldsmusic.org.uk)
- ♿ **Wheelchair access** Yes, the market is accessible but may be difficult to navigate if busy
- 🍴 **Eat and drink** Snacks Patisserie Valerie (37 Brushfield Street, E1 6AA) offers salads, wraps and gorgeous homemade Italian ice cream. Real meal The Breakfast Club (12–16 Artillery Lane, E1 7LS) serves brilliant brunches
- 🚻 **Toilets** In the market and surrounding restaurants and cafés

Letting off steam

There is a small play area beside Christ Church, opposite the market on Commercial Street. Alternatively, head east to Buxton Street, where kids can commune with Bayleaf the donkey, Bentley the goat and friends at **Spitalfields City Farm** (closed Mon; admission free; Buxton Street, E1 5AR; www.spitalfieldscityfarm.org).

Costumed guide at the Museum of the Order of St John

④ Museum of the Order of St John

From nurses to knights

There's something distinctly magical about visiting the historic home of real knights in the heart of London. The building certainly looks the part – built in 1504, it is a remnant of the priory of the Knights Hospitallers, the medieval crusaders who went from helping sick pilgrims in Jerusalem to fighting Saladin.

The museum uses TV screens, armour and artifacts to relay its stirring story of chivalric sacrifice. A separate gallery is devoted to the St John's Ambulance movement, the 20th-century reincarnation of the order, still based here. It may be fairly conventional, but the museum succeeds in bringing history to life.

Letting off steam

The peaceful lawns at **Rotunda Gardens** (West Smithfield, EC1A 9BD) belie its grisly past as an execution site. Those executed include the Scottish knight William Wallace (1305); today there is a jolly new playground.

The Lowdown

- 🌐 **Map ref** 11 C1
- **Address** St John's Gate, St John's Lane, EC1M 4DA; 0207 324 4005; www.museumstjohn.org.uk
- 🚃 **Train** Farringdon **Tube** Farringdon **Bus stop** Farringdon Road, Clerkenwell Road
- 🕐 **Open** 10am–5pm Mon–Sat; closed 22 Dec–1 Jan
- 💲 **Price** Free (optional donation £5)
- 🎫 **Guided tours** 11am and 2:30pm (free) Tue, Fri and Sat
- 🚻 **Age range** 8 plus
- 🏃 **Activities** Challenge Trail (ages 6–11) plus sticker trail for younger kids (free); actor-led interpretation sessions; drop-in craft activities,

3rd Sat of the month, plus school-holiday workshops
- ♿ **Wheelchair access** Main galleries are accessible, but crypt and upper floor are reached via stairs
- 🍴 **Eat and drink** Picnic Benugo (116 St John Street, EC1V 4JS; 020 7253 3499; www.benugo.com) does made-to-order sandwiches and salads for eating in or out Snacks Dose (70 Long Lane, EC1A 9EJ; 020 7600 0382; www.dose-espresso.com) serves up great salads, homemade bread and cakes
- 🛍 **Shop** A small gift shop
- 🚻 **Toilets** Ground floor

Southwark
and the South Bank

The South Bank first blossomed as an arts district in 1951, when it was chosen as the focal point for the Festival of Britain. However, it took another 50 years, and the opening of the London Eye, for the area to finally become a prime visitor destination. Today, it offers an irresistible array of family-friendly attractions, from Shakespeare's Globe and Tate Modern to the National Theatre and IMAX Cinema.

Bloomsbury and
Regent's Park

The City and
the East End

Westminster
and the
West End   **Southwark and
the South Bank**

Kensington,
Chelsea and
Battersea

Highlights

The *Golden Hinde*
Every child loves a pirate fancy-dress party – and there's no more authentic place to enjoy one than aboard Sir Francis Drake's gorgeous treasure galleon. Ahoy, matey *(see p150)*!

Borough Market
The stalls of this bustling market allow brave gastronomes to explore many of the world's cuisines. Pick up a picnic, then head for the tables outside Southwark Cathedral *(see p150)*.

Imperial War Museum
Despite the planes, tanks and guns, what kids will remember

most about this museum are the personal stories, and the mud and madness of its World War I Trench Experience *(see p166)*.

River Thames RIB-boat tour
When sightseeing starts to feel a little sedate, jump aboard this speedboat for a spray-drenched blast past the London Eye and other riverside sights *(see p161)*.

The Old Operating Theatre
On Saturday afternoons, limbs are swiftly lopped off in a bloodcurdling demonstration of Victorian surgery at this museum. Needless to say, most children love it *(see p151)*.

Left Fun and frolics on the Golden Hinde – youngsters come face to face with a buccaneer during a "Pirate Days" activity session Above Marine life at the Sea Life London Aquarium

The Best of
Southwark & the South Bank

For all its imposing parks and squares, London never really had one long, traffic-free promenade – until the 21st-century transformation of the South Bank. A walkway now stretches virtually unbroken along the Thames from Tower Bridge to the London Eye, offering a terrific pleasure trail for families. Runners rush, seagulls soar, speedboats skim… and when the tide goes out, there's even a beach.

A South Bank stroll

Start at Tower Hill Tube station, and cross Tower Bridge to pick up The Queen's Walk past the imposing bulk of **HMS Belfast** (see pp152–3). From here, the City's skyline is visible across the water. At London Bridge, turn left and take the stairs down beside **Southwark Cathedral** (see p150), where Borough Market (see p146) may be in full swing (Thu–Sat) – a great place to gather a picnic for later.

Return to the river, where you'll soon pass a brace of brilliant attractions, **Shakespeare's Globe** (see pp146–7) and **Tate Modern** (see p148), both very welcoming for families. Beyond Blackfriars Bridge, break out your lunch among the craft studios and cafés of **Gabriel's**

Wharf (see p163), then press on past the **Southbank Centre** (see p164–5) to the **London Eye** (see pp160–61), its glass capsules guaranteed to elicit gasps from all. Cross Westminster Bridge to the Tube station and Big Ben – a fitting finale to a River Thames walk.

Dressing-up time

Who do you want to be today? A sea captain or a pirate? Perhaps a fighter pilot or a star of the Elizabethan stage? A clutch of museums along the South Bank offer children the chance to act the part. **Shakespeare's Globe** (see pp146–7) has sound booths where kids can play Juliet or King Lear, and there are occasional drama workshops during matinee performances.

Below The naval gunship HMS Belfast on the Thames

Left Spectacular views from the top of the London Eye
Middle Kids queue for tasty treats from Borough Market
Bottom A performer dazzling a crowd on the South Bank

Younger kids may prefer the **Golden Hinde** (see p150), a replica of Sir Francis Drake's globetrotting Tudor galleon, which holds regular pirate sleepovers for families. Nearby, **HMS Belfast** (see pp154–5) is perhaps the most atmospheric of all, evoking life on a battleship with the help of a lively children's audioguide and the chance to be a pint-sized admiral.

Two further museums, the **Fashion and Textile Museum** (see p156–7) and the **Design Museum** (see p157) will appeal to the more creative youngster interested in design.

The world's a stage

At the southern end of Waterloo Bridge is a true village for the arts, from classical music to comedy, cinema to circus. There is always plenty going on, and families are well catered for, especially during the summer festival season. The highlight is the three-month Watch This Space Festival at the **National Theatre** (see p162), which transforms the riverside into an all-singing, all-dancing performance space, complete with a dedicated children's programme.

Virtually next door, the **Southbank Centre's** (see p164) summer celebration focuses on the Udderbelly pop-up theatre, housed in an upside-down purple cow. The British Film Festival follows in October, at the nearby **BFI** (see pp162–3) – and at any time of year, it offers free film and TV in its Mediatheque suite, plus monthly film-making workshops for kids at the BFI IMAX, Britain's largest cinema screen.

In a weekend

The essential Southwark weekend begins on Saturday morning, gathering cosmopolitan edibles from Borough Market (see p146). Kids love soaking up the sounds, smells and free samples, and Monmouth coffee shop (2 Park Street, SE1 9AB) does all-you-can-eat bread and jam for £3, perfect for elevenses. Afterwards, sign up for a story-filled tour at **Shakespeare's Globe** (see pp146–7) – family fundays are on the second weekend of every month. Picnic by the river, then head off to **Tate Modern** (see p148) for the art trails.

On Sunday, head for the dark side, getting up early to beat the queue at the **London Dungeon** (see p164). Afterwards, if you can stomach it, the nearby George Inn (see p147), an atmospheric old coaching tavern, serves Sunday roast. Then it's off to view the spooky potions and pickled parts at the **Old Operating Theatre** (see p151), which has a herb-handling session at 2pm.

Shakespeare's Globe and around

The Globe is a genuine time-travel experience for children, set in a thatched theatre straight from a picture book. River bus services dock at Bankside Pier, opposite the gates. The theatre is just one of several attractions on the South Bank, so book ahead for the auditorium tour, then build the day around it. Families can happily spend a full day on museum-going, pavement-dining and people-watching – while barely encountering a single car.

Southwark and the South Bank

Shakespeare's Globe

London Eye *p158*

HMS *Belfast p152*

Southwark Cathedral, the oldest cathedral in London, dating from the 7th century

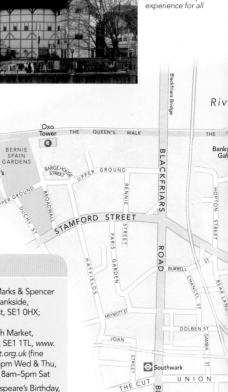

The open-roofed Shakespeare's Globe theatre – a lively experience for all

The Lowdown

🚗 **Train** Blackfriars and London Bridge stations are about a 10-minute walk away; Cannon Street, about 15 minutes away **Tube** London Bridge, Mansion House, Cannon Street **Bus** Southwark Bridge Road: route number 344; Southwark Street: RV1, 381; London Bridge: 17, 21, 35, 40, 43, 47, 133, 141, 149, 343, 521 **River bus** Bankside Pier, en route from Westminster to St Katherine's Dock (020 7936 2033; *www.crownrivercruise. co.uk*); and from London Eye to Greenwich (0870 781 5049; *www.thamesclippers.com*). The Tate to Tate Boat (020 7887 8888; *www.tate.org.uk/ tatetotate*) shuttles between Tate Britain and Tate Modern during gallery opening hours.

ℹ️ **Visitor information** City of London Information Centre *(see pp128–9)*

🛒 **Supermarket** Marks & Spencer Simply Food, Bankside, 90 Southwark St, SE1 0HX; open daily **Market** Borough Market, 8 Southwark St, SE1 1TL, *www. boroughmarket.org.uk* (fine foods), 10am–5pm Wed & Thu, 10am–6pm Fri, 8am–5pm Sat

🎊 **Festivals** Shakespeare's Birthday, the Globe (Apr); Coin Street Festival, Bernie Spain Gardens (Jun–Jul); The Mayor's Thames Festival (Sep); Bankside Winter Festival (Dec)

➕ **Pharmacies** Boots, 8–11 Hays Galleria, SE1 2HD; 020 7407 4276 (7:30am–7pm Mon–Fri, 10am–6pm Sat, 11am–5pm Sun). For 24-hour pharmacies, visit *www.nhs.uk/servicedirectories*

🎢 **Nearest playground** Little Dorrit Park (*www.london-se1.co.uk/places/ little-dorrit-park*); Mint Street Adventure Playground *(see p146)*

0 metres 100
0 yards 100

Testing the torture equipment at the Clink Prison Museum

Tasting delicious Spanish food at Brindisa, Borough Market

Places of Interest

SIGHTS
1. Shakespeare's Globe
2. Tate Modern
3. Clink Prison Museum
4. The *Golden Hinde*
5. Southwark Cathedral
6. The Old Operating Theatre

EAT AND DRINK
1. Borough Market
2. Tate Café
3. Swan at the Globe
4. OXO Tower Brasserie
5. The Rooftop Cafe
6. Gourmet Burger Kitchen
7. Caffè Nero
8. Fish!
9. Frank's Cafe
10. The George Inn

See also Shakespeare's Globe (p147), Tate Modern (p148) and Southwark Cathedral (p151)

WHERE TO STAY
1. Ibis Styles London Southwark Rose
2. London Bridge

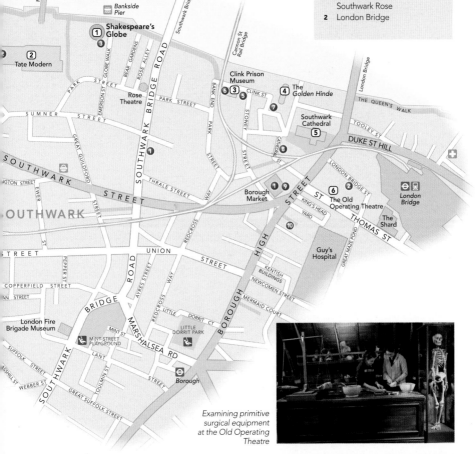

Examining primitive surgical equipment at the Old Operating Theatre

① Shakespeare's Globe

The roar of the greasepaint, the smell of the crowd

In Shakespeare's time, going to the theatre was not the genteel experience it is today. Rival acting troupes competed to attract an audience – who would drink and shout at the actors during plays packed with murder, magic and comedy. The original Globe was built nearby in 1599, after Shakespeare and his company, the Lord Chamberlain's Men, transported a playhouse, timber by timber, across the Thames from Shoreditch. Today's open-air theatre, a near replica, opened in 1997.

Detail from the Globe's gates

Key Features

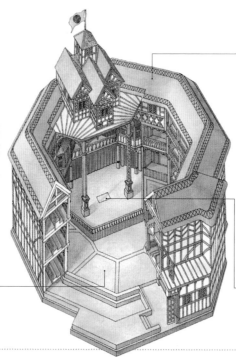

THE GLOBE IN 1600

The actors Until 1661, boys as young as 13 performed the female roles. It is believed that many died early, poisoned by the lead in their make-up.

The plays *Hamlet, Macbeth* and *Julius Caesar* all had their premieres at the original Globe Theatre. Shakespeare often performed minor roles in his own plays.

The audience 3,000 people would cram inside for a play. It cost a penny to watch from the yard – in summer, it got so smelly, these spectators were called "penny stinkards".

THE GLOBE TODAY

The building It uses 16th-century materials, such as hand-made bricks and wooden pegs, not nails. The thatched roof was the first in the city since the Great Fire of London.

The theatre season runs from April to October. After the monthly Child's Play workshops, kids get to sneak in to watch the end of the Saturday matinee.

The stage Look out for trapdoors (above and below), which allow surprise entrances by devils or ghosts in puffs of smoke, or angels and fairies flying down on ropes.

Letting off steam

When the tide is out, get down to the riverside in front of **Gabriel's Wharf** for a bit of beach time (check the tides at *www.pla.co.uk*). There is a stretch of grass in front of nearby Tate Modern, but for swings and slides, head south to **Mint Street**

At Gabriel's Wharf, kids can play on the beach in the centre of the city

Prices given are for a family of four

Adventure Playground (*Lant St, SE1 1QP*), or to **Nelson Square Garden** (*Nelson Square, SE1*), near Southwark Tube station.

Eat and drink

Picnic: under £20; Snacks: £20–40; Real meal: £40–60; Family treat: £60 or more (based on a family of four)

PICNIC Borough Market (*8 Southwark St, Borough, SE1 1TL; www.boroughmarket.org.uk; 11am–5pm Wed & Thu, 10am–6pm Fri, 8am–5pm Sat*) makes foraging for food a gastronomic, globetrotting adventure, though it's not cheap: its classy picnic offerings include Spanish hams and cheeses at

Brindisa (*www.brindisa.com*) and German bread from The Backhaus Bakery (*www.backhaus.co.uk*). **SNACKS** Tate Café (*Tate Modern, Bankside, SE1 9TG; 0207 887 8888; www.tate.org.uk/modern; open daily*) allows one child to eat for free at lunchtime when an adult chooses a main course. The café serves soup, many other savoury dishes, cakes and homemade smoothies. **REAL MEAL** Swan at the Globe (*21 New Globe Walk, SE1 9DT; 020 7928 9444; www.loveswan.co.uk; open daily – check website for times*) is located right next to the theatre with a great view of the river Thames, and specializes in upmarket pub food.

The Lowdown

- **Map ref** 11 D4
  Address 21 New Globe Walk, Bankside, SE1 9DT; 020 7902 1400; www.shakespearesglobe.com

- **Train** Blackfriars, Cannon Street, London Bridge **Tube** London Bridge, Cannon Street
  Bus stop Southwark Bridge Road, Southwark Street
  River bus Bankside Pier

- **Open** Exhibitions: 9am–5:30pm daily; Box Office: 10am–6pm daily

- **Price** Museum: visit £36–52, under-5s free. Theatre tickets from £5–£43

- **Skipping the queue** During the theatre season (late Apr–Oct), auditorium tours are mornings only; afternoon tours focus on the remains of the Rose Theatre, contemporary with the Globe

- **Guided tours** 40-minute tour included in the museum visit

- **Age range** 6 plus

- **Activities** Live demonstrations of stage combat, Elizabethan stage costumes or printing most days in the museum (phone to check). Family activity weekends (2nd weekend of month) and school holiday workshops, free with museum admission

- **Allow** Up to 2 hours

- **Wheelchair access** Yes, via lifts and ramps

- **Café** In the theatre lobby; plus the Swan at the Globe (see below left)

- **Shop** Selling theatre merchandise and souvenirs

- **Toilets** Inside exhibition space

Good family value?
The exhibition is pricey, but there's plenty happening for children, and standing tickets cost as little as £5.

Fresh artisan bread sold at The Flour Station, Borough Market

FAMILY TREAT OXO Tower Brasserie (Barge House St, SE1 9PH; 020 7803 3888; www.harveynichols.com/oxo-tower-london; open daily), eight storeys above the river, feels like dining in the sky: European cooking for grown-ups, spaghetti bolognese or sausages for kids.

Find out more

DIGITAL Watch the BBC's *Shakespeare: the Animated Tales*, collected together at www.ovguide.com/tv/shakespeare_the_animated_tales.htm. For more William Shakespeare activities, including themed word searches, jigsaws and mazes, visit www.folger.edu/shakespeare

Next stop. . .

THE GEORGE INN Head across Southwark to the George Inn (77 Borough High St, SE1 1NH; www.nationaltrust.org.uk/george-inn/) to see London's last surviving galleried coaching tavern. In the days before formal playhouses, actors performed in the cobbled courtyards of inns like this one (note: children are admitted only when accompanied by an adult).

UNICORN THEATRE The Unicorn Theatre (147 Tooley St, SE1 2HZ; 020 7645 0560; www.unicorntheatre.com) is London's dedicated children's playhouse, with family shows plus kids' workshops on Sundays.

The purpose-built Unicorn Theatre, close to Tower Bridge

KIDS' CORNER

Stage craft

There is plenty to get your hands on at the Globe…

- **Elizabethan costumes**
  Find a farthingale, a doublet and a ruff – which parts of the body were they for?

- **Musical instruments.**
  Find a cittern, a sackbut and a tabor – which would you pluck, blow or beat?

Answers at the bottom of the page.

GROSS!

Shakespeare's audiences liked violent scenes, because blood and battle were part of everyday Tudor life. On the way to the theatre, people walked past the heads of criminals, traitors and pirates put on spikes on London Bridge!

Open sesame

The Globe's amazing iron gates are decorated with every plant and animal mentioned in a Shakespeare play. From the river side, see if you can spot a crab, a dolphin and a snake. Which creature completes this sequence: vulture, crow, dove and. . . ?

Answer at the bottom of the page.

Fire! Fire!

Elizabethan special effects included cannons and fireworks to recreate battle scenes. The Globe burnt to the ground in 1613, when a cannon set the roof ablaze. Everyone escaped alive – although one man's trousers caught fire! Can you spot how the theatre is protected from fire hazards today?

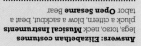

Answers: Elizabethan costumes legs, torso, neck **Musical Instruments** pluck a cittern, blow a sackbut, beat a tabor **Open sesame** Bear

② Tate Modern

Shattering, splattering, exploding… art

There's no need to worry whether children will enjoy Tate Modern. Whether it's a Jackson Pollock splatter painting, Henri Matisse's colourful collages, or Claes Oldenburg's make-believe hamburgers, chances are they have already created something along the same lines at school or in their bedroom. If not, they soon will, after a wander around London's most mind-expanding art gallery. Copying Niki de Saint Phalle, who created her paintings by shooting at them, should probably be discouraged, however.

Housed in the tall-chimneyed former Bankside Power Station, Tate Modern was a smash hit from the moment it opened in 2000, and a £215 million redevelopment has doubled the exhibition space to help soak up its five million annual visitors. The gallery offers masses for children. A dedicated team occupies the family concourse on Level 3 every weekend afternoon, suggesting art trails and challenges for kids aged five and above. The "Interactive Zone" on Level 5 is available full time, with touch-screen consoles and video clips that illuminate and explain the collection. The children's audio tour is strong on quizzes and puzzles, and there's even a "Tate Trumps" game to download as an app for iPhone – collect seven favourite works

then pit them against art chosen by friends. Exploring the gallery is less daunting than it first appears: while there are seven storeys in all, the permanent collection is only on levels 2 and 4, and is grouped by theme into four wings. A great approach is to let kids lead the way, wandering the 20 or so rooms on each floor in search of appealing pieces. Rewarding stops include Room 2 of the "Poetry and Dream" wing, for Dali; Room 1 of "Structure and Clarity" on Level 4, for Matisse; and Room 1 of "Energy and Process" for Malevich. Also look

for Cy Twombly in "Energy and Process" on Level 4. Note that the Tate often loans out or removes work for restoration so works may not always be on display. Don't leave without a visit to the Turbine Hall, right at the bottom, housing a single, huge installation.

Letting off steam

Tate Modern's new extension opens up into a piazza to the south and west of the gallery. The **Millennium Bridge** is a great spot for watching the Thames water traffic.

The Lowdown

- 🌐 **Map ref** 11 C5
  Address Bankside, SE1 9TG; 020 7887 8888; www.tate.org.uk
- 🚗 **Train** Blackfriars, Cannon Street, London Bridge **Tube** Southwark, London Bridge, Cannon Street **Bus stop** Southwark Bridge Road, Southwark Street **River bus** Bankside Pier.
- 🕐 **Open** 10am–6pm Sun–Thu; 10am–10pm Fri–Sat (last admission to exhibitions: 45 mins before closing)
- 💲 **Price** Turbine Hall and permanent collection free; temporary shows charge
- 🚶 **Skipping the queue** The extension should ease weekend congestion
- 🚩 **Guided tours** Free 45-minute tours daily at 11am, noon, 2pm and 3pm, each covering one of the four wings of the permanent collection. There are one-hour tours of temporary shows – times and prices vary

- 👫 **Age range** All
- 🏃 **Activities** Free guided kids' activities (age 5 plus) every Sat & Sun noon–4pm, also Thu & Fri in school holidays. Family zone with art books and materials on Level 0; free art trails (age 5 plus) from information desks on Levels 1 and 2. Kids' multimedia guide from Levels 2 and 3 (£3.50)
- ⏱ **Allow** At least 2 hours
- ♿ **Wheelchair access** Yes
- 🍴 **Eat and drink** *Snacks* Tate Café (Level 1) has good-value lunch deals for under-12s, also sandwiches and pastries. *Real meal* Tate Modern Restaurant (Level 6) has river views and a more ambitious menu; also open for dinner Fri–Sat
- 🛍 **Shops** Levels 0, 1 and 3 selling art books, jewellery, prints and exhibition souvenirs
- 🚻 **Toilets** All levels; baby-changing facilities on Level 0

Above The Millennium Bridge over the Thames links St Paul's and Tate Modern **Left** The heart of Tate Modern is the towering Turbine Hall

Prices given are for a family of four

Waxwork inmate undergoing punishment at the grisly Clink Prison Museum

③ Clink Prison Museum

The original London dungeon

Medieval Southwark was outside the jurisdiction of London's civic authorities, and was a lawless place notorious for bear fights, drinking dens and brothels – all licensed by the bishops of Winchester, whose palace stood here on the south bank of the Thames. A gaol was needed to control the area, and in 1144 the Clink was opened – a place so infamous that its name became a byword for prisons across the land.

Inside the small, dingy cells of this subterranean attraction, waxwork inmates, recorded shrieks and replica torture equipment are used to tell the gory story of crime and punishment up to 1780, when the Clink locked up for the last time. Information boards describe a 12th-century trial by ordeal (walk across red-hot irons without injury and you're innocent)

Clambering over a steam-train climbing frame in Little Dorrit Park, SE1

and the priestly persecutions of Bloody Mary. It is more histrionic than historical, and maybe a bit too spooky for the under-8s. Ghoulish children will enjoy trying on the scold's bridle or placing their head on the executioner's chopping block. Visitors are able to download a picture of their visit afterwards.

Letting off steam

Head south along Bank End Park and Redcross Way to **Little Dorrit Park** (off Little Dorrit Court, SE1), which has play equipment.

The Lowdown

- 🌐 **Map ref 12 E5**
  Address 1 Clink Street, SE1 9DG; 020 7403 0900; www.clink.co.uk
- 🚆 **Train** London Bridge **Tube** London Bridge **Bus stop** Southwark Bridge, Southwark Street, Borough High Street **River bus** Bankside Pier
- 🕐 **Open** Jul–Sep: 10am–9pm daily; Oct–Jun: 10am–6pm Mon–Fri, 10am–7:30pm Sat & Sun
- 💷 **Price** £18
- 🚩 **Guided tours** Groups only
- 🚶 **Age range** 8 plus
- ⏱ **Allow** Up to 1 hour
- ♿ **Wheelchair access** There are nine steps to get down to the musem.
- 🍴 **Eat and drink** Snacks The Rooftop Cafe (28 London Bridge Street, SE1 9SG; www.theexchange.so/rooftop; open Mon–Sat) has great views of London with seasonal selections Real meal Gourmet Burger Kitchen (Soho Wharf, Clink Street, SE1 9DG; www.gbk.co.uk; 11:30am–10pm daily) does mini versions of its burgers for kids.
- 🛍 **Shop** Gift shop selling souvenirs
- 🚻 **Toilets** No

④ The *Golden Hinde*

Ahoy there me hearties!

This beautiful replica of a Tudor galleon sits majestically on the river alongside the cafés and office blocks of Bankside, as if moored there just a minute ago by pirates. Indeed, miniature mutineers swarm aboard regularly, during the pirate days and sleepovers staged for families.

The *Hinde* is a full-size reproduction of Sir Francis Drake's flagship, which circumnavigated the world in the 1570s, discovering California and plundering much Spanish loot along the way. Rewards could be high – after one profitable trip, even a lowly cabin boy became the equivalent of a millionaire.

A rudimentary handout describes the decks, rigging and artillery – but aim to visit at the weekend if possible, when excellent tour

Dressed up and pretending to fire a cannon on the Golden Hinde

guides are on board to help. Sit in Drake's chair in the captain's cabin and marvel at how the cramped quarters once accommodated up to 80 crew – even little ones will need to duck down to explore the gloomy gun deck. Most Saturdays there are costumed family fun days: grab a cutlass and eye-patch and learn how to weigh anchor and fire a cannon.

Letting off steam

Head south along Borough High Street to **Little Dorrit Park** (*off Little Dorrit Court, SE1*).

The Lowdown

- 🌐 **Map ref** 12 E5
  Address Pickfords Wharf, Clink Street, SE1 9DG; 020 7403 0123; *www.goldenhinde.com*
- 🚇 **Train** London Bridge **Tube** London Bridge, Monument **Bus stop** Borough High Street. **River bus** Bankside Pier
- 🕐 **Open** 9am–5:30pm daily
- 💲 **Price** £20, under-4s free
- 🚹 **Skipping the queue** Best to book ahead for a family workshop
- 🚩 **Guided tours** Costumed tours or pirate dress-up days every Sat (family £20, including admission)
- 🚻 **Age range** 5 plus
- 🏃 **Activities** 2-hour pirate workshops for families most Saturdays (plus some weekdays in school holidays) – come in costume. Also regular sleepovers for ages 5–10, accompanied by an adult (£40pp). Call or check website
- ⏱ **Allow** 1 hour for self-guided visit
- ♿ **Wheelchair access** No, due to the steep stairs and low ceilings
- 🍴 **Eat and drink** *Picnic* Caffè Nero (3 Cathedral Street, SE1 9DE; 7am–8:30pm Mon–Fri; 7:30am–9pm Sat & Sun) overlooks the ship, or try the stalls at Borough Market (*see p146*)
- 🛍 **Shop** At the ticket shop selling souvenirs
- 🚻 **Toilets** At the ticket shop

⑤ Southwark Cathedral

Pilgrims, poets and posh provisions

The "archaeology chamber" in Southwark Cathedral's millennium wing is a window on nearly 2,000 years of worship beside London Bridge. A 4th-century Roman religious icon was unearthed here, and there is a stone coffin from the medieval Priory of St Mary Overie.

The church we see today is mostly 14th century. Geoffrey Chaucer's pilgrims in *The Canterbury Tales* began their journey from a nearby tavern, and the fabulous tomb of Chaucer's contemporary John Gower lights up the cathedral's nave with its carousel colours – red, green and gold. Look out for a 500-year-old stone "corpse", emaciated in its shroud – perfect for spooking the children. However, the best known

memorial remembers William Shakespeare, who spent 12 years working at the nearby Globe Theatre – characters from some of his plays cavort in a stained-glass window above.

From Thursday to Saturday, the stalls of Borough Market (*see p146*) lap around the cathedral railings, adding greatly to the atmosphere of the neighbourhood. London's oldest food market was chartered by Edward III in 1406, although it is unlikely to have sold ostrich burgers or Burmese curry powder back then. The market now specializes in delectable ingredients from across Europe and beyond, and sampling the food is encouraged – but steer clear on Saturday mornings after 10am, when the area gets super-busy.

Letting off steam

The cathedral has an outside area with tables, and beyond that there is a small square beside the river.

Gilded Mary and Jesus, a detail of the Great Screen, Southwark Cathedral

The Lowdown

🌐 **Map ref** 12 E5
Address London Bridge, SE1 9DA; 020 7367 6700; www.southwarkcathedral.org.uk

🚆 **Train** London Bridge **Tube** London Bridge, Monument **Bus stop** Borough High Street **River bus** Bankside Pier

🕐 **Open** 8am–6pm Mon–Fri, 8:30am–6pm Sat & Sun; services include choral evensong daily. Borough Market: 10am–5pm Wed & Thu, 10am–6pm Fri, 8am–5pm Sat

💲 **Price** Donations

🚩 **Guided tours** Groups only (adults £5.50; under-11s £3); walking tours also available

🎵 **Activities** Regular concerts

⏱ **Allow** Up to 1 hour

♿ **Wheelchair access** Yes, via lifts or fixed and portable ramps

🍴 **Eat and drink** Snacks The café serves lunch and cakes *Real meal* Fish! (Cathedral Street, SE1 9AL; 020 7407 3803; 11:30am–11pm Mon–Thu, noon–11pm Fri & Sat, to 10:30pm Sun) offers seafood

🛍 **Shop** Selling cathedral souvenirs, cards, books and gifts

🚻 **Toilets** At the west end of Lancelot's Link, near the entrance

The small surgeon's table at the heart of the Old Operating Theatre

gore, inside the attic of 300-year-old St Thomas's Church. It shows off Europe's oldest surviving operating theatre, established in 1822 to serve nearby St Thomas's Hospital, where student surgeons once gathered to watch limbs being chopped off poor patients – without anaesthetics.

Howls of real torment once rang through the rafters here, and the museum's entrance could hardly be spookier – it is reached via a spiral staircase in the church's tower. The first chamber to visit is the Herb Garret, storehouse of the hospital apothecary in centuries past, and stacked with musty animal skins and bizarre potions, much like a witch's pantry. Harry Potter fans will adore the vibe here. The operating room is a creepy space too – literally a theatre, with the surgery table as the stage, steeply banked viewing stands, a box of sawdust to soak up the blood of amputees and a corridor of murderous-looking surgical instruments.

Letting off steam

Little Dorrit Park (see left) has a small playground for children.

⑥ The Old Operating Theatre

The church that dripped blood

This macabre museum makes an interesting counterpoint to the London Dungeon (see p156), just around the corner. Whereas the Dungeon is a schlocky horror show, this is an authentic slice of Victorian

The Lowdown

🌐 **Map ref** 12 E5
Address 9a Saint Thomas Street, SE1 9RY; 020 7188 2679; www.thegarret.org.uk

🚆 **Train** London Bridge **Tube** London Bridge **Bus stop** London Bridge

🕐 **Open** 10:30am–5pm daily

💲 **Price** £13.90

🚶 **Skipping the queue** Capacity is tight, so book ahead for events

👫 **Age range** 7 plus

🏃 **Activities** Free demonstrations, at 2pm Sat and Sun (age 7 plus), might feature herbal medicine or 19th-century speed surgery. There's an imaginative programme of family

activities in the school holidays: call ahead or check website

⏱ **Allow** 1 hour

♿ **Wheelchair access** limited

🍴 **Eat and drink** Snacks Frank's Cafe (132 Southwark Street, SE1 0SW) is a classic cafe serving breakfast and lunch with a couple of outdoor tables *Real meal* The George Inn (77 Borough High Street, SE1 1NH; 020 7407 2056; 11am–10pm daily) serves traditional pub fare

🛍 **Shop** Selling quirky and original gifts and presents with a medical theme

🚻 **Toilets** On entrance level before entering (requires a key)

Picnic under £20; **Snacks** £20–40; **Real meal** £40–60; **Family treat** £60 or more (based on a family of four)

HMS *Belfast* and around

HMS *Belfast*, the most powerful battle cruiser in Britain's World War II fleet, is now a floating museum. Visiting with kids is an immersive experience, but avoid inclement days, and check the website for kid's activities. Back on shore, this pedestrianized strip of riverside is perfect for families. Youngsters with an eye for flair will enjoy the Design or Fashion and Textile Museum.

The Modernist building housing the Design Museum, founded in 1989 and one of the first design museums in the world

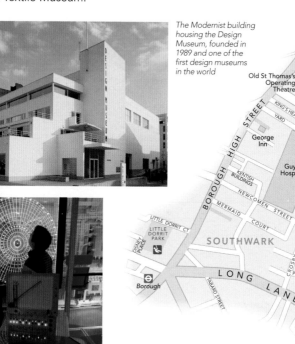

Inside the interactive Operations Room on board HMS Belfast

The Lowdown

🚗 **Train** London Bridge, a five-minute walk away; Tower Gateway (DLR) **Tube** London Bridge, Monument, Tower Hill **Bus** Tooley Street: route numbers 47, 343, 381, RV1; London Bridge: 17, 21, 35, 40, 43, 47, 133, 141, 149, 521 **River bus** London Bridge City Pier, on riverbus route between Woolwich Arsenal and London Eye (0870 781 5049; www.thamesclippers.com)

ℹ️ **Visitor information** City of London Information Centre (see pp128–9)

🛒 **Supermarkets** Marks & Spencer Simply Food, 6 More London Place, SE1 2DA; Costcutter, 134 Tooley Street, SE1 2TU **Markets** Borough Market, see pp144–5; Bermondsey Market, Bermondsey Square, SE1 3UN (mostly food, plus flowers and garden plants), 6am–2pm Fri

🎪 **Festivals** City of London Festival, music and arts (Jun–Jul); the Mayor's Thames Festival, music, arts and markets (Sep)

➕ **Pharmacies** Boots, 8–11 Hays Galleria, SE1 2HD; 020 7407 4276; 7:30am–7pm Mon–Fri; 10am–6pm Sat; 11am–5pm Sun. For 24-hour pharmacies, visit www.nhs.uk/servicedirectories

🛝 **Nearest playground** Tanner Street Park (SE1); Little Dorrit Park (SE1); St John's Churchyard (SE1); Leathermarket Street Gardens (SE1)

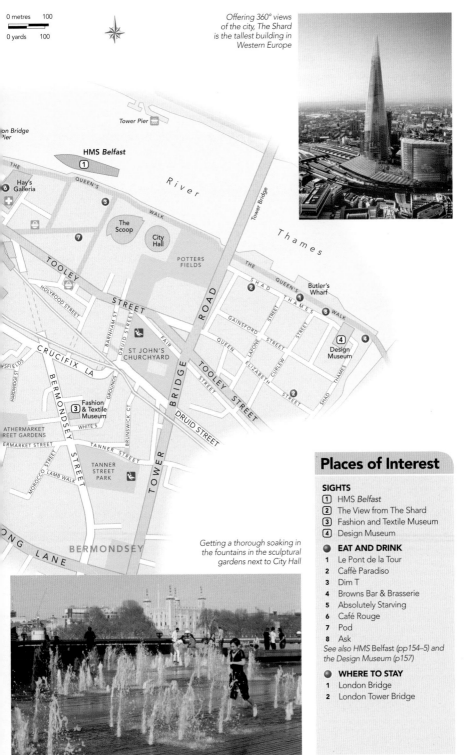

0 metres 100
0 yards 100

Offering 360° views of the city, The Shard is the tallest building in Western Europe

Tower Pier

on Bridge
Pier

HMS *Belfast*
①

THE
Hay's
Galleria
QUEEN'S

River
③
WALK

The
Scoop

City
Hall

Thames

POTTERS
FIELDS

⑦

TOOLEY

HOLYROOD STREET

STREET

BARNHAM ST

DRUID STREET

THE

SHAD
②
THAMES

QUEEN'S
WALK

Butler's
Wharf
⑨

GAINSFORD STREET

STREET

LAFONE STREET

④
Design
Museum
④

QUEEN
ELIZABETH
CURLEW
STREET

ROAD

CRUCIFIX LA

HARDWIDGE ST

WSFIELDS

BERMONDSEY

ST JOHN'S
CHURCHYARD

GROUNDS

TAIR
STREET

TOOLEY
STREET

SHAD
THAMES
②

BRUNSWICK CT

WHITE'S

Fashion
③ & Textile
Museum

ATHERMARKET
REET GARDENS
ERMARKET STREET

TANNER STREET

MOROCCO STREET

LAMB WALK

STREET

TANNER
STREET
PARK

TOWER

BRIDGE

DRUID STREET

ONG
LANE

BERMONDSEY

Getting a thorough soaking in the fountains in the sculptural gardens next to City Hall

Places of Interest

SIGHTS
① HMS *Belfast*
② The View from The Shard
③ Fashion and Textile Museum
④ Design Museum

● **EAT AND DRINK**
1 Le Pont de la Tour
2 Caffè Paradiso
3 Dim T
4 Browns Bar & Brasserie
5 Absolutely Starving
6 Café Rouge
7 Pod
8 Ask
See also *HMS Belfast (pp154–5)* and the Design Museum (p157)

● **WHERE TO STAY**
1 London Bridge
2 London Tower Bridge

① HMS *Belfast*

Action stations – on one of Britain's great warships

She was built in 1938, in the same Northern Irish shipyard as the *Titanic*, but on a quiet day, HMS *Belfast* feels more like the *Marie Celeste*. What could be more atmospheric than exploring a great warship in battle trim, populated only by visitors and the ghosts of the 800 seamen who once manned her? Generators buzz, orders crackle through the speakers and most areas are accessible to children, who can swarm down ladders and along gangways, into gun turrets and mess decks accompanied by the lively audio guide.

Signalling with semaphore flags

The Lowdown

🌐 **Map reference** 12 G5
Address HMS Belfast, The Queen's Walk, SE1 2JH; 020 7940 6300; www.iwm.org.uk

🚗 **Train** London Bridge (a five-minute walk); Tower Gateway (DLR) **Tube** London Bridge, Monument, Tower Hill. **Bus stop** Tooley Street, London Bridge **River bus** London Bridge City Pier, en route between Woolwich Arsenal and London Eye (020 7001 2222; www.thamesclippers.com).

🕐 **Open** Mar–Oct: 10am–6pm daily; Nov–Feb: till 5pm (last admission one hour earlier)

💲 **Price** £38.15–42, under-5s free

🚩 **Guided tours** Free audio guide (also in French, German and Spanish); children's audio guide

👫 **Age range** 7 plus

🏃 **Activities** Family drop-in activities take place on selected weekends and during school holidays. Check website for more information

⏱ **Allow** 2 hours

♿ **Wheelchair access** Limited due to the nature of a warship. See website for details

☕ **Café** The Walrus Café, Zone 3 (open 11am to last admission during weekends and school holidays)

🛍 **Shop** In ticket hall

🚻 **Toilets** On both the upper and main decks, ask staff for the key to the disabled toilets

Good family value?

For maximum value, make time for the hands-on Life at Sea exhibition on Deck 3, with knots to tie and kitbags to lift.

Key Features

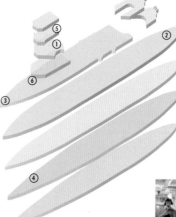

① **Admiral's Cabin** HMS *Belfast* became the flagship of Britain's Far East Fleet, and in the admiral's command room, children can don uniforms and scan for enemy craft.

② **Quarterdeck** The ship's parade ground and exercise yard, this was mainly reserved for officers. It is where visitors board – don't forget to salute!

■ **Bridge** The compass platform at the front was where the captain controlled the ship.

■ **Superstructure** This part of the ship held the gun turrets, funnels, life boats, fore mast and main mast.

■ **Deck Two** This housed a forward mess deck, where the crew would sleep and eat, as well as the officers' mess.

■ **Deck Three** As well as the staff's cabins, this held the chapel, punishment cells, mail room and laundry.

■ **Deck Four** This held the shell room and gun guidance system, as well as the ship's wheel and steering gear.

■ **Deck Five** Home to the forward and aft engine rooms, as well as smaller shells and the submarine detection device.

③ **Anchor** If the electric winch failed, it took 144 men to turn the capstan and raise the ship's main anchor. It is as heavy as an elephant (5.5 tonnes).

④ **Shell Room** The shells line up like giant bowling pins here. They were loaded into a carousel and then hoisted up to the four main gun turrets.

⑤ **Operations Room** In the ship's nerve centre, *Belfast*'s finest hour is re-created – when she helped sink the German battleship *Scharnhorst* at the Battle of the North Cape in 1943.

⑥ **Gun Turret** Swivel in the turret captain's chair and imagine unleashing *Belfast*'s guns on a target 23 km (14 miles) away.

Taking a break in Potters Field Park, right next to Tower Bridge

Letting off steam

Potters Fields Park is a spread of lawn beside Tower Bridge. Behind it, across Tooley Street, **St John's Churchyard**, on Fair Street, has a small play area; at **Tanner Street Park**, further along Tower Bridge Road, is a larger playground. Junior sessions at **White's Grounds Skate Park** (corner of Crucifix Lane & Druid Street, SE1 3JW), cater for ages 11–16: call 020 7525 1102 for details.

Eat and drink

Picnic: £20–30; Snacks: £20–40; Real meal: £45–65; Family treat: £65 or more (based on a family of four)

PICNIC Le Pont de la Tour (36D Shad Thames, SE1 2YE; 020 7403 8403; www.lepontdelatour.co.uk; noon–11pm Mon–Sat, noon–10pm Sun) has a great deli with good bread, a cheese counter and gourmet goodies. Grab a picnic and head to nearby Potters Fields Park where there is plentiful rug-spreading space. **SNACKS** The designer Docklands haunt of Shad Thames has an array of good eateries, including **Caffè Paradiso** (45 Shad Thames, SE1 2NJ; 020 7378 6606; www.pizza paradiso.co.uk; 7am–7:30pm Mon–Fri, 8am–7pm Sat, 8:30am–7:30pm Sun), a Sicilian-style hangout offering piled-high patisserie and proper ice cream. **REAL MEAL Dim T** (2 More London Place, Tooley St, SE1 2DP; 020 7403 7000; www.dimt.co.uk; noon–11pm Tue–Sat, to 10:30pm Sun & Mon), just ashore from HMS Belfast, creates a wide range of Asian-fusion dishes, including Thai curries and crispy duck, while children can choose between a bento box or dim-sum selection basket.

FAMILY TREAT There are posher places along Butler's Wharf, but **Browns Bar & Brasserie** (Shad Thames, SE1 2YG; 020 7378 1700; www.browns-restaurants.co.uk; 8:30am–11pm Mon–Wed, till 11:30pm Thu, till midnight Fri & Sat, 9am–11pm Sun) serves British classics, such as shoulder of lamb or calves' liver and bacon. There's also a two-course children's menu.

Find out more

DIGITAL Learn more about objects from HMS Belfast, including photographs of the ship during World War II Arctic Convoy missions, by searching IWM's collections online at www.iwm.org.uk/collections/search.

Next stop. . .

LONDON FIRE BRIGADE MUSEUM For more heavy-duty hardware, head for the nearby London Fire Brigade Museum (94a Southwark Bridge Rd, SE1 0EG; 020 8555 1200; www.london-fire.gov.uk/london-fire-brigade-museum.asp), which has shiny red engines to admire and uniforms to try on: tours run 10:30am & 2pm Mon–Fri, booking essential (adults £5, children £3).

Examining fire engines from the past at the Fire Brigade Museum

② The View from The Shard

Amazing 360° views of the London skyline

The tallest building in Western Europe, The Shard is designed by architect Renzo Piano. One of the latest skyscrapers to dominate the London skyline, it is 310 m (1,016 ft) high and houses offices, restaurants, the five-star Shangri-La hotel, exclusive residential apartments and the country's highest observation gallery, The View, reached by high-speed lifts. The entrance to The View is via Joiner Street.

Situated near the top of The Shard, on floors 68, 69 and 72, the public galleries feature multimedia displays that provide context to the views. Adults, and especially kids, will enjoy travelling skyward in "kaleidoscopic" lifts that use video screens and mirrors to create the effect of soaring through the iconic ceilings and roofs of London. On arrival at the "cloudscape" on Level 68, head upwards to the triple-height, main viewing gallery at Level 69, where unobstructed 360° views

Visitors enjoying panoramic views of the city from the top of The Shard

of the capital are revealed. The city of London is brought to life through 12 telescopes, enabling people to explore the city around them in real time. These free-to-use instruments also help visitors identify 250 famous landmarks and places of significant interest, while providing information about them in 10 languages. For a profound experience, go to the viewing gallery at Level 72 – the highest habitable level of the building. This level is partially open-air, and is considered the highest vantage point in Western Europe. Visitors are surrounded by giant shards of glass that form the top of The Shard and can listen out for the sounds of the bustling city below.

Letting off steam

Walk east along Tooley Street to **St John's Churchyard** (*Fair Street, SE1*), which has a small playground and grassy areas for picnics.

The Lowdown

- 🌐 **Map ref** 12 F6 **Address** Joiner Street, SE1 9QU; 0844 499 7111; *www.theviewfromtheshard.com*
- 🚊 **Train** London Bridge **Tube** London Bridge **Bus stop** London Bridge: 43, 48, 141, 149, 521
- 🕐 **Open** Apr–Oct: 10am–10pm daily (last entry 8:30pm); Nov–Mar: till 7pm Sun–Wed, till 10pm Thu–Sat
- 💲 **Price** £108–118; book online for reductions. There's a concessionary rate for disabled guests and free access to a registered carer (bookable only by phone)
- 👫 **Skipping the queue** Buy tickets online – it's cheaper – or book in advance by phone (extra charge)
- 👫 **Age range** 7 plus
- ♿ **Wheelchair access** Yes
- 🍴 **Eat and drink** *Snacks* Absolutely Starving (51 Tooley St, SE1 2QN; 020 7407 7417; 7am–9pm Mon–Fri, 9am–8pm Sat & Sun) has a hot buffet. *Real meal* Café Rouge (Hay's Galleria, Tooley St, SE1 2HD; 020 7378 0097; 8:30am–11pm Mon–Fri, 9am–11pm Sat, 9am–10:30pm Sun) has a kids' menu
- 🛍️ **Shop** The Sky Boutique
- 🚻 **Toilets** Ground and floor 68 of The View

③ Fashion and Textile Museum

A glimpse into the world of high fashion

Occupying a distinctive orange and pink building on trendy Bermondsey Street in London Bridge, this superb museum is the brainchild of British textile designer Zandra Rhodes. Primarily aimed at adults, the museum's vibrant colours will ensure that any kids with even the faintest interest in the world of fashion will enjoy themselves here.

The museum's permanent exhibits explore fashion and textile design from 1950 to the present day. There is also a constantly revolving roster of exhibitions covering all aspects of the fashion industry from specific periods, such as 70s Bohemian Chic, to overviews that have included a display of shoes worn by stars over the last century. Frequent exhibitions dedicated to luminaries of the fashion world such as Zandra Rhodes, Tommy Nutter and Sue Timney are also held here. In addition, the museum offers opportunities to participate in workshops on a variety of fashion-related subjects including pattern cutting, crochet, couture techniques and fashion illustration. The majority of these workshops can be pricey and mostly aimed at adults with serious fashion aspirations but there are occasional events suitable for kids, particularly during the school holidays. Take a look at the museum's website for up to date information on kid-friendly workshops and activities.

Fashion and Textile Museum

The Lowdown

🌐 **Map ref** 12 G6

📍 **Address** 83 Bermondsey Street, SE1 3XF; 020 7407 8664; www.ftmlondon.org

🚆 **Train** London Bridge **Tube** London Bridge **Bus stop** Tooley Street & Tower Bridge Road **River bus** London Bridge City Pier

🕐 **Open** 11am–6pm Tue–Sat (till 8pm Thu); 11am–5pm Sun (last admission 45 minutes before closing)

💷 **Price** £25–39, under-12s free

👪 **Age range** 7 plus

⏱ **Allow** 1 hour

♿ **Wheelchair access** Yes

🍽 **Eat and drink** *Picnic* Borough Market for delicious takeaway food. *Snacks* Pod (7 More London Place, SE1 2RT; 020 7407 9048; www.podfood.com; 7am–4:30pm Mon–Fri) offers healthy food such as superfood salads

🛍 **Shop** Near the entrance

🚻 **Toilets** Near the café

One of the ever-changing exhibitions at the Design Museum

walkways were used in Victorian times to wheel tea and spices from the quayside, but now link luxury loft apartments, their courtyards parked with convertibles instead of carthorses. A stroll around here will certainly appeal to kids' imaginations. The Design Museum itself is arranged over three floors of an appropriately cool white building. There is no permanent collection, instead temporary shows focus on avant-garde architecture, furniture or fashion. It can be a bit esoteric for children, but there's a family workshop or tour most months, linked to current exhibitions, while the free under-12s' activity sheet encourages kids to doodle their own designs.

Letting off steam

Walk east to Tower Bridge Road, then up to grassy **Potters Fields Park** (The Queens Walk, SE1 2AA) for great views of Tower Bridge and the Tower of London.

④ Design Museum

A modern temple to design

A big part of the appeal of this museum is its setting on Butler's Wharf, a chunk of London's revitalized Docklands. The approach is along Shad Thames, whose overhead

Letting off steam

The **Butler's Wharf** waterfront is a good place to dash around – it is littered with old anchors that kids will enjoy clambering over. For slightly softer surroundings, head towards Tower Bridge to **Potters Fields Park**.

The Lowdown

🌐 **Map ref** 12 H6

📍 **Address** 28 Shad Thames, SE1 2YD; 020 7403 6933; www.designmuseum.org

🚆 **Train** London Bridge, Tower Gateway (DLR station) **Tube** London Bridge, Tower Hill **Bus stop** Tooley Street, Tower Gateway, Jamaica Road, Tower Bridge **River bus** Tower Pier, St Katharine's Pier

🕐 **Open** 10am–5:45pm daily (last admission: 5:15pm)

💷 **Price** £35 (under-6s free)

👥 **Guided tours** Occasional tours of specific exhibitions, some geared towards families

👪 **Age range** 5 plus

🤸 **Activities** Free activity sheet

available for under-12s. There are Sunday pm workshops for ages 5–11 most months. School holiday courses for age 12-plus focus on specific design disciplines

⏱ **Allow** 1 hour

♿ **Wheelchair access** Yes

🍽 **Eat and drink** *Snacks* The Blueprint Café (www.blueprintcafe.co.uk) in the museum serves gourmet pies and pastries *Real meal* Ask (34 Shad Thames, Butler's Wharf, SE1 2YG; 020 7403 4545; www.askrestaurants.com; 10am–11pm Mon–Sat, 10am–10pm Sun) serves pasta and pizza and has a kids' menu

🛍 **Shop** On the ground floor, selling excellent designer goods

🚻 **Toilets** On the ground floor

London Eye and around

Erected in 2000, the London Eye is a genuine wow for kids, especially if approached on foot from Waterloo station. Book ahead to ride – but not before checking the weather forecast, because rain blots the views. That's good advice for the eclectic South Bank, which can be bleak on a wet day, although it embraces the National Theatre, the London Aquarium and Britain's biggest cinema screen as well as a motley crew of street entertainers.

Southwark and the South Bank

Shakespeare's Globe *p144*

London Eye

HMS *Belfast* *p152*

The London Eye in front of the Sea Life London Aquarium, on the South Bank

Places of interest

SIGHTS

1. London Eye
2. National Theatre
3. BFI Southbank
4. Gabriel's Wharf
5. Southbank Centre
6. Sea Life London Aquarium
7. London Dungeon
8. Captain Kidd's Canary Wharf Voyage
9. Imperial War Museum
10. Florence Nightingale Museum

● EAT AND DRINK

1. Zen Café
2. Zen China
3. Riverside Terrace Café
4. Le Pain Quotidien
5. Canteen
6. Mezzanine
7. The Riverfront
8. Benugo Bar & Kitchen
9. House of Crepes
10. Gourmet Pizza Company
11. Concrete at the Hayward
12. Skylon Restaurant
13. Ned's Noodle Bar
14. Aji Zen Canteen
15. Café Roma
16. The Garden Café
17. Yo! Sushi
18. Troia
See also National Theatre (p162), BFI Southbank (pp162–3) and London Film Museum (p165)

● WHERE TO STAY

1. Park Plaza
2. Premier Inn

Southbank Centre, one of London's popular artistic venues.

0 metres 200

0 yards 200

Oxo Tower

briel's arf

BERNIE SPAIN GARDENS

DUCHY

REET

AQUINAS STREET

HATFIELDS

STREET

WINDMILL STREET

PELL

Waterloo East

OTTON STREET

GREET'S

WALK

CUT

THE

SHORT ST

MITRE RD ST

STREET

Old Vic

WEBBER

VALENTINE PL

LOO

GRAY ST

BARON'S

ROW

STREET

WEBBER ROW

BLACKFRIARS RD

AL STREET

MAN STREET

MORLEY STREET

GERRIDGE ST

ROAD

DODSON STREET

ST GEORGES

CIRCUS

GE

ROAD

St George's Cathedral

ROAD

MBETH

GEORGE'S ROAD

GLADSTONE ST

GARDEN ROW

GERALDINE ST

ALDINE MARY SWORTH PARK

WEST SQUARE

Imperial War Museum

OOK DRIVE

OT SQUARE

Rockets, planes and armoured cars at the Imperial War Museum

Enthralled by an inquisitive ray at the Sea Life London Aquarium

The Lowdown

🚆 **Train** Waterloo, a 5-minute walk away **Tube** Waterloo, Westminster, Lambeth North **Bus** Belvedere Road: route number RV1; York Road: 76, 77, 211, 341, 381, 507; Westminster Bridge: 12, 53, 148, 159, 211, 453 **River bus** London Eye Millennium Pier: riverbus services to Woolwich Arsenal (020 7001 2200; *www. thamesclippers.com*); and to Greenwich via the Tower (020 7740 0400; *www.city cruises.com*). Also services from Westminster Pier (*see p64*)

ℹ **Visitor information** Britain and London Visitor Centre, Waterloo station, SE1 7LY

🛒 **Supermarkets** Costcutter, 17–19 York Road, SE1 7NJ; Sainsbury's, 101 Waterloo Road, SE1 8UL; Iceland, 112–113 Lower Marsh, SE1 7AE **Markets** South Bank Book Market, BFI Southbank, daily; Real Food Market, Royal Festival Hall, Southbank Centre, noon–8pm Fri; 11am–8pm Sat; noon–6pm Sun; Lower Marsh street market, SE1 (mixed stalls), 8am–6pm Mon–Sat (Wed 10am–3pm)

🎌 **Festivals** Coin Street Festival, mixed arts, Bernie Spain Gardens (Jun–Aug); Meltdown Festival, music, Southbank Centre (summer); Watch This Space, family arts, National Theatre (Jun–Sep); The Mayor's Thames Festival (Sep); BFI London Film Festival (Oct)

➕ **Pharmacies** Boots, Waterloo Station, SE1 7LY (7am–10pm Mon–Fri; 8am–10pm Sat; 9am–9pm Sun. For a list of 24-hour pharmacies, visit *www.nhs.uk/service directories*

🛝 **Nearest playgrounds** Archbishop's Park (*Lambeth Palace Road, SE1 7LQ*); Jubilee Gardens (*Belvedere Road, SE1 7XZ*); Geraldine Mary Harmsworth Park (*Kennington Road, SE11*); Bernie Spain Gardens (*Duchy Street, SE1 9NL*)

The Lowdown

🌐 **Map ref** 10 H6
Address County Hall, Westminster Bridge Road, SE1 7PB; 0871 781 3000, *www.londoneye.com*

�"" **Train** Waterloo, a 5-minute walk away **Tube** Waterloo, Westminster **Bus stop** Belvedere Road, York Road, Westminster Bridge **River bus** London Eye Millennium Pier, Westminster Pier

🕐 **Open** Sep–Mar: 10am–8:30pm daily; Apr–Jun: till 9pm; Jul & Aug: till 9:30pm; closed 2 weeks in mid-Jan for maintenance

💲 **Price** £95–119 (book online for 20 per cent discount). Time-flexible and fast-track tickets cost extra

👫 **Skipping the queue** Jul & Aug are busiest; avoid the 11am–3pm peak and arrive 30 minutes before flight time. Fast-track tickets are the same price for adults and children.

🚩 **Guided tours** 3pm daily (includes fast track entry). £23–26.50 per adult, £19–21.50 for ages 4–15, under 4s free

👫 **Age range** 5 plus

👫 **Activities** Free "4D" film experience included in ticket. Kids' puzzle sheet downloadable from website only. In winter, the ice-rink in Jubilee Gardens has a separate charge

⏱ **Allow** 1 hour

♿ **Wheelchair access** Yes (carer can travel for free)

☕ **Café** *Snacks* Zen Café, with outlets beside Jubilee Gardens and inside County Hall, sells snacks and drinks. *Real meal* Zen China inside County Hall is a more grown-up alternative, specializing in traditional Chinese cuisine

🏷 **Shop** At the bottom of the exit ramp, selling souvenirs and visitor photos

👫 **Toilets** Downstairs at County Hall

Good family value?
It's expensive for 30 minutes, but there's a saving for combined admission to sister attractions Madame Tussauds and London Dungeon. On a budget? Consider the OXO Tower (*see p147*) instead.

Prices given are for a family of four

① London Eye
Take a spin over London

How does it feel to be a seagull soaring above London? Find out during a ride on "the world's tallest cantilevered observation wheel". Rising 135 m (443 ft) above the Thames, the London Eye opened as part of the city's millennium celebrations. A serene 30-minute ride in one of its glass capsules offers views stretching 40 km (25 miles) – on a clear day you might even be able to see Windsor Castle!

Key Features

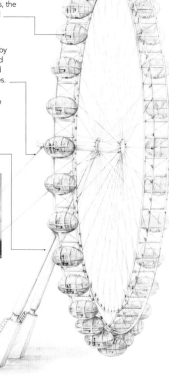

The capsules Each of the 32 capsules weighs 10 tonnes, can hold 25 passengers and rotates at 26 cm (10 in) per second. Celebrity fliers have included Prince Harry, Kate Moss, the Jonas Brothers…and Kermit the Frog!

The spec The wheel cost £70 million, weighs 2,100 tonnes and is supported by two 60-m (197-ft) cables. It was floated up the Thames in sections, assembled and then slowly raised using the cables.

The structure Although no longer the world's tallest observation wheel (the 165-m (541-ft) Singapore Flyer takes that prize for now) it is the largest cantilevered wheel, as it is supported by an A-frame on one side only.

The ride The slow-moving capsules mean the wheel can be boarded without it stopping, and the gentle ascent is entirely unscary.

Extras A 4-minute "4D" cinema show in the ticket hall is free for London Eye travellers. It uses dry ice, bubbles and "real rain" to simulate an aerial journey over London.

The view On a clear day, Windsor Castle, 40 km (25 miles) west of London, is visible – although Wembley Stadium's arch, 12 km (7 miles) away to the northwest, is a better bet.

Imaginative playground at Archbishop's Park, next to Lambeth Palace

Letting off steam

Jubilee Gardens (Belvedere Road, Southbank SE1 7XZ), beside the Eye, has lawns and a playground, and is best for younger children. The colourful **Archbishop's Park** (Carlisle Lane, SE1 7LE), a 10-minute walk away, was designed by children and is probably a better bet. If it's wet, there are hours of mindless pleasure to be had at **Namco Station** inside County Hall (10am–midnight daily; www.namcofunscape.com), which has three beeping, flashing floors of arcade games, dodgem cars and bowling alleys.

Eat and drink

Picnic: under £20; Snacks: £20–40; Real meal: £40–60; Family treat: £60 or more (based on a family of four)

PICNIC For provisions, check out the weekend **Real Food Market** held behind Royal Festival Hall. The hall's **Riverside Terrace Café** (Royal Festival Hall, SE1 8XX; 020 7921 0758; www.southbankcentre.co.uk; 10am–10:30pm daily) becomes an outdoor eating space in summer. **SNACKS Le Pain Quotidien** (Festival Terrace, Belvedere Rd, SE1 8XX; www.lepainquotidien.com; 7:30am–8pm Mon & Tue, to 9pm Wed–Fri, 8am–8pm Sun) offers superior tartines, salads and snacks.

The stylish Canteen restaurant behind the Royal Festival Hall, South Bank

REAL MEAL Canteen (Royal Festival Hall, Belvedere Road, SE1 8XX; 0845 686 1122; www.canteen. co.uk; 8am–11pm Mon–Fri, 9am–11pm Sat, 9am–10pm Sun) serves up a stylish take on English classics (roasts, steak and chips), and its kid's menu offers half portions of most dishes. The restaurant also gives out activity books and there are badges to collect.
FAMILY TREAT Mezzanine (National Theatre, South Bank, SE1 9PX; 020 7452 3600; www. nationaltheatre.org.uk; 5:15–11pm Mon–Sat, plus weekend lunchtimes) is a grown-up Modern European restaurant with a seasonal menu, but it also does half portions for kids and themed food to link with family shows. Green eggs and ham, anyone?

Find out more

FILM The Eye has starred in more than one Hollywood blockbuster. It almost comes crashing down in the 2007 comic-book caper *Fantastic Four: Rise of the Silver Surfer*; while in the 2004 movie *Thunderbirds*, Thunderbird 2 lands right beside it in Jubilee Gardens.

A London Duck Tour amphibious vehicle splashing into the Thames

Next stop. . .

SIGHTSEEING TOURS The Eye is high, but there are several unusual ways to see the city at a faster pace. Spin your own wheels by hiring bikes from the **London Bicycle Tour Company** (from £3.50 per hour; 020 7928 6838; www.londonbicycle. com), at Gabriel's Wharf; get soaked on a spray-drenched 40 mph (65 kph) speedboat ride from the London Eye Pier (020 7928 8933; www.londonribvoyages.com); or see the sights by both land and water on an ingenious, amphibious **London Duck Tour** (020 7928 3132; www.londonducktours.co.uk), starting from Chicheley Street, SE1.

② National Theatre

London's top family arts destination

Britain's largest theatre complex was built on the South Bank in 1976. It was designed by Sir Denys Lasdun in the Brutalist architectural style, with lots of concrete and sharp edges, which people seem to either love or hate. Inside are three auditoria showing a terrific mix of classic drama and new writing, providing something for everyone. It's worth just dropping in, too, as the lobby areas embrace four restaurants, two exhibition spaces (photography figures strongly) and a small stage for free live music before curtain-up most evenings.

Guided tours include a visit to the fan-shaped Olivier Theatre, modelled on ancient Greek theatres, and a glimpse of the scenery work-shops backstage, where children can get up close to props from recent plays, such as Alice the mare, a puppet from the smash-hit show *War Horse*, based on Michael Morpurgo's novel for children. The liveliest time to come is June to September, when the theatre hosts a madcap family performance festival, mostly outdoors and largely free.

Enjoying an auditorium tour at the Olivier Theatre, part of the National Theatre

The theatre is currently undergoing an £83m redevelopment programme called NT Future. The project will transform the theatre's public spaces as well as areas behind the scenes.

Letting off steam

Bernie Spain Gardens *(Upper Ground, SE1 9PP)*, just east along the river, offers grassy spaces. **Jubilee Gardens** *(Belvedere Road, SE1 7XZ)*, in the opposite direction, has a decent playground.

③ BFI Southbank

Britain's largest big-screen experience

Crouching right under Waterloo Bridge, London's art-house cinema hub opened as the National Film Theatre in 1953, and now has four screens, a gallery for celluloid-based art and a very slick cocktail lounge. The programme generally has something for families.

For children who need a screen fix even when sightseeing, there is also the free Mediatheque room: simply choose a booth and access a menu of 2,000 movies and TV shows from the world's biggest screen archive. The children's list spans *Robin Hood* and *The Railway Children* to *Watership Down*. Nearby, the more commercial **BFI IMAX** is contained in a giant glass

The Lowdown

- 🌐 **Map ref** 11 A5
  Address South Bank, SE1 9PX; 020 7452 3000; www.nationaltheatre.org.uk

- 🚗 **Train** Waterloo or Waterloo East (both a 5-minute walk), Charing Cross (10 minutes). **Tube** Waterloo, Embankment **Bus stop** Waterloo Bridge, Upper Ground, Waterloo Road, Stamford Street **River bus** Festival Pier (Westminster to St Katharine's route; 020 7936 2033; www.crownriver.com); London Eye Millennium Pier; Embankment Pier (across Golden Jubilee Bridges).

- 🕐 **Open** 9:30am–11pm Mon–Sat, noon–6pm Sun

- ② **Price** Show tickets vary, from £10–45+; standing tickets are sold on the day only, £5

- 🚩 **Guided tours** Usually 10:15am, 10:30am, 12:15pm, 12:30pm, 5:15pm, 5:30pm Mon–Fri; 10:30am, 12:15pm Sat; 12:30pm Sun. Adults £8.50, under-18s £7.50; call 020 7452 3400

- 👫 **Age range** All

- 🏃 **Activities** Foyer concerts 5:45pm Mon–Sat and lunchtimes Sat & Sun (free). The Big Wall in the main foyer has touch-screen clips and information about current shows. Talks and workshops programme, mostly for adults. Watch This Space festival (Jun–Sep) has events Tue–Sun; Playspace programme runs in school summer holiday

- 🕐 **Allow** Up to 1 hour

- ♿ **Wheelchair access** Yes

- 🍽 **Eat and drink** *Snacks* Lyttelton Café (Ground floor) and Olivier Café (Levels 2–3) serve hot and cold dishes pre-theatre *Real meal* Terrace Bar & Food (Level 2) offers meze-style bites, with a focus on fresh seasonal ingredients

- 🛍 **Shop** On the ground floor selling books, texts, programmes, posters, recordings and gifts

- 🚻 **Toilets** In theatres and foyers

BFI Southbank, a big attraction for film buffs of all ages

drum outside Waterloo Station, where the likes of Harry Potter and Shrek loom 20-m (66-ft) tall on Britain's largest screen. Look out for the monthly Film Funday workshops, where kids get to animate their own movie before the main screening, or dress up as their heroes. A special children's menu is also available at the restaurant.

Letting off steam
Jubilee Gardens *(see left)*.

The Lowdown

🌐 **Map ref** 11 A5
   Address Belvedere Road, SE1 8XT; 020 7928 3232 (IMAX enquiries 020 7928 3232); *www.bfi.org.uk*

🚗 **Transport** See National Theatre *(opposite)*

🕑 **Open** 11am–11pm daily (till 11:30pm Fri & Sat); Mediatheque 1–8pm Tue (from noon Wed–Fri, from 12:30 Sat & Sun)

💷 **Price** Seat prices vary – all tickets cost £6 on Tue. Mediatheque free

👫 **Skipping the queue** Book ahead for Film Fundays (020 7928 3232)

🧑‍🤝‍🧑 **Activities** Film Fundays, usually on last Sun of each month, free with cinema tickets

♿ **Wheelchair access** Yes

🍴 **Eat and drink** *Real meal* The Riverfront (020 7928 0808; *www. riverfrontbarandkitchen.com)* does burgers, salads and grills. *Family treat* Benugo Bar & Kitchen (020 7401 9000; *www. benugobarandkitchen.com)* is more formal, but offers children's dishes on Film Fundays

🛍️ **Shop** Selling postcards, DVDs, BFI merchandise and books, including those for the more serious film connoisseur

🚻 **Toilets** In the foyer

④ Gabriel's Wharf
Boutiques and bicycles

It's heartening that this little oasis of "alternative culture" can thrive in such a go-getting strip of Central London, and that's thanks to Coin Street Community Builders – a gang of residents who banded together in 1984 to save the site from property developers. They've created a perky area of pastel-painted craft studios and cafés right

by the Thames, with lots of appeal for families: it has a giant mural, bicycle hire *(see p161)*, and a bevy of carved wooden beasts, some of them made for tots to ride on. Just beyond looms the Art Deco **OXO Tower**, with a small art gallery on the ground floor, bijou design shops along its balconies and a viewing platform at the summit.

Letting off steam
Bernie Spain Gardens *(Upper Ground, SE1 9PP)*, just east along the river has running-about room.

Some of the pretty, pastel-painted buildings at Gabriel's Wharf

The Lowdown

🌐 **Map ref** 11 A5
   Address 56 Upper Ground, SE1 9PP; 020 7021 1686; *www. coinstreet.org*

🚆 **Train** Blackfriars, Waterloo **Tube** Southwark, Waterloo **Bus stop** Stamford Street, Blackfriars Bridge, Waterloo Bridge, Upper Ground, Waterloo Road **River bus** Blackfriars Millennium Pier, Bankside Pier

🕑 **Open** Shops, studios and Oxo Gallery 11am–6pm Tue–Sun. Restaurants and cafés till late

💷 **Price** Free, including Oxo Gallery and Oxo Tower Walkway

👫 **Age range** All

🧑‍🤝‍🧑 **Activities** Sport and dance drop-in classes are available at the nearby Colombo Centre (34–68 Colombo St, SE1 8DP; 020 7261 1658; *jubileehalltrust.org/colombo/).*

🍴 **Eat and drink** *Snacks* House of Crepes (56 Upper Ground, SE1 9PP; 020 7401 9816; 11am–3pm) is one of several options at Gabriel's Wharf *Real meal* Gourmet Pizza Company (59–65 Upper Ground, SE1 9PP; 020 7928 3188; 11:30am–11:30pm daily) serves traditional Italian dishes and tasty pizzas with inventive toppings

🚻 **Toilets** Next to the Studio 6 bar/restaurant

KIDS' CORNER

Have you seen it?
In 2005, the BFI (British Film Institute) made a list of the "Top 50 films you should see by age 14". Here are 10 of the more famous ones – how many of them have you seen?
1 *Beauty and the Beast*
2 *Billy Elliot*
3 *ET The Extra-Terrestrial*
4 *Finding Nemo*
5 *The Princess Bride*
6 *Jason and the Argonauts*
7 *Star Wars*
8 *Raiders of the Lost Ark*
9 *The Wizard of Oz*
10 *Toy Story*
Download the full list at *www. bfi.org.uk/education/ conferences/watchthis*

GIDDY UP!
War Horse is the National Theatre's most successful play ever. It uses life-size puppets to tell the story of a boy, Albert, and his horse, Joey, who is sold to the cavalry during World War I. Joey is worked by three puppeteers: two inside his body, and one moving his head. He has eight "understudy" legs backstage, in case of breakages!

Up on the roof
When the Oxo Tower was built, the owners wanted to advertise their beef stock product called Oxo, on the outside of the building. But London's city council said no. Take the lift to the amazing viewing platform on the eighth floor, and see if you can spot the clever way they got around this problem. (Answer below).

....

Answer: When lit up the windows spell out the product name – OXO

Picnic under £20; Snacks £20–40; Real meal £40–60; Family treat £60 or more (based on a family of four)

⑤ Southbank Centre

Music, dance, art, poetry, comedy... and purple cows

The Southbank Centre comprises three main venues, the Hayward Gallery, the Queen Elizabeth Hall and the Royal Festival Hall, which together showcase all manner of music, art, dance and performance.

The Hayward Gallery is a contemporary art space that puts on innovative and interactive shows. For example, its 2014–15 "Mirrocity" exhibition let visitors explore the effect the digital revolution has had on our experiences. The Royal Festival Hall, built for the 1951 Festival of Britain, is filled with

The Lowdown

- 🌐 **Map ref** 10 H5
  Address Belvedere Road, SE1 8XX; 020 7960 4200; www. southbankcentre.co.uk. Hayward Gallery: 0844 847 9910
- 🚗 **Train** Waterloo, Waterloo East, Charing Cross **Tube** Waterloo, Embankment **Bus stop** Waterloo Bridge, Upper Ground, Waterloo Road, Stamford Street **River bus** Festival Pier; London Eye Millennium Pier; Embankment Pier.
- 🕐 **Open** Royal Festival Hall 10am–11pm daily; Hayward Gallery noon–6pm Mon (to 8pm Thu & Fri), 11am–7pm Tue, Wed, Sat & Sun. Queen Elizabeth Hall: 5–11:30pm daily
- 💲 **Price** Performances individually priced, likewise Hayward Gallery exhibitions (reductions for ages 12–16; under-12s free)
- 🏃 **Activities** For the full programme, visit www.southbankcentre.co.uk/ find/family. The Waterloo Sunset Pavilion has six monitors showing cartoons suitable for all.
- ♿ **Wheelchair access** All venues
- 🍽 **Eat and drink** Snacks Concrete at the Hayward (Hayward Gallery; 020 7921 0758; noon–6pm Mon 11am–11pm Tue–Thu, 11am–midnight Fri & Sat,) serves toasties Family treat Skylon Restaurant (Royal Festival Hall; 020 7654 7800; noon–2:30pm, 5:30pm–10:30pm Mon–Sat, noon–4pm Sun) offers upmarket food.
- 🛍 **Shops** Festival Terrace sells design-led gifts. Royal Festival Hall shop celebrates the artistic programme. Hayward Gallery offers gifts, books and cards.
- 🚻 **Toilets** All venues

exhibition, performance and eating areas. Its eclectic line-up includes Friday Lunch, a free gig in the Foyer Bar (Level 2), and family workshops.

Each April the Centre stages a summer arts festival in the Udderbelly, a pop-up theatre in Jubilee Gardens set inside a giant upside-down purple cow. The programme includes family shows, music and theatre.

Letting off steam

Jubilee Gardens (Belvedere Road, SE1 7XZ; closed Mon) has a play-ground, and from May–Oct, kids can play in Jeppe Hein's "walk-in fountain" on the Festival Hall terrace.

⑥ Sea Life London Aquarium

Find Nemo and outstare a shark

It is said that we know more about deep space than we do about the deep oceans. After visiting the London Aquarium, that claim seems entirely plausible. Its three floors of tanks showcase more than 500 marine species, including amazing fish that change colour, fish that change sex, fish that glow in the dark, and fish that look like snowflakes, butterflies or boulders.

The aquarium tunnels under County Hall, its galleries snaking through vaults that echo with ambient music, which can feel a bit claustro-phobic at busy times. A walk-through glass tunnel brings children eye to eye with turtles, rays and murderous-looking sand tiger sharks. In other zones, kids may get to stroke a starfish or help out with the daily fish feeds, though interactivity is limited. The big climax is the Shark Walk, which dares visitors to tiptoe over a glass platform right above the killers.

Mesmerising creatures of the deep in the Sea Life London Aquarium

The Lowdown

- 🌐 **Map ref** 10 H6
  Address County Hall, Westminster Bridge Road, SE1 7PB; 0871 663 1678; www.visitsealife.com/London
- 🚗 **Train** Waterloo **Tube** Waterloo, Westminster **Bus stop** Belvedere Road, York Road **River bus** London Eye Millennium Pier.
- 🕐 **Open** 10am–7pm daily (last admission: 1 hour earlier)
- 💲 **Price** £81–94 (10 per cent saving by booking online); under 3s free.
- 🏃 **Skipping the queue** Priority Entrance (more expensive) ticket-holders skip most of the queue.
- 👪 **Age range** 3 plus
- 🏃 **Activities** A variety of feeding sessions available to visitors on Tue, Thu & Sat. Check website for dates, times and fees.
- ⏱ **Allow** Up to 1½ hours
- 🍽 **Eat and Drink** Picnic Ned's Noodle Bar (3E Belvedere Road, SE1 7GQ; 020 7593 0077; noon–11:15pm Mon–Sat, till 10:15pm Sun) does kids' noodle boxes Snacks Aji Zen Canteen (County Hall; 020 7620 6117; noon–11pm Mon–Sat, till 10pm Sun) is another tasty option.
- 🛍 **Shop** Selling gifts and souvenirs
- 🚻 **Toilets** All floors

Letting off steam

Try **Jubilee Gardens** (see left), or spacious **Archbishop's Park** (Carlisle Lane, SE1 7LE), just to the south on Lambeth Palace Road.

⑦ London Dungeon

Gruesome tales of London's grisly past

After 40 years under London Bridge, the Dungeon has moved to a larger space in the vaults beneath County Hall. The all-new attraction brings 1,000 years of authentic British history to life with talented live actors and special effects. Visitors are ushered into the Dungeon through a gloomy labyrinth of torchlit rooms showcasing dark chapters from the city's past – from the Black Death and the Guy Fawkes' conspiracy to blow up Parliament to Sweeney Todd and Jack the Ripper – via dismembered corpses and heads on spikes. There's a generous helping of audience participation: children should stand at the back or expect to be locked in a torture chamber, burnt at the stake or operated on by the butcher surgeon. It's all played for laughs (watch out for chamber pots being emptied from medieval windows) – the young cast act with gusto and the Ripper rooms are especially atmospheric – though younger children might find themselves howling more in terror than delight.

Letting off steam
Jubilee Gardens (see left) and **Archbishop's Park** (see left) have good space for running around and grassy areas for picnics.

The Lowdown

🌐 **Map ref** 10 H6
Address Riverside Building, County Hall, Westminster Bridge Road, SE1 7PB; 0871 423 2240; www.thedungeons.com/london

🚃 **Train** Waterloo **Tube** Waterloo, Westminster **Bus stop** Belvedere Road, York Road, Westminster Bridge **River bus** London Eye Millennium Pier, Westminster Pier

🕐 **Open** 10am–5pm Mon–Wed & Fri (from 11am Thu & till 6pm Sat & Sun). Times vary in holidays.

💲 **Price** £74–79; under 4s free (book online for 30% discount)

👫 **Skipping the queue** Priority entry ticket can be purchased online

👫 **Age range** All (under-16s need to be accompanied by an adult aged 18 years and over)

⏱ **Allow** 90 minutes

♿ **Wheelchair access** Yes

🍴 **Eat and drink** Snacks EAT. (Unit 4, Royal Festival Hall) for sand-wiches and pastries Real Meal Giraffe (Belvedere Road, SE1 8XX; 020 7042 6900) for unusual salads and views over Thames.

🛍 **Shop** At the end of the tour

🚻 **Toilets** After the ticket hall

The thrilling speedboat ride, Captain Kidd's Canary Wharf Voyage

⑧ Captain Kidd's Canary Wharf Voyage
Fun fair speedboat ride

This exhilarating speedboat ride takes the family from the London Eye Millennium Pier to Canary Wharf and back in the flash of an eye. It provides the excitement of a fun fair ride and the educational purposes of a tour past some of the city's most famous riverside sights. The guides recount stories about the sights in an engaging and humorous manner, to ensure that kids and adults alike will come away with some new-found knowledge, and the afterglow of the adrenalin rush.

The trip on the compact low-lying red vessels is not only a joy in the summer but also enjoyable during the colder months as you are provided with top-notch sailing gear safety equipment, such as lifejackets.

Letting off steam
Jubilee Gardens (see left) has a playground or **Archbishop's Park** (see left) have space for kids to run around.

The Lowdown

🌐 **Map ref** 10 H6
Address London Eye Millenium Pier, Westminster Bridge, southbank SE1 7PB; 020 7982 8933; www.londonribvoyages.com

🚃 **Tube** Waterloo
Bus Stop Waterloo Bridge

🕐 **Open** Mar–Sep: 10am–6pm daily; Oct–Feb: 10am–6pm Thu–Sun

💲 **Price** £122–130; under-5s free

⛵ **Guided tours** No

👫 **Age range** all ages

⏱ **Allow** 1 hour

♿ **Wheelchair access** Yes

🍴 **Eat and drink** Picnic Ned's Noodle Bar (3E Belvedere Road, SE1 7GQ; 020 7593 0077; noon–11:15pm Mon–Sat, till 10:15pm Sun) does kids' noodle boxes Real Meal Giraffe (Belvedere Road, SE1 8XX; 020 7042 6900) for unusual salads

🚻 **Toilets** Available for use in The London Eye

German Focke Wulf 190, North American P-51 Mustang and British Spitfire at the IWM

⑨ Imperial War Museum (IWM)

War stories and weaponry

Housed in what used to be the Bethlem Royal Hospital, this enormous museum, which tells the stories of people's experiences of war from World War I to the present day, tries hard not to be too gung-ho about its subject. But some kids (and adults) are bound to coo over the vast main hall, literally filled to the rafters with warplanes, tanks, missiles and other deadly hardware. Highlights include British Field Marshall Bernard Montgomery's tank, a Nazi V2 rocket and a one-man submarine.

The IWM makes a real effort to appeal to families through a changing series of well-thought-out galleries and exhibitions. A Family in Wartime highlights the daily struggles of the Allpress family, who

Memorial to the Soviet dead of World War II, Geraldine Mary Harmsworth Park

lived in Stockwell, London during World War II. Their story has been brought to life through a series of photos and interviews. The displays can be unflinching, but are always accessible, with stories to listen to and games to play such as spot the enemy bomber.

Several galleries explore what life was like at home and abroad during both world wars. An exhibition on the Holocaust, some parts of which might be too graphic for pre-teens (under-11s are not allowed to enter), traces the Nazi persecution and murder of Jews, and you can discover the extraordinary stories of bravery behind the Victoria Cross

Up periscope! Children getting hands-on at the Imperial War Museum

and George Cross in The Lord Ashcroft Gallery. There is also a library with a fascinating archive.

Letting off steam

The IWM is set in **Geraldine Mary Harmsworth Park** *(Kennington Road, SE11)*, which has a café, a fine playground, and an indoor play centre for under-5s – or under-12s during school holidays – which is open 1–4pm weekdays.

The Lowdown

🌐 **Map ref** 17 B2
Address Lambeth Rd, SE1 6HZ; 020 7416 5000; www.iwm.org.uk

🚗 **Train** Waterloo, Elephant and Castle **Tube** Lambeth North, Elephant and Castle, Waterloo **Bus stop** Lambeth Road, Kennington Road, St George's Road

🕐 **Open** 10am–6pm daily, last admission: 5:30pm

💲 **Price** Free; temporary exhibitions individually priced

🚩 **Guided tours** Audio guides for adults and children

👫 **Age range** 6 plus, but some exhibitions may be unsuitable for pre-teens

🤸 **Activities** Family activities take place on certain weekends and during school holidays. Check website for the most up-to-date information

⏱ **Allow** Up to 3 hours

♿ **Wheelchair access** Yes, via Park entrance – sometimes parts of exhibitions are not accessible

🍴 **Eat and drink** *Picnic* Café Roma *(Geraldine Mary Harmsworth Park, SE11)* offers ices, shakes and good-value kids' lunch bags. *Snacks* The Garden Café *(Lambeth Palace Rd, SE1 7LB; 020 7401 8865; www. gardenmuseum.org.uk; 10:30am–4:30pm Mon–Fri, till 5:30pm Sat & Sun)* is part of the Garden Museum, set in the former St Mary-at-Lambeth church. The museum has garden history displays and an art cart for children, and the menu at the homely vegetarian café changes daily according to what's in season. The Kitchen Front Café *(10am–5pm daily)*, inside the museum, serves a selection of home-made British dishes, including stews, pies, salads and sandwiches. The café also has a variety of dishes for children

🛍 **Shop** Lower ground floor, selling books, CDs, posters and gifts

🚻 **Toilets** All floors except third and fourth

Prices given are for a family of four

⑩ Florence Nightingale Museum

Throwing light on the Lady With The Lamp

This one-room museum, beside the ambulance bay at St Thomas's Hospital, deserves top marks for making this woman's extraordinary life story so engaging. Florence Nightingale worked as a nurse during the Crimean War (1853–6), and founded Britain's first school of nursing in 1860. The museum is partitioned into three eye-catching "pavilions": the first hemmed by hedgerows to represent Nightingale's gilded youth; the next clad in Turkish tiles, to evoke the Crimean War; the third a mock-up of the bedroom where she spent most of her later life. She was often ill, but became the most popular woman in Victorian England thanks to her tireless campaigning for health reform. Kids can see the figurines that sold by the thousand to Florence's fans, along with her pet owl (stuffed, of course) and that famous lamp.

Florence Nightingale is a genuinely interesting character, but there are also several gadgets to help keep kids' attention, not least the ingenious "stethoscope" audio guide. Touch-screen challenges invite children to pack a medicine chest with useful kit for the battle-field, or wash their hands then scan them for germs. Elsewhere, short films bring the history of nursing up to date – including a look at the MRSA menace raging through modern hospitals. The Lady With The Lamp would not approve.

The Lowdown

Map ref 16 H1
Address 2 Lambeth Palace Road, SE1 7EW; 020 7620 0374; *www.florence-nightingale.co.uk*

Train Waterloo **Tube** Waterloo, Westminster **Bus stop** Westminster Bridge, York Road, Lambeth Palace Road **River bus** London Eye Millennium Pier, Westminster Pier

Open 10am–5pm daily

Price £17, under-5s free

Guided tours Two tours: one for 7–11 year olds and one for adults. Free audio guides for adults and children aged 7–11

Age range 5 plus

Activities Themed art-and-craft activities in school holidays: check website for details. Kids under 7 can follow Florence's story by following the I-Spy trail

Allow Up to 2 hours

Wheelchair access Yes

Eat and drink *Snacks* Yo! Sushi *(County Hall, Belvedere Rd; 020 7928 8871; 11:30am–10pm Mon–Sat, till 7pm Sun)* *Real meal* Troia *(County Hall, 3F Belvedere Road, SE1 7GQ; 020 7633 9309; noon–11:30pm daily)* is a Turkish diner

Shop Selling a range of quirky souvenirs

Toilets On the ground floor

Letting off steam

Just 3 minutes' walk along Lambeth Palace Road is **Archbishop's Park** *(Carlisle Lane, SE1 7LE)*, with a play-ground, a nature garden and tennis courts (0845 130 8998) for hire.

Using a stethoscope to listen to the audio tour at the Florence Nightingale Museum

KIDS' CORNER

Mission impossible?

Imagine you're a soldier in the trenches. Find answers to these questions about your mission in the IWM Trench Experience:

1 What time will the raid start on enemy lines?
2 What is the signal to go "over the top"?
3 What should you try to bring back with you?

Answers at the bottom of the page.

Evacuate!

More than 1 million British children were evacuated in World War II. It must have been scary but exciting to move to the countryside. Why not imagine you're an evacuee, and write a letter home about what happens to you.

Mary's magic herbs

Mary Seacole, another famous nurse during the Crimean War, treated the soldiers using herbal remedies. Match the plant with the ailment it treated (you can find the answers at the museum).

1 Liquorice	**a** Infection
2 Lemongrass	**b** Diarrhoea
3 Cinnamon	**c** Stomach pain
4 Ginger	**d** Fever

Answers at the bottom of the page.

FLORENCE'S ZOO

Florence Nightingale adored animals. Her tortoise Jimmy roamed the hospital in the Crimea, and the soldiers gave her a puppy. She even had a pet cicada – a kind of beetle – until it was eaten by her owl, Athena! You can see Athena (stuffed) at the museum.

Answers: Mission impossible
1 7:15pm **2** A whistle **3** Enemy prisoners
Mary's magic herbs 1c **2**d **3**a **4**b

Kensington,
Chelsea & Battersea

With its world-class museums and fine parks, this wedge of West London feels like a purpose-built family entertainment zone. And in the 1850s, that is more or less what it was. A new cultural quarter in Kensington rose from the proceeds of the 1851 Great Exhibition, while across the river, plant-hunter John Gibson created Battersea Park for the masses. Tying the two together is the King's Road, lined with designer shops and restaurants.

Bloomsbury and Regent's Park

The City and the East End

Westminster and the West End

Southwark and the South Bank

Kensington, Chelsea and Battersea

Highlights

Science Museum
If you think science is boring, think again. The galleries here are filled with interactive hi-tech wizardry, and the live science shows are a blast (see pp180–81).

Natural History Museum
This great museum's collection runs to 70 million specimens – animals, insects, fossils, plants and skeletons. But beware: the T rex comes alive (see pp182–3)!

Victoria and Albert Museum
There's a maze of galleries here so it can be hard on the feet. If that's the case, take a break in the palatial paddling pool (see p184).

Battersea Park
Meet the monkeys at Battersea Park Children's Zoo, then ape them at London's wildest adventure playground (see pp188–9).

Kensington Palace
There's nowhere more regal to take high tea than Queen Anne's Orangery at Kensington Palace – they even serve a special child's version (see p176).

Harrods
For everything your child never knew they needed – how about a diamond-encrusted Monopoly set, bespoke rocking-horse or a doll in their own image (see p181)?

Left Wooden pirate galleon, the impressive centrepiece of the Diana Princess of Wales Memorial Playground, Kensington Gardens Above Meerkat at Battersea Park Children's Zoo

The Best of
Kensington, Chelsea and Battersea

South Kensington's three famous museums – the Science Museum, the Natural History Museum and the Victoria and Albert Museum (V&A) – represent one of the greatest gatherings of wonders in the world. And they're all free. If the children tire of all this learning, the open spaces of Kensington Gardens and Battersea Park are perfect places to let off steam.

Free for all

This affluent area is one of London's best places for a weekend of free family activities. Start at the **Science Museum** *(see pp180–81)* on Saturday: arrive at 10am to get first go on the Launchpad gallery's hands-on experiments, then see the auditorium's lively shows; after that, hit the basement picnic zone (cheaper than the cafés). Round off with the 3:30pm tour in the Exploring Space gallery.

On Sunday, take in some pageantry as Her Majesty's horse guards trot under Wellington Arch *(see p177)* at 10:30am. Afterwards, feed the ducks on the Serpentine lake *(see p174)* in **Hyde**

Left The Peter Pan-themed Diana Princess of Wales Memorial Playground **Below** *Traditional pedalo fun on the Serpentine*

Life-size model of a blue whale, the largest-ever creature on the planet, at the Natural History Museum

Park, then leave the park via the playground at Edinburgh Gate and head to the **V&A** (see p184), which runs free drop-in family workshops till 5pm.

Wet, wet, wet ...

Who doesn't love making a splash – whether it's running a hand through the water from a pedalo in **Battersea Park** (see p188), or total immersion at the Serpentine Lido (see p174), which is open from Jun–Sep and has a paddling pool for little ones. Or you could try the Peter Pan paddling pool at the Diana Princess of Wales Memorial Playground (see p172) in Kensington Gardens.

The museums get in on the act too: the V&A (see p184) allows summer paddling in its courtyard, while in the basement playroom at the **Science Museum** (see pp180–81), kids can splash around with water. In winter, when the weather's wet, head for the Chelsea Sports Centre pool (see p190) and jump right in.

Encounters with nature

With three great parks and the world's biggest collection of birds, beasts and botany, this area is a great place to introduce children to nature. The main draw is the **Natural History Museum** (see p182–3) – so vast that it warrants a day's exploration. First off, book a place on a behind-the-scenes Spirit Collection Tour and consult the film schedule at the Attenborough Studio. Pick up a free children's backpack from the welcome desk and head off to see prehistoric monsters or cheeky monkeys. From 2:30pm, the Investigate Centre invites families to study real specimens.

There is a meerkat enclosure at **Battersea Park Children's Zoo** (see p190), while just across the Thames, the **Chelsea Physic Garden** (p191)

is another hive of animal activity – its holiday workshops include pond-dipping, creepy-crawly handling and herbalism for beginners.

Season by season

In Hyde Park (see p174), spring begins with a bang, with a 41-gun salute on 21 April for the Queen's birthday. From Easter, pedalos and rowing boats glide over the Serpentine, while at the **Natural History Museum** (see p182–3), they open their wildlife garden and pop-up butterfly house. The Chelsea Flower Show (see p187) bursts into bloom in May.

July sees the **Serpentine Galleries** (see p176) launch their summer season and entertainers perform at the Diana Princess of Wales Memorial Playground (see p174). The Proms, an eight-week summer season of orchestral concerts, begin at the **Royal Albert Hall** (see p185).

Winter is festival time. November brings fireworks in **Battersea Park** (see p188) and the city's Christmas bash, Winter Wonderland, in **Hyde Park** (see p174), with Santa, skating and *glühwein*.

A ring-tailed lemur, one of the popular small primates at Battersea Park Children's Zoo

Kensington Gardens, Hyde Park and around

Inspired by the story of Peter Pan, with its pirate galleon and tree full of pixies, the Diana Princess of Wales Memorial Playground in Kensington Gardens is the perfect place to let imaginations run wild. The playground is situated next to the late Princess's Kensington Palace home, with Hyde Park next door for more outdoor fun. Most kids' stuff is concentrated south of the Serpentine swimming lido, making Knightsbridge, on the Piccadilly Tube line, the best route in.

Kensington, Chelsea and Battersea

Kensington Gardens and Hyde Park

Science Museum
p178

Battersea Park
p186

0 metres   200
0 yards   200

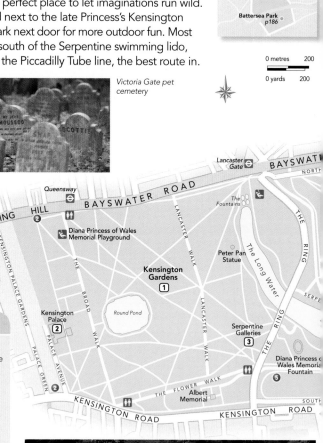

Victoria Gate pet cemetery

The ornate Albert Memorial, Kensington Gardens, commissioned by Queen Victoria after the death of her husband, Albert

Places of interest

SIGHTS
1. Kensington Gardens and Hyde Park
2. Kensington Palace
3. Serpentine Galleries
4. Apsley House

EAT AND DRINK
1. Mount Street Deli
2. Broadwalk Café
3. Serpentine Bar & Kitchen
4. The Cookbook Café
5. Hyde Park Tennis Centre Café
6. Lido Café Bar
7. Hard Rock Café
See also Kensington Palace (p176)

SHOPPING
1. Selfridges

WHERE TO STAY
1. Mandarin Oriental
2. Royal Garden
3. The Parkwood at Marble Arch

Cooling off on a hot day at the Diana Princess of Wales Memorial Fountain

Right The Serpentine Galleries, built in 1934 as a Tea Pavilion, and now home to modern art **Far right** Speakers' Corner in Hyde Park, a bastion of public speaking for 150 years

The Round Pond in Kensington Gardens, popular with wildlife and visitors alike

The Lowdown

🚐 **Rail** Paddington (a 5–10-minute walk) **Tube** Marble Arch, Lancaster Gate, Queensway (all Central Line); Knightsbridge, Hyde Park Corner (both Piccadilly Line) **Bus** Park Lane: route numbers 2, 10, 16, 36, 73, 74, 82, 137, 148, 414, 436; Marble Arch: 6, 7, 23, 98, 113, 159; Bayswater Road: 94, 274, 390; Knightsbridge: 9, 10, 52, 452

ℹ️ **Visitor information** Old Police House, Hyde Park, W2 2UH (www.royalparks.org.uk); Victoria Railway Station (see pp64–5)

🏪 **Supermarkets** Sainsburys Local, Marble Arch Tower, 55 Bryanston Street, W1H 7AA; West One Food Fayre, 85 Duke Street, W1K 5PG **Markets** Bayswater Road Market (art, jewellery), 10am–6pm Sun; Notting Hill Farmers' Market (food), Kensington Church Street, 9am–1pm Sat; Portobello Market 8am–7pm Mon–Sat (fashion, antiques)

🎏 **Festivals** Royal Gun Salutes, near Speakers' Corner (6 Feb, 21 Apr, 2 Jun, 10 Jun and 14 Nov); Barclaycard British Summer Time, music festival with family day (Jun-Jul); Notting Hill Carnival, Aug Bank Holiday weekend; Winter Wonderland, Christmas festival (Nov–Jan)

➕ **Pharmacies** Bliss Chemists, 5–6 Marble Arch, W1H 7EL (9am–11:30pm daily). For 24-hour pharmacies, visit www.nhs.uk/ServiceDirectories

🎪 **Nearest playgrounds** There are three in the parks, at Edinburgh Gate (Hyde Park); Diana Princess of Wales Memorial Playground and Westbourne Gate (both Kensington Gardens)

① Kensington Gardens and Hyde Park
Visit one park and get another one free!

The ever-youthful Peter Pan first sprang to life in Kensington Gardens – his creator JM Barrie lived nearby – and it remains a great place for those who've never really grown up. Along with neighbouring Hyde Park, it offers picnic and play opportunities galore – on both land and water. The LookOut runs arts and crafts programmes inspired by nature, and the Diana Princess of Wales Memorial Walk cleverly links together all the highlights.

Peter Pan statue by the Long Water

Key Features

■ Diana Memorial Walk

Kensington Palace (see p176)

Peter Pan statue

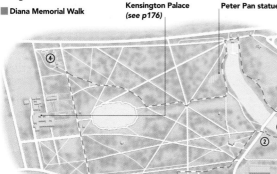

Albert Memorial

① **The Serpentine** Eat beside it, swim in it, row across it, or seek out herons and cormorants in its wilder reaches or swans and geese around its edge.

② **Diana Princess of Wales Memorial Fountain** Created in 2004, in memory of Princess Diana, this is an experiential fountain where kids can dip their toes.

③ **Speakers' Corner** A place for budding orators and eccentrics to address people on any subject they choose. Sunday is the busiest day.

④ **Diana Princess of Wales Memorial Playground** As well as a galleon, there is a music trail and a teepee encampment. Nearby, the ancient Elfin Oak is alive with fairy folk carvings made by Ivor Innes in the 1920s.

The Lowdown

Map ref 8 G4
Address Park Office, Rangers Lodge, W2 2UH; 030 0061 2000; www.royalparks.org.uk.

Tube Marble Arch, Queensway, Lancaster Gate **Bus stop** Black Lion Gate; Marlborough Gate; Marble Arch; Hyde Park Corner; Edinburgh Gate; Royal Albert Hall; Palace Gate

Open Hyde Park: 5am–midnight daily; Kensington Gardens: 6am–dusk daily

Price Free

Guided tours The Royal Parks Foundation run rambles in the parks (www.supporttheroyalparks.org/shop/experiences/filter/walks); 45-minute Albert Memorial tours 1st Sun of month (2pm & 3pm), Mar–Dec (020 7936 2568)

Age range All

Activities The Isis Education Centre runs discovery days in the school holidays (www.supporttheroyalparks.org/explore/isis_education_centre). Serpentine Lido (020 7706 3422) and paddling pool open May: 10am–6pm Sat & Sun; Jun–mid-Sep: 10am–6pm daily (adults £4.60, ages 3–15 £1.10, family ticket £10.50). Hyde Park Tennis & Sports Centre has pay-and-play tennis all year (020 7262 3474). The Boathouse offers boat and pedalo hire, Easter–Oct: 10am–dusk (£29/hour; 020 7262 1330). Solarshuttle boat rides, Mar–Sep: weekends and public hols; Jun–Aug: daily (020 7262 1989; www.solarshuttle.co.uk)

Allow Up to a full day

Wheelchair access There are free electric buggies which give half-hour rides around the park.

Cafés Serpentine Bar & Kitchen (see opposite) or Lido Café Bar (020 7706 7098; www.benugo.com/restaurants/serpentine-bar-kitchen). Snacks at Hyde Park Tennis Centre Café (summer 9am–9pm, winter 10am-4pm; 020 7486 4216) and Broadwalk Café (see right), as well as at kiosks

Toilets At Serpentine Road, the LookOut; Palace Gate, Lancaster Gate, Black Lion Gate, Marlborough Gate (Kensington Gardens)

Good family value?
The park and its three playgrounds are free; swimming and tennis are affordable; only boat hire is pricey.

Prices given are for a family of four

Take cover

If it rains, **Queens Ice and Bowl** (*17 Queensway, W2 4QP; 020 7229 0172; www.queensiceandbowl.co. uk; Mon–Sun 10am–11pm*) is a 2-minute walk north of Black Lion Gate, and offers ice-skating (£41–51; skate hire from £3) and tenpin bowling (£7.50 per person). Alternatively, Kensington's trio of mighty museums (*see pp180–84*) are just a short walk away via Exhibition Road and entirely free.

Youngsters ice-skating at Queens Ice and Bowl

Eat and drink

Picnic: under £30–45; Snacks: under £20; Real meal: £40–65; Family treat: £70 or more (based on a family of four)

PICNIC Delicatessens are more decadent than usual around here. Try Mayfair's **Mount Street Deli** (*100 Mount Street, W1K 2TG; 020 7499 6843, www.themountstreetdeli.co.uk; 8am–6pm Mon–Fri, 9am–5pm Sat*). **SNACKS** **Broadwalk Café** (*020 7034 0722; www.royalparks.org.uk; 8am–8pm in summer, 10am–4pm daily in winter*), by the Diana Princess of Wales Memorial Playground, has a "playcafé" menu for kids.

The Lido Café Bar, on the banks of the Serpentine

REAL MEAL **Serpentine Bar & Kitchen** (*020 7706 8114; www.serpentinebarandkitchen.com; 8am–5pm Mon–Fri, till 7pm Sat & Sun*) overlooks the lake and has a kids menu for £5.

FAMILY TREAT The **Cookbook Café** (*1 Hamilton Place, Park Lane, W1J 3QY; 020 7318 8563, www.cook bookcafe.co.uk; 6:30am–10:30am; noon–3:30pm; 6:30am–10:30pm daily; weekend brunch 12.30pm–3:30pm*) is cool, casual and costly, with hefty Market Table lunches plus a monthly kid's cookery class.

Shopping

The mammouth **Selfridges** department store is nearby (*400 Oxford Street, W1A 1AB; 0800 123400, www.selfridges.com*).

Find out more

DIGITAL A self-guided walk around Hyde Park can be downloaded at *www.royalparks.gov.uk/parks/ hyde-park/things-to-see-and-do/ self-guided-walks.*
FILM The biopic *Finding Neverland* (2004), starring Johnny Depp, used the real Kensington Gardens for the scenes where author JM Barrie first enchanted children with tales of Peter Pan, Wendy and Captain Hook.

Next stop. . .

PORTOBELLO ROAD MARKET
If it's Saturday, walk west from Black Lion Gate to explore Portobello Road Market (*9am–7pm; www. portobelloroad.co.uk*), reputedly the world's biggest antiques jamboree. Children should seek out Mr Punch's Old Toys (*Unit 18, Admiral Vernon Arcade, W11 2DY*) and Victoriana Dolls (*101 Portobello Rd, W11 2QB*).
HYDE PARK STABLES For a canter beside the Serpentine, contact Hyde Park Stables (*63 Bathurst Mews, W2 2SB; 020 7723 2813; www. hydeparkstables.com*), which offers riding lessons on Rotten Row, the 300-year-old royal carriageway. From £79 per hour, beginners welcome.

Putting a pony and young rider through their paces at Hyde Park Stables

② Kensington Palace

A palace full of princesses

It was in 1689 that Kensington Palace first became a royal home, when William of Orange asked architect Christopher Wren to turn a Jacobean manor into a place fit for a king. On 20 June 1837, 18-year-old Princess Victoria woke in her bed here to discover she was queen, and by the 1930s, so many minor royals were quartered in "Princesses' Court" that Edward VIII called it "an aunt heap". But the palace is best known as the long-time home of Diana, Princess of Wales – and as a showcase for her gorgeous array of gowns. William and Kate, the Duke and Duchess of Cambridge, now have an apartment here, too.

Major refurbishment in the last few years has opened up much of the palace, allowing visitors better access to the elegant courtyards, which they can enjoy before touring the highlights of the Royal Ceremonial Dress Collection, with its 12,000 historic garments. Other exhibitions reveal the public and private lives of queens – Mary II, Anne and especially Victoria – and detail the trials and tribulations that come with being a princess, by exploring the lives of Princess Margaret and, of course, Diana.

Letting off steam

Head to the nearby **Diana Princess of Wales Memorial Playground** for a run around (see p174).

The Lowdown

- **Map ref** 7 D5
  Address Kensington Gardens, W8 4PX; 0844 482 7777; www.hrp.org.uk/KensingtonPalace
- **Tube** High Street Kensington, Queensway **Bus stop** Bayswater Road, Knightsbridge
- **Open** Mar–Oct: 10am–6pm daily; Nov–Feb: 10am–5pm daily (last admission: 1 hour earlier)
- **Price** £33–35 (excluding voluntary donation), under-16s free
- **Skipping the queue** Book online to dodge the ticket queue
- **Age range** 5 plus
- **Activities** Free family craft activities in school holidays. Online "games and makes" zone has creative downloadable craft projects. Bookable day workshops for families (check website for details)
- **Allow** Up to 2 hours
- **Wheelchair access** Yes
- **Eat and drink** Snacks The Broadwalk Café (see p175) is lovely when the sun shines Real meal The palace's 300-year-old Orangery is an elegant place for breakfast, a light lunch or afternoon tea (winter: noon–5pm; summer till 6pm). The restaurant has a super kids' menu, and even does a special children's version of afternoon tea
- **Shop** Selling gifts and souvenirs
- **Toilets** On the ground floor

③ Serpentine Galleries

Art in the gardens

These two outstanding – and often underrated – galleries showcase modern and contemporary art. The original gallery looks, from the outside, like a twee 1930s tea pavilion – but step indoors, and surprises lurk. The four stark whitespaces have held exhibitions by Andy Warhol, Damien Hirst and Jeff Koons. Typically, there are five shows a year, and from July to October the gallery spills onto the surrounding lawns, when it invites big names such as Frank Gehry to design a pavilion to host "Park Nights" – a theatre, music and film performance programme. Meanwhile, an artist-led Family Sunday workshop takes place most months, and includes hands-on craft activities.

The second gallery is housed in the Grade II-listed Palladian-style Magazine building across the lake. This satellite gallery, opened in 2012, focuses on young artists, and there is an outdoor Playscape to encourage all ages to play around with art.

The Lowdown

- **Map ref** 8 F6
  Address Kensington Gardens, W2 3XA; 020 7402 6075; www.serpentinegallery.org
- **Tube** Knightsbridge, South Kensington, Lancaster Gate **Bus stop** Knightsbridge
- **Open** 10am–6pm Tue–Sun
- **Price** Free
- **Age range** Call ahead to check suitability of current show
- **Activities** Free Family Sunday workshop most months (noon–5pm). Check website for full programme
- **Allow** 1 hour
- **Wheelchair access** Yes
- **Eat and drink** Snacks Hyde Park Tennis Centre Café (020 7262 3474) offers simple snack fare Real meal Lido Café Bar serves lunches and home-made ice cream (020 7706 7098; www.royalparks.org.uk/hyde-park)
- **Shop** In reception, selling art books and cards
- **Toilets** On the ground floor

The grand entrance gates at Kensington Palace

Prices given are for a family of four

Letting off steam

The galleries are surrounded by open, grassy areas, and there's a playground at the nearby **Serpentine Lido** *(see p174)*.

Children's art workshop at the Serpentine Galleries, a major modern art venue

④ Apsley House

At home with Old Nosey

A door-plate outside Apsley House, known as "Number One, London", says: "To the private apartments of the Duke of Wellington." This mansion on Hyde Park Corner is still part-occupied by descendants of Arthur Wellesley, the first Duke of Wellington, Britain's greatest general and the hero of the Battle of Waterloo (1815). The duke bought the house in 1817, two years after his triumph over Napoleon, and it has been restored to the dazzle of its Regency heyday, filled with the paintings, porcelain and silver given to him by kings and emperors.

Riding along the pleasant bridleways through Hyde Park

In his day, Wellington was said to be "the most famous man in Europe", though his troops nicknamed him "Old Nosey" – and Apsley's jolly children's trail encourages kids to hunt for his aquiline profile all over the house. A giant statue of Napoleon stands in the stairwell, but the highlight is the Waterloo Gallery – with works by Goya, Rubens and Velazquez – where children can lie supine and scan the painted ceiling.

Apsley's front window looks out to Wellington Arch, commissioned by George IV as a grand gateway to Buckingham Palace. An admission fee buys you access to exhibits and a balcony view of the Household Cavalry en route to the Changing the Guard ceremony *(see p70)*.

Letting off steam

Hyde Park is Apsley's back garden and the nearest playground is at the park's Edinburgh Gate.

The Lowdown

- 🌐 **Map ref** 9 B6 **Address** 149 Piccadilly, Hyde Park Corner, W1J 7NT; 020 7499 5676; *www.english-heritage.org.uk/daysout/properties/apsley-house*
- 🚃 **Train** Victoria **Tube** Hyde Park Corner. **Bus stop** Hyde Park Corner
- 🕐 **Open** Apr–Oct: 11am–5pm Wed–Fri; Nov–Mar 10am–4pm Sat & Sun (last admission: 30 minutes before closing). Wellington Arch opens at 10am
- 💲 **Price** £21.10. Joint ticket £23.10 (includes Wellington Arch)
- 👫 **Skipping the queue** The Horse Guards ride through Wellington Arch most days at 10:30am and 11:30am – come early for a view
- 🪧 **Guided tours** Free 15-minute gallery talks daily (times vary)
- 🧍 **Age range** 7 plus
- 🧍 **Activities** Free audio guide. Free children's trail from visitor desk or downloadable online
- ⏱ **Allow** 1–2 hours
- ♿ **Wheelchair access** No, due to unavoidable steps
- 🍽 **Eat and drink** *Snacks* Serpentine Bar & Kitchen *(see p175)* is great for lunches *Real meal* Hard Rock Café (150 Old Park Lane, W1K 1QR; 020 7514 1700; *www.hardrock.com*) is a themed burger joint with an under-11s' menu
- 🛍 **Shop** On the ground floor, selling specialist books and memorabilia
- 🚻 **Toilets** In the basement

Picnic: under £20; **Snacks:** £20–40; **Real meal:** £40–60; **Family treat:** £60 or more (based on a family of four)

Science Museum and around

Prince Albert's dream of a new cultural quarter funded by profits from his 1851 Great Exhibition, ballooned into a trio of colossal free museums south of Hyde Park. From South Kensington Tube station, pedestrian tunnels lead directly to the Science Museum and Natural History Museum, while the Victoria & Albert is just across Exhibition Road. The Science Museum is an especially powerful magnet for kids, using every trick of 21st-century technology to bring its subject to life. This area is a great destination in winter, with almost everything under cover (including indoor playrooms and an IMAX cinema).

Kensington, Chelsea and Battersea

Kensington Gardens and Hyde Park
p172

Science Museum

Battersea Park
p186

Captivated by a statue in the Victoria & Albert Museum

Taking part in a demonstration at the Science Museum

0 metres 200

0 yards 200

Diplodocus skeleton in the Natural History Museum

The Lowdown

🚌 **Tube** South Kensington **Bus** Exhibition Road, South Kensington Tube station: route numbers 14, 49, 70, 74, 345, 414, 430, C1; Kensington Road: 9, 10, 52, 452

ℹ️ **Visitor information** Victoria Railway Station (*see pp64–5*)

🛒 **Supermarkets** Waitrose, Gloucester Arcade, 128 Gloucester Rd, SW7 4SF **Markets** South Kensington Farmers' Market, Bute Street, SW7, 9am–2pm Sat

🎪 **Festivals** Kensington Dollshouse Festival, Kensington Town Hall (May); BBC Proms, Royal Albert Hall (Jul–Sep); London Design Festival, Victoria & Albert Museum (Sep); Harvest Festival, Kensington Gardens (Sep); Festival of Remembrance, Royal Albert Hall (Nov); Winter Wonderland, Hyde Park (Nov–Dec)

➕ **Pharmacies** Boots, 203–205 Brompton Road, SW3 1LA (9am–7pm Mon–Sat; 10am–6pm Sun). Harrods Pharmacy, 87–135 Brompton Road, SW1X 7XL (10am–8pm Mon–Sat; noon–6pm Sun). For 24-hour pharmacies, visit *www.nhs.uk/ServiceDirectories*

🛝 **Nearest playground** Climbing frame at Hyde Park Tennis Centre, near Alexandra Gate; larger playground near Edinburgh Gate

Harrods' Toy Kingdom – guaranteed to excite children young and old

Places of Interest

SIGHTS
1. Science Museum
2. Natural History Museum
3. Victoria & Albert Museum
4. Royal Albert Hall

EAT AND DRINK
1. Partridges
2. Ice Cream Parlour
3. The Burger Bar
4. Verdi Italian Kitchen
5. L'Opera

See also Science Museum (p181), Natural History Museum (p183), Victoria & Albert Museum (p184) and Royal Albert Hall (p185).

SHOPPING
1. Harrods

WHERE TO STAY
1. Crowne Plaza
2. Mandarin Oriental
3. The Beaufort
4. Number Sixteen
5. Beaufort House
6. Fraser Place Queens Gate

① Science Museum
Putting the fizz into physics

Fly with the Red Arrows, fire up a pedal-powered TV set or launch a space probe: the Science Museum offers an explosively entertaining day out. With seven storeys filled with wonders, there's plenty to occupy young and old here. At every turn it's playtime – whether in the Launchpad zone, with its child-friendly experiments, or Antenna, where kids can study scientific breakthroughs. Best of all is the look of the museum – a sci-fi universe of neon-lit galleries that makes just being there an adventure.

Replica of Sir Isaac Newton's telescope

Key features

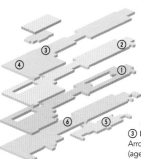

① **Who Am I?** An intriguing interactive gallery using face-morphing, sex-switching gadgets and personality tests to explore human identity.

② **Atmosphere** Play games on the tabletops, walk across oceans and see how the environment adjusts in this climate-change hall controlled by its visitors.

③ **Fly Zone** Soar with the Red Arrows in a "3-D aerobatic experience" (ages 4 plus), or take the controls in a "Fly 360°" simulator (9 plus).

④ **Launchpad** This kids' gallery has lots of hands-on experiments and science shows with audience participation.

Fifth Floor Veterinary History, History of Medicine.

Fourth Floor Glimpses of Medical History.

Third Floor Launchpad, Flight and the Fly Zone, plus Health and 18th-century medicine.

Second Floor Energy, Computers, Mathematics, Ships, Docks and Diving, and Atmosphere.

First Floor Materials, Communication, the Cosmos, Time, Agriculture and Who Am I?

Ground floor Energy and the power of steam, Exploring Space, Making the Modern World and Pattern Pod for families.

Basement The Garden gallery and a display on labour-saving gadgets for the home.

⑤ **The Garden** This basement playroom invites pre-schoolers to get to grips with the material world, via water troughs, junk instruments and a "building site" climbing frame. It's mayhem!

⑥ **Eagle capsule** This full-size replica of the Apollo 11 craft that put Armstrong and Aldrin on the moon in 1969 is in the Exploring Space gallery.

Letting off steam

The museum's own The Garden playroom (ages 3–6, basement) and Pattern Pod (ages 5–8, ground floor) are both rule-free romping spaces. For alfresco action, head 5 minutes along Exhibition Road into **Hyde Park** for tennis, playgrounds and pedaloes. The area between Rotten Row and the South Carriage Drive is set aside for Frisbee and ball games.

The very open and child-friendly spaces of Hyde Park – perfect for picnics

Eat and drink
Picnic: under £20; Snacks: £20–40; Real meal: £40–60; Family treat: £60 or more (based on a family of four)

PICNIC Partridges (17–19 Gloucester Road, SW7 4PL; 020 7581 0535; www.partridges.co.uk; 8am–11pm daily) offers superior cold cuts and nibbles.

SNACKS Ice Cream Parlour (2nd Floor, Harrods, 87–135 Brompton Road, SW1X 7XL; 020 7893 8959; www.harrods.com/content/the-store/restaurants/ice-cream-parlour; 11am–8pm Mon–Sat, 11:30am–6pm Sun).

REAL MEAL The Burger Bar (4th Floor, Harrods, 87–135 Brompton Road, SW1X 7XL; 020 7730 1234; www.harrods.com/content/the-store/restaurants/the-burger-bar; noon–9pm Mon–Sat, noon–6pm Sun) is the store's family diner, with burgers and milkshakes to eat.

FAMILY TREAT The Royal Albert Hall's **Verdi Italian Kitchen** (Door 12, SW7 2AP; 020 7070 4401; www.royalalberthall.com; noon–8:30pm Tue–Sun) is a sleek and grown-up place to dine before (or during) a show. It has free jazz or world music most Friday lunchtimes (noon to 1:30pm) and over Sunday brunch, and an enticing menu for under-12s.

Prices given are for a family of four

The Lowdown

🌐 **Map reference** 14 F2
Address Exhibition Road, SW7 2DD; 0870 870 4868; www.sciencemuseum.org.uk

🚇 **Tube** South Kensington **Bus stop** Exhibition Road, South Kensington Tube station: route numbers 14, 49, 70, 74, 345, 414, 430, C1; Kensington Road: 9, 10, 52, 452

🕐 **Open** 10am–6pm daily (until 7pm during school holidays); last admission 5:15pm; plus 6:45–10pm on last Wed of month (adults only)

💷 **Price** Free. Charges apply for IMAX 3-D cinema (£94–120), simulator rides and some temporary exhibitions

👪 **Skipping the queue** Launchpad is the big draw for kids, so arrive at 10am and head there first. The gallery is quieter when the live science shows are on

🚩 **Guided tours** Free 30-minute tours (ages 13 plus) at 1pm, 2pm and 3pm most days, focusing on specific galleries. Cockroach tours (with costumes) start at 2pm and 4pm at weekends and during Lates each month

👫 **Age range** All

🎭 **Activities** Free 20-minute science shows, seven times daily (ages 7 plus); storytelling (under-7s) weekends at 1:30pm – both in Launchpad. School

holiday shows feature Albert Einstein, aviator Amy Johnson and more. Live science experiments sometimes invite museum-goers to take part in research. World Wonders and Contemporary Art trails for older children are downloadable online. Monthly Science Night sleepovers, usually on Fridays, for ages 7–13 (minimum group size six, including parent/guardian, £45pp)

⏱️ **Allow** Up to a day

♿ **Wheelchair access** Yes, all floors

☕ **Cafés** Energy Café serves buffet-style lunches; Deep Blue Diner is a waiter-service family diner – both on ground floor. Shake Bar (Floor 3) and Media Space Café (Floor 2) do snacks. Picnic area around the museum

🛍️ **Shop** On the ground floor, filled with brain-testing games, toys and clever souvenirs

🚻 **Toilets** All floors except 5

Good family value?
The IMAX cinema and flight simulators charge, but with science shows, family tours and hands-on galleries galore, there is more than enough free stuff to fill a day. To avoid being pestered for pennies for the kids' rides, steer clear of the café next to the Fly Zone.

Find out more
There are entertaining and fact-packed digital mini-sites devoted to the museum's galleries online at www.sciencemuseum.org.uk/onlinestuff, which also has more than a dozen brain-expanding computer games: work out how to help the Energy Ninjas beat climate change, or build cuddly "Things" using chromosomes and genes.

Next stop. . .
ALBERTOPOLIS Explore the museums of Exhibition Road on foot with an architectural scavenger hunt from the Royal Institute of British Architects, downloadable at http://www.architecture.com/Library/DrawingsAndPhotographs/Albertopolis/ExploringSouth Kensington/ScavengerHunt.aspx

HARRODS When little (and big) brains start to ache, there's always Harrods (87–135 Brompton Road, SW1X 7XL), cascading with fairylights. London's most over-the-top department store caters for kids on the fourth floor, with its Toy Kingdom and "children's fashion rooms". The pet department is fun, too, with doggie four-poster beds and cookbooks for cats.

Harrods' Toy Kingdom – where future Formula One stars start out

② Natural History Museum

Life on Earth – in 70 million specimens

Imagine a dinosaur rampaging around a cathedral. That's the scene that confronts children entering the hallowed Central Hall of the Natural History Museum – and it's sure to grip them from the start. A full-size Diplodocus dominates the lobby, and a sharp left turn from here leads into the dinosaur gallery, stalked by scores of skeletal monsters from prehistoric times.

This is just the beginning of the museum's extraordinary expedition through life on Earth. In other halls, a blue whale dangles from the ceiling, leaf ants scurry and an earthquake simulator shakes. On the lower ground floor, the Investigate Centre has shelf after shelf stacked with exhibits for kids to hold and examine. And don't miss the Darwin Centre, housed in a great white cocoon, which uses wall-to-wall digital wizardry to reveal how the museum collects and conserves its 70 million specimens.

Families should begin their visit at the welcome desk in the Central Hall. The free Explorer backpacks guide under-8s on exciting investigations into the natural world, well-equipped with binoculars, magnifying glass and clue book. There are various Discovery booklets as well, themed on mammals, dinosaurs

Key Features

① **Investigate Centre** This invites children aged 7–14 to grab trays loaded with skins, skulls, rocks and bones, and view them under a microscope. Open 3:30–5pm daily, weekends and holidays 11am–5pm.

② **Dinosaur Exhibition** See a giant animatronic Tyrannosaurus rex lunge to life here. The beast was eight times more powerful than a lion, and could have swallowed a human whole.

③ **Treasures** Home to an amazing display of specimens and objects, such as the dinosaur teeth that sparked the discovery of these giant creatures, each of the 22 exhibits here has a fascinating story to tell.

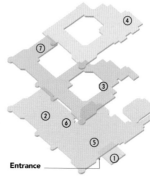

■ **Second Floor**	■ **Ground Floor**
■ **First Floor**	■ **Lower Ground**

Entrance

⑤ **Central Hall** Under the vaulted arches here, the museum's most astonishing exhibits line up, including its famous replica of a *Diplodocus* dinosaur skeleton and a model of the extinct, flightless giant moa bird.

④ **Quake simulator** Walk into a model of a Japanese supermarket and hold on tight as a re-creation of the 1995 Kobe earthquake shudders the floor. Meanwhile, CCTV screens show scenes from the real thing.

⑥ **The Human Biology Zone** Head here for an entertaining skip through the body and brain. Scan microscopic liver cells, wander inside a womb, and have a go at fun memory tests and optical illusions.

⑦ **Darwin Centre** Journey through the centre's amazing eight-storey white cocoon and discover incredible specimens, exciting displays and shows, and also see leading scientists at work.

Prices given are for a family of four

or rocks for children aged 5–7 and 8–11 (£1 each). For pre-schoolers, there's the Bookasaurus dinosaur trail (free). In the Darwin Centre, pick up a NaturePlus smartcard, which allows digital specimens to be scanned during a visit, for online investigation at home.

Science Focus specimen-handling sessions take place in the Darwin Centre and selected other galleries: weekdays 10:45am–2pm, weekends 11:15am–3pm. There are also hands-on nature workshops, which take place at weekends and every day during school holidays from 2–5pm.

Free 30-minute Nature Live shows and talks (for ages 8 and over) run in the Attenborough Studio, daily at 2:30pm, weekends and school holidays at 12:30pm and 2:30pm; the studio also screens nature documentaries daily. Monthly Dino Snores museum sleepovers are open to ages 7–11; £60 per person.

Check the museum website for the school holiday events programme, which typically includes live actors performing in character as famous figures from science. In recent summers, a temporary butterfly house has been erected on the East Lawn

Beehive in the Natural History Museum's Wildlife Garden

(typically Apr–Sep). Finally, there is lots to explore and investigate on the Kids Only web pages, including nature-cams, games and picture galleries.

Letting off steam

The museum's East and West lawns, on Cromwell Road, welcome picnickers, and the neighbouring Wildlife Garden, with its working beehives, pond and wide variety of other natural habitats is a great place to explore and is open from April to October (10am–5pm).

KIDS' CORNER

Speak like a whale

Can you communicate like a whale? Pinch your nose and close your mouth, then say "oh" three times, sending the sound echoing through your skull. That's roughly how whales "speak" – but underwater, their messages can travel up to 100 km (62 miles)!

Flesh eaters!

Curators add 150,000 new specimens to the collection every year, and one team of workers spends every day just munching on meaty carcasses, stripping them down to their bones. Can you guess what they are? For the answer, and to see them in action, visit *www.nhm.ac.uk/kids-only/naturecams.*

DINOSAUR HUNTER

You're never too young to be a naturalist. One little girl became famous for her discoveries – the fossil hunter Mary Anning. When she was just 12, Mary found the first skeleton of an ichthyosaur – a giant sea reptile that lived during the dinosaur era. Look out for Mary's story in the museum's Green Zone.

Monkey puzzle

Can you solve this conundrum? You are a macaque monkey, and you find some tasty grains lying on a beach, but they are all mixed up with the sand. What's an easy way to separate the grains so you can eat them? (Clue: look for a rock pool).

Answer: **Monkey puzzle** Put the mixture in a rock pool. Only the grains will float, then you can scoop them up for lunch.

The Lowdown

🌐 **Map reference** 14 F2
Address Cromwell Road, SW7 5BD; 020 7942 5000; www.nhm.ac.uk

🚗 **Tube** South Kensington (on Circle, District and Piccadilly lines)
Bus stop South Kensington; Exhibition Road

🕐 **Open** 10am–5:50pm daily; last admission 5:30pm. After Hours opening (till 10:30pm, last Fri of month) offers live music, debates, films and food

💲 **Price** Free. Some temporary exhibitions charge

🚶 **Skipping the queue** Spirit Collection tour has limited places: book on arrival at museum, or by phone after 10:15am on the day)

🏁 **Guided tours** Free 30-minute Spirit Collection tour (ages 8 plus) goes backstage at the Darwin Centre up to four times daily. Extended 50-minute tour at 3.15pm weekdays

👫 **Age range** All

🤸 **Activities** Monthly Nature Live Nights open up the museum after hours, mainly for adults (see website)

⏱ **Allow** Up to a day

♿ **Wheelchair access** Yes

☕ **Cafés** The museum's striking galleried restaurant in the Green Zone (11am–3:30pm weekdays, till 4pm weekends and school holidays) serves ploughman's lunches and hot dishes, and offers a hearty children's menu. The Central Café in the Blue Zone does lighter bites and kids' lunch bags, plus there's a basement snack bar and picnic area

🛍 **Shops** There are three. The main shop near the entrance has imaginative nature-themed gifts; Dino Store and Earth Shop sell dinosaur- and planet-themed items

🚻 **Toilets** On all floors

Picnic: under £20; **Snacks:** £20–40; **Real meal:** £40–60; **Family treat:** £60 or more (based on a family of four)

③ Victoria & Albert Museum

A labyrinth of artistic delights

For a first-time visitor, wandering the 145 galleries of the Victoria & Albert Museum (V&A) can feel like being in a very odd dream: turn a corner, and there's a hall hung with the enormous Raphael Cartoons; climb a staircase, and there's a chamber encrusted with Fabergé gems. Room after room is crammed with the world's most dazzling array of decorative arts – glass, ceramics, sculpture, furniture, textiles, silver and more, spanning five continents and 5,000 years. Perhaps it's best to forget the museum map and just roam, so the most dramatic galleries come as a breathtaking surprise. The Cast Courts, for example, are dominated by a towering 30-m (98-ft) replica of Rome's Trajan's Column, chopped in half to fit under the ceiling.

For children, the V&A can be a little overwhelming, especially since most exhibits are presented very conventionally – don't expect the interactive thrills of the Science and Natural History museums. However, the British galleries on Levels 2 and

The entrance of the Victoria & Albert Museum, designed by Aston Webb

4 include a series of ante-rooms with hands-on activities, one for each historical period. These follow a repeating format, with a dressing-up corner (Victorian crinolines, Tudor gauntlets); a design table (weave a tapestry, make a bookplate); and a construction puzzle (piece together a chair, build a model of the Crystal Palace). The museum also hosts a number of free activities every day, including storytelling, arts and crafts, tours and treasure hunts. The bookable family workshops give families an opportunity to learn

from an experienced artist or designer using quality materials (recommended for kids aged 5–12).

The V&A's toy collection is now held at its sister museum in Bethnal Green (see pp206–7), but by way of compensation, objects from the defunct Theatre Museum at Covent Garden are displayed in a suite of rooms on Level 3. These are unmissable with kids; they feature backstage film clips from West End shows, a mock-up of pop diva Kylie Minogue's dressing-room, doll-size models of theatrical sets, and flamboyant costumes from *The Lion King*. There are outfits to try on, too.

Letting off steam

The V&A's majestic courtyard garden has lawns and a summer café – plus what must be London's grandest paddling pool, which welcomes waders during warm weather.

The Lowdown

- 🌐 **Map ref** 14 G2
  Address Cromwell Rd, SW7 2RL; 020 7942 2000, www.vam.ac.uk
- 🚌 **Tube** South Kensington
  Bus stop Exhibition Road, South Kensington tube station
- 🕐 **Open** 10am–5:45pm Sat–Thu; 10am–10pm Fri (selected galleries open late)
- 💷 **Price** Free; some temporary exhibitions charge (all free for under-12s)
- 🏃 **Skipping the queue** Advance booking advised for temporary shows or events, available up to 48 hours ahead (www.vam.ac.uk)
- 🚩 **Guided tours** Private 1 hour 30 minute tours are available daily. The tours cost £17.50 per person and you will need to contact the booking office in advance on 020 7942 2211 to make a booking
- 👫 **Age range** 5 plus
- 🎒 **Activities** Eight different backpacks for ages 5–12, available till 4pm from the information desk as well as Agent Animal bags for under-5s; plus activity trails devoted to

  Tudor and Silver galleries; and Picnic Parties (ages 7–12). Free family Drop-in Design sessions every Sun (10:30am–5pm); free 25-minute Gallery Plays every Sat (11am, 1pm, 3pm). Regular Sat workshops for ages 11–19 on photography, fashion and theatre (www.vam.ac.uk/create), plus school holiday events (www.vam.ac.uk/families)

- ⏱ **Allow** At least 2 hours
- ♿ **Wheelchair access** Yes; building is Grade I-listed – lifts are used to visit all areas and levels
- 🍴 **Eat and drink** *Snacks* L'Opera (241 Brompton Rd, SW3 2EP; 020 7052 9000; www.lopera.co.uk; 10am–11pm), across the road from the museum, is an opulent patisserie-deli *Real meal* The V&A's Café (10am–5:15pm, Fri till 9:30pm), the world's oldest museum restaurant, offers half-price main courses for under-10s
- 🛍 **Shop** Gift and bookshop
- 🚻 **Toilets** On all levels

The Cast Courts in the V&A, housed in two vast galleries, make a real impression

The North Porch of the Royal Albert Hall, viewed from the Albert Memorial

④ Royal Albert Hall

Crown prince of concert venues – home of the Proms

Wagner and Verdi; Einstein and Shackleton; Frank Sinatra and Jay Z; Nelson Mandela and the Dalai Lama; the Beatles and the Rolling Stones – they've all appeared here. Does any concert hall in the world have a roster of greats to rival this one? Squatting like a big pink blancmange on the edge of Kensington Gardens, the Royal Albert Hall is the most instantly recognizable performance space in London – and is every bit as iconic on the inside, as its daily front-of-house tours reveal.

The Hall opened in 1871, fulfilling Prince Albert's vision of a venue "for the advancement of the arts and sciences", and improbably, it is still part-supported by profits from his Great Exhibition of 1851, staged across the road in the Crystal Palace. Best known today for the pomp and circumstance of the annual BBC Proms classical music season, it also hosts rock, jazz, comedy and circus performances, film launches and Masters tennis.

Children will love the glamour of the elliptical auditorium, with its dome full of flying saucers (part of the complex acoustics) – especially since the guided tours approach it via the Queen's retiring rooms behind the royal box. Tours also peek into the balustraded "smoking gallery" up in the eaves, where £5 standing tickets can be had on the day of the show. Note that under 5s are not permitted.

Letting off steam

The green lawns of **Kensington Gardens** are across the road – head north past the Round Pond for the Diana Princess of Wales Memorial Playground (see p174).

The Lowdown

🌐 **Map ref** 14 F1
Address Kensington Gore, SW7 2AP; Box Office: 0845 401 5045; *www.royalalberthall.com*

🚇 **Tube** South Kensington, High Street Kensington **Bus stop** Kensington Rd, Queen's Gate, Exhibition Rd

🕐 **Open** Box office 9am–9pm daily. Performance times vary

💷 **Price** Show tickets vary; from £25

🚶 **Skipping the queue** For tours, advance booking recommended

🚩 **Guided tours** 1-hour tours every 30 minutes, except on matinee days, £12 per adult, under 15s £5. Call 0845 401 5045 to book. For back-stage tours check website

👫 **Age range** 7 plus on guided tours

🎭 **Activities** Occasional free family concerts during school holidays; regular jazz and comedy shows in the Elgar Room, plus Classical Coffee Mornings most Sundays at 11am (charges apply)

♿ **Wheelchair access** Yes, via ramps and lifts

🍴 **Eat and drink** *Real meal* the Elgar Bar & Grill is an informal restaurant *Family treat* Coda offers more formal modern British cooking and a cocktail bar. (both on Level 3, and open two hours before shows)

🛍️ **Shop** Near box office

🚻 **Toilets** In lobby

Battersea Park and around

Battersea Park boasts a Thames-side promenade, a bucolic boating lake, a miniature zoo and the city's most action-packed adventure playground (in the southwest corner). Approach on foot from Sloane Square Tube station (a 10-minute walk), perhaps diverting along Royal Hospital Road to the National Army Museum, which offers an indoor play zone for younger children – handy when it's wet.

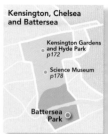

Kensington, Chelsea and Battersea

Kensington Gardens and Hyde Park *p172*

Science Museum *p178*

Battersea Park

The Chelsea Physic Garden, created in 1673 to help with the identification of medicinal plants

The beautiful surroundings at Battersea Park Lake

Boy with a Dolphin, Cheyne Walk, created by David Wynne in 1975

Places of Interest

SIGHTS
1. Battersea Park
2. Battersea Park Children's Zoo
3. National Army Museum
4. Chelsea Physic Garden

● EAT AND DRINK
1. Le Pain Quotidien
2. The Stockpot
3. San Gennaro
4. The Gallery Mess
5. Made in Italy
6. My Old Dutch
See also Battersea Park

(p188), Battersea Park Children's Zoo (p190), National Army Museum (p190) and Chelsea Physic Garden (p191)

● PLACES TO STAY
1. Sydney House

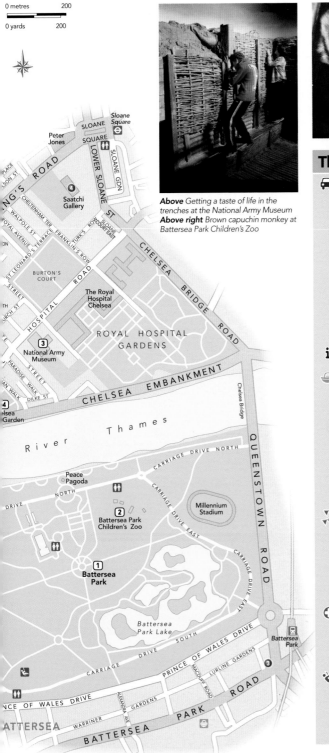

Above *Getting a taste of life in the trenches at the National Army Museum*
Above right *Brown capuchin monkey at Battersea Park Children's Zoo*

The Lowdown

🚃 **Rail** Battersea Park or Queenstown Road (5-minute walk). **Tube** Sloane Square (10 mins), Pimlico (15 mins) **Bus** Chelsea Bridge: route numbers 44, 137, 452; Battersea Park Station: 156, 344; Chelsea Embankment: 170, 360; Battersea Bridge: 19, 49, 319, 345; King's Road: 11, 22, 211 **River bus** Cadogan Pier, on River Taxi route between Blackfriars and Putney, peak hours only Mon–Fri (01342 820600; www.thamesriver services.co.uk/wpb/thames executivecharters.cfm)

ℹ️ **Visitor information** Victoria Railway station, (see pp64–5)

🍽️ **Supermarkets** Waitrose, 196–198 King's Road, SW3 5XP; Tesco Metro, 275–277 Battersea Park Road, SW11 4LU; Here, 125 Sydney Street, SW3 6NR
Markets Battersea High Street Market (mixed), 9am–4pm Sat; Chelsea Antiques Market, King's Road, 2–8pm Wed, 11am–6pm Thu–Sat, 11am–5pm Sun; Pimlico Road Farmers' Market, Orange Square, 9am–1pm Sat

🎉 **Festivals** BADA Antiques & Fine Art Fair, Duke of York Square (Mar); RHS Chelsea Flower Show, Royal Hospital Chelsea (May); Masterpiece Art Fair, Royal Hospital Chelsea (Jun–Jul); Bastille Day, Battersea Park (Jul); Battersea Park fireworks (Nov)

➕ **Pharmacies** Healthchem, 166–168 Battersea Bridge Rd, SW11 3AW; 9am–7:30pm Mon–Fri, 9am–6pm Sat. For 24-hour pharmacies, visit www.nhs.uk/ServiceDirectories

🛝 **Nearest playground** Adventure playground and toddler area inside Sun Gate (southwest corner) in the park; St Luke's Park (see p191)

① Battersea Park
London's best adventure playground

It may lack the royal pedigree of Regent's Park or Kensington Gardens, but Battersea Park has its fair share of exotica. Meet monkeys and meerkats at the children's zoo, take tea beside fantastical fountains, hide behind palms in Britain's original sub-tropical gardens and meditate beside a Japanese peace pagoda. What's more, Battersea is the only major city-centre park with a Thames-side promenade, thronging at weekends with baby buggies, roller-skaters and some of the best-dressed joggers in the world.

Pagoda statue

Key Features

① **Peace Pagoda** Built by Japanese monks in 1984 as a shrine to universal peace, the four gilded sculptures here recount Buddha's path to enlightenment.

Recumbent Cycling Half-bike, half-go-kart, these curious "lie-down" contraptions are rentable for all ages. If that sounds too intrepid, there's a toddlers' train.

② **Pleasure Gardens** During the 1951 Festival of Britain, Londoners flocked to the Battersea Pleasure Gardens for the funfair and flowers. Today, there is a fairytale tea terrace to enjoy.

⑤ **Sub-Tropical Gardens** Created by John Gibson, with finds from his orchid-hunting expeditions in India, this caused a sensation in 1860s London.

③ **Millennium Arena** The park's main sports hub has an eight-lane running track, 19 floodlit tennis courts, all-weather pitches and a gym. It's open to all.

④ **Pump House Gallery** The Victorian engine house now hosts changing exhibitions of contemporary art.

Children's Zoo
(see p190)

⑥ **Boating Lake** A wooded idyll sprinkled with tree-branch bridges, the lake has sculptures by Henry Moore and Barbara Hepworth, a waterside café and boats for hire.

The Lowdown

🌐 **Map reference** 15 A6 **Address** Park Offices, Battersea Park, SW11 4NJ; 020 8871 7530, www.wandsworth.gov.uk/parks

🚗 **Rail** Battersea Park or Queenstown Road **Tube** Sloane Square (Circle and District lines) or Pimlico (Victoria line) **Bus stop** Chelsea Bridge, Battersea Park Station, Chelsea Embankment, Battersea Bridge **River** Cadogan Pier

🕐 **Open** Daily 6:30am–10:30pm

💲 **Price** Park admission free; charges apply for zoo, boating, cycle hire and sports pitches

🚩 **Guided tours** None; self-guided walk leaflets from Park Office (open weekdays only, 9am–5pm)

👫 **Age range** All

🏃 **Activities** Adventure Playground 6:30am–10:30pm daily. Land train runs July–August. Cycle hire weekends and holidays from 10am (from £10 per hour; 020 7498 6543, www.londonrecumbents.co.uk). Boat hire Easter to September, weekends and school holidays only (£15 per half-hour; 020 7262 1330, www.solarshuttle.co.uk). Frequent school holiday art workshops at Pump House Gallery open 11am–4pm Wed–Sun (020 8871 7572, www.pumphousegallery.org.uk). Millennium Arena open weekdays 7am–10pm, 9am–6pm Sat, till 9:30pm Sun (020 8871 7537); tennis bookings (020 8871 7537). Occasional funfairs in school and bank holidays

🕐 **Allow** Half a day

☕ **Cafés** Family-run La Gondola al Parco (near Rosery Gate, open 8.30am–8pm in summer, winter till 4pm; 020 7978 1655; www.batterseapark.org/info/eating/la-gondola-al-parco) does home-style Italian staples and a kids' menu, by the lakeside. The Tea Terrace Kiosk (8:30am–7pm) has snacks; plus weekend sandwich van with picnic tables, outside the adventure playground.

🚻 **Toilets** Near fountains, zoo entrance and adventure playground.

Good family value?
The brilliant playground is free; the zoo, cycling and boating are affordable. What's not to like?

Take cover

The refurbished Adventure Playground, with exciting new equipment, is a fun stop for kids aged 5 to 16 (for opening times, see Lowdown). Just across the river is **Chelsea Sports Centre** (Chelsea Manor Street, SW3 5PL; 020 7352 6985, www.better.org.uk/leisure/chelsea-sports-centre#/) with good-value swimming, including junior lessons (pool open weekdays 6:30am–10pm; Sat 8am–8pm; Sun 8am–10pm).

Eat and drink

Picnic: £30–35; Snacks: £30–50; Real meal: £40–60; Family treat: £60 or more (based on a family of four)

PICNIC Le Pain Quotidien (201 King's Road, SW3 5ED; 020 7486 6154, www.lepainquotidien.co.uk; 7am–9pm Mon–Fri, 8am–9pm Sat, 8am–7pm Sun) serves a wide selection of breads, cakes, pastries and tarts. The light lunches offered include delicious salads and soups.
SNACKS The endless menu at **The Stockpot** (273 King's Road, SW3 5EN; 020 7823 3175; www.stockpotchelsea.co.uk; 9am–11pm Mon–Sat, 11:30am–11pm Sun) should please even the fussiest young palate – there are traditional English dishes as well as a huge range of continental favourites. Takeaways are also available – and it's very cheap for Chelsea.
REAL MEAL South of the park, **San Gennaro** (22 Battersea Park Road, SW11 4HY, 020 7622 0475, www.sangennaro.co.uk; 5– 10:30pm daily) is a super-authentic, super-friendly pizzeria – evenings only, but half-price before 6:30pm.

Enjoying lunch at the Lemon Tree Café in the Battersea Park Children's Zoo

FAMILY TREAT The Gallery Mess (Saatchi Gallery, Duke of York's HQ, King's Road, SW3 4RY; 020 7730 8135, www.saatchigallery.co.uk; 10am–11:30pm Mon–Sat, till 7pm Sun) does deceptively sophisticated comfort food. Daily specials using fresh seasonal ingredients and a constantly changing menu means there is something for everyone. Outdoor dining is available during the summer months. Champion of Damien Hirst and Tracey Emin, the Saatchi is a bastion for provocative new art: while the kids are eating, sneak around the gallery to check if the current show is too shocking for them.

Find out more

DIGITAL Print off a copy of a picture from the colouring gallery, or draw one yourself, and then colour it in to recreate beautiful flowers spotted in Battersea Park: www.coloring-pictures.net/misc-flowers.html

Families enjoying a tour of Stamford Bridge football ground

Next stop. . .

CHELSEA FOOTBALL GROUND
A 20-minute walk via Albert Bridge (or a ride on the number 11 bus from the King's Road) brings the story of association football up to date: from Battersea-based Wanderers FC, who won the first FA Cup back in 1872, to modern-day maestros Chelsea FC. For football lovers, there is the opportunity to have a 1-hour tour of the club's stadium, Stamford Bridge, which run daily from 10am–3pm, except on match-days (£56 and up depending on package, under 5s free; 0871 984 1955, www.chelseafc.com/tours). Nearby Brompton Cemetery (open 8am–6pm daily) is worth a look too, for its Beatrix Potter connections.

② Battersea Park Children's Zoo

Mingle with meerkats and ogle an otter

Chinchillas have the softest fur of any creature on Earth; brown capuchin monkeys smear garlic on their bodies to smell nice; and meerkats can sneak up on scorpions and bite off their stings. This modest menagerie can't compete with London Zoo, with its gorillas and lions, but compensates with intriguing titbits about the behaviour of its cute inhabitants.

The zoo is all about catering for kids – every resident seems to have a name, from Piggle and Wiggle the pigs to Morris and Murray the talking mynah birds – and at weekends children can help feed some of the animals. As well as several small primates, the zoo features child-friendly farm animals, interesting birds from emus to zebra finches, and a Mouse House filled

The Lowdown

🌐 **Map ref** 15 B6
   Address Battersea Park, Chelsea Bridge Gate, SW11 4NJ; 020 7924 5826; www.batterseapark zoo.co.uk

🚗 **Rail** Battersea Park, Queenstown Road **Tube** Sloane Square, Pimlico **Bus stop** Chelsea Bridge, Battersea Park Station, Chelsea Embankment, Battersea Bridge **River bus** Cadogan Pier

🕐 **Open** Apr–Sep:10am–5:30pm daily; Nov–Mar till 4:30pm or dusk (last admission: 30 minutes earlier)

💲 **Price** £28–37

👫 **Age range** 2 plus

🏃 **Activities** Feeding times at weekends and school holidays: otters and meerkats 11am, 2:30pm; monkeys 11:30am, 3pm; farm animals noon and 3:30pm. Storytime Wednesdays in Feb and Mar; drop-in activities during school holidays (check website)

⏱ **Allow** Up to 2 hours

♿ **Wheelchair access** Yes, via ramped entrance

☕ **Eat and drink** Snacks Lemon Tree Café in the zoo serves sandwiches, soup and cakes. Real meal La Gondola al Parco (see p188), beside the boating lake, offers hot dishes

🛍 **Shop** Near the ticket office

🚻 **Toilets** Near the gift shop

The ever-popular meerkat enclosure at Battersea Park Children's Zoo

with pet–size animals; there's also a butterfly garden. Stars of the show are the meerkats, and kids get to crawl through a tunnel into their compound, popping their heads up for a closer view.

Two hours is ample time here, even allowing for a long frolic in the excellent playground, which includes a full-size fire engine to "drive", hay bales to clamber on and an enormous sandpit.

Take cover

The zoo is mostly outdoors, so on a really rainy day, flee across the river for a swim, trampoline or jungle gym at **Chelsea Sports Centre** (Chelsea Manor Street, SW3 5PL).

③ National Army Museum

Tiny troops most welcome

Climbing chronologically through five levels of halls, this museum fills every inch with displays telling the story of the British Army from 1066 to the present. See the skeleton of Napoleon's horse, clamber through a World War I dugout, and light up a toy-soldier war zone to see how Wellington won the Battle of Waterloo. The liveliest areas for children are two Action Zones lined with hands-on kit and quizzes. In Victorian Soldier, a game of chance determines their army rank and whether they'll survive their service. In The World's Army, an interactive map plays out various battles and troop movements from the two world wars. Kids can borrow two prop-packed backpacks themed on World War II spies and military art.

On the face of it, a soft-play area for tots themed on war and conflict is a tricky idea to pull off. Thankfully, the museum's Kids' Zone (for ages 0–8) eschews guns and grenades and sticks to climbing nets, rocking horses and khaki-based dressing-up. It can get a bit manic at weekends, but the room offers a useful safety valve after a tour of the galleries.

Next door to the museum is The Royal Hospital Chelsea, famed as the home of the Chelsea Pensioners since 1682. Christopher Wren's chapel and the Great Hall are free to visit (10am–5pm Mon–Sat; 020 7881 5200; www.ornc.org/visit/ getting-here/opening-times).

Young recruits learning how to fire a rifle at the National Army Museum

The Lowdown

🌐 **Map ref** 15 A5
Address Royal Hospital Road, Chelsea, SW3 4HT; 020 7730 0717; www.nam.ac.uk

🚌 **Tube** Sloane Square **Bus stop** Royal Hospital Road, Chelsea Bridge Road, King's Road **River bus** Cadogan Pier

🕐 **Open** 10am–5:30pm daily

💷 **Price** Free; some temporary exhibitions charge. Kids' zone: £2.50 per child (ages 0–8)

👫 **Skipping the queue** Free Kids' Zone operates on timed ticket system; it is sometimes reserved for private parties – check online

👫 **Age range** Kids' Zone closed for refurbishment until 2016

👫 **Activities** Children's activities will begin again when Kids' Zone reopens in 2016

⏱ **Allow** Up to 2 hours

♿ **Wheelchair access** Yes

🍴 **Eat and drink** *Snacks* Base Café, in the museum, offers a short menu of hot dishes and snacks *Real meal* Made in Italy (249 King's Road, SW3 5EL; 020 7352 1880; www.madeinitalygroup. co.uk; 6–11:30pm Mon, noon–11:30pm Tue–Sat, noon–10:30pm Sun) serves pizza by the metre

🛍 **Shop** Selling gifts, toys and books on military topics

👫 **Toilets** On the Ground and Lower Ground levels

Letting off steam
The Hospital grounds are open 10am – dusk (from 2pm Sun), or cross King's Road to the playground at **St Luke's** (Cale Street, SW3 3QU), where kids can act out their own play battle.

Pomegranates growing in the Chelsea Physic Garden

④ Chelsea Physic Garden

Calling all plant detectives

"Warning!" says the sign at Chelsea Physic Garden. "Many plants here are poisonous and can kill!" London's oldest botanical garden was opened in 1673 by the Worshipful Society of Apothecaries to study medicinal plants, and includes a Poison Bed, a Tropical Corridor and Perfumery, as well as an 18th-century rockery made from Icelandic lava, in its rambling walled plot beside the Thames. It feels like a charming secret garden.

The ingenious Shelf Life display cultivates nearly 100 plants inside the packaging of food and medicines that are made from them, while the main focus for kids is the inventive family sessions sprinkled through the school holidays. These include garden photography, herbal medicine workshops, paper-making, creepy-crawly handling and (best of all) CSI Chelsea, a crime-solving day looking into forensic pathology.

Letting off steam
Head across the river to **Battersea Park** for plenty of room to play.

The Lowdown

🌐 **Map ref** 15 A5
Address 66 Royal Hospital Road, SW3 4HS; 020 7352 5646; www. chelseaphysicgarden.co.uk.

🚌 **Tube** Sloane Square **Bus stop** Royal Hospital Road, Chelsea Bridge Road, King's Road **River bus** Cadogan Pier

🕐 **Open** Apr–Oct: noon–6pm Tue–Fri, 11am–6pm Sun and Bank Holidays; Nov–Mar: 9:30am–4pm or dusk (last admission: 30 minutes earlier)

💷 **Price** £33–43, under-5s free

🎫 **Guided tours** Free most days, times vary

👫 **Age range** Most family activity sessions target ages 7 plus

👫 **Activities** School holiday family programme, themes vary, booking essential (£5.50 per person, including accompanying adult)

⏱ **Allow** 1 hour

🍴 **Eat and drink** *Snacks* Tangerine Dream Café (open from 12:30pm), in the garden, serves home-made hot lunches and afternoon teas *Real meal* My Old Dutch (221 King's Road, SW3 5EJ; 020 7376 5650; www.myolddutch.com; 10am–10:45pm Mon–Sat, 10am–10pm Sun) is a cosy creperie

🛍 **Shop** Selling garden-related products

👫 **Toilets** Beside shop

Beyond
the City Centre

Spread out beyond the city centre are scores of terrifically appealing attractions, including some of London's most-fun museums and its widest, wildest open spaces. For families, several are too good to miss, including toy heaven at the Museum of Childhood, a glimpse into outer space at the Royal Observatory, and the world in one garden at Kew. The Tube, train and bus network makes them all accessible within about an hour.

Highlights

Kew Gardens
Kew invites kids to burrow into a badger's sett, get inside a giant flower, or perch bird-like on the treetop walkway (see p228).

Warner Bros. Studio Tour London – The Making of Harry Potter
Step into the world of Harry Potter and marvel at the sets, costumes and hands-on exhibits (see p218).

Horniman Museum
Among the voodoo shrines and stuffed walruses at this quirky museum, the Music Gallery stands out – touch the table-tops and instruments strike up (see p222).

Wembley Stadium
Touring the stadium is a trip to dreamland for football-crazy kids (and adults), climaxing when they climb those famous steps to view the FA Cup (see p219).

V&A Museum of Childhood
London's noisiest museum? The Museum of Childhood, with its rocking-horse races, Punch & Judy shows and toys (see p208–9).

Royal Observatory
At the Royal Observatory in Greenwich, kids can mastermind a mission to Venus, dodge a meteorite shower or even watch a big-screen Big Bang (see p201).

Left Mudchute Park and Farm, a pastoral corner of London in the shadow of the gleaming skyscrapers of Canary Wharf **Above** The time ball atop Royal Observatory Greenwich, which dominates Greenwich Park's skyline

The Best of
Beyond the City Centre

When it comes to visitor attractions, London's riches extend far beyond the Tower of London, Buckingham Palace and Regent's Park. Families who venture out from the centre will be richly rewarded, whether they go east to hip Hoxton, west into well-to-do Richmond and Kew, north to the pleasure grounds of Hampstead Heath or south to the splendours of Greenwich. Here are some itineraries that will help you pick out the plums.

A Greenwich weekend

If Greenwich were outside London, it would vie with Windsor, Oxford and Bath. There is so much to see here by the Thames. An exciting way to arrive is on the Docklands Light Railway (DLR), gliding through the skyscrapers of Canary Wharf. Hop off for the **Museum of London Docklands** (see p202), where there's a programme of events every Saturday. Carry on to Greenwich for lunch at Discover Greenwich (see p200), then ramble through the **Old Royal Naval College** (see p200) and visit the **Cutty Sark** (see p202).

On Sunday, pick up a picnic at Greenwich Market (see see p198) and head for Greenwich Park. When its playground and pedal boats pall, dip into the free Discover Sundays kids' programme at the **National Maritime Museum** (see p200). For a star-studded finish, book family tickets for a blast into the Sky Tonight at the **Royal Observatory** planetarium (see p201).

Life out east

Beyond the pie-and-mash cliché, East London offers a rich mix of multicultural influences and terrific places to see. The starting point for families is the **V&A Museum of Childhood** (see pp208–9) at Bethnal Green – parents can browse the vintage toys while their kids go nuts in play zones scattered about the building.

Just one Tube stop further east, in Mile End, is the **Ragged School Museum** (see p213), offering an eye-opening Victorian classroom experience; while to the west, the **Geffrye Museum** (see p210) is all historical interiors and family action. Get to the Geffrye by bus (26, 48 or 55), or on foot via **Weavers Fields Adventure Playground** (see p209) and **Hackney City Farm** (see p210). On a sunny day, however, most kids would opt for a bus ride north to London Fields (see p211), with its sparkling outdoor lido. Spooky **Sutton House** (see p212) is also within easy reach.

Below Narrowboats moored on the Hertford Union Canal, in Hackney's Victoria Park

Above The Old Royal Naval College, Greenwich, designed by Sir Christopher Wren **Middle** The Climbers and Creepers indoor playground at Kew Gardens **Bottom** Horse and pony riding for little ones at Richmond Park

Gods and monsters

The **Horniman Museum** (*see pp222–3*), a mish-mash of macabre masks and mad musical instruments – is the kind of place that turns kids on to museum-going. It's easy to fill a whole day here: activities include watching the honey bees and harvest mice in the Nature Base and the lively object-handling sessions every weekend afternoon. The museum is free, and nearby **Dulwich Park** (*see p224*), with its boats, bicycles and café, is great for a lunchtime breather.

The Horniman also combines well with **Crystal Palace Park** (*see pp224–5*), a 30-minute bus ride south (176 or 197). It is full of Victorian character, with Punch & Judy shows in summer, spooky statues left over from Joseph Paxton's Crystal Palace, and the unmissable Dinosaur Court, 30 life-size monsters beside a lake.

Wilderness diary

Yes, metropolitan London does have wilderness, albeit in child-size chunks. To find some, head southwest, where a trio of natural oases offer year-round treats for wildlife-watchers.

Spring is a great time to visit the **WWT London Wetland Centre** in Barnes (*see p230*). Sand martins swoop in from sub-Saharan Africa, Easter is full of fluffy ducklings, and there are walks to hear the dawn chorus. In summer, head to **Richmond Park** (*see p232*), hiring bikes to see Isabella Plantation as the azaleas burst into flaming blooms. In October, the park's red deer spar in their autumn rut. It's never winter inside the steamy glasshouses at **Kew Gardens** (*see p228–9*), and its Tropical Extravaganza fills February with spectacular orchid flowers.

Greenwich and around

They don't quite match Manhattan, but the shiny towers of Canary Wharf make a dramatic splash on London's eastern horizon. Once the world's largest port, this docklands quarter was reborn as a hive of business, entertainment and the high life. Arrive on the Docklands Light Railway (DLR) from Bank or Tower Gateway for a futuristic trip through the skyscrapers. Alight at West India Quay for the Museum of London Docklands; or at Mudchute for its city farm. Royal Greenwich, birthplace of Henry VIII, can be reached by DLR or river bus. Packed with museums and markets – all walkable – it's an irresistible summer's day out.

Places of Interest

SIGHTS

1. Greenwich
2. Old Royal Naval College
3. National Maritime Museum
4. Royal Observatory Greenwich
5. Museum of London Docklands
6. Cutty Sark
7. Mudchute Park and Farm
8. Eltham Palace
9. Firepower Museum
10. Thames Barrier

● EAT AND DRINK

1. Royal Teas
2. Paul Rhodes Bakery
3. Trafalgar Tavern
4. Rivington Grill Greenwich
5. Even Keel Café
6. Goddard's at Greenwich

See also Greenwich Park (p198), Old Royal Naval College (p200), Royal Observatory (p201), Museum of London Docklands (p202), Mudchute Park and Farm (p202), Eltham Palace (p204), Firepower Museum (p204) and Thames Barrier (p205)

● WHERE TO STAY

1. Hilton London Docklands
2. Novotel London Greenwich
3. Ramada London Docklands
4. Fox Apartments

An array of colourful puppets on sale at Greenwich Market

Above *Vanbrugh Castle – a private residence on the borders of Greenwich Park*
Left *Making friends with the goats at Mudchute Park and Farm, Isle of Dogs*

Thames river bus in front of the Old Royal Naval College, Greenwich

The Lowdown

🚗 **Train** Docklands Light Railway (DLR) runs from Bank and Tower Gateway to Cutty Sark and Greenwich stations, via Canary Wharf/Docklands. Mainline trains run to Greenwich and Maze Hill from Charing Cross **Tube** Canary Wharf and North Greenwich (for the O2) are both on the Jubilee Line **River bus** Services run to Greenwich Pier from Westminster and Embankment and stops en route

ℹ️ **Visitor information** Pepys House, 2 Cutty Sark Gardens, SE10 9LW; 0870 608 2000; *www.visitgreenwich.org.uk*

🏬 **Supermarkets** Marks & Spencer Simply Food, 1–2 Cutty Sark Station, SE10 9EJ. **Markets** Greenwich Market (food, crafts, arts) 10am–5:30pm Tue–Sun; Clocktower Market, Greenwich

High Road (vintage, jewellery, books) 10am–5pm Sat–Sun; Blackheath Farmers' Market 10am–2pm Sun

🎭 **Festivals** The London Marathon begins in Greenwich Park (Apr); Greenwich and Docklands International Festival, performance arts (Jun); Great River Race, starting point (Sep)

➕ **Pharmacies** Pharmacy Meridian, 16 Greenwich Church Street, SE10 9BJ (8:30am–5:30pm Mon–Fri; till 1pm Thu); Duncans, 193–195 Greenwich High Road, SE10 8JA (9am–7pm Mon–Fri; 9:30am–4pm Sat). For 24-hour pharmacies, search at *www.nhs. uk/servicedirectories*

🪁 **Nearest playgrounds** Greenwich Park Playground; Millwall Park playground

① Greenwich
Where east meets west

As well as periscopes and telescopes, pedaloes and playgrounds, roaming deer, jewelled lizards, exploding stars, the fastest Victorian tea clipper of its day, and Nelson's bloody breeches, Greenwich is also the official home of Greenwich Mean Time in 1847. So there's not a second to waste: climb to the top of the hill and see the glossy lawns of Greenwich Park spread out below, with space for squirrel-chasing, pedal-boating, and plenty of hands-on history.

A ship's figurehead

Key Features

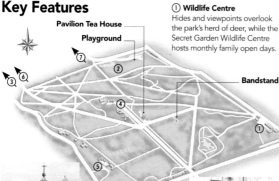

Pavilion Tea House
Playground

① **Wildlife Centre**
Hides and viewpoints overlook the park's herd of deer, while the Secret Garden Wildlife Centre hosts monthly family open days.

Bandstand

② **Boating lake**
Boats and pedaloes are available from Easter to October.

③ **Greenwich Market** From Tuesday to Sunday, the market jumps with stalls selling food, vintage clothing and a variety of arts and crafts.

④ **Royal Observatory**
Home of Greenwich Mean Time and the Prime Meridian of the World, The Royal Observatory is the official starting point for each new day and year.

⑤ **Wernher Collection**
Enamelled skulls and an opal-encrusted lizard pendant shine among the paintings and porcelain collected by diamond magnate Julius Wernher (Sunday-Wednesday, *www.english-heritage.org.uk*).

⑥ **Cutty Sark** Built in 1869, this Victorian tea clipper was the fastest of its day. Following a six-year conservation project, it has been raised 3 m (10 ft), allowing visitors to walk beneath its copper hull and explore its upper decks.

⑦ **Trafalgar Tavern**
This atmospheric old pub teetering on a prow of land above the Thames is Greenwich's unofficial figurehead.

The Lowdown

🌐 **Map ref** 18 H3
Address Greenwich Tourist Information, Pepys House, 2 Cutty Sark Gardens, SE10 9LW; 0870 608 2000; *www.visitgreenwich.org.uk*

🚗 **Train** Greenwich Maze Hill, or Blackheath (mainline); Cutty Sark or Greenwich (DLR) **Tube** North Greenwich, then bus number 188 **Bus stop** Cutty Sark **River bus** Greenwich Pier: on Embankment to Woolwich Arsenal route (0870 781 5049; *www.thamesclippers.com*); plus from Westminster (*www.thamesriverservices.co.uk; www.citycruises.com*)

🕐 **Open Park:** 6am daily (closing times seasonal, 6–9:30pm); closed to traffic 10am–4pm and all day at weekends. Visitor information centre open 10am–5pm

💲 **Price** Free

🚩 **Guided tours** From Greenwich Tourist Information Centre, 12:15pm, 2:15pm daily (£7 per adult; under 16s free)

👫 **Age range** All

🏃 **Activities** Boat hire (Easter–Oct); playground; pay-and-play tennis and golf putting (020 8293 0276); bandstand concerts on summer weekends (*www.royalparks.gov.uk/greenwich-park*). Family open days at Secret Garden Wildlife

Centre, last Sat of month (*www.friendsofgreenwichpark.org.uk*). Full events calendar at *www.visitgreenwich.org.uk*

⏱ **Allow** At least a day

☕ **Cafés** Pavilion Tea House (*see p201*) and Cow and Coffee Bean (*020 8293 07035; www.companyofcooks.com/locations/our-locations/cow-and-coffee-bean*), both in Greenwich Park

🚻 **Toilets** At Discover Greenwich, Royal Observatory, children's playground and Blackheath Gate

Good family value?
Excellent. Vast amounts to do, much of it blissfully free.

Prices given are for a family of four

Letting off steam

Greenwich Park Playground has a Wendy house, scrambling tubes and a sandpit, and the boating lake is right next door. If it rains, Arches Leisure Centre *(Trafalgar Road, SE10 9UK; 020 8317 5020; www.better. org.uk/leisure/arches-leisure-centre#/)* is close by, with family swimming – phone ahead to check times. Both Greenwich Theatre *(Crooms Hill, SE10 8ES; 020 8858 7755; www.greenwich theatre.org.uk)* and Greenwich Picture House *(180 Greenwich High Road, SE10 8NN; 0871 902 5732; www.picturehouses.com/cinema/ greenwich_picturehouse)* have regular family shows and screenings.

Greenwich Park Playground, traditional fun for younger children

Eat and drink

Picnic: £25–35; Snacks: £30–45; Real meal: £55–70; Family treat: £60 or more (based on a family of four)

PICNIC Royal Teas *(76 Royal Hill, Greenwich, SE10 8RT; 020 8691 7240; www.royalteascafe.co.uk)* is a vegetarian café and coffee shop that offers baguettes and delicious cakes and scones.

SNACKS Paul Rhodes Bakery *(37 King William Walk, SE10 9HU; 020 8858 8995; www.rhodesbakery.co. uk)*, the artisan baker, does unbeatable sandwiches, pastries and cupcakes.

REAL MEAL Trafalgar Tavern *(Park Row, SE10 9NW; 020 8858 2909; www.trafalgartavern.co.uk; food served noon–11pm Mon–Thu,*

One of the many enticing artisan food stalls in Greenwich Market

The light, airy and octagonal Pavilion Tea House, Greenwich Park

till midnight Fri & Sat, till 10:30pm Sun) has been serving whitebait platters since the 1830s. They're still on the menu, alongside many other fresh fish dishes, but no longer caught in the Thames.

FAMILY TREAT Rivington Grill Greenwich *(178 Greenwich High Road, SE10 8NN; 020 8293 9270; www.rivingtongreenwich.co.uk; noon–10pm Mon–Fri, 10am–10pm Sat & Sun)* serves smart seafood and home-made British classics (shepherd's pie, bangers and mash, fish fingers).

Shopping

Greenwich Market *(Durnford St, SE10 9HZ; www.greenwichmarket london.com)* has a mind-boggling spread of hot and cold food, especially at weekends. Alongside all the food stalls are jewellery shops, vintage clothing stores, an array of gift and craft stores and lots of lovely toy shops.

Find out more

DIGITAL In 1515, King Henry VIII had a tiltyard built at Greenwich Palace for jousting tournaments. Find out more about the Tudor joust, and have a go online, at: *www.tudorbritain.org/joust*

Next stop...

THE FAN MUSEUM *(12 Crooms Hill, SE10 8ER; 020 8305 1441; www.thefanmuseum.org.uk; 11am–5pm Tue–Sat, noon–5pm Sun; £8–14, under 7s free)* This is the only museum in the world devoted to every aspect of fans and fan-making. The museum is home to a collection of more than 3,500 predominantly antique fans from around the world, dating from the 11th century to the present day.

The symmetrical Thameside façade of the Old Royal Naval College

② Old Royal Naval College

Home for old sea dogs

Set on riverside lawns, with the silver towers of Canary Wharf rising across the water, Sir Christopher Wren's double-domed palace is the best collection of Baroque buildings in Britain. Except this wasn't a palace, it was a residential home for injured soldiers. Queen Mary II commissioned the complex in the 1690s, and until 1869, seamen spent their days here drinking, gambling and dragging their wooden legs to the river and back.

Today, the college's slick Discover Greenwich visitor centre introduces the place's maritime history – it was the Royal Naval College from 1873–1998 – using lots of tactile gadgetry. There's a dressing-up box, self-guided family trails and crafty children's workshops in the school holidays. Daily guided tours specialize in the kind of horrible history that kids love, including the grisly story of how Horatio Nelson returned from the Battle of Trafalgar

in 1805 – preserved inside a barrel of brandy. Nelson's body lay in state in the Painted Hall, London's answer to Rome's Sistine Chapel, which must be the finest dining hall in Europe – the old sailors once ate their mutton and beans here. Tours also visit the College's underground skittle alley, with its musket ball missiles – and don't miss a peep into the quadrangle now occupied by Trinity Laban of Music, where tubas parp and pianos tinkle from every window.

Letting off steam

Greenwich Park's well-equipped children's playground is nearby, just across Romney Road.

③ National Maritime Museum

Dive into the depths of Britain's nautical past

Bigger than the average cruise liner, the National Maritime Museum's central hall – a shiny glass cube full of whirring propellers and winking lighthouses – makes an instant impact on children. Prize exhibits

The Lowdown

- 🌐 **Map ref** 18 G3
  Address Romney Road, Greenwich, SE10 9 NF; 020 8858 4422; *www.rmg.co.uk*
- 🚆 **Train** Cutty Sark (DLR) or Maze Hill (5-minute walk) **Bus** Cutty Sark **River bus** Greenwich Pier
- 🕐 **Open** 10am–5pm daily (last admission 4:30pm)
- 💷 **Price** Free
- 🚩 **Guided tours** Free themed talks in Maritime Galleries daily (times vary). Queen's House offers tours weekdays only (11:30am, 2pm) and free audio guide
- 🧍 **Age range** All
- 🧒 **Activities** Young Explorers' trails downloadable online only. Play Tuesdays for under-5s at 10:30am–12:30pm and 1–3pm weekly (free tickets at welcome desk). Explore Saturdays for over-5s and Discover Sundays for all ages, 11am–4pm. Programme runs daily in school holidays
- ⏱️ **Allow** 2 hours
- ♿ **Wheelchair access** Yes
- 🍽️ **Eat and drink** *Snacks* Museum Café (Level G) and The Brasserie have seasonal menus; Paul Bakery (Level 1) has cakes and sandwiches.
- 🛍️ **Shop** Level G, to right of entrance
- 🚻 **Toilets** Level G and Level 1

from five centuries of nautical history are here, including Prince Frederick's gilded barge, which once propelled Georgian monarchs along the Thames. Upstairs are galleries devoted to explorers, cruise travel and the slave trade, while it's all hands on deck on Level 2, where kids aged 5 to 85 get to hoist flags, load a cargo ship and even fire a cannon. Older children will love the simulation of a sea captain's bridge, which challenges them to steer boats into port. The sea-themed family events schedule divides into sessions for under-5s (Tue) and

The Lowdown

- 🌐 **Map ref** 18 G2
  Address 2 Cutty Sark Gardens, SE10 9LW; 020 8269 4747; *www.ornc.org*
- 🚆 **Train** Cutty Sark (DLR) or Maze Hill (5-minute walk) **Bus** Cutty Sark **River bus** Greenwich Pier
- 🕐 **Open** Grounds 8am–6pm; Discover Greenwich visitor centre, Painted Hall and Chapel, 10am–5pm
- 💷 **Price** Free
- 🚩 **Guided tours** 90-minute tours given by yeoman guides daily, 2pm (£5 per adult, under-16s free)
- 🧍 **Age range** All
- 🧒 **Activities** Family trails (£1 each, or download them from the website). Drop-in craft workshops every Fri in school holidays (small charge); plus

occasional archaeology workshops and shows (check website)

- ⏱️ **Allow** 2 hours
- ♿ **Wheelchair access** Yes
- 🍽️ **Eat and drink** *Picnic* Enjoy a packed lunch or eat food from Greenwich Market *(10am–5:30pm daily)* on the lawns of the ORNC and appreciate the beautiful surroundings. *Real meal* The Old Brewery café-bar *(020 3327 1280; www.oldbrewerygreenwich.com; café 10am–5pm; restaurant 6–11pm)* has a riverside courtyard and children's sandwiches
- 🛍️ **Shop** Discover Greenwich centre sells innovative gifts and souvenirs
- 🚻 **Toilets** Discover Greenwich centre

Playing on one of the huge anchors outside the National Maritime Museum

over-5s (Sat) – both are catered for on Sundays. The museum's Sammy Ofer wing hosts temporary exhibitions and is also home to a café and shop, along with a more upmarket restaurant serving contemporary British cuisine.

It is the museum's artifacts that most capture the imagination, though: Admiral Nelson's bloodstained breeches, cut from his body after Trafalgar; and the snow boots, part-chewed in hunger, from Sir John Franklin's Northwest Passage expedition, lost in the ice in 1847. The adjoining Queen's House, a pearlescent Palladian villa from 1614, shows off the museum's nautical art collection, including Canaletto's celebrated view of Greenwich from across the Thames.

Letting off steam

There is plenty of space to run around in **Greenwich Park** (see p198).

④ Royal Observatory Greenwich

The world's timekeeper

Dominating Greenwich Park's skyline, the Royal Observatory is a Willy Wonka affair, with green onion domes and a red gobstopper on the roof. The gobstopper is actually the "time ball", which drops daily at 1pm to signal the hour to passing ships. The world has been setting its clocks by Greenwich Mean Time since an international conference fixed the

A favourite photo opportunity – astride the Prime Meridian

line of zero longitude here in 1884, making this the official starting point for each new day and year. Today, visitors queue to have a photo taken astride the Prime Meridian.

The observatory hosts a galaxy of exhibitions, from the intricate to the interplanetary. Watchmaker John Harrison's grapplings with the longitude conundrum will confuse most adults, but the astronomy galleries are much more friendly to children, with a film evocation of the Big Bang and a 4.5 billion-year-old meteorite. In the Astronomy Explorers room kids can man the flight deck and send a virtual space probe to Venus. The most memorable part of the visit, though, is the Peter Harrison Planetarium: tilt back in an armchair and watch as worlds appear, stars detonate and universes collapse on the big screen above.

Letting off steam

Head to **Greenwich Park** (see p198).

The Lowdown

🌐 **Map ref** 18 H4
Address Blackheath Avenue, Greenwich, SE10 8XJ; 020 8858 4422; *www.rmg.co.uk/royal-observatory*

🚗 **Train** Greenwich or Maze Hill, both a 15-minute walk **Bus stop** Romney Road **River bus** Greenwich Pier

🕐 **Open** 10am–5pm daily (last admission 4:30pm)

💲 **Price** £22, under-6s free (astronomy galleries free); Planetarium £33

👫 **Skipping the queue** Book ahead for Planetarium shows (020 8312 6608; *www.nmm.ac.uk/tickets*)

🚩 **Guided tours** Most weekdays (free, times vary); audio guide (£3.50)

👫 **Age range** 6 plus

🏃 **Activities** Kids' trail downloadable from website only. Free monthly Space Explorers workshops (Sat, age 6-plus). Planetarium shows include Space Safari (under-7s) and Sky Tonight Live (5-plus), both daily (check website for schedule)

🕐 **Allow** 2–3 hours

♿ **Wheelchair access** Yes, but slightly restricted in some buildings

🍽 **Eat and drink** *Snacks* Astronomy Café overlooking Greenwich Park. *Real Meal* The Pavilion Tea House serves hot and cold meals

🛍 **Shop** In Astronomy Centre and near Meridian Line

👫 **Toilets** In Astronomy Centre and Flamsteed House

Picnic under £20; **Snacks** £20–40; **Real meal** £40–60; **Family treat** £60 or more (based on a family of four)

⑤ Museum of London Docklands

Sailors, slaves and swashbucklers

London's best museum for children? Step forward the Museum of London Docklands which, not content with offering a terrific soft-play area for toddlers, runs weekly Mini Mudlarks sessions for gallery-goers under the age of 2. It shows just how hard the museum tries to engage families.

The museum is set within a Georgian sugar warehouse, built with the profits of the slave trade, and tells the 2,000-year story of wharfside London. Thanks to a series of galleries packed with models, movie clips and touch-screen fun, the place is surprisingly rewarding for children. They will be fascinated by a gibbet cage that was once used to dangle dead pirates above the Thames, and can explore the atmospheric alleyways of Sailortown, a realistic reconstruction of Victorian Wapping, complete with a noisy alehouse and a smelly wild animal emporium.

However, the dedicated children's gallery, Mudlarks, is best saved till last, otherwise it will be impossible to get the children away from its banks of bashing, flashing gadgets and games. Here, they get to hoist cargoes, delve for archaeological finds and even build a scale model of Canary Wharf. Visit on a Saturday, or during school holidays, when the museum's family events programme shifts into top gear with a tumult of Caribbean dancing, cookery demonstrations and computer animation workshops.

Letting off steam

Millwall Park *(Manchester Road, E14)* has a lovely children's playground suitable for all ages.

⑥ Cutty Sark

The classiest tea clipper of all

One of Greenwich's most enduring attractions is back after a complete refurbishment following a devastating fire in 2007. First launched in 1869 the Cutty Sark was the pride of British sailing ships on the lucrative tea trade route to India and the Far East until they were superseded by steam vessels. It is the last surviving clipper in existence and its presence adds an important touch of authenticity to London's most seafaring corner.

The ship has now been raised by three metres, allowing visitors

The Lowdown

🌐 **Address** West India Quay, Canary Wharf, E14 4AL; 020 7001 9844; *www.museumoflondon.org.uk/docklands*

🚗 **Train** West India Quay (DLR). **Tube** Canary Wharf. **Bus** Westferry Circus. **River bus** Canary Wharf Pier, on London Eye–Woolwich Arsenal route (*www.thamesclippers.com*)

🕐 **Open** 10am–6pm daily

💲 **Price** Free

🚩 **Guided tours** Free highlight tours: ask on arrival

👫 **Age range** All

🏃 **Activities** Mudlarks Children's Gallery open 2–5:30pm weekdays; 10am–5:30pm weekends and school holidays. Free Explorer Backpacks for ages 2–5. Download activity sheets from website. Mini Mudlarks sessions (6 months–walking) 3:30–4:30pm Wed. Little Mudlarks (walking–age 5) 11am–noon Wed. Under-5s storytime 11–11:45am, 12–12:45pm & 2–2:45pm Wed. Family events Sat and school holidays (check website for full programme) and book ahead.

⏲ **Allow** Half a day

♿ **Wheelchair access** Yes

🍴 **Eat and drink** Picnic Museum café-bar (*10:30am–5:30pm daily*) serves sandwiches and kids' lunch boxes. Snacks The museum's Rum & Sugar restaurant (*11am–11pm Tue–Thu & Sat, to 1am Thu–Fri, to 6pm Sun*) serves heartier fare and often has special kids' offers.

🛍 **Shop** To left of entrance

🚻 **Toilets** Ground and third floors

The Lowdown

🌐 **Address** King William Walk, Greenwich, SE10 9HT; 020 8312 6608; *www.rmg.co.uk/cuttysark*

🚗 **Train** Cutty Sark (DLR) or Maze Hill (5-minute walk). **Tube** North Greenwich (Jubilee line). **Bus stop** Cutty Sark. **River bus** Greenwich Pier

🕐 **Open** 10am–5pm daily (last admission 4pm)

💲 **Price** £31.50, under-5s free. Combination ticket with Maritime Museum available

👫 **Age range** All

🏃 **Activities** Family activities (free with admission) in school holidays: check website

⏲ **Allow** Up to 2 hours

♿ **Wheelchair access** Yes

🍴 **Eat and drink** Snacks Even Keel Café offers a range of snacks and light meals Real meal Goddard's at Greenwich (*020 8305 9612*) serves traditional pie and mash.

🛍 **Shop** Full of stuff for naval enthusiasts.

🚻 **Toilets** Near café on lower deck

Checking out the nautical displays at the Museum of London Docklands

Prices given are for a family of four

Friendly goats lining up for petting at Mudchute Park and Farm

the unique experience of walking underneath the rock elm hull. The interior has also been refitted to give you the best possible idea of what it was like during its heyday, with all sorts of barrels and other maritime paraphenalia. The outside Main Deck allows you to gaze up at the three huge main masts and admire the intricate rigging.

Lots of interactive features have been added that will delight kids in particular. There is even a theatre on board, where interesting talks and performances take place. Occasional other fun events such as sleepovers are also arranged.

Letting off steam

It's a short walk) to **Greenwich Park** (see pp198), with its playground, boating lake and picnic lawns.

⑦ Mudchute Park and Farm

Dally with Dalai the llama

It is one of the more surreal sights in London: a llama called Dalai trotting around his paddock, with the Canary Wharf skyscrapers behind. Mudchute is one of Europe's largest city farms, home to every bleating, braying animal from a child's colouring book – plus three llamas and a few rare breeds, too.

Arrive on the Docklands Light Railway (DLR) for a truly space-age journey along elevated tracks in driverless trains – it's best

The Lowdown

🌐 **Address** Pier Street, Isle of Dogs, E14 3HP; 020 7515 5901; www.mudchute.org

🚆 **Train** Crossharbour or Mudchute (both DLR). **Bus stop** Crossharbour, Pier Street

🕐 **Open** Farm: 8am–4pm daily; park: open daily

💷 **Price** Free

👫 **Age range** All

🏃 **Activities** Duck walk (9am) and animal round-up (4pm). Drop-in sessions Mon–Wed in school holidays; plus seasonal fundays. Riding lessons available (charged).

⏱ **Allow** 2 hours

♿ **Wheelchair access** Yes, but can be difficult if wet

☕ **Eat and drink** *Snacks* Mudchute Kitchen, beside the farmyard, serves hot food and snacks. Or take a picnic.

🛍 **Shop** Selling animal feed and sometimes eggs from the hens

🚻 **Toilets** In the courtyard

experienced in the front carriage. The farm's noisy donkeys, Dizzy and Snowflake, send a rallying call to visitors walking in from Mudchute or Crossharbour stations, and once inside, there are pastures and parkland to explore, riding stables and a courtyard with exotic aviaries and cuddly rabbits and guinea pigs. Stroking is actively encouraged, just ask a friendly farmhand.

Take cover

The multiscreen **Cineworld Cinema** (0871 200 2000; www.cineworld.co.uk/cinemas/london-west-india-quay/information), on West India Quay, has afternoon shows daily and is the perfect place to sit out the rain. Or head to the lively and engaging **Museum of London Docklands** (see left) for some indoors fun.

The beautifully restored Cutty Sark, in the heart of maritime Greenwich

KIDS' CORNER

Quay questions

Try this Museum of London Docklands quiz...

1 How many arches did London Bridge have in 1440?
2 What did whaleboat captains draw in their journal when they killed a whale?
3 Which continent did trading ships import coffee from?
4 In which year was the slave trade banned in Britain?
5 Where would you go to buy rope in London Docklands?

Answers at the bottom of the page.

GLORIOUS MUD

In Victorian London, "mudlarks" was the name given to poor children who hunted on the slimy banks of the Thames for things to sell. It was an unpleasant job – in those days, the river was awash with broken glass, toilet waste, even dead bodies!

A pig's tale

Have you heard the story of the Tamworth Two? They were a pair of Tamworth pigs, like those at Mudchute Farm, who got out of their truck on the way to market. The brave porkers made a run for it, crossing a river and hiding out in some woods. Newspapers named them Butch and Sundance, after two famous outlaws. They were eventually captured – but by then they were celebrities, so instead of becoming bacon, they lived happily ever after at an animal sanctuary. Oink!

Answers: 1 19 **2** A whale's tail **3** South America **4** 1807 **5** A chandlery

⑧ Eltham Palace

Art Deco dream house

With its gold-plated bathroom, self-vacuuming floors and lemur's bedroom, a tour of Eltham Palace is anything but humdrum. Squatting improbably in one of South London's suburbs, the royal palace began life in 1305 as the grand, moated manor of King Edward II, and its 15th-century Great Hall and Tudor bridge look much as they did when the young Henry VIII played in the grounds. Step inside the adjoining house, though, and there's an even bigger surprise – a decadent Art Deco interior from the 1930s, put together with enormous panache by society high-rollers Stephen and Virginia Courtauld.

The Courtaulds lavished their textile fortune on the house, and the whole place screams glamour: the dining room has a shimmering aluminium ceiling and pink leather chairs; Virginia's vaulted bathroom has an onyx tub and gold taps. A built-in "hi-fi" supplied the jazz soundtrack for their Hollywood-style house parties. Children will be especially captivated by the deluxe living quarters of Mah-Jongg, the couple's pet lemur, who enjoyed such luxuries as central heating and hand-painted wallpaper. Mah-Jongg features heavily in Eltham's activity sheets for kids, and the palace's events programme typically includes Tudor jousting and Art Deco fairs.

Letting off steam

The palace's grounds are a delight, with views over London and lots of places to enjoy a picnic.

The impressive Art Deco interior of Eltham Palace

The Lowdown

🌐 **Address** Royal Artillery Museum, Royal Arsenal, Woolwich, SE18 6ST; 020 8855 7755; www.firepower.org.uk

🚃 **Train** Woolwich Arsenal (mainline and DLR), 5-minute walk
Bus stop Plumstead Road; Woolwich town centre
River bus Woolwich Arsenal Pier, services from Embankment (www.thamesclippers.com)
Car Pay-and-display car park at Plumstead Road entrance

🕐 **Open** 10am–5pm Tue–Sat

💲 **Price** £12.50

🚩 **Guided tours** daily, from admissions desk

👫 **Age range** 7 plus

👟 **Activities** Camo Zone activities cost extra (£1.50 each). There is a busy school holiday events programme – mostly free (check website)

⏱ **Allow** 2 hours

♿ **Wheelchair access** Yes

☕ **Eat and drink** Snacks The Museum Café (020 8312 7138; 9:30am–5pm Mon–Sat) has an appealing bistro vibe and a menu to match

🛍 **Shop** Selling gifts, souvenirs, books, militaria, models and music

🚻 **Toilets** Ground and first floors

⑨ Firepower Museum

Battle stations everyone!

If only all wars were fought with sponge balls. Hopefully, that's the message kids will take away from Firepower, aka the Royal Artillery Museum. Housed in warehouses at Woolwich Arsenal, once England's largest ordnance factory, this is a full-bore celebration of military weaponry, and its interactive Camo Zone squarely targets young children. Prepare to do battle on the sponge-ball firing range, chase along the bungee run and fight it out with radio-controlled tanks – it's great fun for all. Soldiers in combat gear are on hand to supervise.

Elsewhere, the Gunnery Hall bristles with vintage anti-aircraft guns and missile launchers, and visitors can attempt touch-screen missions – shoot down a bomber, or destroy a tank. The History Gallery takes visitors through the story of armaments, all the way "from catapult to rocket", while Fields of Fire is hopefully the closest kids will ever come to being in battle – four big-screens flash archive footage of artillery in action, while smoke fills the room, searchlights beam overhead, there's the sound of anti-aircraft guns, and bombs shake the floor. It's a sobering experience.

There are monthly toy soldier war-game weekends and the

Explore military weaponry throughout history at the Firepower Museum

The Lowdown

🌐 **Address** Court Yard, Eltham, SE9 5QE; 020 8294 2548; www.english-heritage.org.uk/daysout/properties/eltham-palace-and-gardens/

🚃 **Train** Eltham or Mottingham, then 15-minute walk. **Bus stop** Court Road; Eltham High Street. **Car** Free car park off Court Road

🕐 **Open** Apr–Oct: 10am–5pm Sun–Wed; Nov–Mar: 10am–4pm Sun; closed Jan

💲 **Price** £27, under-5s free

🚩 **Guided tours** Free audio guide with admission

👫 **Age range** 5 plus

👟 **Activities** Children's activity sheets, Time Traveller family days with historical themes in school holidays, plus Easter Egg Hunt and Tudor Jousting weekend (Jun)

⏱ **Allow** 2–3 hours

♿ **Wheelchair access** Yes, but parts of garden are uneven

☕ **Eat and drink** Snacks The palace tearoom (10am–4:30pm) serves light lunches and snacks

🛍 **Shop** Selling gifts and souvenirs

🚻 **Toilets** On the ground floor

school holiday programme might involve taking part in simulated army drill, peeking into ration packs, or dressing up in uniform.

Letting off steam

There is space to run around by the riverside. Alternatively, walk west for 10 minutes to the **Waterfront Leisure Centre** in Woolwich High Street (020 8317 5010; www.better.org.uk/ leisure/waterfront-leisure-centre#/), which runs Wild 'n' Wet family swimming sessions every afternoon.

⑩ Thames Barrier

The "sharks" that saved London

London has long been vulnerable to flooding: in 1236 the Thames rose so high that people were able to go boating across Westminster Hall, now part of the Houses of Parliament. But with sea levels inching upwards and tectonic movements tilting the south of England slowly into the sea, something had to be done. The crunch year was 1953, when more than 300 people drowned in floods around the Thames Estuary.

The 520-m- (1,706-ft-) long Thames Barrier became operational in 1982, adding a futuristic new landmark to the riverscape in the form of its seven curvy piers, which line up like shiny steel shark fins advancing on London. The barrier is effectively a tilting dam, swinging up from the riverbed in 10 circular sections whenever surge tides threaten.

The visitor experience is divided by the river. An information centre on the south bank has working models of the barrier in action. To the north, the Thames Barrier Park is a curious landscape of shaped hedgerows, honeysuckle and aerial walkways, perfect for hide-and-seek. Both sides of the river have cafés, playgrounds, and scintillating views,

Above The gleaming Thames Barrier protects London from flooding
Below Among the wave-like manicured hedges at the Thames Barrier Park

but in summer, the fountain plaza tempts most families northwards with its 32 jets of splashing fun.

Letting off steam

There are children's playgrounds on both sides of the river.

The Lowdown

🌐 **Address** Information Centre, 1 Unity Way, Woolwich SE18 5NJ; 020 8305 4188; www.gov.uk/ the-thames-barrier. Thames Barrier Park, North Woolwich Road, E16 2HP

🚗 **Train** Charlton, then 15-minute walk (south side) **DLR** Pontoon Dock (north side) **Bus stop** Holborn College Park; North Woolwich Road; Connaught Bridge

🕐 **Open** Information Centre: 10:30am–5pm Thu–Sun) Park: 7am–dusk daily

💲 **Price** £10–15; under-5s free

🤸 **Activities** To see the barrier closed, visit on a maintenance day (dates listed on website); call to book

⏱ **Allow** 1 hour

♿ **Wheelchair access** Information Centre: largely accessible but access to the river front is restricted as steep stairs lead down from the bank. Park: yes

☕ **Eat and drink** Cafés and picnicking at both sites

🚻 **Toilets** Both sides of river

Flood warning!

How long will the Thames Barrier continue to protect London? Scientists reckon at least another 50 years, but nobody knows for sure. If the barrier failed during a tidal surge, the city would be 2 m (6 ft) deep in water within an hour. You can see how London would look after a flood at www. postcardsfromthefuture. co.uk. Why not draw your own imagined view of your favourite London landmark submerged in water?

V&A Museum of Childhood and around

The Cinderella borough of Hackney is finally having a ball, as young professionals move in prompting the opening of hip shopping and dining venues. Especially vibrant are London Fields, home to a lido, and über-trendy Broadway Market. Families will love the V&A Museum of Childhood in nearby Bethnal Green, offering a full day of play for free – and the Central Line brings visitors virtually to the door. Visit on the first Sunday of the month, when the Ragged School Museum, one Tube stop further, stages Victorian lessons.

Places of interest

SIGHTS

1. V&A Museum of Childhood
2. Geffrye Museum
3. Hackney City Farm
4. Hackney Museum
5. Sutton House
6. Discover
7. Ragged School Museum

EAT AND DRINK

1. Broadway Market
2. L'Eau à la Bouche
3. The Gallery Café
4. E Pellicci
5. Frizzante
6. The Grocery
7. Treacle
8. Caffè Theatro
9. Tre Viet
10. Bouchon Fourchette
11. King Eddie's VII
12. The Palm Tree

See also V&A Museum of Childhood (p208), Geffrye Museum (p210), Sutton House (p212), Discover (p212) and Ragged School Museum (p213)

WHERE TO STAY

1. Boundary Rooms
2. Crowne Plaza Shoreditch
3. Town Hall Apartments

Feeding the ducks in a peaceful corner of Victoria Park

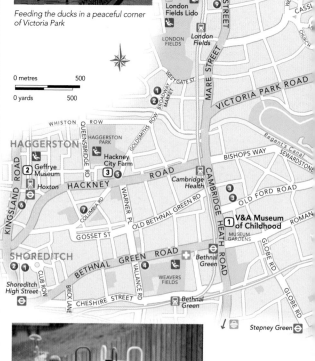

0 metres 500
0 yards 500

Fashion dolls on display at the V&A Museum of Childhood

Playing on the brightly coloured equipment in Haggerston Park playground

The Lowdown

One of the many exhibits packed into the Hackney Museum

🚗 **Train** Bethnal Green, Cambridge Heath, London Fields or Hackney Downs (all from Liverpool Street); Stratford **Tube** Bethnal Green, Mile End, Stratford (all Central line) **Bus** number 388 runs to Bethnal Green from Embankment via Liverpool Street; number 254 to Bethnal Green and Hackney from Aldgate

ℹ️ **Visitor information** 020 8356 3500, *www.hackney.gov.uk/ leisure-culture; www. destinationhackney.co.uk*

🚤 **Supermarkets** Tesco, 55 Morning Lane, Hackney, E9 6ND **Markets** Broadway Market (food, fashion, crafts), 7:30am–7pm Sat; Columbia Road Flower Market, 8am–3pm Sun; Backyard Market (vintage fashion, bric-a-brac), 11am–6pm Sat, 10am–5pm Sun

🎏 **Festivals** Great Spitalfields Pancake Race, Brick Lane (Shrove Tuesday); Big Write, Stratford, children's books (Mar); Bonfire Night, Victoria Park (Nov)

➕ **Pharmacies** Boots, 426 Bethnal Green Road, E2 0DJ (8am–7pm Mon–Fri, 9am–6pm Sat, 11am–5pm Sun). For 24-hour pharmacies search at *www.nhs. uk/servicedirectories*

🤸 **Nearest playgrounds** Weavers Fields Adventure Playground (*Mape St, E2*); London Fields (*West Side, E8 3EU*); Mile End Park (*Grove Rd, E3 5BH*); Victoria Park playground (*Grove Rd, E3 5SN*)

Playing games at the interactive Discover Children's Story Centre

The mid-20th-century room at the Geffrye Museum

① V&A Museum of Childhood
The grandest playroom in London

Children want to play with toys, not just look at them, and that's tricky when the toys include a queen's doll's house, an 18th-century puppet theatre and the very first Mickey Mouse doll. The Museum of Childhood solves the problem by creating "activity stations" between its display cases, where kids can ride a rocking horse, jump in a sandpit or put together a robot. The impressive building – a huge Victorian pavilion with plenty of space and pink iron balconies – helps set the tone.

Classic Barbie with matching luggage

Key features

First floor This houses the Childhood galleries, which explore the social history of childhood.

Ground floor This floor is divided into two galleries – Moving Toys and Creativity.

① **Queen Mary's Doll's House** Part of a large collection, this was furnished personally by Queen Mary. Look for the tiny telephone – ultra-modern in 1910!

② **Vintage pedal car** A perfect replica of an open tourer, this has working lights, a horn and a turning starter handle. It would have cost a fortune in the 1920s.

③ **Game Boy** Hand-held games took off in 1989 with the Nintendo Game Boy, which sold 118 million. The Moving Toys gallery looks at toy technology from zoetropes onwards.

④ **Dolls** This collection of over 4,000 dolls dates back to 1300 BC and includes well-known favourites such as Cabbage Patch Kids, Barbie and Tiny Tears.

⑤ **Venetian Puppet Theatre** This huge 18th-century theatre provided entertainment for an aristocratic Venetian family.

⑥ **Victorian seaside** This gallery has a sandpit for toddlers, overlooked by a 100-year-old Punch & Judy theatre and a booth for kids to stage their own shows.

⑦ **Construction Toys** Meccano, Lego and Mr Potato Head all feature in this impressive collection of 20th-century construction kits.

The Lowdown

Address Cambridge Heath Road, E2 9PA; 020 8983 5200; www.museumofchildhood.org.uk

Train Cambridge Heath (five-minute walk) or Bethnal Green (10-minute walk) **Tube** Bethnal Green (Central line) **Bus stop** Cambridge Heath Road

Open 10am–5:45pm daily (last admission 5:30pm)

Price Free

Skipping the queue Major events bookable up to two weeks in advance (check website)

Guided tours Free family tours on Saturdays and Sundays during term time. Daily activities vary

Age range 3 plus

Activities Kids' trails with a variety of themes; drop-in storytelling and art sessions. Montessori Family Packs for under-5s, plus toddler sessions. Tours and activities available every weekend and on school holidays, check the website for details

Allow Half a day

Wheelchair access Yes

Café Benugo Café, in the main hall, serves simple hot lunches and salads. There are also picnic tables indoors and outside.

Shop Ground floor, selling books, stationery, gifts and pocket money toys

Toilets Lower ground floor

Good family value?
Excellent – even the temporary exhibitions are free. Bring some change though, as some toys can be set in motion with a 20p coin.

Picnic area within the grounds of the V&A Museum of Childhood

Letting off steam

Museum Gardens, right next door, has lawns but no playground. For a playground, you need **Weavers Fields** (*Viaduct St, Vallance Road, E2 6HD*), a 10-minute walk away off Bethnal Green Road, where a terrific staffed adventure playground has climbing frames, rope swings, an indoor playroom and tuck shop (3:30–6:30pm Tue–Fri on school days, 11am–6pm Mon–Fri during holidays; plus noon–5pm Sat; noon–3pm Sun). To the east, **Victoria Park** (*Grove Road, Bow, E3 5TB*) is in easy striking range, with its scrumptious lakeside café (*www. towerhamlets.gov.uk/victoriapark*).

Eat and drink

Picnic: under £20; Snacks: £20–40; Real meal: £20–40; Family treat: £60 or more (based on a family of four)

PICNIC Broadway Market (*south of London Fields, E8 4QL; www. broadwaymarket.co.uk; 9am–5pm Sat*), a 15-minute walk or a short bus ride north of the museum, is an excellent source of provisions, with over 80 stalls, a cosmopolitan restaurant scene and the French deli **L'Eau à la Bouche** (*www. labouche.co.uk; open daily*) selling delicious continental classics.
SNACKS The Gallery Café (*21 Old Ford Road, E2 9PL; 020 8980 2092; http:// thegallerycafe.wordpress.com; open daily*) is a buzzing,

super-cheap veggie and vegan café with good chips and even better cakes.
REAL MEAL Grandest of all the East End "greasy spoon" cafes, **E Pellicci** (*332 Bethnal Green Road, E2 0AG; 020 7739 4873; 7am–4pm Mon–Sat*) has been run by the same Italian family for a century, and is still serving good-value English and Italian dishes. The breakfasts here are deservedly renowned.
FAMILY TREAT Frizzante (*1a Goldsmiths Row, E2 8QA; 020 7739 2266; www.frizzanteltd.co.uk; 10am–4:30pm Tue–Sun plus occasional Thu evenings*) is a fashionable diner at Hackney City Farm (*see p210*), with gorgeous rustic Italian cuisine and hip toddlers scurrying underfoot. Its Thursday dinners are extra special.

Shopping for sweet picnic treats at a stall in Borough Market.

Find out more

DIGITAL The museum's kids' pages are busy with lots of activities to download, cut out and make. There are kaleidoscopes, thaumatropes, jumping jacks and paper dolls, among others (*www. museumofchildhood.org.uk/ learning/things-to-do*).

Next stop...

POLLOCK'S TOY MUSEUM
Unlock another trove of toys from yesteryear at Pollock's Toy Museum in Bloomsbury (*see p104*).

Enjoying the Italian dishes on offer at Frizzante, Hackney City Farm.

An elegant drawing room at the Geffrye Museum

Bella, a British saddleback pig, at the Hackney City Farm

② Geffrye Museum

The ghosts of London past

On paper, it sounds like a bizarrre choice for a family day out in London: a procession of roped-off living rooms revealing how carpets, sideboards and wallpaper have evolved from 1600 to the present day. But the Geffrye Museum has one of the hardest-working children's programmes anywhere, from its monthly Saturday Specials with activities such as portrait painting, spider handling and animation workshops, to its five-week Christmas Past season, when the halls are well and truly decked with historical holly. Family audio guides, quiz trails and activity packs are available every weekend, and there's a refreshing commitment to all age groups, from toddlers to teens. Choose a day when there is lots happening, tell the kids they're going to be travelling back in time to Tudor England, and they'll be gripped.

The museum is set in a cute quadrangle of 18th-century almshouses, its front pathway lit by ghostly furniture, the work of installation artist Kei Ito. Indoors, 11 set-dressed rooms chart the changing face of middle-class décor, from a 1630 merchant's parlour to a 1998 loft apartment. From April till October, the museum's immaculate period gardens host picnic parties, steel bands and other festivities.

Letting off steam

The Apples & Pears Adventure Playground *(28 Pearson Street, London E2 8EL; school days: 3–6pm Tue–Fri; holidays: 9:30am–4pm Mon–Fri; 10am–4pm every Sat; 020 7729 6062)* is a supervised play area just a 5-minute walk away.

③ Hackney City Farm

Meet Larry the showbiz donkey

One field does not a farm make, but hats off to the enterprising band of locals who transformed this postage stamp-sized piece of land in one of London's most congested boroughs. Created in 1984 on the site of a derelict lorry park, the farm now has calves, goats, sheep, pigs, rabbits, geese and chickens (not forgetting Larry the donkey, star of the small screen), plus a thriving crafts studio and a cottage garden growing seasonal vegetables.

Feeding time is at 4pm and there's a clutch of courses for all ages, from felt-making and yoga to beekeeping and green living, plus regular afternoon pottery sessions for children. It's worth visiting just for lunch at the sparkling Frizzante café, whose zesty Italian food has made it a dining destination in its own right.

Letting off steam

Haggerston Park *(Audrey Street, London, E2 8QH)* is on the doorstep, with its pond, ping-pong, BMX track, sports areas and playground.

Enjoying the children's playground at Haggerston Park, Hackney

The Lowdown

🌐 **Map ref** 6 G4
Address 136 Kingsland Road, E2 8EA; 020 7739 9893; www. geffrye-museum.org.uk

🚃 **Train** Hoxton, 5-minute walk
Tube Old Street (Northern Line), then number 243 bus or 15-minute walk; Hackney Central and Hackney Downs **Bus stop** Kingsland Road; Hackney Road

🕐 **Open** 10am–5pm Tue–Sun; bank hols (Mon)

💲 **Price** Free; £13–16 per adult for special exhibitions, under-16s free

👫 **Skipping the queue** For Saturday Special activities at 10:30am and 2pm, arrive 30 minutes early to secure a place

🚩 **Guided tours** Audio guide (£3), children free

👫 **Age range** 3 plus

👪 **Activities** Free family audio guide (ages 5–11) and activity backpacks (ages 3–5), weekends and holidays only. Free family days first Sat of month (ages 5–16), plus full school holiday programme. Website has recipes and garden design games

🕐 **Allow** 1–2 hours

♿ **Wheelchair access** Yes, except for Restored Almshouses Exhibition

🍴 **Eat and drink** *Picnic* The Grocery (54–56 Kingsland Road, E2 8DP) offers upmarket picnic fare *Snacks* The museum's restaurant serves half-price, home-cooked children's dishes

🛍 **Shop** Selling high-quality gifts and books relating to interiors

👫 **Toilets** On all floors

The Lowdown

🌐 **Address** 1a Goldsmiths Row, E2 8QA; 020 7729 6381; *www.hackneycityfarm.co.uk*

🚆 **Train** Cambridge Heath, 10-minute walk **Tube** Bethnal Green (Central Line), 15-minute walk **Bus stop** Hackney Road

🕙 **Open** 10am–4:30pm Tue–Sun, plus bank holidays

💲 **Price** Free

👫 **Age range** All

🏃 **Activities** Self-guided tour leaflet has animal information and activities (£1). Feeding time 4pm; drop-in pottery twice weekly (£5, 2–4pm Wed or 11am–1pm & 2–4pm Sun). Summer holiday workshops include puppet-making

⏱ **Allow** 1 hour

♿ **Wheelchair access** Yes; contact Farm Manager beforehand

🍽 **Eat and drink** *Snacks* Treacle (110-112 Columbia Rd, E2 7RG; 020 7729 0538; www.greatcakeplaces.com; noon–5pm Sat, 9am–4pm Sun), part of Columbia Road flower market, recreates bygone British baking *Real meal* Frizzante cafe *(see p209)* serves tasty children's dishes.

🚻 **Toilets** On ground floor

④ Hackney Museum
The world on your doorstep

Hackney promises to be the hippest place in London, thanks to its rich stew of cultural influences, and this bright and breezy local museum does a tasty job of stirring the pot, especially for families, though it might be a bit unsafe in

Hands-on exhibits captivate at the Hackney Museum

the evening. The overarching theme of the museum is the 1,000-year history of people who have settled here, and the touchy-feely tone begins with the very first exhibit – a replica Saxon boat that kids can load up with goods. Elsewhere, they get to step into an East End pie-and-mash shop, play conductor on a vintage London bus, and race against the clock to make matchboxes – just as hundreds of poverty-stricken children did in 19th-century Hackney. There are drop-in dance, storytelling and art workshops in school holidays, often coinciding with a temporary show – the summer exhibition is always a hive of hands-on interactivity.

If it's sunny, combine a snoop around the museum with a splash at London Fields Lido, a short walk away via Richmond Road. Open every day, this is the city's only Olympic-size heated outdoor pool.

Letting off steam
As well as the Lido *(020 7254 9038; www.gll.org)*, **London Fields** has tennis courts, ping-pong, a paddling pool and two playgrounds. Also nearby is St John at Hackney Churchyard *(Lower Clapton Road, E5 0PD)*, with its neat play area.

The Lowdown

🌐 **Address** 1 Reading Lane, E8 1GQ; 020 8356 3500; www.hackney.gov.uk/cm-museum.htm

🚆 **Train** Hackney Central, five-minute walk; Hackney Downs (10 minutes) **Bus stop** Mare Street

🕙 **Open** 9:30am–5:30pm Tue–Fri (Thu till 8pm); 10am–5pm Sat

💲 **Price** Free

🍴 **Guided tours** Free Tea and Tour 3pm Wed. Occasional local history walks (call to check)

👫 **Age range** 3 plus

🏃 **Activities** Interactive exhibits, dressing-up and toddler reading corner. Free drop-in crafts and

storytelling events in school holidays, 2–4pm Wed–Thu

⏱ **Allow** 1 hour

♿ **Wheelchair access** Yes

🍽 **Eat and drink** *Snacks* Caffè Theatro (316 Mare Street, E8 1HY) has cool décor and great cakes *Real meal* Tre Viet (245–249 Mare Street, E8 3NS; 020 8533 7390; www.treviet.co.uk; noon–11pm Sun–Thu, till 11:30 Fri & Sat) is a good-value Vietnamese eatery

🛍 **Shop** Selling books, souvenirs and pocket-money toys

🚻 **Toilets** On ground floor

Time-travel challenge
Exploring the Geffrye Museum is a bit like being a time-traveller. Can you spot these three objects?
• A polar bear
• Some birds under glass
• A clay bottle with a face on it.
See if you can include all three in an adventure story about a child who journeys back to the past. Or look for Sam the dog in the Victorian time-travel game on the museum's website: *www.geffrye-museum.org.uk/kidszone*.

Room of the future
Which of the rooms at the Geffrye Museum would you like to live in? Maybe you'd prefer life in the future? What would a room from the year 2050 look like? Draw a picture of it when you get home.

Dare you to eat it!
After exploring the pie-and-mash shop at Hackney Museum, head down to nearby Broadway Market. There you'll find F. Cooke's, where East Enders have been eating this traditional London dish since 1900. The dish consists of a minced-beef pie with a scoop of mashed potato. Watch out for the bright green "liquor" that's poured over the top, made by adding parsley to the water used to boil eels.

Eeyore!
How do donkeys bray? The "eeee" sound comes from a deep intake of breath and the "ore" is made when they breathe out again through their nose. Try it yourself!

⑤ Sutton House

A Tudor manor in 21st-century London

Oak panelling, echoing flagstones, roaring fires… Sutton House couldn't look more Tudor if Henry VIII himself was at the banqueting table, tossing chicken legs over his shoulder. Built in 1535 by Sir Ralph Sadler, Henry's Secretary of State, it's the last relic of the once-rural Hackney village.

There is plenty to engage kids, including the 16th-century kitchen, with food to handle and smells to sniff, and three "treasure chests" full of hands-on historical goodies – they include Elizabethan codes to crack, Jacobean jigsaws, and even a "dance mat" on which to perfect your 17th-century moves. The Sutton House stewards are ever ready to share a spine-tingling ghost story, while the mechanic's yard is being transformed into an imaginative outdoor play space, with an old Hackney cab and ice-cream van. Admission is cheap by National Trust

Atmospheric 16th-century room at Sutton House

standards, and free altogether on the last Sunday of the month, when there's a family day themed on music or meals, spooks or squatters (a room of "squatter art" has been preserved from the 1980s). In the summer holidays, there might even be a jousting tournament in the courtyard.

Letting off steam

The house's play area (with picnic tables) is free to all; or head to nearby St John's Churchyard, which has a tots' playground.

⑥ Discover

A stroll in storyland

Shock! Crisis! Emergency! The planet Squiggly Diggly is running out of stories, and a friendly alien named Hootah has been sent to Earth to gather some. That's the backstory for the Discover Children's Story Centre, a one-of-a-kind walk-through wonderland of enchanted towers, secret caves and wishing trees, with lashings of dressing-up and acting-out to help ensure a happy ending. On the Story Trail, children wander wide-eyed among £6 million-worth of multi-sensory play gear designed to spark the imagination: they might bump into a giant, dress up as a princess, sit down for a tea party, or make

The Lowdown

- 🌐 **Address** 2 & 4 Homerton High Street, Hackney, E9 6JQ; 020 8986 2264; www.nationaltrust.org.uk/sutton-house/
- 🚆 **Train** Hackney Central, 10-minute walk; Hackney Downs, 15-minute walk **Bus stop** Homerton High Street; Lower Clapton Road; Morning Lane
- 🕐 **Open** noon–5pm Wed–Sun
- 💲 **Price** £6.30
- 🚩 **Guided tours** First Sun of month, 3pm (free)
- 👫 **Age range** 5 plus
- 🏃 **Activities** Free family days monthly – call or check website for dates
- ⏱ **Allow** 2 hours
- ♿ **Wheelchair access** Yes; adapted toilet located close to entrance
- 🍽 **Eat and drink** *Snacks* Georgian Tearoom serves hot snacks and cakes *Real meal* Bouchon Fourchette (171 Mare St, E8 3HR; 020 8986 2702; www.bouchonfourchette.co.uk/main; 5am–10pm Mon, 9am–10pm Tue–Thu & Sun, 9am–11pm Fri & Sat) is an authentic French bistro
- 🛍 **Shop** Selling gifts and Trust goods; also secondhand books
- 🚻 **Toilets** Close to entrance

Prices given are for a family of four

The Lowdown

- 🌐 **Address** 383–387 High Street, Stratford, E15 4QZ; 020 8536 5555; www.discover.org.uk
- 🚆 **Train** Stratford (DLR and mainline trains), 5-minute walk **Tube** Stratford (Central and Jubilee lines), 5-minute walk **Bus stop** Stratford Bus Station; High Street; Stratford Centre
- 🕐 **Open** 10am–5pm Tue–Fri, 11am–5pm Sat & Sun (open daily during school holidays)
- 💲 **Price** £18, under-2s free
- 🏃 **Skipping the queue** Book ahead for the frequent literature and art events
- 👫 **Age range** 3–11
- 🏃 **Activities** Free storytelling sessions every weekend (11:30am, 2:30pm), and in school holidays (11:30am, 1pm, 2:30pm), plus programme of workshops (see website)
- ⏱ **Allow** 2 hours
- ♿ **Wheelchair access** Yes
- 🍽 **Eat and drink** *Snacks* The centre's café has organic snacks and home-made cupcakes *Real meal* King Eddie's VII (47 Broadway, Stratford, E15 4BQ; 020 8534 2313; www.kingeddie.co.uk; noon–11pm Mon–Wed, to 9pm Sun) serves traditional British dishes
- 🛍 **Shop** Selling pocket-money toys, gifts and classic picture books
- 🚻 **Toilets** On the ground floor

Getting hands-on and stirring imaginations at the Discover Centre

Learning the Victorian way at the Ragged School Museum

a spoon puppet and put on a show. Friendly "story builders" are on hand to help them compose their own tall tales; and in case they can't quite believe it themselves, a bank of TV screens shows their progress in storyland.

There is more make-believe in the Story Garden outside, with its pirate ship, space craft, trick mirrors and giant musical instruments; while interactive shows in the Story Studio profile popular kids' characters. Weekend storytelling sessions culminate in the Big Write festival each March, which throngs with well-known writers and illustrators.

Letting off steam
The garden is one big energetic adventure, with a slide and activities.

⑦ Ragged School Museum
Back to school, Victorian style

In Victorian London, children didn't just do without toys and books, they often lacked shoes and a shirt. More than half were illiterate, and one in three funerals were for children under five. A young Dubliner, Thomas Barnardo, was so shocked by the poverty he saw in the East End, he set about rescuing orphans and setting up "ragged schools" to educate them – including this one, in a canalside warehouse in Mile End.

Today, a Victorian education is delivered here again by strict-but-fair Miss Perkins, in full 1870s garb, who scratches the alphabet on her blackboard for pupils aged five to 85. The monthly lessons are a real eye-opener for kids – especially those with poor handwriting, who

may end up standing in the corner wearing a dunce's hat.

The school has also re-created an East End kitchen from 1900, with a mangle, a tin bath and other hands-on hardware. Top marks for interactivity, but the museum must do better on opening times.

Letting off steam
Just along Rhodeswell Road lies **Mile End Park playground** (*Locksley St, Limehouse E14 7EJ*), with its castle to conquer and "riverbed" sandpit. Older kids might favour the swimming pool at Mile End Leisure Centre (*190 Burdett Road, E3 4HL; 020 8709 4420*), just opposite.

The Lowdown

🌐 **Address** 46–50 Copperfield Rd, E3 4RR; 020 8980 6405; *www.raggedschoolmuseum.org.uk*

🚗 **Train** Limehouse (DLR), 10-minute walk **Tube** Mile End (Central, Hammersmith & City, District lines), 10-minute walk **Bus stop** Ben Jonson Road; Burdett Road; Mile End Road

🕐 **Open** 10am–5pm Wed–Thu, plus 2–5pm first Sun of month

💷 **Price** Free

👫 **Age range** 5 plus

🏃 **Activities** Free 45-minute history lessons (all ages), 2:15pm and 3:30pm first Sun of month. Free themed activities for under-13s, usually led by eminent Victorians, Wed–Thu in school holidays.

⏱ **Allow** 1 hour

♿ **Wheelchair access** Yes

☕ **Eat and drink** *Snacks* Museum café has decent snacks *Real meal* The Palm Tree (*127 Grove Road, Mile End, E3 5BH; 020 8980 2918*) is a good pub for a canal-side lunch

🛍 **Shop** Selling vintage toys

🚻 **Toilets** No

Kenwood House and around

Aside from its Georgian mansion, Kenwood House, this locale is light on visitor attractions. But there's one compelling reason to make the train ride north: Hampstead Heath, a world of playgrounds, pools and woodland. Kenwood combines well with Golders Hill Park and lunch at The Spaniards Inn (Northern Line to Golders Green, then bus number 210). Or alight at Hampstead, pick up a picnic and hike to the Heath. Consider, too, a visit to Wembley Stadium (Jubilee Line) or the RAF Museum (Northern Line), a little further out of town.

Places of interest

SIGHTS

1. Kenwood House
2. Warner Bros. Studio Tour London – The Making of Harry Potter
3. RAF Museum
4. Wembley Stadium

● EAT AND DRINK

1. The Hampstead Butcher
2. Golders Hill Park Refreshment House
3. The Spaniards Inn
4. Gaucho

See also Kenwood House (p216), Warner Bros. Studio Tour London – The Making of Harry Potter (p218), RAF Museum (p218), Wembley Stadium (p219)

● WHERE TO STAY

1. Premier Inn, Hampstead
2. Quality Hotel Hampstead
3. La Gaffe

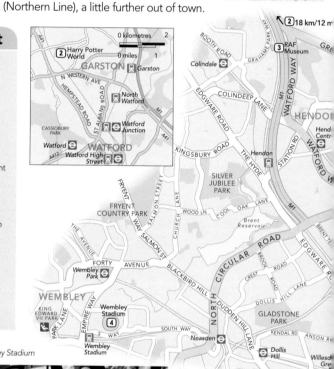

Enjoying the atmosphere at Wembley Stadium

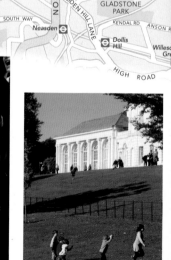

Playing on the landscaped lawns around Georgian Kenwood House

The RAF Museum has dozens of historic aircraft, including the legendary Battle of Britain Spitfire and Hawker Hurricane

Getting hands-on with the inmates of the Butterfly House, Golders Hill Park

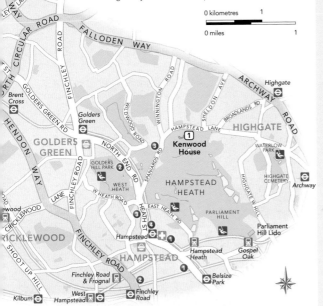

0 kilometres 1

0 miles 1

Kite-flying on Parliament Hill, Hampstead Heath

The Lowdown

🚗 **Train** For Hampstead Village and Parliament Hill (southern side of the Heath), take mainline trains to Gospel Oak and Hampstead Heath from Camden Road station **Tube** For Kenwood House and Highgate, take the Northern Line (High Barnet branch) to Archway, Highgate or Golders Green stations

ℹ️ **Visitor information** www.lovecamden.org

🛒 **Supermarkets** Tesco Express, 27 Heath Street, Hampstead, NW3 6TR; Sainsbury's, 614 Finchley Road, Golders Green, NW11 7RX **Markets** Hampstead Community Market, Hampstead High Street, 10am–6pm Mon–Sat; Parliament Hill Farmers' Market, Highgate Road, 9am–2pm Sat; Archway Market, Holloway Road (crafts), 10am–5pm Sat

🚩 **Festivals** Hampstead Heath Easter Fair (also at Whitsun & August Bank Holiday); Proms at St Jude's (Jun); Kenwood Picnic Concerts (Jun–Aug); Hampstead & Highgate Literary Festival (Sep); Hampstead Heath Conker Championships (Oct)

➕ **Pharmacies** Boots, 40 Hampstead High Street, NW3 1QE (8:30am–6:30pm Mon–Sat, 11am–6pm Sun), or see www.nhs.uk/servicedirectories

🛝 **Nearest playgrounds** Parliament Hill (Hampstead Heath); Golders Hill Park (West Heath Avenue, NW11 7QP or North End Road, NW3 7HA); King Edward VIII Park; Waterlow Park

① Kenwood House
The big house on the Heath

With its manicured lawns, ornamental lakes, stables and kitchen garden, Kenwood is a gentleman's country estate, 6 km (4 miles) from London's West End. It's an authentic slice of Georgian England, where Robert Adam's Neo-Classical interiors and Humphrey Repton's picturesque park survive more or less intact from the late 1700s. Immediately to the south stretches Hampstead Heath, a hinterland frequented by wild swimmers, kite-fliers, Frisbee-throwers and tree-climbers. It is a big blast of freedom for families.

Picnicking outside Kenwood House

Key Features

The Orangery · Dressing room · The library

The Library, with its ostentatious painted ceiling, colourful friezes and colonnades, is one of Robert Adam's masterpieces.

Picnic concerts are staged in Kenwood's grounds on Saturday evenings in summer. In recent years the bill has featured Blondie and music by Vivaldi, usually with a fireworks finale.

Rembrandt self-portrait (1661) This picture is a highlight of Kenwood's collection of old masters, which also includes Vermeer's The Guitar Player and paintings by Hals, Turner and Gainsborough.

The park was remodelled in the 1790s under the guidance of Humphrey Repton. Its meandering lakeside walks are designed to spring picturesque "surprises".

The Lowdown

🌐 **Address** Hampstead Lane, NW3 7JR; 020 8348 1286; www.english-heritage.org.uk/daysout/properties/kenwood/

🚗 **Train** Gospel Oak or Hampstead Heath **Tube** Golders Green (Northern line), then bus 210 or H3; or Archway (Northern line), then bus 210 **Bus stop** Hampstead Lane **Car** West Lodge car park (pay-and-display); free parking on Hampstead Lane

🕐 **Open** House: 10am–5pm daily; Estate: from 8am (closing time varies with season)

💲 **Price** Free; some temporary exhibitions charge

🚩 **Guided tours** Yes, times vary (small charge applies)

👫 **Age range** 6 plus

🤸 **Activities** Occasional holiday crafts sessions; Easter Egg trails; bat-spotting walks on summer evenings. Picnic concerts programme Jun–Aug (www.picnicconcerts.com)

⏱ **Allow** Up to 2 hours

♿ **Wheelchair access** Ground floor and toilets only

☕ **Café** Set in Kenwood's servants' wing, the Brew House Cafe (020 8341 5384; 9am–4pm) serves breakfasts and lunches on the terrace; the Steward's Room serves home-baked bites

🛍 **Shop** On the ground floor

🚻 **Toilets** On the ground floor

Good family value?
It's free, and so is the Heath

Hampstead Heath
First recorded in Saxon times and once the stalking ground of highwaymen, "The Heath" still has a wild streak. A swathe of sandstone hills and wooded glades, it runs from Kenwood House in the north to Parliament Hill, its view of London protected by law. Summer kite-fliers and winter sledgers gather here, at the bottom (near Gospel Oak station), there are playgrounds, a paddling pool and a lido.

Sampling the wares at Parliament Hill Farmers' Market

Letting off steam

Kenwood's own grounds have grass to sprawl on and trees to scramble up. Hampstead Heath's best playground *(9am–dusk; 020 7433 1917)* is in the far south, near the Nassington Road entrance, with a sandpit and paddling pool. There is an adventure playground for older children nearby, plus the lido swimming pool – unheated *(open 7am–6pm May–Sep, 7am–noon Sep–Apr)*. Accompanied children aged eight and over can also swim in the reedy bathing ponds on the eastern fringe of Hampstead Heath. From Kenwood House, a handy playtime option is **Golders Hill Park** *(West Heath Avenue, NW11 7QP; 020 7332 3511; 7:30am–dusk)*, with its petting zoo, deer, butterfly house and playground. Get there via a short bus ride from Kenwood towards Golders Green Station.

Eat and drink

Picnic: under £25; Snacks: £25–40; Real meal: £50–65; Family treat: £70 or more (based on a family of four)

PICNIC The Hampstead Butcher *(56 Rosslyn Hill, NW3 1ND; 020 7794 9210; www. hampsteadbutcher.com)* does good cold cuts, cheeses and ready-to-eat picnic hampers.
SNACKS Golders Hill Park Refreshment House *(020 8455 8010; open 9am–6pm Mon–Sat)* has a terrace, good cakes and home-made ice cream. For a café

on Hampstead Heath, try the one at Parliament Hill Fields (off Highgate Road; *020 7485 6606; 9am–4:30pm)*.
REAL MEAL The Spaniards Inn *(Spaniards Road, NW3 7JJ; 020 8731 8406, www.thespaniards hampstead.co.uk; food daily from noon)* has a large and splendid garden, a traditional British menu and barbecues and hog roasts sizzling away on summer weekends.
FAMILY TREAT Gaucho *(64 Heath Street, NW3 1DN; 020 7431 8222; www.gauchorestaurants.co.uk; noon–11pm Mon–Thu; noon–11:30pm Fri & Sat; 10am–11:30pm Sun)*, between Hampstead Tube station and the Heath, has funky cowhide decor and specializes in Argentine steaks.

Find out more

DIGITAL A leaflet with three walking trails on the Heath is downloadable from *www. cityoflondon.gov.uk*: click on "Forests, Parks & Gardens"; "Hampstead Heath"; "Visitor information and map", then "Download the trail leaflet".
FILM Kenwood House features prominently in the 1999 romantic comedy *Notting Hill*, starring Julia Roberts and Hugh Grant.

Next stop...

POETS' CORNER Two tiny museums south of the Heath add weight to Hampstead's reputation as a hotbed of literature and the arts. Burgh House *(New End Square, NW3 1LT; 020 7431 0144; www.burghhouse. org.uk)* is a Queen Anne mansion once frequented by Rudyard Kipling; while Keats House *(10 Keats Grove, NW3 2RR; 020 7332 3868; www. keatshouse.cityoflondon.gov.uk)* is where the eponymous poet wrote *Ode to a Nightingale*. Both run occasional family events.

Hampstead's 400-year-old, oak-panelled tavern, The Spaniards Inn

② Warner Bros. Studio Tour London – The Making of Harry Potter

A simply wizard tour!

Here at Warner's studio, even though there are no thrilling rides and only a few hands-on interactive gadgetry, children will be spellbound by the original scenery, costumes and props that were used in the filming of all eight Harry Potter movies.

The Making of Harry Potter studio tour is by timed ticket and is largely self-guided, though friendly and knowledgeable staff are always on hand. Among the sets en route are the iconic Great Hall at Hogwarts School of Witchcraft and Wizardry, Professor Dumbledore's study, Hagrid's hut, the Gryffindor common room and Diagon Alley, complete with Ollivanders wand shop and the Weasley brothers' joke emporium. Hagrid's motorcycle and Harry's Nimbus 2000 are also on display. Kids will be delighted to know that

Set of the Great Hall, part of the Warner Bros. Studio Tour, Leavesden Studios

they can ride broomsticks here as well. The tour also offers glimpses into the off-camera world of the film-makers, including how animatronics and green-screen effects brought the monsters and marvels of Harry's world to life.

Letting off steam

The studio has a backlot, which offers plenty of space for kids to run about in. They can also explore the Knight Bus, 4 Privet Drive and Hogwarts Bridge here.

The Lowdown

🌐 **Address** Warner Bros. Studio Tour, Studio Tour Drive, Leavesden, WD25 7LR; 08450 840 900; www.wbstudiotour.co.uk

🚗 **Train** Watford Junction station, then shuttle buses run every 30 minutes to attraction (£2pp return) **Car** Free parking on site

🕐 **Open** Daily; first tour: 10am, last tour starts at 4:30pm and 6:30pm (varies with season); closed Dec 25 & Dec 26

💲 **Price** £101, under-4s free (tickets must be bought in advance)

👤 **Skipping the queue** Book the earliest tour available

👫 **Age range** All ages

👫 **Activities** Hand-held audio-visual guide available in eight languages includes facts, interviews and unseen footage (£4.95)

⏱ **Allow** 3.5 hours, arrive 20 minutes before the tour starts

♿ **Wheelchair access** Yes

🍴 **Eat and drink** *Snacks* The on-site Studio Café (*9:30am–closing time*) serves soups, salads and sandwiches; there is a food court midway through the tour

🛍 **Shop** Selling an extensive range of merchandise

🚻 **Toilets** Several throughout

③ RAF Museum

Fighter pilot playtime

Many kids want to be a fighter pilot when they grow up. Few actually make it, so here's the next best thing: a whole hangar full of interactive flying games and challenges at the Royal Air Force Museum in Hendon. Its Aeronauts Centre has 40 hands-on experiments that cunningly disguise principles of science as play: climb into a helicopter cockpit and take the controls; grab a hang-glider bar and manoeuvre through the air; or grapple with pilot aptitude tests.

The Lowdown

🌐 **Address** Grahame Park Way, NW9 5LL; 020 8205 2266; www.rafmuseum.org.uk/london

🚗 **Train** Mill Hill Broadway, 15-minute walk **Tube** Colindale (Northern line), 10-minute walk **Bus stop** Grahame Park Way; Lanacre Avenue **Car** Parking on site (from £3 for 0–3 hours)

🕐 **Open** 10am–6pm. Our Finest Hour show runs hourly, 1–5pm

💲 **Price** Free, except flight simulator (£3) and 4-D theatre (£4)

🚩 **Guided tours** Free volunteer-led tours, times vary. Audio guide to selected galleries available by download only

👫 **Age range** 6 plus; Eurofighter simulator min height 107 cm (3 ft 6 in)

👫 **Activities** Some activity sheets and audio guides available from website, plus worksheets. Family activity programme focuses on Commonwealth Day (Mar), Armed Forces Day (Jun) and the Battle of Britain (Sep), plus half-term holiday workshops

⏱ **Allow** Half a day

♿ **Wheelchair access** Yes, although getting in aircraft will be difficult

🍴 **Eat and drink** *Snacks* Wessex Café has helicopters and home-made snacks; *Real meal* Echo Alpha Tango serves a health-conscious kids' menu

🛍 **Shop** Selling a variety of aviation-themed gifts

🚻 **Toilets** By the entrance

The museum is spread across the former Hendon Aerodrome, the century-old birthplace of British aviation. Giant hangars house more than 100 full-size flying machines, from Sopwith Camels to cruise missiles, many suspended

Getting up close to one of the many planes on display at the RAF Museum

dogfight-style from the rafters. The Milestones of Flight gallery gives a literal overview of aircraft history from its "control tower" balcony, and other highlights include a sound and light show – Our Finest Hour – bringing alive the Battle of Britain, a "4-D" theatre experience aboard an American B-17 bomber, and a Eurofighter Typhoon flight simulator, soaring at twice the speed of sound.

Letting off steam
There are lots of grassy picnic grounds at the museum.

④ Wembley Stadium
Ninety minutes of glory

After a controversial £750 million rebuilding, the "new" Wembley Stadium has resumed its mantle as the spiritual home of football, with 90,000 seats and a 133-m (436-ft) arch that curves like a rainbow above the North London skyline. As well as the FA Cup final each May, Wembley hosts international rugby, American football, rock concerts and the 2012 Olympic football finals.

For footie-mad kids (and adults), a trip here is akin to a pilgrimage, and the 90-minute guided tours won't let them down. They get to follow in the footsteps of their heroes on matchday – from the England team's dressing-room and warm-up area, through the tunnel to pitch-side, where they'll be greeted by the cacophonous roar of a piped-in crowd. After a sit down in the manager's dugout, it's up the famous steps to the Royal Box for a feel of a replica FA Cup. For the adults, there's also a video of historic highlights and a look at some

Going behind the scenes at Wembley Stadium

famous Wembley relics, including the crossbar that helped England win the 1966 World Cup.

Letting off steam
Brought your own ball along? For a good kick-about, head west via Dagmar Avenue to **King Edward VII Park** *(Park Lane, Wembley, HA9 7RX)* which has grassy space, football pitches and a playground.

Out and about on the pathways of King Edward VII Park

The Lowdown

🌐 **Address** Wembley National Stadium, HA9 0WS; 0844 980 8001 (booking line: 0800 169 9933); www.wembleystadium. com/Wembley-Tours.aspx

🚗 **Train** Wembley Stadium station. **Tube** Wembley Park (Metropolitan and Jubilee lines) **Bus stop** Olympic Way, Empire Way, Wembley Park Station **Car** Green Car Park, Engineers Way

🕐 **Open** Tours run most days (check website), departing 10am–4pm. Sometimes only a 60-minute "mini tour" is offered, missing out dressing rooms and pitch-side

💲 **Price** £45, under-5s free

🚻 **Skipping the queue** Advance booking strongly advised; arrive 30 minutes before tour

🚻 **Age range** 6 plus

🏃 **Activities** Quiz sheets can be downloaded from the website's Groups and School Visits page

⏱ **Allow** 2 hours

♿ **Wheelchair access** Yes

🍴 **Eat and drink** *Snacks* A café at the entrance serves sandwiches and snacks

🛍 **Shop** Selling football and Wembley souvenirs

🚻 **Toilets** At start of tour

Horniman Museum and around

If the Horniman Museum was in Central London, it would be on every family's must-see itinerary. A treasure chest of strange marvels, it has everything from voodoo charms to mummy cases, live bees to stuffed apes and a skull-covered hat. The museum is near Forest Hill, a 15-minute train ride from London Bridge station. The P4 bus route runs from the Horniman to South London's other star attraction: Dulwich Picture Gallery, whose old masters come to life at ArtPlay family workshops. Better still, walk there across Dulwich Park, where the Pavilion Café is a super sunny-day lunch option.

Picnicking on the lawns surrounding the ornate Victorian conservatory at the Horniman Museum

Enjoying a ride through Dulwich Park on the recumbent bicycles available for hire

Places of interest

SIGHTS
1. Horniman Museum and Gardens
2. Dulwich Picture Gallery
3. Crystal Palace Park

● EAT AND DRINK
1. The Teapot
2. The Pavilion Café
3. The Dartmouth Arms
4. The Herne Tavern

See also Horniman Museum and Gardens (p223), Dulwich Picture Gallery (p224) and Crystal Palace Park (p225)

Getting up close to one of the many life-size dinosaurs that lurk at Crystal Palace Park

0 metres 500
0 yards 500

The Lowdown

🚗 **Train** For the Horniman Museum, go to Forest Hill from London Bridge. Crystal Palace Station is served by Victoria and London Bridge; nearby Penge West Station from London Bridge only. West Dulwich station from Victoria; North Dulwich Station from London Bridge. **Bus** Number 185 runs to the Horniman Museum from Victoria Station via Dulwich; number 176 runs from Tottenham Court Road via Trafalgar Square, Waterloo, Dulwich and the Horniman to Crystal Palace Park

ℹ️ **Visitor information** 020 8297 8317; www.lewisham.gov.uk; www.southwark.gov.uk

🛒 **Supermarket** Sainsbury's, 34–48 London Road, Forest Hill, SE23 3HF. **Markets** North Cross Road Market, East Dulwich (food, crafts, jewellery), 9am–5pm Sat; Dulwich College Farmers' Market, 9am–1pm fourth Sun of month

🎌 **Festivals** Dulwich Festival, music, arts, walks (May); Bonfire Night, Crystal Palace Park (Nov)

➕ **Pharmacies** Boots, 21–23 Dartmouth Road, SE23 3HN (9am–5:30pm Mon–Sat). For 24-hour pharmacies, search at www.nhs.uk/servicedirectories

👟 **Nearest playgrounds** Triangle Playground (London Road, Forest Hill, SE23 3PH); Dulwich Park Playground (College Road, SE21 7BQ); Crystal Palace Park playground (Thicket Rd, SE20 8DT)

Getting creative at one of the kids' art classes at Dulwich Picture Gallery

① Horniman Museum and Gardens
Mummies, magic amulets and a merman

A Victorian tea trader, Frederick Horniman gathered an eclectic collection of objects from across the British Empire. His museum bursts with artefacts from the wildest childhood imagination: a totem pole, a torture chair, magic amulets, mummies, even a merman. Apart from being child-friendly, there is the universally popular Aquarium as well as exhibits that appeal to older age groups. It hosts some of London's most exotic "Busy Bee" play sessions, which could involve sharks' teeth, ritual masks or thumb pianos.

Goliath Beetle in the Nature Base

Key Features

■ **First Floor** Natural History Balcony

■ **Ground Floor** Natural History Gallery, Hands On Base, Education Centre, café and shop

■ **Lower Ground Floor** Temporary Exhibitions, Music Gallery, African Worlds Gallery and Centenary Gallery

■ **Basement** An aquarium reveals what lives in ponds, in coral reefs and the Amazon rainforest.

Entrance _____

① **Haitian voodoo shrine** This gloriously gaudy altar is loaded with strange offerings: make-up, dolls, posters, perfume, skulls. Haitians believe spirits are everywhere, even in discarded objects.

② **Igbo Ijele mask** Piled with figurines and feathers in fantastic colours, this towering mask is Africa's largest. It is worn at the lively ijele ceremony in Nigeria.

③ **Music Gallery** Touch the tabletops to hear sound clips from the dazzling instruments collection.

④ **Tlingit totem pole** Carved in cedar, the Horniman totem pole guards the entrance. It depicts the Alaskan legend of a girl who married a bear.

⑤ **Nature Base** Here you can observe a live honey bee colony, watch the scampering harvest mice and scrutinize beetles under a microscope.

⑥ **Aquarium** The aquarium features 15 displays, from a British pond to a Fijian coral reef. For kids, the seahorses are the stars.

Letting off steam

Draped across the summit of Forest Hill, with panoramic views over London, the museum's grassy grounds include award-winning display gardens, which opened in 2012. Other highlights include the

The vast sandpit at the Triangle, opposite the Horniman Museum

Prices given are for a family of four

historic bandstand, a picnic area, the animal walk with alpaca and rabbits and the mile-long nature trail on the site of an old railway line. For a traditional playground, cross London Road to the **Triangle**, which has a sandpit, a climbing wall and a tea kiosk.

Eat and drink

Picnic: under £20; Snacks: £20–40; Real meal: £40–60; Family treat: £60 or more (based on a family of four)

PICNIC The Teapot (56 London Road, SE23 3HF; 020 8699 2829) is a dapper little tearoom and deli, handily placed halfway

between Forest Hill station and the museum.

SNACKS The Pavilion Café in Dulwich Park (College Road, SE21 7BQ; 020 8299 1383; 8:30am–5:30pm, weekends from 9am) is a lovely spot for coffee and home-baked cakes, and their lunchtime specials have an Italian flavour.

REAL MEAL The Dartmouth Arms (7 Dartmouth Road, SE23 3HN; 020 8488 3117; www.thedartmoutharms. com; food served noon–3:30pm, 6:30pm–10pm Sun–Fri, noon–10pm Sat) is a friendly gastro-pub with several dishes available in smaller portions, ideal for kids. It is near Forest Hill station.

The Lowdown

- **Address** 100 London Road, Forest Hill, SE23 3PQ; 020 8699 1872; www.horniman.ac.uk

- **Train** Forest Hill, 10-minute walk **Bus stop** London Road; Sydenham Hill

- **Open** 10:30am–5:30pm daily; gardens 7:15am–sunset Mon–Sat, from 8am Sun

- **Price** Free. Aquarium £22; some temporary exhibitions charge

- **Skipping the queue** Busy Bee tickets available at 10:45am, 11:30am & 12:15pm on Wed & Fri, 12:30pm at weekends

- **Age range** 3 plus

- **Activities** Free family activities every weekend afternoon: mix of drop-in "discovery for all" sessions (2–3:30pm) and ticketed art workshops and object-handling (11:45am–12:30pm, 1–1:45pm, 1:30–2:15pm, 2:45–3:30pm). Free family storytelling every first Sunday of month (2:15pm & 3:30pm). Frequent sessions on school

holiday weekdays, too (check website). Half-hour Busy Bee crafts and story sessions for under-5s every Wed and Fri (10:45am, 11:30am & 12:15pm). Download age-graded activity sheets and learning packs before visiting at: www.horniman.ac.uk

- **Allow** At least half a day

- **Wheelchair access** Yes, both museum and gardens

- **Café** The museum's café has excellent variety for kids; on a sunny day, eat in the ornate Victorian conservatory

- **Shop** Selling toys, musical instruments and books inspired by the museum's collection

- **Toilets** By café and on Lower Ground Floor

Good family value?
Absolutely tremendous. Unlike many London museums, even the café is affordable.

This stuffed walrus dominates the Natural History Gallery

FAMILY TREAT The Herne Tavern *(2 Forest Hill Road, SE22 0RR; 020 8299 9521; www.theherne.net; noon–11pm Mon–Thu; noon–2am Fri & Sat; noon–midnight Sun)* is more restaurant than pub, with a children's menu of grilled chicken, linguine, sausages or scampi. Kids eat for free Monday to Friday when an adult main is purchased. It's at East Dulwich: take the 363 bus from the Horniman.

"Marine mash-ups" and a living dinosaur trail.

For behind-the-scenes footage from the Horniman, including an X-ray view of its famous "merman", visit the museum's YouTube channel *(www.youtube.com/user/horniman)*. Find the Horniman on Facebook and Twitter *(@HornimanMuseum)* and follow the walrus himself *(@HornimanWalrus)*.

Find out more
DIGITAL The museum's official website *(www.horniman.ac.uk)* has activity packs and trails, including "Flights of Fancy",

Next stop...
CRYSTAL PALACE PARK Head here for an afternoon of fun amoung the dinosaurs and playgrounds, or visit the Sports Centre in wet weather.

KIDS' CORNER

Twang!
As the museum's thongaphone proves, musical instruments can be made from anything. Here's how to make a shoebox lute:

1 Take an old shoebox and carefully cut a round hole in the lid.
2 Stretch five or six rubber bands around the box, so they run across the hole. Use thick and thin ones.
3 Place a pencil under the bands at each end of the box, to make a "bridge", and your lute is ready to strum! Add more instruments to your orchestra at *www.ehow.com/videos-on_5019_make-musical-instruments-kids.html*.

Don't touch!
Can you spot the poison dart frogs in the aquarium? The golden poison frog is the deadliest frog species of all, with enough toxin to kill 20,000 mice. Just touching one could kill you!

Chasing shadows
Sundials use the sun's shadow to tell the time. How many different ones can you find in the Horniman grounds? There are 10 to find – including one that needs you to work it!

Real or fake?
Why isn't the walrus wrinkly? Because when he was stuffed in the late 19th century, no one had seen a live walrus, so they didn't know how full he should be. Other than being overstuffed, he's the real thing though! Nearby you'll see a merman – or is it? Actually it's a combination of a fish's body and a fierce head made from paper and clay. Now that's REALLY creepy!

② Dulwich Picture Gallery
Old masters and leafy grounds

With its cloistered gardens, chapel and mausoleum, this looks precisely the kind of place that wouldn't welcome children, but appearances can be deceptive. London's oldest public gallery is crammed with priceless portraits – from 17th-century saints to 18th-century courtesans – which were gathered in the 1790s for the King of Poland, who was promptly overthrown, leaving his new collection homeless. Architect Sir John Soane (see p94) stepped in, and with his interlinked halls lit by skylights, created the template for art galleries the world over. There are works by Canaletto, Constable, Raphael and Rubens here – and free drawing trails help visitors to unpick their secrets.

The real joy for families, though, is the inspiring array of hands-on art classes that are offered here. On the first and last Sundays of the

The Lowdown

🌐 **Address** Gallery Road, SE21 7AD; 020 8693 5254; www.dulwichpicturegallery.org.uk

🚃 **Train** North Dulwich or West Dulwich, both a 10-minute walk away **Bus stop** College Road; Dulwich College

🕐 **Open** 10am–5pm Tue–Fri, 11am–5pm Sat–Sun (last admission 4:30pm)

💷 **Price** £10–12, under-18s free; temporary exhibitions extra

🧍 **Skipping the queue** Book half-term and after-school courses in advance: 020 8299 8732

🚩 **Guided tours** 3pm Sat and Sun (free); multimedia iGuide (£3)

👫 **Age range** 8 plus

👫 **Activities** Free quiz and drawing trails (ages 4–12). Family ArtPlay drop-in, 2–4pm first and last Sun of month (charges apply); also Wed in school holidays. Half-term workshops (ages 6–8 and 9–11, charges apply). Jazz evenings and films in summer

⏱ **Allow** 1–2 hours

♿ **Wheelchair access** Yes

🍽 **Eat and drink** Real meal The Café opens 30 minutes earlier than the gallery and has a children's menu and celebrated afternoon teas Snacks The Pavilion Café in Dulwich Park (see p222) is also a good bet

🛍 **Shop** Selling art-related gifts, books and toys

🚻 **Toilets** On the ground floor

Left Hanging out paintings to dry at Dulwich Picture Gallery
Below Enjoying the playground in Dulwich Park

month, drop-in ArtPlay sessions encourage grown-ups and their children to work creatively together – drawing cartoons, making bunting or block-printing, perhaps. There is more of the same every Wednesday afternoon in summer, when the gallery gardens are transformed into a giant arty picnic. There are also half-term workshops for ages 6–11, and after-school art clubs for 7–18s.

The 15-minute zip out of town to leafy Dulwich Village feels like a magical journey into the heart of the countryside, and once sated with old masters, children get to cross the road into attractive Dulwich Park, with its boating lake, bike hire and adventure playground.

Letting off steam
The gallery gardens are open for picnics and playtime – no "keep off the grass signs" here. **Dulwich Park** (020 8693 8635; www.southwark.gov.uk/info/461/a_to_z_of_parks/1296/dulwich_park) has a playground, cycle hire (020 8299 6636; www.londonrecumbents.co.uk/bikes_we_hire.html; 10am–5pm, last hire 4:30pm) and turn-up-and-play tennis.

③ Crystal Palace Park
The land that time forgot

Television, theme parks and the Girl Guides – a fine trio of inventions, especially if you happen to be a child, and all were hatched here in one of London's most history-packed parks. So it's great that Crystal Palace is finally getting a new lease of life after years in the doldrums, with plans afoot for a multi-million pound makeover that will restore it to something like the popular pomp of its Victorian heyday.

The park was created by master gardener Joseph Paxton (1803–65) to house his mammoth Crystal Palace, which was moved here pane by pane from Hyde Park after hosting the 1851 Great Exhibition. Perched on a ridge overlooking the city, it had extensive pleasure grounds and fountains higher than Nelson's Column, and thousands flocked to visit. However, the Crystal Palace burnt down in 1936: look out for its ghostly terraces, and the odd statue of a sultan or sphinx. But one

Dinosaur-spotting in the Dinosaur Court at Crystal Palace Park

KIDS' CORNER

Stop, thief!
At Dulwich Picture Gallery, find the portrait of Jacob de Gheyn III, by Rembrandt. This is the world's most stolen painting! In 1983 a cat burglar lowered himself through a skylight and spirited it away. Where do you think the police finally found it?
a Tied to a bicycle
b Under a graveyard bench
c In a train station luggage rack

Answer at the bottom of the page.

Eureka!
Three great ideas that started in Crystal Palace Park...

1) Theme parks
Crystal Palace had the world's first dinosaur sculptures – Victorian visitors flocked to walk among them, and bought small models as souvenirs. Look out for the iguanodon – in 1853, the Dinosaur Court opened with a grand dinner served inside its belly!

2) Television
John Logie Baird, who invented television, beamed the first television shows from his Crystal Palace studio in 1935. You can't miss the giant TV mast that still stands here – at 219 m (719 ft) it's the fourth tallest thing in London.

3) Girl Guides
The Guides started here in 1909, when a group of girls marched on a Boy Scout rally and demanded to join. See if you can find the Guide badges hidden inside the park's hedge maze.

of the park's original wonders is still a huge draw for families – its Dinosaur Court, an army of 30 life-size prehistoric monsters that stalk the boating lake. Installed in 1853 by the sculptor Benjamin Waterhouse Hawkins and the pioneering palaeontologist Richard Owen, these models were a sensation in their day, prefiguring Darwin's *Origin of the Species* and staking a claim for Crystal Palace as the world's first "theme park".

Pick up a guide from the park information centre and go hunting for Iguanodons and Pterodactyls – dino-mad kids will enjoy pointing out the anatomical errors exposed by 150 years of science. The nearby children's playground boasts a dinosaur climbing frame, and the park also has a small farmyard with alpacas and a reptile room, plus one of the biggest hedge mazes in the country. Add the indoor facilities at the sports centre, the spiritual home of British athletics, and there's easily enough to warrant a train ride out from the city centre. Soon, there should be more entertainment, too – the Crystal Palace masterplan promises tropical glasshouses, a treetop walkway, even a revival of one of Paxton's 1850s fountains.

Take cover
The park is dominated by the **National Sports Centre** (*Ledrington Road, SE19 2BB; 020 8778 0131; www.better.org.uk/leisure/crystal-palace-national-sports-centre#/*), which has an Olympic-size indoor swimming pool, tennis courts and a climbing wall. The centre's training pool is reserved for 2-hour family-only swimming most days.

Alternatively, visit the museum that tells the story of Paxton's original Crystal Palace (*020 8676 0700; www.crystalpalacemuseum.org.uk; open 11am–3pm, weekends and bank holidays only*).

The Lowdown

- 🌐 **Address** Crystal Palace Park, Thicket Road, SE20 8DT; 020 8313 4471; www.bromley.gov.uk. Access via Thicket Rd, Crystal Palace Park Rd and Ledrington Rd
- 🚕 **Train** Crystal Palace, 2-minute walk; Penge West, 5-minute walk; **Bus stop** Crystal Palace Station; Penge West Station
- 🕐 **Open** 7:30am–dusk Mon–Fri, from 9am Sat & Sun (to 9pm May–Aug). Information Centre (near Thicket Road entrance) open 9am–5:30pm Mon–Fri
- 💲 **Price** Free
- 🚩 **Guided tours** Dinosaur trail leaflet from information centre, which has a small history display
- 🚻 **Age range** All
- 🏃 **Activities** Playground and dinosaur area near Thicket Road gate, plus hedge maze (free). Most weekends, keepers at Crystal Palace Park Farm (noon–4pm Mon, Tue & Thu–Sun; 020 8659 2557). Ranger-led pond-dipping and Easter egg hunts in school holidays (call to check). National Sports Centre hosts school holiday activity or sports schools (ages 6–15; www.gll.org/holidayactivities)
- ⏱ **Allow** Up to half a day
- ♿ **Wheelchair access** Yes
- 🍴 **Eat and drink** Snacks Park café (Thicket Road entrance; 020 8776 5422; 9am–seasonal closing) offers fast food, snacks and drinks
- 🚻 **Toilets** Near Thicket Road entrance

Picnic under £20; Snacks £20–40; Real meal £40–60; Family treat £60 or more (based on a family of four)

Kew Gardens and around

Glossy, well-groomed and handily located at the end of the District line, Richmond and Kew offer a breath of fresh air for families overcome by the pace of the city. Kids will delight in the gardens' attractions and they will love Richmond Park – especially its deer. For Kew, alight at the tube station, pick up a picnic and tour the gardens on the Explorer Bus. For Richmond Park, take bus number 65 or 371 from Richmond station. Several stately homes are close, too: try the riverside walk from Richmond to haunted Ham House.

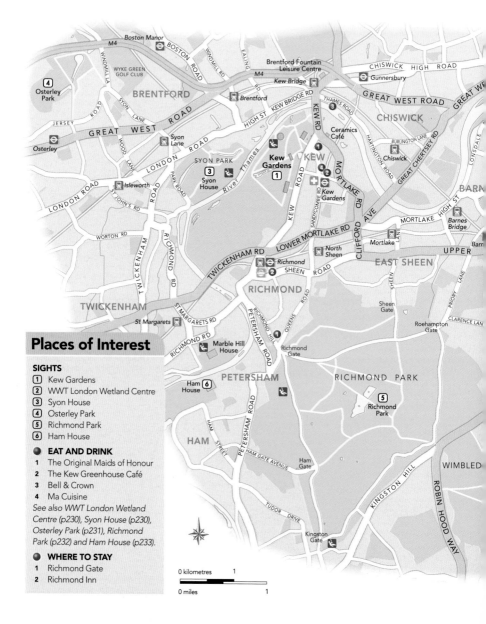

Places of Interest

SIGHTS
1. Kew Gardens
2. WWT London Wetland Centre
3. Syon House
4. Osterley Park
5. Richmond Park
6. Ham House

● EAT AND DRINK
1. The Original Maids of Honour
2. The Kew Greenhouse Café
3. Bell & Crown
4. Ma Cuisine

See also WWT London Wetland Centre (p230), Syon House (p230), Osterley Park (p231), Richmond Park (p232) and Ham House (p233).

● WHERE TO STAY
1. Richmond Gate
2. Richmond Inn

0 kilometres 1

0 miles 1

Above *The Great Conservatory at Syon House*
Right *Delicious treats on display at The Original Maids of Honour*

Above *Interactive play area, Climbers and Creepers, at Kew Gardens*

The Lowdown

🚗 **Train** Kew Bridge and Richmond, both served by trains from Waterloo (via Barnes). Richmond and Kew Gardens (North London Line) **Tube** Kew Gardens, Richmond (both District Line)

ℹ️ **Visitor information** 020 8891 1411; *www. visitrichmond.co.uk*

🛒 **Supermarkets** Waitrose, 4 Sheen Road, Richmond, TW9 1AE. **Markets** Richmond Farmers' Market, Heron Square, 11am–3pm Sat

🚩 **Festivals** Tropical Extravaganza, Kew Gardens (Feb); Holi Hindu Festival of Colour (Mar); Kew Summer Swing picnic concerts (Aug); Richmond Riverside Festival, world music and dance (Aug); Great River Race, finish point (Sep); Richmond Literature Festival (Nov)

➕ **Pharmacies** Lloyds, 19–21 Station Parade, Kew, TW9 3PS (8:30am–7pm Mon–Fri, 9am–6pm Sat, 10am–2pm Sun). For 24-hour pharmacies, search at *www.nhs.uk/ servicedirectories*

👟 **Nearest playgrounds** Climbers and Creepers, Kew Gardens (*near Brentford Gate*); Petersham Gate, Richmond Park (*Petersham Rd, TW10 5HS*); Marble Hill Adventure Playground, Marble Hill Park (*Richmond Rd, TW1 2NL*)

Youngsters riding ponies through Richmond Park

① Kew Gardens
The world's most famous garden

Founded more than 250 years ago, the Royal Botanic Gardens – a treasure trove of lakes, mini-temples, nature trails and playgrounds – is a delightful place to spend time. Kew's Victorian glasshouses offer a botanical world tour, but even better is just dawdling in the dappled glades around Queen Charlotte's Cottage, or admiring the peacocks at the Waterlily Pond. Little visitors can burrow in a badger sett and climb into the treetops – and if that doesn't tire them out, there's an exhilarating plant-themed playhouse.

Oriental Pagoda

Key Features

① Treetop Walkway Clamber into the branches of Kew's arboretum for giddying views. The walkway is designed to sway in the wind.

② Palm House The tropical plants here drip in the steamy atmosphere of Kew's hottest glasshouse. In the basement aquarium, don 3-D glasses and go "swimming with plankton".

③ Temperate House The world's biggest Victorian glasshouse is also home to the world's tallest "house plant", reached via ornate iron balconies.

④ Climbers and Creepers Fall prey to the slippery pitcher plant or wriggle into a field-mouse nest in this ingenious indoor playground. Outside, the Treehouse Towers has a zip-wire and rope bridges.

Queen Charlotte's Cottage

⑤ Evolution House Waterfalls crash and insects hum on this trip through primordial swamps back to the age of the dinosaurs. Watch out for monster millipedes!

Brentford Gate

Elizabeth Gate

Victoria Gate

Waterlily Pond

Lion Gate

⑥ Princess of Wales Conservatory Look out for Venus flytraps and the world's largest flower in one of 10 climatic zones. Portholes give a close-up view of the fishponds.

⑦ Badger Sett Expect muddy kneecaps after a crawl inside this child-size badgers' home. Nearby, the Nature Hide and Stag Beetle Loggery explore more native wildlife.

Take cover

Kew's glasshouses, aquariums and indoor playroom offer rainy-day diversions – plus there's a toddler corner in the White Peaks Shop. On nearby Kew Green, the Ceramics Café offers drop-in pottery painting (1A Mortlake Terrace, TW9 3DT; 020 8332 6661, www.ceramicscafe.com/studio-locations/kew; 10am–6pm), while just south of Kew Gardens, Pools on the Park (Twickenham Rd, Richmond, TW9 2SF; www.spring health.net/richmond/index.html) has indoor and outdoor pools (from 6:30am Mon–Fri; 8am Sat & 7am Sun; closing times vary, check website).

Prices given are for a family of four

Eat and drink

Picnic: under £25; Snacks: £25–45; Real meal: £45–65; Family treat: £60 or more (based on a family of four)

PICNIC The Original Maids of Honour (288 Kew Road, Kew, TW9 3DU; 020 8940 2752, www.the

"Maids of Honour" pastries, which gave the popular Kew bakery its name

originalmaidsofhonour.co.uk; 8am–6pm Mon–Fri; from 8:30am Sat & Sun) is a Kew institution, said to date back to Tudor times. It offers tearoom treats, smart lunches and pre-packed picnics of varying extravagance.

SNACKS The Kew Greenhouse Café (1 Station Parade, Richmond TW9 3PS; 020 8940 0183, www. thekewgreenhousecafe.com; 8am–5:30pm) is a traditional English café, between the Tube and Victoria Gate, serving pasta, quiches, eggs on toast and home-made cakes.

REAL MEAL Bell & Crown (11–13 Thames Road, W4 3PL; 020 8994 4164; www.bell-and-crown.co.uk;

The Lowdown

- 🌐 **Address** Royal Botanic Gardens, Kew, Richmond, Surrey, TW9 3AB; 020 8332 5000; www.kew.org

- 🚗 **Train** Kew Gardens, 5-minute walk; or Kew Bridge, 10 minutes **Tube** Kew Gardens (District Line) **Bus stop** Kew Gardens, Kew Bridge Station **Car** Parking at Brentford Gate (£6.50 per day) **River bus** Kew Pier, Apr–Sep, four services daily to and from Westminster (020 7930 2062; www.wpsa.co.uk)

- 🕐 **Open** Apr–Aug: 9:30am–6:30pm; Sep–Oct: 9:30am–6pm; Oct–Jan: 9:30am–4:15pm; Feb–Mar: 9:30am–5:30pm. Last admission 30 minutes earlier, weekends close an hour later; Evolution House: closed for renovation (check website for details)

- 💲 **Price** £30; under-16s free

- 🚩 **Guided tours** Explorer Bus tours the gardens between 11am–3pm (duration 40 minutes, £10–13). Free walking tours daily from Victoria Plaza, 11am and 1:30pm; plus themed tours

- 👫 **Age range** All

- **Activities** Cimbers and Creepers

(ages 3–9); Treehouse Towers (up to 11). Kids' Kew guidebook (£3.95) has stickers and garden trails. Tropical Extravaganza festival in February (orchids etc); Kew the Music picnic concerts in July

- 🕐 **Allow** Up to a day

- ♿ **Wheelchair access** Mostly. Aquarium and top-level galleries not accessible, but garden paths and most buildings are. Explorer Bus can take one wheelchair.

- ☕ **Café** The Orangery is self-service, with children's portions and afternoon teas; White Peaks Café serves simpler family fare and ice cream next to the play area; Victoria Plaza Café sells sandwiches and snacks. In summer, Pavilion Restaurant has outdoor BBQ and salad buffet. All offer a kids' lunchbox

- 🛍️ **Shop** Selling plant-related and cookery items; children's toy/gift shop near play area

- 🚻 **Toilets** At main attractions

Good family value?
Free admission for under-17s, and there's almost nothing to pay for once inside.

food: 11am–11pm Mon–Sat, noon–10:30pm Sun) is one of a pleasant strip of popular riverside pubs just across Kew Bridge that boast good pub grub for families. **FAMILY TREAT Ma Cuisine** (The Old Post Office, 9 Station Approach, Kew, TW9 3QB; 020 8332 1923, www.macuisinebistrot. co.uk; noon–10pm Sun–Thu, till 10:30pm Fri & Sat) is a neat French bistro with a very relaxed and welcoming atmosphere, as well as a Michelin Bib Gourmand for its authentic French food.

The "Flying fox" zipwire at Treetop Towers, outside Climbers and Creepers

Find out more

DIGITAL On the Kew Gardens website, the Climbers and Creepers zone has colouring, stories and virtual plant-growing games for ages 3–6: www.kew. org/climbersandcreepers. Older kids can learn how to grow mango plants and make smoothies, at www.plantcultures.org/activities.

Next stop...

KEW PALACE Inside the Royal Botanic Gardens is a playhouse of princesses. Kew Palace (0844 482 7777; www.hrp.org.uk/kewpalace; 10am–5:30pm, from 11am Mon; Mar–Sep) looks like an overgrown doll's house – which is apt, since it was bought by King George III as a nursery for his children. It is the smallest surviving royal palace, and its highlights include a 200-year-old "baby house" built by the Georgian princesses themselves. Admission costs extra (£6), though accompanied under-16s get in free of charge.

② WWT London Wetland Centre

London's best duck pond

Opened in 2000, London Wetland Centre has been a conservation triumph – an ugly-duckling reservoir site transformed into a beautiful wilderness of lagoons and pasture just 6 km (4 miles) from Westminster. Thousands of waterbirds live here, including exotic duck species such as grey-and-gold feathered wigeons, which graze the fields like sheep; and shovelers, which swim in manic circles to create a vortex to bring their food to the surface.

The indoor Discovery Centre is all about engaging children, with its underwater pond camera and poo-shooting exhibit, demonstrating how reed beds filter dirty water. The all-action adventure playground has frogs to bounce on and rubber ducks to race, and kids can wander out into the wetlands to watch for

Whistling ducks by the water at the London Wetland Centre

water voles and admire the reserve's eco-friendly lawnmowers – a trio of cute frizzy-wigged highland cattle. There is warden-led bird feeding each afternoon, while the family events programme fills every weekend and school holiday with nestbox-building, pond safaris and (at Easter) egg candling – a fascinating glimpse inside a duck egg as it develops. But what young ones will appreciate most, perhaps, is the immense feeling of space, and the glorious London skyline stretched across a far horizon.

Take cover

The interactive Discovery Centre, pond zone and "bird airport" observatory offer at least an hour's weatherproof entertainment.

③ Syon House

Costume drama heaven

Gleaming like a gold ingot beside the Thames, this is outer London's last bastion of aristocratic England – still home to the Dukes of Northumberland after more than 400 years. It's easy to imagine the house as a stage set, and on the big screen it has starred in both *Gosford*

Little dippers looking for waterborne wildlife at the London Wetland Centre

The Lowdown

- 🌐 **Address** Queen Elizabeth's Walk, Barnes, SW13 9WT; 020 8409 4400; www.wwt.org.uk/visit-us/london
- 🚗 **Train** Barnes or Barnes Bridge, 15-minute walk. **Tube** Hammersmith, then number 283 bus. **Bus stop** Wetland Centre or Red Lion. **Car** Free parking on site
- 🕐 **Open** Apr–Oct: 9:30am–6pm; Oct–Mar: 9:30am–5pm (last admission 1 hour earlier)
- 💷 **Price** £29–32, under-4s free
- 🚩 **Guided tours** 11am, 2pm (free), plus noon at weekends
- 👫 **Age range** All
- 👫 **Activities** Bird feeding 3pm daily. Free family activities (30–60 mins) weekends and holidays, plus Animal Discovery weekends. Occasional evening bat walks (age 8 plus, £10 per person).
- 🕐 **Allow** Half a day
- ♿ **Wheelchair access** Yes, apart from Wildside Hide (steps)
- 🍴 **Eat and drink** *Snacks* Water's Edge Café sells cakes and hot lunches from 9:30am–4:30pm
- 🛍 **Shop** Selling books, eco items, bird feeders/boxes and souvenirs
- 👫 **Toilets** Ground floor near café and in the car park

The Lowdown

- 🌐 **Address** Brentford, Middlesex, TW8 8JF; 020 8560 0882; www.syonpark.co.uk
- 🚗 **Train** Kew Bridge, then bus 237 or 267; or Brentford, then 15-minute walk. **Tube** Gunnersbury (District line) then bus 237 or 267. **Bus stop** Brent Lea. **Car** Free car park
- 🕐 **Open** House: mid-Mar–Oct: 11am–5pm Wed Thu, Sun (last admission 4pm); Gardens: 10:30am–5pm daily and winter weekends
- 💷 **Price** £27, under-5s free
- 🚩 **Guided tours** Occasional guided garden walks
- 👫 **Age range** 8 plus
- 👫 **Activities** Garden cinema, Aug; Enchanted Woodland evening openings, Nov; craft fairs
- 🕐 **Allow** Up to 2 hours
- ♿ **Wheelchair access** Garden paths are accessible, as is ground floor of the house (via chair lift)
- 🍴 **Eat and drink** *Snacks* Refectory Café sells a range of snacks and light lunches
- 🛍 **Shop** Small gift shop and garden centre
- 👫 **Toilets** On the ground floor

Park and *The Madness of King George*. Meanwhile, its stellar cast of real-life characters includes Henry VIII and Sir Walter Raleigh, Indian chiefs and Gunpowder Plotters.

Explore the epic suite of rooms designed for the first duke by Robert Adam (1728–92), who gave him the gilded gods, silk hangings and wedding-cake ceilings he had seen in Neo-Classical Italy. There is also the domed Great Conservatory – so grand it inspired Joseph Paxton's Crystal Palace (see pp224–5) – and the extensive grounds modelled by "Capability" Brown (1716–83). For kids, the ornamental arboretum is especially bewitching during Syon's

The Neo-Classical Northumberland family dining room at Syon House

The Great Conservatory at Syon House, built of gunmetal, Bath stone and glass

"Enchanted Woodland" season, when it twinkles with more than 1,000 lights. Younger children can be humoured with the promise of a romp at Snakes and Ladders, a soft-play centre in the grounds.

Letting off steam
Syon House has extensive gardens as well as a lake that is a haven for a variety of wildlife. There is also an ice house, which was in use in 1760–61. At that time it took two days to fill it with ice from the lake. The ice was used to make desserts such as ice creams and sorbets.

④ Osterley Park
A very big banker's bonus
In 1761, when wealthy banker Sir Francis Child wanted a flashy new look for his family pile at Osterley Park, there was only one man to call – the style guru extraordinaire, Robert Adam. He didn't just add a Roman portico, stuccoed stairways and the 40-m (131-ft) Long Gallery to the Elizabethan mansion, he

designed new carpets, new furniture, fireplaces and ceilings. The result is a "palace of palaces", a glimpse of how Britain's super-rich bankers lived 250 years ago.

What's great for children is that the rooms "below stairs" at Osterley remain pretty intact, too: in the vaulted servants' hall, they can get to grips with antique kitchen gear, don servants' mob caps and aprons, and watch spooky film projections of Georgian maids and footmen at work. A hand-held audio-visual guide just for kids stars Tweeny the serving girl, who leads the way from room to room, filling fireplaces and fetching water. Osterley's panoramic parkland is open daily all year round – but aim to visit on one of the monthly family discovery days, when it's busy with history trails, crafts and stories.

Letting off steam
The beautiful lake-filled park is prime picnic country: pick up a walks leaflet from the house.

The magnificent mansion at Osterley Park, seen from across the Garden Lake

---

The Lowdown

🌐 **Address** Jersey Road, Isleworth, Middlesex TW7 4RD; 020 8232 5050; *www.nationaltrust.org.uk/osterley*

🚗 **Train** Isleworth, 30-minute walk **Tube** Osterley (Piccadilly line), 15-minute walk **Bus stop** Jersey Road (number H28); Hammersmith (H91, 15-minute walk) **Car** Parking £3.50

🕐 **Open** House Mar–Oct: noon–4:30pm Wed–Sun (till 3:30pm Mar); Nov–mid Dec: noon–3:30pm Sat & Sun. Garden Mar–Oct: 11am–5pm Wed–Sun; Nov: noon–3:30pm Sat & Sun. Park 8am–7:30pm daily

💷 **Price** House and garden: £24.75; garden only: £1–; park free

🚩 **Guided tours** Audiovisual guide includes family trail; occasional themed tours and parkland walks (charges apply, see website)

👫 **Age range** 6 plus

🏃 **Activities** Family Discovery Days last Sun of month, noon–4pm; children's activities on Thu pm in school holidays, 1–4pm; both free with admission

⏱ **Allow** 2 hours

♿ **Wheelchair access** No

🍴 **Eat and drink** *Snacks* Stables Café *(11am–5pm Wed–Sun; Nov noon–4pm)* serves home-cooked lunches and teas

🛍 **Shop** Selling gifts; also a farm shop selling flowers and vegetables

🚻 **Toilets** Close to stableyard

Picnic under £20; **Snacks** £20–40; **Real meal** £40–60; **Family treat** £60 or more (based on a family of four)

⑤ Richmond Park

Hills, hinds and Henry VIII

Gibbet Wood, Bone Copse, Leg of Mutton Pond… the names of the natural features in this park are rich with romance and they describe the place well: it is the wildest tract of country in London. Richmond is the largest royal park and remains much the same as when Charles I put a 13-km (8-mile) wall around it in 1637 and 2,000 deer were released for him to hunt. Some of the oak trees the king knew are here still, and so are the deer: 650 reds and fallows, a great draw for children – though it's best not to get too close, especially during the autumn rut, when they spar for supremacy.

The best way in for families is from Richmond, for the playground at Petersham Gate and Pembroke Lodge Café, set in a Georgian mansion. Walk off the cakes with a hike up Henry VIII's Mound to take in the view to St Paul's Cathedral: some say the king stood watch here for the signal that his marriage to Anne Boleyn had been terminally severed.

A colourful performance at the Polka Theatre in Wimbledon

Above Children's playground near Petersham Gate, Richmond Park
Below Magnificent male red deer under the trees at Richmond Park

There is year-round cycle hire inside Roehampton Gate, on the east side, and the park's other sporting options include power-kiting, horse riding and fishing in Pen Ponds. Isabella Plantation, with its azaleas and maze of streams and bridges, looks sensational in spring and autumn, and the hide-and-seek potential goes on for miles.

Take cover

Take the 493 bus from Richmond or Roehampton to the **Wimbledon Lawn Tennis Museum** (*Church Rd, SW19 5AE; 020 8946 6131; www. wimbledon.com/visiting/museum; 10am–5pm daily; £42–70, under-5s free, stadium tours extra*), which has interactive exhibits, including the "ghost" of John McEnroe. Or stay on the bus and visit the **Polka Theatre** (*240 The Broadway, Wimbledon SW19 1SB; 020 8543 4888; www. polkatheatre.com; 9:30am–4:30pm Wed–Fri, from 10am Sat & Sun; book ahead - check website*) for under-14s, with a busy roster of live drama (twice daily Tue–Sat), a playground and a dressing-up corner with rocking horses and storybooks.

The Lowdown

🌐 **Address** Holly Lodge, Richmond Park, Richmond, TW10 5HS; 0300 061 2200; www.royalparks. org.uk/parks/richmond-park

🚗 **Train** Richmond, then bus 65 or 371; or Norbiton, then 15-minute walk to Kingston Gate **Tube** Richmond (District Line), then bus. **Bus stop** North side: 33, 190, 337, 391, 419, 485, R68. South: 85, 263, K3. East: 72, 493. West: 65, 371 **Car** Six free car parks

🕐 **Open** Park: from 7am Mar–Sep; from 7:30am Oct–Feb (closes half an hour before dusk). Park office: open weekdays 8:30am–4pm. Visitor centre: Pembroke Lodge (Richmond Gate) open 10am–4pm Fri–Sun (till 3pm Nov–Feb)

💲 **Price** Free

🎫 **Guided tours** Free garden walks and history rambles most months (dates vary, check website)

👫 **Age range** All

🏃 **Activities** Playgrounds at Petersham and Kingston Gates. Cycle hire at Roehampton Gate (10am–5pm Mon–Fri, till 7pm weekends and school holidays; from £4 per hour; 0705 020 9249; www.parkcycle.co.uk). Power-kiting lessons (020 7870 7700; www.kitevibe.com); fishing permits (Jun–Mar; 020 8940 3209); pay-and-play golf (020 8876 1795); for riding stables, see park website

⏱ **Allow** Up to a day

🍵 **Eat and drink** *Snacks* The park's Roehampton Café (*9am–5pm daily*) sells snacks and ices. Plus kiosks at Broomfield Hill and Pen Ponds. *Real meal* Pembroke Lodge Café in the park (*020 8940 8207; summer: 10am–5:30pm; winter till dusk*) has a full restaurant menu, with children's dishes, and outdoor seating

🚻 **Toilets** All main gates

Prices given are for a family of four

⑥ Ham House

The most haunted house in London?

With its riverside gardens, children's treasure map and gaggle of ghosts, it's hard to think of a more appetizing stately home for families than Ham House. The main draw is its dreamy setting, with lawns running down to an especially bucolic stretch of the Thames. The house itself is a time capsule, little changed since the 1670s, when the ruthless and beautiful Duchess of Lauderdale schemed her way to the top of Stuart society. A prime mover in the secret Sealed Knot society, which restored Charles II to the throne, the duchess filled Ham's halls with exuberant furniture and art.

What will interest kids, though, is not the duchess's legacy, but the fact she may still be in residence. Staff and visitors sometimes hear the tap-tap-tap of her silver cane and glimpse her King Charles spaniel scampering along the corridors. Regular ghost tours complement an imaginative spread of children's stuff here: a dedicated Discovery Room, complete with treasure map for investigating the house; garden trails; and al fresco storytelling, cinema and theatre every summer.

On sunny days, walk to Ham from Richmond station along the Thames Path (download the route at *www.nationaltrust.org.uk/hamhouse*) or hop on the historic foot-ferry across to the north bank, where Marble Hill House (Richmond Rd, Twickenham, TW1 2NL; 020 8892 5115; *www.english-heritage.org.uk*) shimmers like a mirage above the water. A masterpiece Palladian mansion, Marble Hill has a weekend programme for families.

Letting off steam

Children can run wild in the garden's labyrinthine wilderness of hedges and summerhouses.

The Lowdown

- 🌐 **Address** Ham Street, Richmond, TW10 7RS; 020 8940 1950; *www.nationaltrust.org.uk/hamhouse*
- 🚗 **Train** St Margarets or Twickenham, then 10-minute walk and foot ferry (10am–6pm or dusk, Feb–Oct, plus winter weekends); Richmond, then 30-minute riverside walk, or bus 65 or 371 **Tube** Richmond (District Line) **Bus stop** Ham Street, Sandpits Road **Car** Free parking nearby
- 🕐 **Open** Apr–Oct Noon–4pm Sat–Thu; Feb, Mar and Nov: guided tours only, 11:30am–3:30pm. Garden, shop and café: 10am–5pm daily
- 💲 **Price** House and garden: £25. Garden only: £11
- 🎫 **Guided tours** Feb, Mar and Nov only: 30-minute tours of selected rooms. Garden tours all year round (call for times). "Servants' Tours", Apr–Oct, Tue (charged)
- 👫 **Age range** All
- 🧒 **Activities** Interactive Discovery Room, quiz trail and garden trails. Art Cart craft activities Apr–Oct, Sun. Occasional family ghost tours (ages 5 plus; book ahead). Easter egg hunts; summer cinema and theatre in the gardens; Christmas events for families
- ⏱ **Allow** 2 hours
- ♿ **Wheelchair access** Limited: steps and narrow doorways inside – lift available; gravel paths outside
- 🍴 **Eat and drink** *Snacks* The luscious Orangery Café does its own baking, and has a kids' corner
- 🛍 **Shop** Selling local and unusual gifts and souvenirs
- 🚻 **Toilets** In courtyard

The beautifully kept kitchen garden at Ham House

Day Trips

London packs in enough history for several cities – but to really breathe the atmosphere of Henry VIII's England, nowhere beats Hampton Court Palace. Families get to dress, act and even eat and drink the period. Windsor, by contrast, is all about the modern monarchy, with a majestic castle, parkland, a school for princes and one of Britain's best theme parks. Do what the Queen does and come for the whole weekend.

Highlights

Play the king
Hampton Court's live history experience includes free cloaks, so kids can dress up and explore Henry VIII's magnificent home (see p236–7).

Eat like a Tudor
The palace kitchens regularly re-create dishes from 500 years ago – sometimes available to try at the Tiltyard Café (see p237).

Get lost!
People have been losing themselves in Hampton Court Maze for 300 years, and three new forks have made it more fiendish than ever (see p236).

See monarchy in miniature
Displayed at Windsor Castle, Queen Mary's Dolls' House is an exquisite creation and the world's most opulent – a snapshot of royal life in the 1920s (see p238).

Ride with the royals
The royal family love riding in Windsor Great Park. In the absence of horses, saddle up and explore by hiring bicycles from Windsor (see p239).

Visit toyland
Windsor's Legoland is totally geared for pre-teens, with its "pink-knuckle" roller coasters and splashing water rides (see p241).

Left As well as thrilling rides, there are tamer entertainments at Legoland, such as Miniland, a Lego reconstruction of landmarks from around the world
Above A collection of sporting caps in the museum at Eton College

① Hampton Court Palace
Where Henry VIII still rules

Children need to be on their best behaviour at Hampton Court, in case they run into its former owner in one of his tempers. Henry VIII, everyone's favourite bad-boy monarch, caroused here with his 1,000-strong court and his six wives, and still roars through the Great Hall most days, as part of an interactive history experience. As the aroma of roasting meat wafts from the kitchens, families get to dress as 16th-century courtiers in miniature costume dramas – velvet cloaks are available from the Information Centre.

Falconry display in the grounds

Key features

The maze The world's most famous maze was planted for William III in 1690. But don't follow the map at the entrance – it's wrong!

Young Henry VIII Exhibition Sporting hero, musician, dancer… before becoming a bloated tyrant, Henry was a "lusty and brave prince". These hands-on displays trace his early years.

Wine Fountain This was re-created by studying archaeological remains found in Base Court in 2008. As in Henry VIII's day, it can serve wine.

Haunted Gallery It's said Queen Catherine Howard still wails in the corridor through which she was dragged by Henry's guards in 1541.

Great Vine Planted by "Capability" Brown in 1768, this vine produced an amazing 383 kg (745 lb) of sweet black grapes in 2001.

Tudor Kitchens The kitchens had 55 rooms and 200 kitchen hands. On certain weekends, costumed "food archaeologists" re-create banquets based on 500-year-old recipes.

Fountain Court In 1689, William and Mary hired Christopher Wren to execute a Baroque makeover here, in a bid to outdazzle Versailles.

Great Hall Shakespeare's company performed here for James I in 1603. The walls are hung with splendid tapestries of *The Story of Abraham*.

Letting off steam

The grounds go on forever, with the maze, formal gardens and the 20th Century Garden, great for hide-and-seek. For under-5s, there's a soft-play room off Base Court. To the north and within walking distance, **Bushy Park** (Hampton Court Road, Hampton, TW12 2EJ) has a playground, while to the west lies the open-air

Deer in Bushy Park, within walking distance of Hampton Court

Prices given are for a family of four

Hampton Swimming Pool *(High Street, Hampton, Middlesex, TW12 2ST; www.hamptonpool.co.uk; open daily).*

Eat and drink

Picnic: under £20; Snacks: £20–40; Real meal: £45–65; Family treat: £60 or more (based on a family of four)

PICNIC There are picnic tables in the 20th-Century Garden, or else spread a rug in the Tiltyard or Wilderness gardens. **The Pheasantry Cafe** *(Woodland Gardens in Bushy Park, TW11 OEQ; 020 8943 1347; from 9am–6pm)* offers hearty breakfasts as well as cakes and pastries.

SNACKS In an area originally used for jousting by Henry VIII, Hampton Court's **Tiltyard Café** has meal deals on its home-made children's food and serves Tudor dishes on the first weekend of the month. There's also a playroom for younger kids.

REAL MEAL Jamie's Italian *(19–23 High Street, Kingston, KT1 1LL; 020 3326 4300; www.jamieoliver. com/italian/kingston; noon–11pm; till 10:30pm Sun)*, stands out among the chain restaurants across the river in Kingston upon Thames, for atmosphere. Kids dine free from the children's menu on weekdays.

FAMILY TREAT Jin Jin *(8 Charter Quay, Riverside, Kingston, KT1 1HR; 020 8549 3510; noon–10pm Mon–Fri; till 11pm Sat & Sun)* offers flavourful Asian food: the downstairs noodle bar is best for families.

The Lowdown

🌐 **Address** East Molesey, Surrey, KT8 9AU; 0844 482 7777; *www.hrp.org.uk/hamptoncourtpalace*

🚗 **Train** Hampton Court Station (trains from London Waterloo) **Bus stop** Trophy Gate, Hampton Court Station **River bus** Services run Apr–Oct from Westminster, Kew and Richmond (www.wpsa.co.uk or www.turks.co.uk) **Car** Park at Hampton Court Palace, Hampton Court Green or Hampton Court Station

🕐 **Open** Apr–Oct: 10am–6pm; Nov–Mar: 10am–4:30pm (last admission one hour earlier). Gardens open one hour later.

💷 **Price** £45–49, under-5s free; maze only: £14–16; gardens only: £12, under-16s free

🧍 **Skipping the queue** Book ahead online to skip the ticket queue – it's a little cheaper, too.

🚩 **Guided tours** Costumed tours and dramatic vignettes daily (free, times vary). Four themed audio tours for adults, plus four for children. Occasional evening ghosts tours on Fri and Sun (ages 12 plus)

👫 **Age range** 3 plus

🏃 **Activities** Range of age-graded children's trails, with prizes; plus audio tours for ages 6 plus (all free). Tudor cloaks in all sizes available from Information Centre. Cookery

weekends in Henry VIII's kitchens (see website for dates), plus additional live interpretations in school holidays, which might include Tudor etiquette, falconry displays, jester shows and jousting. Chapel Royal open for services daily. Hampton Court Music Festival (Jun) and Flower Show (Jul)

⏱ **Allow** A full day

♿ **Wheelchair access** Most of the routes are accessible via a lift. There are some shallow stairs, but doorways are wide. There are scooters for the gardens

☕ **Café** Both Tiltyard Café (*see left*), in grounds, and Privy Kitchen Coffee Shop, inside the Palace, offer light lunches and a children's menu

🛍 **Shop** Four – Barracks, Tudor Kitchens, Garden and Henry – selling a vast array of themed gifts, books and toys

🚻 **Toilets** Main car park, Tiltyard Café, Base Court, Fountain Court

Good family value?
It's quite expensive, but apart from the Tower of London, no heritage attraction in Britain does a better job of keeping families entertained all day.

Find out more

DIGITAL The Palace's website has Tudor crafts and recipes to try, plus interviews with expert curators. Learn how tapestries are conserved, make your own Henry VIII bonnet, or take on the king himself in virtual combat: *www.hrp.org.uk/HamptonCourt Palace/educationandcommunity/learning/funandgames.aspx.*

Next stop. . .

THEME PARKS AND THEATRE
With a car, two top theme parks are in striking distance. **Thorpe Park** (*Staines Road, Chertsey, Surrey KT16 8PN; 0871 663 1673; www.thorpepark.com*), 16 km (10 miles) west, has white-knuckle roller-coasters.
Chessington World of Adventures (*Leatherhead Rd, Chessington, Surrey, KT9 2NE; 0871 663 4473; www.chessington.com*), 10 km (6 miles) to

the south, is better for younger children. Both parks are big and a whole day is needed when visiting. **The Rose Theatre** (*24–26 High St, Kingston, KT1 1HL; 020 8174 0090; www.rosetheatrekingston.org*) puts on classy children's shows in school holidays, and has storytelling (under 5s) most Fridays at 11:15am – check website for dates and fees.

The Tiltyard Café sometimes serves Tudor dishes, and has a playroom

② Windsor Castle
Her Majesty's fairytale fortress

Bristling with turrets and suits of armour, the world's oldest occupied castle stands theatrically on a hilltop by the River Thames. The Queen stays here regularly – though presumably she doesn't use all 1,000 rooms. Non-royal visitors should pick up a free audio guide (a kids' version is available too) and tour the State Apartments, Chapel and Art Gallery. Children also enjoy the marching guardsmen, carriage rides and all-round holiday atmosphere of the little riverside town of Windsor, below the castle.

Royal Standard

Key Features

Round Tower The oldest part of the castle, this was built of wood in the 1070s by William the Conqueror. A guided tour climbs 200 steps to the top (over-10s only).

Royal Standard When the Queen's flag flies from the Round Tower, Her Majesty is at home.

① **Queen Mary's Dolls' House** The world's most luxurious doll's house was designed by architect Sir Edwin Lutyens in the 1920s, and took 1,500 artists and craftsmen three years to complete.

St George's Chapel This is a Gothic wonder from the 15th century. Light from the stained-glass windows illuminates the tombs of Henry VIII and Charles I.

Changing the Guard Everything stops in Windsor High Street when the castle guard marches through at 10.45am most mornings. The ceremony happens in the castle's Lower Ward.

State Apartments Furnished with gilt, crystal, antiques and armour, these rooms also have priceless art: look out for works by Rembrandt, Rubens, Canaletto and Gainsborough.

② **Long Walk** If the weather is dry, horse-drawn carriages trot along the Long Walk, which leads down to Windsor Great Park (from 12:30pm; Easter–Oct: daily; Nov–Easter: Sat & Sun).

The Lowdown

🌐 **Address** Castle Hill, Windsor, SL4 1NJ; 020 7766 7304; *www.royalcollection.org.uk/visit/windsorcastle*

🚗 **Train** Windsor & Eton Central, served by trains from Paddington via Slough; or Windsor & Eton Riverside, direct from Waterloo (journey time: 40 minutes–1 hour) **Coach** Green Line daily from London's Victoria Coach Station (*www.greenline.co.uk*) **Car** Use long-stay parking in Windsor town centre (charged)

🕐 **Open** Mar–Oct: 9:45am–5:15pm; Nov–Feb: 9:45am–4:15pm (last admission 75 minutes earlier). State Apartments closed very occasionally (check ahead). St George's Chapel open Mon–Sat, and for services only on Sun

💲 **Price** £50 (less when State Apartments are closed), under-5s free. Plus £2 per ticket booking fee

👥 **Skipping the queue** Buy tickets direct from the Royal Collection (online or from castle ticket office) for one year's free re-admission

🚩 **Guided tours** Free 2-hour audio-tour, plus children's version (ages 7–11). Frequent 30-minute tours of Castle Precincts daily (free with admission). Aug–Sep only: 45-minute Conquer the Tower Tour for ages 11 plus (£68); 30-minute Great Kitchen Tour (£16), check website for dates, pre-booking essential.

👫 **Age range** 5 plus

🏃 **Activities** Free kids' audio-guide plus activity sheets for ages 5–7 and 7–11 (also downloadable from website). Art activities in Moat Room, first Sat every month. School-holiday programme may include special children's tours, storytelling, object-handling and armour design (check website). Changing the Guard ceremony: Apr–Jul: 11am daily; Aug–Mar: alternate days; no ceremony on Sun

⏱ **Allow** 2–3 hours

♿ **Wheelchair access** Yes, but there are steps to the main entrance and to St Georges Chapel. There is a lift inside the castle. The outside areas can be uneven.

Prices given are for a family of four

Letting off steam

Playtime and picnicking are not smiled upon inside the castle grounds, though there are endless lawns and trees to run among along the Long Walk, south of the castle. The nearest playground is at **Bachelors Acre**, off Victoria Street.

Eat and drink

Picnic: under £20; Snacks: £20–40; Real meal: £45–65; Family treat: £65 or more (based on a family of four)

PICNIC Cinnamon Cafe *(The Old Booking Hall, Windsor Royal Station SL4 1PJ; 01753 857879; www. cinnamoncafe.com)*, en route from the train station to the castle, whips up delicious breakfasts and cakes.
SNACKS Extreme Motion and Windsor Skate Park Café *(Alexandra Gardens, Alma Rd, Windsor, SL4 5HZ; 01753 830220; www.extrememotion. com/coffee-shop/)* serves sandwiches and pizza. It has rails and ramps for all ages, mini-golf, a bungee trampoline and bike hire – good for exploring Windsor Great Park *(see p240)*.
REAL MEAL Gastropub the **Riverhouse** *(10 Thames Side,*

Playing cricket on the Long Walk, which runs south from Windsor Castle

Bouncing around on a trampoline in Alexandra Gardens, Windsor

Windsor, SL4 1QN; 01753 620010; www.windsor.gov.uk/food-and-drink/rivershouse-restaurant-and-bar-p282301; food: noon–10pm) is a child-friendly option with a lovely Thames-side terrace and a special £7 menu for under-10s.
FAMILY TREAT Gilbey's *(82–3 High Street, Eton, Windsor SL4 6AF; 01753 854921; www.gilbeygroup. com; noon–10pm)* serves smart modern-British fare with an emphasis on seasonal ingredients. It also has delicious afternoon teas.

Find out more

DIGITAL Explore Queen Mary's Dolls' House in every tiny detail at this interactive mini-site: *www.royalcollection.org.uk/ queenmarysdollshouse.*

Next stop...
BOAT TRIPS

Among the raft of River Thames cruises offered from Windsor Promenade, 5 minutes from the castle, are 40-minute return trips with **French Brothers** to Boveney Lock, with views of Eton College *(daily Mar–Oct, plus some winter weekends; 01753 851900; www. boat-trips.co.uk)*. Or try **Salters Steamers** *(01865 243 421, www. salterssteamers.co.uk)*.

A leisurely tour down the Thames aboard the French Brothers' boat

---

Café None on site; ice cream and water available from North Terrace

Shop There are three shops, all selling Royal- and castle-themed souvenirs and gifts

Toilets Courtyard and North Terrace

Good family value?
Far from cheap, but just about worth it when combined with the town and Windsor Great Park *(see p240)*. Aim to visit when children's activities are scheduled, and avoid Sundays, when there's no Changing the Guard and St George's Chapel is closed to visitors. Visit again within 12 months for free.

③ Windsor Great Park

Where the royals ride out

He gallops across the Great Park at midnight on a black stallion, wearing a ghoulish antler headdress and with a pack of hell-hounds in his wake. No, it's not the Duke of Edinburgh, but Herne the Hunter, a legendary ghost from Windsor folklore – and he is not the only exotic apparition in this 13th-century hunting park, which stretches south of the castle. There's also a Canadian totem pole to discover, rising incongruously beside Virginia Water, the park's large ornamental lake. The nearby "Roman temple" was picturesquely assembled in 1818 by George IV, with columns taken from Leptis Magna, a major city of the Roman Empire in what is now Libya.

Windsor Great Park is a vast expanse of woods, ponds and pasture, with deer, formal gardens, the royal polo club and more. The

The Deer Park, just one area of the vast Windsor Great Park

Long Walk stretches south into the park from Windsor Castle – but it's a 1- or 2-hour walk to reach the Savill Garden, where, a visitor centre offers a good café, carriage rides and occasional holiday activities for children. A better bet is to hire bikes from Windsor and cycle here on National Cycle Route 4, which largely avoids busy roads. Or go by car, parking either at the Savill Garden or Virginia Water.

Letting off steam

The park's playground is at **Obelisk Lawn**, near the Savill Garden car park, with a shipwreck to scramble on and a sandpit to jump around in.

④ Eton College

Classes for the upper classes

"Etonians should not be approached, shouted at or photographed", says the Eton College website – though children can be forgiven one small giggle at the tail-coated young gentlemen who promenade like penguins around the School Yard. Founded in 1440 by King Henry VI, Eton is the world's most prestigious boys' school, having produced 19 British prime ministers, including David Cameron. Princes William and Harry also studied here – the fees are close to £30,000 per year.

The college is best approached on foot across the river from Windsor

The Lowdown

- 🌐 **Address** The Savill Garden, Wick Road, Englefield Green, Surrey TW20 0UU; 01784 435544; *www.theroyallandscape.co.uk*
- 🚗 **Train** Windsor & Eton Central, Egham or Virginia Water for Savill Garden **Car** Free parking on A332 south of Windsor. Pay car parks at Savill Garden (free with garden admission), Valley Gardens, Wick Road, Virginia Water Gate and Blacknest Gate
- 🕐 **Open** Park: 7am–dusk. Savill Garden: Mar–Oct: 10am–6pm; Nov–Feb: 10am–4:30pm (last admission 30 minutes earlier)
- 💷 **Price** Windsor Great Park free. Savill Garden: summer £26; winter £31 (under-6s free)
- 🚩 **Guided tours** Groups only
- 👫 **Age range** All
- 🖐 **Activities** Seasonal treasure trails and activities for families in some school holidays. Open-air theatre

and opera (Jun–Aug); carriage rides from Savill Garden on selected spring and summer weekends (check website for details)

- 🕐 **Allow** Half a day
- 🍽 **Eat and drink**
  Snacks Refreshments at Windsor Great Park post office and (seasonal) kiosks at Obelisk Lawn, Blacknest Gate, Totem Pole and Virginia Water car park *Real meal* Savill Garden Restaurant (01784 485 402; Mar–Oct: 10am–6pm; Nov–Feb till 4:30pm) has home-made kids' meals and lunchboxes
- 🛍 **Shop** Savill Garden visitor centre, selling gifts, toys, books, garden items, wildlife and eco products, and the Duchy Original range
- 👫 **Toilets** Savill Garden, Valley Gardens, Virginia Water car park

The Lowdown

- 🌐 **Address** Windsor, SL4 6DW; 01753 370 100; *www.etoncollege.com*
- 🚗 **Train** Windsor & Eton Riverside, then 15-minute walk **Car** Arrive from north via Slough Road, or (preferably) walk from Windsor
- 🕐 **Open** By guided tour only (no tours until 2016 – check website)
- 💷 **Price** £24–34
- 🚩 **Guided tours** 1-hour tours at 2pm and 3:15pm
- 👫 **Age range** 8 plus
- 🕐 **Allow** 1–2 hours
- ♿ **Wheelchair access** Mostly – there is a chairlift to the chapel and cobbled surfaces outside
- 🍽 **Eat and drink** Picnic Tastes (92 High St, Eton, SL4 6AF; 01753 641 557; 10am–6pm Tue–Sat) is a super deli; eat your picnic in Windsor Park. *Snacks* Zero 3 (21 High St, Eton, SL4 6BL; 01753 864725) serves good-value food to eat in
- 🛍 **Shop** In Eton High Street, selling school-related items
- 👫 **Toilets** Brewhouse Yard

and through Eton village. Tours are offered twice daily in season, covering the school's stately main quadrangle, cloisters and 15th-century chapel. The highlight is the very first school-room, preserved from the 1400s and carved with the graffiti of later students Robert Walpole, Percy Shelley and others. The guides happily field questions about the quirks of college life past and present – and children who fail to pay attention can be pointed towards the little museum at the end of the tour. It displays the cane and "swishing block" employed by infamous headmaster Dr Keate, who once flogged almost the entire school.

Eton students in tail-coats relaxing in between lessons

Viking River Splash ride, one of many attractions at Legoland

Letting off steam

Home Park playground *(Romney Lock Road, off King Edward VII Avenue)*, just across the footbridge in Windsor, was given to the public by Queen Victoria.

⑤ Legoland
Tiny-brick wonderland

Pack swimsuits and sunglasses before heading for Windsor's super-popular brick-themed fun park. The swimsuits are for the assorted splash rides, which include simulated jet skis and a super-fast water slide. The shades are for the sheer multi-coloured intensity of it all: Legoland packs in 10 zones of stunt shows, children's theatre, rollercoasters and model-building, all loosely inspired by the classic toy box building blocks.

The focus is on pre-teens, especially ages 5–10, with a handful of mildly thrilling rides plus lots of junior race-car driving, balloon races and submarine adventures (among real-life sharks). Purists will enjoy Miniland, with its intricate Lego landmarks. The whole thing is fiendishly expensive; seek out online ticket deals, and try not to visit at holiday times, when the queues stretch almost to Denmark.

The Pirates' Training Camp playground at Legoland

Letting off steam

Kids with any energy left should head for the climbing apparatus at Pirates' Training Camp or DUPLO Playtown, both in Legoland.

The Lowdown

🌐 **Address** Winkfield Road, Windsor, SL4 4AY; 0871 2222 001; www.legoland.co.uk

🚗 **Train** Windsor & Eton Central or Windsor & Eton Riverside, then shuttle bus (charged; from 10am till 30 minutes after park closes) **Coach** Green Line service daily from London Victoria (www.greenline.co.uk) **Car** 3 km (2 miles) from Windsor on B3022; parking fee

🕐 **Open** Mar–Nov: call for details (closing time varies with season)

💷 **Price** £140–184; book online for reductions

🚶 **Skipping the queue** Book online to skip the ticket queue. Ride queues peak noon–3pm; for a hefty extra charge, Q-Bot devices enable visitors to reserve slots on selected rides

👫 **Age range** 3–12 years

🎭 **Activities** Stunt performances, puppet plays and 4-D cinema shows in Imagination Theatre. Programme might include events with kids' TV characters, laser spectaculars and Hallowe'en fun and fireworks

⏱ **Allow** A full day

♿ **Wheelchair access** Yes

🍽 **Eat and drink** More than a dozen outlets in park, such as Mexican Cantina and Pirate's BBQ, many offering healthy meal deals for kids

🛍 **Shop** Throughout the park; the Big Shop is at the entrance, selling Lego® products

🚻 **Toilets** In car park and throughout the park

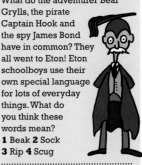

Picnic under £20; **Snacks** £20–40; **Real meal** £40–60; **Family treat** £60 or more (based on a family of four)

Where to Stay in London

London's hotels are much more child friendly than they used to be. Today, even the grandest have family rooms and restaurants with children's menus. As alternatives to traditional hotels, B&Bs or small hotels offer more informal accommodation and apartments can make a flexible and good-value option.

AGENCIES

At Home in London
020 8748 2701; www. athomeinlondon.co.uk

This agency specializes in B&B accommodation in private homes in central and suburban London. It has more than 80 homes on its books, all carefully chosen and regularly inspected. The website search engine is organized according to London Transport zones 1 (very central) and zones 2/3 (further out).

London Bed & Breakfast Agency
020 7586 2768; www.londonbb.com

An agency offering B&B in private houses, and some apartments, covering central, north (a particularly good selection here), south and west London. It prides itself on paying attention to visitors' individual requirements. Hosts welcome families with children aged five and over.

London Home to Home
020 8769 3500; www. londonhometohome.com

This friendly B&B agency offers good quality family accommodation in private houses in central, north and west London. Rooms are comfortable and well maintained, and rates include a generous breakfast. The usual minimum stay is two nights.

London House
0845 834 0244; www.london-house.com

Gold-standard service, a wide choice and value for money are at the heart of this online business's success. It has made finding family-friendly accommodation across the city one of its specialities, with apartments, B&Bs and hotels on its books.

Westminster and the West End

HOTELS

Brown's
Map 9 D4

33 Albemarle Street, W1S 4BP; 020 7493 6020; www.brownshotel.com

The kindly staff at London's oldest hotel go out of their way to make children feel at home. Afternoon tea is a must in the iconic English Tea Room, where Rudyard Kipling wrote *The Jungle Book*. Kids' treats include a Brown's bear to snuggle up with and DVDs to watch.

£££

Stylish bedroom in London' oldest hotel, Brown's

Duke's
Map 9 D5

35–36 St James's Place, SW1A 1NY; 020 7318 6576; www.dukeshotel.com

This traditional Mayfair hotel offers plenty to keep boredom at bay, from storybooks to designated TV channels and PlayStation games. The special menus are always popular and usually rounded off with Duke's signature Knickerbocker Glory ice cream. Delicious picnic boxes can be supplied for lunch on the move.

£££

The Goring
Map 15 C2

15 Beeston Place, SW1W 0JW; 020 7396 9000; www.thegoring.com

Owned and run by the Goring family for four generations, this London institution prides itself on giving a warm welcome to its "VI (little) Ps". Treats include a bedtime story library, a gift bag and a visit to the kitchen, where children get to don aprons and chef's hats and decorate cakes.

£££

Dolphin House
Map 16 E5

Dolphin Square, SW1V 3LX; 020 7834 3800; www.dolphinsquare.co. uk/dolphin-house/

Part of the 1930s Dolphin Square development by the river in Pimlico, this offers a good choice of apartments. Among the main selling points are the 18-m (59-ft) indoor pool and extensive grounds, which include a tennis court – ideal for little ones to let off steam.

££

Rosewood London Hotel
Map 10 H2

252 High Holborn, WC1V 7EN; 020 7829 9888; www. rosewoodhotels.com/en/london

This impressive hotel is approached through an imposing arch to a Neo-Classical courtyard. It is well placed for Covent Garden and West End theatre trips. A fun family package includes a city "Duck Tour" on land and water in an amphibious vehicle. Prams are available for a fee.

£££

The entrance of The Goring hotel, a short walk from Buckingham Palace

BED & BREAKFAST

B&B Belgravia and Studios@82
Map 15 C3

64–66 Ebury Street, SW1W 9QD;
020 7259 8570; www.bb-belgravia.com
Handy for Victoria Station, this
popular B&B is conspicuous for its
fresh appearance and laid-back
approach. Bedrooms are decorated
in earthy tones, with small but smart
glass-partitioned bathrooms.
Studios@82 next door provides
good family accommodation. Hot
drinks, fruit and shortbread are on
tap. Cots and high chairs available.

££

A modern kitchen in the Athenaeum Apartments

Lime Tree
Map 15 C3

135–7 Ebury Street, SW1W 9QU; 020
7730 7865; www.limetreehotel.co.uk
With the same postcode as the
Queen (well, Buckingham Palace),
this is a brilliantly located, simply
furnished and comfortable island of
good value. Rooms are bigger than
prices suggest and the welcoming
staff give sound advice on travel,
dining and making the most of what
London has to offer. Please note, it
is not suitable for under-5s.

££

Luna Simone
Map 16 E3

47–49 Belgrave Road, SW1V 2BB; 020
7834 5897; www.lunasimonehotel.com
Fresh looking and contemporary,
this hotel was established in 1970
and is now run by the original
owner's sons. Rooms are
comfortable – there is just enough
space for the family to sprawl –
and there are shiny bathrooms
with power showers. It's a friendly
place and a cooked breakfast is
included in the price of the room.

££

Strand Palace Hotel
Map 10 H4

372 Strand, WC2R 0JJ; 020 7379
4737; www.strandpalacehotel.co.uk
This large, four-star hotel offers
contemporary accommodation in
the heart of the West End. Covent
Garden, Leicester Square, Piccadilly,
Trafalgar Square and Buckingham
Palace are all within walking
distance. Somerset House is a
stone's throw away and an ideal
spot for children to run around.
Room facilities include Wi-Fi, iPod
docking stations and DVDs.
Afternoon tea is served daily.

££

Taj 51 Buckingham Gate
Map 16 E1

SW1E 6AF; 020 7769 7766;
www.51-buckinghamgate.com
Close to Buckingham Palace, this
five-star hotel, with its butler service,
Michelin-starred Quilon restaurant,
spa and stunning courtyard garden,
exudes luxury. All rooms include an
iPod docking station, Wi-Fi, DVD
player and library, and there is
complimentary access to a fitness
centre as well. Some suites come
with fully-equipped kitchenettes.

£££

SELF-CATERING

44 Curzon Street Apartments
Map 9 C5

44 Curzon Street, W1J 7RF; 020 7373
6265; www.44curzonstreet.co.uk
Built in 1908 as a gentlemen's pied-
à-terre, this is one of three salubrious
apartment buildings in the vicinity
under the same ownership. Their
style is traditional English and cosy.
Kitchens are extremely well
equipped, though there's no
shortage of local restaurants.

£££

*Comfortable, contemporary rooms in
the Luna Simone hotel*

Athenaeum Apartments
Map 9 C6

116 Piccadilly, W1J 7BJ; 020 7499
3464; www.athenaeumhotel.com/
apartments.aspx
They come at a bit of a price, but
these roomy apartments benefit
from the facilities of the nearby
luxurious Athenaeum Hotel, while
allowing families a bit of space and
total independence. With prior
notice, the Kids' Concierge will
keep your apartment stocked with
children's essentials such as games
and age-appropriate DVDs. Check
out the half-term and holiday offers.

£££

Citadines Prestige Holborn-Covent Garden
Map 10 H2

94–99 High Holborn, WC1V 6LF;
020 7395 8800; www.citadines.com/
*en/uk/london/holborn_covent_*
garden.html
What these apartments lack in
space, they make up for in quality
furnishings (everything sparkles
following a comprehensive
refurbishment) and a handy
location (on the borders of Holborn
and Covent Garden). Pleasant
touches include a welcome tray,
mineral water, tissues and bedroom
slippers. Air conditioning makes
summer stays more comfortable.
Pets are welcome (additional fee).

££

Price Guide
The following price ranges are based on
one night's accommodation in high
season for a family of four, inclusive of
service charges and any additional taxes.
£ Under £150 **££** £150–250 **£££** over £250

Key to symbols *see back cover flap*

The kitchen and sitting area of one of the SACO – Holborn apartments

Flemings Apartments   Map 9 C5
7–12 Half Moon Street, W1J 7BH;
020 7499 0000; www.flemings-
mayfair.co.uk
Attached to Flemings Hotel but with their own entrance in Clarges Street, these ten serviced apartments in the heart of Mayfair are smart without being too precious. Helpful hotel staff are happy to arrange outings, from picnics and cycle rides in Green Park to tickets for Premier League football matches.

££££

Bloomsbury & Regent's Park
HOTELS
Bedford   Map 10 G1
83–95 Southampton Row,
WC1B 4HD; 020 7278 7871;
www.imperialhotels.co.uk/bedford
If one visit to the British Museum isn't enough, the pick of the Imperial group's six Bloomsbury hotels is just around the corner. Interesting local walks are featured on its website, and sightseeing tours further afield leave from the

Traditional English furnishings in a Mayfair apartment

nearby Royal National Hotel. The on-site Café London offers a child-friendly menu.

££

The Landmark   Map 8 H1
222 Marylebone Road, NW1 6JQ;
020 7631 8000; www.
landmarklondon.co.uk
Well placed for an early start at Madame Tussauds, the Planetarium or Sherlock Holmes Museum, this red-brick Victorian building was originally a railway hotel. It now boasts a stunning atrium with towering palm trees, where after-noon tea is served. Families won't feel cramped because the bedrooms are huge at this five-star hotel.

££££

The Langham   Map 9 D2
1C Portland Place, W1B 1JA;
020 7636 1000; www.london.
langhamhotels.co.uk
This luxurious West End hotel offers family packages, including a shopping expedition to Hamleys toy store or a day at London Zoo, plus a complimentary family movie to watch on your return. If your kids are picky eaters, the one-bedroom apartment has its own kitchenette.

££££

Marriott Regent's Park   Map 2 G1
128 King Henry's Road, NW3 3ST;
020 7722 7711; www.marriott.com/
hotels/travel/lonrp-london-marriott-
hotel-regents-park
In leafy north London, within striking distance of Regent's Park, London Zoo, Primrose Hill and Camden

Lock Market, this Marriott is perennially popular with families. Reasons include the large, airy bedrooms with sliding patio doors on to small balconies, lovely indoor pool, helpful concierges, and excellent weekend rates.

££

BED & BREAKFAST
Alhambra   Map 4 G5
17–19 Argyle Street, WC1H 8EJ;
020 7837 9575; www.alhambrahotel.
com
An affordable, hospitable base in the King's Cross area, particularly useful for Eurostar travellers. In an 1840s building with a modern interior, it is a family-run affair and has been for 50 years. Rooms are on the small side, but squeaky clean. The owner cooks irresistible full English breakfasts.

££

Arosfa   Map 10 F1
83 Gower Street, WC1E 6HJ;
020 7636 2115 www.arosfalondon.
com
Guests are made to feel like part of the family at this simple Bloomsbury B&B, where the genial staff keep the rooms spotlessly cleans and tidy. Be aware that some bedrooms have minuscule bathrooms. Four nearby Tube stations bring the whole city conveniently within reach.

££

The Arosfa has neat, if compact, bedrooms

Arran House   Map 10 F1
77–79 Gower Street, WC1E 6HJ;
020 7636 2186; www.arranhotel-
london.com
People fall so comprehensively for this family-run B&B that they just keep coming back. The 200-year-old house has kept its original features intact and exudes old-fashioned charm. There's a sitting room with TV and leather sofas, seating in the garden for

The attractive Georgian façade of Arran House

summer picnics, plus a fridge and laundry for guests' use.

🛏 🚼 ⚐   ££

Blandford   Map 9 B1
80 Chiltern Street, W1U 5AF; 020 7486 3103; www.capricornhotels. co.uk/hotel_blandford/index.php
The most charming in the small Capricorn chain is perfectly placed for the shops and a visit to Madame Tussauds. It's also next to Regent's Park and the well appointed rooms have all been refurbished. The English breakfast here is guaranteed to get you through the day.

🛏   ££

Euro   Map 4 G5
53 Cartwright Gardens, WC1H 9EL; 020 7387 4321; www.eurohotel.co.uk
This is a good hotel to choose if you have a budding tennis star in the family – guests can use the courts in Cartwright Gardens (reservations at reception). Of the clutch of modest hotels that occupy the fine former merchants' houses in this Georgian crescent, the Euro stands out for its service and competitive rates.

🛏   ££

Hart House   Map 9 A2
51 Gloucester Place, W1U 8JF; 020 7935 2288; www.harthouse.co.uk
For families seeking fair prices but more character than a chain, this B&B provides plain, reliable accommodation in a Georgian house that once sheltered French nobility during the Revolution. The staff are attentive, and the rooms spotless. If you tire of the shops, the Wallace Collection is nearby.

🛏   ££

Jesmond Dene   Map 4 G5
27 Argyle Street, WC1H 8EP; 020 7837 4654; www.jesmonddenehotel. co.uk
Mostly small rooms, even smaller bathrooms (some microscopic, some shared) and a few steep stairs to

negotiate, but (and it's a big but) the friendly, thoughtful staff, the cleanliness, the breakfasts, the free Wi-Fi and, above all, the price for this central, King's Cross location keep families coming back.

🛏   ££

Lincoln House   Map 9 A2
33 Gloucester Place, W1U 8HY; 020 7486 7630; www.lincoln-house-hotel. co.uk
A trustworthy alternative to Hart House – in the same road but closer to Oxford Street. Bedrooms are modest, with tiny bathrooms, but have a number of treats, including five-star Hypnos mattresses, satellite TV, unlimited tea and coffee and free Wi-Fi. Air conditioning has been fitted in two-thirds of the rooms.

🛏   ££

PUB WITH ROOMS
New Inn   Map 2 G3
2 Allitsen Road, NW8 6LA; 020 7722 0726; www.newinnlondon.co.uk
Close to Regent's Park and the canal, the price, the good-natured welcome and the spotless, ample rooms above this pub are hard to beat. If sleep before midnight is vital, check the live music forecast before booking (usually at weekends). The pub serves breakfasts, light meals and good Sunday roasts.

    ££

The New Inn pub, just steps from Regent's Park

SELF-CATERING
23 Greengarden House   Map 9 C3
St Christopher's Place, W1U 1NL; 020 7935 9191; www. greengardenhouse.com
St Christopher's Place is distinctive and lined with fashionable shops, restaurants and cafés (many with outdoor tables and chairs). These apartments are in pleasant, modern surroundings, with weekday maid service, double glazing and a first-day survival kit for families.

🚼   £££

Europa House   Map 2 E5
79A Randolph Avenue, W9 1DW; 020 7724 5924; www. europahouseapartments.co.uk
With children in tow, Little Venice has great appeal – it's away from the hurly-burly and has a colourful canal and pretty bridges. Europa House has 14 comfortable, airy apartments, large, leafy communal gardens and a children's playground. Frazzled parents can order groceries, take-aways or an in-house massage.

🚼 ⚐   £££

SACO – Holborn   Map 10 H1
72–84 Lamb's Conduit Street, WC1N 3LT; 117 970 6999; www. sacoapartments.com
Exceptionally comfortable and with all mod cons, these award-winning apartments are in a vibrant part of the city. Eclectic boutiques, restaurants, delicatessens and cafés characterize the area, and children can scamper around Coram's Fields, a playground with slides, a flying fox and pets' corner. Not for very light sleepers.

🚼   £££

The City & the East End
HOTELS
Apex City of London   Map 12 G4
1 Seething Lane, EC3N 4AX; 0845 365 0000; www.apexhotels.co.uk/ hotels/city-of-london
Early birds can get to the Tower as soon as the gates open from this modern hotel situated just minutes away. There are complimentary kids' menus for under-13s and under-18s can stay free in their parents' room. The pristine rooms have comfortable beds and plenty of storage for the family paraphernalia.

    £££

Grange City   Map 12 G4
8–14 Cooper's Row, EC3N 2BQ; 020 7863 3700; www.grangehotels. com
The greatest draw of this hotel is the fabulous 25-m (82-ft) swimming pool, something of a rarity in London, with generous children's hours, particularly at weekends. The hotel restaurant also has a kids' menu. Grange City is close to the Tower, with splendid views of it from some of the rooms.

🛏 🚼   £££

Key to symbols *see back cover flap*

The Hoxton
Map 6 F6

81 Great Eastern Street, EC2A 3HU; 020 7550 1000; https://thehoxton. com

The huge ground-floor space here incorporates a reception, shop, sitting room, bar, the Hoxton Grill restaurant, Internet café and two blazing fires. The place has a real buzz that characterizes the local area. Working on budget airline principles, the earlier you book, the less you pay. There are occasional sales, when rooms are offered for just £1.

££

Close to the Tower of London, Hamlet (UK) offers basic accommodation

SELF-CATERING
Cheval Calico House
Map 12 E3

42 Bow Lane, EC4M 9DT; 020 7489 2500; www.chevalresidences.com/ our-london-residences/cheval-calico-house

Cheval Residences have several apartment buildings in London; Calico House offers the best value for money. Flats are attractive yet practical, with little luxuries such as goose-down duvets and Frette linen. Close to St Paul's Cathedral, the location is bustling during the week and quite peaceful at weekends. Seven days minimum rent.

£££

Eagle Court
Map 11 C1

10–11 Britton Street, EC1M 5QD; www.eaglecourt-apartments. co.uk (online booking only)

Clerkenwell is a reinvigorated district that is fun for families, with child-oriented restaurants and the Little Angel (puppet) Theatre in nearby Islington. Eagle Court has clean, modern accommodation at excellent rates if booked in advance. Weekly maid service and 24-hour phone support.

££

Hamlet (UK)
Map 12 H5

Nightingale House, 50 Thomas More Street, E1W 1UA & Burr Close, E1W 1ND; 01462 678037; www.hamletuk. com

Arriving at the Tower early to avoid the crowds is painless for guests staying at these modest one- and two-bedroom apartments in St Katharine's Dock. The area was redeveloped in the 1970s and is now surrounded by shops and restaurants. Kids will love the activity of the marina as the pleasure boats come and go. Minimum seven-night stay.

£££

Market View by BridgeStreet
Map 11 C2

15 West Smithfield, EC1A 9HY; 0800 278 7338; www.bridgestreet. com/Market_View_by_Bridgestreet_ Worldwide.htm

Of BridgeStreet's City apartment buildings, this restored Victorian red-brick block provides the best family accommodation. Ranging from studios to three bedrooms, all have sensible hardwood floors and furniture, and superb views of the still working Smithfield Meat Market. Lots of restaurants in this lively area.

££

Southwark & the South Bank
HOTELS
69 The Grove
Map 16 H5

69 Vauxhall Grove, SW8 1TA; 07796 874 677; www.69thegrove.com

Set in a quiet Victorian square close to Vauxhall Tube station and several main bus routes into the West End, this townhouse has excellent travel

The elegant exterior of the London Bridge hotel

connections. The building has been elegantly remodelled by its helpful owner/managers to offer a choice of smart rooms including apartments for families and groups of up to eight people. Free Wi-Fi, toiletries and an iPod dock/alarm clock all add to the comfort. There is a minimum three-night stay.

££

Church Street
29–33 Camberwell Church Street, SE5 8TR; 020 7703 5984; www. churchstreethotel.com

A lively one-off, this Latin American-inspired sanctuary in multi-ethnic Camberwell is owned and was designed by two artistic brothers. It has an informal tapas restaurant and large colourful rooms, furnished with wrought-iron beds and Mexican art. Buses 176 and 185 go from here to the excellent Horniman Museum.

££

Comfortable sitting area in one of Market View by BridgeStreet's apartments

Ibis Styles London Southwark Rose
Map 11 D5

43–47 Southwark Bridge Road,
SE1 9HH; 020 7015 1480;
www.ibis.com/gb/hotel-7465-
ibis-styles-london-southwark-rose/
index.shtml

The UK's first All Seasons includes
all the latest technology in its
bargain-priced rooms, such as
Wi-Fi and flat-screen TVs. With the
Globe, the National Theatre and
Tate Modern only minutes away,
it is a perfect choice for families
of culture vultures.

££

London Bridge
Map 12 E6

8–18 London Bridge Street, SE1
9SG; 020 7855 2200; www.
londonbridgehotel.com

If the London Dungeon features on
your "to do" list, this welcoming
and intimate hotel in an interesting
central area could hardly be better
located. The enticing lobby sets the
scene, while rooms are restful with
neat black-and-white bathrooms.
The hotel is much larger than it
appears from the outside and
contains three restaurant/bars.

£££

Park Plaza County Hall
Map 10 H6

1 Addington Street, SE1 7RY; 0844
415 6760; www.parkplaza.com/
london-hotel-gb-se1-7ry/gbcounty

This vast 398-room high-rise
giant is handily located for such
must-visit sights as the London Eye
and Aquarium. Its smart Spectrum
restaurant boasts a breathtaking setting below a 14-storey glass atrium.
Studios, ideal for families, have a
living area with plasma TV (movies
on demand) and kitchenette.

££

Premier Inn London County Hall
Map 10 H6

Belvedere Road, SE1 7PB; 0871 527
8648; www.premierinn.com/en/check
Hotel/LONCOU/london-county-hall

Two under-16s stay for free when
sharing with their parents in this well-
kept hotel. Geared to family life, this
reasonably priced hotel offers high
chairs, additive-free kids' meals and
activity packs. It also has an enviable
location opposite Westminster.

£

BED & BREAKFAST
Kennington B&B
Map 17 B4

103 Kennington Park Road, SE11
4JJ; 020 7735 7669; www.
kenningtonbandb.com

This B&B in an impeccably renovated
Georgian townhouse is a standard
setter: it scores top marks for location,
price, welcome and comfort. It has
adjoining rooms, perfect for families
with young children, and is virtually
on the doorstep of Kennington Tube
station, giving easy access to the rest
of London. Babysitting and English
courses are available for a fee.

££

SELF-CATERING
London Tower Bridge
Map 12 H6

The Circle, Queen Elizabeth Street,
SE1 2JJ; 020 8674 7069; www.
londontowerbridgeapartments.co.uk

It may be tricky to find, but once
you're here, this building offers an
agreeable refuge from the bustle.
Hard-to-match prices, colourful
furnishings and plenty of space for
lounging add to the all-round appeal
of these apartments. Patronize the
local deli, bakery and Borough
Market (Wed–Sat), then cook up a
feast in the well-kitted-out kitchen.

££

*Smart lobby of the Crowne Plaza
Kensington*

Kensington, Chelsea & Battersea
HOTELS
Crowne Plaza Kensington
Map 14 E2

100 Cromwell Road, SW7 4ER; 0871
942 9022; www.ihg.com/crowneplaza/
hotels/gb/en/london/lonke/hoteldetail

Probably the best-value hotel in
Kensington, this is just a short stroll
from the Science and Natural History
museums and a favourite with
families. Although the Cromwell
Road is a busy thoroughfare, once
inside, or in the large garden, all is
calm. Guests who decide to eat out
are spoiled for choice.

££

Mandarin Oriental Hyde Park
Map 9 A6

66 Knightsbridge, SW1X 7LA; 020
7235 2000; www.mandarinoriental.
com/london/

From mini bathrobes, books and
crayons to popcorn on demand,
children want for nothing at this
luxurious Edwardian pile on the
edge of Hyde Park and bang
opposite Harvey Nichols. The
smart interior is part contemporary,
part traditional, with a stunning
ballroom where in the 1930s, the
Queen learned to dance.

£££

Rafayel on the Left Bank

34 Lombard Road, SW11 3RF; 020
7801 3600; www.hotelrafayel.com

You'll find large rooms with
remarkably comfortable beds
in this glossy, eco-friendly hotel.
If the kids wake up hungry in the
night, there's 24-hour room service.
There's also pampering for parents
in the spa and gym; a free shuttle
bus to and from Clapham Junction
and Clapham Common; and the
kind staff will organize cycling and
kayaking trips.

££

The luxurious Mandarin Oriental, near Hyde Park and Sloane Street

Key to symbols *see back cover flap*

The elegant interior of The Beaufort hotel

Royal Garden
Map 7 D6

2–24 Kensington High Street, W8 4PT; 020 7937 8000; www. royalgardenhotel.co.uk

Favoured by footballers and rock bands, this is a hotel for celebrity spotting. However, the attraction for families is having Kensington Gardens, with the Diana Memorial Playground, Peter Pan statue and Round Pond, as their backyard. The hotel provides bread for feeding the ducks.

£££

BED & BREAKFAST
Amsterdam
Map 13 C3

7 Trebovir Road, SW5 9LS; 020 7370 5084; www.amsterdam-hotel. com

In a quiet street around the corner from Earl's Court Road Tube station, this prize-winning townhouse B&B has decent-sized and reasonably priced family rooms – these are at a premium in this area, so book early. Breakfast is served by smiling staff in a bright, pretty room with crisp tablecloths. The garden is especially lovely in summer.

££

The Beaufort
Map 14 H1

33 Beaufort Gardens, SW3 1PP; 020 7584 5252; www.thebeaufort. co.uk

This privately owned hotel offers 29 comfortable, tastefully decorated bedrooms, a relaxed atmosphere and a very classy Knightsbridge address. Be sure to return from shopping or sightseeing in time for tea and mouth-watering home-made scones, served from 3–5pm and included in the room price. There's also a great choice of excellent restaurants nearby.

£££

The Cranley
Map 14 E3

10 Bina Gardens, SW5 0LA; 020 7373 0123; www.the cranley.com

A night spent here feels more like staying with friends than in a hotel: it's a traditional, luxurious home-from-home with plenty of personal touches, such as an honesty bar and turn-down service. A highlight of the day is afternoon tea, served on the front terrace in summer and by the fire in winter. There are family offers from time to time.

££

Darlington Hyde Park
Map 8 G2

111–117 Sussex Gardens, W2 2RU; 020 7460 8800; www.darlingtonhotel.com

The area around Paddington is full of B&Bs, many of them rather dubious. However, here is a superior one, well located for the train station and Heathrow Express, as well as Oxford Street's shops. Although some family rooms are on the lower-ground floor, they still feel bright and breezy. Fridges in the rooms are a bonus.

££

Hyde Park Rooms
Map 8 G2

137 Sussex Gardens, W2 2RX; 020 7723 0225; www.hydeparkrooms.com

In business for more than 30 years, this modest family-run B&B offers no-frills accommodation plus a generous breakfast at unbeatable prices for central London. Guests are guaranteed a warm welcome from the owner and staff, and although rooms are simple and not all have en-suite facilities, they are certainly spick and span.

£

Lavender Guesthouse
18 Lavender Sweep, SW11 1HA; 020 7585 2767; www. thelavenderguesthouse.com

Simply decorated and equipped, but squeaky clean and very friendly, this guesthouse is in a quiet suburban area but is only a short walk from Clapham Junction (7 minutes by train from Victoria). Rooms are small (but prices are smaller) and there is a 3-night minimum stay. The sunny garden is filled with flowers and shrubs.

£

The Nadler Kensington
Map 13 D3

25 Courtfield Gardens, SW5 0PG; 020 7244 2255; www.base2stay. com

Occupying a smart townhouse in a rather salubrious corner of Earl's Court, this 65-room, 4-star, boutique hotel offers exceptional value. By editing out unnecessary extras, a stay here offers guests convenience, flexibility and affordable luxury. Free Wi-Fi and a mini kitchen in every room.

££

New Linden
Map 7 C3

59 Leinster Square, W2 4PS; 020 7221 4321; www.newlinden.com

Not far from Portobello Road, this converted townhouse has 50 pristine and carefully designed rooms. Floors are wooden; walls plain with the occasional modern painting; and beds have distinctive headboards and colourful covers. The staff couldn't be friendlier, and rooms are good value, especially as the excellent buffet breakfast is included in the price.

£

Number Sixteen
Map 14 F3

16 Sumner Place, SW7 3EG; 020 7589 5232; www.firmdalehotels. com/hotels/london/number-sixteen/

Tim and Kit Kemp, who own Firmdale Hotels, have the knack of creating places to stay that not only look stunning but are easy going and smooth running. Number Sixteen is no exception. Extras include 24-hour room service, a DVD library, honesty bar and freshly-squeezed orange juice for breakfast.

£££

Park City Grand Plaza Kensington
Map 13 D2

18–30 Lexham Gardens, W8 5JE; 020 7341 7090; www.parkcitylondon.co.uk

Tucked away behind Cromwell Road, which runs in an almost straight line from Hammersmith to Harrods, the award-winning Park City spreads itself through seven substantial houses. Once the little ones are in bed, the grown-ups can enjoy a nightcap in Ruby's Cocktail Bar (which also serves lunchtime snacks).

£££

The Parkwood at Marble Arch
Map 8 H3

4 Stanhope Place, W2 2HB; 020 7402 2241; www.parkwoodhotel.com

This is a tranquil oasis close to, but a world apart from, the frenzy of Marble Arch. Tasteful prints hang on the walls of the spacious, cheerfully decorated bedrooms, some of which have handsome iron bedsteads. There are no hidden costs, and the price, which includes a full English breakfast, represents terrific value for money.

££

Rhodes
Map 8 F3

195 Sussex Gardens, W2 2RJ; 020 7262 0537; www.rhodeshotel.com

The current owners of the Rhodes have been at the helm since 1978 and take great pride in their friendly, eclectic B&B in an elegant Georgian house, which was first opened before World War II. Double glazing keeps the rooms beautifully quiet;

the ones at the top are a fairly steep climb, but there are willing members of staff to help with luggage.

£

Apartment in Allen House, off Kensington High Street

Royal Park
Map 8 F3

3 Westbourne Terrace, W2 3UL; 020 7479 6600; www.theroyalpark.com

The name is apt: Hyde Park is only a few minutes' walk south from this smart, traditional little hotel. Families can arrange to have interconnecting rooms, where breakfast is served in bed each morning. It may be pricey, but extras, such as Wi-Fi and use of a guest computer are included.

£££

Sydney House
Map 14 G3

9–11 Sydney Street, SW3 6PU; 020 7376 7711; www.sydneyhousechelsea.com

Plumb between the shops of the King's Road and the museums of South Kensington, this is a cool but cosy Georgian townhouse that has undergone a chic makeover. Rooms have pale walls, blonde-wood floors, flat-screen TVs and comfy

beds. It has charming staff and fair prices (look out for special offers).

££

Trebovir
Map 13 C3

18–20 Trebovir Road, SW5 9NH; 020 7373 6625; www.trebovirhotel.com

In the same street as the Amsterdam and occupying two 19th-century white stucco houses, this revamped small hotel has some double-height windows, which make the interior feel light and airy. A number of rooms have traditional bathrooms, while others have tiny pods, so be sure to check first. The best rates just drop it into the inexpensive bracket.

£

SELF-CATERING

The Apartments
Map 15 A3

36 Draycott Place, SW3 2SA; 0843 218 5060; www.theapartments.co.uk

These luxuriously appointed and spacious apartments are ideal for longer stays and families looking for a more homely feel. The apartments all have fully equipped kitchens and features include iPod docking stations, plus a weekly maid and linen service.

£££

Beaufort House
Map 14 H1

45 Beaufort Gardens, SW3 1PN; 020 7584 2600; www.beauforthouse.co.uk

Just a 5-minute hop from Harrods toy department, these exclusive one- to four-bedroom apartments overlook a Knightsbridge cul-de-sac. Each one is handsomely furnished and boasts a top-of-the-range kitchen and bathroom. Facilities include iPod docking stations and an extensive DVD collection.

£££

Castletown House
Map 13 A4

11 Castletown Road, W14 9HE; 020 7386 9423; www.castletownhouse.co.uk

If these were a short distance east, inside the Royal Borough of Kensington and Chelsea, prices could be double. Choose between studios (a tight fit), and one- or two- bedroom apartments with delightful courtyards. The owners are on hand to welcome and help.

££

Sydney House, located between the King's Road and the Natural History Museum

Key to symbols *see back cover flap*

Dolphin House Apartments
Map 16 E4

Chichester Street, SW1V 3LX; 020 7798 6890; www.euracom.co.uk/london_apartments_westminster.htm

Offering some of the nicest of the many serviced apartments that can be booked through Euracom throughout the city, this former hotel is in a quiet but central location and constitutes great value. There's a minimum 2-night stay.

£

Fraser Place Queens Gate
Map 14 E2

39B Queen's Gate Gardens, SW7 5RR; 020 7969 3555; http://london-queensgate.frasershospitality.com

Ideal for families planning a visit to the dinosaurs at the Natural History Museum, these apartments are well designed, and with wipeable surfaces, they are available per night. Home entertainment includes cable TV, DVD and CD players. Daily maid service and 24-hour reception.

 £££

Oyster Wharf

Oyster Wharf, 18 Lombard Road, SW11 3RR; 020 7183 3680; www.oysterwharfsuites.co.uk

These luxury serviced apartments, just 8-minutes' walk from Clapham Junction Station, are equipped with microwaves, dishwashers, refrigerators and washing machines. Foldaway beds can be provided for an additional fee. Facilities include free Wi-Fi, TVs and DVD players.

££

Royal Court Apartments
Map 8 F3

51 Gloucester Terrace, W2 3DQ; 020 7402 5077; www.royalcourtapartments.co.uk

Managed by the Paddington Hotel opposite, these apartments range from the modest and old-fashioned to the sleek and refurbished (reflected in the price). Families will be comfortable with two bedrooms, a sitting room and kitchen.

££

Space Apart Hotel
Map 7 D3

36–37 Kensington Gardens Square, W2 4BQ; 020 7908 1340; www.aparthotel-london.co.uk

These are an outstanding choice for families, with everything on demand, from Wii games to potties. The excellent management is hands-on and the wide-open spaces of Hyde Park are on the doorstep. The apartments (some duplex) are enlivened by quirky details (such as zebra-print carpets) and have the latest Bosch appliances, practical but attractive furniture and clever storage.

 ££

Beyond the Centre

HOTELS

Boundary Rooms
Map 6 G5

2–4 Boundary Street, E2 7DD; 020 7729 1051; www.theboundary.co.uk

There is plenty of space to spread out in the bedrooms at Terence Conran's typically stylish converted Victorian printworks in buzzy Shoreditch. Have breakfast and snacks in the congenial Albion, a café-cum-bakery (open 8am–midnight) and, in summer, eat on the rooftop (which hums at weekends) with the whole City on display.

 ££

Crowne Plaza Shoreditch
Map 6 G6

100 Shoreditch High Street, E1 6JR; 020 7613 9800; www.ichotelsgroup.com/h/d/cp/925/en/hd/lonsd

Handy for east visiting families, who can eat breakfast with a view in the top-floor Globe restaurant, or nip around the corner to Leila's Shop (15 Calvert Avenue), a Spitalfields' institution. With Brick Lane, Columbia Road and Spitalfields all within striking distance, this is a recommended option for market enthusiasts. Rooms are bland, but spacious.

 ££

Novotel London Greenwich, close to the Old Royal Naval College

Hilton London Docklands

265 Rotherhithe Street, SE16 5HW; 020 7231 1001; www.hilton.co.uk/docklands

With a complimentary ferry service to and from Canary Wharf Tube station, getting around from this riverside hotel could hardly be easier. The rather utilitarian family rooms are a decent size, but if you need two because of your children, the second room will be half price. There is also a small pool.

 £££

The Premier Inn, Hampstead has on-site parking

Novotel London Greenwich
Map 18 E4

173–85 Greenwich High Road, SE10 8JA; 020 7660 0682; www.novotel.com/gb/hotel-3476-novotel-london-greenwich/index.shtml

This branch of the ubiquitous hotel chain stands out for the warmth of its staff and the comfort and cleanliness of its rooms. The company aims to make families a priority, and this hotel comes equipped with a PlayStation 3 and two Apple computers. The splendid breakfast will set you and the family up for a day of sightseeing in Greenwich.

 ££

Premier Inn, Hampstead

215 Haverstock Hill, NW3 4RB; 0871 527 8662; www.premierinn.com

Fairly convenient for the sights of the West End (via the Northern Line from Belsize Park tube) and close to the attractive outdoor spaces of Hampstead Heath and Kenwood House, this Premier Inn has smart, contemporary public areas and an on-site Thyme restaurant and Costa Coffee. Bedrooms are quiet, if slightly smaller than average for this chain. It looks a bit dull on the outside, but is made more cosy by attentive service at reception.

 £££

Dining and sitting area of one of the Glenthurston self-catering apartments

Ramada London Docklands
ExCeL, 2 Festoon Way, Royal Victoria Dock, E16 1RH; 020 7540 4820; www.ramadadocklands.co.uk
A cut above the usual chain hotels and handy for City Airport and the DLR, which zooms into the heart of the City in minutes. The best suites overlook Victoria Dock and have their own kitchenettes. Alternatively, forget cooking and try the tasty Italian dishes on offer at the hotel's Stresa restaurant. Free parking.

£

Richmond Gate
152–58 Richmond Hill, TW10 6RP; 0844 855 9121; www.richmondgate.com
This elegant, 4-star hotel occupies a stunning 18th-century building at the top of Richmond Hill. The hotel has a country-house feel and is steps from London's largest park, the river and the centre of Richmond, with its shops and theatres. Guests can use the pool at the health club next door. Highly-rated food.

££

BED & BREAKFAST
Forest Lodge
70 Drax Avenue, West Wimbledon, SW20 0EY; 020 8946 3253; www.thewimbledonbedandbreakfast.com
Located in a large house, Forest Lodge is a family-run bed and breakfast close to Wimbledon Common. Rooms are bright and sunny with pleasant decor. Guests can use the indoor pool all year round. Amenities include free Wi-Fi, flat-screen TVs and parking. Cots are also available.

££

Quality Hotel Hampstead
5 Frognal, NW3 6AL; 020 7794 0101; www.qualityhampstead.com
"Olde worlde" it is not, but it does have proper bathrooms, decent-sized, comfortable bedrooms, lifts to every floor and free parking. It is also close to Finchley Road tube and bus routes into the centre. Staff are knowledgeable and helpful; breakfasts are generous. A variety of tempting local restaurants nearby.

££

Richmond Inn
50–56 Sheen Road, TW9 1UG; 020 8940 0171; www.richmondinnhotel.com
Aspiring botanists and their parents will enjoy being so close to Kew Gardens, while theatre buffs should know that many West End productions try out in Richmond first. The clean, well-equipped bedrooms may be slightly suburban for some but there are elegant marble-covered bathrooms, which are something of a treat. Helpful 24-hour staff, a good choice of local restaurants and free parking.

££

SELF-CATERING
Fox Apartments
Warehouse K, Western Gateway, ExCeL Centre, E16 1DR; 020 7558 8859; www.foxapartments.com
A superb conversion of a 170-year-old warehouse next to an official Olympic venue and handy for the DLR. Exposed brickwork, warm neutral colours, two bathrooms, small patios and simple stylish fixtures and fittings make these duplexes a great find in Docklands. There is some airport noise, but it's not a huge problem.

£££

Glenthurston
30 Bromley Road, SE6 2TP & 27 Canadian Ave, SE6 3AU; 020 8690 3092; www.londonselfcatering.co.uk
For energy-filled young ones, there are swings, a trampoline and grass to run around on in the gardens of these neighbouring Victorian houses, as well as a pool table and an indoor swimming pool. These simple, cheerful apartments are perfect for families. There are direct buses to Greenwich and the Horniman Museum, and a good

train service into town. Only week-long lets are available.

£

Sanctum
Map 1 C3
1 Greville Road, NW6 5HA; 020 7644 2100; www.sanctum-international.com
There is little doubt that you get more space for your money even a short distance out of the centre. A three-minute walk from Kilburn Park Tube station (and a direct route to Oxford Circus), this circular space-age building houses 43 light, handsomely furnished apartments, with well-appointed kitchens and first-class management.

£££

Town Hall Apartments
8 Patriot Square, E2 9NF; 020 7871 0460; www.townhallhotel.com
Just a five-minute walk from the V&A Museum of Childhood, the Town Hall Apartments are a happy combination of imposing Edwardian architecture and striking contemporary furnishings. The beautifully designed apartments have state-of-the-art facilities, such as wet rooms, and enjoy those of the hotel, including pool and gym. Hotel staff are obliging.

£££

RESTAURANT WITH ROOMS
La Gaffe
107–111 Heath Street, NW3 6SS; 020 7435 8965; www.lagaffe.co.uk
Above its own cheerful family-run Italian restaurant in Hampstead's village atmosphere, near the Heath and Kenwood House, La Gaffe has cosy, pleasing rooms with serviceable bathrooms. There are very friendly, hospitable staff, who are prepared to go the extra mile to help, and, of course, wonderful home-cooked Italian food.

£

La Gaffe restaurant and rooms in the centre of Hampstead village

Key to symbols *see back cover flap*

The distinctive "Gherkin" building
towering over the City of London

London
MAPS

London City Maps

The map below shows the divison of the 18 pages
of maps in this section, as well as the main areas
covered in the sightseeing section of this book.
The smaller inset map shows Greater London
and the areas covered in Beyond the City Centre.

BELSIZE PARK

HIGHBURY

1

2

3

CAMDEN

4

5

QUEEN'S
PARK

ST. JOHN'S
WOOD

ISLINGTO

KING'S
CROSS

REGENT'S
PARK

FINSBUF

MAIDA
VALE

7

8

9

MARYLEBONE

BLOOMSBURY

10

11

PADDINGTON

HOLBORN

SOHO

COVENT
GARDEN

NOTTING
HILL

MAYFAIR

ST JAMES'S

SOUTH
BANK

HYDE
PARK

13

KENSINGTON

14

15

WESTMINSTER

Thames

16

17

LAMBETH

EARLS
COURT

CHELSEA

HAMMERSMITH

Thames

PIMLICO

VAUXHALL

KENNINGT

BATTERSEA

STOCKWELL

0 kilometres   1

0 miles   1

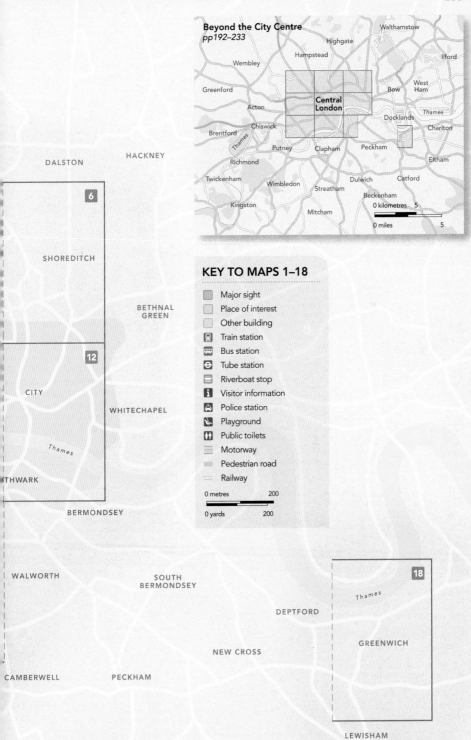

Beyond the City Centre
pp192–233

Walthamstow
Highgate
Hampstead
Wembley
Ilford
Greenford
Bow
West Ham
Acton
Central London
Thames
Docklands
Chiswick
Charlton
Brentford
Thames
Peckham
Eltham
Putney
Clapham
Richmond
Twickenham
Dulwich
Catford
Wimbledon
Streatham
Beckenham
Kingston
Mitcham

0 kilometres 5
0 miles 5

DALSTON
HACKNEY

6

SHOREDITCH

BETHNAL GREEN

12

CITY
WHITECHAPEL

Thames

THWARK

BERMONDSEY

KEY TO MAPS 1–18

- Major sight
- Place of interest
- Other building
- 🚆 Train station
- 🚌 Bus station
- Ⓔ Tube station
- 🛥 Riverboat stop
- ℹ Visitor information
- 👮 Police station
- 🧗 Playground
- 🚻 Public toilets
- Motorway
- Pedestrian road
- Railway

0 metres 200
0 yards 200

WALWORTH
SOUTH BERMONDSEY

18

Thames

DEPTFORD

GREENWICH

NEW CROSS

CAMBERWELL
PECKHAM

LEWISHAM

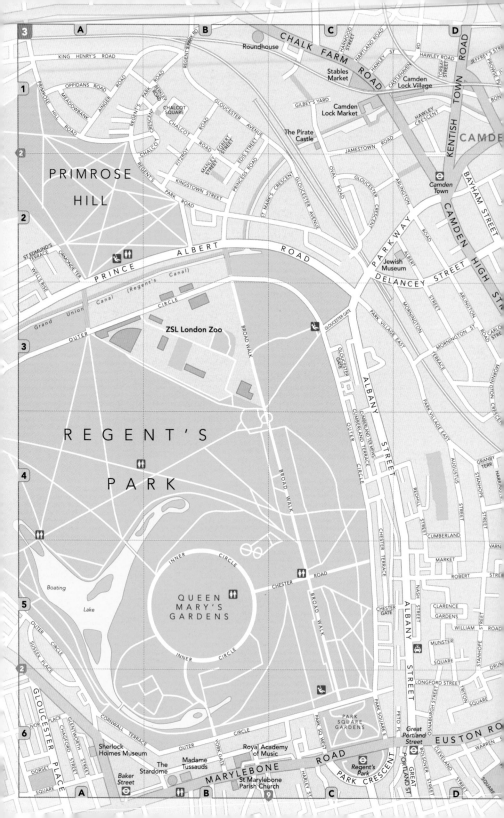

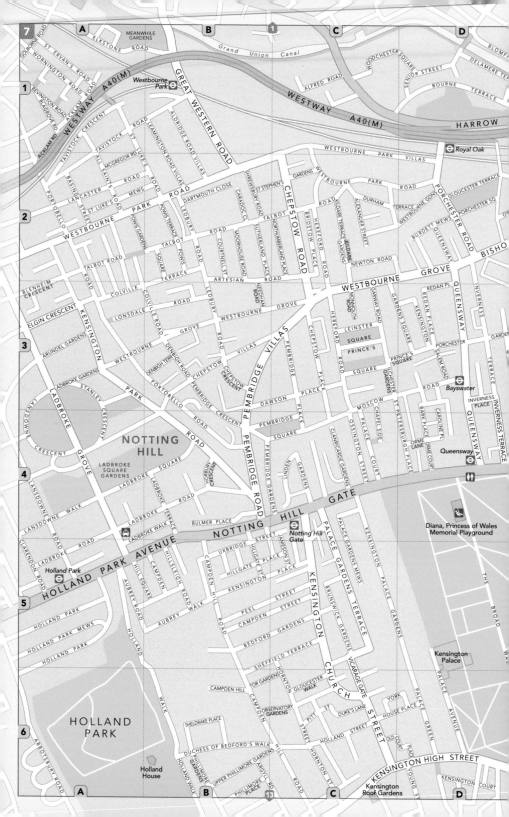

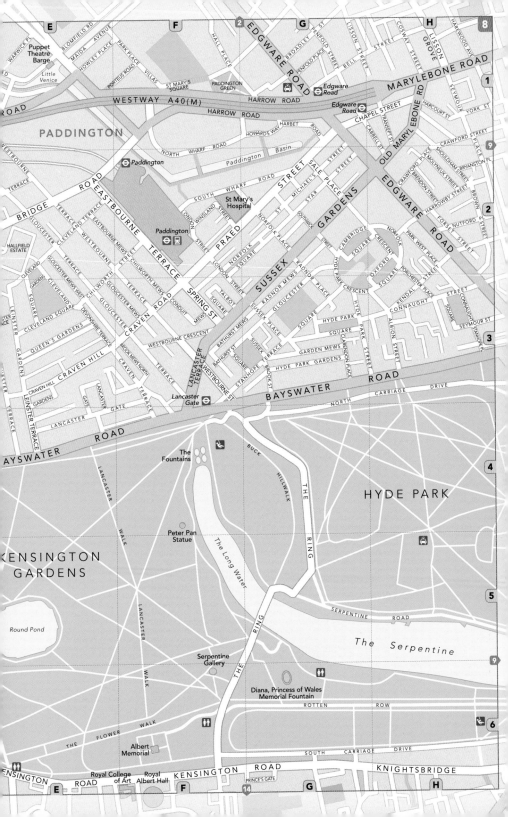

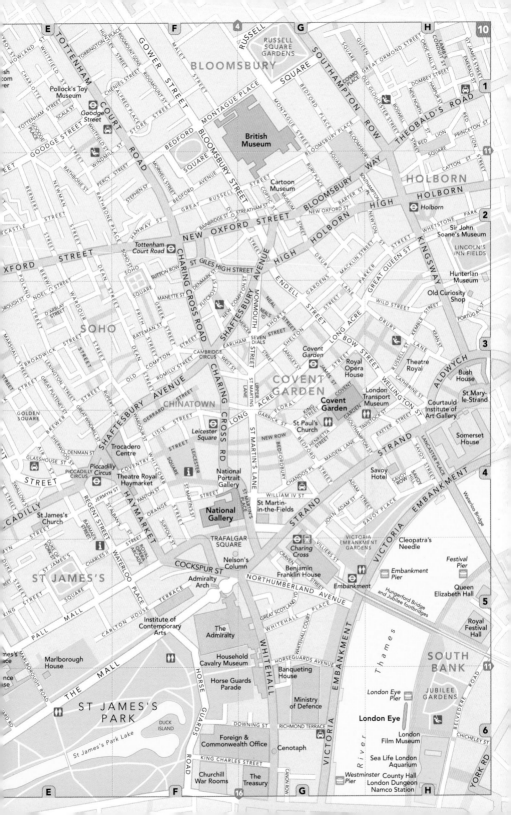

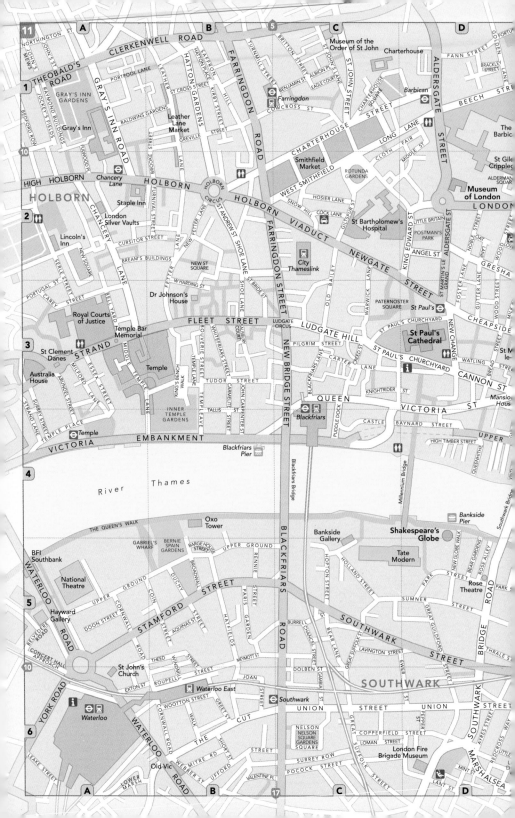

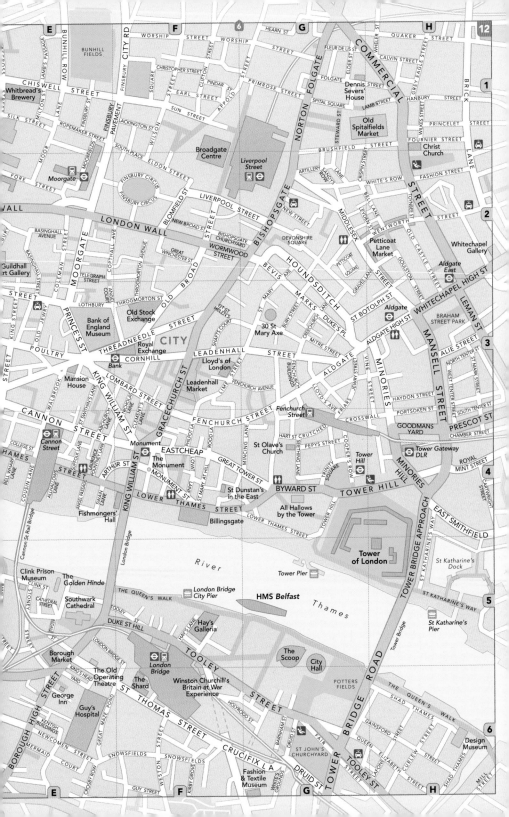

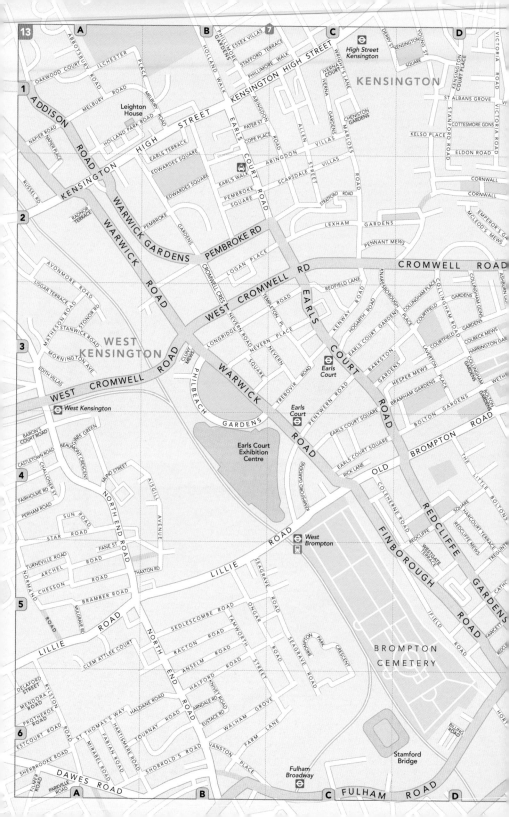

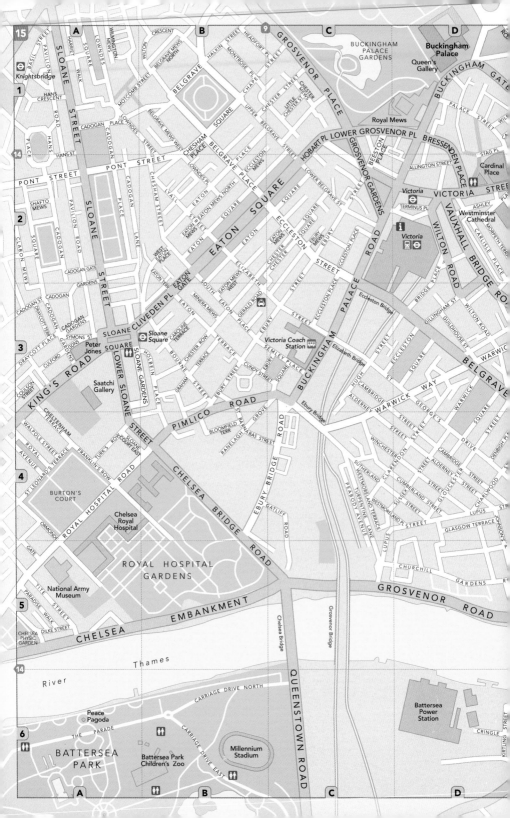

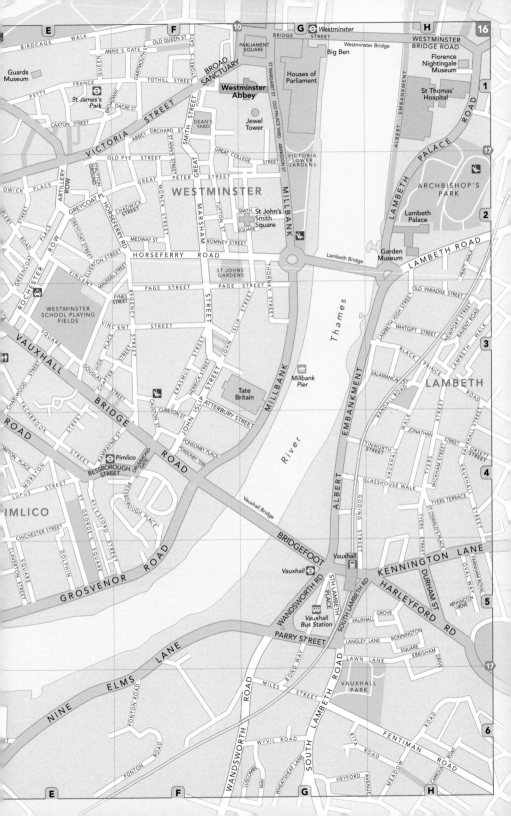

London Maps Index

Index

Acknowledgments

Dorling Kindersley would like to thank the following people whose help and assistance contributed to the preparation of this book.

Main Contributor
Journalist Vincent Crump, an Oxford English graduate, has worked widely across most spheres of written journalism: on staff for trade magazines, regional newspapers and consumer magazines, and latterly as a freelance writer and editor, principally on travel. Most of his recent work has been as resident UK travel specialist for the *Sunday Times Travel* section and *Sunday Times Travel Magazine*, for whom Vincent has been writing and editing for 10 years. This is his first book.

Introducing London & Where to Stay
Written by Leonie Glass.

Additional Photography
Max Alexander, Demetrio Carrasco, Tim Draper, Steve Gorton, Dave King, Stephen Oliver, Rough Guides/Victor Borg, Chris Stowers.

Cartography
Maps on pages 196–7, 206–7, 214–15, 220–21, 226–7 are derived from © www.openstreetmap.org and contributors, licensed under CC–BY–SA; see creativecommons.org for further details.

Additional Design and Editorial Assistance
ASSISTANT EDITOR Claire Bush
JACKET DESIGN Tessa Blindoss, Louise Dick
ICON DESIGN Claire-Louise Armitt
READERS Scarlett O'Hara, Anna Streiffert
FACT CHECKER Karen Villabona
PROOFREADER Huw Hennessy
INDEXER Helen Peters
With thanks to Douglas Amrine for his help in developing this series.

Revisions Team
Ashwin Raju Adimari, Karen D'Souza, Maria Edwards, Caroline Elliker, Kaberi Hazarika, Bharti Karakoti, Tanya Mahendru, Catherine Palmi, Susie Peachey, Marianne Petrou, Khushboo Priya, Nikky Twyman, Ajay Verma

Photography Permissions
Dorling Kindersley would like to thank all the museums, galleries, churches and other sights that allowed us to photograph at their establishments.
Terri and Sir Richard Raleigh at 44 Curzon Street Apartments, Apple UK Press Office, Nicolas at Arosfa B&B, Hélène Muron for Barbican Film Sunday, Finoa Vella at Battersea Park Children's Zoo and Lemon Tree Café, Benjamin Pollock's Toyshop, Britain at War, British Music Experience, Paul and Sarah at Brown's Brasserie, Sophie Darley at Browns Hotel, Brunel Museum, Burgh House, Camden Arts Centre, Cartoon Museum, Shannon Hermes at Charles Dickens Museum, Jess Walker at Davis Tanner for Chelsea Football Club and all at the club, The Clink Museum, Crystal Palace Museum, Crystal Palace Sports Center, DR Johnson's House, Lettie McKie at Dulwich Picture Gallery, Farady Museum and the Royal Institution, Fire Brigade Museum, Florence Knightingale Museum, Gemma Colgan at the Foundling Museum, Lorenzo & Giuseppe at La Gaffe, Garden Museum, Guards Museum, Nancy Loader at Geffyre Museum, Vikki at Giraffe, Golders Hill Butterfly House, Amelia Atkinson at The Goring, Hany Kirollos at Gourmet Burger Kitchen Windsor, Guildhall Art Gallery, Jo Wilkinson and Madeleine McClure at Hamleys, Richard Brindley at Hard Rock Café, Harrods, Tim Powell at Historic Royal Palaces, Sarah Beckett at the Horniman Museum, Household Cavalry Museum, Hunterain Museum, Imperial War Museums, Alison Bledge at Legoland®, Sophie Lilley at The London Eye, London Film Museum, Wendy Neville at London Transport Museum, Nicola Kalimeris at Museum of London, Becca Hubbard at National Army Museum, Claire Gilbey at Natural History Museum, Old Operating Theatre Museum and Herb Garret, Malida at Original Maids of Honour, Gren Middleton at Puppet Theatre Barge, Royal Air Force Museum, Bryony Phillips at Royal Botanic Gardens Kew, Royal Observatory Greenwich, SACO – Holborn, St Paul's Cathedral, Nicola Osmond-Evans at Science Museum, Serpentine Gallery, Snook's Fun Store, Syon House, Theatre Royal Drury Lane, Unicorn Theatre, Joanna Bolitho at V&A Museum of Childhood, Amy Randall at the Wallace Collection, Dean and Chapter of the Collegiate Church of St Peter Westminster, WWT London Wetland Centre, Zoological Society of London (ZSL).

Picture Credits
a = above; b = below/bottom; c = centre;
f = far; l = left; r = right; t = top.

The publisher would like to thank the following for their kind permission to reproduce their photographs:

ALAMY IMAGES: The Art Gallery Collection/*The Execution of Lady Jane Grey* 1833 Hippolyte (Paul) Delaroche 80cra; Robert Bird 80tr; Mike Booth 184br; Greg Balfour Evans 20bl; Keith Mayhew 218tc; John Warburton-Lee Photography 178cl.

BATTERSEA PARK CHILDREN'S ZOO: 187tl.

THE BRIDGEMAN ART LIBRARY: Index/Bymuseum, Oslo, Norway 54cra.

BRITISH AIRWAYS: Newscast 20–1.

THE TRUSTEES OF THE BRITISH MUSEUM: 103tc, 103cla; Alan Hills 103ca.

CHESSINGTON WORLD OF ADVENTURES/MERLIN ENTERTAINMENTS GROUP: 49bl.

CORBIS: Demotix/David Mbiyu 46br, /James Gourley 18bl, /P Nutt 18br; EPA/Frantzesco Kangaris 11t; Eurasia Press/Steven Vidler 55cb; Jason Hawkes 252–3; Heritage Images 78bl; Robbie Jack 91tl; Pawel Libera 58–9; Reuters/A.J. Sisco 17cl; SuperStock/Clive Sawyer PCL 8–9.

DESIGN MUSEUM: Gilbert McCarragher 157tc.

DORLING KINDERSLEY: Jamie Marshall Collection 30bl; Courtesy of The Science Museum 180tr; Park Lane Group Young Artists' Concert 164bl.

DREAMSTIME.COM: Nanisub 193c; Padmayogini 16br, 17br; Tamara Kulikova 203bc.

EDF ENERGY LONDON EYE: 160bc.

© ENGLISH HERITAGE PHOTO LIBRARY: 204clb, 216cl, 216c, 216cr.

EUROLINES: 21bc.

GAMBADO CHELSEA: 48br.

GETTY IMAGES: 19br; AFP 62br, /Carl de Souza 19bl; Express/Stan Meagher 57crb; Imagno 80cr; Chris Jackson 72c; Christopher Lee 16bl; Clive Rose 63t; Oli Scarff 15bl; SuperStock 80c; Time & Life Pictures/ Mansell 56tr.

GLENTHURSTON SELF CATERING APARTMENTS: Andrew Hatfield 251tl.

THE GOLDEN TREASURY BOOKSHOP: 43bl.

THE GOVERNOR & COMPANY OF THE BANK OF ENGLAND: 129cr.

IMPERIAL WAR MUSEUMS: 154crb.

WWW.KIDSROLLERBLADINGLESSONS.CO.UK: 13b.

THE KOBAL COLLECTION: Walt Disney Pictures 131bc.

LONDON BOROUGH OF CAMDEN: 48bl.

LONDON CITY AIRPORT: Andrew Baker 20bc.

LONDON RECUMBENTS: 188cl.

MADAME TUSSAUDS/LONDON: 114tc.

THE MAYOR'S THAMES FESTIVAL: Barry Lewis 15br. NATIONAL PORTRAIT GALLERY, LONDON: Colin Streater 79tl.

THE NATIONAL TRUST PHOTO LIBRARY ©NTPL: Arcaid/Richard Bryant 233bl; Andrew Butler 231cb; Geoffrey Frosh 212tc; David Levenson 44br.

POLKA THEATRE: © Robert Workman 47br, 232tr.

REGENT'S PARK OPEN AIR THEATRE: Tristram Kenton 14bl. NATURAL HISTORY MUSEUM, LONDON: 182cl.

REX FEATURE: Mark Thomas 24br.

RIPLEY'S BELIEVE IT OR NOT: 85tl.

ROYAL ALBERT HALL: © Marcus Ginns 2009 185tl.

THE ROYAL COLLECTION © 2011 HER MAJESTY QUEEN ELIZABETH II: 238cr; John Freeman 74crb; Derry Moore 74cla, 74clb.

ROYAL NATIONAL THEATRE: Simon Annand 162tr.

ROYAL OPERA HOUSE: Sim Canetty–Clarke 45br.

SHAKESPEARE GLOBE TRUST: Pawel Libera 146cl, Rocco Redondo 146cr.

SIR JOHN SOANES MUSEUM: Derry Moore 94tc.

SOMERSET HOUSE: © Gideon Mendel 13tr, 93t.

ST PAUL'S CATHEDRAL: Peter Smith 130cra.

SUPERSTOCK: Photononstop 156br.

THORPE PARK/MERLIN ENTERTAINEMENTS GROUP: 49tl.

TRAVEL PICTURES: Charles Bowman 27clb.

THE VIEW FROM THE SHARD: 153tr, 156tc.

VISIT GREENWICH: 198cl, 198c.

WESTFIELD LONDON: 41bl.

Jacket images: Front: 4CORNERS: Justin Foulkes cb; ALAMY IMAGES: Martin Bond tr, Jacek Nowak tc, Steve Vidler cb; GETTY IMAGES: Grant Faint tl, Jon Arnold tr; SUPERSTOCK: Roberto Herrett/Loop Images tc; Dave Povey/Loop Images tl; Back: ALAMY IMAGES: Veryan Dale tr; AWL IMAGES: Alan Copson tl, Julian Love tc; Spine: CORBIS: Sylvain Sonnet t.

All other images © Dorling Kindersley
For further information see: www.dkimages.com

SPECIAL EDITIONS OF DK TRAVEL GUIDES

DK Travel Guides can be purchased in bulk quantities at discounted prices for use in promotions or as premiums. We are also able to offer special editions and personalized jackets, corporate imprints, and excerpts from all of our books, tailored specifically to meet your own needs.
To find out more, please contact:
(in the United States) **specialsales@dk.com**
(in the UK) **travelguides@uk.dk.com**
(in Canada) **specialmarkets@dk.com**
(in Australia) **penguincorporatesales@penguin randomhouse.com.au**

Chesham ⓜ Chalfont & Latimer ≈
Amersham ≈
Chorleywood
Rickmansworth
West Ruislip ○
Hillingdon ⓑ Ruislip
Uxbridge ⓑ Ickenham Ruislip Manor
Eastcote
Ruislip Gardens Rayners Lane
South Ruislip ≈ South Harrow
Northolt Sudbury Hill
Greenford ○ Sudbury Town
Alperton
Perivale
Hanger Lane
Park Royal
North Ealing
Ealing Broadway ○ ≈
Ealing Common
South Ealing
Northfields
Boston Manor
Osterley
Hounslow East
Hounslow Central
Heathrow Terminals 1, 2, 3 Hounslow West
Hatton Cross
Heathrow Terminal 4 ✈
Heathrow Terminal 5

Watford
Croxley
Moor Park
Northwood
Northwood Hills
Pinner
North Harrow
West Harrow
South Harrow

≈ Watford Junction ⓑ
Watford High Street ≈
≈ Bushey ○
Carpenders Park ⓑ
Hatch End ≈
Headstone Lane ≈
≈ Harrow & Wealdstone
Kenton
Harrow-on-the-Hill

Edgware ⓑ
Burnt Oak
Stanmore Colindale
Canons Park Hendon Central
Queensbury Brent Cross
Kingsbury

Northwick Park
Wembley Park
South Kenton
North Wembley
≈ Wembley Central ⓑ
Stonebridge Park
Harlesden
Willesden Junction

Neasden
Dollis Hill
Willesden Green
Kilburn ✝

Golders Green
Hampstead

Finchley Road & Frognal
West Hampstead ≈

Kensal Rise Brondesbury
Kensal Green
Queen's Park Kilburn South
High Road Hampstead
Finchley Road
Swiss Cottage
St. John's Wood

Kilburn Park
Maida Vale
Warwick Avenue
Royal Oak
Westbourne Park

Edgware
Paddington Road Marylebone ≈

Baker Street
Great Portland Street
Euston

Ladbroke Grove
Latimer Road

Edgware Road
Bayswater

Warren Street
Regent's Park

East White
Acton City
West North
Acton Acton Wood Lane
Acton Central
Shepherd's Bush Market
South Acton
Acton Town
Chiswick Park
Goldhawk Road
Turnham Stamford Ravenscourt
Green Brook Park
Gunnersbury
Kew Gardens
Richmond ≈

Shepherd's Bush ≈
Holland Park
High Street Kensington
Kensington (Olympia)
Hammersmith
Barons Court
West Kensington

Notting Lancaster Bond
Hill Gate Gate Street
Queensway Marble Arch
Hyde Park Corner
Knightsbridge
Gloucester Road
Earl's South
Court Kensington

Oxford Circus
Tottenham Court Road
Green Park
Piccadilly Circus
St. James's Park
Sloane Square
Victoria ≈ Westminster ≈

≈ West Brompton
Fulham Broadway ⓑ
Parsons Green
Putney Bridge ⓑ
East Putney
Southfields ⓑ
Wimbledon Park ≈
⛴ ≈ Wimbledon ⓑ

Pimlico
Imperial Wharf ⛴
River Thames
✝ Waterloo ⛴ ≈

Vauxhall ⛴ ≈
≈ Clapham Junction ⓑ
Wandsworth Road
Clapham High Street
Clapham North
Clapham Common
Clapham South
≈ Balham
Tooting Bec
Tooting Broadway
Colliers Wood
South Wimbledon
Morden ⓑ

Oval
Stock

MAYOR OF LONDON

🌐 tfl.gov.uk   ℹ 24 hour travel information
0343 222 1234*

✉

*Service and network charges may apply. See tfl.gov.uk/terms for details.